T0211123

Lecture Notes in Computer Science 13533

More information about this series at https://link.springer.com/bookseries/558

Aurora González-Vidal ·
Ahmed Mohamed Abdelgawad · Essaid Sabir ·
Sébastien Ziegler · Latif Ladid (Eds.)

Internet of Things

5th The Global IoT Summit, GIoTS 2022
Dublin, Ireland, June 20–23, 2022
Revised Selected Papers

 Springer

Editors
Aurora González-Vidal ⓘ
University of Murcia
Murcia, Spain

Ahmed Mohamed Abdelgawad ⓘ
Central Michigan University
Mount Pleasant, MI, USA

Essaid Sabir ⓘ
University of Quebec at Montreal
Montreal, QC, Canada

Sébastien Ziegler ⓘ
IoT Forum
Mandat International
Geneva, Switzerland

Latif Ladid ⓘ
University of Luxembourg
Esch-sur-Alzette, Luxembourg

ISSN 0302-9743   ISSN 1611-3349 (electronic)
Lecture Notes in Computer Science
ISBN 978-3-031-20935-2   ISBN 978-3-031-20936-9 (eBook)
https://doi.org/10.1007/978-3-031-20936-9

This Springer imprint is published by the registered company Springer Nature Switzerland AG
The registered company address is: Gewerbestrasse 11, 6330 Cham, Switzerland

Preface

This volume contains the papers presented at the 5th edition of The Global IoT Summit (GIoTS 2022). GIoTS 2022 was co-located with the IoT week and held during June 20-23, 2022 in Dublin. GIoTS is an international conference established to attract and present the latest research results on the Internet of Things (IoT). It intends to select the best papers through a systematic peer review process.

GIoTS 2022 drove its focus on multiple critical innovations that affect today's research and real-world application space and will enhance our IoT ecosystem. This edition put new efforts into attracting innovative researchers from diverse cross-disciplinary areas to address challenges in the emerging discipline with several workshops organized around the conference. Industry leaders, academics, professionals, government officials and student discussed and fostered knowledge in emerging technologies, business cases and social impacts in this technological area by the means of various activities.

The program consisted of 33 technical papers, selected from 75 submissions, aggregated into technical track sessions and workshops such as:

- IoT Enabling Technologies,
- IoT Applications, Services and Real Implementations
- IoT Experimental Results and Deployment Scenarios
- IoT Security, Privacy and Data Protection
- End-user and Human-centric IoTincluding IoT MultimediaSocietal Impacts and Sustainable Development

Four workshops and Industry forum sessions on hot and emerging topics were held:

- W1: 4th Workshop on Internet of Things Security and Privacy (WISP)
- CITIES2030 Blockchain Food Supply Chain
- GIoTS Industry. Forum – Cross-Border Corridors: 5G for Connected and Automated. Mobility
- IPv6-based 5G, IoT, Cloud Computing Industry

We were also honored to include three invited talks by distinguished researchers:

- Latif Ladid (Founder and President, IPv6 Forum and University of Luxembourg, Luxembourg)
- Craig Wright (Founder and Chief Scientist, nChain, UK)
- Patrick Wetterwald (Cisco Systems, France)

We would like to congratulate everyone who helped make GIoTS 2022 successful.

September 2022

Aurora Gonzalez-Vidal
Ahmed Mohamed Abdelgawad
Essaid Sabir
Sébastien Ziegler
Latif Ladid
Bala Krishna Maddali
Mirko Presser

Organization

General Chair

Sébastien Ziegler — IoT Forum, Switzerland

Technical Program Committee Chairs

Ahmed Mohamed Abdelgawad	Central Michigan University, USA
Bala Krishna Maddali	GGS Indraprastha University, India
Mirko Presser	Aarhus University, Denmark
Essaid Sabir	University of Quebec at Montréal, Canada

Steering Committee

Franck Boissière	European Commission
Srdjan Krco	DunavNET, Serbia
Latif Ladid	IPv6 Forum and University of Luxembourg, Luxembourg
Mirko Presser	Aarhus University, Denmark
Essaid Sabir	University of Quebec at Montréal, Canada
Antonio Skarmeta	University of Murcia, Spain
Sébastien Ziegler	IoT Forum, Switzerland

Technical Program Committee

Cristina Alcaraz Tello	University of Malaga, Spain
Ramon Alcarria	Universidad Politecnica de Madrid, Spain
Gianmarco Baldini	Joint Research Centre European Commission, Italy
Martin Bauer	NEC Europe Ltd, Germany
John A Beattie	Information Catalyst, UK
Paolo Bellavista	University of Bologna, Italy
Nabil Benamar	Moulay Ismail University, Morocco
Zakaria Benomar	University of Messina, Italy
Jorge Bernal Bernabe	University of Murcia, Spain
Igor Bisio	University of Genoa, Italy
Jens-Matthias Bohli	Hochschule Mannheim, Germany
Christopher Brewster	TNO, Greece
Arne Bröring	Siemens AG, Germany

Paul-Emmanuel Brun	Airbus Defence and Space, France
Davide Brunelli	University of Trento, Italy
Daniel Burmeister	University of Lübeck, Germany
Maria Calderon	Universidad Carlos III de Madrid, Spain
Ioannis Chatzigiannakis	Sapienza University of Rome, Italy
Pin-Yu Chen	IBM T J Watson Research Center, USA
Zhuo Chen	InterDigital Communications, USA
Philippe Cousin	eGlobalMark, France
Soumya Kanti Datta	EURECOM, France
Ciprian Dobre	Politehnica University of Bucharest, Romania
Julian Dreyer	Osnabrück University of Applied Sciences, Germany
Xenofon Fafoutis	Technical University of Denmark, Denmark
Xinxin Fan	IoTeX, USA
Nikos Fotiou	Athens University of Economics and Business, Greece
Alexandros Fragkiadakis	Institute of Computer Science, FORTH, Greece
Janusz Furtak	Military University of Technology, Poland
Dan Garcia-Carrillo	University of Murcia, Spain
Dominique Genoud	HES-SO Valais-Wallis, Switzerland
Alireza Ghasempour	ICT Faculty, USA
Maurizio Giacobbe	University of Messina, Italy
Raffaele Giaffreda	FBK CREATE-NET, Italy
Aurora González-Vidal	University of Murcia, Spain
Christoph Grimm	Kaiserslautern University of Technology, Germany
Jayavardhana Gubbi	TCS Research and Innovation, India
Nour Haidar	University of La Rochelle, France
José Luis Hernandez Ramos	European Commission Joint Research Centre, Belgium
Chun-Ying Huang	National Chiao Tung University, Taiwan
Antonio Iera	University of Calabria, Italy
Dimosthenis Ioannidis	Information Technologies Institute, Greece
Isam Ishaq	Al-Quds University, Palestine
Atman Jbari	Mohammed V University in Rabat, Morocco
Nikos Kalatzis	Neuropublic S.A., Greece
Carlos Kamienski	Universidade Federal do ABC, Brazil
Sye Loong Keoh	University of Glasgow, United Kingdom (Great Britain)
Ahmed Khattab	Cairo University, Egypt
Rahul Kher	G H Patel College of Engineering and Technology, India

Pavlos Kosmides	National Technical University of Athens, Greece
Ernö Peter Kovacs	NEC Europe Laboratories GmbH, Germany
Srdjan Krco	DunavNET, Serbia
Thomas Krousarlis	Inlecom Innovation, Greece
Dennis Labitzke	University of Lübeck, Germany
Dmitrij Lagutin	Aalto University, Finland
Franck Le Gall	Easy Global Market, France
Danh Le Phuoc	Technical University of Berlin, Germany
Francesco Longo	Universita di Messina, Italy
Konstantinos Loupos	Inlecom Innovation, Greece
Rafael Marin-Perez	University of Murcia, Spain
Juan A. Martinez	University of Murcia, Spain
Sara Nieves Matheu García	University of Murcia, Spain
Yasser Mawad	Universität zu Lübeck, Germany
Roc Meseguer	Universitat Politècnica de Catalunya, Spain
Fabrizio Messina	University of Catania, Italy
Florian Michahelles	Siemens Corporation, USA
Enzo Mingozzi	University of Pisa, Italy
Alejandro Molina Zarca	University of Murcia, Spain
Septimiu Nechifor	Siemens SRL, Romania
Jordi Ortiz	University of Murcia, Spain
Carlos E Palau	Universitat Politecnicade Valencia, Spain
Raul Palma	PSNC, Poland
Georgios Z. Papadopoulos	IMT Atlantique, France
Maulika S. Patel	G H Patel College of Engineering and Technology, India
Shashikant Shantilal Patil	SVKMs NMIMS, Mumbai, India
Thinagaran Perumal	Universiti Putra Malaysia, Malaysia
Dirk Pesch	University College Cork, Ireland
Tom Pfeifer	IoT Consult Europe, Germany
Ivana Podnar Zarko	University of Zagreb, Croatia
Henrich C. Pöhls	University of Passau, Germany
George C. Polyzos	Athens University of Economics and Business, Greece
Athanasios Poulakidas	Intrasoft, Greece
Mirko Alexander Presser	Aarhus University, Denmark
Muhammad Waqas Rehan	University of Lübeck, Germany
Sérgio L. Ribeiro	CPQD, Brazil
Rodrigo Roman	University of Malaga, Spain
Domenico Rosaci	Mediterranea University of Reggio Calabria, Italy
Domenico Rotondi	FINCONS SpA, Italy
Ioanna Roussaki	National Technical University of Athens, Greece

Giuseppe Ruggeri	University of Reggio Calabria, Italy
Jorge Sá Silva	University of Coimbra, Portugal
Luis Sanchez	University of Cantabria, Spain
Jesus Sanchez-Gomez	University of Murcia, Spain
Claudio Savaglio	University of Calabria, Italy
Neetesh Saxena	Cardiff University, UK
Corinna Schmitt	Universität der Bundeswehr München, Germany
Dhananjay Singh	Hankuk University of Foreign Studies, South Korea
Rana Pratap Sircar	Ericsson, India
Vasilios A. Siris	Athens University of Economics and Business, Greece
Ali Hassan Sodhro	Linkoping University, Sweden
Rute C. Sofia	Fortiss, Germany
Cesar Alexandre Souza	University of São Paulo, Brazil
Orazio Tomarchio	University of Catania, Italy
Rafael Torres Moreno	University of Murcia, Spain
Sergio Trilles	Universitat Jaume I, Spain
Thomas Usländer	Fraunhofer IOSB, Germany
Andrea Vinci	ICAR CNR, Italy
Konstantinos Votis	Information Technologies Institute, Centre For Research and Technology Hellas, Greece
Yunsheng Wang	Kettering University, USA
Hung-Yu Wei	National Taiwan University, Taiwan
Konrad Wrona	NATO Communications and Information Agency, The Netherlands
Stavros Xynogalas	National Technical University of Athens, Greece
Narges Yousefnezhad	Aalto University, Finland
Anastasios Zafeiropoulos	National Technical University of Athens, Greece
Arkady Zaslavsky	Deakin University, Australia
Sherali Zeadally	University of Kentucky, USA
Mengchu Zhou	New Jersey Institute of Technology, USA
Zbigniew Zielinski	Military University of Technology, Poland

Contents

IoT Security, Privacy and Data Protection

IoT Pilots, Testbeds and Experimentation Results

IoT Enabling Technologies

Overview of Drone Communication Requirements in 5G

Radheshyam Singh$^{(\boxtimes)}$ (iD), Kalpit Dilip Ballal$^{(\boxtimes)}$ (iD),
Michael Stübert Berger$^{(\boxtimes)}$ (iD), and Lars Dittmann$^{(\boxtimes)}$ (iD)

Department of Photonics Engineering, Technical University of Denmark,
Kgs. Lyngby, Denmark
{radsi,kdiba,msbe,ladit}@fotonik.dtu.dk

Abstract. The ease of use and flexibility provided by drones or Unmanned Aerial vehicles (UAV) is attracting different industries and researchers across domains (e.g., delivery, agriculture, security, etc.). Although maintaining a reliable and secure command and control communication channel is still an open challenge and primary limitation for using drones. Satellite and 5G are considered viable solutions for drone communication. In this survey paper, we have explored specifications and proposed enhancements in cellular technology specified by 3GPP to command and control UAVs. It also describes the required network Quality of Service (QoS) parameters for drone communication. Such as end-to-end latency to send and receive a command and control message (C2), reliability, and message size. Along with these, it also emphasizes defining the reliability in terms of communication and navigation of UAVs, based on cellular technology 5G additional investigation and standardization should be executed.

Keywords: 5G cellular technology · Unmanned aerial vehicle · Drones · Latency · Coverage · 3GPP

1 Introduction

We live in a technological era and try to develop a world where essential services can be operated and controlled autonomously-for example, autonomous cars, buses, trains, etc. Researchers, educational institutes, and some giant tech companies are attentively looking into the field related to UAVs, in general, known as drones. Drones are prominently emerging technology and attracting people to develop some usage scenario. This technology is still in the developing phase in terms of mass acquiescence for formulating and implementing, but drones have already broken the conventional obstacles and proved their importance in several fields. For instance, delivering a parcel and medical help where a human can not reach or is incapable of performing in a timely manner, along with these it has been used to keep an eye on the military area. Several use cases are there, where unmanned aerial vehicles are considered as feasible tools [1,2].

Acceptance of UAVs applications and innovations across the industries hopped from sluggish level to active level, because gradually businesses have

© The Author(s), under exclusive license to Springer Nature Switzerland AG 2022
A. González-Vidal et al. (Eds.): GIoTS 2022, LNCS 13533, pp. 3–16, 2022.
https://doi.org/10.1007/978-3-031-20936-9_1

started to see the potential, comprehensive scope, and worldwide reach in drone based applications. Drones can be operated and controlled remotely via an application installed on smartphones or autonomously. They can provide services and support with or without manpower and conserve efforts, energy, and, most importantly, time. All these points are very attractive to the industries and research groups to invest their time and resources to get the profitable business based on drones [3].

As we know, drones or UAVs can be used for a variety of applications such as surveillance, data gathering, environment monitoring, aerial photography, delivery, etc. Along with these, it provides real-time data to help the industry design real-time operations. A report published in "Fortune Business Insights" about unmanned aerial vehicles or drones shows that the global service market based on drones was 7.12 billion USD in 2020. An unfortunate situation like COVID-19 boosted the market and allowed further investigation related to applications based on UAVs. The drone-based market is projected to escalate from 9.56 billion USD to 134.89 billion USD by 2028 [4]. A Germany-based company, "Drone Industry Insights," has forecasted that the drone market will be 41.3 billion USD by 2026. Figure 1 shows the commercial drone scale and business forecast by 2026. They have also divided the drone business market into three segments [5].

1. **Hardware:-** This segment includes the industries which are generating the revenue from providing the tools, components, hardware, and systems associated with unmanned aerial vehicles. This sector acquires 16.4% revenue of total drone business sector [5].
2. **Software:-** This segment holds the 4.3% revenue of the drone market. This revenue is generated from providing the software for drone communication, navigation, fleet planning, computer vision, control, and management system [5].
3. **Drone based Services:-** The drone-based service sector produces a huge part of the revenue. This segment generates 79.3% revenue for the drone business market [5].

This survey paper aims to find out the supporting capability of cellular technology, primarily of 5G for the drones or UAVs based applications. Along with this, it will also fill the gap between the researcher in academia and on going trends in giant tech industries by providing a comprehensive analysis. In this survey paper, the following questions are investigated and attempted to address with appropriate answers.

– What are the near-future potential applications of drones and which are the giant tech companies exploring this field?
– What are the requirements for drone based applications?
– What are the technical enhancements executed or proposed by the 3rd Generation Partnership Project (3GPP) standards, especially for the UAVs based applications?
– How 5G cellular technology can support and contribute to enhance drone communications and applications?

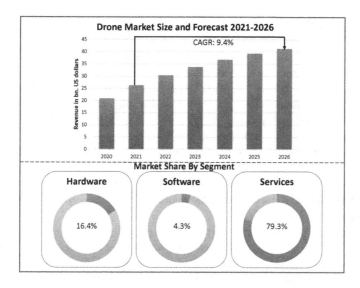

Fig. 1. Drone market projection 2021–2026 [5]

The structure of this paper is as follows, Sect. 2 gives the information about the drone based applications and which multinational companies are looking into the drone based business. Essential parameters for drone based communication are explored in Sect. 3. These parameters include the government's rules and regulation along with technical requirements for drone based applications. Information about some previous research works, challenges, and findings in reference to drones or UAVs are given in Sect. 4. Section 5 demonstrates the role of 5G cellular technology for drones or UAVs. The conclusion of this survey paper is given in Sect. 6.

2 Applications of Drones

This section will explore the applications of drones and which corporations are investing their time, money, and resources to design and develop a potential application using drones or UAVs. Drone or UAV based applications can be deployed in several sectors. Based on some ongoing developments and used cases, we have divided drone based applications into the following sectors-

1. **Delivery of Products:-** Since 2013 Amazon has created a research and development team to leverage the drones for delivering their packages. Amazon has now a drone based application that can deliver packages in the range of 24 Km and the delivery drone is capable to deliver a package of approximately 2.5 kg. In 2018 Amazon is awarded a patent for its UAVs application by US patent [6]. Google's parent company Alphabet is working in the field of UAVs based package delivery applications under the project name "Wing". Alphabet executed its first UAVs flight test in Australia in the year 2014 [8].

In the year 2021, Wing has delivered more than 140,000 packages to customers [7].

Uber has published a white paper to investigate the future on-demand air transportation, and they were more anxious to design and developed an autonomous air travel [10]. But in the year 2018 company has shifted its interest to develop a more efficient drone based application for the food delivery business. DHL is working on UAVs since 2013 to use a quadcopter to deliver small packages [9]. Like Amazon, Walmart is also exploring this field and has opened an incubator in Austin, Texas in 2018. The central objective of this tech incubator is to develop drone or UAV based applications. JD.com China's one of the largest e-commerce retailers is testing drones since 2016 to deliver the products. In the year 2019 company has delivered its first product in Indonesia [8].

2. **Security and Inspection:-** Drones are considered as one of the feasible solutions for the sectors where security and inspection of a site or product are necessary. FedEx is using UAVs to deliver the aircraft's parts to the ground engineers and along with this, the drone will inspect the runways at the airports. Since 2016, IBM is developing an application to visualize natural disasters in real-time, using IBM's Cloud, drones, and cognitive computing technologies [11]. GE provides UAVs to inspect the tools and equipment installed in the field of energy and manufacturing sector [12]. A British-based airline enterprise easyJet is using UAVs since 2015 to perform an inspection of aircraft to detect damages [8].

3. **Entertainment:-** Drones are making the entertainment sector more realistic. To shoot a movie's scene a drone with a high-resolution camera is used by the movie craters. Intel has designed and developed light-weighted fleets of UAVs. Which are used in concerts, sports opening ceremony events, and for the entertainment purpose [13]. The UK-based broadcasting company British Broadcasting Corporation (BBC) is using drones for news broadcasting since 2013 [8].

4. **Internet Connectivity:-** In 2014 Facebook announced a project "Aquila". The objective of this project is to provide internet connectivity using lightweight UAVs. Based on the estimation given by a telecom company Otelco installing fiber optic cables costs 22000 USD per mile. This was the reason behind deploying UAVs for internet connectivity, which is less expensive than installing fiber optic cables [8]. Facebook had carried out a successful test flight of Aquila in the year 2017 at an altitude of 3000 ft, but in the year 2018 Facebook terminated this project [14].

5. **Maps and Navigation:-** In the year 2012 Apple created its maps, but it disappointed Apple's customers because the maps were imprecision and they were not competent to show the location directions. Apple uses drone technology to improve the gathering and transmitting of visual and geographical real-time data [15]. In this way Apple eliminated the flaws from the Apple maps [8].

6. **Agriculture:-** Microsoft and DJI are working together on a project "Farm-Beast" since 2015. The purpose of this project is to gather agricultural

data such as soil moisture, temperature, infected crops, and other important parameters which could help to increase crop productions [8].

Table 1. Drone based applications [8].

Application sector	Company	Drone based application	Starting year of R&D	Application is developed/under development
Delivery	Amazon	Home deliveries of products with in 24 KM of range	2013	Developed
	Alphabet	For delivery	2014	Application is developed got the air-carrier certification from FAA and have legal permission to deliver the products
	Uber	Forfoods delivery	2018	Under Development
	JD.com	For delivery	n/a	Developed
	UPS	For delivery the vaccines	2016	Developed
	Walmart	For delivery	2016	Under Development
	DHL	For delivery	2013	Under Development
Security and inspection	FedEx	Drones for maintaining aircraft and inspecting runway	N/a	Application is developed, soon FedEx will use UAVs at Memphis International Airport
	GE	Inspection of manufacturing sectors	2014	Developed
	EasyJet	To inspect the aircrafts	2015	Under Development
	IBM	To Visualize the natural disaster in real-time	2016	Under Development
Entertainment	Intel	For entertainment purposes like light shows, dancing drones, etc.	N/a	Application is developed, used for the sports, concerts and entertainment
	BBC	Real-time news brodcasting	2013	Developed
Maps and navigation	Apple	To enhance the maps and navigation	2012	Developed
Internet connectivity	Facebook/Meta	To provide internet connectivity	2014	Terminated the program in the year 2018
Agriculture	Microsoft and DJI	To gather the agricultural data	2015	Under Development

3 Essential Parameters for Drone Communication and Navigation

To fly a drone for any kind of application there are some specific rules and regulations, and they are applied on both hobbyist applications as well as commercial operations. European Aviation Safety Agency (EASA) has developed these rules to make drone operations more secure and regulated. This section will discuss the EASA rules for drone flights. Along with this, it will also elaborate on the technical parameters that are essential for drone communication and navigation based on 5G cellular technology.

3.1 Government Rules and Regulations

Following are brief information about EASA regulations which are followed by the European Union member states along with Norway, Iceland Liechtenstein and United Kingdom [16].

- Drone should not be flown above 120 m or 400 ft above the ground surface.
- Drones operations are prohibited under 150 m of a crowded area.
- Drones having weight less than 250 g (A1 Drones), can be operated over the people. Drones having a weight of more than 250 g but less than 2 Kg (A2-Drones) must have to operate at least 50 m away from people. Drones having more than 2 kg weights should be operated well away from people.
- Drone operators should have a license to operate the drones.

- No drones operations inside 1 km perimeter of airbase without permission.
- While flying the drones operators have to look always at the drones to avoid any kind of incursions. They should look at the screen to just adjust the frame to capture the shot or to check battery [17]. If the operator is flying drones in line-of-site in that case operating distance should not be more than 500 m.

Depending upon the countries and regions there are more other rules. Drone operations in Beyond Visual Line of Sight (BVLOS) have more strict rules and regulations. Government officials are still looking thoroughly into this, to develop a secure infrastructure for UAVs applications.

3.2   Technical Parameters

To achieve secure and reliable communication for drones using a cellular communication system, drones have to exchange the information with the pilot, nearby other drones or UAVs, and principally with the air traffic control system. This mechanism is called UAV Control and Non-payload Communication (CNPC) [19]. simultaneously, depending upon the applications, a drone has to transmit or receive information on a timely basis related to the assigned task, such that images, videos, and data packets from ground entities to the drone and vice-versa. This operation is known as payload communication [20]. To deploy the UAVs application on a large scale the International Telecommunication Union (ITU) has categorized the CNPC in the following section:

1. **UAV Command and Control Communication (C2):**- This type of communication includes UAV or drone's status, a real-time control signal from pilot to UAV, and flight command updates.
2. **Air Traffic Control (ATC) Relay Communication:**-Communication between the air traffic control system and UAV operator via ATC relay.
3. **Communication for Detect and Avoid Collision:**- Capability to sense and avoid collision from nearby UAVs and territory.

Payload communication and CNPC require different set of spectrum. Table 2 and Table 3 represents the network key points for UAV's communication. These communication parameters are specified in Release 17 by the 3GPP standards.

UAV Control and Non-payload Communication:- Table 2 represents the required QoS parameters for the CNPC communication. Here, uplink (UL) data transmission represents UAV to network side messages and downlink (DL) data transmission represents network to UAV side messages. Control and command communication is duplex communication and it may be integrated with video for controlling the operation of UAVs. Therefore, when a C2 message is sent with video, the required end-to-end latency is 1 s. A positive acknowledgment message for downlink transmission is necessary in this mode. On the other hand, when a C2 message is sent without video, end-to-end latency would be less than 40 ms. This mode also requires a positive acknowledgment in downlink transmission. To communicate with the ATC relay, end-to-end latency should not be more than 5 s. To sense and avoid the collision with other UAVs and territories, the delay for the uplink transmission should be less than 140 ms and in downlink transmission required delay is 10 ms. In this mode, the reliability of the network should be 99.99% for the uplink transmission and 99% for the downlink transmission. However, network reliability should be 99.9% for the rest of the communication mode [18].

Table 2. UAV control and non-payload communication requirements [18].

Control and non-payload communication	Message interval (UP/DL)	Message size (UP/DL)(byte)	Max UAV speed (km/h)	End-to-end latency (UP/DL)	Reliability (UP/DL)	ACK (UP/DL)
Control & Command message (without video)	1 s/ >= 1 s	84–140/100	300	1 s/1 s	99.9%	Not required/Required
Control & Command message (With Video)	40 ms/40 ms	84–120/24	60	40 ms/40 ms	99.9%	Not required/Required
Communication with UTM or ATC	1 s/1 s	1500/10K	300	5 s/5 s	99.9%	Required/Required
Detect & Avoid collision with other UAV	500 ms/500 ms	4K/4K	50	140 ms/10 ms	99.99%/99%	Required/Required

UAV Payload Communication:- The 5G cellular technology shall be capable to transmit data collected by the entity which are installed on UAVs, such as a camera to transmit images, videos, and data files. Depending upon the applications, UAVs require different uplink and downlink quality of service (QoS). Table 3 represents the UAV payload communication requirements. To transmit real-time video using a UAV up to 100 m above ground level requires a 100 Mbps data rate for uplink transmission and 600 Kbps for downlink transmission. The allowed latency is 200 and 20 ms for uplink and downlink transmission respectively. Using a UAV for surveillance needs 20 ms of end-to-end latency in both uplink and downlink transmission. The essential data rate for this kind of application is 120 Mbps for uplink and 50 Mbps for downlink transmission. For controlling an UAV through HD video where the speed of the UAV is less than 160 km/h, the required uplink data rate is 25 Mbps and the downlink data rate is 20 Mbps. For this kind of application, end-to-end latency is 100 and 20 ms for uplink and downlink transmission [18] respectively.

Table 4 represents the communication requirements for the different drone based use cases. These requirements are published by the China Mobile in a "4G+, 5G UAV white paper" [20].

3.3 3GPP Vision

In this section, we will discuss the UAV requirements described in the 3GPP Release 17 [18]. The following section provides an overview of communication services for UAVs and problems in unmanned aviation.

Table 3. UAV payload communication Requirements [18].

UAV applications	Above ground level (m)	Max UAV speed (km/h)	End-to-end latency (UP/DL)(ms)	Data Rate (UP/DL)
8K Video Real-Time Broadcasting	<100	60	200/20	100 Mbps/600 kbps
4X4K AI Surveillance	<200	60	20/20	120 Mbps/50 Mbps
Remote UAV Controller Through HD Video	<300	160	100/20	25 Mbps/300 kbps

Table 4. Communication Requirements for drone based applications [20].

Drone based application sector	Coverage height (m)	End-to-end latency (ms)	Throughput requirements (UL/DL)
Delivery of goods	100	500	200 kbps/300 kbps
Videography and image capturing	100	500	30 Mbps/300 kbps
Security and inspection	100	3000	10 Mbps/300 kbps
Drone fleet show	200	100	200 kbps/200 kbps
Agriculture	300	500	200 kbps/300 kbps
Rescue mission	100	500	6 Mbps/300 kbps

1. **Mobility Management:** 5G network should be able to relatively quickly adapt to the mobility pattern of UAV during an active session. This primarily includes maintaining IP addresses and reducing packet loss and interruption time while performing handover at relatively high speeds.
2. **Security:** 3GPP has paid special attention towards maintaining high-security standards for UAV communication. Some of the features include encrypting data exchanges between UAV and Unmanned Traffic Management (UTM) and blocking data from unreliable UAV. 5G should be able to provide confidentiality regarding personally identifiable information from UAV, and 5G should also be able to support various levels of integrity and privacy protection.
3. **Priority, QoS, and Policy Control:** 5G communication systems should be able to provide different priority levels to the services which may share the same QoS characteristics but varying levels of priority. It should also be able to provide mechanisms for measuring E2E QoS and the dependability of the network and different services offered.
4. **Positioning Services and Remote Identification:** Accurate identification of the location of a UAV in the cell is an extremely important feature of the 5G system. 3GPP systems should provide a way to validate the position reported by the UAV utilizing 3GPP and non-3GPP positioning systems. The

network should also be able to provide UE identity by means of IMEI, IMSI, IP, etc. UE capabilities and other flight-related information at any given time.

5. **UAS Traffic Management:** 5G network should be able to traffic manage the communication between UAV and UTM with a maximum latency of 500ms. The network should be able to carry out short-range message transfer (up to 600m) such as position and collision avoidance data intra-network as well as inter-networks with less than 100ms of latency at a relative speed of 320 km/h

6. **Service Performance Requirements:** The 3GPP system should be able to provide network-related Key Point Indicators (KPIs) (UL/DL data, packet drop, latency, etc.) for payload (e.g., images, real-time video, sensory information, etc.) as well as non-payload related services (e.g., C2, telemetry, etc.) offered by the system.

4   Related Work

In this section, some previous research works and findings are given. We have divided these findings based on cellular technical parameters, which play a significant role in communicating and navigating the drones.

– **Security:** Authentication and key agreement, data integrity, cryptographic algorithm, etc. are the key elements of the 5G security standards. 5G standard significantly improves consolidated authentication procedure than the one used in 4G. Apart from the network-provided security improvements, it is also crucial to provide different ways to encrypt the application data. One such approach is described in [25] by integrating blockchain into 5G communication by implying permission blockchain technology for decentralized data management system.

– **Latency:** The latency constraints imposed by the 5G standard for supporting critical applications is very high. For instance, a remote UAV controller through HD videos has a latency budget of 20 ms, whereas an 8K video live broadcast at 100 Mbps has a budget of 200 ms. The requirements get even stricter when it comes to command and control UAV applications. UAV terminated control messages have a maximum latency budget of 10 ms in an autonomous flight. Xiaopan Zhu and et al. [21] have managed to successfully implement a Clustering method for large-scale drone swarms to reduce the latency. The OPNET model can effectively form different sizes of clusters to improve the transmission efficiency and ability to execute the task. Xiangwang Hou and et al. [22] describes a distributed fog computing architecture for improving the latency and reliability of wireless communication. Another method described in the 3GPP standards is to use Network-slicing to improve the network's performance and reduce the latency of the communication.

– **Bitrate:** Most commonly described application of the use of drones is to stream high-quality video for surveillance, remote inspection, etc. In order to transfer HQ video from a drone to an application server, the communication system should be able to provide high bitrate in the Uplink direction. The

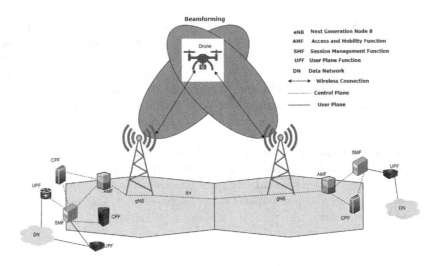

Fig. 2. Operation of UAV over cellular coverage-5G

use of millimeter-wave (mmWave) frequency band for communication will definitely help in achieving high bitrates; however, the performance is susceptible to obstacles and beam misalignment. Woongsoo NA and et.al [23] their work proposes a deep-learning-based TCP (DL-TCP) model that can quickly adapt to the TCP conjugation and window sizing by prediction based on the network performance. DL-TCP shows much higher network throughput and stability than just using TCP for the data transfer.

– **Wireless Coverage:** Bin Li et al. have explored some potential challenges for drone communication in [24]. One of the crucial challenges in UAV based application is to provide reliable coverage to command, control, and navigate. To ensure reliable coverage in a particular direction beamforming technique is feasible. It uses multiple antenna array to transmit uniform signal to one direction. It helps to enhance signal strength, data transfer speed and avoid the interference [28]. H.C Nguyen et al. have surveyed that beamforming solution has capability to increase the Signal to Interference plus Noise Ratio (SINR) in both uplink and downlink transmission [29]. Drones have possibility to detect higher number of interfering signals from the cellular base stations deployed in the vicinity [26,27]. This is because of elevated height. Interference due to multiple neighbouring or line of sight base stations can be mitigated using the beamforming technique. Figure 2 shows the operation of a drone over cellular coverage using beam-forming mechanism.

5   Role of 5G in Drone Applications

Critical use cases and applications of drone have stringent requirements on the reliability and efficiency of the communication technology used. The advance-

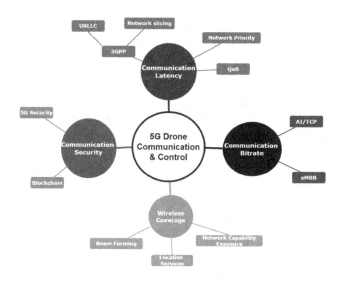

Fig. 3. Summary of communication and control of UAV over 5G

ments and improvements offered by the 5G technology make it an excellent candidate to be used as a control and data communication technology for drones. 5G offers guaranteed service and data delivery. 5G being a WAN technology makes it also easy to scale up the deployment of the application. Unlike other RF-communication technologies, the use of a private spectrum helps in controlling the interference and noise in the communication channel. 5G also offers enhancement to communication security, which is important from a critical application perspective.

Table 5 shows the network KPIs of 5G cellular technology. It has data rate up to 10 Gbps and 20 Gbps for uplink and downlink transmission respectively. The promised latency of 5G network is less than 1 millisecond and reliability is 99.999%. It can connect 100x number of devices per unit area [31]. 5G standalone system also includes the functionality of Ultra-Reliable Low Latency Communications (URLLC) and enhanced Mobile Broadband (eMBB). In Release 16, 3GPP has enhanced URLLC and able to reduce the latency up to 0.5 ms [32]. To design and develop a drone based application on cellular based command,

Table 5. 5G network key point indicators [30,31].

Service parameter	Network KPI	Section
Peak data rate	DL: 20 Gbps, UL: 10 Gbps	EMBB
Throughput	DL: 100 Mbps, UL: 50 Mbps	EMBB
Latency	4 ms for eMBB, 1 ms For URLLC	EMBB, URLLC
Reliability	99.9999%	URLLC

control and navigation, the required communication QoS are summarised in the Table 2 and 3. These standardized parameters are given by 3GPP. If we compare these QoS with 5G, we can say that the 5G communication system can support drone based applications. Figure 3 shows some substantial specifications of 5G, that can be utilized to strengthen drone communication and control.

Based on 3GPP documentation reliability depends upon packet loss in uplink transmission. Mentioned in release 15, reliability is defined as successfully delivery of X bytes of data packet with-in acceptable delay. Where delay is the time taken to deliver the data packet from layer 2 of radio protocol transmitting ingress point to layer 3 of radio protocol receiving egress point at adequate signal strength. In general, URLLC vision defined by 3GPP is $1 - 10^{-5}$, which means in available coverage, for a single transmission, probability of successful delivery of packet data unit should be 99.999% in 1 ms of time interval [33]. Whereas, if we define the reliability in terms of drone community or drone based application, network connectivity should be available for 99.999% of time. Hence, it can be inferred that cellular network operator and application developer based on drones they have different terms for defining reliability.

It concludes, requirements specified by 3GPP are expressly overlaying user plan. Therefore, to develop an application using 5G as communication backbone with UAVs, end-to-end latency and reliability requirements of specific application should also be taken into consideration. The mentioned specification of reliability is inadequate to outline the variety of use cases such as enhanced Vehicle to Everything (eV2X) and drone communication and navigation based on 5G cellular communication [34]. In summary, defining reliability is critically important for communication and navigation of drones. There should be common parameters which will be used to define the reliability for cellular based drone communication.

6   Conclusion

In this paper, the authors have given an overview of drone communication requirements and challenges for the upcoming 5G standard and 3GPP vision for UAV communication. We have described improvements supported in the 3GPP Release 17, and related works and techniques to achieve them. The paper goes over the essential parameters for drone communication and navigation as well as provides an overview of rules and regulations imposed by governmental bodies in different regions at the time of writing this article. Although there are several improvements both in the 5G standards as well as by individual researchers to provide better UAV communication, there is still further field testing required before autonomous drones can be deployed for various industrial applications.

Acknowledgement. This survey paper is a part of a project "5G ENABLED COMMUNICATION INFRASTRUCTURE FOR UNMANNED AERIAL SYSTEMS (5G GENIUS)", which is supported and funded by Innovation Fund Denmark (IFD). Authors would like to acknowledge the assistance of University of Southern Denmark (SDU).

References

1. Valavanis, K.P., Vachtsevanos, G.J.. (eds.): Handbook of Unmanned Aerial Vehicles. Springer, Dordrecht (2015). https://doi.org/10.1007/978-90-481-9707-1
2. Beard, R.W., McLain, T.W., Small Unmanned Aircraft: Theory and Practice. Princeton Univ. Press, Princeton (2012)
3. Drone technology uses and applications for commercial, industrial and military drones in 2021 and the future. https://www.businessinsider.com/drone-technology-uses-applications?r=US&IR=T. Accessed 22 Feb 2022
4. The global drone services market is projected to grow from $9.56 billion in 2021 Report ID: FBI102682. https://www.fortunebusinessinsights.com/drone-services-market-102682. Accessed 23 Feb 2022
5. Global Drone Market Report 2021–2026 New insights on the commercial drone market and an updated model for the drone market report. https://droneii.com/product/drone-market-report. Accessed 22 Feb 2022
6. Amazon's drone delivers its first packages. https://www.dr.dk/nyheder/viden/tech/amazons-drone-leverer-sine-foerste-pakker. Accessed 22 Feb 2022
7. 2021: The year that drone delivery took off. https://blog.wing.com/2021/12/2021-year-that-drone-delivery-took-off.html. Accessed 25 Feb 2022
8. From Retailers To Insurance Providers, Here Are 20 Corps Using Drone Tech Today Published by CBINSIGHTS (2019). https://www.cbinsights.com/research/report/corporations-drone-technology/. Accessed 23 Feb 2022
9. Heutger, M., Kückelhaus, M., Report by DHL.: Unmanned Aerial Vehicles and DHL perspective on implications and use cases for the logistics industry
10. Fast-Forwarding to a Future of On-Demand Urban Air Transportation. https://uberpubpolicy.medium.com/fast-forwarding-to-a-future-of-on-demand-urban-air-transportation-f6ad36950ffa. Accessed 25 Feb 2022
11. Drone Deploy- Helps businesses take off by harnessing the power of drone technology. https://www.ibm.com/case-studies/c848309d42496w67. Accessed 25 Feb 2022
12. GE Introduces new company to develop next generation unmanned traffic management. https://www.ge.com/news/press-releases/ge-introduces-new-company-develop-next-generation-unmanned-traffic-management. Accessed 25 Feb 2022
13. Drone Light shows powered by intel. https://www.intel.com/content/www/us/en/technology-innovation/intel-drone-light-shows.html. Accessed 23 Feb 2022
14. Facebook abandons its Project Aquila flying internet plan.https://www.bbc.com/news/technology-44624702. Accessed 23 Feb 2022
15. Apple Confirms It Is Using Drones to Improve Apple Maps. https://gadgets360.com/transportation/news/apple-confirms-drone-usage-on-apple-maps-with-privacy-standards-in-place-1850205. Accessed 23 Feb 2022
16. Easy Access Rules for Unmanned Aircraft Systems (Regulation (EU) 2019/947 and Regulation (EU) 2019/945) revision from September 2021
17. EU has passed a uniform set of drone rules, paving the way for easier flight. https://www.dpreview.com/news/6070763652/eu-has-a-uniform-set-of-drone-rules. Accessed 25 Feb 2022
18. Unmanned Aerial System (UAS) support in 3GPP, 3GPP TS 22.125 v17.2.0 (12/2020). https://portal.3gpp.org/desktopmodules/Specifications/SpecificationDetails.aspx?specificationId=3545. Accessed 25 Feb 2022
19. Characteristics of unmanned aircraft systems and spectrum requirements to support their safe operation in non-segregated airspace, ITU (2009). ITU Tech. Rep. M.2171.M Series

20. Wu, Q., Zeng, Y., Zhang, R.: UAV Communications for 5G and Beyond, UAV Definitions, Classes, and Global Trend, pp. 3–16. Wiley, IEEE Press (2020)
21. Zhu, X., Bian, C., Chen, Y., Chen, S.: A low latency clustering method for large-scale drone swarms. IEEE Access **7**, 186260–186267 (2019). https://doi.org/10.1109/ACCESS.2019.2960934
22. Hou, X., Ren, Z., Wang, J., Zheng, S., Cheng, W., Zhang, H.: Distributed fog computing for latency and reliability guaranteed swarm of drones. IEEE Access **8**, 7117–7130 (2020). https://doi.org/10.1109/ACCESS.2020.2964073
23. Na, W., Bae, B., Cho, S., Kim, N.: DL-TCP: deep learning-based transmission control protocol for disaster 5G mm wave networks. IEEE Access **7**, 145134–145144 (2019). https://doi.org/10.1109/ACCESS.2019.2945582
24. Li, B., Fei, Z., Zhang, Y.: UAV communications for 5G and beyond: recent advances and future trends. IEEE Internet Things J. **6**(2), 2241–2263 (2019). https://doi.org/10.1109/JIOT.2018.2887086
25. Kang, J., Xiong, Z., Niyato, D., Xie, S., Kim, D.I.: Securing data sharing from the sky: integrating blockchains into drones in 5G and beyond. IEEE Network **35**(1), 78–85 (2021). https://doi.org/10.1109/MNET.011.2000183
26. Van Der Bergh, B., Chiumento, A., Pollin, S.: LTE in the sky: trading off propagation benefits with interference costs for aerial nodes. IEEE Commun. Mag. **54**(5), 44–50 (2016). https://doi.org/10.1109/MCOM.2016.7470934
27. Bucur, M., Sorensen, T., Amorim, R., Lopez, M., Kovacs, I. Z, Mogensen, P.: Validation of large-scale propagation characteristics for UAVs within urban environment. In: 2019 IEEE 90th Vehicular Technology Conference (VTC2019-Fall), pp. 1–6 (2019). https://doi.org/10.1109/VTCFall.2019.8891422
28. 5G IN A NUTSHELL - Air-Met Scientific, Narda Safety Test Solutions GmbH, L3HARRIS
29. Nguyen, H.C., Amorim, R., Wigard, J., KováCs, I.Z., Sørensen, T.B., Mogensen, P.E.: How to ensure reliable connectivity for aerial vehicles over cellular networks. IEEE Access **6**, 12304–12317 (2018). https://doi.org/10.1109/ACCESS.2018.2808998
30. 3GPP Release 15 Overview 3rd Generation Partnership Project (3GPP) members meet regularly to collaborate and create cellular communications standards. https://spectrum.ieee.org/3gpp-release-15-overview. Accessed 27 May 2022
31. ETSI TS 122 261 V15.5.0 (2018–07). 5G; Service requirements for next generation new services and markets (3GPP TS 22.261 version 15.5.0 Release 15)
32. A 5G Americas White Paper, 3GPP Releases 16 & 17 & Beyond, Jan 2021
33. ETSI TR 138 913 V15.0.0 (2018–09). 5G; study on scenarios and requirements for next generation access technologies (3GPP TR 38.913 version 15.0.0 Release 15)
34. Popovski, P., et al.: Wireless access in ultra-reliable low-latency communication (URLLC). IEEE Trans. Commun. **67**(8), 5783–5801 (2019). https://doi.org/10.1109/TCOMM.2019.2914652

Accurate Indoor Positioning Based on Beacon Weighting Using RSSI

Yuuki Takagi[1]([✉])[iD] and Takayuki Kushida[2][iD]

[1] Tokyo University of Technology Graduate School, Hachioji-shi, Tokyo, Japan
`g21210300d@edu.teu.ac.jp`
[2] Tokyo University of Technology, Hachioji-shi, Tokyo, Japan
`kushida@acm.org`

Abstract. Bluetooth Low Energy (BLE) is one of the technology for indoor positioning. The coordinates in indoor positioning are calculated from the radio signal strength, although distance errors occur between the measured and calculated positions. This paper proposes the method for selecting BLE beacons in multi-point positioning for distance error reduction. The proposed method consists of Learning and Calculation Phase. The correct values used in the proposed method are the values measured with the tape measure. The Learning Phase obtains features from the RSSI distribution of each beacon and uses them to compute the coordinates in the Calculation Phase. The Calculation Phase is used for navigation with an allowable distance error of 0.5 [m] based on a person's shoulder width. The proposed method calculates the typical value from the Learning Phase based on the probability that it fits within the distance error range of 0.5 [m]. The calculated position uses the logarithmic approximation to convert the beacon's radio signal strength to the distance. The experiment for measuring the distance error compares the proposed method calculated, the existing method calculated by two-dimensional three-point positioning, and the tape measure-based method. The number of combinations in three-point positioning was also changed to compare the accuracy. The mean distance error compared to the value measured with a tape measure was 1.337 [m] for the existing method and 0.449 [m] for the proposed method. The proposed method is 66.3% less distance error than the existing methods.

Keywords: Internet of Things · Bluetooth low energy · Indoor positioning · Multi-point positioning

1 Introduction

Bluetooth Low Energy (BLE) is one of the extensions to the Bluetooth specification. BLE beacons are popular in general because they are low cost, low power consumption, and ease of deployment [6]. The global indoor location market size is expected to grow from USD 7.0 billion in 2021 to USD 19.7 billion by 2026 [3]. However, BLE beacon technology is sensitive to radio waves from other devices

A. González-Vidal et al. (Eds.): GIoTS 2022, LNCS 13533, pp. 17–28, 2022.
https://doi.org/10.1007/978-3-031-20936-9_2

and causes distance errors in positioning because its frequency is based on 2.4 [GHz] radio band. The distance error is also caused by desks, chairs, and people. BLE provides several kinds of parameters related to location estimation and received radio signal strength indicator (RSSI). This paper focuses on RSSI, and accurate indoor location estimation requires RSSI converted to actual length.

The rest of this paper is organized as follows. Section 2 describes the related studies for improving the accuracy of indoor positioning using RSSI. Section 3 describes preliminary arrangements, the calculation of the coordinates, and the use-case scenario. Section 4 describes the software architecture created and the experiment method. Section 5 describes the evaluation. Section 6 describes the challenges of this study and analysis the proposed method. Section 7 concludes the paper with some final remarks.

2   Related Studies

Zixiang et al. proposed the fingerprinting method based on the RSSI ranking of BLE [5]. Their method used Kendall Tau Correlation Coefficient. The RSSI ranking was calculated by relating the radio wave location to multiple iBeacon devices placed in the store. The experimental results showed that mean of the distance error was 0.87 [m]. Their results were only done in one room. The architecture needs to be adaptable to multiple locations.

Zhu et al. proposed the method that combines RSSI-based offline learning with online positioning [4]. The offline learning used the classified linear approximation based on the log-normal distribution model. The propagation model of RSSI was learned to reduce the effect of different beacon locations on positioning accuracy. A Gaussian filter was designed for pre-processing the received signals. The online positioning utilized the weighted sliding window. The weighted sliding window was used for online positioning to reduce the variation of the real-time signal. The localization algorithm based on Taylor series expansion reduces the error of target coordinates by the ordinary least squares method. The results showed that the probability of positioning errors is less than 1.5 [m] was more than 80%. The indoor positioning method is known as PDR [1].

Thai-Mai et al. proposed an indoor positioning system using iBeacon and smartphone sensors [2]. The method estimated the initial position by converting RSSI to distance and using the median filter and triangulation method. The position determination utilized fingerprinting method. The results show that the error was less than 1.8 [m] with more than 90% probability.

This method needs improvement because it is not adaptable to each environment, and the error is more than 1 [m]. Indoor navigation in tight hallways requires that the distance error be less than 0.5 [m].

3   Proposed Method

This study aims to reduce the distance error compared to the existing method using three-point positioning of two-dimension. The proposed method is based on the probability of an RSSI value within the 0.5 [m] error range of the typical value per 1 min. The typical value in this paper is the statistically defined standard value in the ever-changing RSSI that can be converted to the distance. In addition, there are two major phases in the proposed method. The first phase obtains RSSI from each installed beacon, and the weights are calculated while selecting representative values from the frequency distribution. This paper defines the first phase as the "Learning Phase." The second phase is to select several optimal beacons within the range that can be detected by the IoT device and calculate the distance error with multi-point positioning. This paper defines the second phase as the "Calculation Phase."

Learning Phase

The Learning Phase calculates the weights by numericizing the differences between each beacon. The beacons have the same standard but different radio wave output strengths and the features are acquired by quantifying the difference. The process is handled in two ways. The first is to convert RSSI to distance using the logarithmic approximation formula. The second is to calculate the Confidence Level for beacon selection in multi-point positioning.

The first process is described in the following sentences. The logarithmic approximation calculates the distance between each beacon and the IoT device from the RSSI. The radio signal strength decays with a shape closer to convex than the Friis transmission formula. The actual distance in this paper is measured using a tape measure. The logarithmic approximation is shown in Fig. 1.

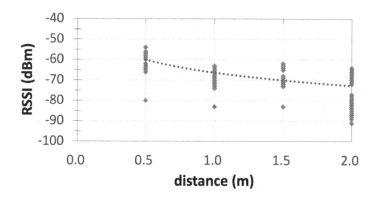

Fig. 1. Logarithmic approximation formula for pre-processing.

Figure 1 shows RSSI values on the y-axis and the distance between the beacon and the IoT device on the x-axis. The data is collected at four different distances from 0.5 [m] to 2 [m]. The device collects data about 400 times in 10 min at each distance. The polynomial for the conversion between RSSI and distance is based on the natural logarithm approximation. The Learning Phase calculates the coefficient of approx. 9.1 and the intercept of approx. −24.3 for $LN(x)$ in Fig. 1. The radio signal strength is decayed as the distance between the transmitter and receiver increases. The attenuation of the radio signal strength is approximated as the convex downward asymptote. Each beacon creates a different polynomial to convert the RSSI value to distance. The different polynomials reduce the distance error due to individual differences. The index for selecting beacons is called Confidence Level (CL) in the proposed method. CL is calculated from three processes. A summary of the three processes is shown in Fig. 2.

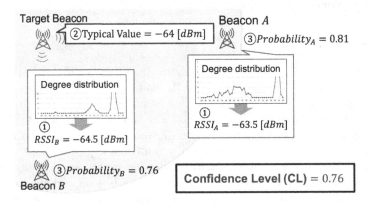

Fig. 2. Calculation of the Confidence Level.

The first (①) is to get RSSI at each beacon for a while and calculate the Typical Value. The Typical Value is calculated for all beacons, with the currently calculating beacon as the target beacon. The Typical Value of the i-th beacon in the proposed method is called $RSSI_i$. $RSSI_i$ is the mean of the maximum number of each split. Figure 3 shows the process of calculating the Typical Value from the frequency plot with the number of RSSI collections on the y-axis and the radio signal strength on the x-axis. The value is set to 1 if it increases, −1 if it decreases, and 0 if it is unchanged compared to the previous value.

$$\text{Typical Value} = ROUND\left(\frac{1}{beaconN}\sum_{i=1}^{beaconN} RSSI_i\right) \tag{1}$$

$$\text{Confidence Level (CL)} = MIN(Probability_A, Probability_B, ...) \tag{2}$$

$RSSI_i$ is the mean value of the $split_i$, including mode. The second (②) is to set the Typical Value for the target beacon by calculating the mean of $RSSI_i$. The number of beacons is $beaconN$, and the mean value of each beacon is $RSSI_i$. The Typical Value of the target beacon is described by the formula (1). The third (③) is that it calculates CL from the probability of receiving the Typical Value. CL is the percentage of the number of RSSI that fall within the specified range. The Calculation Phase is as follows. The RSSI value equal to 0.5 [m] is calculated based on the value of the Learning Phase. The proposed method uses the range of ±2 [dBm]. The number of RSSI in the range of ±2 [dBm] from the Typical Value is counted, and the overall percentage is calculated.

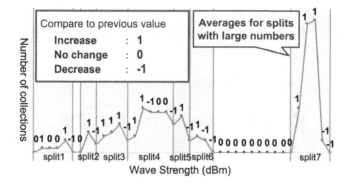

Fig. 3. Calculation of the Typical Value for each beacon.

CL is calculated for all placed beacons. CL is calculated for the beacons within the range of the correct RSSI to distance conversion among the placed beacons. The flow from ① to ③ of the proposed method is defined as the Learning Phase. Finally, the Learning Phase impacts RSSI as little as possible.

Calculation Phase

The proposed method selects beacons based on two parameters to calculate multi-point positioning. The first parameter is the measured value that is not changed easily based on the Learning Phase. The second parameter is close to an IoT device that receives radio signal strength.

The process has three steps. The first is to calculate the weights based on CL calculated in the Learning Phase and the distance between the beacon and the IoT device. The second is to select beacons based on the weights to calculate the coordinates of IoT devices by multi-point positioning. The third is to select the number of beacons with the minor distance error in the multi-point positioning.

The case of nine beacons is shown in Fig. 4. The radio signal strength of BLE becomes smaller as the distance between the IoT device and each beacon increases, and the value of RSSI becomes an evident change. CL and distance define the weights used for calculation in the proposed method.

The IoT device has a limited range that can convert the distance to RSSI. This range is shown by the circle centered on the IoT device. The limited range is the orange circle shown in Fig. 4, and the radius is defined as R. This radius R is calculated by converting the radio signal strength to distance based on the RSSI collected during the Learning Phase.

In this case, Beacon1, 6, and 8 are not used for multi-point positioning. The case of four-point positioning is shown in Fig. 5. The four-point positioning is calculated by selecting four beacons. Each beacon is sorted in descending order of weight (distance and CL). The number of beacons to be used is selected from three to six for increased weight in the case of Fig. 5.

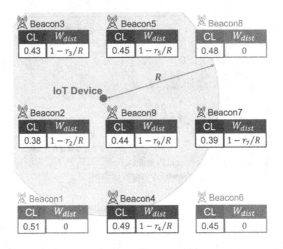

Fig. 4. Calculation of the weight for each beacon.

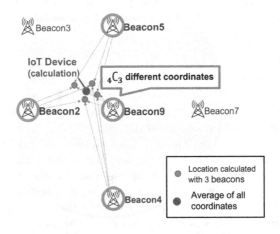

Fig. 5. Selecting beacons for multi-point positioning.

The result of coordinates at least needs three beacons to calculate, which means there is a $_nC_3$ combination of coordinates when running the mean of the calculation process. The four-point positioning calculates the mean of four different coordinates. The proposed method is based on three dimensions and assumes that the radio signal strength propagates spherically around three beacons. The IoT device user is assumed to be at the point of intersection with the sphere. An overview of the coordinate calculation is shown in Fig. 6.

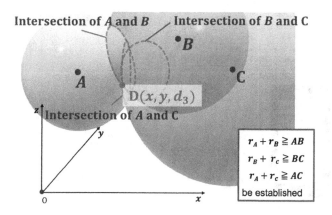

Fig. 6. Point of intersection with the three spheres.

A's x, y and z coordinate is a_1, a_2 and a_3. B's x, y and z coordinate is b_1, b_2 and b_3. C's x, y and z coordinate is c_1, c_2 and c_3. Formulas (3)-(5) show how to calculate the BLE beacons A, B, and C radius.

$$(x - a_1)^2 + (y - a_2)^2 + (z - a_3)^2 = r_A^2 \tag{3}$$

$$(x - b_1)^2 + (y - b_2)^2 + (z - b_3)^2 = r_B^2 \tag{4}$$

$$(x - c_1)^2 + (y - c_2)^2 + (z - c_3)^2 = r_C^2 \tag{5}$$

$$(2a_1 - 2b_1)x + (2a_2 - 2b_2)y + (2a_3 - 2b_3)z \\ = r_B^2 - r_A^2 + (a_1^2 + a_2^2 + a_3^2) - (b_1^2 + b_2^2 + b_3^2) \tag{6}$$

$$(2b_1 - 2c_1)x + (2b_2 - 2c_2)y + (2b_3 - 2c_3)z \\ = r_C^2 - r_B^2 + (b_1^2 + b_2^2 + b_3^2) - (c_1^2 + c_2^2 + c_3^2) \tag{7}$$

$$(2a_1 - 2c_1)x + (2a_2 - 2c_2)y + (2a_3 - 2c_3)z \\ = r_C^2 - r_A^2 + (a_1^2 + a_2^2 + a_3^2) - (c_1^2 + c_2^2 + c_3^2) \tag{8}$$

Formulas (6)–(8) show how to calculate the plan, including the intersection of the three spheres. The coordinate calculation uses two of the formulas (6)–(8). The variables become x and y by inserting the IoT device's z coordinate d_3.

Use-Case Scenario

The proposed method can be used for indoor navigation, such as shopping malls. The indoor navigation system determines the position in real-time. An image of the navigation system is shown in Fig. 7.

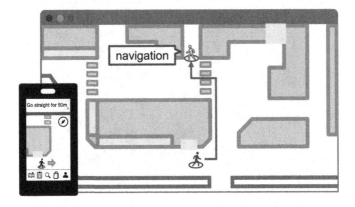

Fig. 7. Navigation in shopping malls using smartphone or browser.

The Use-case scenario of the proposed method requires two preconditions. The user carries around an IoT device such as a smartphone. The user can visually find his location on the map through the browser. The user uses the proposed method based on these two assumptions. The IoT device receives the radio wave from the beacon and acquires the radio signal strength. The radio signal strength is converted to RSSI and sent to the server. The server then converts the RSSI into the distance and calculates the coordinates on the map. Real-time indoor positioning can be achieved by repeating the proposed method.

4   Implementation and Experimentation

An overview of the implementation is shown in Fig. 8. The implementation of the proposed method has three major components.

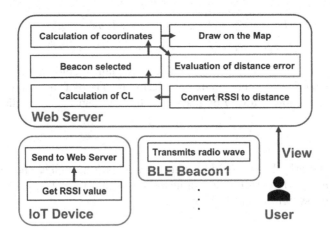

Fig. 8. Overview of software.

The first is the IoT device that obtains RSSI from the received radio wave and sends it to the Web Server. The software is implemented using the ESP32 equipped with MicroPython. The second is the BLE beacon which sends radio waves. The developed software is deployed in one IoT device and nine BLE beacons. The third is the Web Server that calculates the coordinates and shows them on the map. The web software is implemented on Python3 and Flask. The RSSI value sent by the ESP32 is received by the Flask software and stored in MongoDB. The RSSI is collected from MongoDB and converted to distance using the polynomial.

The experimental environment consisted of four tables and a center stand. Nine beacons transmitting radio waves and one receiving device are installed. The layout is shown in Fig. 9.

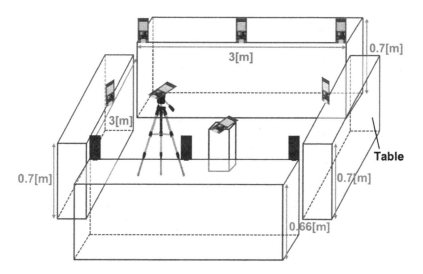

Fig. 9. Layout of the experimental environment.

The tables are at two different heights, 0.7 [m] and 0.66 [m]. The difference is used to check the three-dimensional calculation. Beacons are also placed in the center to check the effect of distance and radio signal strength.

5   Results and Evaluation

Figure 10 shows the distance error variation obtained at the four positions in the experiment. The location of the IoT device is at coordinates (1, 1), (1, 2), (2, 1), (2, 2) in Fig. 10. The graph shows the number of beacons used and the distance error. The results in Fig. 10 was 75% reproducible.

The ESP32 was placed, as shown in Fig. 9, and measurements were taken. The distance error calculations used 15622 records in the Learning Phase and at least 3000 records for each coordinate in the Calculation Phase. The evaluation method compares the distance error of the proposed method with existing methods.

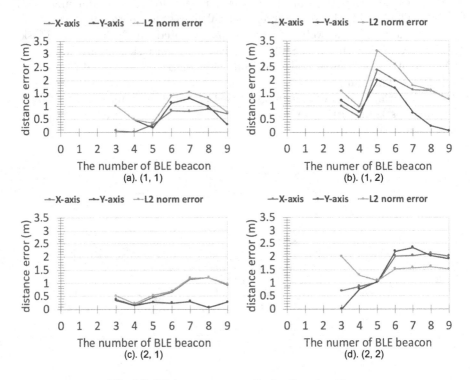

Fig. 10. Distance error results for four locations.

The comparisons are made between the three-point positioning of the proposed method, the existing three-point positioning using the Learning Phase, and the three-point positioning of the existing method. The proposed method has two phases: the Learning and Calculation phases. The proposed method is compared to existing methods to describe the most affected process. The error calculation method uses L2 norm error. The calculated coordinates and the actual position are defined as the points of the cuboid. The distance error can be calculated as the straight line linking the points. The existing method calculates the distance error using the Euclidean distance. The number of pieces with the bit of distance error changed at different acquisition times. The distance error due to the number of pieces decreased until the halfway point, and then it tended to increase again. The optimal number from Fig. 10 is 5 for (a), (d) and 4 for (b), (c). The optimal number of devices varies by location. This graph shows that three or nine pieces increase the distance error by three or more than the number of pieces with the smallest distance error. The optimum number of pieces needs to be found between four and eight. The existing method had a mean distance error of 1.337 [m], and the proposed method had a mean distance error of 0.449 [m]. The proposed method can reduce 66.3% of the distance error.

6   Discussions

Figure 10 shows the results obtained at 75% probability in the experiment. This means that there is 25% probability of obtaining a very different distance error, which needs to be reduced to a lower probability. Figure 11 showed the results when the experiment included a large number of outliers.

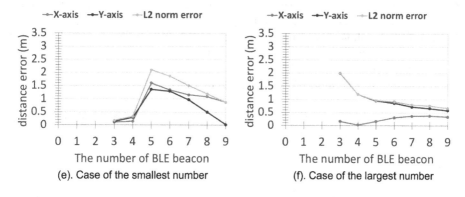

Fig. 11. Case with the large number of outliers.

The lowest distance error was calculated when the number of devices placed was the smallest in (e) and the largest in (f). The result in (e) is because the devices selected in the fourth and fifth cases contained a large number of outliers. The result in (f) is because the difference in RSSI distribution obtained in the Learning Phase and the Calculation Phase appeared.

The Learning Phase can be improved in a few ways to increase the probability of correct results. The leading cause of distance error for multi-point positioning is the conversion from RSSI to distance. The error should be as small as possible on converting from RSSI to distance. The Learning Phase requires obtaining accurate coefficients of logarithmic approximation based on the more number of RSSI values. The exact number of RSSI values is determined as the number of RSSI values increases, increasing the reproducibility of Fig. 10. The solution for improving accuracy in the Learning Phase is selecting the best splits among RSSI values. The proposed method selects splits that contain mode, although the acquired RSSI values include outliers. Selecting the correct splits without the outliers can reduce the distance error.

It can also improve the small allowance range used in the Learning Phase. The impact is small and is unlikely to include outliers. However, it is difficult to calculate the RSSI deviation due to radio wave interference. The proposed method uses the minimum value of the 0.5 [m] change (± 2 [dBm]) collected in the Learning Phase. The allowable RSSI range can be changed for more accurate CL calculations depending on the distance.

7 Conclusion

This paper focuses on reducing the distance error of indoor positioning using RSSI in BLE. The proposed method was defined by the Learning Phase and the Calculation Phase to reduce the distance error. The Learning Phase calculated the weights by numerically differentiating between each beacon. The Calculation Phase proposed the beacon selection method for multi-point positioning. The beacon selection method is based on the number of RSSI values obtained within the specified threshold range per unit of time. The paper examines the results between the existing methods and proposed methods. The mean distance error on the existing method was 1.337 [m], and the proposed method was 0.449 [m]. The proposed method reduces 66.3% of the distance error.

Acknowledgment. This work was supported by JSPS KAKENHI Grant Number JP20K11776.

References

1. Beauregard, S., Haas, H.: Pedestrian dead reckoning: a basis for personal positioning. In: Proceeding of the 3rd Workshop on Positioning, Navigation and Communication (2006)
2. Dinh, T.M.T., Duong, N.S., Sandrasegaran, K.: Smartphone-based indoor positioning using BLE iBeacon and reliable lightweight fingerprint map. IEEE Sens. J. **20**(17), 10283–10294 (2020)
3. Market, I.: Indoor location market by component (hardware, solutions, and services), technology (ble, uwb, Wi-Fi, rfid), application (emergency response management, remote monitoring), organization size, vertical, and region - global forecast to 2026. Marketsandmarkets.com (2021)
4. Jianyong, Z., Haiyong, L., Zili, C., Zhaohui, L.: RSSI based bluetooth low energy indoor positioning. In: 2014 International Conference on Indoor Positioning and Indoor Navigation (IPIN), pp. 526–533 (2014)
5. Ma, Z., Poslad, S., Bigham, J., Zhang, X., Men, L.: A BLE RSSI ranking based indoor positioning system for generic smartphones. In: 2017 Wireless Telecommunications Symposium (WTS), pp. 1–8 (2017)
6. Subhan, F., et al.: Experimental analysis of received signals strength in Bluetooth Low Energy (BLE) and its effect on distance and position estimation. Trans. Emerg. Telecommun. Technol. **33**, e3793 (2019)

Adaptive Data-Driven Routing for Edge-to-Cloud Continuum: A Content-Based Publish/Subscribe Approach

Ivan Čilić[✉] and Ivana Podnar Žarko[✉]

University of Zagreb Faculty of Electrical Engineering and Computing,
Zagreb, Croatia
{ivan.cilic,ivana.podnar}@fer.hr
https://www.fer.unizg.hr/en

Abstract. The concept of Edge-to-Cloud Continuum aims to significantly reduce overall traffic to the cloud by enabling IoT data processing as close as possible to the data sources, either on near- or far-edge devices. In this highly dynamic environment, where IoT devices and edge nodes are constantly changing their state and location, services running on edge nodes have to be scheduled, deployed and managed to ensure high service availability with appropriate Quality of Service (QoS) parameters. However, once services are deployed in the edge-to-cloud continuum, the question arises how to ensure continuous data delivery from IoT devices to the appropriate services for further processing, either on edge devices or in the cloud. In this paper, we propose a general architecture for adaptive data-driven routing in the edge-to-cloud continuum and introduce an implementation of this architecture using the content-based publish/subscribe approach. We evaluate the given implementation against a real-world use case scenario for federated learning in an edge-to-cloud environment hosting digital twins. The performance evaluation of this scenario shows that our implementation efficiently adapts to service failures and reconfigures the edge-to-cloud environment with minimal latency and without data loss, while preserving data privacy and security. In addition, the experiments show that our solution is stable in an environment with IoT data sources generating data at high frequency.

Keywords: Internet of Things · Edge computing · Data streaming · Publish/subscribe · Federated learning · Digital twin

1 Introduction

The majority of Internet of Things (IoT) data traffic is transmitted today over the Internet to cloud servers for processing/storage, causing network congestion and slowing down the overall processing cycle and responsiveness to events

This work has been supported by Croatian Science Foundation under the project IP-2019–04-1986.

detected in local smart environments. The concept of Edge-to-Cloud Continuum (ECC) aims to reverse this trend by enabling processing of IoT data as close as possible to the data sources, either on near- or far-edge devices, so that the overall traffic to the cloud is substantially reduced.

Devices are organized hierarchically into layers in the ECC, starting with IoT devices, i.e., resource-constrained devices hosting sensors/actuators, at the bottom layer. IoT devices are connected to neighboring gateway nodes and local devices in the far-edge layer. Far-edge nodes are in close proximity to IoT devices, either within the same local network or one hop away, and are also resource-constrained. Near-edge is the following ECC layer, consisting of more powerful compute nodes, e.g., a local micro-cloud with a few server racks, followed by the cloud at the top layer with virtually unlimited resources within data centers [2]. In this hierarchical multi-tier environment, each layer offloads the upper layer by taking over some of its functionalities, e.g., data processing or control over the entities of a lower layer. Compute nodes placed higher up in this hierarchy are assumed to be further away from IoT devices in terms of network distance, and are in general more powerful in terms of computational and network resources compared to devices at the lower layers [8]. Moreover, there is a possibility for edge nodes to connect to other nodes at the same layer so as to share the processing tasks and optimize the placement of services within a given layer. By extending the cloud with additional compute nodes in the ECC, cloud processing and storage capabilities are brought closer to the end devices. The ECC thus offers the following benefits to IoT solutions [12]: reduced overall Internet traffic, improved responsiveness and shorter processing cycles, enhanced security with privacy control, and lower operational costs.

In a highly dynamic edge-to-cloud environment where IoT devices and edge nodes are continuously changing their state and possibly also their location, the services running on the edge nodes have to be scheduled, deployed and managed to ensure high service availability with appropriate Quality of Service (QoS) parameters. In our previous work [19], we focused on QoS-aware orchestration of services for continuous optimal service placement on compute nodes within edge environments with volatile QoS parameters. However, once services are deployed in an ECC, the question arises on how to ensure continuous data delivery from IoT devices to the corresponding services running in the ECC, while taking into account the dynamic nature of the edge-to-cloud environment. Moreover, data-driven routing between compute nodes at different levels of the continuum hierarchy is required since, on the one hand, the processing output of one node becomes the input to another node, which is typically higher up in the hierarchy. On the other hand, the invocations of actuation functions or device reconfiguration events (e.g., updates of sensing frequency) are sent in the opposite direction down the hierarchy, and typically require high responsiveness to events.

In this paper, we focus on enabling *adaptive data-driven routing in the ECC* without incurring significant overhead to resource-constrained IoT devices and services deployed in the ECC. Our routing solution is based on the content-based publish/subscribe approach [1,6], which enables continuous data delivery from IoT devices (data producers) to services (data consumers) running in the ECC that express interest in receiving specific data. In addition, content-based publish/subscribe enables seamless reconfiguration of the ECC in the event of a compute node/service failure or service relocation without data loss. Our routing solution differs from standard publish/subscribe solutions by introducing a mechanism that allows data producers to influence who receives their data: We limit the number of data consumers for a given data producer and deliver data only to those consumers that meet the producer's QoS requirements.

Our contribution can be summarized as follows:

- We propose a general architecture for adaptive data-driven routing in the ECC to ensure continuous data delivery to IoT services requiring specific data for further processing, while maintaining high QoS for IoT devices and associated services.
- We present an implementation of the proposed architecture which employs the content-based publish/subscribe approach.
- We evaluate the given implementation through a real-world use case using federated learning in an edge-to-cloud environment hosting digital twins. Performance evaluation of the implemented adaptive data-driven routing solution for the edge-to-cloud continuum is performed in an emulated network environment using the Imunes network emulator [17]. Evaluation results demonstrate that our implementation efficiently reacts to dynamic changes of the edge-to-cloud continuum, including service failures, with low latency as the main QoS parameter, and without data loss while preserving data privacy and security. Moreover, the performance evaluation shows that our solution is stable in an environment with IoT data sources generating data with high frequency.

The paper is organized as follows. Section 2 provides an overview of related work in the field of data routing in ECC. Section 3 introduces the general architecture for adaptive data-driven routing in the ECC, and Sect. 4 presents the implementation of the architecture using the content-based publish/subscribe approach. Section 5 demonstrates how the presented implementation can be utilized in an IoT digital twin environment which applies federated learning, and Sect. 6 provides the evaluation results and QoS measurements from our implemented case study to demonstrate the benefits of our solution. Finally, Sect. 7 provides the conclusion and lists future work.

2 Related Work

The problem of service orchestration and placement in ECC is a well-known research topic [10,15,16]. However, the problem of continuous and efficient data routing in ECC, which comes into play once scheduling is performed, is still underexplored. We have identified only the following three papers in this field which are comparable to our solution. The importance of IoT data routing in ECC is highlighted in [8], which proposes a context-aware routing scheme that monitors the behavior of ECC nodes—whether they accept particular data or not—to decide whether to skip certain nodes in the ECC hierarchy and forward the data directly to nodes which typically accept it. The authors have a similar goal of reducing the communication latency. However, our solution is quite different, as the content-based publish/subscribe approach ensures that IoT data is delivered only to nodes that need it for further processing. This has the advantage of significantly reducing latency and overall communication traffic in the ECC, as routing is optimized for node- and service-specific processing tasks and resources. Routing can also be changed seamlessly and with a short delay to respond to changes in the ECC. Another relevant approach for routing of IoT data is presented in [5]. It uses Semantic Routing Trees (SRT) which allow a node to efficiently determine whether any of the nodes below it in the ECC hierarchy will participate in a given query over an attribute [11]. The authors propose a novel approach for parent node selection when building a SRT to reduce communication overhead. Their solution maintains a highly volatile network topology to optimize queries for specific IoT data. Our solution similarly enables data routing based on specific data attributes, with the main difference being that we use the publish/subscribe approach, unlike their solution based on ad hoc queries. Moreover, our solution can route the same data to multiple services, with an adaptive solution to select the top-K services based on specific QoS parameters, while their solution optimizes routing to a single data consumer. Pham et al. [13] propose a hierarchical publish/subscribe network for the ECC focused on latency-sensitive IoT applications. Their system delivers IoT data to interested subscribers using topic-based subscriptions that are propagated through publish/subscribe brokers under the coordination of a central system coordinator. To compare, our solution also utilizes the publish/subscribe mechanism to provide continuous data delivery without a direct connection between data producer and data consumer in a ECC. However, we propose a fully decentralized approach that does not require an external coordinator since all the routing information is shared among distributed nodes, while we allow a data producer to limit the number of consumers receiving data to save network bandwidth and processing power. Also, we support content-based subscriptions to provide a fully interoperable environment where a subscriber shows interest in specific data attributes and their value ranges.

3   Adaptive Data-Driven Routing Architecture for the ECC

One of the main challenges of edge computing is to constantly ensure high QoS of services deployed within the ECC, while lowering the communication and operational costs. Since compute nodes and IoT devices are part of a heterogeneous and dynamic environment, a routing mechanism is required to support continuous data delivery from IoT devices to services running in the ECC, while enabling real-time failure recovery and relocation of services. In this section we propose an adaptive data-driven routing architecture for the ECC and introduce its main building blocks.

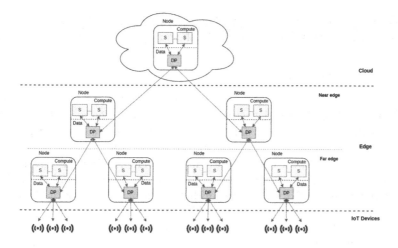

Fig. 1. Adaptive data-driven routing architecture for the edge-to-cloud continuum.

We propose the following four main building blocks of the adaptive data-driven routing architecture for the ECC, as shown in Fig. 1: 1) IoT device (D), 2) IoT service (S), 3) data proxy (DP), and 4) node (N).

An *IoT device* is a constrained device with limited resources (typically Class 1 device as classified in RFC 7228 [3]) that performs at least one of the following tasks: It may sense the environment to generate measurements/data, send the generated data to a compute node, or perform actuation functions. An IoT device is connected to the Internet through a gateway since it is a resource-constrained device requiring an additional compute node to receive and (pre)process the generated data or to make a decision about invoking an action to be performed by the actuator.

An *IoT service* is responsible for receiving data from IoT devices, data processing/storage, and sending of actuation commands to IoT devices. An IoT service is assigned either to IoT devices or IoT services from the underlying layer that can also generate output data for further processing up the ECC hierarchy. The IoT service must be autonomous, stateless, and portable to keep edge service migrations short and service availability high. The best technology for an easy-to-migrate service implementation is container virtualization because once a service is packaged, it can be easily migrated with reduced startup time compared to other methods. We use it in our implementation study.

A *data proxy* is the most important component in our system which delivers the data to the target services within the ECC or propagates messages to IoT devices. This component has to be autonomous and able to quickly adapt to changes in the dynamic edge-to-cloud environment. Its main functions are explained in the following two subsections.

A *node* is the compute node of the ECC which hosts services at a data layer and compute layer. The data layer is responsible for data routing and running a data proxy, while the compute layer is in charge of running IoT services. This node must be able to start a required service with short delay and can run on any available resource within the ECC: at the far edge, near edge or in the cloud.

3.1 ECC Topology Setup

A hierarchical network of data proxies is responsible for data routing between IoT devices and services which act as clients to DPs. There are two types of DP clients: data producers and data consumers. Data producers must provide a semantic description of the data they are producing, and data consumers must provide a description of the data they are interested in. A DP client is responsible to connect to the DP as either a data consumer or producer, and the DP will handle the data routing. IoT devices and IoT services act as both producers and consumers in this architecture. If an IoT device generates data that must be processed by an IoT service, it is a producer, and the IoT service is a consumer of data. However, an IoT service can act as a producer when it generates new data by processing received data, which is then forwarded to other services, or it can generate data in the form of an action to be performed by an IoT device, in which case the IoT device acts as a consumer.

Data proxies are interconnected in a hierarchical topology, as already shown in Fig. 1, where each DP has exactly one parent in the upper layer of the hierarchy. A parent DP is chosen based on the following criteria: network distance between the child and the parent DP; and the parent DP's load.

When a new node joins the network, it must first determine the layer in which it will operate. The cloud node is the first node to enter the network and must be statically configured. As a result, a new node can become either a far or near edge node. If the node is connected to the public network, it is designated as a near edge node. Otherwise, it acts as a far edge node. After determining its layer, the node queries the system for the nearest upper layer nodes to which it can connect. Then it examines the load of the identified nodes and chooses its parent, i.e., the node with the lowest number of connected child DP's, or the closest one in terms of network distance. If the node loses connection to its parent DP, the process is repeated.

Clients (IoT devices and services) begin connecting to the system once the ECC topology has been set up. To produce or consume data, clients, both producers and consumers, must connect to their DPs. IoT services use a simple DP discovery mechanism as they connect to the DP running on the same node. IoT devices use a DP discovery mechanism similar to the one used by nodes joining the network. First, an IoT device looks for a far edge node in its private network and, if one is found, connects to this DP. Otherwise, it retrieves the closest near edge nodes and chooses the node with the lowest load.

3.2 Data Routing Mechanism

The routing within the network of DPs is performed based on the parameters defined by a producer. When connecting to a DP, the producer becomes a data source and specifies the following:

- *data description*: semantic description of the data which will be produced.
- *consumer limit*: the maximum number of consumers allowed to receive the data.
- *QoS requirements*: the requirements that are taken into account when selecting an appropriate consumer or consumers for the producer's data, such as latency, throughput or security.

Algorithm 1. Initial routing setup

Require: *producer, dataDescription, consumerLimit, qos*
1: *consumers* ← *getInterestedConsumers(dataDescription)*
2: **if** *consumers.size ¿ 0* **then**
3:     *consumersSorted* ← *filterAndSortConsumersByQos(consumers, qos)*
4:     *producerConsumers* ← *markTopKConsumers(consumersSorted, consumerLimit)*
5:     *storeProducerConsumers(producer, producerConsumers)*
6:     **return** *activateProducer(producer)*
7: **end if**

Algorithm 1 defines the initial routing setup performed by a DP. When a producer provides a description of the data to its assigned DP, the DP propagates the description to all DPs in the system which compare the producer's description with the description of the data that their consumers are interested in and return interested consumers to the assigned DP. After that, the assigned DP filters and and sorts interested consumers based on the producer-defined QoS parameters. The consumer's approximate QoS level is calculated using the information received from other DPs or an external entity. For example, the number of network hops from the consumer to the producer can be used to estimate latency. After the consumers are sorted, the top-K consumers are selected as data destinations respecting the consumer limit, and the entire sorted list of consumers is also stored by the DP to quickly adapt to possible consumer failures/relocations within the ECC. Finally, if at least one consumer is selected as a data destination for the producer, the producer is activated and can begin sending data to the DP. Otherwise, there is no need to produce and route data through the ECC if there are no consumers requiring the data. Note that a special mechanism can be set up to start an adequate service for processing producer data in the ECC, but this mechanism is outside the scope of this paper as it relates to service orchestration and scheduling.

Algorithm 2 defines a procedure for a DP to route the received data to the top-K consumers. After retrieving the list of top-K consumers, the DP forwards the data to the consumer if it is directly connected to the DP or to the next DP on the shortest path to the consumer's DP. To reduce the overhead of computing the top-K consumers when new data is produced, the routing algorithm retrieves the list of previously computed top-K consumers for a given producer and forwards the data to them. If the desired QoS level for the producer is not achieved, the producer can re-trigger the setup procedure (Algorithm 1), which updates the list of top-K consumers. If a producer relocates and a new DP is assigned to the

---

Algorithm 2. Data routing

Require: $producer, data$

1: $topKConsumers \leftarrow getTopKProducerConsumers(producer)$
2: **for** $consumer \in topKConsumers$ **do**
3:    **if** $consumer.assignedDP == currentDP$ **then**
4:       $forwardData(data, consumer)$
5:    **else**
6:       $forwardData(data, getNextDP(consumer))$
7:    **end if**
8: **end for**

---

producer, another setup procedure is triggered on the newly assigned DP, and the data will be automatically re-routed to the new top-K consumers.

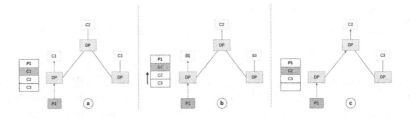

Fig. 2. Failure recovery mechanism.

One of the key requirements of the proposed architecture is failure recovery, which is illustrated in Fig. 2 where consumer limit is set to one. To ensure real-time failure recovery, as previously defined, producer's DP maintains a complete and sorted list of all consumers which are interested in data produced by producer P_1 and meet its QoS, as illustrated in Fig. 2.a, where the data from P_1 is forwarded through its DP to C_1. When a consumer fails or exits the system, e.g., C_1 as shown in Fig. 2.b, this information is propagated from the consumer's DP to the producer's DP (which is the same DP in Fig. 2.b). The unavailable consumer is removed from the DP's list of consumers maintained for P_1, and the next consumer in the list is marked as the selected consumer for consuming P_1's data. Subsequently, the produced data is forwarded by producer's DP to the DP on the path to the new consumer, as depicted in Fig. 2.c where P_1's DP forwards P_1's data to C_2's DP which delivers it to C_2 for processing/storage. Note that P_1 is unaware of the entire reconfiguration process which is performed by the network of DPs.

4   Content-Based Publish/Subscribe for Adaptive Data-Driven Routing

Publish/subscribe is a messaging pattern for continuous data delivery in distributed environments, where the data is delivered from data producers, *pub-*

lishers, to data consumers, *subscribers*, based on their subscriptions. Considering the key requirement of the proposed architecture, i.e. continuous data delivery to the target services which are dynamic, we concluded that the publish/subscribe mechanism is perfect for implementing adaptive data routing for the ECC, since no direct connection between a consumer and a producer of the data is required, and the data can be easily forwarded to a new consumer via publish/subscribe brokers in case of consumer failure or relocation. Content-based publish/subscribe is a type of publish/subscribe middleware where subscribers subscribe to the specific content, i.e., the specific attribute properties of the data events [6]. We chose this approach to implement the proposed architecture because we want to enable interoperable IoT environments where the same data can be consumed by various services in different domains, which is enabled by content-based subscriptions. Based on our previous research results [1,14] and the lack of existing publish/subscribe solutions with native support for both hierarchical topology and content-based subscriptions which limit the number of subscribers to top-K according to publisher preferences, we decided to implement our original content-based publish/subscribe solution in line with the requirements of adaptive data routing in the ECC.

Publish/subscribe solutions use three main entities which can easily be mapped to components in the proposed architecture: publisher, subscriber and broker. Publisher can be mapped to data producer, subscriber to data consumer and broker functionality is provided by data proxies. We use the the standard *publish-subscribe-notify* communication pattern enhanced with an *announce* message in our solution. A *data producer* performs all functionalities of a publisher in the proposed architecture. It can announce itself as a data source using the *announce* message which lists the data attributes that the producer will publish, consumer limit and QoS parameters. For example, in our use case we are minimizing latency and limiting the geographical area where the data may be consumed in line with privacy and security requirements of a data producer. The data is published by a *publish* message sent to its DP; the DP propagates the message further to relevant DPs and data consumers. A *data consumer* shows interest in specific attributes and their values using the *subscribe* message which is submitted to its DP. A *data proxy* integrates a publish/subscribe broker which is the key entity that routes all messages and published data to the target subscribers. Brokers residing within DPs form a hierarchical network topology following the rules defined for creating a DP network specified in Sect. 3.1.

The routing of messages in the network of DPs is performed in the following way. The DP receives subscribe messages from its consumers and holds them in the local storage. When a producer sends an *announce* message to start producing data, its DP forwards the message via broadcast to be delivered to all DPs in the system. Each DP, when receiving the *announce* message, checks if the announcement matches its local subscriptions and, if it does, the subscription is propagated to the source DP using the *subscribe* message. The source DP collects the subscriptions, filters them and sorts by the QoS requirements, and activates the producer. When the producer sends a *publish* message, its DP selects the top-K subscriptions from the the producer's list and forwards the data to the relevant consumers through the DP network using the *notify* message. If the desired QoS level of the destination service falls below a certain threshold for the producer or the producer has changed its location, the producer restarts the announcement process so that its DP can re-calculate the top-K subscriptions. Failure recovery is implemented in line with the example illustrated in Sect. 3.2. The assigned DP holds a list of subscriptions for the announcement of its producer. If one of the consumers disconnects from the network, all of its subscriptions are removed from the announcement subscriptions list and the next subscriptions move forward in the list. If one of the removed subscriptions is one of the top-K subscriptions, the next subscription in the list becomes the top-K subscription and a path from the producer towards the respective consumer is enabled within the network of DPs.

5   Case Study: Federated Learning for Digital Twins

Federated learning (FL) is a machine learning technique where a shared global model is trained on a set of distributed devices with the coordination of a central server [9]. Local devices, i.e. workers, train the model only on local data and forward local model updates to a central server for model aggregation, which increases security and privacy of the data set and reduces network traffic.

The motivating example for our case study is the work by Zhou et al. [18] which points out the necessity for load balancing and data scheduling between different FL clients. The solution identifies four control decisions: i) admission control - accepting or denying newly arrived data; ii) load balancing - distributing data to different edge nodes; iii) data scheduling - scheduling data for execution; iv) accuracy tuning - selecting accuracy for the local model computation. Our adaptive streaming solution can ensure continuous data delivery to FL clients and support admission control. Additionally, it can activate or deactivate data producers based on the needs of FL clients, and facilitate load balancing by routing data to the appropriate consumers selected based on consumer load. To highlight another important characteristic of our solution, *latency-aware routing*, in the case study we implement a digital twin solution based on FL which is modeled by Gupta et al. [7]. The authors propose a hierarchical FL model for smart healthcare where each patient is represented by a digital twin (DT). As patient data demands high privacy, the models are only trained on FL clients running on hospital servers, and only model updates are shared globally. Finally, patient DTs are updated after a global model update has been received.

In the case study shown in Fig. 3, IoT devices generate data which is sent to a service that maintains a digital twin (DT) for a device. The DT compares the received data with the digital representation of the device and takes action if the current reported state does not match the desired state of the device. The action to be taken is sent to the device. In addition, the DT service filters all outliers and sends the filtered data to its local model client (LMC) for training. When a sufficient data volume is received by the LMC, it performs training and sends

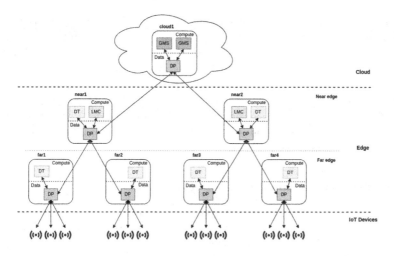

Fig. 3. Case study: digital with with FL.

local model updates to the global model server (GMS) running in the cloud for model aggregation. The GMS aggregates all model updates, combines them into a new model, and propagates the new model to all local clients. An LMC can also perform predictions based on the received data and can update a digital twin based on prediction results.

DT services are primarily placed on far edge nodes to minimize response latency, but they can also be placed on near edge nodes for redundancy, if far edge nodes fail. LMC's are placed on near edge nodes, while the GMS is placed in the cloud and replicated for redundancy. When a device connects to the network, it sends the announcement which contains the attributes of the data which will be generated, consumer limit set to one so that only one DT processes its data, and latency as the QoS parameter so that its DT service is chosen to act in the shortest time possible. DT services also serve as data sources for LMCs, and create announcements specifying the attributes of the data which will be sent after processing, set the consumer limit to one so that only one LMC performs the training on it, and limit the geographical area where the data can be consumed to increase privacy and security. Finally, LMC announces its attributes which relate to local model updates, doesn't set the consumer limit so the data will end up in all GMS nodes in the cloud for redundancy, and no QoS parameters are specified if there are no specific requirements for choosing a particular GMS node (they are replicas in our use case scenario).

6   Evaluation Study

Since the ECC environment is very dynamic and highly distributed, it is desirable to use a network simulation tool to simulate network delays and failures. For this purpose, we used the Imunes network emulator/simulator. Imunes is an integrated multiprotocol network emulator/simulator based on the FreeBSD and

Linux operating system kernel, partitioned into several lightweight virtual nodes that can be interconnected via kernel-level links to form arbitrarily complex network topologies [17]. Imunes is used to simulate network delays and failures between ECC nodes and devices which are emulated as Docker containers. The implemented topology follows the one shown in Fig. 3: It consists of one cloud node (*cloud1*), two near edge nodes (*near1*, *near2*), four far edge nodes (*far1*, *far2*, *far3*, *far4*) and four devices, one per each far edge node. The delay between the far and the near edge node is set to 10 ms and the delay between the near edge and cloud node is set to 50 ms.

6.1   Performance Evaluation Scenarios

Three scenarios are designed for the DT case study to demonstrate and test our routing solution. Scenario *S1* investigates the failure recovery mechanism by simulating DT service failures. The scenario starts at t_1 with a device, connected to node *far1*, generating data which is processed by the DT instance running also on *far1*. Then, at t_2, the DT instance is terminated and the traffic is re-routed to the DT instance running on the node *near1*. Finally, at t_3, the DT instance on the near edge node crashes and the data is re-routed to the backup DT running in the cloud.

Scenario *S2* demonstrates the ability of the ECC to quickly adapt to QoS changes. Similarly to scenario *S1*, a device connected to *far1* starts generating data at t_1 which is processed by the DT instance on *far1*. However, the instance fails at t_2 and the data is re-routed to a DT instance running on *cloud1*. Each DT instance is implemented so that it periodically sends receipt confirmation message back to a device which generated the data. This message is used by the device to determine the RTT between the device and a DT instance to check whether the QoS requirements are met. When RTT increases and reaches a value over 100 ms, the device triggers a re-routing procedure by sending a new *announce* message, as explained in Sect. 4. When the device starts the re-announcement process at t_3, a new DT instance is found on the node *near1* and the data is re-routed to this DT instance which meets the device's QoS requirements.

Scenario *S3* demonstrates the privacy-aware characteristic of our solution, as it is vital for any FL-based use case. To continuously ensure data privacy, a DT instance limits the geographical area where the data may be consumed by a LMC (*far1*, *far2*, *near1*). When *S3* starts at t_1, the DT running on *far1* is connected to the LMC on *near1*. The LMC instance fails at t_2, and even though there is another LMC instance on the node *near2*, the data is not delivered to this instance due to privacy restrictions, meaning that the instance is not in the allowed area. Finally, a new LMC instance is started at t_3 on *far2* which is in the allowed area, and the data is automatically re-routed to this instance.

6.2   Evaluation Results

Figure 4 shows the RTT between the device and DT for scenario *S1*. We can observe that after t_1 RTT is around 10 ms when the device is connected to the far edge node running its DT, while it increases to approx 35 ms after t_2 because the new DT instance is running on a near edge node. Finally, after reconfiguration at t_3, the RTT increases again as the new DT instance is running in the cloud.

Figure 5 shows the RTT between the device and DT for scenario *S2*. We can observe that after t_2 RTT increases significantly since the newly assigned DT instance is running in the cloud. As the device observes that the RTT is higher than its threshold of 100 ms, the device triggers a new announcement procedure at t_3 and the RTT decreases as the processing instance is running on the near edge node.

Figure 6 illustrates the RTT between the DT and LMC for scenario *S3*. The graph shows that after t_2 the data is not being sent to LMC as there is no LMC instance which meets the privacy requirement. Finally, at t_3, the data is again being sent and processed as a new instance has been found which meets the privacy requirements. All evaluation results show that re-routing introduces an overhead of approximately 30 ms which only affects the first message sent to the consumer. Considering the high generating frequency of the device, set at 10 ms, this overhead may be even lower at lower frequencies, as the system has more time to respond.

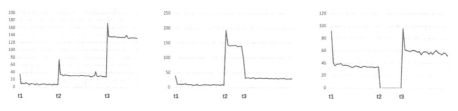

Fig. 4. Scenario *S1*.   **Fig. 5.** Scenario *S2*.   **Fig. 6.** Scenario *S3*.

7   Conclusion and Future Work

Once the services are deployed in the ECC, the question arises how to ensure continuous data delivery from IoT devices to the appropriate services for further processing, either on edge devices or in the cloud. In this paper, we proposed a general architecture for adaptive data-driven routing in the ECC and presented an implementation of this architecture using the content-based publish/subscribe approach that enables seamless reconfiguration of the ECC in case of a compute node/service failure or service relocation without data loss. Finally, we tested the implementation using a real-world use case with digital twins and FL, and the results have shown that our implementation efficiently responds to dynamic changes of the ECC.

Another key challenge for ECC is to ensure secure interactions within the environment considering its heterogeneity so in our future work we aim to design an appropriate authentication and access control mechanism for our routing solution. Furthermore, to provide a fully automated ECC environment, we intend to integrate our solution into an ECC orchestration platform, such as K3s [4], where our data proxy component will be used to provide continuous data routing between clients and services.

References

1. Antonić, A., Marjanović, M., Pripužić, K., Podnar Žarko, I.: A mobile crowd sensing ecosystem enabled by CUPUS: cloud-based publish/subscribe middleware for the Internet of Things. Futur. Gener. Comput. Syst. **56**, 607–622 (2016)
2. Arulraj, J., Chatterjee, A., Daglis, A., Dhekne, A., Ramachandran, U.: eCloud: a vision for the evolution of the edge-cloud continuum. Computer **54**(5), 24–33 (2021)
3. Bormann, C., Ersue, M., Keränen, A.: Terminology for Constrained-Node Networks. RFC 7228 (2014)
4. Cloud native computing foundation: K3s. https://k3s.io/
5. Giouroukis, D., Jestram, J., Zeuch, S., Markl, V.: Streaming data through the IoT via actor-based semantic routing trees. Open J. Internet Things **7**(1), 59–70 (2021)
6. Gupta, A.K., Sahin, O.D., Agrawal, D., Abbadi, A.E.: Meghdoot: content-based publish/subscribe over P2P networks. In: Middleware, pp. 254–273 (2004)
7. Gupta, D., Kayode, O., Bhatt, S., Gupta, M., Tosun, A.S.: Hierarchical federated learning based anomaly detection using digital twins for smart healthcare (2021)
8. Karagiannis, V., Frangoudis, P.A., Dustdar, S., Schulte, S.: Context-aware routing in fog computing systems. IEEE Trans. Cloud Comput. 1–1 (2021)
9. Konečný, J., McMahan, H.B., Yu, F.X., Richtárik, P., Suresh, A.T., Bacon, D.: Federated learning: strategies for improving communication efficiency (2016)
10. Krivic, P., Kusek, M., Cavrak, I., Skocir, P.: Dynamic scheduling of contextually categorised Internet of Things services in fog computing environment. Sensors **22**(2), 465 (2022)
11. Madden, S.R., Franklin, M.J., Hellerstein, J.M., Hong, W.: TinyDB: an acquisitional query processing system for sensor networks. ACM Trans. Database Syst. **30**(1), 122–173 (2005)
12. Openfog Consortium: OpenFog Reference Architecture for Fog Computing (2017)
13. Pham, V.N., Nguyen, V., Nguyen Tri, T., Huh, E.N.: Efficient edge-cloud publish/subscribe broker overlay networks to support latency-sensitive wide-scale IoT applications. Symmetry **12**(1), 3 (2019)
14. Podnar Žarko, I., Antonić, A., Marjanović, M., Pripužić, K., Skorin-Kapov, L.: The OpenIoT approach to sensor mobility with quality-driven data acquisition management. In: Podnar Žarko, I., Pripužić, K., Serrano, M. (eds.) Interoperability and Open-Source Solutions for the Internet of Things, pp. 46–61. Springer International Publishing, Cham (2015). https://doi.org/10.1007/978-3-319-16546-2_5
15. Salaht, F.A., Desprez, F., Lebre, A.: An overview of service placement problem in fog and edge computing. ACM Comput. Surv. **53**(3), 1–35 (2020)
16. Santos, J., Wauters, T., Volckaert, B., De Turck, F.: Resource provisioning in fog computing: From theory to practice †. Sensors **19**(10), 2238 (2019)
17. University of Zagreb: IMUNES. http://imunes.net/
18. Zhou, Z., Yang, S., Pu, L., Yu, S.: CEFL: online admission control, data scheduling, and accuracy tuning for cost-efficient federated learning across edge nodes. IEEE Internet Things J. **7**(10), 9341–9356 (2020)
19. Čilić, I., Podnar Žarko, I., Kušek, M.: Towards service orchestration for the cloud-to-thing continuum. In: 2021 6th International Conference on Smart and Sustainable Technologies (SpliTech), pp. 01–07 (2021)

Online Decentralized Frank-Wolfe: From Theoretical Bound to Applications in Smart-Building

Angan Mitra[1,3], Nguyen Kim Thang[2], Tuan-Anh Nguyen[1(✉)],
Denis Trystram[1], and Paul Youssef[1]

[1] University Grenoble-Alpes, Saint-Martin-d'hères, France
{tuan-anh.nguyen,paul.youssef}@inria.fr, denis.trystram@imag.fr
[2] IBISC, University of Evry, University Paris-Saclay, Evry-Courcouronnes, France
kimthang.nguyen@univ-evry.fr
[3] Qarnot Computing, Paris, France
angan.mitra@qarnot-computing.com

Abstract. The design of decentralized learning algorithms is important in the fast-growing world in which data are distributed over participants with limited local computation resources and communication. In this direction, we propose an online algorithm minimizing non-convex loss functions aggregated from individual data/models distributed over a network. We provide the theoretical performance guarantee of our algorithm and demonstrate its utility on a real life smart building.

1 Introduction

The popularity of sensors and IoT devices has the potential of generating and equivalently accumulating data in order of Zeta bytes [15] annually. High throughput, low latency, data consumption, networking dependencies are often the key metrics in designing high-performance learning algorithms under the constraint of low powered computing. In recent times, there has been an alternate trend to process data on cloud or dump into a centralized database. Commonly known as edge computing, the new paradigm embraces the idea of using interconnected computing nodes to reduce high bandwidth consuming data uploads, privacy preservation of data and knowledge on the fly.

Smart building applications typically have a profound implication on environment in terms of energy savings, reduction of green house emission, etc. Predicting the future often forms the basis of corrective actions taken by such apps and can be regarded as a predominant use-case of machine learning. Usually the data is generated across multiple zones from heterogeneous sensors and forms a setting of decentralized learning. In recent times, the hardware-software interface has benefited from advances in network communication coupled with edge

Supported by the Multidisciplinary Institute in Artificial Intelligence, Univ.Grenoble Alpes, France (ANR-19-P3IA-0003).

computing. Thus deploying a machine learning model in site and processing data on the fly has become a realistic alternative of sending data to a centralised data base. Optimizing problems to maintain robust solutions under the uncertainty of future is a nice to have feature for such cyber physical systems. Contrary to the classical train-test-deploy framework, online learning offers continual learning where during run time, a batch of sensor data has the potential to update an AI model on site.

This work aligns with the edge computing paradigm by proposing an online and decentralized learning algorithm. Online learning helps better adapt to the uncertainty of the future where the data pattern continually changes over time. The designed algorithm repeatedly chooses a high-performance strategy given a set of actions compared to the best-fixed action in hindsight. Instead of having a centralized mediator, the decentralized setting promotes peer-to-peer knowledge exchanges while prohibiting data sharing between learners. Many proposed online decentralized algorithms use gradient descent-based methods to solve constraint problems. Such an approach requires projection into the constraint set that usually involves intensive computation, which is not best suited in the context of sensors and IoT. We aim to design a competitive, robust algorithm in the decentralized and online setting that has the flexibility of being projection-free.

Problem Setting. Formally, we are given a convex set $\mathcal{K} \subseteq \mathbb{R}^d$ and a set of agents connected over a network represented by a graph $G = (V, E)$ where $n = |V|$ is the number of agents. At every time $1 \leq t \leq T$, each agent $i \in V$ can communicate with (and only with) its immediate neighbors, i.e., adjacent agents in G and takes a decision $\boldsymbol{x}_i^t \in \mathcal{K}$. Subsequently, a batch of new data is revealed exclusively to agent i and from its own batch, a non-convex cost function $f_i^t : \mathcal{K} \to \mathbb{R}$ is induced locally. Although each agent i observes only function f_i^t, agent i is interested in the cumulating cost $F^t(\cdot)$ where $F^t(\cdot) := \frac{1}{n} \sum_{j=1}^n f_j^t(\cdot)$. In particular, at time t, the cost of agent i with the its chosen $\boldsymbol{x}_i^t$ is $F^t(\boldsymbol{x}_i^t)$. The objective of each agent i is to minimize the total cumulating cost $\sum_{t=1}^T F^t(\boldsymbol{x}_i^t)$ via local communication with its immediate neighbors.

When the cost functions f_i^t are convex, a standard measure is the *regret* notion. An online algorithm is $R(T)$-*regret* if for every agent $1 \leq i \leq n$,

$$\frac{1}{T}\left(\sum_{t=1}^T F^t(\boldsymbol{x}_i^t) - \min_{o \in \mathcal{K}} \sum_{t=1}^T F^t(\boldsymbol{o})\right) \leq R(T)$$

As the cost functions in the paper are not necessarily convex, we consider a stationary measure on the quality of solution based on the Frank-Wolfe gap [11], and that can be considered the counter-part of the regret in the non-convex setting. Specifically, we aim to bound the *convergence gap*, for every agent $1 \leq i \leq n$:

$$\max_{o \in \mathcal{K}} \frac{1}{T} \sum_{t=1}^T \langle \nabla F^t(\boldsymbol{x}_i^t), \boldsymbol{x}_i^t - \boldsymbol{o} \rangle \tag{1}$$

In the same spirit as the regret, the measure of convergence gap compares the total cost of every agent to that of the best stationary point in hindsight. Note that when the functions F^t are convex, the convergence gap is always upper bounded by the regret. Moreover, when the problem becomes offline, i.e., all F^t are the same, the convergence gap measures the speed of convergence to a stationary solution.

1.1 Our Contribution

The challenge in designing robust and efficient algorithms for the problem is to resolve the following issues together: the uncertainty (online setting, agents observe their own loss functions only after choosing their decisions), the partial information (decentralized setting, agents know only its own loss functions while aiming to minimize the cumulating cost), and the non-convexity of the loss functions. As a starting point, we consider the Meta Frank-Wolfe (MFW) algorithm [3] in the (centralized, convex) online setting and the Decentralized Frank-Wolfe (DFW) algorithm [22] in the decentralized (offline) setting. However, these algorithms work either in the online setting or in the decentralized one but not both together. The difficulty in our problem, as mentioned earlier, is to resolve all issues together.

In the paper, we present algorithms, subtly built on MFW and DFW algorithms, that achieves the convergence gap of $O(T^{-1/2})$ and $O(T^{-1/4})$ in cases where the exact gradients or only stochastic gradients of loss functions are available, respectively. Note that in the former, the convergence gap of $O(T^{-1/2})$ asymptotically matches the best regret guarantee even in the centralized offline settings with convex functions. Besides, one can convert the algorithms to be projection-free by choosing appropriate oracles used in the algorithm. This property provides a flexibility to apply the algorithms to different settings depending on the computing capacity of local devices. Our work applies to online neural network optimization amongst a group of autonomous learners. We demonstrate the practical utility of our algorithm in a smart building application where zones mimic learners optimizing a temperature forecasting problem. We provide a thorough analysis of our algorithms in different angles of the performance guarantee (quality of solutions), the effects of network topology and decentralization, which are predictably explained by our theoretical results.

1.2 Related Work

Decentralized Online Optimization. Authors [24] introduced decentralized online projected subgradient descent and showed vanishing regret for convex and strongly convex functions. In contrast, Hosseini et al. [10] extended distributed dual averaging technique to the online setting using a general regularized projection for both unconstrained and constrained optimization. A distributed variant of online conditional gradient [8] was designed and analyzed in [26] that requires linear minimizers and uses exact gradients. However, computing exact gradients may be prohibitively expensive for moderately sized data and intractable when a closed-form does not exist. In this work, we go a step ahead in designing a distributed algorithm that uses stochastic gradient estimates and provides a better regret bound than in [26].

Learning on the Edge. Over the year, edge computing has become an exciting alternative for cloud-based learning by processing the data closer to end devices while ensuring data confidentiality and reducing transmission. [23] proposes a distributed framework for non-i.i.d data using multiple gradient descent-based algorithms to update local models and a dedicated edge unit for global aggregation. Another popular approach is to reduce the memory size of classical machine learning models to meet edge resource constraints. [20] and [18] similarly takes this idea by building a tree-based learning framework with a considerable reduction in memory using compression and pruning. At the same time, [6] introduce an edge-friendly version of k-nearest neighbor [5] by projecting the data into a lower-dimensional space. Besides traditional machine learning algorithms, adapting deep learning models to work on edge devices is an emerging research domain. In [4,14], the authors propose a pruning technique on convolutional network for faster computation while preserving the model ability. Another approach using weight quantization is proposed in [21]. The current dominant paradigm is federated learning [12,16], where offline centralized training is performed through a star network with multiple devices connected to a central server. However, decentralized training is more efficient than centralized one when operating on networks with low bandwidth or high latency [9,13]. In this paper, we go one step further by studying arbitrary communication networks without a central coordinator and the local data (so local cost functions) evolve.

Thermal Profiling a Building. Usually, building monitoring sensors are distributed across a building and thus acts as a scattered data lake with potentially heterogeneous patterns. Indoor temperature is an important factor in controlling Heating Ventilation Air Conditioning systems that maintain ambient comfort within a building [7]. Typically such embedded systems run in anticipatory mode where temperature prediction [2] of controlled building zones helps in maintaining thermal consistency. A multitude of factors effect the thermal profile like outdoor environment, opening/closing of windows, number of occupants, etc, which are hard to get and often rely on intrusive mechanisms to gather the data. Researchers have utilized deep learning models [25] in the context of online learning of temperature, but lack the benefit of interacting with multiple similar sensors. This study seeks to generate a thermal profile of a building by only utilizing temperature data from multiple zones of a building in order to extract patterns about thermal variation. The proposed methodology not only processes data on the fly [1], but also identifies meaningful topological data exchange networks that can best predict multi zonal temperature settings.

2   Conditional Gradient Based Algorithm

In this section, after introducing and recalling useful notions, we will first provide an algorithm for the setting with exact gradients. Subsequently, building on the salient ideas of that algorithm, we extend to the more realistic setting with stochastic gradients.

2.1   Preliminaries and Notations

Given an undirected graph $G = (V, E)$, the set of neighbors of an agent $i \in V$ is $N(i) := \{j \in V : (i, j) \in E\}$. Consider a symmetric matrix $W \in \mathbb{R}_+^{n \times n}$ defined as follows. The entry W_{ij} has a value of

$$
W_{ij} = \begin{cases} \dfrac{1}{1 + \max\{d_i, d_j\}} & \text{if } (i, j) \in E \\ 0 & \text{if } (i, j) \notin E, i \neq j \\ 1 - \sum_{j \in N(i)} W_{ij} & \text{if } i = j \end{cases}
$$

where $d_i = |N(i)|$, the degree of vertex i. In fact, the matrix W is doubly stochastic, i.e $W\mathbf{1} = W^T\mathbf{1} = \mathbf{1}$ and so it inherits several useful properties of doubly stochastic matrices. We use boldface letter e.g. x to represent vectors. We denote x_i^t as the decision vector of agent i at time step t. We suppose that the constraint set $\mathcal{K}$ is a bounded convex set with diameters $D = \sup_{x,y \in \mathcal{K}} \|x - y\|$.

A function f is β-*smooth* if for all $x, y \in \mathcal{K}$:

$$
f(y) \leq f(x) + \langle \nabla f(x), y - x \rangle + \frac{\beta}{2}\|y - x\|^2
$$

or equivalently $\|\nabla f(x) - \nabla f(y)\| \leq \beta\|x - y\|$. Also, we say a function f is G-*Lipschitz* if for all $x, y \in \mathcal{K}$

$$
\|f(x) - f(y)\| \leq G\|x - y\|
$$

In our algorithm, we make use of linear optimization oracles where its role is to resolve an online linear optimization problem given a feedback function and a constraint set. Specifically, in the online linear optimization problem, at every time $1 \leq t \leq T$, one has to select $u^t \in \mathcal{K}$. Subsequently, the adversary reveals a vector d^t and feedbacks the cost function $\langle \cdot, d^t \rangle$. The objective is to minimize the regret, i.e., $\frac{1}{T}\left(\sum_{t=1}^T \langle u^t, d^t \rangle - \min_{u^* \in \mathcal{K}} \sum_{t=1}^T \langle u^*, d^t \rangle\right)$. Several algorithms [8] provide an optimal regret bound of $\mathcal{R}^T = O(1/\sqrt{T})$ for the online linear optimization problem. These algorithms include the online gradient descent algorithm or the follow-the-perturbed-leader algorithm (projection-free). One can pick one of such algorithms to be an oracle resolving the online linear optimization problem.

2.2   An Algorithm with Exact Gradients

Assume that the exact gradients of the loss functions f_i^t are available (or can be computed). The high-level idea of the algorithm is the following. In the algorithm, at every time t, each agent i executes L steps of the Frank-Wolfe algorithm where every update vector (for iterations $1 \leq \ell \leq L$ where the parameter L will be chosen later) is constructed by combining the outputs of linear optimization oracles $\mathcal{O}_{j,\ell}$ and the current vectors of its neighbors $j \in N(i)$. During this execution, a set of feasible solutions $\{x_{i,\ell}^t : 1 \leq \ell \leq L\}$ is computed. The solution x_i^t for each agent $1 \leq i \leq n$ is then chosen uniformly at random among $\{x_{i,\ell}^t : 1 \leq \ell \leq L\}$. Subsequently, after communicating and aggregating the information related to functions f_j^t for $j \in N(i)$, the algorithm computes a vector $d_{i,\ell}^t$ and feedbacks $\langle d_{i,\ell}^t, \cdot \rangle$ as the cost function at time t to the oracle $\mathcal{O}_{i,\ell}$ for $1 \leq \ell \leq L$. The vectors $d_{i,\ell}^t$'s are subtly built so that it captures step-by-step more and more information on the cumulating cost functions. The formal description is given in Algorithm 1 and a detailed proof of Theorem 1 is given in [17]

Algorithm 1. Online Decentralized algorithm

Input: A convex set $\mathcal{K}$, a time horizon T, a parameter L, online linear optimization oracles $\mathcal{O}_{i,1}, \ldots, \mathcal{O}_{i,L}$ for each agent $1 \leq i \leq n$, step sizes $\eta_\ell \in (0,1)$ for all $1 \leq \ell \leq L$

1: **for** $t = 1$ to T **do**
2:    **for** every agent $1 \leq i \leq n$ **do**
3:       Initialize arbitrarily $x_{i,1}^t \in \mathcal{K}$
4:       **for** $1 \leq \ell \leq L$ **do**
5:          Let $v_{i,\ell}^t$ be the output of oracle $\mathcal{O}_{i,\ell}$ at time step t.
6:          Send $x_{i,\ell}^t$ to all neighbours $N(i)$
7:          Once receiving $x_{j,\ell}^t$ from all neighbours $j \in N(i)$, set $y_{i,\ell}^t \leftarrow \sum_j W_{ij} x_{j,\ell}^t$.
8:          Compute $x_{i,\ell+1}^t \leftarrow (1 - \eta_\ell) y_{i,\ell}^t + \eta_\ell v_{i,\ell}^t$.
9:       **end for**
10:       Choose $x_i^t \leftarrow x_{i,\ell}^t$ for $1 \leq \ell \leq L$ with probability $\frac{1}{L}$ and play x_i^t
11:       Receive function f_i^t
12:       Set $g_{i,1}^t \leftarrow \nabla f_i^t(x_{i,1}^t)$
13:       **for** $1 \leq \ell \leq L$ **do**
14:          Send $g_{i,\ell}^t$ to all neighbours $N(i)$.
15:          After receiving $g_{j,\ell}^t$ from all neighbours $j \in N(i)$, compute $d_{i,\ell}^t \leftarrow \sum_{j \in N(i)} W_{ij} g_{j,\ell}^t$ and $g_{i,\ell+1}^t \leftarrow \left(\nabla f_i^t(x_{i,\ell+1}^t) - \nabla f_i^t(x_{i,\ell}^t) \right) + d_{i,\ell}^t$.
16:          Feedback function $\langle d_{i,\ell}^t, \cdot \rangle$ to oracles $\mathcal{O}_{i,\ell}$. (The cost of the oracle $\mathcal{O}_{i,\ell}$ at time t is $\langle d_{i,\ell}^t, v_{i,\ell}^t \rangle$.)
17:       **end for**
18:    **end for**
19: **end for**

Theorem 1. *Let $\mathcal{K}$ be a convex set with diameter D. Assume that functions F^t (possibly non convex) are β-smooth and G-Lipschitz for every $1 \leq t \leq T$. Then, by choosing the step size $\eta_\ell = \min\left(1, \frac{A}{\ell^\alpha}\right)$ for some $A \geq 0$ and $\alpha \in (0,1)$, Algorithm 1 guarantees that for all $1 \leq i \leq n$:*

$$\max_{o \in \mathcal{K}} \frac{1}{T} \sum_{t=1}^{T} \mathbb{E}_{\boldsymbol{x}_i^t}\left[\langle \nabla F^t(\boldsymbol{x}_i^t), \boldsymbol{x}_i^t - o \rangle\right] \leq O\left(\frac{GDA^{-1}}{L^{1-\alpha}} + \frac{AD^2\beta/2}{L^\alpha(1-\alpha)} + \mathcal{R}^T\right)$$

where $\mathcal{R}^T$ is the regret of online linear minimization oracles. Choosing $L = T$, $\alpha = 1/2$ and oracles as gradient descent or follow-the-perturbed-leader with regret $\mathcal{R}^T = O\left(T^{-1/2}\right)$, we obtain the gap convergence rate of $O\left(T^{-1/2}\right)$.

2.3   Algorithm with Stochastic Gradients

We extend the previous algorithm to the setting of stochastic gradients estimates. As only stochastic gradient estimates are available, we use a variance reduction technique in order to upgrade Algorithm 1 to its stochastic version (Algorithm 2). The difference between the two algorithms is stochastic gradient estimation and an additional step for variance reduction. After making the decision, the agent receives an unbiased gradient to perform updates and communication to obtain stochastic estimates $\widetilde{\boldsymbol{g}}_{i,\ell}^t$ and $\widetilde{\boldsymbol{d}}_{i,\ell}^t$ of $\boldsymbol{g}_{i,\ell}^t$ and $\boldsymbol{d}_{i,\ell}^t$, respectively. (Note that the stochastic variables are denoted by the same letter as its exact counterpart with an additional tilde symbol.) Then the agent uses Step 17 in Algorithm 2 to get the reduced variance version $\widetilde{\boldsymbol{a}}_{i,\ell}^t$ of $\widetilde{\boldsymbol{d}}_{i,\ell}^t$. The function $\langle \widetilde{\boldsymbol{a}}_{i,\ell}^t, \cdot \rangle$ is then feedbacked to the oracle.

The formal description is given in Algorithm 2 in which all previous steps are the same as Algorithm 1 and the additional variance reduction step is marked in red. A detailed proof of Theorem 2 can be found in [17].

Algorithm 2. Stochastic online decentralized algorithm

. . .

12: Receive function f_i^t and an unbiased gradient estimate $\widetilde{\nabla} f_i^t$
13: Set $\widetilde{\boldsymbol{g}}_{i,1}^t \leftarrow \widetilde{\nabla} f_i^t(\boldsymbol{x}_{i,1}^t)$
14: **for** $1 \leq \ell \leq L$ **do**
15:     Send $\widetilde{\boldsymbol{g}}_{i,\ell}^t$ to all neighbours $N(i)$.
16:     After receiving $\widetilde{\boldsymbol{g}}_{j,\ell}^t$ from $j \in N(i)$, compute $\widetilde{\boldsymbol{d}}_{i,\ell}^t \leftarrow \sum_{j \in N(i)} W_{ij} \widetilde{\boldsymbol{g}}_{j,\ell}^t$ and set $\widetilde{\boldsymbol{g}}_{i,\ell+1}^t \leftarrow \left(\widetilde{\nabla} f_i^t(\boldsymbol{x}_{i,\ell+1}^t) - \widetilde{\nabla} f_i^t(\boldsymbol{x}_{i,\ell}^t)\right) + \widetilde{\boldsymbol{d}}_{i,\ell}^t$.
17:     $\widetilde{\boldsymbol{a}}_{i,\ell}^t \leftarrow (1 - \rho_\ell) \cdot \widetilde{\boldsymbol{a}}_{i,\ell-1}^t + \rho_\ell \cdot \widetilde{\boldsymbol{d}}_{i,\ell}^t$.
18:     Feedback function $\langle \widetilde{\boldsymbol{a}}_{i,\ell}^t, \cdot \rangle$ to oracles $\mathcal{O}_{i,\ell}$. (The cost of the oracle $\mathcal{O}_{i,\ell}$ at time t is $\langle \widetilde{\boldsymbol{a}}_{i,\ell}^t, \boldsymbol{v}_{i,\ell}^t \rangle$.)
19: **end for**

Theorem 2. *Let $\mathcal{K}$ be a convex set with diameter D. Assume that for every $1 \leq t \leq T$.*

1. *functions f_i^t are β-smooth and G-Lipschitz,*
2. *the gradient estimates are unbiased with bounded variance σ^2,*
3. *the gradient estimates are Lipschitz.*

Then, choosing the step-sizes $\eta_\ell = \min\{1, \frac{A}{\ell^{3/4}}\}$ for some $A \geq 0$, we have for all $1 \leq i \leq n$,

$$\max_{o \in \mathcal{K}} \mathbb{E}\Big[\frac{1}{T}\sum_{t=1}^{T}\mathbb{E}_{\boldsymbol{x}_i^t}\left[\langle \nabla F_t\left(\boldsymbol{x}_i^t\right), \boldsymbol{x}_i^t - o\rangle\right]\Big] \leq O\left(\frac{DG + 2ADQ^{1/2}}{L^{1/4}} + \frac{2AD^2\beta}{L^{3/4}} + \mathcal{R}^T\right)$$

Choosing $L = T$ and oracles with regret $\mathcal{R}^T = O\left(T^{-1/2}\right)$, we obtain the convergence gap of $O\left(T^{-1/4}\right)$.

3   Experiments

The data-set used for experimentation comes from a 7 storey building with 24 sensor equipped zones [19]. The zone-wise knowledge exchange happens through the edges of an undirected graph of n nodes participating in the learning process. For every round t, each node i receives a batch $\mathcal{B}_i^t$ of 32 time-series sequences corresponding to a look-back period 13 timestep to predict the temperature of the next timestep. We extract the data from March 7th to April 20th for training, set L equal to 360, $\alpha = 0.95$ and $A = 1$. A min-max scaler is used to normalize the data and we apply a rolling window with stride 1 on the original time series. Each node is embedded with a model built from a two-layers long-short-time-memory (LSTM) network followed by a fully connected layer. Denote the output of the model i for a data sequence b at time t by $\hat{y}_{i,b}^t$ and its ground truth by $y_{i,b}^t$. Consider the ℓ_1 loss as the objective function:

$$\mathcal{L}(\hat{y}_{i,b}^t, y_{i,b}^t) = \begin{cases} \dfrac{(\hat{y}_{i,b}^t - y_{i,b}^t)^2}{2} & \text{if } |\hat{y}_{i,b}^t - y_{i,b}^t| \leq 1 \\ |\hat{y}_{i,b}^t - y_{i,b}^t| - \frac{1}{2} & \text{otherwise.} \end{cases}$$

Consider the constraint set $\mathcal{K} = \{\boldsymbol{x} \in \mathbb{R}^d, \|\boldsymbol{x}\|_1 \leq r\}$, where $\boldsymbol{x}$ is the model's weight, d its dimension and $r = 1$. The (normalized) loss incurred by the data of agent i is $\frac{1}{|\mathcal{B}_i^t|}\sum_{b \in \mathcal{B}_i^t} \mathcal{L}(\hat{y}_{i,b}^t, y_{i,b}^t)$. The global loss function incurred by the overall data is

$$F^t(\boldsymbol{x}) = \frac{1}{|\cup_{i=1}^n \mathcal{B}_i^t|} \sum_{b \in \cup_{i=1}^n \mathcal{B}_i^t} \mathcal{L}(\hat{y}_{i,b}^t, y_{i,b}^t),$$

that can be written as $F^t(\boldsymbol{x}) = \frac{1}{n}\sum_{i=1}^n f_i^t(\boldsymbol{x})$ where $f_i^t(\boldsymbol{x}) = \frac{1}{|\mathcal{B}_i^t|}\sum_{b \in \mathcal{B}_i^t} \mathcal{L}(\hat{y}_{i,b}^t, y_{i,b}^t)$. Note that the non-convexity here is due to the non-convexity of $\hat{y}_{i,b}^t$ as a function of $\boldsymbol{x}_i^t$. In the following section, if not specify otherwise, we call *loss* the temporal average of the global loss function F^t defined as $\frac{1}{T}\sum_{t=1}^T F^t$.

3.1   Prediction Performance

Figures 1a and 1b show the loss and gap values for different network sizes. The implementation justifies our theoretical results about the convergence of the gap. Besides, we also observe the convergence of loss value, an expected implication of the gap convergence. We set M the number of prediction points between the 21st and 24th of April and n the number of zones within one configuration. We use the mean absolute error (MAE $= \frac{1}{nM} \sum_{i=1}^{n} \sum_{m=1}^{M} |\hat{y}_{i,m} - y_{i,m}|$) and mean square error (MSE $= \frac{1}{nM} \sum_{i=1}^{n} \sum_{m=1}^{M} (\hat{y}_{i,m} - y_{i,m})^2$) as a measure between the prediction and the ground truth. We observe that increasing nodes in a network does not always lead to better online performance. In-fact, a 7 node configuration achieves the lowest MSE (0.65) and MAE (0.78) for floors 6 and 7. We see a 40 % drop in MSE and 20 % reduction in MAE for floor 6 zonal models when 3 extra peers from floor 7 joined the group. We observe 19 % and 25 % increase in MSE and MAE values by adding zonal nodes from floor 7 to a 10 node group. This can be best argued by the fact that the top floor of a building has a non identical thermal variation with the rest of the storeys.

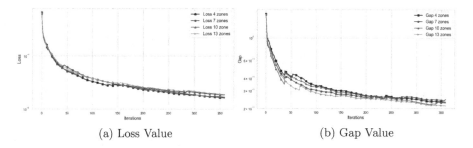

| (a) Loss Value | (b) Gap Value |

Fig. 1. Loss and Gap values of different network size on complete topology *(Plot on log-scale)*

3.2   Effect of Network Topology

We study the effect of topology in learning for a 7 node configuration with a complete, cycle and line graph containing 28, 7 and 6 edges respectively and with 13 nodes having 78,13 and 12 edges respectively. For both 7 (Table 1a) and 13 (Table 1b) node configurations, we observe that the complete graph yields the least amount of prediction error, mean absolute error $\in [0.66, 1.3]°C$. However we note the peculiarity that the line graph can perform better than a cycle graph and has roughly a 10% error margin compared to the complete configuration.

3.3   Effect of Decentralization

We are interested in understanding the role of decentralization in terms of accuracy of zonal learners. Let $L_{MFW}(t)$ be the loss from Meta Frank Wolfe

Table 1. Temperature forecasting performances on different network topologies

Topology	Metric	Mean	Var	Max	Min
Cycle	MAE	1.09	0.48	1.80	0.56
Cycle	MSE	0.78	0.21	1.09	0.52
Complete	MAE	**0.77**	**0.38**	**1.47**	0.27
Complete	MSE	**0.64**	**0.20**	**1.04**	0.39
Line	MAE	0.81	0.53	1.95	**0.24**
Line	MSE	0.66	0.28	1.26	**0.34**

(a) Impact of Topology on 7 learners configuration.

Topology	Metric	Mean	Var	Max	Min
Cycle	MAE	1.51	1.46	6.16	0.36
Cycle	MSE	0.94	0.38	1.90	0.48
Complete	MAE	**1.26**	**0.82**	3.64	**0.32**
Complete	MSE	**0.85**	**0.27**	1.50	**0.42**
Line	MAE	1.38	0.91	3.17	0.50
Line	MSE	0.90	0.35	**1.66**	0.49

(b) Impact of Topology on 13 learners configuration.

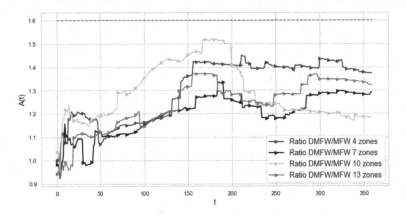

Fig. 2. Loss ratio of decentralized and centralized Meta Frank-Wolfe on different network size.

(MFW) at time t. The approximation ratio $A(t) = \frac{L_{DMFW}(t)}{L_{MFW}(t)}$ at time t represents how worse is our decentralized version compared to a centralized optimization. $A(t) \leq B_{max}$ will mean our algorithm performs no worse than B_{max} times of the MFW. On Fig. 2, we plot the ratio $A(t)$ for a 13 node network and show that $A(t) \leq 1.4$. The 7 node network has the closest approximation bounded by 1.35 which can be explained by earlier insights on performance accuracy. We notice that the 10 node network performs worse till $t = 200$ and after $t \geq 250$ or 21 h, the approximation ratio becomes close to centralised version with less than 20% error.

4   Concluding Remarks

We proposed an online algorithm minimizing non-convex loss functions aggregated from local data distributed over a network. We showed the bounds of the convergence gap in both exact and stochastic gradient settings. In complement to the theoretical analysis, we run experiments on a real-life smart building dataset. The results make our offerings valuable for learning in distributed settings.

References

1. Abdel-Aziz, H., Koutsoukos, X.: Data-driven online learning and reachability analysis of stochastic hybrid systems for smart buildings. Cyber Phys. Syst. **5**(1), 41–64 (2019)
2. Cai, M., Pipattanasomporn, M., Rahman, S.: Day-ahead building-level load forecasts using deep learning vs. traditional time-series techniques. Appl. Energy **236**, 1078–1088 (2019)
3. Chen, L., Hassani, H., Karbasi, A.: Online continuous submodular maximization. In: Proceedings 21st International Conference on Artificial Intelligence and Statistics (AISTAT) (2018)
4. Chiliang, Z., Tao, H., Yingda, G., Zuochang, Y.: Accelerating convolutional neural networks with dynamic channel pruning. In: 2019 Data Compression Conference (DCC), p. 563 (2019)
5. Cover, T.M., Hart, P.E.: Nearest neighbor pattern classification. IEEE Trans. Inf. Theory **13**(1), 21–27 (1967)
6. Gupta, C., et al.: ProtoNN: Compressed and accurate kNN for resource-scarce devices. In: Precup, D., Teh, Y.W. (eds.) Proceedings of the 34th International Conference on Machine Learning. Proceedings of Machine Learning Research, vol. 70, pp. 1331–1340. PMLR (2017)
7. Gupta, S.K., Kar, K., Mishra, S., Wen, J.T.: Distributed consensus algorithms for collaborative temperature control in smart buildings. In: 2015 American Control Conference (ACC), pp. 5758–5763. IEEE (2015)
8. Hazan, E.: Introduction to online convex optimization. Found. Trends Optim. **2**(3–4), 157–325 (2016)
9. He, L., Bian, A., Jaggi, M.: Cola: decentralized linear learning. In: Advances in Neural Information Processing Systems, pp. 4536–4546 (2018)
10. Hosseini, S., Chapman, A., Mesbahi, M.: Online distributed optimization via dual averaging. In: 52nd IEEE Conference on Decision and Control, pp. 1484–1489 (2013)
11. Jaggi, M.: Revisiting Frank-Wolfe: projection-free sparse convex optimization. In: Proceedings of the 30th International Conference on Machine Learning (2013)
12. Kairouz, P., McMahan, H.B., Avent, B., Bellet, A., et al.: Advances and Open Problems in Federated Learning. Foundations and Trends® in Machine Learning **14**(1), (2021)
13. Lian, X., Zhang, C., Zhang, H., Hsieh, C.J., Zhang, W., Liu, J.: Can decentralized algorithms outperform centralized algorithms? A case study for decentralized parallel stochastic gradient descent. In: Advances in Neural Information Processing Systems, pp. 5330–5340 (2017)
14. Lin, J., Rao, Y., Lu, J., Zhou, J.: Runtime neural pruning. In: Guyon, I., et al. (eds.) Advances in Neural Information Processing Systems, vol. 30. Curran Associates, Inc. (2017)
15. MacCarthy, M.: In defense of big data analytics. The Cambridge Handbook of Consumer Privacy, pp. 47–78 (2018)
16. McMahan, B., Ramage, D.: Collaborative machine learning without centralized training data. Google Research Blog 3 (2017)
17. Mitra, A., Thang, N.K., Nguyen, T.A., Trystram, D., Youssef, P.: Online Decentralized Frank-Wolfe: from theoretical bound to applications in smart-building (2022)
18. Nan, F., Wang, J., Saligrama, V.: Pruning random forests for prediction on a budget. In: Lee, D., Sugiyama, M., Luxburg, U., Guyon, I., Garnett, R. (eds.)

Advances in Neural Information Processing Systems, vol, 29. Curran Associates, Inc. (2016)

19. Pipattanasomporn, M., et al.: Cu-bems, smart building electricity consumption and indoor environmental sensor datasets. Sci. Data **7**, (2020)

20. Shotton, J., Sharp, T., Kohli, P., Nowozin, S., Winn, J., Criminisi, A.: Decision jungles: compact and rich models for classification. In: Burges, C., Bottou, L., Welling, M., Ghahramani, Z., Weinberger, K. (eds.) Advances in Neural Information Processing Systems, vol. 26. Curran Associates, Inc. (2013)

21. Simons, T., Lee, D.J.: A review of binarized neural networks. Electronics **8**(6), 661 (2019)

22. Wai, H., Lafond, J., Scaglione, A., Moulines, E.: Decentralized frank-wolfe algorithm for convex and nonconvex problems. IEEE Trans. Autom. Control **62**(11), 5522–5537 (2017)

23. Wang, S., et al.: When edge meets learning: Adaptive control for resource-constrained distributed machine learning. In: IEEE INFOCOM 2018 - IEEE Conference on Computer Communications, pp. 63–71 (2018)

24. Yan, F., Sundaram, S., Vishwanathan, S.V.N., Qi, Y.: Distributed autonomous online learning: regrets and intrinsic privacy-preserving properties. IEEE Trans. Knowl. Data Eng. **25**(11), 2483–2493 (2013)

25. Zamora-Martinez, F., Romeu, P., Botella-Rocamora, P., Pardo, J.: On-line learning of indoor temperature forecasting models towards energy efficiency. Energy. Build. **83**, 162–172 (2014)

26. Zhang, W., Zhao, P., Zhu, W., Hoi, S., Zhang, T.: Projection-free distributed online learning in networks. In: Proceedings of the 34th International Conference on Machine Learning, pp. 4054–4062 (2017)

IntellIoT: Intelligent IoT Environments

Arne Bröring[1]([✉]), Vivek Kulkarni[1], Andreas Zirkler[1], Philippe Buschmann[1],
Konstantinos Fysarakis[2], Simon Mayer[3], Beatriz Soret[4], Lam Duc Nguyen[4],
Petar Popovski[4], Sumudu Samarakoon[5], Mehdi Bennis[5], Jérôme Härri[6],
Martijn Rooker[7], Gerald Fritz[7], Anca Bucur[8], Georgios Spanoudakis[2],
and Sotiris Ioannidis[9]

[1] Siemens AG, Technology, Munich, Germany
arne.broering@siemens.com
[2] Sphynx Analytics Ltd., Nicosia, Cyprus
[3] University of St. Gallen, St. Gallen, Switzerland
[4] Aalborg University, Aalborg, Denmark
[5] University of Oulu, Oulu, Finland
[6] EURECOM, Sophia Antipolis, France
[7] TTTech Computertechnik AG, Vienna, Austria
[8] Philips Research, Eindhoven, Netherlands
[9] Technical University of Crete, Chania, Greece

Abstract. Traditional IoT setups are cloud-centric and typically focused around a centralized IoT platform to which data is uploaded for further processing. Next generation IoT applications are incorporating technologies such as artificial intelligence, augmented reality, and distributed ledgers to realize semi-autonomous behaviour of vehicles, guidance for human users, and machine-to-machine interactions in a trustworthy manner. Such applications require more dynamic IoT environments, which can operate locally without the necessity to communicate with the Cloud. In this paper, we describe three use cases of next generation IoT applications and highlight associated challenges for future research. We further present the IntellIoT framework that comprises the required components to address the identified challenges.

Keywords: Internet of Things · Artificial intelligence · Autonomous systems · Human-computer interaction · Trust

1 Introduction

In today's Internet of Things (IoT) deployments, cloud-based platforms are typically central points of data collection and processing. However, this cloud-centric IoT model has limitations [13,16,27]: (i) unreliable cloud connectivity impedes dependable end-to-end applications (ii) limited bandwidth restricts the amount of data that can be processed (iii) high round-trip times prevent real-time operation, (iv) high cost of data transport and intake, as well as (v) privacy and trust concerns. Moreover, typical hierarchical setups of IoT cloud platforms (vi)

A. González-Vidal et al. (Eds.): GIoTS 2022, LNCS 13533, pp. 55–68, 2022.
https://doi.org/10.1007/978-3-031-20936-9_5

hinder use cases with dynamically changing context due to lacking self-awareness of the individual subsystems and the overall system.

To enable next generation IoT applications, these issues can be overcome through localized IoT environments comprised of heterogeneous devices (e.g., edge computers as well as resource-constrained devices) that can collaboratively execute semi-autonomous IoT applications, which include functions for sensing, acting, reasoning, and control. However, since IoT applications cannot be completely autonomous in what they decide and act, they need to keep the human-in-the-loop for control and optimization of their Artificial Intelligence (AI).

In this paper, we derive research challenges from three key classes of Next Generation (NG) IoT use cases: 1) a fleet of agricultural vehicles (e.g., tractors) is semi-autonomously operated in conjunction with supporting devices (e.g., drones), 2) patients are semi-autonomously guided by artificial advisors based on IoT device input; and 3) semi-autonomous machine-to-machine collaboration in industrial plants (e.g., robot arms and machinery). In all three use case areas, a human expert plays a key role in controlling, monitoring and teaching AI-enabled autonomous systems.

The remainder of this paper is organised as follows: Sect. 2 presents the three use case classes from agriculture, healthcare and manufacturing. Section 3 describes the IntelIIoT framework to enable NG IoT application development. Section 4 presents current research around key enablers to fulfill the vision and highlights associated research challenges. Section 5 concludes this paper and points to future work.

2   Next Generation IoT Use Cases

Due to the dimensions of variability, we selected three distinct use cases that stand exemplary for a broad range of NG IoT applications.

2.1   Autonomous Operation of *Agriculture* Vehicle Fleets

Figure 1 describes the use case of a semi-autonomous agricultural vehicle fleet. This use case entails the provision of new functionalities (e.g., AI algorithm implementations) for IoT applications by technology providers (e.g. tractor manufacturers) via step (1). A human operator (Farmer or Agriculture fleet management) specifies a goal for autonomous activities (e.g., ploughing or spraying a certain farm field) of the tractor on an Edge infrastructure as depicted in step (2). From the defined goal, a plan for IoT application instantiation is derived and a deployment of the required functions to the involved devices, e.g., tractor or drones shown in step (3), is triggered. Next, the deployed AI operates the involved vehicles, which includes dealing with blockages or other adversarial events using sensors of the vehicle (e.g., cameras or LIDAR) via step (4). This can be facilitated by sensing the environment from multiple neighbouring vehicles to collectively train their models and identify objects in a faster and more robust manner. The sensed data can also serve as a training dataset for continually improving the underlying AI models.

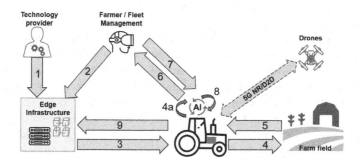

Fig. 1. IntelIIoT-enabled NG IoT agriculture use case.

If an obstacle is detected and the tractor cannot determine how to traverse it (step 5), then control of the tractor is handed over to a human operator (step 6). Data from the cameras and sensors is transmitted to the human operator who can use AR/VR technology to have a surround view of the situation. Direct and indirect strategies for taking over remote control are both necessary for step (7): Direct interaction with the tractor (i.e. remotely driving the vehicle) requires a reliable and high-speed connection enabling real-time interaction between operator and tractor. Indirect control with VR tooling aims to identify a feasible trajectory around the tractor, and control is given back to the tractor, while the human operator supervises the tractor remotely while it traverses the newly defined trajectory correctly. Based on the input from the human operator, the vehicle can refine its AI models by continually learning (step 8) how to overcome such obstacles in the future in addition to potentially sharing the learned model with other vehicles.

In the future, service providers will also offer such semi-autonomous vehicles (e.g., to provide farming services). Then, contractual agreements need to be set up using distributed ledger technology (DLT) (e.g., ownership of the farmer's land needs to be confirmed). This information will constitute a digital evidence that the field owner authorized the requested services and the area in which the smart equipment operates. Storing performed agricultural activities back in the DLT as historic evidence (step 9) can then be utilized in business models.

2.2   Collaborative Intelligence for Remote Patient Monitoring

Advances in AI and in IoT-enabled systems may lead to significant benefits in healthcare, enabling physicians to efficiently improve patient outcomes, safety and comfort, for instance by leveraging the new technology to remotely guide their patients through recovery and rehabilitation at home. The solution empowers patients to focus on their recovery, giving them the confidence that they are safe, that the tools can support and inform them all the way, and that their physicians are always in the loop when needed.

Figure 2 describes a system that leverages IoT device inputs to give clinical experts accurate information on the health status of their patients and provides AI-assisted recommendations and interventions to patients, with clinical expert oversight. Patient users are equipped with wearable sensing devices measuring relevant data that is transferred to a personal IoT device (e.g., smart watch) (step 1). The AI on board of this IoT device analyses the data in step (2) to identify the need for interventions or recommendations, according to the initial AI model and the intervention workflows previously defined as goals by the clinicians in charge of the patient. The model is applied on the collected data, and when the need for an intervention is detected, either a recommendation is sent to the patient (step 3a), or the case is escalated to involve a clinician, leading to the human-in-the-loop (step 3b). Privacy and security-compliant exchange is thereby crucial. The system may further implement a model for monitoring and diagnosing technical issues with the constrained devices (step 4).

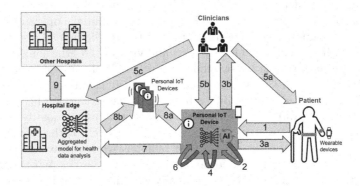

Fig. 2. IntelIIoT-enabled NG IoT healthcare use case.

In the IntelIIoT solution, when an escalation takes place and a clinical expert is notified, the clinician may decide to contact the patient as shown (step 5a), respond to the personal device (step 5b), or raise an alarm (step 5c). The clinician provides feedback which is used to validate and re-train the AI model locally on the personal IoT device (step 6). Model updates are then contributed to the aggregated model at the edge infrastructure (e.g., of a hospital) (step 7). This distributed AI can be implemented using federated learning and the model update is communicated to all IoT devices, either in a device to device fashion (step 8a) or through distribution of the aggregated model (step 8b). Further, federated learning can be done between hospitals (step 9). All the involved communications and interactions need to be covered by state-of-the-art security and privacy provisions, catering for the intricacies of the private-sensitive user data. Digital consent management to drive the interactions of the system (patients, clinicians, devices) can be managed e.g. via smart contracts.

2.3   Autonomous Collaboration of *Production* Machines

This use case (Fig. 3) describes an example of machine to machine collaboration. A customer of a shared manufacturing plant orders a product by specifying a manufacturing goal (step 1). In step (2), a machine orchestration and associated process plan is determined to manufacture the desired product from a workpiece. The event-based process planner monitors the manufacturing process and reacts when the health state of a machine changes. If the process planner cannot find a solution for the manufacturing goal on its own (step 3) it can request support from a human plant operator or eventually customer. In step (4), a robot or AGV is tasked to transport the workpiece to the next production step and manufacturing process data is sent to involved machines. As these machines may be operated by the plant owner or a third-party operator, contractual arrangements need to be set up, for which a distributed ledger is used. Further, comprehensive security mechanisms are applied to ensure privacy and security of customer data.

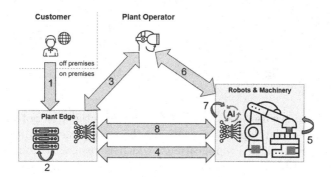

Fig. 3. IntellIoT-enabled NG IoT manufacturing use case.

In step (5), a local AI on board of the robot decides how the robot picks a workpiece and places it in the next machine. If the confidence-level of the local AI is low and it cannot pick and place the workpiece, it can request support from a human plant operator or machine owner again (step 6). Utilizing AR/VR technology, the human can virtually grab the workpiece to support the robot. A tactile communication needs to be established for this interaction, under consideration of security and privacy. Additionally, 3D cameras can be used to generate an accurate enough reconstruction of the surroundings and the robot itself which allows the full control and visual information about the parameters of the robot. For grabbing and haptic feedback to the user, special user input devices (e.g., a stylus or glove) are needed. If support from a remote operator is needed, a tactile communication may not be possible through long-distance internet connection. Hence, the operator would be able to control a virtual robot, rendered in the local edge, with delayed movement of the real robot. From the human handling of the work piece, local AI on the robot re-trains itself (step 7), and federates the learned process parameters to other robots through model update on edge (step 8).

3   A Next Generation IoT Framework: The IntelIIoT Approach

Analyzing the above use cases, a pattern of NG IoT applications can be extrapolated, as shown in Fig. 4: NG IoT applications generally consist of multiple heterogeneous devices that collaborate in a semi-autonomous way through AI. Users interact with the system to provide knowledge and thereby may (re-)train the AI. Interaction among the devices and with the user may have to happen in a tactile way, with low latencies and high bandwidth.

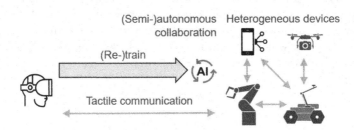

Fig. 4. Pattern of an NG IoT Application.

Tackling the above use cases in a holistic manner is the driver of the IntelIIoT project[1]. It aims to develop a framework for the management of intelligent IoT environments and their IoT applications, which is realized through an architecte comprising three building blocks (see Fig. 5): (a) distributed, self-aware, & semi-autonomous **IoT applications**; (b) a **human-in-the-loop** to define and support the autonomy in (a), and (c) an efficient, reliable and trustworthy **computation and communication infrastructure** that enables (a) & (b).

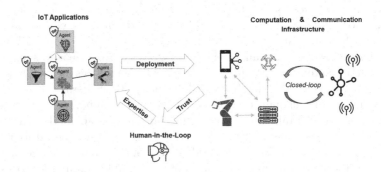

Fig. 5. IntelIIoT concept for enabling intelligent IoT environments.

---

[1] http://intelliot.eu.

3.1 Distributed, Self-aware, Semi-autonomous IoT Applications

Autonomous software agents of a novel hypermedia-based multi-agent system (HyperMAS) [8] execute IoT applications. Interoperable access to agents and functions is given through standardized interfaces that are hosted by IoT or edge devices, e.g., based on W3C Web of Things specifications [20]. Using these functions as building blocks, software agents can autonomously create distributed IoT applications and execute these applications while flexibly reacting to environment dynamics. To further facilitate IoT application development, interoperability is supported through components that are able to translate between communication technologies, protocols and vocabularies. Software agents are self-aware and observe each other, e.g., to detect and autonomously mitigate failures. They participate in a distributed ledger to enable contractual relations and monetization. Leveraging reinforcement and federated learning [22], distributed AI is enabled by on-device training and inference that are subject to the device's resource constraints.

3.2 Autonomy Defined by a Human-in-the-Loop

The human-in-the-loop provides expertise to the IoT environment and is therefore crucial to the system: At design time, the human defines goals and requirements. Then, a mechanism automatically deducts and translates an IoT application workflow into IoT/edge device interactions with associated network constraints. At runtime, the human observes the AI-enabled autonomous behavior and provides input [14] to improve it. For that, the human needs to leverage tactile interactions through AR/VR to refine the model and avoid blockages by e.g., teaching an industrial robot how to handle a product.

3.3 Efficient, Reliable and Trustworthy Computation and Communication Infrastructure

Intelligent IoT environments must operate upon a communication and computation infrastructure capable of flexibly supporting the capabilities described in 3.1 & 3.2 above, whereby resource-constrained IoT devices and more powerful edge assets must be efficiently managed, optionally integrating cloud-based services, and also supporting complex, cost-intensive computations (e.g., AI inference/training, as well as AR rendering). Edge resources will be diverse [28], e.g., Multi-access Edge Computing (MEC) offered through 5G functionalities, or an industrial edge offered by networked computing devices in a manufacturing plant. Computation & communication form a closed-loop system through which the infrastructure will be optimized in an integrated way (i.e., deployment of application functions on IoT/edge resources must be optimized under consideration of network constraints, and the network must be dynamically managed and reconfigured to optimally serve the purpose of the application and the IoT/edge devices). The infrastructure will enable ultra-reliable and low-latency communication through dynamic network management, through heterogeneous network technologies (e.g., 5G NR [17], NB-IoT [15], or D2D [1]). The wireless front end will be specifically designed to support communication requirements of advanced techniques, such as DLTs and federated learning. Finally, security & privacy assurance concepts will be included by design to ensure reliability and overall trustworthiness of the developed solution.

3.4   Bringing All Together - The IntellIoT High-Level Architecture

Integrating the above concepts, a high-level view of IntellIoT's logical architecture has been derived, shown in Fig. 6. The three key concepts highlighted (i.e., Collaborative IoT, Human-in-the-loop and Trustworthiness) are prominently featured in the architecture.

In total, five core component groups have been identified, with individual components falling into one of the following groups:

- **Collaborative IoT enablers**: Components that realize IntellIoT's Collaborative IoT pillar, focusing on the cooperation of various semi-autonomous entities to execute IoT applications.
- **Human-in-the-Loop enablers**: Components involved in IntellIoT's Human-in-the-Loop pillar, which focuses on involving the human in the process; e.g., to solve complex situations.
- **Trust enablers**: Components that are part of IntellIoT's Trust pillar. This pillar focuses on privacy, security, and ultimately building trust into the IntellIoT framework.
- **Infrastructure management**: The computation & communication infrastructure and its management capabilities, enabling the deployment and management of edge applications.
- **Use-Case deployment**: Components which are use case-specific, (i.e., pertaining to the use case environment deployment), such as edge devices, edge apps, and edge AI models.

For more details on the individual components comprising the architecture, we defer the reader to the publicly-available architecture specification of IntellIoT [9].

4   State of the Art and Research Challenges

To achieve its vision, IntellIoT improves the state of the art in the related research areas; the key enablers and resulting research challenges are highlighted in the subsections that follow.

4.1   Autonomy and Distributed Intelligence

Next generation IoT applications require a paradigm shift from classic ML to distributed, low-latency and reliable ML at the wireless network edge [22]. Federated learning (FL) is a decentralized learning technique where private-sensitive

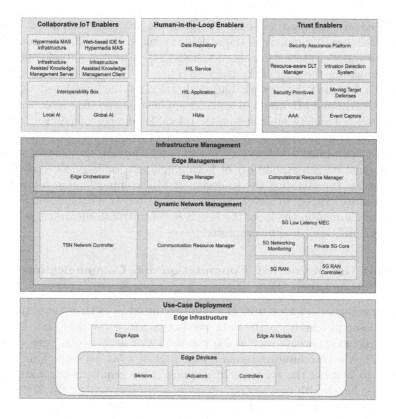

Fig. 6. IntelIIoT high-level architecture.

training data is distributed across learning agents [19]. Agents share their local models, instead of the training data, reducing communication latencies during ML training. Nevertheless, except few works, such as [7,26], most of the existing literature assumes ideal client-server communication conditions, overlooking channel dynamics and uncertainties. FL uses stochastic gradient decent (SGD) techniques (e.g., elastic SGD, entropy SGD) for local training, each with its own intrinsic characteristics (computation requirements, accuracy etc.). However, the impact of different ML algorithms in real-world applications is an open research area. The continual discovery and interaction of agents within their environment requires the use of multi-agent Reinforcement Learning (RL). Furthermore, the branch of deep RL (DRL) [5] addresses issues arising from the larger state dimensions. Model-free, value/policy-based, and actor-critic RL within DRL exhibit efficient and accurate decision-making capabilities over classical RL. Yet the aspects of computation-communication limitations and privacy in distributed multi-agent RL are still not well-understood and require further investigation. The involvement of a human expert in data collection, training, testing, and validation is the fundamental philosophy behind the human-in-the-loop for ML. With distributed AI techniques, the interaction between the agents and the human needs to consider time sensitivity, learning procedure and ability to control and train/teach remotely in the scalable systems. Hence, it is mandatory to investigate various transfer learning methods [24] as well as suitable optimizers and the human-in-the-loop of the training [14].

For the IntelIoT framework and realization of the envisioned use cases (Sect. 2), distributed ML needs to consider application-specific target accuracies and worst-case training latencies under tolerable number of failures (reliability and robustness guarantees), wireless resources availability, on-device energy, storage, or computing restrictions. In addition, studying the control stability (plant, string, swarm- stabilities) of both single and multi-agent systems will be mandatory. Investigating the co-design of ML, communication-computation and control are crucial for developing novel distributed AI solutions. For fully enabling the human-in-the-loop, the fusion between transfer learning, optimization and FL/RL are being incorporated.

4.2 Next Generation IoT Computation and Communication Infrastructure

IoT applications are moving from the cloud to the edge, so that computing happens in closer proximity to the data producers and consumers [28]. Relevant solutions include concepts such as fog computing or multi-access edge computing (MEC), where computing resources are part of a 5G network. This has the potential to address the concerns of response time requirements, battery life constraints, bandwidth cost saving, or safety and privacy (e.g., [13,27]). In NG IoT applications, a key challenge for the computation infrastructure is to decide on which computing resource to handle a specific workload (e.g., execute an AI algorithm). There are multiple existing allocation strategies, e.g., [6,21], which optimize different performance metrics, e.g., response time, bandwidth, availability, or energy consumption. Therefore, components are needed for advanced, dynamic resource management which can be flexibly applied in various private edge environments. IntelIoT develops a mechanism for optimized allocation of workloads to computing resources (i.e., mapping of IoT applications to devices). It consists of a flexible algorithmic framework that builds on prior work [23] and is adjustable to different optimality criteria at runtime. Further, it needs to be dynamically adapting to network changes based on high-level application requirements [4]; i.e., establishing closed-loop infrastructure management.

While IoT/edge devices can provide the computation side of the infrastructure, the communication side needs to be driven by advanced networking technologies, such as 5G New Radio (NR) and its extensions towards private networks and Industrial IoT. Further, 5G eV2X, as a complete redesign of the LTE V2X, can play a role for cooperative automated mobility and 'sidelink' device-to-device (D2D) [1] communications, e.g., between robots and machines. For "tactile" communication links, a major challenge is to design a steer-/control-based communication framework for real-time transmission of haptic information (touch, motion, etc.) in addition to conventional audio-visual and data traffic. The provided solutions need to enable efficient spectrum usage [3] in downlink, with massive sensory feedback on the uplink, targeting 1ms downlink, 10ms uplink with 99.99% availability. In order to support ultra-reliable and low latency (URLL) communication towards TSN for 5G Industrial IoT, 5G mmWave radio (with fiber data speed, real-time reactivity and massive sensorics capacity) [12] as well as support for IEEE TSN, are being investigated. Regarding distributed networking support, functions for ad-hoc scheduling capabilities for enhanced D2D communication do not include a specific scheduler, hence, IntelIIoT develops a wireless TSN-grade D2D scheduler providing deterministic QoS for decentralized computing in the IoT context.

Building on the computation and communication infrastructure, IoT artifacts need to be able to discover and interact with one another. A first major step towards this goal has been the Web of Things (WoT) [20], where interactions between devices are based on the Web architecture. Crucially, however, interoperability on the semantic level is a central requirement in the future evolution of the Web. Based on efforts of the W3C WoT, new means to use hypermedia for designing evolvable Web APIs and general-purpose clients are being explored. IntelIIoT will build up on these developments towards integrating them with research on multi-agent systems (MAS) towards enabling a hypermedia-based MAS (HyperMAS) [8] that are vertically and horizontally scalable with respect to the number of agents, devices, and interactions among these components. It will support self-aware agents within IoT environments and semi-autonomous IoT systems.

4.3   Humans and Trust in Intelligent IoT

The wide adoption of IoT technologies in a plethora of domains, necessitates considering security, privacy, and trust requirements early in the design phase [10]. Even securely initialised devices can be compromised, allowing attackers to affect connected devices, the network, or collaborative applications. Trust-based mechanisms can be used to defend against such attacks by monitoring the behaviour of each participant. An IoT deployment must also have the intelligence to protect itself proactively, e.g., through Moving Target Defence (MTD) techniques [25], where AI-driven agents periodically alter the network topology and/or configuration to counter attacks. Thereby, security assurance evaluations for IoT systems are still in their infancy (e.g., [2]). Therefore, IntelIIoT provides security and trustworthiness by design, via a combination of: (i) an evidence-based continuous security assurance, integrating hybrid assessments which considers different attack surfaces and vulnerabilities; ii) trust-based computing mechanisms that will act as distributed intrusion detection system, and (iii) MTD strategies with security-context aware processes.

Supporting these security and trust mechanisms, IntelIIoT uses distributed ledger technologies (DLT) to encode transaction logic and policies, which include the requirements and obligations of the party requesting access to an IoT resource as well as its provider [18]. This can lead to a wave of novel applications, enabling trusted access to IoT resources. Therefore, the state-of-the-art is being progressed in three aspects (building on previous work [11]): (1) circumventing devices' resource constraints; (2) advancing uplink-dominated IoT network designs; (3) providing interoperability with third-party devices. In IoT, an edge gateway with DLT solutions is equipped with the necessary computational intelligence. Yet, devices in a blockchain should keep a copy of the DLT record, which can be large and increasing over time and limits the scalability of the system. Moreover, the transactions associated with smart contracts require two-way communication traffic, which violates the common assumption that the IoT systems are dominated by an uplink traffic. An IoT/edge device in a blockchain network should be capable of verifying information in the blockchain, which is associated with the downlink traffic. Therefore, the IntelIIoT framework provides an architecture that aims at trading off complexity of the device, achieved trust and network capabilities, and maintain the trust when a device belongs to a third party.

5   Conclusions and Future Work

The key contributions of this paper is the analysis of three classes of Next Generation IoT use cases, the extrapolation of a common pattern, the presentation of the IntelIIoT framework, and the postulation of key research challenges associated with it. All three use cases are based on semi-autonomous behaviour of the IoT system. Multiple heterogeneous devices are interacting and autonomous control of their collaboration is provided through AI, which can be (re-)trained through human intervention. This pattern can be assumed for many next generation IoT applications.

The described *pattern* spreads over three key areas: (1) providing the distributed artificial intelligence for autonomous behaviour, (2) providing efficient and reliable communication and computation resources, and (3) incorporating the human (by providing trust in the system) and learning from his input. The described framework of IntelIIoT addresses all three fields. The presented high-level architecture combines software components to realize functionalities required by these fields. The full implementation of this architecture is currently in process. Thereby, the key research challenges that are being faced are outlined and describes the further path of research for this project and beyond.

Acknowledgment. This work has received funding from the European Union's Horizon 2020 research and innovation programme H2020-ICT-56–2020, under grant agreement No. 957218 (Project *IntelIIoT*).

References

1. Ansari, R.I., et al:. 5G D2D networks: techniques, challenges, and future prospects. IEEE Syst. J. **12**(4), 3970–3984 (2017)
2. Di Martino, B., Li, K.-C., Yang, L.T., Esposito, A. (eds.): Internet of Everything. IT, Springer, Singapore (2018). https://doi.org/10.1007/978-981-10-5861-5

3. Bennis, M., Debbah, M., Poor, H.V.: Ultrareliable and low-latency wireless communication: tail, risk, and scale. Proc. IEEE **106**(10), 1834–1853 (2018)
4. Bröring, A., Seeger, J., Papoutsakis, M., Fysarakis, K., Caracalli, A.: Networking-aware IoT application development. Sensors **20**(3), 897 (2020)
5. Bu, F., Wang, X.: A smart agriculture IoT system based on deep reinforcement learning. Futur. Gener. Comput. Syst. **99**, 500–507 (2019)
6. Cardellini, V., Grassi, V., Presti, F.L., Nardelli, M.: Optimal operator placement for distributed stream processing applications. In: Proceedings of the 10th ACM International Conference on Distributed and Event-based Systems, pp. 69–80. ACM Press (2016)
7. Chen, M., Yang, Z., Saad, W., Yin, C., Poor, H.V, Cui, S.: A joint learning and communications framework for federated learning over wireless networks. IEEE Trans. Wireless Commun. **PP**, 1–1 (2020)
8. Ciortea, A., Mayer, S., Gandon, F., Boissier, O., Ricci, A., Zimmermann, A.: A decade in Hindsight: the missing bridge between multi-agent systems and the world wide web. In: Proceedings of the 18th International Conference on Autonomous Agents and Multi Agent Systems, pp. 1659–1663. International Foundation for Autonomous Agents and Multiagent Systems (2019)
9. IntellIoT consortium. Deliverable D2.3 - High level architecture (first version). https://intelliot.eu/wp-content/uploads/2021/10/D2.3-High-level-architecture-first-version.pdf
10. Conti, M., Dehghantanha, A., Franke, K., Watson, S.: Challenges and opportunities, Internet of Things security and forensics (2018)
11. Danzi, P., et al.: Communication aspects of the integration of wireless IoT devices with distributed ledger technology. IEEE Netw. **34**(1), 47–53 (2020)
12. Giordani, M., Polese, M., Roy, A., Castor, D., Zorzi, M.: Initial access frameworks for 3GPP NR at mmWave frequencies. In: 2018 17th Annual Mediterranean Ad Hoc Networking Workshop (Med-Hoc-Net), pp. 1–8. IEEE (2018)
13. Ha, K., Chen, Z., Hu,W., Richter, W., Pillai, P., Satyanarayanan, M.: Towards wearable cognitive assistance. In: Proceedings of the 12th Annual International Conference on Mobile Systems, Applications, and Services, pp. 68–81. ACM (2014)
14. Holzinger, A., et al.: Interactive machine learning: experimental evidence for the human in the algorithmic loop. App. Intell. **49**(7), 2401–2414 (2019)
15. Hsieh, B.Z., Chao,Y.H, Cheng, R.G., Nikaein, N.: Design of a UE-specific uplink scheduler for narrowband Internet-of-Things (NB-IoT) systems. In: 2018 3rd International Conference on Intelligent Green Building and Smart Grid (IGBSG), pp. 1–5. IEEE (2018)
16. Islam, M.M, Morshed, S., Goswami. P.: Cloud computing: a survey on its limitations and potential solutions. Int. J. Comput. Sci. Iss. (IJCSI) **10**(4), 159 (2013)
17. Kaltenberger, F., Souza, G.D., Knopp, R., Wang, H.:The OpenAirInterface 5G new radio implementation: current status and roadmap. In: WSA 2019; 23rd International ITG Workshop on Smart Antennas, pp. 1–5. VDE (2019)
18. Khan, M.A., Salah, K.: IoT security: review, blockchain solutions, and open challenges. Futur. Gener. Comput. Syst. **82**, 395–411 (2018)
19. Konečný J., McMahan, B.H., Ramage, D., Richtárik, P.: Federated optimization: distributed machine learning for on-device intelligence. arXiv preprint arXiv:1610.02527 (2016)
20. Kovatsch, M., Matsukura, R., Lagally, M., Kawaguchi, T., Toumura, K., Kajimoto, K.: Web of Things (WoT) Architecture (2019). https://w3c.github.io/wot-architecture

21. Mohan, N., Kangasharju, J.: Edge-Fog cloud: a distributed cloud for Internet of Things computations. In: 2016 Cloudification of the Internet of Things (CIoT), pp. 1–6. IEEE (2016)
22. Park, J., Samarakoon, S., Bennis, M., Debbah, M.: Wireless network intelligence at the edge. Proc. IEEE **107**(11), 2204–2239 (2019)
23. Seeger, J., Bröring, A., Carle, G.: Optimally self-healing IoT choreographies. ACM Trans. Internet Technol. (TOIT) **20**(3), 1–20 (2020)
24. Sun, L., Peng, C., Zhan, W., Tomizuka, M.: A fast integrated planning and control framework for autonomous driving via imitation learning. In: Dynamic Systems and Control Conference, vol. 51913, p. V003T37A012. American Society of Mechanical Engineers (2018)
25. Xiong, X.-L., Yang, L., Zhao, G.-S.: Effectiveness evaluation model of moving target defense based on system attack surface. IEEE Access **7**, 9998–10014 (2019)
26. Yang, H.H., Liu, Z., Quek, T.Q., Poor, H.V.: Scheduling policies for federated learning in wireless networks. IEEE Trans. Commun. **68**(1), 317–333 (2019)
27. Yi, S., Hao, Z., Qin, Z., Li, Q.: Fog computing: platform and applications. In: 2015 Third IEEE Workshop on Hot Topics in Web Systems and Technologies (HotWeb), pp. 73–78. IEEE (2015)
28. Yousefpour, A., et al.: All one needs to know about fog computing and related edge computing paradigms: a complete survey. J. Syst. Architect. **98**, 289–330 (2019)

An Interoperable Framework for Heterogeneous IoT infrastructure to Unlock Data Value

Wei Qingsong, Yang Yechao, Lu Sifei, Juniarto Samsudin,
Renuga Kanagavelu, Zhang Haibin, and Farzam Farbiz[✉]

A-STAR, Institute of High Performance Computing, Singapore 138632, Singapore
{wei_qingsong,Farzam_Farbiz}@ihpc.a-star.edu.sg

Abstract. While there are currently multiple commercial IoT and IIoT platforms available in the market (e.g., Siemens MindSphere, Microsoft Azure, PTC Thing-Worx, Amazon AWS), the key problem in using these platforms is lack of interoperability and flexibility in data exchange among these platforms. Each of these platforms promotes its own IoT infrastructure, and they have their proprietary protocols and interfaces, with incompatible standards, formats, and semantics that create closed ecosystems. To address above mentioned interoperability issue, we proposed an IoT interoperability framework to support different layers of heterogeneous sensors, edge devices, on-premise platform and even cloud platforms, so as to unlock data value.

Keywords: Internet of Things · Interoperability · OPC-UA · Data model · Provision server

1 Introduction

The Internet of Things (IoT) [1, 2, 10–15] advancements in connectivity, communication technology and real-time data analysis have opened the possibility of integrating the traditional operational technology (OT) of a manufacturing plant with the Information Technology (IT) systems. The integration between OT and IT in the manufacturing industry provides a huge opportunity for a more efficient manufacturing process on factory floor, seamless supply chain, efficient product and machine maintenance, as well as flexible and agile adaption to dynamic customer demands [16–20]. Industry 4.0 [1] refers to the trend of bringing IoT technology to the manufacturing industry towards digital transformation for smart manufacturing. With the adoption of Industry 4.0, it is projected that manufacturing machines are fully interconnected, monitored by sensors, and powered by advanced machine learning techniques.

There are a number of IoT platforms available in the market (e.g., Siemens Mind-Sphere [3], Microsoft Azure [4], PTC ThingWorx [5]). Each of these platforms promotes its own IoT infrastructure, proprietary protocols and interfaces, incompatible standards, formats, and semantics that create closed ecosystems (sometimes called silos). It is challenging to communicate with each other and connect to devices/platforms of different vendors. Interoperability refers to the ability for systems or their individual components

© The Author(s), under exclusive license to Springer Nature Switzerland AG 2022
A. González-Vidal et al. (Eds.): GIoTS 2022, LNCS 13533, pp. 69–81, 2022.
https://doi.org/10.1007/978-3-031-20936-9_6

communicate with each other, regardless of their manufacturers or technical specifications. Lack of interoperability among different platforms is a barrier of collaborations across companies. In addition, device interoperability is the key to bridge OT and IT for information exchange between heterogeneous devices and integration of new devices into any IoT platform.

In this paper, we propose a layered IIoT interoperability framework, which is composed of 3 layers. The bottom layer is for shopfloor with data capture from different machines and an Edge Gateway for data store, process and transfer. Middle layer is mainly for on-premise IoT platform with functions of data model, storage, process, visualization and analytics, as well as smart cloud adapters. The top layers are for cloud IoT platform such as Azure IoT Cloud, Amazon IoT Cloud, and Siemens Mindsphere. This proposed framework is able to automatically connect and interoperate sensors, edge devices, machines and platforms based on real-time and interactive parameters setting and configuration updates.

2   Problem Statement

As shown in Fig. 1, IoT interoperability can be classified into different layers [2, 7–9, 21, 22].

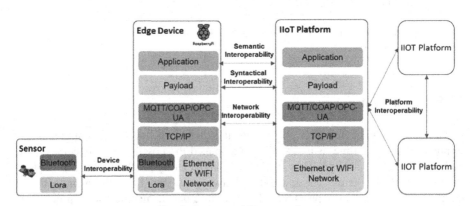

Fig. 1. Interoperability overview

Device interoperability is the key function to bridge OT and IT so that data can be collected and transferred for comprehensive process. IoT edge devices run applications to collect or process data with reduced latency. However, they require costly manual deployment and intervention which result in low efficiency and delayed software update. With the number of devices increasing, it becomes challenging to manage and deploy IoT devices in an automatic and scalable way. In addition, edge device presents hardware diversity e.g., Raspberry PI is based on 64bits ARMv8 processor, NVIDIA Jetson Nano is based on ARM Cortex-A57, and Intel Edison is based on Intel Atom processor. How to provide an abstract for portable application deployment to hide the hardware difference on edge device is a challenge?

In today's IoT systems, new sensor hardware is added to the existing system as it scales. This adds complexity and confusion if no proper housekeeping is implemented. The definition of housekeeping in this aspect refers to the syntax and semantics of the data and finally how they are synchronized.

Most of existing IoT platforms lack interoperability to seamlessly work with each other for establishing a big industrial IoT ecosystem. This results in vertical silos in IoT ecosystems and scarce reusability of technical solutions. On-premise IIoT platform provides on-site IoT services with guaranteed privacy, while Cloud IIoT platform offers public IoT services with various functions and scalable resources. Hence, the interoperability between an on-premise platform and a cloud platform is essential to take advantages between them and enable redundancy, flexibility and cost saving.

To address above mentioned interoperability issue, we proposed IoT interoperability framework to support different layers of heterogeneous sensors, edge devices, on-premise platform and even cloud platforms, so as to unlock data value.

3 Proposed Framework Architecture

This section introduces the details of Industry Internet of Things (IIoT) Interoperability Implementation Architecture which provides a generic framework to address the implementation challenges of IIoT interoperability.

Considering the diversity of data source, data volume, data format, machine, device, and platform, we are facing challenges to implement an interoperable and cost effective IIoT system. We propose a framework to address those challenges, and provide solution for Interoperability on different layers.

As shown in Fig. 2, the proposed architecture comprises of three layers with security firewall between layers.

- **The bottom layer**: it is in shopfloor with data capture from different machines, and an Edge Gateway for data store, process, as well as protocol translation in Edge computing. Industrial automation data is captured from diverse automation devices, software applications and some legacy devices. Leveraging on OPC-UA [6] and IT-centric communication protocols (such as SNMP, ODBC, and web services), it provides users with a single source for industrial data. Edge computing in this layer helps to connect, process and publish data using OPC-UA protocol. The OPC-UA protocol could achieve semantic interoperability and syntactic interoperability. One additional feature of this bottom layer is that edge analytics is flexible to integrate with Edge computing.
- **The middle layer**: it is mainly for on premise IIoT platform which could support most IIoT requirements such as data model, data storage, data process, data visualization and data analytics. In this layer, it also provides smart cloud adapters which are specific to Azure Cloud, Amazon Cloud and any other cloud platforms. Provisioning server and fleet management server are optional. Some sophisticated IIoT platforms could support device provision and fleet management with code configuration. In this layer, data can also be transferred to and exchange with enterprise systems such as ERP, MES, SCADA systems.

- **The top layer**: it is cloud IIoT platform such as Azure IoT Cloud, Amazon IoT Cloud, and Siemens Mindsphere. All of them provide stream processing, data storage and data analytics. Data is collected from the middle layer's smart cloud adapter for each cloud IoT platform. Enterprise could benefit from the advance machine learning tools, data processing tools, visualization tools and many other cloud services in this layer.

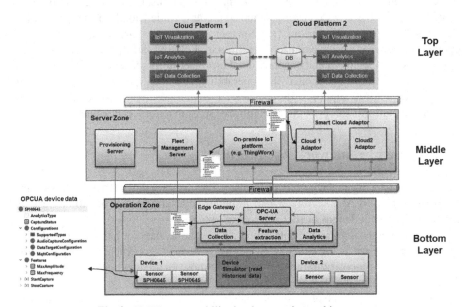

Fig. 2. IIoT Interoperability implementation architecture

With the layered concept, the proposed architecture is able to increase interoperability of the solution among different machines, software, and IIoT platforms. The flexible device connectivity feature could connect to many types of industry devices, while Edge processing could handle large volume and high frequent data. The OPC-UA interface between the bottom layer and the middle layer could provide high interoperability with many IIoT platforms and Industry systems such as ERP, MES, SCADA and PLCs. The layered concept also enhances the security and helps the integration with IT systems. One more feature of this architecture is that it can integrate different proprietary IIoT on premise platforms or cloud IIoT services to provide a solution to enterprise users.

The Smart Cloud Adaptor is a key component to implement connection to cloud platforms. It is specific to Azure Cloud, Amazon Cloud or any other cloud platforms. For example, Azure IoT Edge comprise of Edge runtime, Edge Hub, OPC publisher and customized analytics or processing modules. It could subscribe OPC-UA data and use Edge hub to send it to cloud Azure IoT hub. Amazon AWS IoT Greengrass comprises of Greengrass connector, SiteWise Connector for OPC-UA, Greengrass Core MQTT Broker and custom Lambda function. It will send data to cloud AWS IoT Core or AWS IoT SiteWise.

The OPC-UA protocol in the middle layer could achieve semantic interoperability and syntactic interoperability through the data model that we present in the next section. In the bottom layer, device or sensors could support OPC-UA or just use native protocols. Edge OPC-UA server sends OPC-UA data to the middle layer. The synergy of the OPC-UA infrastructure to exchange such industry information models enables interoperability at the semantic level.

4   Data Model

The data model defines common interfaces on top of OPC-UA Device Information Model with below common data structures [6]:

1) Sensor device configuration information.
2) Sensor device data capturing information and methods.
3) Sensor device on-edge data analysis algorithm.
4) Sensor device firmware information.

Applications can be built to configure, control, and read/write different sensor devices with the OPC-UA data model, without knowing sensor device specific information.

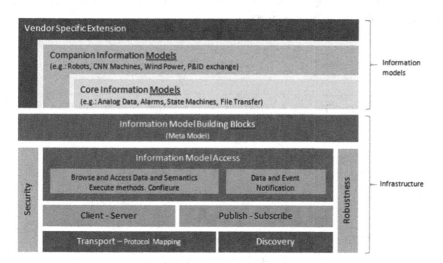

Fig. 3. OPC UA Data Model

As showed in Fig. 3, OPC UA is built on the following Infrastructure:

• Information Modelling Access which comprises the means to expose object-based Information Models in an Address Space and the Services to access this information. OPC UA infrastructure exchanging such industry information models enables interoperability at the semantic level.

- Client-Server communication with full range of information model access is available via services and follows the design paradigm of service-oriented architecture (SOA).
- Publish-Subscribe (PubSub) provides an alternative mechanism for data and event notification.
- Transport which defines protocol mappings that allow establishing a connection and exchanging well-formed messages between OPC UA Applications.
- Discovery which allows Clients to find OPC UA Servers, their supported protocols, security policies and other capabilities.
- Security and Robustness, which are integrated into Transport and Information Access.

OPC UA achieves connectivity interoperability by Transport and Discovery layer and syntactic interoperability by Information Modelling Access layer. Information Models are layered on top of the infrastructure. OPC UA provides a framework that can be used to represent complex information as Objects in an AddressSpace which can be accessed with standard services. These Objects consist of Nodes connected by References. Different classes of Nodes convey different semantics. For example, a Variable Node represents a value that can be read or written. A Method Node represents a function that can be called. Every Node has number of Attributes including a unique identifier called a NodeId and non-localized name called as BrowseName. To represent the information model design with different type of nodes and relationships between nodes, OPC UA uses notations showing in Fig. 4 to design information model with elements directly mapping to Nodes in the AddressSpace.

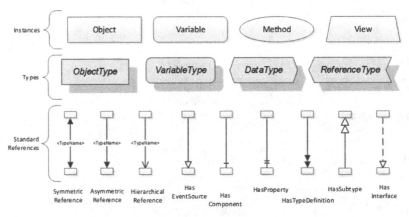

Fig. 4. Information model

4.1 Devices Information Model

Figure 5 depicts the main components (ObjectTypes) of the base device model defined by OPC-UA, with the data types described below.

- The TopologyElementType is the base of ObjectType for elements in a device topology. Its most essential aspect is the functional grouping concept.

- The ComponentType ObjectType provides a generic definition for a Device or parts of a Device where parts include mechanics and/or software. DeviceType is commonly used to represent field Devices.
- The ConfigurableObjectType ObjectType implements the configurable component and is used when an Object or an instance declaration needs nothing but configuration capability.
- The FunctionalGroupType is subtype of the OPC UA FolderType, used to structure Nodes like Properties, Parameters and Methods according to their application.

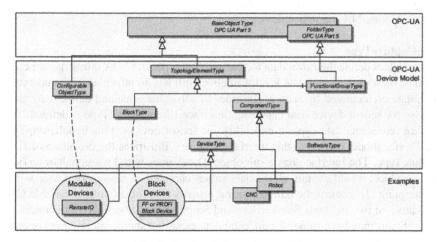

Fig. 5. Devices Information Model

4.2 Interface Model

Interfaces are ObjectTypes that represent a generic feature. The Interface model specifies the rules and mechanisms. Some general rules for defining Interfaces are as follows:

- Interface ObjectTypes shall be abstract subtypes of the BaseInterfaceType ObjectType.
- InstanceDeclarations on an Interface shall only have ModellingRules Optional or Mandatory.
- Interfaces shall not be the source of HasInterface References.
- The first letter of an Interface should be 'I'.

Clients can detect the implementation of Interfaces by filtering for the HasInterface Reference into the Browse Service request.

4.3 OPC-UA Interfaces ObjectType for Sensor Device

To abstract different sensor devices functions, features, and requirements with a common data model, three Interface ObjectTypes are defined in the next subsections.

IConfigurationType
This interface represents functions of sensor device configurations. An example of this kind of configuration is sample rate for an audio sensor device. ConfigurableObjectType from Device model is used in this interface. Figure 6 shows the definition of IConfigurationType. The Interface has a sub object Configurations with ConfigurableObjectType. This sub object would be used as a placeholder to hold all configuration variables or objects supported by the sensor device.

IDataCaptureType
Sensor devices define their own data format and data type. OPC-UA infrastructure could exchange these data at semantic level. But client still has no information to understand which data are captured by sensors. In order to solve this issue and define a common behavior for sensor device data capturing, interface IDataCaptureType is defined. This interface represents data capture capability for sensor devices. FunctionalGroupType from Device model is used in this interface. Figure 7 illustrates the definition of IDataCaptureType. The Interface has a sub object DataValues with FunctionalGroupType. This sub object would contain all the data values captured by the sensor device within one sampling. To control the data capturing process from client side, a variable CaptureStatus and two methods StartCapture and StopCapture are defined in the interface. CaptureStatus may have values for different data capturing status: idle, running or error. According to this variable value, client may call method StartCapture or StopCapture to start or stop data capturing.

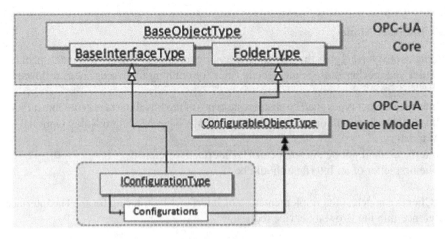

Fig. 6. IConfigurationType

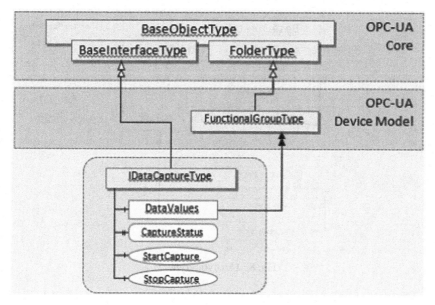

Fig. 7. IDataCaptureType

IAnalyticsType

This interface represents data processing functionality of the device connected to the sensor. For instance, sensor raw data could be processed by classification, sorting or calculations to generate new features. Figure 8 illustrates the definition of IAnalyticsType.

The interface defines a variable AnalyticsType which is used to indicate the type of data processing. For instance, "FFT" AnalyticsType could be used for audio sensor to capture PWM data format and generate frequency spectrum features. This can be set by user from OPC-UA client side and OPC-UA server at the IoT edge device side will switch to the new analytics type if the function is supported.

The Interface has another sub object Features which is a FunctionalGroupType defined by Device Information Model. Similar to DataValues for IDataCaptureType, this object type holds all the features generated by the data processing function specified by IAnalyticsType for one data analytics round. One or multiple data sampling could be used within one analytics round to generate one set of features.

SensorDeviceType

To represent a sensor device in OPC-UA address space, An ObjectTypes SensorDevice-Type is defined. Figure 9 illustrates the definition of SensorDeviceType. SensorDevice-Type is sub ObjectTypes of DeviceType from Device Information Model, and it would inherit all the properties, variables, and objects from DeviceType.

SensorDeviceType implements three Interfaces ObjectTypes: IConfigurationType, IDataCaptureType and IAnalyticsType. An actual sensor device object does not need to implement all three interfaces. To support which interfaces depends on the sensor data type, device capability and requirement.

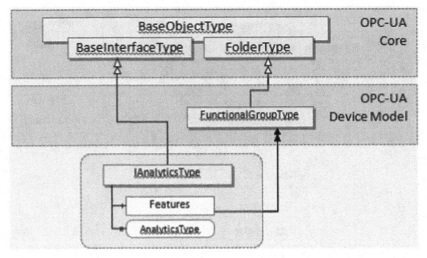

Fig. 8. IAnalyticsType

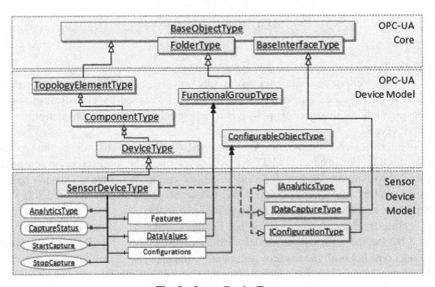

Fig. 9. SensorDeviceType

5 Provisioning Server for Fixable Device Connectivity

Device connectivity is one of the key enablers of IoT interoperability. With the number of devices increasing, it becomes challenging to manage and deploy a fleet of IoT heterogeneous devices in an automatic and scalable manner. To address this issue, we developed Flexible Device Connectivity as shown in Fig. 10. In particular, a provision server is developed for deploying IoT applications for heterogeneous devices. It supports flexible sensor-edge-platform connection, remote application deployment, automatic model update, secure device connection and management by fully leveraging container technology.

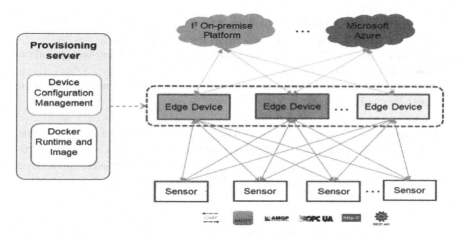

Fig. 10. Overview of flexible device connectivity

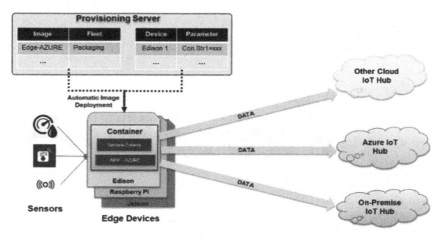

Fig. 11. Design of provision server

Figure 11 shows the details of provision server and its working mechanism. Provision server is designed by fully leveraging container with following functions:

- Enable IoT device management and configuration to deploy and manage device in scale way with support of device fleet management and interactive web interface to add and configure sensor/devices
- Support different networking protocols (e.g., CoAP, MQTT, AMQP, OPC UA and Rest API) including low level device-edge and edge-platform communication.

- Connect edge devices to various platforms including Azure IoT cloud and On-premise IoT platforms, and enable re-directing the data to different platform on-the-fly.
- Support automatic application deployment for uploading software and data analytics models on remote devices.
- Apply light-weight container technology to reduce network traffic and footprint requirement by only updating container deltas with small footprint.
- Support wide variety of chipset architectures and thus enable software portability across different hardware platforms
- Embedded security and authentication support for network communication, using secure token and certificate.

The interface of provision server is shown in Fig. 12. A number of devices, grouped in to multiple fleets, are managed through the interactive interface. User can configure application containers with different parameters, push software updates, check device status, view logs, and so forth. In addition, it also support automatic and remote machine learning (ML) model deployment on edge device.

a.   Status and information of device list

b.   Deploy image to a fleet of devices

Fig. 12. Interface of the flexible device connectivity

6   Conclusion

We proposed a layered IIoT interoperability framework, which is composed of 3 layers. In the middle layer, there is a provisioning server for adaptive system configuration, lightweight container for remote deployment, as well as automatic application update and quick failure recovery mechanisms. With this framework, sensors, edge devices, machines, platforms are automatically connected and interoperated, according to real-time and interactive parameters setting and configuration file updates. Data model is also proposed to enable sematic interoperability.

References

1. Rojko, A.: Industry 4.0 concept: background and overview. Int. J. Interact. Mob. Technol. **11**(5), 77–90 (2017)
2. Noura, M., Atiquzzaman, M., Gaedke, M.: Interoperability in Internet of Things: taxonomies and open challenges. Mob. Networks Appl. **24**(3), 796–809 (2018). https://doi.org/10.1007/s11036-018-1089-9
3. Siemens MindSphere. https://siemens.mindsphere.io/en
4. Microsoft Azure. https://azure.microsoft.com/en-us/
5. PTC ThingWorx. https://www.ptc.com/en/resources/iiot/product-brief/thingworx-platform
6. OPC UA. https://opcfoundation.org/
7. Risteska Stojkoska, B.L., Trivodaliev, K.V.: A review of Internet of Things for smart home: challenges and solutions. J. Cleaner Prod. **140**, 1454–1464 (2017)
8. Chifor, B.C., Bica, I., Patriciu, V.V., Pop, F.: A security authorization scheme for smart home Internet of Things devices. Futur. Gener. Comput. Syst. **86**, 740–749 (2018)
9. Poslad, S., Ma, A., Wang, Z., Mei, H.: Using a smart city IOT to incentivise and target shifts in mobility behaviour—Is it a piece of pie? Sensors (Switzerland) **15**, 13069–13096 (2015)
10. Sherly, J., Somasundareswari, D.: Internet of Things Based Smart Transportation Systems. Int. Res. J. Eng. Technol. **2**, 1207–1210 (2015)
11. Elijah, O., Rahman, T.A., Orikumhi, I., Leow, C.Y., Hindia, M.N.: An overview of Internet of Things (IoT) and data analytics in agriculture: benefits and challenges. IEEE Internet Things J. **5**, 3758–3773 (2018)
12. Yin, Y., Zeng, Y., Chen, X., Fan, Y.: The internet of things in healthcare: an overview. J. Ind. Inf. Integr. **1**, 1–13 (2016)
13. Kantarci, B., Mouftah, H.T.: Trustworthy sensing for public safety in cloud-centric Internet of things. IEEE Internet Things J. **1**, 360–368 (2014)
14. Atzori, L., Iera, A., Morabito, G.: The Internet of Things: a survey. Comput. Networks **54**(15), 2787–2805 (2010)
15. Da Xu, L., He, W., Li, S.: Internet of things in industries: a survey. IEEE Trans. Ind. Inform. **10**(4), 2233–2243 (2014)
16. Shi, W., Cao, J., Zhang, Q., Li, Y., Xu, L.: Edge computing: vision and challenges. IEEE Internet Things J. **3**(5), 637–646 (2016)
17. Shi, W., Dustdar, S.: The promise of edge computing. Computer **49**(5), 78–81 (2016)
18. Lyu, L., Bezdek, J.C., He, X., Jin, J.: Fog-embedded deep learning for the Internet of Things. IEEE Trans. Ind. Inform. **15**, 4206–4215 (2019)
19. Jiang, L., Lou, X., Tan, R., Zhao, J.: Differentially private collaborative learning for the IoT edge. In: International Workshop on Crowd Intelligence for Smart Cities: Technology and Applications (CISC) (2018)
20. Almeida, F., Oliveira, J., Cruz, J.: Open standards and open source: enabling interoperability. Int. J. Softw. Eng. Appl. **2**(1), 1–11 (2011)
21. ITU-T Y.2060 standard. https://www.itu.int/rec/T-REC-Y.2060-201206-I
22. Kalatzis, N., et al.: Semantic interoperability for IoT platforms in support of decision making: an experiment on early wildfire detection. Sensors **19**(3), 528 (2019)

Task Offloading in Computing Continuum Using Collaborative Reinforcement Learning

Alberto Robles-Enciso$^{(\boxtimes)}$ and Antonio F. Skarmeta

Department of Information and Communications Engineering, University of Murcia,
30100 Murcia, Spain
{alberto.roblese,skarmeta}@um.es

Abstract. One of the challenges in the Computing Continuum paradigm is the optimal distribution of the generated tasks between the devices in each layer (cloud-fog-edge). In this paper, we propose to use Reinforcement Learning (RL) to solve the Task Assignment Problem (TAP) at the edge layer and then we propose a novel multi-layer extension of RL (ML-RL) techniques that allows edge agents to query an upper-level agent with more knowledge to improve the performance in complex and uncertain situations. We first formulate the task assignment process considering the trade-off between energy consumption and execution time. We then present a greedy solution as a baseline and implement our two RL proposals in the PureEdgeSim simulator. Finally, several simulations of each algorithm are evaluated with different numbers of devices to verify scalability. The simulation results show that reinforcement learning solutions outperformed the heuristic-based solutions and our multi-layer approach can significantly improve performance in high device density scenarios.

Keywords: Internet of things · Edge computing · Computing continuum · Task offloading · Resource allocation · Reinforcement learning

1 Introduction

Latency-critical applications are a major concern in today's networks as they are saturated by a large number of devices continuously sending tasks. The edge computing paradigm is able to minimise end-user latency but has limited computing capacity, therefore to improve its performance, Computing Continuum proposes the combination of the edge and the cloud in a single interconnected workflow. However, to make efficient use of devices it is necessary to define a computation-offloading framework. Each edge device receives tasks with specific requirements and has to decide whether to perform the computation itself or offload the task to another edge node or the cloud.

© The Author(s), under exclusive license to Springer Nature Switzerland AG 2022
A. González-Vidal et al. (Eds.): GIoTS 2022, LNCS 13533, pp. 82–95, 2022.
https://doi.org/10.1007/978-3-031-20936-9_7

This problem is the *"task assignment problem"* and is a combinatorial optimization problem defined as the process of determining where the computation of each task is performed in order to minimise certain parameters, such as the aforementioned latency and energy consumption. In our article we designed an edge computing architecture in which edge devices receive tasks and can process them locally or send them either to another edge device, to the fog server or the cloud. The main contributions of this work as the following:

- We define the task assignment problem in edge computing as an optimisation problem with a trade-off between latency and energy consumption.
- We introduce a reinforcement learning algorithm for the task offloading decision. Each edge device will be an RL agent that can decide to compute its tasks locally or send them to the edge, fog or cloud layer.
- We propose a novel RL approach based on a multi-layer system in which the RL agents of the devices can delegate the offloading decision to an agent of a higher layer.
- The performance of the proposal is compared with a Greedy and single-layer RL algorithm, showing that the proposed solution is superior to the other algorithms.

This paper is organized as follows. In Sect. 2 we explore the state of the art of the task assignment problem. In Sect. 3 we formulated the assignment problem with its main components. In Sect. 4 we introduce a simple reinforcement learning algorithm and propose our novel multi-layer RL approach. Finally, in Sect. 5 we evaluate the proposed algorithms and present the results.

2 Related Work

The task assignment problem can be solved by several methods using very different techniques [4] such as convex optimization techniques, Lyapunov optimization [13], Hungarian algorithm [7] and novel genetic algorithms [19]. In addition, new methods based on dynamic programming and machine learning [17] techniques have emerged, such as reinforcement learning (RL) and neural network reinforcement learning (Deep RL). Nonetheless, it is difficult to find optimal solutions to the task assignment problem, especially given the prohibitive computational complexity in IoT devices, so in practice heuristic-based techniques or methods that search for suboptimal solutions are often used.

One of the most common techniques are greedy algorithms, which provide sub-optimal solutions but at a low computational cost. In some cases, it is possible to achieve solutions very close to the optimal solution [11,20]. Similarly, an alternative approach to solving optimisation problems are algorithms based on metaheuristics, the most popular are Genetic Algorithms which are inspired by the process of natural selection [5,6].

On the other hand, Reinforcement Learning (RL) is a novel technique based on machine learning that is not part of the well-known supervised and unsupervised learning paradigms. The purpose of reinforcement learning is to learn an optimal, or near-optimal, policy that maximizes the reward function and provides an optimal set of actions for different agent states and environmental conditions. RL algorithms learn iteratively through the immediate rewards they receive each time they perform an action based on their state [9,16].

In some cases, it is not possible to make use of a reinforcement learning algorithm directly, such as in scenarios where the agents' state is a large number of variables, making Q-Learning algorithms inefficient, or even when the state variables are not discrete. To address these limitations, researchers propose the use of neural networks to model the agent's learning process [2,18]. In general, Reinforcement Learning and Deep RL algorithms have a common problem, the convergence time. This type of algorithm requires a series of iterations to reach the optimal solution, and in some cases using random factor policies may take even longer to reach the optimal solution [3].

Finally, some approaches in the literature use other novel techniques to solve TAP. In [12] Dadmehr Rahbari and Mohsen Nickray use classification and regression trees to solve the problem. In [1] Mainak Adhikari et al. design a delay-dependent priority-aware offloading (DPTO) strategy for scheduling and processing tasks, generated from IoT devices to suitable computing devices. In [8] Lindong Liu et al. propose a supervised machine learning approach to solve the TAP based on classification data mining technique.

3   Task Assignment Problem

Computing continuum systems are composed of a large number of heterogeneous devices with different characteristics and roles. Some devices have high computational power and serve as a host for processing tasks, while others with lower computational power constantly generate tasks for the applications they run. This forms a layered architecture where devices are separated into levels according to their role.

On top of this architecture appears a flow of offloaded tasks, as some lower-capacity devices decide to send tasks to more powerful devices for processing. We define a task as an indivisible piece of computation generated by a particular application, which has its own characteristics and constraints such as maximum latency, data size and computational resources required. One of the key components of these architectures is the Task Assignment Problem since it is necessary to determine the best possible distribution of tasks between devices at each layer.

3.1   System Model

Our proposed system consists of devices that are separated into three layers, depending on their role, Fig. 1 shows the proposed offloading architecture. The layer closest to the users is the edge layer, which consists of heterogeneous edge devices that might have an intermittent connection and a dynamic position. This layer has the lowest latency and computational capacity, and is where tasks are generated from the edge devices that host IoT applications. Tasks can be processed locally or sent to devices in any of the three layers according to the decision of the offloading algorithm.

The fog layer is the middle layer where fog Servers are deployed. Fog Servers are small datacenters with intermediate computational capacity located between edge devices and the cloud, hence they have intermediate latency.

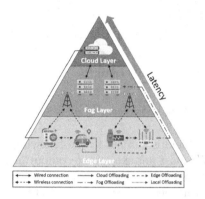

Fig. 1. Edge computing architecture.

The upper layer is the cloud layer, which has very high computational capacity and medium-high latency. The cloud acts as a single device, but in real deployments it is typically a large number of high-performance computers in a datacenter, therefore its computational capacity can be very high. However, their latency is also high due to the distance to end-users.

In the edge layer each edge device executes an offloading algorithm that decides, using the local information of the device, where it offloads the tasks it generates. We call to the decision-making system that uses the perception of the environment an agent.

3.2 Problem Definition

As shown above, a device can decide to execute a task locally ($a = 0$) or send it to a adjacent node ($a = 1$), a fog server ($a = 2$) or the cloud ($a = 3$), resulting in a specific cost as a weighted sum of execution time and energy consumption.

We formulate the cost of our optimization problem as a piecewise function that depends on the offloading action, which we define in detail in a paper still under revision. In a real environment, it may be possible that the offloading process fails ($a = -1$), so it is necessary to define a penalty cost δ in the segmented function Eq. 1.

Therefore, our proposal consists of designing an optimisation scheme in which the cost resulting from the allocation of tasks ($\boldsymbol{K}$) produced by a device $\boldsymbol{d}$ is minimised. Therefore, each device $\boldsymbol{d}$ aims to perform the best possible assignment of actions for each task $\boldsymbol{k}$ to minimise the resulting cost of all assignments.

The optimization problem is formulated in Eq. 2.

$$C_{d,k}(a) = \begin{cases} C_{d,k}^l & \text{if } a \text{ is equal to } 0 \\ C_{d,k}^m & \text{if } a \text{ is equal to } 1 \\ C_{d,k}^f & \text{if } a \text{ is equal to } 2 \\ C_{d,k}^c & \text{if } a \text{ is equal to } 3 \\ \delta_d & \text{if } a \text{ is equal to } -1 \end{cases} \tag{1}$$

$$G_d = \min_{a_k} \sum_{k=1}^{K} C_{d,k}(a_k) \tag{2}$$

subject to:

$$\sum_{k=1}^{K'} T_{mips}^{d,k} \leqslant D_{mips}^d, \forall k, \ L_{d,k} \leqslant T_{dl}^{d,k}, \ a_k \in \{-1,0,1,2,3\}$$

The optimization problem is subject to the following constraints: The tasks assigned to a device (K') must not exceed the computing capacity of the device, no task must exceed its maximum latency (deadline) and the possible actions that can be taken are error, local processing, offload to an adjacent node, offload to the fog layer and offload to the cloud layer.

4   RL-Based Task Offloading Algorithm

To solve the TAP defined in Eq. 2 we use a reinforcement learning approach based on Tabular Q-Learning. Each edge device runs its own reinforcement learning algorithm to explore the optimal task offloading policy by minimizing the long-term cumulative discounted cost. Figure 2 shows an overview of our agent.

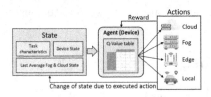

Fig. 2. Q-Learning agent.

When a task is received, the agent will decide offloading action ($a_t \in A = \{0,1,2,3\}$), whenever possible, whether to process the task locally (*action 0*), send it to a nearby node (*action 1*), send it to the fog layer (*action 2*) or send it to the cloud (*action 3*). The decision will depend on the environment, which is based on the characteristics of the task, the state of the device and the last average state of fog and cloud.

The learning process uses a Q-Value table to store and query the value of the Q-function for each state-action. When an action is performed, the new Q-Value in the table is updated according to the following one-step Q update formula:

$$Q(s_t, a_t) = (1 - \alpha) Q(s_t, a_t) + \alpha (C_t + \gamma \min_a Q(s_{t+1}, a)) \tag{3}$$

The reward obtained after the execution of an action is a piecewise function of two elements that depends on the execution time of the task. If the execution time of the task $(T^t_{end} - T^t_{start})$ is less than its deadline (T^t_{dl}), the reward obtained is a weighted sum between the execution time and the energy consumption of the task (T^t_{energy}). Otherwise, the reward is the same but multiplied by a penalty δ factor.

$$C_t = \begin{cases} (T^t_{end} - T^t_{start}) + \beta T^t_{energy} & T^t_{end} - T^t_{start} < T^t_{dl} \\ \delta \cdot ((T^t_{end} - T^t_{start}) + \beta T^t_{energy}) & \text{otherwise} \end{cases} \tag{4}$$

The reward function only considers energy and execution time, all other parameters are part of the state and do not need to be included as they will have an indirect impact on the latency.

In this basic RL approach, each device works independently using its local information and aggregated global information. Thus, decisions are made according to the local state and knowledge of the agent. However, the biased view of the environment and the lack of knowledge in the early stages of the algorithm causes low performance in complex situations. To overcome this drawback, we propose to allow the RL agent of a device to delegate the offloading decision to a upper level agent in case it does not have enough information. The upper level agent, e.g. deployed in the fog layer, will decide according to its knowledge and the global state of the system. The offloading decision will be sent to the querying device and both the local and the upper level agent will learn from the reward obtained after executing the action. Figure 3 shows the process of the offloading query.

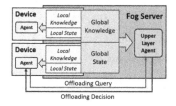

Fig. 3. Offloading query process.

In this enhanced architecture, both edge devices and fog servers run an independent RL algorithm that can collaborate between layers. The offloading query allows a passive knowledge transfer from fog agents to edge agents, especially useful when an edge agent starts with no knowledge and performs queries to learn from the decisions of the upper level agent.

We extend the functionality of the RL algorithm to include in the set of feasible actions of edge devices the new offloading query action. Edge devices and fog servers execute the same algorithm but with different behaviour, as they have a different view of the environment.

The edge device agent now has the action $(A \cup \{4\})$ of performing the offloading query. When a reward is received for an action queried to a fog server, it is considered to have a higher value since it is assumed that the upper agent will take better decisions. Also, the Q-Value of the query action is penalized as it is used to decrease the probability of being selected while increasing the agent's local knowledge. On the other hand, the upper layer agent waits to receive offloading queries from other agents and uses its own knowledge and view of the current state, including cloud and fog realtime CPU usages, to take an offloading decision and send it back. As a result, a reward will be obtained from the execution of the offloading action that will improve the knowledge of both the agent who made the request and the upper layer agent.

Algorithm 1: ε-greedy Multilayer Q-Learning Algorithm

Parameters: discount factor γ, learning rate α, exploration rate ε, penalty factor δ, query reward factor ρ and query use penalty ω

```
1  begin
2      for each step t do
3          Observe actual state s_t
4          Determine feasible action set A' from A
5          isQuery ← false
6          e ← random number from [0,1]
7          if e < ε then
8          |   a_t ← randomly select an action from A'
9          else
10         |   a_t ← arg min  Q(s_t, a)
           |           a∈A'
11         end
12         if a_t is to ask a fog server then
13         |   isQuery ← true
14         |   Send the offloading request to a fog server
15         |   a_t ← get the fog server decision
16         end
17         Execute or send the offloading action a_t
18         Wait for the task to be completed
19         Observe new state s_{t+1}
20         Calculate reward C_t by (4)
21         if isQuery then
22         |   C_t ← ρ · C_t
23         |   C_t^q ← ω · t · C_t
24         |   Update Q(s_t, 4) using (3) with C_t^q
25         end
26         Update Q(s_t, a_t) according to (3) with C_t
27     end
28 end
```

The proposed multilayer solution to the offloading problem based on ε-greedy Q-Learning is shown in Algorithm 1. As mentioned before, all devices run the same algorithm but with their own view of the state and their own knowledge. This means that each device will manage an independent Q-Table that will be trained locally. In addition, the upper layer agent will take advantage of all interactions with the devices to update their global status.

5   Performance Evaluation

In this section we will evaluate our proposed solution compared to a greedy and a single layer reinforcement learning approach in a simulated edge computing environment. We will perform simulations to compare the performance of each algorithm using a set of metrics. The simulation results are available in our GitHub repository [15].

5.1   Methodology

The purpose of our evaluation is to obtain enough data to fairly compare the offloading algorithms. Therefore, we will make use of an edge computing simulator to test the behaviour of the algorithms from low-density to high-density device scenarios. The output of each simulation will be a set of metrics used to determine the performance of the algorithm in the specific simulation scenario. To prevent inaccurate results caused by the random component of the simulator, the metrics will be calculated by averaging the result of several simulations on the same conditions.

5.2   Experiment Setup

The evaluation has been performed on a modified version of PureEdgeSim v4.2 [10], the source code of our extension is available on GitHub [14]. The simulated edge computing scenario consists of three layers of devices (edge-fog-cloud) randomly distributed over an area of 200×200 metres.

To verify the scalability of the proposed algorithms, the number of edge devices in each simulation is increased by 10 until 200. Each simulation lasts 10 min and is executed 10 times per configuration to calculate the average result. The bandwidth of the connection between devices is 100 megabits per second at the edge and fog layers, while the connection to the cloud layer is 20 megabits per second. The maximum range of the wireless connection of the edge devices is 40 m. The simulation parameters of the PureEdgeSim environment are summarised in Table 1.

5.3   Metrics

To compare the performance of each algorithm we define the following benchmark metrics:

– **Task Success Rate:** The percentage of the tasks that finish their execution over the total. A task is not considered to complete its execution correctly if its execution time exceeds its deadline or if the offloading process fails. This metric is one of the most important for the evaluation.
– **Average Total Time:** The total time required to complete successfully a task, which includes the execution time and the time to send the task to the processing node. This metric is especially useful for comparing the latency incurred by each algorithm.

Table 1. PureEdgeSim simulation parameters

Simulation Parameter	Value
Simulation duration	10 min
Number of averaged simulations	10 per configuration
Min number of edge devices	10
Max number of edge devices	200
Simulation area	200 m × 200 m
Edge and Fog Bandwidth	100 Mbps
Cloud Bandwidth	20 Mbps
Edge devices range	40 m

- **Complete Average Total Time:** Same as **Average Total Time** but also considering the time wasted on tasks that were not executed successfully.
- **Failed tasks due to latency:** The number of tasks that have failed because their execution time exceeds their maximum allowed latency.
- **Average CPU Usage per device:** Average CPU usage of a device. Useful to determine how much the computational resources of the devices are used.
- **Average Energy Consumption per Device:** Average power consumption of one device.

5.4   Compared Methods

We have implemented in the simulator three algorithms to evaluate their performance. The greedy solution will serve as a reference for comparison with the single-layer RL algorithm and our proposed multi-layer guided RL.

In addition, we designed three methods based on the implementations of the reinforcement learning solutions explained in previous sections. The first one is the basic implementation of a RL algorithm that runs locally on each device without external knowledge, in the tests we will denote it as *"Local RL"*. The second and third methods are the same implementation of the multi-layer RL algorithm but with different initial conditions. The *"RL Multilayer Empty"* version starts each simulation with all Q-Tables (knowledge) of the devices completely empty, while *"RL Multilayer"* version uses on the fog servers the Q-Table resulting from the previous simulations, with the same configuration, to simulate the behaviour of a system that starts with knowledge to improve initial performance. The parameters used by both methods are summarised in Table 2.

Table 2. Reinforcement learning algorithm parameters

Parameter/RL Algorithm	Single	Multi
Learning rate α	0.6	0.6
Latency-Energy Trade-off β	0.003	0.003
Discount factor γ	0.3	0.3
Failure penalty δ	1000	1000
Average CPU refresh rate	60 s	60 s
Query reward factor ρ	-	0.2
Query use penalty ω	-	10
Initial Q-Value	200	200
Initial Query Q-Value	-	10

5.5 Experimental Results and Analysis

In this section we will show the most important results of the simulations performed for each algorithm and configuration. Each of the subfigures of 4 represents the metrics that were defined to make the comparison between algorithms.

One of the most critical results is the success rate in task execution, since in practice this has the most negative impact on the end-user. Figure 4a shows the success rate resulting from each algorithm when performing the simulation.

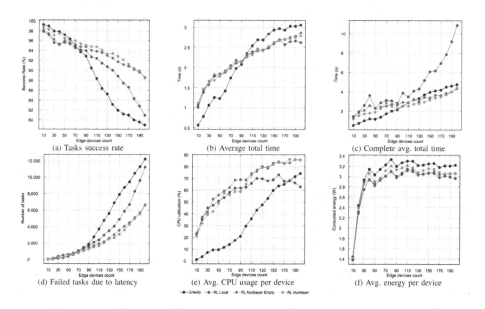

(a) Tasks success rate   (b) Average total time   (c) Complete avg. total time

(d) Failed tasks due to latency   (e) Avg. CPU usage per device   (f) Avg. energy per device

Greedy   RL Local   RL Multilayer Empty   RL Multilayer

Fig. 4. Simulations results

As we can see, in low device density scenarios, the greedy method outperforms the others until it reaches a medium density, 70 devices, where its success rate starts to drop. In the high device density scenarios the performance of the greedy method and the RL single-layer are very low while both multi-layer methods are able to keep an acceptable performance.

This behaviour is due to the fact that in low device density scenarios there are not a large number of tasks and most of them can be executed by the fog and cloud servers without saturation, so the heuristics of the greedy method gives a better result than the reinforcement learning algorithms. When a medium density of devices is reached, the appropriate use of resources becomes more relevant and algorithms using reinforcement learning techniques are able to adapt dynamically to keep the success rate as high as possible. In high density scenarios with a large number of tasks the optimal use of processing nodes is critical, therefore the greedy method cannot achieve good results and even the single-layer RL method cannot improve the result. In contrast, multi-layer RL methods achieve a high success rate due to the possibility of delegating offloading decisions to higher level agents. In fact, the best success rate is achieved with multi-layer RL method that start with the Q-Table of the fog servers filled with the values learned from previous simulations since it allows to provide useful knowledge to the devices in the early stages of the learning process.

The average time required to complete a task for each algorithm and number of devices is shown in Fig. 4b. Similar to the success rate, the average total time of the greedy algorithm drastically changes its performance based on the number of devices, while reinforcement learning algorithms slowly change the average total time. The three RL methods provide a similar average total time as this metric only considers tasks that have successfully completed their execution.

If we consider the time lost due to tasks that do not execute correctly because of latency, we can see in Fig. 4c the real impact of the algorithm's actions when deciding to do an unsuitable offloading. The behaviour of the greedy algorithm is similar to Fig. 4b, but the single-layer RL method substantially increases the time in high device density scenarios as the impact of bad decisions in complex situations is very high. In contrast, multi-layer RL methods avoid the initial uncertainty by delegating the decision, thereby making better offloading decisions that reduce latency failures as can be seen in Fig. 4d.

One more relevant result that can be analysed is the average CPU usage per device, which indicates the degree of utilization of the system's computational resources. A proper distribution of tasks among the devices results in a high average CPU usage per device as resource utilisation is maximised. In contrast, low CPU usage indicates that the algorithm is saturating a few devices while many others are idle. As shown in Fig. 4e, which represents the simulator output for this metric, the two multi-layer RL methods stand out from others, and the greedy method shows a low use of computational resources.

Similarly, the performance of algorithms can be measured in terms of their energy consumption as this is one of the components of the optimization problem, Fig. 4f shows the average energy consumption per device obtained from the simulations. The greedy algorithm presents the highest energy consumption while the RL algorithms show the lowest energy consumption.

After having seen the performance of the algorithms in different simulator scenarios, we can conclude that the greedy algorithm offers acceptable performance in low and medium device density scenarios. However, as device density increases, more complex methods must be applied to maintain system performance. Reinforcement learning algorithms are able to adapt to complex scenarios at a low computational cost, thus providing the best results in simulations. Furthermore, our multi-layer approach stands out from other methods because in complex high-density scenarios it shows high performance in the most important metrics. This improvement is due to enhanced offloading decision system by using external knowledge and serves as evidence of the good performance of our multi-layer RL proposal. Therefore, reinforcement learning algorithms are good methods for solving the task assignment problem and our proposal is a useful and easily applicable extension to any RL algorithm to improve its performance.

6   Conclusion

In this paper, we have presented the task assignment problem as a key component of collaborative edge computing architectures. As shown in the first section, there are several methods for solving TAP, but those based on artificial intelligence are the most promising. Reinforcement learning is presented as a solution for the task offloading process in our proposed three-layer edge-fog-cloud architecture.

In this work we have studied different configurations to understand the impact of task distribution and limited vision of RL agents and how this impacts the performance behaviour of the algorithm in complex situations. To overcome these drawbacks, we propose a novel extension of reinforcement learning techniques that allows agents to query an upper-level agent with more knowledge and a broader view of the environment.

We have implemented our proposals together with a greedy alternative in a modified version of PureEdgeSim simulator and performed several tests to compare the performance of each algorithm in different situations following a set of metrics, providing access to the results and simulations for reproducibility. The experimental results showed that, compared with the greedy and classical RL algorithms, under multiple conditions, our proposed multilayer RL algorithm achieved much better performance in scenarios with a high number of devices and tasks.

Acknowledgments. This work was supported by the FPI Grant 21463/FPI/20 of the Seneca Foundation in Region of Murcia (Spain), partially funded by project PID2020–112675RB–C44 and PTAS–20211009 MCIN/AEI/10.13039/501100011033 and by the "European Union NextGenerationEU/PRTR".

References

1. Adhikari, M., Mukherjee, M., Srirama, S.: DPTO: a deadline and priority-aware task offloading in fog computing framework leveraging multilevel feedback queueing. IEEE Internet Things J. **7**, 5773–5782 (2020)
2. Alfakih, T., Hassan, M., Gumaei, A., Savaglio, C., Fortino, G.: Task offloading and resource allocation for mobile edge computing by deep reinforcement learning based on SARSA. IEEE Access **8**, 54074–54084 (2020)
3. Argerich, M.F., Fürst, J., Cheng, B.: Tutor4RL: guiding reinforcement learning with external knowledge. In: AAAI Spring Symposium: Combining Machine Learning with Knowledge Engineering (2020)
4. Bellendorf, J., Ádám Mann, Z.: Classification of optimization problems in fog computing. Futur. Gener. Comput. Syst. **107**, 158–176 (2020). https://doi.org/10.1016/j.future.2020.01.036
5. Ghanavati, S., Abawajy, J., Izadi, D.: An energy aware task scheduling model using ant-mating optimization in fog computing environment. IEEE Trans. Serv. Comput. **15**(4), 2007-2017 (2020)
6. Jia, Z., Yu, J., Ai, X., Xu, X., Yang, D.: Cooperative multiple task assignment problem with stochastic velocities and time windows for heterogeneous unmanned aerial vehicles using a genetic algorithm. Aerosp. Sci. Technol. **76**, 112–125 (2018). https://doi.org/10.1016/j.ast.2018.01.025
7. Liang, J., Long, Y., Mei, Y., Wang, T., Jin, Q.: A distributed intelligent hungarian algorithm for workload balance in sensor-cloud systems based on urban fog computing. IEEE Access **7**, 77649–77658 (2019). https://doi.org/10.1109/ACCESS.2019.2922322
8. Liu, L., Qi, D., Zhou, N., Wu, Y.: A task scheduling algorithm based on classification mining in fog computing environment. Wirel. Commun. Mobile Comput. **2018**, 1–11 (2018). https://doi.org/10.1155/2018/2102348
9. Liu, X., Qin, Z., Gao, Y.: Resource allocation for edge computing in IoT networks via reinforcement learning. In: ICC 2019–2019 IEEE International Conference on Communications (ICC), pp. 1–6 (2019)
10. Mechalikh, C., Taktak, H., Moussa, F.: Pureedgesim: a simulation framework for performance evaluation of cloud, edge and mist computing environments. Comput. Sci. Inf. Syst. **18**, 42 (2020). https://doi.org/10.2298/CSIS200301042M
11. Rahbari, D., Nickray, M.: Low-latency and energy-efficient scheduling in fog-based IoT applications. Turk. J. Electr. Eng. Comput. Sci. **27**, 1406–1427 (2019)
12. Rahbari, D., Nickray, M.: Task offloading in mobile fog computing by classification and regression tree. Peer-to-Peer Netw. Appl. **13**, 104–122 (2020)
13. Ren, C., Lyu, X., Ni, W., Tian, H., Song, W., Liu, R.P.: Distributed online optimization of fog computing for internet of things under finite device buffers. IEEE Internet Things J. **7**(6), 5434–5448 (2020). https://doi.org/10.1109/JIOT.2020.2979353
14. Robles-Enciso, A.: Pureedgesim RL extension (2021). https://github.com/alb1183/ML-RL-PureEdgeSim
15. Robles-Enciso, A.: ML-RL Simulations results (2022). https://github.com/alb1183/ML-RL-simulations
16. Sen, T., Shen, H.: Machine learning based timeliness-guaranteed and energy-efficient task assignment in edge computing systems. In: 2019 IEEE 3rd International Conference on Fog and Edge Computing (ICFEC), pp. 1–10 (2019)

17. Shakarami, A., Ghobaei-Arani, M., Shahidinejad, A.: A survey on the computation offloading approaches in mobile edge computing: a machine learning-based perspective. Comput. Netw. **182**, 107496 (2020). https://doi.org/10.1016/j.comnet.2020.107496
18. Wang, J., Zhao, L., Liu, J., Kato, N.: Smart resource allocation for mobile edge computing: a deep reinforcement learning approach. IEEE Trans. Emerg. Top. Comput. **9**(3), 1529–1541 (2019)
19. Wen, Z., Yang, R., Garraghan, P., Lin, T., Xu, J., Rovatsos, M.: Fog orchestration for internet of things services. IEEE Internet Comput. **21**(2), 16–24 (2017). https://doi.org/10.1109/MIC.2017.36
20. Zhang, G., Shen, F., Liu, Z., Yang, Y., Wang, K., Zhou, M.T.: FEMTO: fair and energy-minimized task offloading for fog-enabled IoT networks. IEEE Internet Things J. **6**(3), 4388–4400 (2019). https://doi.org/10.1109/JIOT.2018.2887229

Assessing Efficiency Benefits of Edge Intelligence

Nicola Lenherr[1], René Pawlitzek[2], and Bruno Michel[1(✉)]

[1] IBM Research – Europe, 8803 Rueschlikon, Switzerland
bmi@zurich.ibm.com
[2] OST Ostschweizer Fachhochschule, CH-9471 Buchs, Switzerland

Abstract. The recent focus on deep learning accuracy ignored economic and environmental cost. Introduction of Green AI is hampered by lack of metrics that balance rewards for accuracy and cost and thus improve selection of best deep learning algorithms and platforms. Recognition and training efficiency universally compare deep learning based on energy consumption measurements for inference and deep learning, on recognition gradients, and on number of classes. Sustainability is assessed with deep learning lifecycle efficiency and life cycle recognition efficiency metrics that include the number of times models are used.

Keywords: Deep learning · Sustainability · Edge · Green AI · Accuracy · Accelerator

1 Introduction

Artificial Intelligence (AI) and machine learning (ML) have revolutionized how industries address data deluge. Stagnating performance of CPUs [1] has triggered specialized computing architectures where frequently used functions are accelerated rebalancing performance and flexibility [2, 3]. Since 8 years, AI considerably improved accuracy in deep learning (DL) models but training cost increased $300,000\times$ which is not sustainable. The focus on accuracy ignores sustainability [4] which asks for a stronger focus on Green AI [7]. Low-power accelerators are crucial for edge ML since inference accounts for 90% cost [1]. DL progress requires efficient balancing of flexibility, number of classes, and accuracy. DL is inherently compute-intensive: The flexibility that outperforms expert models makes it expensive, scaling faster than necessary [10]. Computing time for training grows as square of data points and fourth power of performance, while inference energy grows with the square of classes. DL excels because of over-parametrization, while regularization makes the complexity tractable. Graphic Processors (GPU)- and ASIC-based DL led to widespread adoption, but computing grew faster, at $10\times$ pa. Since 2012 [6].

To identify energy-efficient CNNs, accurate runtime, power, as well as energy models and measurements are important. Common metrics for CNN complexity are too crude to predict energy consumption since it depends on architecture and hardware platform. The Energy-Precision Ratio (M) rewards both accurate and energy efficient CNN architectures. It uses the classification error (Error) with adjustment exponent alpha, and energy consumption per data item (EPI). Higher α enlarges the importance of accuracy over energy consumption but for a fair comparison the number of classes (Cl) has to be included in an assessment. Edge computing proliferated due to reduced latency, bandwidth, improved availability, and better privacy. With federated learning (FL) clients compute an update with local data and communicate this for model aggregation. Communication cost is reduced by structured updates [8–11]. FL preserves privacy by distributed training deep neural networks (DNNs) on local data to optimize global models by averaging trained gradients [12, 13]. FL is heavy on batteries, but a two-layered process provides 20% energy savings [14]. Mobile inference reduces latency with billions of operations. Frequent inferences drain batteries unless compressed models, minimize data transfer, and offloading reduces consumption. Quantization is also efficient in reducing computation and communication.

2 Methods

2.1 Devices, Models, and Frameworks

To cover a wide accelerator spectrum, we used: (1) the Intel MovidiusX processor (NCS2) [16], (2) the Google Coral Dev Board (TPU) [15], (3) the Nvidia Jetson (JNA) [17], (4) a RPi4, and (5) a Windows workstation as reference (Fig. 1A). We tested different models of vastly different complexity: 1) Heart rate variability parameters (HRV par): The model distinguishes between 4 stress classes. The data consists of RR intervals used for training of a two-layer MLP model with 128 neurons followed by a dense layer of 4 and a SoftMax activation. 2) Heart rate variability from RR intervals: The model is a 1D CNN applied on the raw RR intervals [18]. 3) Environmental Sound Classification (ESC) contains 2000 5 s clips recorded with 44.1 kHz separated into 50 different classes [19] from which we used 30. 4) Image Classification: To be comparable to literature three image classification model architectures were included: MobileNet (V2, 1.0), ResNet-50 and VGG-16, trained on the ImageNet dataset with image input size 224×224 pixels and 1000 distinct classes [20].

2.2 Power and Energy Measurements

A inference latency measurement consists of a starting and an ending time-stamp defining the latency in milliseconds. For USB powered devices the metering device [21] was plugged between power adapter and USB port. For other devices power was recorded with the Smart-me [22] (Fig. 1A f and g). Inference duration and power consumption measurements were logged with timestamps. The inference power was calculated with start and end timestamps. For comparison between devices baselines recorded average power consumption for 40 s (~100 data points) while idling. The amount was subtracted from the power recorded during the inference to calculate the energy. Inferences are run repeatedly with the same data and power consumption is recorded after a delay to remove ramp-up effects. Timestamps are stored afterwards to avoid I/O influence on the measurement. A good baselining process improves the accuracy of power measurements in small and even more in larger multi-user, multi-tenant Cloud systems. A baseline measurement is done every time before a measurement is taken on all platforms with the assumption that background processes do not considerably change during the monitored process. Spurious activities happen, but statistically cancel since baselines and measurements are repeated often and averaged (Fig. 1B).

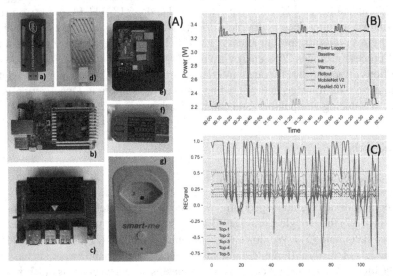

Fig. 1. A) Platforms used and of the tools for acquisition of electrical power consumed: a) Movidius NCS2, b) Coral Dev board c) Coral Dev Sick, d) Jetson Nano, e) Raspberry Pi4, f) Joy-IT UM25C, g) SmartMe. (B) Power measurement graph showing how the baseline was recorded to isolate the energy associated with inference and/or training. The line colors show the different phases (init, green; warmup, red; rollout, violet; and power logger, blue) that were isolated from the inference process of MobileNet V2 (yellow), or ResNet-50 V1 (brown) to improve the accuracy. (C) Process to determine recognition gradient for Top-1 (blue line) up to Top-5 image classification tasks. The values for Top-1 are higher because to determine the gradient, accuracies are divided by N for Top-N predictions (Color figure online).

2.3   Recognition Gradient

Evaluation metrics are important: Accuracy (*acc*) or error rate (*err*) are simple to compute for multi-class/label problems and easy-to-use but biased to majority class data. *Acc* evaluates the quality based on percentage of correct predictions over total number of instances. *Err* evaluates percentage of incorrect predictions [23]. Where Tp is true positive, Tn is true negative, Fn is false negative, and Fp is false positive. Alternative metrics are F-Measure and geometric-mean. Recognition gradient (*RECgrad*) is the probability difference between best and second-best class or the gradient between Tp and next best probability. For a Fp the gradient $Tp - Fp$ becomes negative. For search results the gradient is calculated similar to classifications. *RECgrad* including the 95% confidence interval are calculated statistically from > 100 test cases (Fig. 1C and Fig. 2d). The confidence intervals are typically of the order of 30%. To reduce the confidence intervals more test cases would be needed which were not available in this study. In 1–20% where no true label is found, the gradient is subtracted. This approach makes *RECgrad* more stable and useful compared to classical accuracy calculations when a large number of test cases is used. *RECgrad* is used both with recognition and training efficiency. While top 5 accuracy is a more balanced assessment for single events, the statistical analysis reaches a better result for top 1 analyses. As expected, the risk for a top-1 miss is higher than for a top-5 miss but this is compensated by higher values.

3 Results

DL models for image, audio, and HRV data are compared on accelerated platforms. 2D image data is computationally more demanding than 1D audio data (44 kHz) and heart rate or heart rate variability data (1 Hz). The complexity difference is more than 10000× which is also reflected in the power consumed. We start out with a comparison of energy consumption for inference and learning.

3.1 Energy and Accuracy

Figure 2A shows that large models (brown) consume more energy than medium (violet) and small (red) models. The factor is >6'500 between the largest (VGG-16) on Cloud and the smallest (MobileNet) on TPU. This factor becomes 300'000 when audio (green) and HRV pars (blue) are included. On the same platform (NCS2, JNA) the inference energy E_{inf} varies from 578 mJ (large), over 186 mJ (medium) to 70 mJ (small). This factor is larger on TPU. Small image recognition models save 10-1000× energy, albeit at slightly smaller accuracies, but the accuracy difference is much smaller than the energy consumption difference. Accuracy wise ESC30 is low and VGG-16 high on the *M* graph (Fig. 2a). But VGG-16 classifies 1000 while ESC only 30 classes. Energy measurements with our method are very accurate of the order of 1 and up to 15% of a few cases (Fig. 2a) with a standard deviation that is much smaller than confidence intervals found for *RECgrad* (Fig. 2d).

The comparison is unfair since TPUs use quantization. The NCS2 and JNA consume 2x more energy for the large model, and 10–20× more for the small MobileNet model. The power consumption of Cloud is 100× larger for VGG-16 and >1000× larger for MobileNet irrespective whether computed on GPUs or CPUs. This is due to the added data transfer energy to the Cloud (70 kB for Images, 50 kB for sounds, and 0.5 kB for RR). The transfer energy for a GB from a Mobile/IoT device to the cloud is 202 J/Mbyte [24, 25]. Inference comparisons between platforms are unfair for models with different accuracies. It would be better to balance energy consumption and accuracy.

3.2 Energy-Precision Ratio

Energy-Precision ratio M compares models and platforms including accuracy [7]. *M* with ($a = 4$, Fig. 2b) provides a better angle than energy consumption and nicely compares models trained on the same dataset. However, it fails on datasets with different *Cl*: 1000 (image), 30 (audio), and 4 (RR). Selecting among 4 classes is simpler leading to low *M* than among 1000 classes. Due to the low E_{inf}, HRV pars (blue) reaches a low M value. The lowest M is reached by the ESC30 model because the accuracy is high. M is more than $1000\times$ lower on the same platform than VGG-16 and $100\times$ lower than MobileNet. M is high on ARM and server CPU/GPUs. Discussions based on energy-precision graphs do not enable a far better understanding on model, library, and platform efficiency than energy consumption.

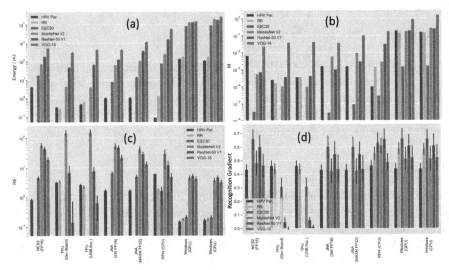

Fig. 2. (a) Inference energy in mJ for stress recognition from HRV pars (blue), or raw HRV (orange), ESC-30 sounds (green), and image recognition for MobileNet model (red), ResNet-50 (violet) and VGG-16 (brown). The left column is from the NCS2 (16 bit), the next two from TPU (Board/Stick), the fourth from the JNA at 5W (16 bit) and the fifth form JNA at full power (32bit), the sixth from the RPi 4 platform, and the final two from a Windows PC (GPU/CPU). (b) Energy precision ratio M for α = 4 which emphasizes accuracy over power consumption, (c) Recognition efficiency RE calculated using Eq. 1. M in (b) and RE in (c) are shown for the same models and platforms with the same colors as in (a). (d) Recognition gradients used for the RE determination are shown with 95% confidence intervals (Color figure online).

3.3 Recognition Efficiency

For this reason, we introduce the "Recognition Efficiency" (*RE*) as follows:

$$RE = \frac{RECgrad \times Cl}{\sqrt[2]{Einf}} \qquad (1)$$

where REC_{grad} is the recognition gradient, Cl the number of classes and E_{inf} the energy in mJ for the inference computation. *RE* uses the square root of energy. Figure 2c shows a superior *RE* of MobileNet (red) on TPU followed by JNA low power, NCS2, JNA MAXN, the ARM on RPi4. *RE* is much lower for Cloud. ResNet-50 model (violet) is on par with the accelerated platforms while Cloud performs 10× worse. For ResNet-50 the TPU performs less than JNA and NCS2. For the VGG-16 model (brown) the TPU board performs 100× worse than NCS2 and Jetson. Still JNA and NCS2 are 3–6× better than Cloud. The audio (green) and time-based models, are ranked as follows: RE is even among accelerated platforms except for Cloud. ESC 30 RE is 10× better on RPI4 than on Cloud which also performs 30× worse than the best accelerated platform. For the HRV Par (blue) with 4 classes the TPU performs 4x better than the NCS2. Surprisingly, RE of HRV Par is high on the RPi4 and the Cloud performs two orders of magnitude worse. The RE confidence intervals are around 30% (black bars) and are comparable among models and platforms with a few exceptions: VGG on TPU and most models on RPI4 are larger due to memory management issues. While image recognition models were optimized, we show that RE compares maturity/efficiency on best recognition for the least amount of inference energy.

3.4 Cloud-Centric and Federated Learning

E_{train} is similar to E_{inf}, but with 4–6 orders of magnitude larger power consumptions. E_{inf} is more important because it is used much more often. Training large and medium size models takes weeks on Cloud consuming MWh - too big for edge systems. The only approach accessible for smaller systems is FL with several edge systems and an integrating server for ESC50, RR, and HRV. Training on systems that generate data (camera, Mobile Hub) and receive labels, reduces the energy wasting movement of data to Cloud and leaves personal data with the owner. Table 1 shows E_{train} on Cloud and on edge systems. REC_{grad} applied to training leads to the training efficiency (TE):

$$TE = \frac{(RECgrad \times Cl)^2}{\sqrt[2]{Etrain}} \tag{2}$$

where REC_{grad} is the recognition gradient, Cl the number of classes and E_{train} the energy in kJ for DL training. TE scales with the square of energy invested. With the 4th power of accuracy TE rewards models that distinguish among many classes with a good REC_{grad}. For a complete evaluation, inference and training need to be combined with a usage factor. The combined term is called deep learning lifecycle efficiency ($DLLCE$):

$$DLLCE = 1 / (E_{train}/(E_{inf} \, x \, F) +) \tag{3}$$

where E_{train} is the training energy, E_{inf} the inference energy, and F the factor how more often inference is used. $DLLCE$ shows that E_{train} is larger than E_{inf} but with often used models the investment is amortized and $DLLCE$ approaches 1 for large F. Table 1 shows that E_{train} is 1000–10'000× larger than E_{inf} and is reflected as inverse square root of TE. TE in Eq. 2 rewards a steep REC_{grad} and large Cl to distinguish different models because data volume for training and model size increase more than linearly with Cl. REC_{grad} decreases with Cl. E_{train} is for the last training and not for model development.

E_{train} for HRV pars, RR raw, and ESC50 was measured while E_{train} for MobileNet, ResNet-50, and VGG-16 is from literature [26, 27]. Table 1 shows a higher RE on JNA compared to Cloud. For the RPi4 only the HRV pars model is more efficient while the RR and ESC50 models perform worse. Current FL with many epochs leads to higher E_{train} since we have not reduced the model communication overhead like few-shot learning [18]. FL requires more epochs for the same accuracy. Federated Averaging, Federated Stochastic Variance Reduced Gradient, and CO-OP on the MNIST dataset show a similar accuracy with the same training epochs with IID data [28]. Trainings were not possible on NCS2 and TPU since these devices are too much limited.

Table 1. Training/Life cycle energy and efficiency

Platform	Model	Etrain (kJ)	TE	Etrain FL (kJ)	TE FL
RPi 4	HRV pars	0.461	5.06	2.73	1.89
	RR raw	15.84	1.23	18.74	1.27
	ESC 30	83.25	1.7	104.9	1.66
JNA	HRV pars	0.12	8.88	2.79	1.87
	RR raw	0.606	7.06	10.34	1.71
	ESC 30	10.45	5.26	42.9	2.60
Cloud /	HRV pars	1.58	2.48		
PC /	RR raw	3.71	2.86		
Work	ESC 30	31.1	3.05		
station	MobileNet V2	14578	95.9		
	ResNet-50-V1	604800	21.4		
	VGG-16	392000	18.6		

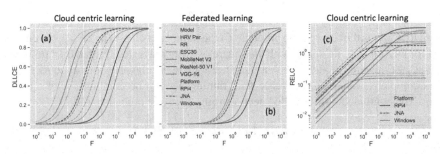

Fig. 3. Deep learning lifecycle efficiency (left) for centralized and (right) FL approaches as function of number of uses (F). Training on Cloud (dotted) need longer amortization than on JNA or RPi4 (solid, dashed). Small models (HRV pars, blue and RR, brown) are quickly amortized. ESC30 models trained on Cloud (green, solid) need much more to amortize training. (bottom) Recognition efficiency (RE) over the entire lifecycle (left) for centralized and (right) federated learning approaches as function of number of uses (F). With models and platforms as in DLLC (Color figure online).

E_{train} of VGG-16 and ResNet-50 require weeks of training on multi-GPU clusters. This improves for MobileNet that is optimized for low network complexity so that *RE* becomes high. E_{train} for FL is higher leading to a 10× shift of the HRV pars curve on RPi4 (blue, solid) towards higher F. Unfortunately, we cannot give values for E_{train} FL on Cloud (Table 1 right columns). Because these values are not published.

3.5 Life Cycle Aspects

Figure 3 shows the life cycle efficiency of image, sound, and stress recognition as function of F: With > 100'000× uses E_{train} reduces RE by <10% but with <100× uses the energy consumption is 100× enlarged. For Cloud training (Fig. 3, *left*), E_{train} for ESC30 is 3.1 million x larger than E_{inf} with a $DLLCE = 0.03$ for 1000 uses. ESC30 needs > 1'000'000 uses so that training adds <5% overhead. For ESC30 on JNA (green, dotted line) E_{train} is 1000× larger than E_{inf}. If used 1000× the E_{train} overhead is 20%. For direct use of RR-intervals E_{train} is fully amortized to<1% overhead with 100 uses. For HRV pars on JNA E_{train} needs 1000 uses for a full amortization. FL is not more efficient because models are as large as datasets. The lifecycle energy consumed for a DL application is calculated by E_{inf}. Multiplied by F and divided by $DLLCE$. Curves in Fig. 3 are drawn using DLLCE (*Eq. 3*) and F sweeping from 100 to 10,000,000.

Table2 shows $DLLCE$ for 10'000 uses in kJ and for 100 million uses in MJ which is very small for HRV pars on RPi4 and JNA and 10× larger on Cloud. For ESC-30 the ratio is: JNA 8× smaller compared to RPi4 and 10× smaller than on Cloud. $DLLCE$ omits model development needing vast hyper-parameter tuning with grid searches. In such cases AI model lifecycle energy exceeds 200'000 MJ, more than the energy a car uses in its lifetime. No detailed information about hyper-parameter tuning is available in literature; for this reason, we have not included number of development and tuning cycles in the E_{train} and total energy values).

Figure 3c,d show how RE varies with included training energy:

$$RE_{LC} = \frac{RECgrad * Cl}{\sqrt[2]{Einf/Etrain/F}} \tag{4}$$

The lifecycle recognition efficiency (RE_{LC}) rewards efficient models ($RE_{LC} > 1$) like HRV pars (blue) or RR intervals (yellow) on RPi4 (solid) or JNA (dashed). MobileNet on Cloud (red dotted) and ResNet on Cloud (violet dotted) reach this threshold only at $F > 10'000'000$. Most models need >100'000× uses before the training energy is deprecated. Below that most models are E_{train} dominated. Models with intermediate RE_{LC} (0.1–1) are ESC 30 on JNA (green dashed) and VGG-16 on Cloud (brown dotted). In the worst category (RE_{LC} <0.1) are ESC30 model on Cloud and rarely used image analysis models (VGG-16 and ResNet50, $F < 1$ Million). The situation is similar also for FL trained models because data for inference remain on the edge and E_{inf} dominates. F was selected from 100–10'000'000 in Fig. 3 since for most models the transition from training to inference energy domination happens in this range.

Figure 4b shows the effective recognition efficiency that is reached by a given implementation as function of number of uses. The range varies from 1000 to 100 billion (10^{11}). It becomes clear that sophisticated models have to be used very often in between retraining in order to reach the pure inference efficiency as given in Fig. 4a. The curves for all models and platforms show three different phases (1) a linear increase, (2) a transition

Table 2. Training/Life Cycle Energy and Efficiency

Plat-form	Model	DLLCE 10'000	DLLCE 100'000'000	Energy (kJ) 10'000	Energy(MJ) 100'000'000
RPi4	HRV pars	0.044	0.975	0.462	0.0093
	RR raw	0.029	0.945	15.85	0.148
	ESC 30	0.950	0.995	84.01	7.690
JNA	HRV pars	0.288	1	0.135	0.112
	RR raw	0.248	1	0.646	0.399
	ESC 30	0.248	1	10.69	2.331
Cloud /	HRV pars	0.677	1	2.914	13.36
PC /	RR raw	0.554	1	5.352	16.45
Work	ESC 30	0.850	1	112.0	809.4
station	MobileNet	0.509	1	486.0	1261
	ResNet	0.014	0.830	604934	1947
	VGG-16	0.019	0.891	392150	1894

where the slope is gradually reduced, and (3) a flat phase to the right of the transition phase. Phase 1 is training energy dominated, while phase 3 is inference energy dominated. Thus, efforts to reduce training energy will move the transition phase towards the left or lower number of uses. If models are implemented on efficiency accelerated edge platforms, the phase 3 levels will be reduced to lower RE while the transition will move to the right or to higher number of uses.

Going through a few examples can better explain the mechanism. The model and platform combination with the earliest transition from training energy domination to inference energy domination (green dotted, 1000'10'000) is the ESC30 model on windows because inference in the cloud is inefficient. If the inference is done on a non-accelerated edge platform (RPi4) then RE_{LC} improves but the transition shifts to the right (green solid, 1–10 million). A very similar transition is also observed for the HRV Par. Model (blue dotted and solid), here the improved going to the RPi4 platform is very impressive (RE_{LC} going from 0.15 to 6). MobileNetV2 reaches a RE_{LC} of 5 when inference is done in the cloud (red, dotted) but reaches $RE_{LC} = 150$ when the inference is done on the Edge TPU platform (red, dash-dotted). Here the transition from training to inference domination changes from 1–10 million in Cloud to 10 billion for the Edge TPU platform. For VGG-16 the RE_{LC} values are lower ($RE_{LC} = 0.65$ on edge TPU and 3 on Cloud brown dash-dotted and dotted) because the too large complexity reduces the gains for edge inference.

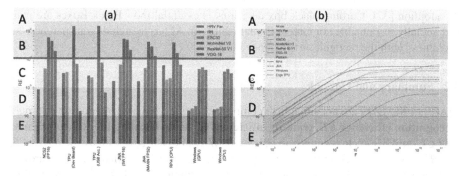

Fig. 4. (a) Recognition efficiency shown for the same models and platforms with the same colors as in Fig. 2. *RE* above 100 is class A(green), *RE* between 10 and 100 is class B (blue), *RE* from 1 to 10 is class C (yellow), *RE* below 1 is class D (orange), and *RE* below 0.1 is class E (red). This is valid for all models, libraries, and platforms. (b) Recognition efficiency over the entire lifecycle (*RE_LC*) for centralized learning approaches as function of number of uses (*F*). Training on Cloud (dotted) need longer amortization than on JNA or RPi4 (solid, dashed). Small models (HRV pars, blue and RR, brown) are quickly amortized. ESC30 models trained on Cloud (green, solid) need much more to amortize training (Color figure online).

4 Discussion, Summary, and Outlook

4.1 Discussion

Accelerated edge systems contribute to Green AI to render DL sustainable. Edge systems reach similar accuracies like but spend 1000–10'000× less energy. Recently, models were optimized only for performance or accuracy which caused non-sustainable Red AI. New universal metrics are needed that establish a better balance between accuracy and energy. A linear comparison between accuracy and energy is unfair, but with the square root energy term for inference and with 0.25 power for training a better assessment is possible. To enable universality, we additionally introduced the number of classes a model distinguishes so that with *RE* the most efficient models, libraries, and platforms that improve efficiency of DL can be selected. The universal *RE* and *TE* metrics were introduced since ML efficiency evaluation lacked accurate, universal tools [24, 54]. CNNs improved accuracy at the cost of strongly increased energy consumption leading to VGG-16 but MobileNet started to revert this trend [29]. Networks have to be selected that meet optimizing needs on energy and satisficing needs on accuracy. Accuracy is the optimizing metric, because it needs to correctly detect an object. The time and energy is the satisficing metric [30]. On edge devices, Once-for-All (OFA) outperforms state-of-the-art NAS methods while reducing many orders of magnitude GPU hours and CO_2 emission [31].

Leader boards avoid disclosure of AI's environmental costs but to accelerate transition to Green AI transparency needs to be enforced by only allowing results that document energy demand and overall efficiency. Measuring the carbon footprint of computing and publishing this information is important to raise awareness about the implications of

AI adoption [32]. Curbing black box decisions is essential too - Black Boxes are neither socially responsible nor Green. Explainability in AI has to include transparency on usefulness with the recognition efficiency metric.

4.2 Summary and Outlook

MACS or MADDS are not suitable to compare efficiency, but new metrics are optimal: **Recognition efficiency RE, training efficiency TE, deep learning lifecycle efficiency $DLLCE$, and life cycle recognition efficiency RE_{LC}.** For a lifecycle assessment $DLLCE$ and RE_{LC} show how close the efficiency is compared to the inference or RE, rewarding lean models that are used frequently between re-training. Red AI optimizes the performance independent of the energy demand which is an optimizer approach which – with respect to human development would not have allowed survival. Thus, there is a need to switch to a satisficer approach to direct Red AI towards a Green AI to save the climate and our survival. To develop in this direction, we need metrics that allow satisficer decisions: These are recognition efficiency RE, training efficiency TE, deep learning lifecycle efficiency $DLLCE$, and Life cycle recognition efficiency RE_{LC}.

Over the last years, the computational power of smartphones and tablets has grown dramatically, reaching desktop computers available not long ago [34–36]. DSPs, GPUs, NPUs and dedicated AI cores enable AI and DL-based computations. Android Neural Networks API, an Android C API has enabled a widespread use of DL on smartphones. In the next years all high-end chipsets will get enough power to run DL models which will result in more AI projects targeting mobile devices as the main platform for deployment. Progress on the software stack is slower: There is still only TensorFlow Lite, providing functionality and ease of deployment, while also having a large developer community. Due to limitations of Android and IoS with respect to implementation of mostly Python based leading AI solutions a study including mobile platforms will have to be carried out as part of a later study.

Following the quote from Peter Drucker: "If you can't measure it, you can't improve it" a universal metric is needed [33, 37]. Our work is crucial to drive Red AI towards green AI. **Based on these metrics, a similar standard like Energy Star for appliances and computers can be created:** RE above 100 is class A (green), RE between 10 and 100 is class B (blue), RE from 1 to 10 is class C (yellow), RE from 0.1 to 1 is class D (orange), and RE below 0.1 is class E (red). This is valid for all models, libraries, and platforms (see Fig. 4). As technology develops thresholds for class A will increase reaching 1000 in the near future. To support large number of uses for a model the classification has to be done on the lifecycle recognition efficiency RE_{LC}.

References

1. Reuther, A., Michaleas, P., Jones, M., Gadepally, V., Samsi, S., Kepner, J.: Survey and Benchmarking of machine learning accelerators. In: 2019 IEEE High Performance Extreme Computing Conference (HPEC). arXiv:1908.11348v1
2. Horowitz, M.: Computing's Energy Problem (and What We Can Do About It). In: 2014 IEEE International Solid-State Circuits Conference Digest of Technical Papers (ISSCC). IEEE, 2014, pp. 10–14. http://ieeexplore.ieee.org/document/6757323/

3. Hennessy, J.L., Patterson, D.A.: A new golden age for computer architecture. Comm. ACM **62**(2), 48-60 (2019)https://dl.acm.org/doi/10.1145/3282307
4. Schwartz, R., Dodge, J., Smith, N.A., Etzioni, O.: "Green AI" (2019). arXiv:1907.10597v3
5. Cai, E., Juan, D.C., Stamoulis, D., Marculescu, D.: NeuralPower: predict and deploy energy-efficient convolutional neural networks. In: Proceedings of Machine Learning Research 77, pp. 622–637. ACML (2017)
6. Thompson, N.C., Greenewald, K., Lee, K., Manso, G.F.: The Computational Limits of Deep Learning (2020). arXiv:2007.05558v1
7. Zhou, Z., Chen, X., Li, E., Zeng, L., Luo, K., Zhang, J.: Edge intelligence: paving the last mile of artificial intelligence with edge computing (2019). arXiv:1905.10083v1
8. Zhang, X., Wang, Y., Lu, S., Liu, L., Xu, L., Shi, W.: OpenEI: an open framework for edge intelligence (2019). arXiv:1906.01864v1
9. Konecny, J., McMahan, H.B., Yu, F.X., Suresh, A.T., Bacon, D.: Federated learning: strategies for improving communication efficiency (2017). arXiv:1610.05492v2
10. McMahan, H.B., Moore, E., Ramage, D., Hampson, S., Arcas, B.A.: Communication-efficient learning of deep networks from decentralized data. In: Proceedings of the 20th International Conference Artificial Intelligence and Statistics (AISTATS), Fort Lauderdale, FL (2017)
11. Deng, S., Zhao, H., Fang, W., Yin, J., Dustdar, S., Zomaya, A.Y.: Edge intelligence: the confluence of edge computing and artificial intelligence (2020). arXiv: 1909.00560v2
12. Das, A., Brunschwiler, T.: Privacy is whatwe care about: experimental investigation of federated learning on edge devices. In: Proceedings of First International Workshop on Challenges in Artificial Intelligence and Machine Learning for IoT, pp. 39–42 (2019)
13. Kasturi, A., Ellore, A.R., Hota, C.: Fusion learning: a one-shot federated learning, ICCS 2020. LNCS **12139**, 424–436 (2020)
14. Xu, Z., Li, L., Zou, W.: Exploring federated learning on battery-powered devices, ACM TURC, May 17–19, Chengdu, China (2019)
15. Edge TPU: Coral DEV.https://coral.ai/docs/dev-board/datasheet/
16. NCS2.https://ark.intel.com/content/www/de/de/ark/products/140109/intel-neural-compute-stick-2.html
17. Jetson.www.nvidia.com/de-de/autonomous-machines/embedded-systems/jetson-nano/
18. Klingner, S., et al: Firefighter virtual reality simulation for personalized stress det., KI (2020)
19. Inoue, T., Vinayavekhin, P., Wang, S., Wood, D., Greco, N., Tachibana, R.: Domestic activities classification based on CNN using shuffling and mixing data augmentation, detection and classification of acoustic scenes and events (2018)
20. Sandler, M., Howard, A., Zhu, M., Zhmoginov, A., Chen, L.C.: MobileNetV2: inverted residuals and linear bottlenecks (2019). https://arxiv.org/pdf/1801.04381.pdf
21. Joy-IT, Germany. https://joy-it.net/de/products/JT-UM25C)
22. (Rotkreuz, Switzerland. https://web.smart-me.com/en/project/smart-me-plug-2/
23. Hossin, M., Sulaiman, M.N.: A review on evaluation metrics for data classification evaluations. Int. J. Data Min. Knowl. Manage Process (IJDKP) **5**,(2), 1–11 (2015)
24. Coroama, V.C., Hilty, L.M.: Assessing internet energy intensity: a review of methods and results. Environ. Impact Assess. Rev. **45**, 63–68 (2014)
25. Pihkola, H., Hongisto, M., Apilo, O., Lasanen, M.: Evaluating the energy consumption of mobile data transfer–from technology development to consumer behaviour and life cycle thinking. Sustainability **10**, 2494 (2018)
26. Hodak, M., Gorvenko, M., Dholakia, A.: Towards Power Efficiency in Deep Learning on Data Center Hardware. In: IEEE Big Data 2019 Conference (2019)
27. You, Y., Zhang, Z., Hsieh, C.-J., Demmel, J., Kreutzer, K.: ImageNet training in minutes (2018). https://arxiv.org/abs/1709.05011
28. Nilsson, A., Smith, S., Ulm, G., Gustavsson, E., Jirstrand, M.: A performance evaluation of federated learning algorithms. DIDL 2018, Dec. 10–11, Rennes, France (2018)

29. Sze, V., Hsin, Y., Yang, T.J., Emer, J.S.: Efficient processing of deep neural networks: a tutorial and survey. Proc. IEEE **105**(12), 2295–2329 (2017)
30. Shankar, Structuring your machine learning projects (2020). https://medium.com/structuring-your-machine-learning-projects/satisficing-and-optimizing-metric-24372e0a73c
31. Cai, H., Gan, C., Wang, T., Zhang, Z., Han, S.: Once-for-all: train one network and specialize it for efficient deployment. ICLR (2020). https://arxiv.org/abs/1908.09791
32. Brevini, B.: Black boxes, not green: mythologizing artificial intelligence and omitting the environment. July–December: 1–5 Big Data Society, **7**, 2053951720935141 (2020)
33. https://www.growthink.com/content/two-most-important-quotes-business
34. Ignatov, A., et al.: AI benchmark: running deep neural networks on android smartphones. In: Leal-Taixé, L., Roth, S. (eds.) Computer Vision – ECCV 2018 Workshops. ECCV 2018. Lecture Notes in Computer Science, vol. 11133, pp. 288–314. Springer, Cham (2019). https://doi.org/10.1007/978-3-030-11021-5_19
35. Mastroianni, C., et al.: Special issue on edge intelligence for sustainable smart environments. IEEE Trans. Green Commun. Netw. 6(1), 234–237 (2022)
36. Savaglio, C., Gerace, P., Di Fatta, G., Fortino, G.: Data mining at the IoT edge. In: 2019 28th International Conference on Computer Communication and Networks (ICCCN). IEEE, pp. 1-6 (2019)
37. Lenherr, N., Pawlitzek, R., Michel, B.: New universal sustainability metrics to assess edge intelligence. Sustain. Comput.: Inf. Syst. **31**, 100580 (2021)

IoT Applications, Services and Real Implementations

A Smart IoT Gateway Capable of Prescreening for Atrial Fibrillation

Eoin Flanagan[1]([✉]) [iD] and Robert Sadleir[2] [iD]

[1] FTI Consulting, The Academy, 42 Pearse Street, Dublin, Ireland
`eoin.flanagan22@mail.dcu.ie`
[2] School of Electronic Engineering, Dublin City University, Dublin, Ireland
`robert.sadleir@dcu.ie`

Abstract. Atrial fibrillation (AF) is a cardiac arrhythmia occurring when the atria lose their normal rhythm causing the heart to beat erratically. The estimated number of individuals with atrial fibrillation globally in 2010 was 33.5 million. Despite continued research in this area there is no universal standard for detecting atrial fibrillation. The majority of published detectors rely on manual classification techniques that are implemented on standalone devices. This paper proposes a dual convolutional neural network (CNN) based AF detection system. The proposed system transforms 5 s windows of electrocardiogram data to two-dimensional images via a stationary wavelet transform to serve as CNN inputs. The dual CNN system implements a model tailored for an IoT gateway device to prescreen arrhythmia cases locally. Less obvious arrhythmia cases are transferred to a secondary model hosted on a cloud server for further prediction. Local classification of AF reduces the overheads for cloud storage capacity and transfer of data. The proposed runtime system ultimately received an F1 score of 0.94 when evaluated using previously unseen data.

Keywords: Internet of Things · Deep learning · Convolutional neural network · ECG · Atrial fibrillation

1 Introduction

Atrial fibrillation (AF) is a cardiac arrhythmia caused by erratic sinoatrial node activity which leads to irregular heart rhythm. Capturing the heart cycle via an electrocardiogram (ECG) reveals the cycles' comprising elements, called PQRST waves, which can be seen in Fig. 1. AF can be diagnosed via an ECG due to irregular morphology of PQRST waves and inconsistency of wave intervals. The most recent worldwide study into the prevalence of AF performed by the World Health Organisation found that the condition was estimated to affect 33.5 million people globally [6]. Predictions indicate that 6–12 million people will be affected by atrial fibrillation in the USA by 2050 and 17.9 million people in Europe by 2060 [5,13,17]. Left untreated AF can lead to complications such as blood clots, strokes and heart failure.

A. González-Vidal et al. (Eds.): GIoTS 2022, LNCS 13533, pp. 111–123, 2022.
https://doi.org/10.1007/978-3-031-20936-9_9

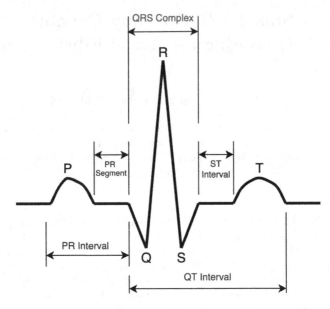

Fig. 1. Typical PQRST wave comprising of P-wave, Q-wave, R-wave, S-wave and T-wave.

Traditionally there are two forms of AF detection techniques;

1. Atrial activity analysis-based i.e., morphology analysis of P wave absence or F wave presence.
2. Ventricular response analysis-based methods i.e., time between peaks of consecutive beats, typically RR intervals.

Some traditional classification techniques have demonstrated high scoring metrics on test data. Machine learning techniques are becoming more popular and increasingly, deep learning based solutions are proposed [10,18]. Such works have achieved accuracy comparable to that of traditional feature-based approaches. Deep learning solutions are amongst the best-in-class detectors developed for use with the following datasets: MIT-BIH Atrial Fibrillation Database (AFDB), MIT-BIH Normal Sinus Rhythm Database (NSDB), MIT-BIH Arrhythmia Database (ADB) and the Computers in Cardiology Challenge (C3) 2001 and 2017 databases. The discussion that follows is based on the fact that deep learning solutions provide the best methods to detect AF.

The research outlined in this paper was motivated by the lack of mobile or IoT based deep learning AF detection systems. The proposed system implements a dual deep learning model for detection of AF with an F1 score of 0.94 on test data which is in line with previously published detection mechanisms and also with the findings in [10], which states that ensembles of multiple approaches can achieve greater results. The system utilises a model on a local IoT device and a backup cloud model. The combination of both models allows for local classification in the majority of cases with dual prediction being used in more difficult cases. This reduces the server requirements needed to host multiple clients and ensures that potentially sensitive information is not being sent to the cloud unnecessarily.

1.1   Existing Techniques for AF Detection

Described traditionally AF is detectable by examining R peak time intervals [7,16,23]. Some detectors collect RR intervals and use techniques such as Shannon entropy [7,15,27] or root mean square of successive differences [15] and symbolic dynamics [27,28] to identify AF. Wave morphology can be used to detect the lack of P waves due to F waves oscillating about the baseline during AF episodes, as described in [3,14,21]. It can be beneficial to combine both interval and morphology based approaches, as demonstrated in [2]. This allows handling of ectopic beats, a problem that hinders interval techniques, and handling of signal noise, a problem that effects the wave morphologies captured. Machine learning detection methods have also been shown to achieve excellent results [1,8]. A machine learning based detector has been adapted into a mobile to cloud infrastructure by Cheng et al. [4], with a possible opportunity to improve the level of specificity that can be achieved. There are a number of deep learning based methods capable of detecting AF [12]. A convolutional neural network (CNN) system by Xia et al. is the best performing detector on the AFDB [26]. These authors implement a stationary wavelet transform (SWT) to convert input from the time domain to the time-frequency domain. The time-frequency data is used as an input array to a two-dimensional (2D) CNN resulting in sensitivity, specificity and accuracy metrics of 98.79, 97.87 and 98.63% respectively. Another detector that utilises some of these techniques was proposed by Wu et al. [25], and they reported equally high levels of performance. The objective of the research outlined in this paper was to create a detector with performance metrics similar to the detector proposed by Xia et al. and implement it in a system with an architecture similar to the detector proposed by Cheng et al.

2   Data Preparation

2.1   Data Source

The AFDB is used as the only data source for this project. This data source has 25 instances of dual channel ECG recordings spanning 9 h. Only 23 of the recordings contain an ECG trace. The 23 recordings were split into *training*, *validation* and *test* datasets on a per record basis while attempting to keep approximately matching numbers of AF and healthy data in each dataset. The split was performed on a per patient basis i.e., each source recording is designated to a mutually exclusive subset. This split prevents data from the same patient existing in multiple subsets. The training data contained 13 recordings, the validation data contained 6 recordings and the test data contained 4 recordings. Each recording is split into 5 s adjacent windows of ECG data leading to a total of 332,122 instance of 5 s data across all datasets. Of that total; the training data contained 76,090 AF instances and 113,214 healthy instances, the validation data contained 36,386 AF instances and 48,403 healthy instances and the test data contained 20,027 AF instances and 38,003 healthy instances.

2.2 Prepossessing

The source recordings originate from a standard two lead ECG acquisition system and have undergone no previous signal processing [9]. Using signal processing techniques will remove unwanted artifacts from the signal. The main sources of these artifacts which are outlined in [11] are summarised below.

1. Baseline wander caused by the respiration and movement of the subject, thus baseline wander is an artifact in most cardiac ECG data. This is a low frequency artifact that affects ECG data by moving the trace away from 0 V during times of no heart activity.
2. Powerline interference due to electromagnetic fields caused by electrical powerline interference with the monitoring device. This causes noise in the range of 50–60 Hz and can severely effect wave morphology, thus affecting classifications of arrhythmias.
3. Myoelectric noise interfering with the ECG signal is caused by the electrical activity generated by muscles. Myoelectric noise is difficult to eliminate because the frequency of the noise is not predictable.

To eliminate these artifacts a zero phase second order Butterworth bandpass filter is implemented in the range of 0.5–50 Hz. The effect of this filter can be seen in Fig. 2. To alleviate the data set imbalances and improve model generalisation 4,900 augmented AF training instances were created using the approach outlined in [24] i.e.;

1. Jittering and off centering by addition of Gaussian noise to the signal with a 0.2 mean and variance of 0.02. This adds slight variance to the values of individual data points and moves the mean of the entire signal away from 0.
2. Dynamic time warping by stochastically compressing the length of the array values. The resulting empty indexes are zero padded to maintain the 5 s windows. This results in a slight increase in PQRST frequency.
3. Array reversing by flipping the data in the window.

In order to transform the images into 2D, a modified SWT was implemented. The SWT allows a time invariant and multiresolutional analysis of an input signal by implementing a series of high and low pass filters, the output at each stage is upsampled by zero padding between adjacent elements to maintain the original input length [19]. Equations (1) and (2) and Fig. 3 all describe the process of the recursive SWT of signal X_k, where G_n and H_n are low and high pass filters. Detail and approximation coefficients of the SWT are represented by V_n and W_n. The outputs of the SWT were reshaped into squares and converted to RGB images with inter-area interpolation, which can be seen in Fig. 4.

$$V_i(x) = \sum_n G_n V_{i-1}(x - 2^{i-1}n) \tag{1}$$

$$W_i(x) = \sum_n H_n V_{i-1}(x - 2^{i-1}n) \tag{2}$$

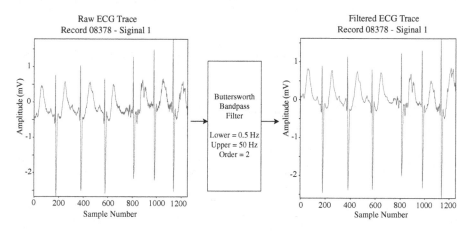

Fig. 2. The effect of Butterworth bandpass filtering on Record 08378 from the AFDB.

3 Deep Learning Models

3.1 Development

The two models were designed with different architectures to generate a non-overlapping classification strategy to reduce the likelihood of both models making the same misclassification. The final classification would be categorised by the highest softmax P-valve achieved by a committee of classifiers. Training took place on the Google Colab Pro environment using the Keras API. The various models created throughout the design process were trained three times and the median performance was taken as representative.

The cloud model architecture can be seen in Table 1. This model was trained for 100 epochs. All models were trained using the Adam optimiser with learning rate of 0.01. Each model consists of multiple convolutional blocks and a fully connected block at the head of the model. The cloud model uses 5×5 convolution and a larger input image and max pooling is utilised at the end of all three convolutional blocks. Regularisation was attained during model training by implementing dropout with a P value of 0.5 and the application of the Image-DataGenerator class to flip instances on their vertical axis to create additional synthetic training data.

The local IoT model is designed to minimise computational load on the embedded device. It was trained for 50 epochs and the architecture as can be seen in Table 2, contains two convolutional blocks each with two subblocks. The subblocks contain stacked convolutions with 3×3 kernels before pooling. The double 3×3 convolution achieves the same receptive field as the single 5×5 convolution used in the cloud model but uses fewer parameters. As the depth of the network increases the features extracted become more representative of the input data. Global max pooling is utilised to implement feature wide pooling along all 24 input maps, resulting in the most useful features being selected

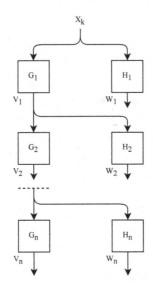

Fig. 3. Representation of the tree structure of a multi-level SWT.

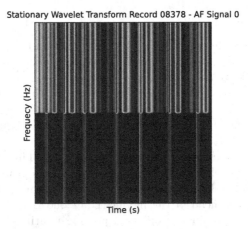

Fig. 4. SWT coefficient response converted to RGB image.

and reducing the total number of parameters in the system. The local model incorporates additional regularisation techniques via the application of ridge regression to the kernel (weights) and to the activity (output) of a layer in the fully connected subblocks. Both models utilise the softmax function which returns an array of two probability scores, which sum to one.

Table 1. Cloud model architecture.

Layer	Block	Outputs	Pooling Size
$Conv2D_0$	1	251, 251, 16	5×5
Batch Normalisation		251, 251, 16	
Max Pooling		83, 83, 16	2×2
Relu		83, 83, 16	
$Conv2D_1$	2	79, 79, 16	5×5
Batch Normalisation		79, 79, 16	
Max Pooling		26, 26, 16	2×2
Relu		26, 26, 16	
$Conv2D_2$	3	22, 22, 16	5×5
Batch Normalisation		22, 22, 16	
Max Pooling		7, 7, 16	2×2
Relu		7, 7, 16	
Flatten	FC	784	
Dense		50	
Relu		50	
Dropout (0.5)		50	
Dense		2	
Softmax		2	

3.2 Deployment

The cloud model is hosted on an EC2 virtual server. Cloud model deployment is achieved using a docker container of TensorFlow Serving. The cloud model is converted from Keras to TensorFlow and the docker container launches Tensor-Flow Serving which hosts the model. The runtime system can be seen in Fig. 5. The user specifies a test recording to analyse. The program loads 5 s of ECG data from both signals and applies bandpass filters and the SWTs to achieve images for each signal source and predictions are made. If the difference in predicted value is less than an empirically determined threshold of 0.7 the cloud model is utilised. Then the argmax of the 8 attained prediction values is the final classification.

3.3 Gateway

The gateway was initially deployed and tested using a desktop machine but the model was developed with a view to deploying it on an embedded Linux device, where the device acts as a gateway that makes local predictions after receiving data from a separate wearable ECG monitor. The desktop runtime system is capable of loading data, preprocessing and making local predictions in approximately 80 ms consistently. In cases where the backup cloud model was

Table 2. IoT model architecture.

Layer	Block	Outputs	Pooling size	Regularisation
Conv2D$_0$	1.0	127, 127, 12	3 × 3	
Batch normalisation		127, 127, 12		
Relu		127, 127, 12		
Conv2D$_1$	1.1	127, 127, 12	3 × 3	
Batch normalisation		127, 127, 12		
Relu		127, 127, 12		
Max pooling		63, 63, 12	2 × 2	
Conv2D$_2$	2.0	63, 63, 24	3 × 3	
Batch normalisation		63, 63, 24		
Relu		63, 63, 24		
Max pooling		31, 31, 24	2 × 2	
Conv2D$_3$	2.1	31, 31, 24	3 × 3	
Batch normalisation		31, 31, 24		
Relu		31, 31, 24		
Global max pooling		24		
Flatten	FC	24		
Dropout (0.5)		24		
Dense		48		L2 Kernel & Activity (0.005)
Dropout (0.5)		48		
Relu		48		
Dense		48		
Softmax		2		

utilised, the time taken for prediction typically increased to 800 ms due to the time necessary for handshake i.e. transmission, cloud operations and receipt of data. When deployed on a Raspberry Pi 4, it is estimated that the time taken to load, preprocess and make local predictions will increase to 240 ms. In cases where the cloud model is required it is estimated that the maximum prediction time will not exceed 2.5 s. This system has been designed to predict new AF instances every five seconds as new data becomes available from a wearable device and the estimated prediction times stated using local and cloud models suggest that the proposed system should be capable of real-time operation on an embedded Linux device.

4   Results

In this paper, two CNN models have been proposed with individual performance metrics on the test dataset seen in Table 3. Both local IoT and cloud models were optimised using the validation set until there was no consistent improvements gained. Most improvements came from reducing overfitting by strategically eliminating model parameters. During the evaluation of the runtime system the threshold to utilise the cloud model was set at 0.7. If either

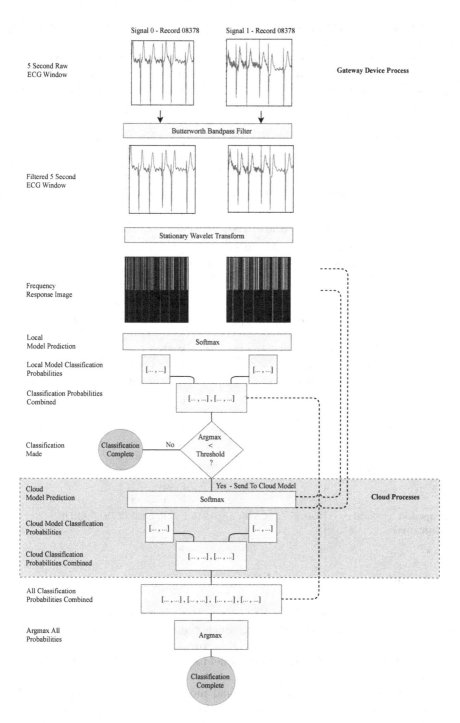

Fig. 5. Runtime flow overview of classification system proposed.

local IoT model prediction score have a difference less than the threshold, the cloud model is also used.

As shown in Table 4, the proposed runtime system results have been compared with a range of other notable high scoring detectors in the literature. The other detectors have been created using a range of traditional and deep learning techniques.

Table 3. Model F1 results.

Class	Local	Cloud	Dual Local & Cloud
AF positive	0.95	0.92	0.94
Healthy	0.94	0.96	0.95
Accuracy	0.90	0.90	0.94
Macro avg	0.94	0.94	0.94
Weighted avg	0.94	0.94	0.94

Table 4. Comparison between the proposed method and previous works.

Detector	Sensitivity	Specificity	Accuracy	F1	Method	Dataset
Xia et al. [26]	0.987	0.978	–	–	SWT, CNN	AFDB
Wu et al. [25]	0.983	0.988	–	–	CWT, CNN	AFDB, ADB
Singh et al. [22]	–	–	0.875	–	ECG Image, CNN	ADB
Lee et al. [15]	0.982	0.977	–	–	Time Varying Coherence, Shannon Entropy	AFDB, NSDB
Babaeizadeh et al. [2]	0.93	0.98	–	–	Interval Markov, P-wave Morphology	AFDB
Proposed (Runtime)	0.953	0.940	0.946	0.945	SWT, Dual CNN	AFDB

5   Analysis

The CNN input equates to 5 s of ECG data, this allows for classification much faster than the majority of detectors, which typically need 30 s of ECG data. And although there have been 1D AF detectors implemented such as [20], the task of creating a robust classification model using just 5 s of 1D input data does not appear to be possible.

The F1 performance of each individual model on the test dataset is 0.90, meaning that these detectors could be considered suitable for use independently of each other. The dual model system improves the F1 score to 0.94. The proposed model achieves performance levels that are in line with some of the best performing deep learning-based detectors in the literature as seen in Table 4, noting that differing evaluation strategies make it difficult to compare techniques directly. In the majority of systems, a single model is forced to choose a category for a single input. In this case, each 5 s event generates two features from the temporally aligned ECG signals, implementing an ensemble of model predictions allows for the model with the greatest probability value to decide the final classification. The hypothesis regarding the implementation of two contrasting model architectures in order to prevent double misclassification has proven to be effective. An investigation into misclassifications found that many are located within adjacent samples of ECG data and thus correspond to the same false positive event. The AFDB dataset contains no patient specific information; it is unknown if patients suffer from atrioventricular blocks, are fitted with a pacemaker or take heart rate controlling medicine. Further information on this would potentially improve the classification performance of this system.

The detector by Lee et al. [15] can be considered the true best performing detector on the AFDB. This detector implements RR intervals in two adjacent windows; during normal rhythm there is a high spatial coherence between windows, if AF occurs the spatial coherence drops, and Shannon entropy between windows is utilised to make classifications. The detector by Babaeizadeh et al. [2] implements both RR interval and wave morphology yet achieved an inferior performance in comparison to the detector by Lee et al. Perhaps a dynamic method to change between RR interval or morphology-based classification depending on the noise levels within the signals will yield an improved performance.

6   Conclusions

The proposed system achieves a level of performance that is in line with some of the best performing detectors in the literature, however, it is developed specifically for use in an IoT setting and is deployed as a distributed committee of classifiers which makes it unique when compared to the other previously published detectors.

The opportunity exists to eliminate dataset imbalances by artificially creating AF data using a Generative Adversarial Network. These networks can be used to generate independently and identically distributed synthetic ECG data. ECG QRS complexes have been artificially generated but a system that extends multiple beats into data that resembles AF requires a higher level of abstraction. Such a system did not exist at the time of writing and will be the subject of further research in this area.

References

1. Asgari, S., Mehrnia, A., Moussavi, M.: Automatic detection of atrial fibrillation using stationary wavelet transform and support vector machine. Comput. Biol. Med. **60**, 132–142 (2015)

2. Babaeizadeh, S., Gregg, R.E., Helfenbein, E.D., Lindauer, J.M., Zhou, S.H.: Improvements in atrial fibrillation detection for real-time monitoring. J. Electrocardiol. **42**(6), 522–526 (2009)
3. Censi, F., et al.: P-wave morphology assessment by a Gaussian functions-based model in atrial fibrillation patients. IEEE Trans. Biomed. Eng. **54**(4), 663–672. (2007). Conference Name: IEEE Transactions on Biomedical Engineering
4. Cheng, S., Tamil, L.S., Levine, B.: A mobile health system to identify the onset of paroxysmal atrial fibrillation. In: 2015 International Conference on Healthcare Informatics, pp. 189–192 (2015)
5. Chugh, S.S., et al.: Worldwide epidemiology of atrial fibrillation: a global burden of disease 2010 study. Circulation **129**(8), 837–847 (2014)
6. Chugh, S.S., et al.: Worldwide epidemiology of atrial fibrillation. Circulation **129**(8), 837–847 (2014)
7. Dash, S., Chon, K.H., Lu, S., Raeder, E.A.: Automatic real time detection of atrial fibrillation. Ann. Biomed. Eng. **37**(9), 1701–1709 (2009)
8. De Giovanni, E., Aminifar, A., Luca, A., Yazdani, S., Vesin, J.M., Atienza, D.: A patient-specific methodology for prediction of paroxysmal atrial fibrillation onset. In: 2017 Computing in Cardiology (CinC), pp. 1–4. iSSN: 2325-887X (2017)
9. Goldberger, A., et al.: PhysioBank, PhysioToolkit, and PhysioNet: components of a new research resource for complex physiologic signals. **101**(23), e215–e220 (2000). https://physionet.org/content/afdb/
10. Hong, S., Zhou, Y., Shang, J., Xiao, C., Sun, J.: Opportunities and challenges of deep learning methods for electrocardiogram data: a systematic review. Comput. Biol. Med. **122**, 103801 (2020)
11. Kameenoff, J.: Signal processing techniques for removing noise from ECG signals. Biomed. Eng. Res. **1**(1), 1 (2017). publisher: JScholar Publishers
12. Khan, A.H., Hussain, M., Malik, M.K.: Arrhythmia classification techniques using deep neural network. Complexity **2021**, 1–10 (2021). https://doi.org/10.1155/2021/9919588
13. Krijthe, B.P., et al.: Projections on the number of individuals with atrial fibrillation in the European Union, from 2000 to 2060. Eur. Heart J. **34**(35), 2746–2751 (2013)
14. Ladavich, S., Ghoraani, B.: Rate-independent detection of atrial fibrillation by statistical modeling of atrial activity. Biomed. Signal Process. Control **18**, 274–281 (2015)
15. Lee, J., Nam, Y., McManus, D.D., Chon, K.H.: Time-varying coherence function for atrial fibrillation detection. IEEE Trans. Biomed. Eng. **60**(10), 2783–2793 (2013)
16. Logan, B., Healey, J.: Robust detection of atrial fibrillation for a long term telemonitoring system. In: Computers in Cardiology, pp. 619–622. iSSN: 2325-8853 (2005)
17. Miyasaka, Y., et al.: Secular trends in incidence of atrial fibrillation in olmsted county, minnesota, 1980 to 2000, and implications on the projections for future prevalence. American Heart Association. Circulation **114**(2), 119–125 (2006). publisher: American Heart Association
18. Murat, F., et al.: Review of deep learning-based atrial fibrillation detection studies. Int. J. Environ. Res. Public Health **18**(21), 11302 (2021). https://doi.org/10.3390/ijerph182111302
19. Nason, G.P., Silverman, B.W.: The stationary wavelet transform and some statistical applications. In: Antoniadis, A., Oppenheim, G. (eds.) Wavelets and Statistics, pp. 281–299. Lecture Notes in Statistics, Springer, New York (1995). https://doi.org/10.1007/978-1-4612-2544-7_17

20. Pourbabaee, B., Lucas, C.: Automatic detection and prediction of paroxysmal atrial fibrillation based on analyzing ecg signal feature classification methods. In: 2008 Cairo International Biomedical Engineering Conference, Cairo, Egypt, pp. 1–4. IEEE (2008)

21. Ródenas, J., García, M., Alcaraz, R., Rieta, J.J.: Wavelet entropy automatically detects episodes of atrial fibrillation from single-lead electrocardiograms. Entropy **17**(9), 6179–6199 (2015). Publisher: Multidisciplinary Digital Publishing Institute

22. Singh, S., Sunkaria, R., Saini, B., Kumar, K.: Atrial fibrillation and premature contraction classification using convolutional neural network. In: 2019 International Conference on Intelligent Computing and Control Systems (ICCS), pp. 797–800 (2019). https://doi.org/10.1109/ICCS45141.2019.9065716

23. Tateno, K., Glass, L.: Automatic detection of atrial fibrillation using the coefficient of variation and density histograms of RR and delta RR intervals. Med. Biol. Eng. Comput. **39**(6), 664–671 (2001)

24. Um, T.T., et al.: Data augmentation of wearable sensor data for Parkinson's disease monitoring using convolutional neural networks. In: Proceedings of the 19th ACM International Conference on Multimodal Interaction, pp. 216–220. ICMI 2017, Association for Computing Machinery, New York, USA (2017)

25. Wu, Z., Feng, X., Yang, C.: A Deep learning method to detect atrial fibrillation based on continuous wavelet transform. In: 2019 41st Annual International Conference of the IEEE Engineering in Medicine and Biology Society (EMBC), pp. 1908–1912. iSSN: 1558–4615 (2019)

26. Xia, Y., Wulan, N., Wang, K., Zhang, H.: Detecting atrial fibrillation by deep convolutional neural networks. Comput. Biol. Med. **93**, 84–92 (2018)

27. Zhou, X., Ding, H., Ung, B., Pickwell-MacPherson, E., Zhang, Y.: Automatic online detection of atrial fibrillation based on symbolic dynamics and Shannon entropy. Biomed. Eng. Online **13**(1), 18 (2014)

28. Zhou, X., Ding, H., Wu, W., Zhang, Y.: A real-time atrial fibrillation detection algorithm based on the instantaneous state of heart rate. PLoS ONE **10**(9), e0136544 (2015). publisher: Public Library of Science

Internet of Things with Web Technologies Solution for Flood Notification in São Paulo

Reinaldo Ferraz[1(✉)], Carlos Rafael Gimenes das Neves[2(✉)], and Jefferson Silva[3(✉)]

[1] NIC.br, São Paulo, Brazil
reinaldo@nic.br
[2] ESPM, São Paulo, Brazil
carlos.neves@espm.br
[3] PUC-SP, São Paulo, Brazil
silvajo@pucsp.br

Abstract. The present study aimed at developing a system capable of collecting atmospheric data from physical sensors distributed throughout the city of São Paulo and to notify users in real-time, to provide people with early flood warnings. In addition to the development of this system, this study also aimed to show, via a real-life case study, how the use of web technologies, coupled with the Internet of Things, could help solve the day-to-day problems of large cities.

Keywords: Flood alert · Web technologies · IoT

1 Introduction

Unlike the Internet, which is the network that directly or indirectly connects computers around the world, the World Wide Web (WWW) is an information system that includes documents and other resources present in the network through a single address, using a standardized format known as Uniform Resource Locators (URL). Berners-Lee[1] conceived the first version of the WWW in 1989, as an attempt by the European Organization for Nuclear Research (CERN) to solve a problem they, as well as other institutions around the world, faced daily: allowing their members to access different but interrelated documents stored in different locations (Berners-lee 1992).

In 1991, CERN physicists carried out the first public demonstration of this idea, still only with texts, during the ACM Hypertext 91 Conference.[2] To ensure that the WWW could grow and reach the largest possible audience, in April 1999, CERN opened the source code for the software responsible for implementing the WWW protocol.

Although the WWW is a system that allows information to be shared between computers in different locations, its initial use was almost entirely based on man-machine interactions, with human beings in control, sending commands to a computer program, known as a browser, which in turn made requests to other computers in search of resources

---

[1] https://www.w3.org/People/Berners-Lee/.

[2] https://www.w3.org/Conferences/HT91/Overview.html.

A. González-Vidal et al. (Eds.): GIoTS 2022, LNCS 13533, pp. 124–134, 2022.
https://doi.org/10.1007/978-3-031-20936-9_10

like documents. This interaction ends up assigning different roles to those involved in the communication. The party that actively makes the request, in this case, the browser, is known as the client. The party that passively waits to receive requests and answer client queries is known as a server. Thus, the interactions that occur via the WWW follow the classic client-server paradigm (Comer 2016).

This entire process underwent an enormous evolution in the following decades. Not only has the speed of data transmission within the network increased substantially but the processing speed and storage capacity of the computers involved in communication have also experienced staggering growth (Comer 2016) and (Höller 2014).

Furthermore, the increase in computational power was followed by the miniaturization of the electronic circuits with which traditional computers were created. This enabled the construction of small electronic equipment that was capable, not only of sending and receiving information but also of processing the information autonomously, without having to send it to another larger computer only for processing purposes. In other words, small electronic devices were no longer limited to capturing and sending data; they were now able to process their data. Thus, it became possible for two devices to communicate directly without the need for human intervention, giving rise to the concept of machine-to-machine communication, or M2M (Höller 2014).

Although there are other simpler and much older forms of communication between devices dating back to the early 1900s, the first M2M interactions to use more sophisticated protocols began in the late 1990s and early 2000s. They took place between industrial sensors and digital instrumentation and did not require the use of the Internet or the WWW, using other proprietary protocols, via wired or wireless means (Höller 2014).

In general, the term M2M is used to describe any communications between two devices that do not require human intervention to interpret the data received and produce a response, although humans are usually involved in analyzing the data produced. Unlike the basic operation of the WWW, M2M communications may or may not follow the client-server paradigm, since each device involved can actively send requests and information to the other (Höller 2014).

Although there were machines capable of communicating with other physically distant machines, most of the initial M2M communications between small devices occurred in the same physical environment, or nearby physical environments, because of the absence, at the time, of miniature circuits capable of allowing communications through other means and protocols, such as the Internet or the WWW. This scenario would only change significantly thanks to a new wave of circuit miniaturization that occurred between the mid-1990s and the mid-2000s (Fleisch 2010).

With the emergence of these new circuits, it became possible to load basic computer functionalities into small mobile devices, such as the ability to communicate using more elaborate protocols such as the TCP/IP protocol and the HTTP protocol, which are the basis of communication on the WWW (Tanenbaum 2011). For demonstration purposes only, at a technology fair in England, and still far from commercial production, the first embedded device to connect to the WWW was an electric toaster created by John Romkey in 1990 (Maschietto 2021). However, it would not be long before industrial processes evolved to allow the mass production of miniature devices effectively capable of communicating with each other over the Internet and the WWW, materializing the term Internet of Things (IoT), which was created in 1985 by Peter T. Lewis (Bernardi 2017).

Although the use of the WWW and the HTTP protocol had already become commonplace in distributed systems in the mid-2000s, the advent of devices with significant computational power has brought forth a range of new means of communication and protocols, some open, another proprietary, such as the MQTT protocol (Maschietto 2021). The emergence of different protocols can be justified, in part, because of the needs inherent to the different contexts in which the devices are immersed. Each of these communication protocols seeks to simplify the issues of the media in which they are inserted. However, this comes at an additional cost to the distributed system as a whole: each device must be able to understand the information input and output protocols, which sometimes forces two or more different protocols to exist on the same device or requires the presence of other intermediate devices just to translate one protocol into another.

A scenario that exemplifies this mix of different protocols is that of a traditional WWW system, involving a server and different clients using the HTTP protocol, which also needs to communicate with distributed IoT devices using protocols other than HTTP. In this case, the webserver would need to be able to interpret protocols other than HTTP, increasing the complexity of its development, or even creating security gaps by requiring it to communicate with intermediate systems responsible for translating sensor information from one protocol to another.

Thus, the present study seeks to demonstrate the technical feasibility of creating a system for the WWW, or simply a web system, in which the server communicates directly with both human clients from any part of the world and with autonomous IoT devices distributed throughout a city, always through the HTTP protocol, dispensing with the need for other systems or intermediate devices to translate information between different protocols.

2 Objective

To develop a proof of concept of a large-scale data collection, monitoring, and distribution system using open protocols and WWW standard definitions.

3 System Architecture

The development of the proof of concept of the present study resulted in the creation of six distinct artifacts:

1. An application programming interface (API) encoded in JSON standard (ECMA, 2017) to transmit atmospheric and rainfall data via HTTP protocol;
2. IoT devices that act as sensors that monitor atmospheric and rainfall conditions of where they are installed and report this information to the central web server through the proposed API;

3. A central web server responsible for receiving, processing, and storing the information received in a database through the proposed API, in addition to making the stored data available to two other web applications, also through the same API;
4. A web application that allows users to receive notifications about floods coming from the sensors and provides manual notifications about floods in their region of the city of São Paulo, which are then relayed in real time to other registered users;
5. A second web application, a public website, which displays the consolidated weather information received from the IoT sensors;
6. An administrative web interface that manages the registration of IoT sensors in the system.

3.1 API, Sensors, and Web Server

The first step in developing the system's proof-of-concept was to create an API to standardize communication between the different IoT devices and the system's central web server. This version of the system connected sensors from the São Paulo Flood Warning System (SAISP) and Pluvi.On, a private company that provides access to rainfall sensors in several regions of Brazil.

The data obtained from the SAISP sensors are fed into the history of reported rainfall in the Metropolitan Region of São Paulo and can be accessed publicly at https://www.saisp.br/historic/index.jsp?C=N;O=D. The SAISP sensors consist of multiple radars and devices of public agencies of the city of São Paulo. The raw data is sent to a web service that receives, processes, compiles it, and then offers it publicly in a user-friendly way at https://www.saisp.br/online/ and https://www.saisp.br/online/prec_acum_sabesp/.

The measurements sent by the SAISP sensors contain the sensor identifier, its name, address, geographical location, a textual description of the type of sensor, the sensor installation date, the rainfall values measured in the period, and a marking with the date and time of the measurement.

The sensors provided by Pluvi.On collect information about rainfall, temperature, wind, and other atmospheric characteristics. Because they belong to a private company, 23 of the sensors located in the city of São Paulo were accessed by hiring the company's service for the duration of this proof of concept.

Each measurement sent by the Pluvi.On sensors contains the sensor identifier, its name, description, and geographical location, a textual description of the type of sensor, the sensor installation date, temperature, relative humidity, precipitation intensity and volume, wind speed and direction, and a marking with the date and time of the measurement.

All sensor data is encoded on the device itself in JSON standard (ECMA 2017) before being transmitted to the system's web server, following the architectural style of Representational State Transfer (REST) (Fielding 2000). The web server, in turn, receives, decodes and stores the data in a database. The sensors, the web server, the two web applications, and the administrative web interface all use the same data standard and follow the specifications of the same system standard API, simplifying communication among all parts of the system.

The system API was developed based on the OpenAPI Specification (OpenAPI initiative 2021). The OpenAPI specification (OEA) defines a standard, which is a language-agnostic interface for any type of REST API that allows humans and computers to discover and understand the service's resources without the need to access the source code, documents, or network traffic inspection. When the system is properly defined, consumers of remote services can understand and interact with this service with a minimal amount of implementation logic (OpenAPI initiative 2021).

The web server, built in Perl language with the Catalyst framework, exposes parts of the API publicly, while keeping other parts of the API private, available only to the two web applications and the administrative web interface.

The publicly exposed part of the API only allows the sensors to communicate with the web server. This allows the safe connection of sensors belonging to government organizations, such as SAISP sensors, of third-party companies, such as Pluvi.On, and also those of any other enthusiasts wanting to build their own sensors, as long as they follow the standards of the API used in the project.

The private part of the API allows for the complete manipulation of the data in the database. Thus, the two web applications and the administrative web interface can send information, query data, and even manipulate sensor configurations remotely.

3.2 Notifications Web Application

The fourth artifact of the system's proof of concept, the web application that allows users to receive and send notifications about floods in their region of the city of São Paulo, was also developed using only open WWW standards.

Because it is an application, and not a web page with the features of a document, the concept of progressive web applications (PWA) was used (Google 2020). A PWA is not an API or a specific tool, but a software development methodology that allows the development of hybrid applications, coupling traditional well-consolidated web techniques with features that were once found only in applications native to the system, whether on personal computers or smartphones.

A PWA could be at risk of not working properly on older browsers, or on certain operating systems, because it merges traditional, established features with new ones. However, the methodology foresees this scenario, which is why it bears the word "Progressive" in its name. PWAs adapt to the browsers on which they run, with regard to several variables, including user input, such as mice or touch screens, screen size and many other attributes. At the other extreme, they also adapt to lack of specific features, a scenario where PWAs do not fail completely, but only cease to offer such feature to users (Google 2020).

There is no need to publish or download PWAs in app stores, because they are accessed through browsers, like regular web pages. However, for convenience, it is possible to create shortcuts to quickly access them on device desktops (Google 2020). Even when run from inside browsers, all PWAs can work disconnected from the Internet, thanks to recent data storage techniques in browser caches, coupled with the use of service workers, who can access and manipulate this data (W3C 2021 B).

Because the application allows users to send manual notifications, which are then retransmitted to other users registered in the system, and because the users that receive the notifications do not keep the application open on their browsers at all times, two APIs were used: Push API (W3C 2021 A), which allows applications to receive messages even when they are in the background, and Notification API (Whatwg 2021), which enables applications to display screen notifications even when they are running in the background.

To send manual notifications and also receive notifications about floods, users must create a basic registration, including their name, e-mail and phone number, just to ensure the uniqueness of the registration. The application, shown in Fig. 1, also collects the geographical location of the users, but only when they create a manual flood notification. In addition to the basic registration data, users must also choose the regions of the city (North, South, East, West and Center) about which they wish to receive notifications.

Fig. 1. Home screen of the application on a smartphone.

In a future version of the system, all flood notifications, both those coming from SAISP and those from Pluvi.On sensors, like those sent by users, will be forwarded to an administrative center that will verify their validity before the system sends it to all users who have expressed an interest in the flood regions. However, during the proof of concept, all notifications were sent directly to users, without prior validation by an administrative center. The application (in Portuguese) can be accessed at https://pwa-radardoalagamento.nicdev.com.br.

3.3 Public Website

The fifth artifact of this system's proof of concept, the public website, was created to present all the sensor data in the form of tables, along with graphs to assist in data visualization. In addition to sensor data, the public website also displays all the manual notifications sent in by registered users. The purpose of the website is to make the data public, serving as the basis for the creation of other projects, also using open WWW standards.

The website's layout is simple, allowing easy navigation, and displaying the data divided into two categories:

- Sensors: Displays all SAISP and Pluvi.On sensors connected to the platform, along with the raw data received from them.
- Regions: Displays all manual notifications sent in by users, separated by regions of the city of São Paulo. The data of users who send in notifications is not publicly displayed, for privacy reasons.

In addition to allowing users to view the data on the screen, the website also allows the same data to be downloaded in structured CSV or JSON files. The website (in Portuguese) can be accessed at https://website-radardoalagamento.nicdev.com.br/.hy.

3.4 Administrative Web Interface

The sixth artifact of the system's proof of concept is the administrative web interface, which was developed using the Vue.js framework. It manages sensor registration and controls their notifications. It also enables the management of all manual notifications sent in by system users, in addition to creating and sending out other notifications to all users registered in the system. Manual management of notifications is a necessary feature because the system does not yet have automatic routines to control the notifications.

Figure 2 shows the screen of the administrative web interface, which displays all the sensors registered in the system and the latest data received by them, and provides access to a button that forces the system to send a flood notification from a specific sensor, as if the sensor has made this notification.

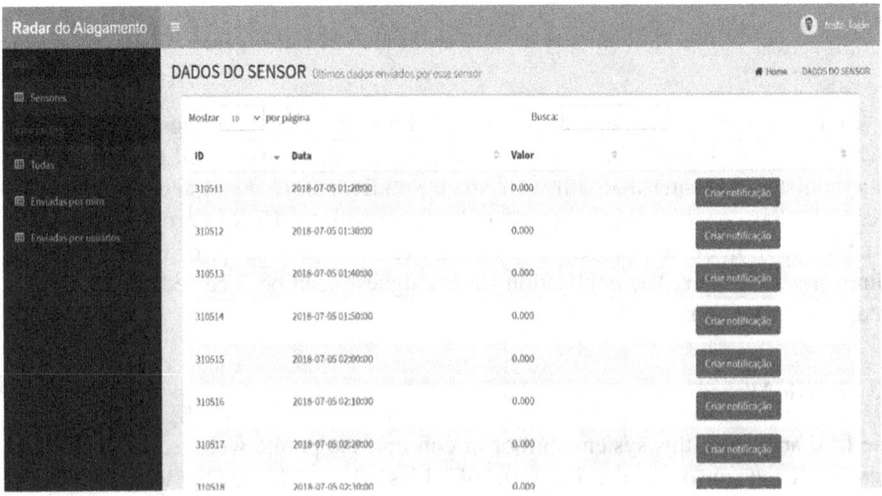

Fig. 2. Administrative web interface screen.

Because the administrative web interface provides access to a sensitive part of the system, with destructive operations, access is password-protected and limited to only a few users.

4 Results

A total of 383,048 measurements were taken from 38 sensors installed throughout the city of São Paulo. Of the 38 sensors, 11 belong to SAISP, for which 330,416 measurements were collected between November 24, 2017 and July 5, 2018. The other 27 sensors belong to Pluvi.On, and they collected 52,632 measurements between October 3, 2018 and March 8, 2019.

The SAISP sensors sent their measurements to the web server every 10 min, regardless of the weather situation. Therefore, 122,807 of the 330,416 measurements taken by the SAISP sensors were taken at times without any precipitation. This was unlike the Pluvi.On sensors, which reported measurements to the server twice an hour, but only when some type of precipitation or adverse atmospheric condition had been detected.

SAISP's 11 sensors reported only the number of millimeters of precipitation accumulated between each measurement, while Pluvi.On's 27 sensors captured a range of information from the region, such as wind speed, maximum and minimum temperature, and precipitation intensity. The total measurement counts for each sensor, together with their locations, are shown in Table 1. The Pluvi.On sensors are indicated with the word PLUVION. Figure 3 presents a map with the sensors' geographical locations.

In addition to sensor measurements, the system received 200 manual notifications of floods, on a test basis, from team members and guests. The notifications are distributed as follows, according to the administrative regions of the city of São Paulo:

- Center: 22 alerts;
- East: 38 alerts;
- North: 15 alerts;
- West: 62 alerts;
- South: 63 alerts.

Table 1. Summary of measurements gathered by sensors

Legend (map)	Measurements	Latitude	Longitude	Sensor description
1 blue	29580	− 23.5660583	− 46.7558577	Precipitation Radar Jaguar Basin
1 red	840	− 23.521969	− 46.709967	PLUVION_41C514-PLUVION_41C514
2 blue	29580	− 23.6051334	− 46.8128505	Precipitation Radar - P1-Tizo Park
3 Blue	29580	− 23.5834923	− 46.7718237	Precipitation Radar - P2 - Springs
4 blue	29580	− 23.5766225	− 46.6898323	Precipitation Radar - P3 - Jacarezinho

(continued)

Table 1. (*continued*)

Legend (map)	Measurements	Latitude	Longitude	Sensor description
5 blue	29580	− 23.5722249	− 46.7564377	Precipitation Radar- P4 - Água Podre
6 blue	29580	− 23.5517223	− 46.7394049	Precipitation Radar - P5 - Kentiki
7 Blue	29580	− 23,5808440	− 46,7567142	Precipitation Radar - P6 - Sapê
A	32106	− 23.5732336	− 46.7792928	Córrego Itaim - Rua Joaquim L. Veiga
B	32090	− 23.5680505	− 46.7591848	Córrego Jaguaré - Rua Jorge Ward
C	29582	− 23.5591155	− 46.6982622	FCTH-USP
D	29578	− 23.5570464	− 46.7328786	Córrego Jaguaré -Polytechnic School
E	2864	− 23.510784	− 46.776861	PLUVION_41C496
F	2547	− 23.559442	− 46.735154	PLUVION_41C484
G	2236	− 23.52783	− 46.679356	PLUVION_41C517
G	573	− 23.52783	− 46.679356	PLUVION_41C501
H	2869	− 23.51266	− 46.794101	PLUVION_41BF05
I	2597	− 23.528092	− 46.733469	PLUVION_41D2C7
J	2173	− 23.521997	− 46.695152	PLUVION_41C523
J	474	− 23.521997	− 46.695152	PLUVION_41D2B0
K	2770	− 23.529876	− 46.743841	PLUVION_41C48F
L	2170	− 23.539581	− 46.718342	PLUVION_41C488
L	597	− 23.539581	− 46.718342	PLUVION_41C594
M	2458	− 23.521593	− 46.725474	PLUVION_41C47E
N	2775	− 23.526528	− 46.686099	PLUVION_41C493
O	2581	− 23.506822	− 46.691231	PLUVION_41C533
P	2755	− 23.49237	− 46.756206	PLUVION_41C48B
Q	2716	− 23.536563	− 46.737348	PLUVION_41C539
R	2787	− 23.535594	− 46,707332	PLUVION_41C48A
S	2310	− 23.558464	− 46.754273	PLUVION_41C51A
T	2481	− 23.544205	− 46.696453	PLUVION_41C516
U	2438	− 23.538147	− 46.756859	PLUVION_41C505
V	2514	− 23.507489	− 46.733895	PLUVION_41C47D
W	1651	− 23.525927	− 46.684601	PLUVION_41C527
X	348	− 23.553709	− 46.659391	PLUVION_41BF0D
Y	646	− 23.529051	− 46.666418	PLUVION_41CD05
Y	545	− 23.529051	− 46.666418	PLUVION_41C486
Z	917	− 23.526829	− 46.710391	PLUVION_41C59F

5   Future Work

The next step of the project is to analyze the data received from the sensors to create an appropriate model, giving the system the ability to send users accurate, automatic flood notifications, and allowing other government services, such as flood protection actions, to be fed by the system's data and notifications.

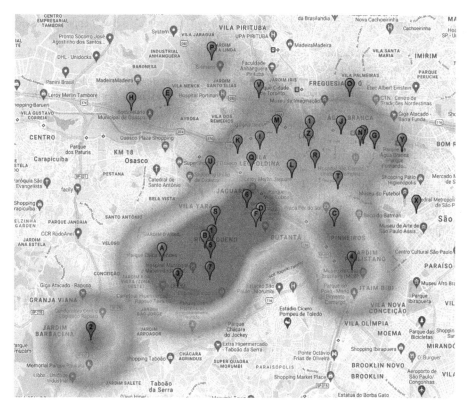

Fig. 3. Map of sensor locations

Another future improvement of the system is the creation of mechanisms, in terms of both software and procedures, that allow users to create their own sensors and connect them to the system through the API, expanding the area monitored by the system.

References

Bernardi, L., Sarma, S., Traub, K.: The Inversion Factor: How to Thrive in the IoT Economy. 1st edn. MIT Press, Cambridge (2017)

Berners-lee, T., et al.: World-Wide Web: the information universe. Electron. Networking Res. Appl. Policy **2**(1), 52–58 (1992)

Comer, D.: Redes de Computadores e Internet. 6th edn. Bookman, Porto Alegre (2016)

ECMA. Standard ECMA-404: The JSON data interchange syntax, 2nd edn. ECMA International (2017). https://www.ecma-international.org/publications-and-standards/standards/ecma-404. Accessed 6 Dec 2021

Fielding, R.: Chapter 5: Representational State Transfer (REST). Architectural Styles and the Design of Network-based Software Architectures (Ph.D.). University of California, Irvine. (2000). https://www.ics.uci.edu/~fielding/pubs/dissertation/rest_arch_style.htm. Accessed 8 Dec 2021

Fleisch, E.: What is the Internet of Things? An economic perspective. Econ. Manage. Finan. Markets **5**(2), 125–157 (2010)

Google. Progressive Web Apps. Google (2020). https://web.dev/progressive-web-apps/. Accessed 8 Dec 2021

Höller, J., et al.: From Machine-To-Machine to the Internet of Things: Introduction to a New Age of Intelligence, 1st edn. Academic Press, Oxford (2014)

Maschietto, L., et al.: Arquitetura e Infraestrutura de IoT. 1st edn. Sagah, Porto Alegre (2021)

OpenAPI initiative. OpenAPI Specification. Version 3.1.0. (2021). https://github.com/OAI/OpenAPI-Specification/blob/main/versions/3.1.0.md. Accessed 8 Dec 202

Tanenbaum, A.: Redes de Computadores, 5th edn. Pearson, Porto Alegre (2011)

Tsiatsis, V., et al.: Internet of Things: Technologies and Applications for a New Age of Intelligence, 2nd edn. Academic Press, Oxford (2018)

W3C. Push API. W3C (2021 A). https://www.w3.org/TR/push-api/. Accessed 20 Dec 2021

W3C. Service Workers Nightly. W3C (2021 B). https://w3c.github.io/ServiceWorker/. Accessed 20 Dec 2021

Whatwg. Notifications API. WHATWG (2021). https://www.w3.org/TR/notifications/. Accessed 20 Dec 2021

Wi-Monitor: Wi-Fi Channel State Information-Based Crowd Counting with Lightweight and Low-Cost IoT Devices

Takekazu Kitagishi$^{(\boxtimes)}$, Ge Hangli , Takashi Michikata ,
and Noboru Koshizuka

The University of Tokyo, Tokyo, Japan
{kitagishi.takekazu,ge.hangli,takashi.michikata,noboru}@koshizuka-lab.org
https://www.koshizuka-lab.org/

Abstract. Crowd counting is of great importance to many applications in various scenarios. Wi-Fi Channel State Information (CSI)-based crowd counting is a highly accurate privacy-conscious method. However, the problem with CSI-based crowd counting is the size and cost of the CSI collecting tool. Most studies benefiting from CSI collection use laptops with specific Network Interface Cards (NICs). The size and cost of the laptops restrict the practicability of such systems and limit active repositioning and mobility of the devices. This research aims to realize highly accurate CSI-based crowd counting using only one pair of lightweight and low-cost IoT devices. The devices are very agile and can easily be deployed even in space-limited environments. However, they have the disadvantage of poor data transportation compared to laptops. We compensate for this drawback by adjusting the deployment location, using multiple preprocessing methods depending on the situation, and standardizing the data for each subcarrier. We conducted evaluations of crowd counting in two representative scenarios. For the scenario of crowd sizes of 0, 1, 2, and 3 persons, when we used a weighted moving average (WMA) filter and phase sanitization as the preprocessing methods, the accuracy was 70.3%. When we used percentage of nonzero elements (PEM) and a moving average (MA) filter as the preprocessing methods, the accuracy was 84.6%. For the scenario of crowd sizes of 0, 5, 10, 15, and 20 persons, when we used a WMA filter and phase sanitization as the preprocessing methods, the accuracy was 76.5%. When we used PEM and a MA filter as the preprocessing methods, the accuracy was 75.9%. We found that the appropriate preprocessing method differs between the case of a small number of people and the case of a large number of people.

Keywords: Wi-Fi sensing · Channel state information · Crowd counting · ESP32 · Deep neural network

1 Introduction

Crowd counting is of great importance to many applications in various scenarios. For example, building management systems can adjust the light and ventilation according to the occupancy level and optimize energy consumption. Crowd counting can also help avoid infection with Covid-19.

Vision-based recognition has been widely deployed in many public places for crowd counting [1]. However, this method has limitations in terms of privacy and user acceptance. Non-image-based solutions typically leverage radio devices to locate objects, such as RFID tags [2] and mobile phones [3], but they require people to carry devices for surveillance. Several device-free approaches have been proposed to tackle the problem, utilizing sensor nodes [4], wireless sensor networks [5]. However, they require setting up a dedicated infrastructure for surveillance. The high cost hinders their broad deployment.

Channel state information (CSI) has the potential to overcome the drawbacks above. This information describes how a signal propagates from the transmitter to the receiver. We can count the number of people in the environment by extracting characteristics of human movements from the CSI. This method can use the existing Wi-Fi infrastructure, which results in a low deployment cost.

However, the size and cost of CSI collecting tools are limitations of this method. Most studies related to CSI collection use laptops with specific Network Interface Cards (NICs). The size and cost of the laptops restrict the practicability of such systems and limit active repositioning and mobility of the devices.

Because of this problem, this research aims to realize highly accurate CSI-based crowd counting using only one pair of lightweight and low-cost IoT devices. The devices are very agile and can easily be deployed even in space-limited environments. However, they have the disadvantage of poor data transportation compared to laptops. We compensate for this drawback by adjusting the deployment location, using multiple preprocessing methods depending on the situation, and standardizing the data for each subcarrier.

We conducted evaluations of crowd counting in two representative scenarios. The contributions of this work are summarized as follows.

1. The solution is based on only one pair of lightweight IoT devices. This system reduces the time and effort required to deploy and maintain it and makes it more portable and easy to place.
2. We evaluated crowd counting for about 20 people. This evaluation enabled us to verify the usage scenario in laboratories and meeting rooms where privacy and confidentiality are required.
3. We found that the appropriate preprocessing method varied depending on the number of people and the room's scale.

The rest of the paper is organized as follows. In Sect. 2, we review CSI-based crowd counting. We also review related work on CSI-based crowd counting and CSI-based sensing with lightweight and low-cost devices. In Sect. 3, we explain the problems of the existing CSI-based crowd counting studies and the limitations of lightweight IoT devices. In Sect. 4, we discuss the objective of this research and present the proposed system design. In Sect. 5, we evaluate the performance of the proposed system and discuss the experimental results. Finally, in Sect. 6, we conclude the paper.

2   Background and Related Work

2.1   CSI-Based Crowd Counting

CSI characterizes how wireless signals propagate from the transmitter to the receiver at certain carrier frequencies [6]. We can realize CSI-based crowd counting by capturing characteristics of human movements in CSI through machine learning.

CSI represents the amplitude attenuation and phase shift of the Wi-Fi signal from the transmitter and the receiver. The link between each pair of transmitting and receiving antennas has multiple subcarriers. The signals in the link between the transmitting and receiving antennas can be expressed as follows:

$$Y(t) = H(t)X(t) + N, \tag{1}$$

where $X(t)$ and $Y(t)$ are the vectors of the transmitting and receiving signals on each subcarrier of the link, $H(t)$ is the CSI matrix, t is the time point, and N is the noise vector.

The CSI amplitude and phase are affected by the presence and movement of people in the environment. Each CSI value has a channel frequency response (CFR) at each subcarrier. The CFR can be expressed as follows:

$$h(f;t) = \sum_{n}^{N} a_n(t)e^{-j2\pi f \tau_n(t)}, \tag{2}$$

where $h(f;t)$ is the CFR, $a_n(t)$ is the amplitude attenuation factor, $\tau_n(t)$ is the propagation delay, and f is the carrier frequency. This equation shows that the displacements and movements of the transmitter, receiver, and surrounding objects and humans affect the CSI amplitude and the phase.

Using the CSI, we can build a machine learning model that represents the number of people in the environment. Collected CSI values include a lot of noise due to hardware/software errors and environmental inferences. We need to remove the noise through various preprocessing methods before we build a machine learning model to infer the number of people with high accuracy.

2.2   Related Work

CSI-Based Crowd Counting. Several studies have conducted CSI-based crowd counting. First, we review the equipment used in the experiments, preprocessing, machine learning model, experimental environment, and accuracy.

Liu et al. [7] performed the first study that used machine learning for CSI-based crowd counting. They used one laptop with three receiving antennas and one router with two transmitting antennas. The experimental environment was indoors, in their lab. For preprocessing, they used the weighted moving average (WMA) filter and the Butterworth filter for the amplitude and phase sanitization for the phase. For model, they used a deep neural network (DNN). The accuracy was 78.0% for five people.

Zhao et al. [8] constructed an integrated system that detects people entering the room and counts the number of them. They used one laptop with three receiving antennas and one router with two transmitting antennas. They constructed a CNN + LSTM model after preprocessing the amplitude with the WMA filter and the phase with phase sanitization. The average accuracy was 85.2% for five people.

Xi et al. [9] proposed a metric percentage of nonzero elements (PEM), which describes the variance of CSI, for CSI-based crowd counting. They conducted experiments indoors and outdoors using one laptop as a transmitter and three laptops as receivers. They placed the laptops at each of the four corners. In the indoor experiment, 98% of the results were within the counting error of ± 2. In the outdoor experiment, 70% of the results were within the counting error of ± 2.

Sandaruwan et al. [10] performed CSI-based crowd counting outside using two pairs of an ESP32 and a NodeMCU. The amplitudes were preprocessed with an exponentially weighted moving average filter, and the phases were preprocessed with phase sanitization. Then, DNN and 1D-CNN models were built to count the number of people. The accuracy was 79% for 12 people.

CSI-Based Sensing with Lightweight and Low-Cost Devices. In recent years, lightweight and low-cost CSI collecting tools have been proposed. We review CSI-based sensing works with lightweight and low-cost IoT devices.

Hernandez and Bulut [11] and Atif et al. [12] presented a method for enabling a standalone ESP32 microcontroller to access CSI data directly. ESP32 is lightweight ($<10\,g$) and low cost ($<\$\,10$); therefore, their contribution extended the practicability and scalability of CSI-based sensing.

Hernandez and Bulut [11] also pointed out that the performance of CSI-based sensing varies depending on the device location. The classification accuracy of the direction of human movement changed by 29.4% depending on the location of the ESP32. In experiments conducted by Liu et al. [7] and Zhao et al. [8], the CSI recording equipment was placed near the center of the room. This location could have been chosen due to the size and weight limitations of the laptops. This point could be utilized to improve the accuracy of crowd counting.

3   Problems

The problem with CSI-based crowd counting is the size and cost of CSI collecting tools. Most of the CSI-based research used laptops with specific NICs. The size and cost of laptops restrict the practicability and scalability of such systems. On the other hand, lightweight and low-cost IoT devices that collect CSI have limitations of poor data transportation.

We compared the characteristics of CSI collecting tools, such as the size, cost, and frequency, used in previous studies. We compared the following tools based on 570 papers listed on the tools' websites [11–14]: (i) the Linux 802.11n CSI Tool for Intel 5300 NIC, (ii) the Atheros CSI Tool for a range of Atheros NIC, (iii) the ESP32-CSI-Tool for the ESP32, and (iv) Wi-ESP for the ESP32. We must

Table 1. Comparison of tools for collecting CSI.

Tool	Specific NIC + laptop	ESP32
Proportion	99.1 %	0.9 %
Size	>30 cm × 20 cm	<5.0 cm × 3.0 cm
Weight	>1 kg	<10 g
Cost	$ 10+ laptop	<$ 10
Bandwidth	Up to 1000 Hz	Up to 650 Hz
No. of antennas	3	1

consider that NICs cannot work alone and to run, require a direct connection to either a laptop or a desktop computer. Of the 570 papers, 99.1% used laptops, while 0.9% used ESP32s. On the other hand, the difference in size and cost between laptops and ESP32s is considerable. Laptops are >30 cm × 20 cm, > 1 kg, and $ 100, while ESP32s are <5.0 cm × 3.0 cm, <10 g, and <$ 10. These results were summarized in Table 1.

We also compared the data transportation of laptops and ESP32s. The sampling bandwidth of the ESP32 is limited to approximately 650 Hz, while that of NICs is up to approximately 1000 Hz. Although human movements, such as walking, are not fast enough to require 650 Hz to capture, sampling bandwidth is critical because packet loss can prevent enough samples from capturing the characteristics of movements. Moreover, only one antenna is attached to the ESP32, while three antennas are attached to laptops. The smaller number of antennas results in less CSI data transportation because today's Wi-Fi devices are equipped with multiple input multiple output (MIMO), which raises throughput by using multiple antennas simultaneously when transmitting Wi-Fi signals.

4   System Design

This research aimed to realize highly accurate CSI-based crowd counting using only one pair of lightweight and low-cost IoT devices. We compensate for the disadvantage of poor data transportation by adjusting the deployment location, using multiple preprocessing methods depending on the situation, and standardizing the data for each subcarrier.

We use one pair of lightweight and low-cost IoT devices as the transmitter and the receiver and use the CSI data collected by the receiver. We remove noise from the raw data with two methods and standardize the distribution of the data for each subcarrier. We use a DNN as a machine learning model. An overview of the system is shown in Fig. 1.

4.1   CSI Data Extraction

A pair of lightweight and low-cost IoT devices are the transmitter and the receiver, and the CSI data collected by the receiver is used. We set the IoT

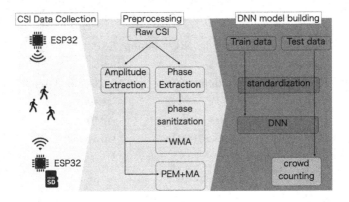

Fig. 1. Wi-Monitor framework.

devices on opposite sides of the rooms. Before we remove the noise from the raw CSI data, we need to calculate the CSI amplitude and phase.

Lightweight IoT devices decrease the restriction on the deployment location, which enables us to set the transmitter and the receiver on opposite sides of the room easily. Hernandez and Bulut [11] pointed out that the classification accuracy of the direction of human movement changed by 29.4% depending on the location of the transmitter and the receiver. This result implies that the accuracy of crowd counting could vary depending on the devices' deployment location.

The data acquired by ESP32 must be converted into amplitude and phase. They are given in imaginary and real numbers for each subcarrier. Although the ESP32 provides CFR values for 64 OFDM subcarriers, 10 subcarriers have null values, and the first two do not vary with time [15]. We calculate the CFR amplitude and phase for each of the effective 52 subcarriers using the following equations for $1 \leqq k \leqq 52$:

$$A_{k,t} = \sqrt{(x_{k,t}^2 + y_{k,t}^2)}, \tag{3}$$

$$\phi_{k,t} = tan^{-1}(\frac{x_{k,t}}{y_{k.t}}), \tag{4}$$

where $A_{k,t}$ and $\phi_{k,t}$ are the amplitude and the phase of the CFR, respectively, and $x_{k,t}$ and $y_{k,t}$ are the imaginary and real parts of the kth subcarrier CFR, respectively, at time t.

4.2 Noise Removal

We used two types of preprocessing methods: WMA/phase sanitization proposed in [7,8] and PEM proposed in [9] and a moving average (MA) filter. The original CSI amplitude and phase information extracted from ESP32s is noisy due

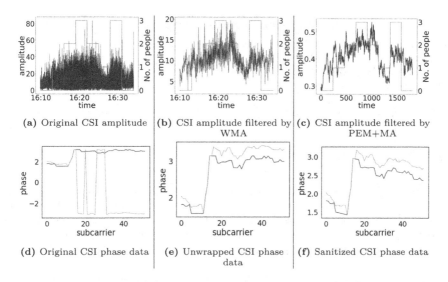

Fig. 2. Preprocessing on data of some subcarriers.

to hardware/software problems and environmental interfaces, which prevent us from inferring the number of people with high accuracy. The original and pre-processed amplitude and phase are shown in Fig. 2.

Weighted Moving Average Filter/Moving Average Filter. We utilized the WMA and MA algorithms to remove the noise. WMA provides more weight the more recent the value, while MA provides the same weight in a window. The formula is as follows:

$$A_t' = \frac{1}{m + (m-1) + ... + 1}[mA_t + (m-1)A_{t-1} + ... + A_{t-m+1}], \qquad (5)$$

$$A_t'' = \frac{1}{m}[A_t + A_{t-1} + ... + A_{t-m+1}], \qquad (6)$$

where A_t' and A_t'' are the value filtered by WMA and MA at time t, and m is the weighted relationship between current values and historical values. Figure 2(a), Fig. 2(b), and Fig. 2(c) illustrate this process.

Phase Sanitization. Hardware/software noise, such as the carrier frequency offset (CFO) and the sampling frequency offset (SFO), affect original phase information. To cancel these offsets, we looked at adjacent time samples and adjacent subcarrier samples, assuming that the phase offsets are the same across the packets and subcarriers. We show the complete algorithm in Algorithm 1.

Algorithm 1 Phase Sanitization

Require: collected Phase data: P_M; the number of subcarriers: Sub;
Ensure: Sanitized Phase Data: P_C;
 1: $U_p = unwrap(P_M)$;
 2: $y = mean(P_M, 2)$;
 3: **for** $i = 1$ to Sub **do**
 4:    x $(0 : Sub - 1)$;
 5: **end for**
 6: $p = polyfit(x, y, 1)$;
 7: $yf = p(1) * x$;
 8: $P_c = P_M - yf$;

The raw phase values are wrapped within the range of $[-\pi, \pi]$ due to the rotational nature of the phase. Assuming that the actual phase is continuous to some extent between adjacent subcarriers, we unwrapped the CSI phases according to an algorithm based on [16]. Figures 2(d) and 2(e) illustrate this process.

To remove the CFO and the SFO, we utilize a simple linear transformation. The phase P_M we get can be expressed as follows:

$$P_M = P + 2\pi \frac{m_i}{N} \Delta t + \beta + N, \qquad (7)$$

where P is the genuine phase, Δt is the time lag due to the SFO, β is the unknown phase offset due to the CFO, and N is the noise. Assuming that the phase offsets are the same across the adjacent packets and subcarriers, we can remove Δt and β by using a simple linear transformation based on an algorithm in [17]. We show the results in Fig. 2(f).

PEM. PEM represents the variation of CSI data in a subcarrier, which was proposed in [9]. This method is divided into three steps: transform the CSI amplitude values into two-dimensional matrices, dilate the elements in the matrix, and calculate the percentage of nonzero elements in the matrix. In the following explanation, C_d is a matrix of the acquired CSI amplitude values, S is the number of subcarriers, C_{max} and C_{min} are the maximum and minimum values in C_d, $\mathbb{M}$ is a newly created matrix, M is the number of rows of $\mathbb{M}$, D is the dilation coefficient, and P is the number of packets.

First, the CSI amplitude values on each subcarrier are transformed into a two-dimensional matrix. For each subcarrier i and for every P sample in the acquired CSI data, we make a matrix of $M \times P$ ($\mathbb{M}$), whose elements are initialized to 0. For each subcarrier i, we convert the CSI value $C_d[i][j](1 \leqq j \leqq P)$ into integers k by $k = \lceil \frac{C_{ij} - C_{min}}{C_{max} - C_{min}} (M - 1) \rceil + 1$, and then we set the elements in row k and column j in $\mathbb{M}$ to 1. One of the elements in each column is changed to 1, and all the other elements in the column remain 0. Then, the value j is moved in the range of $1 \leqq j \leqq P$. The distance of the row numbers (k) between adjacent columns becomes larger when the CSI amplitude values take dramatic turns.

Algorithm 2 PEM

Require: $C_d; S; C_{min}; C_{max}; M; D; P;$
Ensure: $\mathbb{P};$
 1: **for** $i = 1 : S$ **do**
 2:     **for** $j = 1 : P$ **do**
 3:         $k = \lceil \frac{C_{ij} - C_{min}}{C_{max} - C_{min}} (M - 1) \rceil + 1;$
 4:         **for** $u = -D : D$ **do**
 5:             **for** $v = -D : D$ **do**
 6:                 **if** $1 \leq j + u \leq P \& 1 \leq k + v \leq M$ **then**
 7:                     $\mathbb{M}[i + u][j + v] = 1;$
 8:                 **end if**
 9:             **end for**
10:         **end for**
11:     **end for**
12:     **for** $l = 1 : P$ **do**
13:         **for** m=1:M **do**
14:             $Ones = Ones + \mathbb{M}[l][m];$
15:         **end for**
16:     **end for**
17:     $\mathbb{P} = Ones/(P \times M);$
18: **end for**

Second, we transform the elements around elements 1 to 1. This process is called matrix dilation. We transform the elements within a distance of D from the elements 1 to 1. There is less overlap of dilated elements when the CSI amplitude values change more sharply. Less overlap results in more elements becoming the element 1 in $\mathbb{M}$.

Finally, we calculate the percentage $\mathbb{P}[i]$ of the nonzero elements in the matrix $\mathbb{M}$, which is the PEM of the ith subcarrier. The value $\mathbb{P}[i]$ becomes larger when significant changes in CSI amplitude values often occur.

The complete algorithm is shown in Algorithm 2. Figures 2(a) and 2(c) illustrate this process.

4.3 DNN Model Building

We employ a DNN with N fully connected hidden layers with $K_i(i = 1, 2, ..., N)$ neurons on layer i. We took this crowd counting problem as a regression task. Before the model building, we standardize the data distribution for each subcarrier. The distribution of the acquired CSI data is different for each subcarrier. In the DNN, features with a larger scale distribution of the values disproportionately impact the model. Standardizing the distribution of features could improve the accuracy.

5   Evaluation

We conducted evaluations of crowd counting in two representative scenarios. The first testbed was in a corridor with crowds of 0, 1, 2, and 3 people, and the

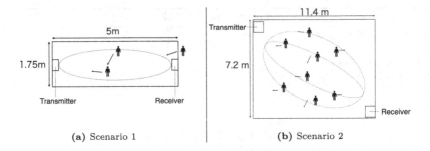

(a) Scenario 1   (b) Scenario 2

Fig. 3. The testbeds.

second testbed was in a rectangular meeting room with crowds of 0, 5, 10, 15, and 20 people, as illustrated in Fig. 3. We found that the appropriate preprocessing method varies depending on the number of people and the room's scale.

In each testbed, two ESP32s (one was the TTGO T8 V1.8, and the other was the ESP32-DevKitC ESP-WROOM-32) formed the transmitter and receiver pair, each working in the 2.4 GHz band. The chosen DNN model had three hidden layers with neurons of [100, 100, 100]. While the training data were collected, the participants walked casually in the Wi-Fi-covered area without any restrictions or limitations on their movements.

5.1   Scenario 1: In a Corridor

The first testbed was in a corridor in front of our laboratory with up to three people, as illustrated in Fig. 3(a). When the counting error was within ±0.5, the data were labeled "correct". The proportion of "correct" data in the test data was defined as "accuracy". We conducted model training and evaluations numerous times on the same parameter and calculated the mean accuracy. When we used WMA and phase sanitization as the preprocessing methods, the mean accuracy was 70.4%. When we used PEM and MA as the preprocessing methods, the mean accuracy was 84.2%. We found that PEM was suitable for preprocessing when the number of people was small.

Both ESP32s were set on chair seats at a height of 0.5 m. The number of people was changed in the following order: 0, 1, 2, 3, 2, 1, 3, and 0. Data were collected for 3 min for each group. The first four scenes were used as training data and the last four scenes as test data.

Results. In the case of WMA and phase sanitization, after 96 model builds and evaluations, the mean accuracy was 70.4%; the highest accuracy was 75.4%, and the lowest accuracy was 64.8%. In the round when the accuracy was 70.3%, which was closest to the average accuracy, the number of correct answers and the number of predictors were compared, as shown in Fig. 4(a), Fig. 4(c).

In the case of PEM and MA, after 62 rounds of model builds and evaluations, the mean accuracy was 84.2%; the highest accuracy was 90.5%, and the lowest

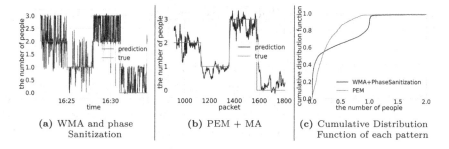

(a) WMA and phase
Sanitization

(b) PEM + MA

(c) Cumulative Distribution
Function of each pattern

Fig. 4. Comparison of the predicted values and the true number of people in Scenario 1.

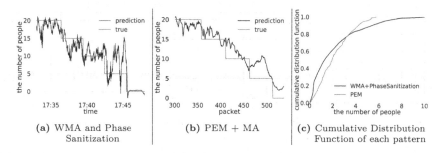

(a) WMA and Phase
Sanitization

(b) PEM + MA

(c) Cumulative Distribution
Function of each pattern

Fig. 5. Comparison of the predicted values and the true number of people in Scenario 2.

accuracy was 77.2%. In the round when the accuracy was 84.6%, which was closest to the average accuracy, the number of correct answers and the number of predictors were compared, as shown in Fig. 4(b), Fig. 4(c).

Discussion. PEM and MA were more accurate than WMA and phase sanitization. Therefore, we conclude that preprocessing using PEM and MA is more suitable for crowd counting in small rooms with few people.

5.2   Scenario 2: In a Meeting Room

The second testbed was in a meeting room with up to 20 people, as illustrated in Fig. 3(b). When the counting error was ± 2.5, the data were labeled "correct". The proportion of "correct" data in the test data was defined as "accuracy". We conducted model training and evaluations numerous times on the same parameter and calculated the mean accuracy. When we used WMA and phase sanitization as the preprocessing methods, the mean accuracy was 76.5%. When we used PEM and MA as the preprocessing methods, the accuracy was 75.9%. We found that WMA/phase sanitization was suitable for preprocessing when the number of people was large.

Both ESP32s were set on desks at a height of 1.0 m. The number of people was changed in the following order: 0, 5, 10, 15, 20, 22, 20, 15, 10, 5, and 0. Data were collected for 3 min each. The first five scenes were used as training data and the last five as test data.

Results. In the case of WMA and phase sanitization, after 59 rounds of model builds and evaluations, the mean accuracy was 76.5 %; the highest accuracy was 83.7 %, and the lowest accuracy was 67.2 %. In the round when the accuracy was 76.5 %, which was closest to the average accuracy, the number of correct answers and the number of predictors were compared, as shown in Fig. 5(a) and Fig. 5(c).

In the case of PEM and MA, after 50 rounds of model builds and evaluations, the mean accuracy was 75.9 %; the highest accuracy was 89.4 %, and the lowest accuracy was 55.1 %. In the round when the accuracy was 75.9 %, which was closest to the average accuracy, the number of correct answers and the number of predictors were compared, as shown in Fig. 5(b) and Fig. 5(c).

Discussion. WMA/phase sanitization were more accurate than PEM and MA, and the accuracy range was much smaller for the WMA/phase sanitization pattern. For PEM and MA, the accuracy was 55.1 % in one case, although we used the same parameters as when the average accuracy was maximized. This low accuracy could be problematic in practice.

The significant accuracy variations for PEM and MA could be due to the small amount of data. PEM preprocessing requires a large amount of data. It may be that the PEM pattern could not capture the characteristics of human movement in Scenario 2. Increasing the amount of data would be required.

5.3   Discussion

The evaluation results for crowd counting showed that appropriate preprocessing method differs between the case of a small number of people and the case of a large number of people. One possible reason is that the features that largely affect crowd counting are different depending on the situation. For a few people, the CSI variations caused by human movement were effective. For many people, the CSI values themselves caused by the presence of people were effective. These reasons may be related to the Fresnel zone.

A Fresnel zone is one of a series of ellipsoidal regions between and around a transmitter and a receiver. Their boundaries represent the line that the difference in the propagation distance is $n\lambda/2$ $(n = 1, 2, 3...)$ between the radio waves that travel in a straight line from the transmitter to the receiver and the radio waves that arrive at the receiver after being reflected by obstacles. These elliptical lines are illustrated in Fig. 3. Waves reflected within an even number of Fresnel zones are out of phase π with the direct wave. Therefore, the amplitude of the wave lowers. However, waves reflected within an odd number of Fresnel zones do the opposite, raising the wave's amplitude.

The reason for the difference in the appropriate preprocessing method between the case of a small number of people and a large number of people could be as follows. Models for CSI and the number of people would be affected by two factors: the attenuation of the Wi-Fi signal due to reflections on people, and the fluctuations in the Wi-Fi signal by people movement between adjacent Fresnel zones. The attenuation is extracted by WMA/phase sanitization, while PEM extracts the fluctuation. In the case of a small number of people, the effect of reflections on people would be small, while the effect of fluctuations would be large. As the number of people becomes large, the effect of fluctuations could reach equilibrium, and the effect of reflections on people could become large.

6 Conclusion

This paper proposed a CSI-based crowd counting method with one pair of lightweight and low-cost IoT devices. We evaluated the proposed method in two scenarios and found that for crowd sizes of 0 1, 2, and 3 people, the counting error was ± 0.5 people for 84.6 % of the cases, and for crowd sizes of 0, 5, 10, 15, and 20 people, the counting error was ± 2.5 people for 76.5 % of the cases.

Acknowledgments. We would like to thank all the participants in the experiments. We also thank Masahiro Matsui and Yusuke Sasaki for their assistance with developing the prototype in the early stages of research. Our research was conducted at Mitsui Fudosan UTokyo Laboratory, a joint research project between Mitsui Fudosan Co., Ltd. and The University of Tokyo. We gratefully acknowledge the kind support of Mitsui Fudosan Co., Ltd.

References

1. Li, M., Zhang, Z., Huang, K., Tan, T.: Estimating the number of people in crowded scenes by mid-based foreground segmentation and head-shoulder detection. In: 2008 19th International Conference on Pattern Recognition, Tampa, FL, USA, pp. 1–4. IEEE (2008). https://doi.org/10.1109/ICPR.2008.4761705
2. Ni, L.M., Liu, Y., Lau, Y.C., Patil, A.P.: LANDMARC: indoor location sensing using active RFID. In: Proceedings of the First IEEE International Conference on Pervasive Computing and Communications, 2003. (PerCom 2003), Fort Worth, TX, USA, pp. 407–415. IEEE (2003). https://doi.org/10.1109/PERCOM.2003.1192765
3. Weppner, J., Lukowicz, P.: Bluetooth-based collaborative crowd density estimation with mobile phones. In: 2013 IEEE International Conference on Pervasive Computing and Communications (PerCom), San Diego, CA, USA, pp. 193–200. IEEE (2013). https://doi.org/10.1109/PerCom.2013.6526732
4. Choi, J., Ge, H., Koshizuka, N.: IoT-based occupants counting with smart building state variables. In: 2020 IEEE 29th International Conference on Enabling Technologies: Infrastructure for Collaborative Enterprises (WETICE), Bayonne, France, pp. 171–176. IEEE (2020). https://doi.org/10.1109/WETICE49692.2020.00041
5. Doong, S.H.: Spectral human flow counting with RSSI in wireless sensor networks. In: 2016 International Conference on Distributed Computing in Sensor Systems (DCOSS), Washington, DC, USA, pp. 110–112. IEEE (2016). https://doi.org/10.1109/DCOSS.2016.33

6. Tse, D., Viswanath, P.: Fundamentals of Wireless Communication. Cambridge University Press, New York (2005)

7. Liu, S., Zhao, Y., Chen, B.: WiCount: a deep learning approach for crowd counting using WiFi signals. In: 2017 IEEE International Symposium on Parallel and Distributed Processing with Applications and 2017 IEEE International Conference on Ubiquitous Computing and Communications (ISPA/IUCC), Guangzhou, China, pp. 967–974. IEEE (2017). https://doi.org/10.1109/ICCCN.2018.8487420

8. Zhao, Y., Liu, S., Xue, F., Chen, B., Chen, X.: DeepCount: crowd counting with Wi-Fi using deep learning. J. Commun. Inf. Networks 4(3), 38–52 (2019). https://doi.org/10.23919/JCIN.2019.8917884

9. Xi, W., et al.: Electronic frog eye: counting crowd using WiFi. In: IEEE INFOCOM 2014-IEEE Conference on Computer Communications, Toronto, ON, Canada, pp. 361–369. IEEE (2014). https://doi.org/10.1109/INFOCOM.2014.6847958

10. Sandaruwan, R., Alagiyawanna, I., Sandeepa, S., Dias, S., Dias, D.: Device-free pedestrian count estimation using Wi-Fi channel state information. In: 2021 IEEE International Intelligent Transportation Systems Conference (ITSC), Indianapolis, IN, USA, pp. 2610–2616. IEEE (2021). https://doi.org/10.1109/ITSC48978.2021.9564725

11. Hernandez, S.M., Bulut, E.: Lightweight and standalone IoT-based WiFi sensing for active repositioning and mobility. In: 2020 IEEE 21st International Symposium on A World of Wireless, Mobile and Multimedia Networks (WoWMoM), Cork, Ireland, pp. 277–286. IEEE (2020). https://doi.org/10.1109/WoWMoM49955.2020.00056

12. Atif, M., Muralidharan, S., Ko, H., Yoo, B.: Wi-ESP-a tool for CSI-based Device-Free Wi-Fi Sensing (DFWS). J. Comput. Des. Eng. 7(5), 644–656 (2020). https://doi.org/10.1093/jcde/qwaa048

13. Halperin, D., Hu, W., Sheth, A., Wetherall, D.: Tool release: gathering 802.11n traces with channel state information. ACM SIGCOMM CCR 41(1), 53 (2011)

14. Xie, Y., Li, Z., Li, M.: Precise power delay profiling with commodity WiFi. In: Proceedings of the 21st Annual International Conference on Mobile Computing and Networking, pp. 53–64. MobiCom 2015, ACM, New York, USA (2015). https://doi.org/10.1145/2789168.2790124

15. Espressif Systems: ESP-IDF programming guide (2021). https://docs.espressif.com/projects/esp-idf/en/latest/esp32/. Accessed 2 Feb 2022

16. Jiang, W., Liu, Y., Lei, Y., Wang, K., Yang, H., Xing, Z.: For better CSI fingerprinting based localization: a novel phase sanitization method and a distance metric. In: 2017 IEEE 85th Vehicular Technology Conference (VTC Spring), Sydney, NSW, Australia, pp. 1–7. IEEE (2017). https://doi.org/10.1109/VTCSpring.2017.8108351

17. Sen, S., Radunovic, B., Choudhury, R.R., Minka, T.: You are facing the Mona Lisa: spot localization using PHY layer information. In: Proceedings of the 10th International Conference on Mobile Systems, Applications, and Services, pp. 183–196. MobiSys 2012, Association for Computing Machinery, New York, USA (2012). https://doi.org/10.1145/2307636.2307654

Design of a Next-Generation Interoperable Cognitive Port Solution

Andreu Belsa Pellicer[1]([✉]) [ID], Matilde Julian Segui[1] [ID], Achilleas Marinakis[2] [ID],
Anastasios Nikolakopoulos[2] [ID], Vrettos Moulos[2] [ID], Héctor Iturria[3] [ID],
José Antonio Clemente[3] [ID], Xhulja Shahini[4] [ID], Tristan Kley[4] [ID],
Andreas Metzger[4] [ID], Miguel Bravo[5] [ID], Paolo Calciati[5] [ID],
Christos-Antonios Gizelis[6] [ID], Filippos Nikolopoulos-Gkamatsis[6] [ID],
Konstantinos Nestorakis[6] [ID], Ignacio Lacalle[1] [ID], Carlos E. Palau[1] [ID],
and Santiago Cáceres[5] [ID]

[1] Department of Communications, Universitat Politècnica de València,
Camino de Vera, s/n 46022, Valencia, Spain
{anbelpel,majuse,iglaub}@upv.es, cpalau@dcom.upv.es
[2] National Technical University of Athens, School of Electrical and Computer
Engineering, 9 Iroon Polytechniou St Athens, 15780 Athens, Greece
{achmarin,tasosnikolakop,vrettos}@mail.ntua.gr
[3] Prodevelop, Carrer del Cronista Carreres, 13, Entresuelo 46003, Valencia, Spain
{hiturria,jclemente}@prodevelop.es
[4] paluno - The Ruhr Institute for Software Technology, Universität Duisburg-Essen,
Gerlingstraße 16, 45127 Essen, Germany
{xhulja.shahini,tristan.kley,andreas.metzger}@paluno.uni-due.de
[5] ITI (Computing Technological Institute), Camino de Vera, S/N, Edif. 8G - Acc. B -
4a Planta, 46022 Valencia, Spain
{mbravo,pcalciati,scaceres}@iti.es
[6] IT Innovation Center OTE Group, 99 Kifissias Ave., 15124 Marousi, Athens, Greece
cgkizelis@cosmote.gr, {fnikolop,knestorak}@ote.gr

Abstract. Ports are essential nodes in global maritime trade. As such,
their efficency is key to ensure sustainable supply chains across the world.
Current studies point interoperability and data integration as the next
milestones to achieve efficient, smart ports. DataPorts aims at covering
those gaps, delivering an industrial data platform bearing in mind seaports' involved actors' needs. With DataPorts, transportation and logistics companies will leverage the current data deluge to offer cognitive
services. This paper describes the technical design of such a platform
and how it enables the acquisition, homogenization, and processing of
the heterogeneous data, judiciously handled to generate advanced data-
exhaustive services. Finally, it presents a practical usage example aimed
to improve the business processes in the port of Valencia.

Keywords: Interoperability · Artificial Intelligence · Seaports

Supported by H2020 Project DataPorts.

A. González-Vidal et al. (Eds.): GIoTS 2022, LNCS 13533, pp. 149–160, 2022.
https://doi.org/10.1007/978-3-031-20936-9_12

1   Introduction

The future of the port industry points towards the *smart ports*: this term defines an innovative port that possesses a competitive advantage thanks to technological innovations. A *smart port* should be able to automate as many services and operations as possible, using intelligent data-driven systems. To become so, Port Authorities need to have a digital transformation strategy, adopting IoT technologies producing valuable data from multiple sources (including sensors) [1]. In the seaports of the future, IoT and 5G technologies are key enablers for data transmission and data traffic management. The data generated by IoT sensors drive the service creation for fleet traffic management, asset tracking and shipping containers monitoring, logistics operations, environmental condition monitoring, inventory management, access and parking control or operational safety and security, among other purposes. This allows the smart port authorities to offer valuable services and attract new clients. Adopting IoT approaches will bring ports closer to real automation in an increasingly data-driven market, where numerous stakeholders and users may benefit from [2].

Although the exchange of data from several sources opens a new range of possibilities, such as the provision of innovative Artificial Intelligence (AI) services, it involves technical requirements that must be met [3]. First, it needs a platform capable of overcoming all the technical challenges related with the acquisition, aggregation, processing and analysis of the data coming from different sources. Second, it needs a secure and trusted platform offering efficient and effective data sharing among stakeholders, in addition to a reliable source of truth that guarantees the quality, validity and veracity of the data, including procedures and policies for data governance. From this need appears the DataPorts project, which has been funded by the European Commission within the frame of the H2020 Big Data Value PPP programme. The project relies on the experience of its partners to address the identified open challenges in the sector and cover the technology gaps as described in the previous paragraph. This paper describes how DataPorts enables the new generation of cognitive data-supported services addressing more open, connected and transparent frameworks that provide intuitive interactions, learning capabilities, data processing and analytic services under a protected environment for maritime ports.

2   Context, Motivation and Related Work

DataPorts aims to design and implement a seaport-oriented technological platform that will enrich and enhance the existing digital infrastructures with some of the most advanced state-of-the-art technological innovations. It will be deployed in two European seaports (Valencia and Thessaloniki), where it is expected to boost the data value chain to an upper level and solve real port constrains. The DataPorts platform intends to interconnect the cluster of heterogeneous digital infrastructures currently present in digital seaports into a unique integrated ecosystem. Besides, the platform tries to establish the policies and rules for a reliable and trusted data sharing. It also includes novel Big Data Analytics services

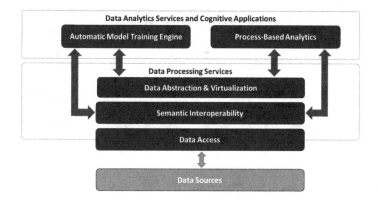

Fig. 1. Overview of the proposed solution.

to solve some of the most important seaport challenges regarding data management and data mining. Finally, DataPorts aims to enable the establishment of a single Data Space for all European seaports, thus collaborating with the EC global challenge of generating a Common European Data Space [4]. These objectives entail several relevant technical challenges regarding the scalability of the solution, the heterogeneity of the data sources, whose volumes of data are unknown, and the data governance mechanisms, among others.

This paper presents a use case from the Port of Valencia to illustrate the use and advantages of the DataPorts platform. The Port of Valencia is mainly specialized in containerized merchandise traffic, for which it has three big terminals managed by the most important shipping lines in the world. Moreover, it also manages other types of freight traffic, such as liquid and solid bulk and ro-ro cargo. The port also receives a significant number of cruise ships annually. From a technical point of view, the Port of Valencia has been involved in several relevant research projects in the areas of IoT [2] and Big Data [5].

3   Design of the Proposed Solution

The proposed solution consists of three main building blocks (Fig. 1): i) the *Data Access Component*, which provides access to the different data sources connected to the DataPorts platform, ii) the *Data Processing Services*, which act as the functional connection between the data sources and the Data Analytics services provided by the platform and iii) the *Data Analytics and Cognitive Applications*, which provide mechanisms to develop cognitive services using AI technologies.

3.1   Data Access Component

The Data Access Component (DAC) distributes data to the upper layers and provides an interface to manage and run agents that integrate data into the DataPorts platform. The component is divided into two sub-components (Fig. 2):

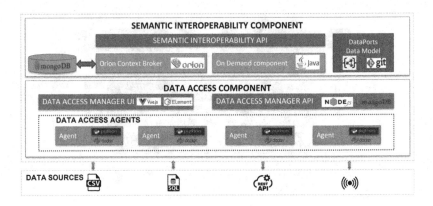

Fig. 2. Data Access Component implementation.

- **Agents:** Set of software components that perform the initial movement of data from its source to the platorm. The agents have been developed using pyngsi [6], which is a NGSI Python framework intended to build FIWARE NGSI Agents and was developed within the context of H2020 Project PIXEL [7].
- **Data Access Manager:** Manages the agents available in the platform. To do so, it provides a REST API to interact directly with the agents and a UI that displays the information regarding the agents as well as the results of the actions executed over them via the API. In addition, it offers an SDK with a series of predefined templates to facilitate the creation of agents. The UI was developed using Element [8] or vue-element-admin [9]. The REST API was developed in Node.js following the MVC pattern [10] and makes use of the Docker API to manage agents as containers and MongoDB to store the templates used to build the agents with the SDK functionality. The specification of the API is done in Swagger.

The DAC enables the direct management of data sources on the platform. This feature of the platform brings other benefits such as the possibility to create instances of the different data sources or to delete those that are no longer of interest. It simplifies the process of creating agents (it is quick and visual), and it allows managing the information in a centralised way. The DAC allows the users to control the data sources available on the platform, how often the data will be retrieved, as well as to see the actionable data and subscriptions.

3.2   Data Processing Services

This block is composed by the Semantic Interoperability Component and the Data Abstraction and Virtualization Component. These components work closely with the DAC to provide input data to the Data Analytics Services.

Semantic Interoperability Component. This component acts as a middleware that distributes the data coming from the agents to the different components of the platform. It enables semantic interoperability by providing a unified API to access the data, as well as a common data model to allow a shared understanding of the information.

Regarding the implementation (Fig. 2), the Orion Context Broker [11], which is part of the FIWARE ecosystem and provides a NGSI interface, is the core element of the Semantic Interoperability Component. In the context of the Data-Ports platform, Orion receives data from the agents, provides a publish/subscribe interface and a common data format and keeps a local registry of the available data sources and agents. In addition, a custom On Demand component has been implemented to enable access to the historical data because Orion only stores the last value of an entity. The Semantic Interoperability Component exposes a common API to access the data and metadata. Finally, the DataPorts Data Model is hosted in a Git repository, which contains the JSON schema documents describing the syntax and JSON-LD context documents, which provide a unique definition of the terms by mapping them to URIs and the documentation. The data model reuses concepts from existing data models and ontologies, such as the FIWARE Smart Data Models [12], the UN/CEFACT data model [13], the SAREF ontology [14] and the IDSA Information Model [15].

Data Abstraction and Virtualization. This component (DAV) is responsible for duly pre-processing, cleaning, and filtering the incoming historical data, storing them to a scalable data lake, and delivering them as data ponds to any potential consumers, such as the analytics components of the platform (Fig. 3). Data ponds are a subset of the data lake that focuses on a particular topic. They are created by applying specific filtering actions (rules), defined by the recipients, in order to retrieve only the portion of data they are interested in, thus minimizing the processing and the network workload [19]. In addition, DAV transforms the data into the requested format, such as Parquet or CSV, and also exposes useful metadata for all the pre-processed datasets, via a RESTful API.

To execute the processing tasks, DAV relies on Apache Spark, which is a unified analytics engine for large-scale data processing. The structure of the data lake is based on MongoDB, along with its sharding and replication features to ensure scalability and availability, while Kubernetes is the orchestration platform to manage the shards and replicas. Regarding the exposure of the data, Apache Nifi is used due to its flow-based programming philosophy.

The goal of DAV is to introduce a middleware based on the Data as a Service notion, which aims at improving the productivity of developers in creating data-intensive applications, by abstracting the details on data access and storage [20]. Following that notion, developers just define the content and format of the data, leaving to the middleware the burden of retrieving, storing, processing and serving them, putting also special emphasis on data quality and performance.

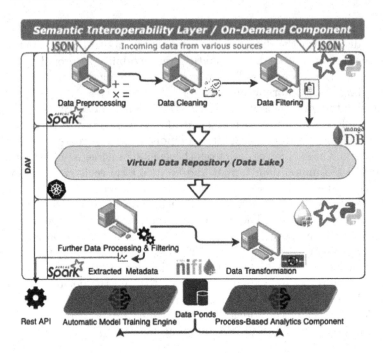

Fig. 3. Data Abstraction and Virtualization (DAV) functionalities and technologies.

3.3 Data Analytics Services and Cognitive Applications

The *Data Analytics Services* and *Cognitive Applications* are advanced features to extract and provide real-world insights from seaports' data. Their main goal is to upgrade the current port domain scenario by implementing advanced AI capabilities, thus enabling the exploitation of the data ecosystem to enhance the understanding of business processes and KPIs. Consequently, port operators will be enabled to apply state-of-the-art data analytics and machine learning techniques to predict new intrinsic patterns and tendencies previously unknown, without the necessity of having deep technical background in Big Data Analytics.

Automatic Model Training Engine. This component creates cognitive services oriented to tackle port's business needs. It is composed of a robust training engine capable of automatically searching the best Machine Learning (ML) model from a vast collection of state-of-the-art algorithms to make predictions of a desired KPI from a port-oriented dataset available at the DataPorts platform. For that, the training engine generates a set of advanced data pipelines to thoroughly manage the data by performing techniques such as data cleansing, features selection and hyperparameters optimization. Following a distributed approach, the instances of such pipelines are concurrently run, drastically reducing the processing time. Finally, the selected model is packaged into a REST service and deployed as a Cognitive Service able to make predictions over new incom-

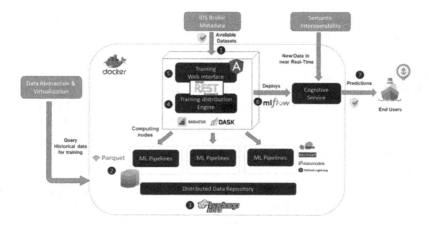

Fig. 4. Architecture of the Automatic Model Training Engine.

ing data. The component also provides a Training Web Interface that allows potential users, who may not have a technical background, to interact with the component and create new Cognitive Services to perform predictions over DataPorts datasets. The technological approach followed with the component is based on the implementation of some of the most suitable Big Data Analytics technologies currently available. To implement this component, parallelization, compression, data processing, distribution, and deployment frameworks were utilized, as showed in Fig. 4.

The Automatic Model Training Engine tries to fill the gap of the lack of AI capabilities in ports by introducing an automatic tool that implements state-of-the-art ML technologies to enhance the understanding of their business process and KPIs. Hence, it facilitates the design of data analytics services that support the configuration of predictive models from the data available at the platform.

Process-Based Analytics. This component provides advanced capabilities to monitor and adapt running business processes in the port domain. To this end, the Process-based Analytics Component (PBAC) combines different state-of-the-art ML techniques, in particular reinforcement learning and explainable AI. Examples of business processes in the port domain are the flow of vessels within the port's service area and the transport operation for containers. In a transport operation process scenario, the goal of PBAC is to monitor processes' delivery time, notifying process managers about potential delays and suggesting adaptations to prevent them. By proactively predicting the future states of the ongoing process, the PBAC component provides forward-looking perspectives and decision support for terminal and process operators. It thereby facilitates proactive management of port processes, assisting port authorities in their decision-making. The PBAC leverages the prediction models trained as part of the Automatic Model Training Engine (AMTE) and connects the outcomes of this prediction model with two novel sub-components, each of which utilises a different, complementary set of ML techniques:

Explainable Predictive Process Monitoring: This sub-component explains the forecasts made by the prediction model trained in the AMTE component [16]. Predictive business process monitoring is usually performed via deep learning models, such as the LSTMs. Although such models consistently achieve higher prediction accuracy than simple models, a major drawback is their lack of interpretability, which limits their adoption in practice. By using recent explainable AI techniques, this sub-component helps answering the question "why was this prediction made?".

Prescriptive Process Monitoring: For this sub-component, an approach was devised based on Online Reinforcement Learning to resolve a fundamental trade-off between prediction accuracy and prediction earliness [17]. This sub-component provides indicators that estimate the reliability of individual predictions made by the predictive models of the AMTE component. Such reliability estimates quantify the likelihood of a correct prediction, which provides additional information for decision making. Process managers should obviously only make decisions based on *accurate* predictions, although adaptations typically have non-negligible latencies. Thus, process managers should act sufficiently early, i.e., with enough lead time for the adaptation to become effective [18]. This sub-component, thus, helps answering the question "when to adapt?".

Regarding the implementation (Fig. 5), the Reinforcement Learning agent used for Prescriptive Process Monitoring is based on the proximal policy optimisation (PPO) algorithm, implemented using Tensorflow. It is trained at runtime by using the prediction model outcomes created from real-time process data. To implement the Explainable Process Monitoring sub-component, authors have developed the Loreley technique [16]. Loreley is a model-agnostic explainable AI technique that generates explanations in the form of counterfactuals. The output of the PBAC is made available through a user interface and a REST API to facilitate its integration into existing port solutions. The API of the PBAC was implemented using Django and the Django REST framework.

4   Use Case Driven Validation

The DataPorts platform will be validated in different scenarios of the project's pilot use cases. In this paper, one of those scenarios is presented to illustrate how the components of the platform work together. In this scenario, the Port of Valencia makes use of the Data Analytics services of the DataPorts platform to generate predictions based on the vessel calls in order to improve transport operation management processes.

4.1   Provision of Data

The interaction between the components of the platform is highlighted using the Port Community System (PCS). This data source provides, among other,

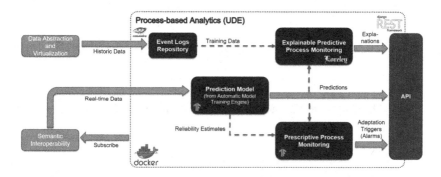

Fig. 5. Architecture of the Process-based Analytics Component (PBAC).

Fig. 6. Data Access Component UI for managing the agent for the historical data.

information about real-time and historical vessel port calls (PCS traffic data). The first step of the scenario is to acquire and register those data, along with their metadata. For that reason, data access agents were developed (more specifically, an agent for the historical data and another for the real-time data). Figure 6 shows the UI of the DAC and the agent developed for the historical data.

These agents are also responsible for performing the translation of the information into the common data model, which is provided by the Semantic Interoperability component. The latter offers a common API to show the metadata of the available data sources and agents as well as to provide access to the data. Therefore, DAV component calls that API to retrieve the historical PCS traffic data. It then proceeds to pre-process and clean them for quality purposes. However, the analytics components might need to consume only specific data ponds of the PCS traffic dataset. For example, the Status of a port call can be Estimated, Authorized, Operational, or Completed; but the Authorized vessels are not useful for the analytics performed by the Automatic Model Training Engine (AMTE). Consequently, when AMTE asks DAV to retrieve the data, it attaches the corresponding filtering rule, along with the request. The rules follow the subject-operator-object syntax and are structured in JSON format (Fig. 7).

```
{
    "name":"status_not_authorized",
    "rule":{
        "subject_column":"Status",
        "operator":"!=",
        "object":"Authorized"
    }
}
```

Fig. 7. Data Abstraction and Virtualization filtering rule.

4.2   Data Analytics

Automatic Model Training Engine. The Automatic Model Training Engine
provides an easy-to-use Web Interface to allow an automated creation of new
cognitive services, which selects the best ML model to make predictions over a
specific port KPI (see Fig. 8). The tool also allows the user to manage existing
cognitive services, explore the ML models associated with a trained cognitive
service and interactively analyse the results of a trained cognitive service.

Fig. 8. Training Web Interface of AMTE.

The training data needed by the ML models is provided by the Data Access
component and the metadata is offered by DAV, so the details of the available
datasets can be displayed in the Web Interface. Also, the training data is pre-
processed and delivered in parquet format by the DAV component. Once the
cognitive service is created with the training data, new predictions over new
real-time incoming data might be performed thanks to the injection of such
data by the Semantic Interoperability component.

Process-Based Analytics. As part of the Port of Valencia use case scenario,
the PBAC combines data from the port's AIS system, which tracks the movement
of vessels within the port area, and data about the arrival and departure forecasts
of vessels. From this data the PBAC constructs a business process trace for each

ship scheduled to arrive at the port, where each trace is completed when the respective vessel leaves the port. PBAC leverages the prediction models trained by the AMTE component to predict the outcome of business processes, such as the time of departure of vessel after it has entered the port. A positive outcome is achieved when the vessel leaves the port ahead or in its planned time of departure. Conversely, a vessel being delayed constitutes a negative outcome, also called a violation. The end users of the PBAC may thus use the PBAC outcomes to proactively schedule port services. The PBAC allows end users to interact via its user interface and API. End users can 1) request and receive business process metadata, 2) request/receive predictions and explanations for historical business process instances, and – when interacting via the API – 3) subscribe to a specific business process to receive real-time outcomes.

The PBAC receives historical data from the DAV component, which is already pre-processed (structured, cleaned, formatted). Using the historical data and the predictive model of the platform, the PBAC trains its ML models. After training, the PBAC receives real-time data from the Semantic Interoperability component, which is similarly pre-processed and provided in the same format as specified for the historical data. Using the real-time data instances, the PBAC creates its results, immediately making them available through its user interface and API, both for querying as well as for notifying subscribers.

5   Future Work and Conclusions

This paper highlights how maritime ports can leverage the huge amount of data generated by many heterogeneous sources using a set of technical components and, as a result, boost their evolution to smart and cognitive ports. This includes a Semantic Approach for Data Acquisition, Sharing and Pre-processing to pave the way for creating Novel Cognitive and AI-Based Services aimed at solving specific problems of the port.

Future versions of the platform will integrate components devoted to the creation of a secure data platform that allows sharing the information not only between port agents but also with other ports. As a result, port companies will be able to collaborate with each other to optimise port operations. The final version of the platform, which will integrate the prototype presented in this paper and the components that guarantee security and data governance, will be delivered during 2022. This follows the overall timeline of the EC global objective of creating a Common European Data Space for all maritime ports of Europe.

Acknowledgements.. Research leading to these results received funding from the European Union's Horizon 2020 research and innovation programme under grant agreement no. 871493 (DataPorts).

References

1. Inkinen, T., et al.: Technological trajectories and scenarios in seaport digitalization. Res. Transp. Bus. Manag. **41**, 100633 (2021)

2. Giménez, P., Llop, M., Meseguer, J., Martin, F., Broseta, A.: INTER-LogP: INTER-IoT for smart port transportation. In: Palau, C.E., et al. (eds.) Interoperability of Heterogeneous IoT Platforms. IT, pp. 257–277. Springer, Cham (2021). https://doi.org/10.1007/978-3-030-82446-4_9
3. Nagel, L., Lycklama, D.: Design Principles for Data Spaces. Position Paper. Version 1.0. Berlin (2021). https://doi.org/10.5281/zenodo.5105744
4. Data sharing in the EU - common European data spaces (new rules). https://ec.europa.eu/info/law/better-regulation/have-your-say/initiatives/12491-Data-sharing-in-the-EU-common-European-data-spaces-new-rules-_en. Accessed 27 May 2022
5. Transforming Transport. https://transformingtransport.eu/sites/default/files/2017-07/TT_BROCHURE_WEB.pdf. Accessed 21 April 2022
6. pyngsi. https://pypi.org/project/pyngsi/. Accessed 21 April 2022
7. PIXEL Project. https://pixel-ports.eu/. Accessed 21 April 2022
8. Element. https://element.eleme.io/#/en-US. Accessed 21 April 2022
9. vue-element-admin. https://panjiachen.github.io/vue-element-admin-site/. Accessed 21 April 2022
10. MVC. https://towardsdatascience.com/everything-you-need-to-know-about-mvc-architecture-3c827930b4c1. Accessed 21 April 2022
11. FIWARE Orion Context Broker. https://fiware-orion.readthedocs.io/en/master/. Accessed 21 April 2022
12. FIWARE Smart Data Models. https://www.fiware.org/smart-data-models/. Accessed 21 April 2022
13. The UN/CEFACT Smart Container Business Specifications. https://www.unece.org/fileadmin/DAM/cefact/brs/BRS-SmartContainer_v1.0.pdf Accessed 26 April 2022
14. SAREF ontology. https://saref.etsi.org/. Accessed 21 April 2022
15. International Data Spaces Information Model. https://github.com/International-Data-Spaces-Association/InformationModel. Accessed 21 April 2022
16. Huang, T., et al.: Counterfactual explanations for predictive business process monitoring. In: Information Systems - 18th European. Mediterranean, and Middle Eastern Conference, EMCIS 2021, Virtual Event, December 8–9, 2021, Proceedings, pp. 399–413. Springer, Cham, Switzerland (2021). https://doi.org/10.1007/978-3-030-95947-0_28
17. Metzger, A., Kley, T., Palm, A.: Triggering proactive business process adaptations via online reinforcement learning. In: Fahland, D., Ghidini, C., Becker, J., Dumas, M. (eds.) BPM 2020. LNCS, vol. 12168, pp. 273–290. Springer, Cham (2020). https://doi.org/10.1007/978-3-030-58666-9_16
18. Metzger, A., Franke, J., Jansen, T.: Ensemble deep learning for proactive terminal process management at the port of duisburg duisport. In: vom Brocke, J., Mendling, J., Rosemann, M. (eds.) Business Process Management Cases vol. 2, pp. 153–164. Springer, Heidelberg (2021). https://doi.org/10.1007/978-3-662-63047-1_12
19. Moulos, V. et al.: A robust information life cycle management framework for securing and governing critical infrastructure systems. Inventions 3(4), 71 (2018). https://doi.org/10.3390/inventions3040071
20. Psomakelis, E. et al.: A scalable and semantic data as a service marketplace for enhancing cloud-based applications. Future Internet 12(5), 77 (2020). https://doi.org/10.3390/fi12050077

Conceptual Framework of Contact-Less Consumer Products Industry During and Post-pandemic Era

Radhya Sahal[1]([⊠]) , Saeed. H. Alsamhi[2], and Kenneth N. Brown[1]

[1] School of Computer Science and IT, University College Cork, Cork, Ireland
rsahal@ucc.ie, k.brown@cs.ucc.ie
[2] Technological University of the Shannon: Midlands Midwest, Athlone, Ireland
salsamhi@ait.ie

Abstract. The COVID-19 era has reshaped the world regarding the contact-less economy, healthcare systems, remote work environment, people's lifestyle and their daily routines, etc. The consumer products (CP) industry is being impacted due to the behaviours of consumers during self-quarantine. This accelerates adopting digital transformation and upgrading the business models for the contact-less CP industry. Accordingly, this study provides a step toward the contact-less CP industry during and post-pandemic. First, we have proposed a conceptual framework for the contact-less CP industry that aims to bring together the key advanced technologies (e.g., Digital Twin (DT), blockchain, AI, cloud computing, 5G, and robots). The combination of the advanced technologies provides data monitoring, transparency, traceability, automation, and data sharing among consumers and CP partners. The proposed framework will enable a more contact-less personalized interaction that will work towards higher levels of consumer satisfaction while maintaining contact-less economy growth. Then, we have described how the proposed framework can be applied for contact-less delivery services for the CP industry during and post-pandemic.

Keywords: Contact-less · Blockchain · Digital twin · Consumer products industry · COVID-19 · Post pandemic

1 Introduction

For more than two years, the COVID-19 worldwide pandemic has persistently continued to affect the lives of millions in several countries. Therefore, to combat the COVID-19 pandemic, the governments announced some restrictions such as self-quarantine, lockdown, and practising social distance. However, these restrictions have changed the way people live; people work, study from home and shop from home. Therefore, the COVID-19 restrictions cause a big challenge for marketing industries and force them to rapidly adapt to contact-less marketing to meet consumer needs while maintaining their expectations to achieve desired growth. Consequently, digital transformation for companies has been accelerated by the COVID-19 pandemic [1,2]. Furthermore, during and post-pandemic era likely also come with some significant challenges, which leads the companies to rethink their business models [3,4].

The consumer products (CP) industry provides consumers with everything from food, beverages, toiletries, personal care, and small appliances. It is considered one of the industries which adopt digital transformation technologies. According to the Deloitte CP industry outlook survey at 2022 [5], the CP industry is one of strong financial performance, which has derived a more significant revenue in the last year. Most consumers are shifting from a go-to-market manner to a contact-less marketing manner during pandemic time according to the change circumstances [6]. Regarding consumer behaviour during the COVID-19 pandemic, the authors in [3] have addressed the impact of COVID-19 on consumer behaviour, strategic decision-making, and marketing policies for short-term and long-term actions. Also, the authors in [7] have proposed a methodological toolkit to assess the purchasing behaviour of online consumers during the COVID-19 pandemic. They have concluded that consumers have become more aware of shopping and more experts for making meaningful purchases. Crosta et al. [8] have focused their studies on psychological factors and consumer behaviour during the COVID-19 pandemic. They administered an online survey during the first peak period of the contagion in Italy. The authors have concluded that the consumer's behaviour is changed due to the pandemic, which raises marketing opportunities that contribute to economic growth. Also, there is more extensive study has been done on 55 countries in the first peak of the pandemic by Ulpiano et al. [9]. The study's empirical results have proved that exigency motivation is positively linked to purchasing essential goods.

Consequently, this shifting to the contact-less shopping paradigm raises challenges for the CP companies at the post-pandemic time to satisfy their consumers' needs and keep their business growth rate. Some CP industry challenges include supply chain (e.g., labour shortage, delayed delivery due to difficulties with international transportation, out of stock products), consumer preferences (e.g., personalized needs and privacy), transparency, offering online platforms for CP companies and so on. Furthermore, trust is critical since consumers won't engage and share data with companies they don't trust. Consequently, the changes during and post-pandemic contact-less society significantly need transforming strategies to combat the COVID-19 outbreak and deal with the new circumstances. In addition, these changes have required adopting new technologies that open the door for researchers to investigate different contact-less solutions during and post-pandemic.

Regarding adopting digital transformation technologies for online marketing during the COVID-19 pandemic, the authors in [10] have introduced a design of a resilient, transparent, and sustainable supply chain. The proposed design aims to develop localization, agility, and digitization characteristics using blockchain technology and circular economy principle capabilities during the COVID-19 pandemic. Also, Pratiksha et al. [11] have proposed a blockchain-based framework to enable the traceability of products in the supply chain to help prevent the spread of the coronavirus. The blockchain is used to track delivery personnel's medical test status and trace the travel history of delivery personnel to different locations. Alsamhi *et al.* [12] have proposed a framework based on blockchain and multi-robot collaboration to provide a tactical solution for combating the COVID-19 pandemic. The blockchain network enables multi-robot to fight COVID-19 collaboratively and efficiently by sharing information autonomously and accessing each other's data. Furthermore, the authors of [1] introduced blockchain-empowered DTs to combat COVID-19 by supporting DTs collaboration for decentralized alerts during COVID-19.

The authors in [13] have addressed the management of delivery for the food supply chain in COVID-19. They have used blockchain technology to maintain data sharing and improve decentralized distribution among competing supply chain partners. Burgos *et al.* [14] have addressed the COVID-19 pandemic's impact on the food retail supply chain with the help of a discrete-event simulation methodology using the DT of the anyLogistix supply chain. The authors confirmed the importance of DT in the supply chain to provide end-to-end visibility for the food retail supply chain. Sahal *et al.* [15] have proposed a framework to fulfill the DTs collaboration requirements for smart transportation. They have discussed how the framework is applied for logistics services during the COVID-19 pandemic for the consumers who prefer a safer and faster delivery method.

On the other hand, some research related to social manufacturing (SM) is related to the contact-less CP industry. The SM is a new business model to connect nearly everyone, and everything [16]. Also, the SM concept has been raised recently to support the sharing participation among individuals in the production of physical goods. Substantially, the SM concept comes to support the product personalized customization based on the customer's requirements [17,18]. In comparison, the contact-less CP industry concept empowers contact-less services to provide autonomous, secure contact-less solutions for the CP industry during and post-pandemic.

Because only a few publications exist in the CP industry regarding shifting to online marketing during the COVID-19 pandemic, the end-to-end contact-less concept has not yet been a focus in the literature to date. This motivates us to consider different emerging technologies to deliver an end-to-end contact-less framework for the CP industry during and post-pandemic. Consequently, combining the emerged technologies (e.g., DTs, blockchain, AI, cloud computing, 5G, and robots) empowers contact-less services for the CP industry. The data derived across the stages of the contact-less CP industry can be accessed and shared by stakeholders, retailers, organizations, or countries. The products could be tracked at every stage of the supply chain, meeting consumer demands with minimal wastage and contact-less. Figure 1 depict the high-level of contact-less remote applications for CP industry to combat COVID-19 and empower contact-less economy. To the best of our knowledge, there is no framework based on the contact-less CP industry proposed to deliver contact-less services to mitigate the unnecessary risk of people contacting during and post-pandemic. Therefore, this research work introduces a conceptual framework for the contact-less CP industry. Our main contributions to this paper can be summarized as follows:

– We propose a conceptual framework for the contact-less CP industry that aims to bring the combination of advanced technologies (e.g., DT, blockchain, AI, cloud computing, 5G, and robots). Furthermore, the proposed framework aims to support the contact-less CP industry by providing data monitoring, transparency, traceability, automation and data sharing among consumers and CP partners.
– We describe how the proposed framework can be applied for contact-less delivery service for the CP industry during and post-pandemic.

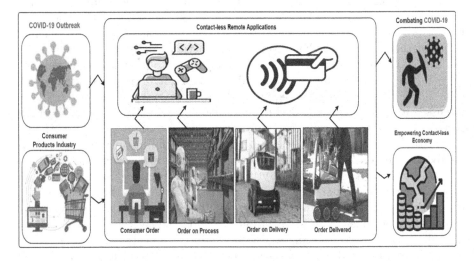

Fig. 1. The high-level of contact-less remote applications for the CP industry to combat COVID-19 and empower contact-less economy.

The remainder of this paper is organized as follows: The proposed conceptual framework of the contact-less CP industry is introduced in Sect. 2. Next, the description of the contact-less delivery service for the CP industry is provided Sect. 3. Finally, the open challenges, discussion and conclusion are presented in Sect. 4 and 5 respectively.

2   Conceptual Framework of Contact-Less Consumer Products Industry

A combination of the emerged technologies (e.g., DT, blockchain, AI, cloud computing, 5G, and robots) has the benefits of empowering a contact-less economy by supporting contact-less industries during the COVID-19 post-pandemic era.

In Fig. 2, we have described the proposed conceptual framework of the contact-less CP industry. The proposed framework's merit is exploiting the emerged industrial technologies' capabilities to provide autonomous, secure contact-less solutions for the CP industry during and post-pandemic. Four layers are used to equip the conceptual framework for the contact-less CP industry with the intelligence of marketing data. As seen in Fig. 2, the four layers are the physical layer which contains the CP industry participants, the DTs layer, the driver industrial technologies layer and the applications layer. These layers will be elaborated flowingly. Further details of how these layers can work together to provide end-to-end contact-less delivery service for the CP industry are demonstrated in Sect. 3.

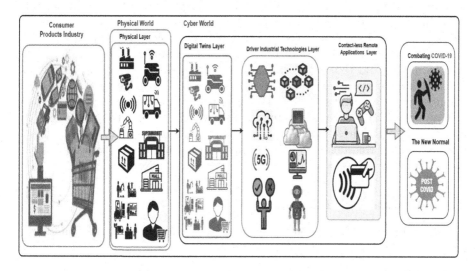

Fig. 2. The proposed conceptual framework for the contact-less CP industry during and post-pandemic.

2.1 Physical Layer

The physical layer contains all nodes involved in the CP industry, ranging from the factory to the consumer. These nodes could be grouped into different categories, including supply chain, in-store and human participants. The supply chain participants can be factories, assets, warehouses, suppliers, products, monitoring devices (e.g., CCTV and sensor devices), robotic devices and auto-cars. The nodes for the in-store category are products on shelves, malls, supermarkets, and delivery robots. Finally, the human participants can be the people who can contribute by using their operational data (e.g., consumers, decision-makers, workers, employees, HR, security staff and so on).

2.2   Digital Twins Layer

The digital twins, digital models, and digital shadows are making the manufacturing revolution which makes our lives easier. These three concepts are used interchangeably in the digitization world. Regarding our work, we are using the DT concept to provide a virtual representation of products, processes, consumers, and other participants within the CP supply chain. Then, these DTs collaborate to automate the contact-less CP industry. The collaborative DTs of products, processes, consumers and other participants within the CP supply chain increase the speed of the contact-less CP industry. Furthermore, the DTs provide real-time data for the tracking stage of the products applicable to logistic companies, supply-chain managers, in-store processes, equipment sensors, purchasing, delivering, etc. Therefore, this layer is responsible for defining DTs within the CP industry at different stages (e.g., the products from being manufactured to being consumed) by providing multiple collaborative DTs with up-to-date operational and marketing data. The data-driven DTs collaborations help to understand the DT status, interact with other DTs at the edge level, learn from other DTs, and share common semantic knowledge within industrial manufacturing systems [19]. The DT-driven data are used as inputs for predictive models to predict the potential risks within the product lifecycle. The intelligence of DT-driven data help makes a timely decision to avoid product wastage and delayed delivery, reduce shipping cost and maximize profits of the contact-less CP industry.

2.3   Industrial Technologies Layer

This layer briefly highlights emerging industrial technologies' role in building a concert contact-less solution for the CP industry.

- **AI technology:** Pairing AI with DTs technologies creates new efficiencies for the contact-less CP industry. The AI technologies (e.g., machine learning (ML) and deep learning (DL)) could be applied using data-driven DTs. The ML/DL techniques provide predicted potential risks to the CP industry, such as product wastage, corrupted products, and estimated delivery [20,21]. Furthermore, AI technologies can build an intelligent experience engine based on the consumer experience to provide more insights and personalised recommendations for consumer satisfaction. For example, the author in [22] has proposed a prediction model for anticipating the consumers' behaviour using ML methods during the COVID-19 pandemic. Also, the authors in [23] have conducted a comprehensive analysis based on evolutionary computing. Then, they have proposed a dynamic algorithm for gaining valuable insights into semiconductor manufacturing processes.
- **Blockchain:** The blockchain network connects multiple DTs of the participants within the contact-less CP industry using distributed ledger technology (DLT). The DT-based blockchain network increases traceability capability to monitor products by affording end-to-end flow of information about

the products. Also, the DT-based blockchain network offers distributed operational data management and secure data sharing across contact-less CP industry participants [15, 24]. Blockchain technology has been used to combat COVID-19 by supporting decentralization for multi-robot collaboration [12]. Also, blockchain technology is used to enable the traceability of products in the supply chain and help prevent the spread of the coronavirus [11].

- **Cloud/edge computing:** Due to large volumes of CP industry data generation, the operational data analysis is performed on computing paradigms such as cloud and edge computing. Furthermore, both remote cloud resources and local edge resources leverage extra computing capabilities for real-time analysis within the contact-less CP industry [25].

- **5G technology:** The 5G technology offers many benefits for the contact-less CP industry by providing reliable, high connectivity private networks and real-time interaction with consumers that open the doors to online business models within the contact-less CP industry [26]. Moreover, online shopping based on powerfully connectivity empowers personalized interactions that make consumers' lives easier and more convenient. It also helps combat pandemics by limiting people's contact and virus spread. The 5G and B5G technology capabilities may be successfully used to address COVID-19 difficulties both now and in the post-COVID-19 period. The authors of [27] highlighted the utilization of 5G e-health and digital services during and post pandemics.

On the other hand, the authors of [28] highlighted the role of 5G networks in empowering AI in the prediction of future pandemic outbreaks and enhancing the digitization to develop a pandemic resilient society. Substantially, because AI approaches are often data-driven, providing support for significant device connections and IoT networks via (Massive Machine-Type Communications) mMTC services in 5G networks would give enough data for AI model training and deployment. Furthermore, AI technologies are often computationally heavy. Therefore, advancements in memory and processor technology and the inclusion of caching and edge computing in 5G would aid in adopting and using AI technologies. Moreover, the software-defined nature of 5G networks and associated architectures like network slicing, network function virtualization, data-control plane separation, and so on would make AI approaches for intelligent and dynamic network management and orchestration easier to implement.

- **Data visualization:** The industrial data visualization tools provide useful dashboards to visualize and track the products based on the DTs operational data in real-time. Also, the visualization tools allow the decision-makers within the contact-less CP industry to conclude insights more quickly for reducing costs and achieving maximum cash flow.

- **Robot technology:** Robot technology plays a vital role in combating COVID-19 by reducing human interaction, monitoring, and delivering goods within in contact-less CP supply chain [12]. Furthermore, the multi-robots collaborate to achieve a contact-less CP industry by integrating with other technologies within the proposed framework, such as DTs, decentralized blockchain networks, efficient 5G connections and powerful AI engines. The authors of [29] introduced the role of robotics in healthcare domains for combating COVID-19. Moreover, the space robots and ground robots collaborations play a vital role in combating COVID-19 and reducing the outbreak with the help of blockchain technology [30]. Furthermore, the authors of [31] proposed the hospitality industries treat the uncertainties by using service robots. Therefore, the service-based robots will support the contact-less CP industry by providing better and more efficient service than humans.

– **Decision making:** Good decisions make great products and competitive services, save time and maximise profit which delivers value for consumers and the business within the CP industry. In the case of the contact-less CP industry, distributed decision-making algorithms are needed to empower contact-less services and prepare for the new changes of the post-pandemic world. In particular, the consensus algorithms are used to improve the contact-less CP industry by utilising the agreement of most nodes regarding the potential risk to notify the decision-makers within the CP supply chain. Some examples of the use of the consensus algorithms include Proof of Work (PoW), Practical Byzantine Fault Tolerance (PBFT), Proof of Stake (PoS), Proof of Burn (PoB), Proof of Capacity, and Proof of Elapsed Time.

2.4 Contact-Less Remote Applications Layer

The contact-less remote applications can be used in all CP industry solutions at different levels, from the product being manufactured to being delivered and consumed (e.g., online shopping, contact-less payment, zero-touch delivery, remote tracking and so on). Furthermore, the contact-less remote applications pave the way for the post-pandemic future and contribute to contact-less economy growth.

3   Contact-Less Delivery Service for Consumer Products Industry During and Post-pandemic Era

The contact-less delivery service describes how the proposed conceptual framework could be applied to provide a complete delivering service to the consumer from the beginning to the end. In particular, the goal of the contact-less delivery service is to deliver the contact-less CP industry's services efficiently with high quality and security to satisfy the consumers. The contact-less delivery service can also serve people in the quarantine areas and residential areas by utilizing the intelligence of data generated by the participants (e.g., malls, medical suppliers, people, robots, drones, etc.) [12,15]. In the contact-less delivery service, a consumer (e.g., quarantined person) makes an online order for delivery, e.g., food, beverages, medicine, toiletries, personal care, .etc. Figure 3 depicts the high-level of mapping our the proposed framework to the contact-less delivery service. Further details are elaborated following. Then, a detailed mapping of our proposed framework to provide end-to-end contact-less delivery service for the CP industry is discussed.

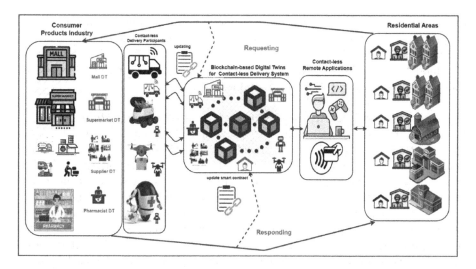

Fig. 3. The contact-less delivery service for CP industry during COVID-19 and post-pandemic era.

Digital Twins Collaboration in Contact-Less Delivery Service. DTs represent the participants collaborating to provide a complete, efficient, high quality and secure delivery service in the contact-less delivery service. The core participants of the contact-less delivery services include malls, suppliers, supermarkets, people, robots, auto-driver cars, drones,.etc. These participants could be represented in interoperable and collaborative DTs to show high visibility of the contact-less delivery service without physical interactions to limit contacting and coronavirus outbreaks. In addition, the DTs are collaborating to track the contact-less delivery service among the participants. The DTs' collaboration can understand each DT's status, interact with other DTs, learn from other DTs, and share common semantic knowledge across geographically delivery services. Furthermore, the DT-based data is used to allow data visualization. For example, the visualized contact-less delivery products enable consumers to track their orders. Also, it will enable the managers and decision-makers to conclude insights for actionable decisions.

On the other hand, there are different data models for the DTs in contact-less delivery services based on the requirements of each participant. In particular, the DTs for the contact-less delivery service are represented the data generated from sensors attached to products containers, robots, and drones to capture real-time data about delivered products and report on-time data about environmental changes. For example, the DTs of the warehouse are used to monitor the weather, e.g., temperature and humidity in the warehouse for storing safety products. For physical assets such as malls, suppliers, and supermarkets, DT models represent information about them, such as their locations and product storage. For example, the product's availability is updated in real-time to help the management department in-store to request the products from the nearest supplier in case of the product is out of stock. Also, the DT model represents the delivery robots used to serve the consumer by transporting ordered products. The models of the delivery robot DT have information about the robot status, the product condition, the location, and so on [12].

Blockchain and Operational Contact-Less Delivery Data Sharing.
Blockchain technology is required to provide high quality, secure connectivity, decentralized, traceability, and tracking transactions for safe communication between delivery robots, food suppliers, and in-stores [12]. In particular, DLT is needed to provide high-quality, secure connectivity to improve the security and safety of the communications between the participants of the contact-less delivery service. For example, DLT is used to acquire secure real-time data exchange and analysis across multiple participants, such as detecting attack vectors for stealing robots. In addition, DLT can implement collaborative DTs that allows data of delivery service sharing among multiple DTs in a decentralized contact-less delivery system. Therefore, sharing DTs-based data among DLTs can offer high data reliability in product delivery, faster access, high availability, and collaboration among contact-less delivery participants.

Data-Driven Digital Twins Based Predictive Analytics. In such a contact-less delivery service, the examples of the potential risks within the decentralized delivery service include faults with robots and drones, lack of products, etc. To avoid the potential fault risk of the movable assets, including auto-cars, robots and drones, monitoring DT-based data is required from these assets, including location, speed, and sensing environment. The real-time collected data from DTs of the auto-cars, robots and drones could be fitted into the data-driven DTs-based predictive analytics to predict the potential fault to perform early maintenance for these movable assets and avoid any delay in the delivery service. DT-based data acquisition can also identify any spoof attack vectors during the robots travelling to deliver products to the quarantine/residential areas. On the other hand, to assess the potential risk of lacking products, products available within the retails are evaluated based on the locations and the real-time demand. The decision-makers can direct the request to the closest in-stores to avoid delayed delivery services. Furthermore, these potential risks of lacking products can help decision-makers better supply plans and increase money flow within the contact-less CP industry.

Decision Making in Contact-Less Delivery Service. A consensus is a decision-making process in the contact-less delivery service to avoid the potential risks, including fault diagnosis and lack of products. Using collaborative DTs provides a better understanding of potential risks for the delivery system and facilitates consensus-building among participants involving the decision-makers. Multiple participants represented in DTs are divided into various consensus sets. The consensus mechanism is chosen based on the potential risk scenario (e.g., hijacking and theft of robots, faulty auto-cares, robots, drones, harmful products, expired food, and so on). The consensus algorithms will then be used to agree on the potential risk provided by collaborative DTs to notify the decision-makers about the potential risk that could delay the contact-less delivery service.

4   Open Challenges and Discussion

Right now, the contact-less CP industry is still a vision for the future of the contact-less economy. However, many challenges stand in developing a concrete contact-less CP industry. Therefore, we will explore some of those challenges and ways of addressing them.

Privacy and Regulation. The security and privacy associated with consumers are challenging within the contact-less CP industry because of the risk of sensitive marketing data created from consumers' preferences. Therefore, the contact-less CP industry should analyze consumers' data locally using federated learning and then share only the model to the blockchain instead of sending the raw data. Thus, the issue of security can be solved by using blockchain technology, while privacy can be solved by using federated learning. Combining both techniques can significantly enhance the security and privacy of the contact-less CP industry.

Security. Data security is crucial for the contact-less CP industry due to hacker attacks. Consumers must be confident that their data is secure, transparent, and accessible. Blockchain technology can be applied to the contact-less CP industry to protect consumers' accounts access. However, blockchain technology faces various security and trust issues, such as attacks against consensus mechanisms and propagation processes [32].

Timing, Speed, and Response. Timing and speed are tricky for delivering products. Also, time enhances decision-making and reaction times for consumer demands requiring high accuracy to avoid long delivery delays.

Data Modeling. Standardization is essential for designing a contact-less CP industry system. The fully connected contact-less CP industry participants need to use standard models to define each participant based on the relevant schema. The schema is determined based on the corresponding physical assets and the communication behaviour within the CP supply chain. These standards are complex to facilitate DTs of CP participants for interactions and collaboration. Furthermore, these standards can range from the file format of the data storage to the details of how the DTs are communicating within the CP industry at different stages (e.g., the products from being manufactured to being consumed) [33].

5   Conclusion

This paper introduces a conceptual framework for the contact-less CP industry due to COVID-19 and post-pandemic. The proposed framework's merit is exploiting the emerged industrial technologies' capabilities to provide autonomous, secure contact-less solutions for the CP industry during and post-pandemic. Four layers are used to equip the conceptual framework for the contact-less CP industry, including the physical layer, which contains the CP industry participants, the DTs layer, the driver industrial technologies layer and the applications layer. Consequently, the CP companies can effectively execute their business functions for the post-pandemic through an efficient combination of technologies within the proposed framework. Furthermore, we have described a contact-less delivery service during COVID-19 and post-pandemic, together with a detailed mapping of our proposed framework. In future, more work is required to be done to improve contact-less services in different sectors (e.g., hospitality industry) by utilizing the improvement in the robot, 5G, blockchain and so on.

Acknowledgement. This research has emanated from research supported by a research grant from Science Foundation Ireland (SFI) under Grant Number SFI/16/RC/3918 (CONFIRM), and Marie Skłodowska-Curie grant agreement No. 847577 co-funded by the European Regional Development Fund.

References

1. Sahal, R., Alsamhi, S.H., Brown, K.N., O'Shea, D., Alouffi, B.: Blockchain-based digital twins collaboration for smart pandemic alerting: decentralized covid-19 pandemic alerting use case. Comput. Intell. Neurosci. **2022** (2022)
2. Li, S.: How does covid-19 speed the digital transformation of business processes and customer experiences? Rev. Bus. **41**(1), 1–14 (2021)
3. Hoekstra, J.C., Leeflang, P.S.: Marketing in the era of covid-19. Ital. J. Mark. **2020**(4), 249–260 (2020)
4. Bhatti, A., Akram, H., Basit, H.M., Khan, A.U., Raza, S.M., Naqvi, M.B.: E-commerce trends during covid-19 pandemic. Int. J. Future Gener. Commun. Networking **13**(2), 1449–1452 (2020)
5. Deloitte: 2022 consumer products industry outlook. https://www2.deloitte. com/content/dam/Deloitte/us/Documents/consumer-business/us-deloitte-2022-consumer-products-industry-outlook.pdf
6. Sheth, J.: Impact of covid-19 on consumer behavior: will the old habits return or die? J. Bus. Res. **117**, 280–283 (2020)
7. Gu, S., Ślusarczyk, B., Hajizada, S., Kovalyova, I., Sakhbieva, A.: Impact of the covid-19 pandemic on online consumer purchasing behavior. J. Theor. Appl. Electron. Commer. Res. **16**(6), 2263–2281 (2021)
8. Di Crosta, A., et al.: Psychological factors and consumer behavior during the COVID-19 pandemic. PLoS ONE **16**(8), e0256095 (2021)
9. Vázquez-Martínez, U.J., Morales-Mediano, J., Leal-Rodríguez, A.L.: The impact of the covid-19 crisis on consumer purchasing motivation and behavior. Eur. Res. Manage. Bus. Econ. **27**(3), 100166 (2021)

10. Nandi, S., Sarkis, J., Hervani, A.A., Helms, M.M.: Redesigning supply chains using blockchain-enabled circular economy and covid-19 experiences. Sustain. Prod. Consumption **27**, 10–22 (2021)

11. Mittal, P., Walthall, A., Cui, P., Skjellum, A., Guin, U.: A blockchain-based contactless delivery system for addressing covid-19 and other pandemics. In: 2021 IEEE International Conference on Blockchain (Blockchain), pp. 1–6. IEEE (2021)

12. Alsamhi, S.H., Lee, B.: Blockchain-empowered multi-robot collaboration to fight covid-19 and future pandemics. IEEE Access **9**, 44173–44197 (2021). https://doi.org/10.1109/ACCESS.2020.3032450

13. Abdullah, D., Rahardja, U., Oganda, F.P.: Covid-19: decentralized food supply chain management. Syst. Rev. Pharm **12**(3), 142–152 (2021)

14. Burgos, D., Ivanov, D.: Food retail supply chain resilience and the covid-19 pandemic: a digital twin-based impact analysis and improvement directions. Transp. Res. Part E: Logistics Transp. Rev. **152**, 102412 (2021)

15. Sahal, R., Alsamhi, S.H., Brown, K.N., O'Shea, D., McCarthy, C., Guizani, M.: Blockchain-empowered digital twins collaboration: smart transportation use case. Machines **9**(9) (2021). https://doi.org/10.3390/machines9090193,https://www.mdpi.com/2075-1702/9/9/193

16. Wang, F.Y., Shang, X., Qin, R., Xiong, G., Nyberg, T.R.: Social manufacturing: a paradigm shift for smart prosumers in the era of Societies 5.0. IEEE Trans. Comput. Soc. Syst. **6**(5), 822–829 (2019). https://doi.org/10.1109/TCSS.2019.2940155

17. Xiong, G., et al.: From mind to products: towards social manufacturing and service. IEEE/CAA J. Automatica Sin. **5**(1), 47–57 (2018). https://doi.org/10.1109/JAS.2017.7510742

18. Shang, X., et al.: Social manufacturing for high-end apparel customization. IEEE/CAA J. Automatica Sin. **5**(2), 489–500 (2018). https://doi.org/10.1109/JAS.2017.7510832

19. Sahal, R., Alsamhi, S.H., Breslin, J.G., Brown, K.N., Ali, M.I.: Digital twins collaboration for automatic erratic operational data detection in Industry 4.0. Appl. Sci. **11**(7) (2021). https://www.mdpi.com/2076-3417/11/7/3186

20. Kapteyn, M.G., Knezevic, D.J., Willcox, K.: Toward predictive digital twins via component-based reduced-order models and interpretable machine learning. In: AIAA Scitech 2020 Forum, p. 0418 (2020)

21. Sahal, R., Breslin, J.G., Ali, M.I.: Big data and stream processing platforms for Industry 4.0 requirements mapping for a predictive maintenance use case. J. Manufac. Syst. **54**, 138–151 (2020). https://doi.org/10.1016/j.jmsy.2019.11.004,

22. Safara, F.: A computational model to predict consumer behaviour during covid-19 pandemic. Comput. Econ. **59**, 1–14 (2020)

23. Ghahramani, M., Qiao, Y., Zhou, M.C., O'Hagan, A., Sweeney, J.: AI-based modeling and data-driven evaluation for smart manufacturing processes. IEEE/CAA J. Automatica Sin. **7**(4), 1026–1037 (2020). https://doi.org/10.1109/JAS.2020.1003114

24. Hasan, H.R., et al.: A blockchain-based approach for the creation of digital twins. IEEE Access **8**, 34113–34126 (2020)

25. Borodulin, K., Radchenko, G., Shestakov, A., Sokolinsky, L., Tchernykh, A., Prodan, R.: Towards digital twins cloud platform: microservices and computational workflows to rule a smart factory. In: Proceedings of the10th International Conference on Utility and Cloud Computing, pp. 209–210 (2017)

26. Almalki, F., et al.: Green IoT for eco-friendly and sustainable smart cities: future directions and opportunities. Mob. Networks Appl. 1–25 (2021)

27. Siriwardhana, Y., Gür, G., Ylianttila, M., Liyanage, M.: The role of 5G for digital healthcare against covid-19 pandemic: opportunities and challenges. ICT Express **7**(2), 244–252 (2021)
28. Abubakar, A.I., Omeke, K.G., Ozturk, M., Hussain, S., Imran, M.A.: The role of artificial intelligence driven 5G networks in covid-19 outbreak: opportunities, challenges, and future outlook. Front. Commun. Networks **1**, 575065 (2020)
29. Raje, S., et al.: Applications of healthcare robots in combating the covid-19 pandemic. Appl. Bionics Biomech. **2021** (2021)
30. Alsamhi, S.H., Lee, B., Guizani, M., Kumar, N., Qiao, Y., Liu, X.: Blockchain for decentralized multi-drone to combat covid-19 and future pandemics: framework and proposed solutions. Trans. Emerg. Telecommun. Technol. **32**, e4255 (2021)
31. Mukherjee, S., Baral, M.M., Venkataiah, C., Pal, S.K., Nagariya, R.: Service robots are an option for contactless services due to the covid-19 pandemic in the hotels. Decision **48**(4), 445–460 (2021)
32. Zhang, P., Zhou, M.: Security and trust in blockchains: architecture, key technologies, and open issues. IEEE Trans. Comput. Soc. Syst. **7**(3), 790–801 (2020). https://doi.org/10.1109/TCSS.2020.2990103
33. Rasheed, A., San, O., Kvamsdal, T.: Digital twin: values, challenges and enablers from a modeling perspective. IEEE Access **8**, 21980–22012 (2020)

Blockchain for Economy of Scale in Wind Industry: A Demo Case

Parwinder Singh[1], Kristoffer Holm[1], Michail J. Beliatis[1(✉)] (ID), Andrei Ionita[2],
Mirko Presser[1], Prinz Wolfgang[2], and René C. Goduscheit[1]

[1] Aarhus University, 7400 Herning, Denmark
{mibel,goduscheit}@btech.au.dk
[2] Fraunhofer FIT, Schloss Birlinghoven 1, 53757 St. Augustin, Germany

Abstract. This paper summarizes the key findings of a qualitative study based on feedbacks of experts from the wind industry followed by a demo case of blockchain technology. This study includes investigation on mapping of supply chain and commodity products related end-to-end life cycle associated data and operational events. Furthermore, identification and blueprinting of the requirements have been pursued for enabling traceability at various stages of their life cycle utilizing blockchain. In this study context, blockchain offers digital traceability of operational events and associated data sharing with complete immutability, ownership, confidentiality, trust, and transparency across distributed supply chain which comprises of multiple stakeholders. In addition, digital technology intervention like IoT has been leveraged to support quality of operations in quantitative manner through real time data driven digitized operations. Thereby, providing economy of scale over operations execution on commodity products in wind industry. This study has focused only on bolts and fasteners associated commodity products and related supply chain. However, this provides a steppingstone foundation for future which can be scaled and mapped to any other commodity product and related supply chain in wind industry. Finally, this study also presents a demonstrator developed in a controlled lab environment to demystify the use of blockchain technology in related manufacturing and supply chain setups of the wind industry.

Keywords: Blockchain · IIoT · Bar code · QR code · Digitalization · lifecycle · Digital traceability · Sustainability · Supply chain · Business

1 Introduction

The hype around blockchain technology in industry4.0 [1] is well established [2, 3], but its utility in a practical and operational settings is limited [4]. To better understand how the technology may be useful for specific industry sectors, projects which involve qualitative analysis of stakeholders for problems identification and realization of demo cases are typically running at national/European level in controlled environments. This paper presents the finding of such project, named as *"UnWind"*, focusing on wind industry in Denmark. As goals of this case study project, first an investigation of the wind turbine industry's value supply chain is conducted to identify and map processes with

© The Author(s), under exclusive license to Springer Nature Switzerland AG 2022
A. González-Vidal et al. (Eds.): GIoTS 2022, LNCS 13533, pp. 175–186, 2022.
https://doi.org/10.1007/978-3-031-20936-9_14

their potential benefits from blockchain technology. Second, an active collaboration has been done with companies/stakeholders of value chain who will get potential benefits from the findings of the first activity. This was done to consider their perspective and associated real world challenges to build a business use case and prototype demonstrator. Finally, the actual realization of a demonstrator with blockchain technology as a solution has been developed for the challenges identified during a series of workshops with the collaborated stakeholders/companies.

For this study, qualitative data was collected in the period January 2020 to March 2022 using an action research-inspired approach [5] with dual-focus on academia and practice. The qualitative data was collected through 10 unstructured interviews, 15 semi-structured interviews and 17 development workshops in which the industrial partners from the wind turbine industry have been interviewed/observed.

The Fastener project, which is an industry born initiative and closely connected to goals of UnWind project, seeks to standardize the procurement procedure for bolts and fasteners to simplify the buyer-supplier relationship between fastener/bolt supplier and wind turbine manufacturers (the buyer). From the bolt/fastener supplier's perspective this is intended to make the production setup simpler as they will no longer have to live up to individual demands from each of the turbine manufacturers. From the turbine manufacturer's perspective, the situation is improved due to reduction of the bull-whip effect as production errors at the supplier end are reduced and by extension the chance of delays in delivery is lessened as well. From both the buyer and supplier's perspective, there is also an added advantage of increasing batch sizes of fasteners, meaning economy of scale will be beneficial. In addition, there is less risk in storing backup components in warehouses, as there are more potential users of the safety stock if all bolts and fasteners are made to fit in with the standard schematics of all the wind turbine manufacturers production schemes. An important question arises here is that how these bolts and fasteners components are tied to blockchain context. The answer to that lies in the part of their procurement standardization process which also guides on how components in wind industry operations are traced across the value chain throughout the years. Practically, there is no need for high level traceability on all fasteners/bolts, as only larger fasteners are of critical importance for the wind turbine's operational performance. For this reason, the traceability standardization only applies to larger fasteners (8 + mm in thickness). To map the fasteners from the physical world to the blockchain in the digital world, a gateway technology in the form of Quick Response (QR) codes is utilized. Practically, each batch of fasteners will have a unique QR-code and through QR-code the information on the given batch of bolts is then digitally tied and stored to the blockchain. The way that each individual fastener becomes identifiable comes in the next steps of its life cycle.

1.1   The Fastener Lifecycle: Events and Data-Points in the Blockchain

The Fig. 1 is illustrating the lifecycle of the fastener it goes through and the events that occur in its journey along with their data points that are logged and traced into the blockchain through the scanning of the QR-codes. The lifecycle consists of two major phases; 1) *Manufacturing and installation* of the fasteners (prior to the operational start of the turbine) and 2) *Service and decommissioning* of the fasteners (post operational start of the turbine).

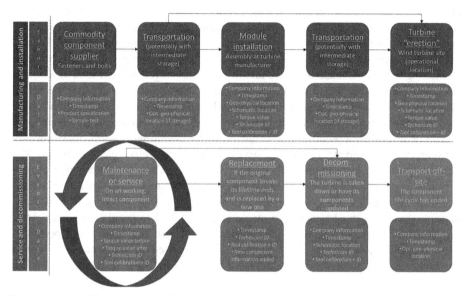

Fig. 1. An overview of events and data-points in the supply chain and life cycle of common products such as bolts used in wind industry

It should be noted that each event in the two phases can be considered a block of information (or transactions) in the chain of events making up the lifecycle of the fasteners thus forming the basis of representing these blocks in blockchain system. Two consistent data points that are recorded at every event, per transaction level, in the lifecycle, is a timestamp and a digital notation of the organization uploading the new event/operations. The first phase, where elements are marked blue (top row) on Fig. 1, starts with the supply chain associated events for each fastener and ends after the fastener is installed in the fully assembled turbine. As touched upon earlier, the first event ties to the manufacturing of the fasteners (also called *commodity component tier one supplier*) and includes data points containing information on product specifications and a sample (quality) test performed on each batch of bolts produced at the manufacturer end. Second comes the *transportation event* of the fasteners, which includes geo-physical data for the relocation sites. This relocation may either lead directly to a *turbine erection event* (i.e., where the turbine is put under operation) or the fasteners may be sent to the *module installation* which then subsequently be *transported* to the *turbine erection* site. Regardless of whether there is module installation event or not, new data is logged into the blockchain when the fastener is no longer an individual component, but a part of a larger schematic (as a module or in the fully assembled turbine). This new data consists of registering the schematic location of the fastener, the value of torque with which the fastener is tightened and potentially the identification (ID) of the service technician who performs the installation operation of the fastener into turbine.

The second phase consists of events in the fastener's lifecycle that occur during the turbine's operational period and is illustrated with green and orange (3rd row) boxes. As opposed to the events that occur in the first phase, this second phase includes repeated events of maintenance or service, in which similar information may be updated repeatedly over 20–30 years in which the turbine remains operational. When maintenance is performed on the fasteners, several data-points are logged and updated in the blockchain. The torque value during each service cycle is registered, the information of technician facilitating the maintenance is logged and in case, a smart tool is used such as a digital wrench, the ID and calibration value of the tool is also logged. If everything occurs as intended, this event will occur regularly until the end of the turbine's life after which the fastener will be decommissioned along with the turbine, resulting in the logging and update of several data points again. In the case of a *replacement event,* which occurs between the *maintenance* and *decommissioning phase, there is a need to replace the broken fastener with a new one in the physical world.* This results in addition of new lifecycle to the blockchain based on the new fastener's lifecycle events (all the information logged as per phase 1). In principle, the replacement protocol can also occur multiple times and this has not been included in the Fig. 1 to avoid complexity. After this, the final event, which is marked as orange color (last box in 3rd row), occurs in the fastener lifecycle wherein the component is transported away and (ideally) sent to recycling, at a location which is logged into the blockchain as the final entry.

2   Business and Sustainability Implications of Blockchain Technology in Large Scale Wind Turbine Setups

Economies of scale: One of the primary points of the associated business case of the UnWind blockchain solution is to create the ideal conditions for turbine manufacturers to take advantage of economies of scale, so that turbines are cheaper to build as such, making the renewable energy production cheaper and more desirable for investments. Bolt/fastener suppliers also take advantage in the economy of scale as developing larger batches are cheaper, less time consuming and with fewer production risks in comparison to produce smaller batches of varying bolts/fasteners. This initial use case of the wind industry leveraging blockchain exclusively focused on bolts and fasteners which are considered commodity (non-compete) items amongst the turbine manufacturers. However, the intention is to expand the principle for all other critically important components of the turbine involved in the supply chain to improve their operational functionality in terms of quality, ownership, transparency, and monitoring.

The key selling point of the blockchain is tied to how the technology enables traceability across organizational bounds in the value chain [3]. By registering each event in commodity components lifecycle, it becomes easier to pinpoint where malfunctions occur or errors are made on the turbine's components – and most importantly, it enables actions to be taken faster and more accurately. For example, if a technician while performing maintenance on a turbine finds a fastener is broken, while it is still valid for its lifetime span, the technician can report this to be a potential issue with a replacement event in the component lifecycle. Via the blockchain this latest event can then be identified, and the responsible company can be informed, and other tasks can also be double-checked at other locations where fasteners are being used thereby enabling a more proactive approach to perform maintenance and service. Similarly, it may be found that a component issue tracks all the way back to a batch at the supplier level in which case the blockchain data can be utilized to identify other locations of fasteners from that batch and test if they also need replacement or maintenance service.

In extension of the traceability argument, the recording of events and product details also enables transparency [2] in what is inside the turbines meaning it is easier for service organizations to bring the right tools and equipment, as well as the rightfully certified personnel to perform tasks. One key issue in the wind turbine industry today (that is particularly expensive and time-consuming for offshore turbines) is that technicians are sent to perform tasks to turbine sites, only to realize upon arrival that they are either not properly certified or equipped to be able to perform their job. Furthermore, service contracts are rarely withheld by one company over the turbine's lifetime, meaning it is critical to pass reliable, accurate information to the companies taking over. However, since the original service provider is done with their commitment, they currently have little incentive to pass on information properly to their replacement. Even more critical is the fact that service contracts will often be taken over by competitors of the original service providers, meaning there may be reluctance to provide the competitor with accurate information. The blockchain, however, enables transparency through its data point registration, removing (or at least minimizing) the risk of inaccurate or lackluster documentation for former events.

Sustainability: Overall, the characteristics of a blockchain can enable better maintenance and monitoring for wind turbines, reducing production downtime which in turn enables more energy production per turbine over its lifetime, meaning each turbine has a larger amount of value that can help pay back the initial investment of the turbine. This translates to a lower levelized cost of energy for wind-based power generation, thereby improving the conditions of the industry. In other words, blockchain is an opportunity for wind turbine manufacturers to collaborate with their immediate competitors (other wind turbine manufacturers) to better compete with other energy producing industries like solar [6], fossil or nuclear fuels. In other words, blockchain technology holds promise to improve sustainability aspects for the service part of the wind industry [7], in addition to other ways this technology is perceived to be an enabler for more sustainable practices [8].

3 Realization of Demonstrator in Controlled Environment

To realize the system context of blockchain contribution in wind turbine supply chain industry, a demo has been designed and developed in a controlled lab environment known as *DigiMicroFactory* Lab at department of Business Development and Technology, Aarhus University in Herning, Denmark. Typically, as discussed earlier, wind turbine industry is based on supply chain consisting of multiple stakeholders, workflows, events, data points, and their supplied services or commodities. The different stakeholders that are involved, but are not limited to - wind manufacturers, first tier vendors, services operations staff. There are different system operations associated to the supply chain workflow, such as transportation, assembly, installation, service (replacement/modifications) maintenance and de-commissioning of wind turbine components [9]. This needs to be performed by the relevant service personnel or engineer at specific value chain lifecycle events either at the onsite or remote location. Each of these operations are associated with lots of data which is usually stored in traditional internet web (including cloud) enabled IT systems based on the inputs of service engineer[10]. Some of these inputs are collected based on output/outcome of mechanical operations directly or via digital systems placed in support to mechanical operations. The service engineer records the output/outcome and enters them in the system interface manually. This human intervention is often prone to errors. For example, consider a scenario wherein a bolt needs to be fastened by wrench (normal or digital) and engineer applies a force on the bolt to be tightened up for the target torque. The service engineer interprets the outcome (i.e., success or failure) of the operation, based on his cognitive skills and updates the system related user interface qualitatively. Therefore, many such mechanical operations where end-to-end digital intervention is not present are often prone to human errors. Additionally, such small errors could cost heavily in energy production running phase of the wind turbine, in terms of down time due to failed operations, quality compromised, missing proactive handling of incorrect operations, and incorrect interpreted information flow to different stakeholder that may leads to conflicting situations and inappropriate action flows. As explained earlier in Fig. 1, the service and maintenance aspects of the wind turbine case are really where the complexity comes to grow and are also the potential areas of issue in the value chain.

For the service technicians to both gain and give value to the blockchain solution, they must be able to interact with the solution, and this requires a user interface and backbone technologies in which the technicians can read and update the blockchain data without necessarily understanding the technology. Practically, the technicians will interact with the blockchain by scanning the Bar/QR-code with a tablet/mobile, which will give them access to either a website or an application through which the relevant information can be accessed and updated. Furthermore, there are multiple IT web systems (referred to as traditional/legacy systems/applications) involved and active from many years, such as delivery tracking, inventory management, service management, quality metrics etc. These systems run in the organizational boundaries, as they belong to different stakeholders, thus creating multiple data silos as well. To overcome this situation, their information or data sharing needs inter-organizational related cross functional system interfaces development. These interfaces should be abstracted and converged into a unified data format among all stakeholders in a trusted, traceable, and transparent manner. At the same time, their organization boundaries need to be protected and defended with complete trust and security. These objectives pose data integration, security, integrity and ownership challenges among different systems and their stakeholders. Therefore, there is need to build a novel framework in place, which can address these challenges and fulfill the relevant objectives at their design level. This is exactly what has been achieved through the developed blockchain enabled unwind demonstrator system concept presented in this paper.

3.1 Overall High-Level Architecture

The high-level architecture of the unwind demo concept is illustrated in Fig. 2. The assumption for the design architecture is the single commodity component operation support i.e., fastener or bolt related value chain in wind industry. The operational use case is a scenario of bolt fastening in wind turbine assembly with capabilities of digital recording its fastening operations with trust to support quality. In the architecture, the following functional layers are shown from the operations point of view:

a) **Wind Turbines at onsite location** – These are the target entities to perform operations upon in the wind turbine supply chain. To build a turbine at onsite, it needs transportation of components like bolts, blades, rotors, motors, electronics equipment, poles etc. Once they transported, then there is a assembly and installation workflow of components needs to be executed. Here, it is assumed that all operations are performed onsite with end-to-end digital traceability in support of mechanical operations. This wind turbine related operational data at onsite acts as a data source.

b) **IoT Edge Device (Bolt/fasten control)** – This is the system interface available at onsite to support turbine operations digitally. In our architecture, it is the kind of bolt fasten control system which monitors the bolt screw operations and related data and then send this data towards systems in upstream flow in real time. These types of systems can communicate with wind turbine systems using internet (e.g., via 5G/LTE/Wi-Fi) and radio (Bluetooth, LoraWan [11], etc.) interfaces and are available close to the wind turbine [12]. That is why it has been referred as IoT edge device in the given architecture. This also gives the scope of improving operations, in terms of low latency, aligned to edge computing goals in future [13, 14].

c) **Traditional organizational level centralized systems:** These are the enterprise level IT web enabled systems (usually enterprise resource planning – ERP - applications) which belong to different stakeholders. These systems record data coming from onsite locations for various events in value chain, process and store them in their databases. It is important to mention here, that the architecture supports the traditional systems flow as is, since they are functional and can save on investments made already and offer ease of work over familiar system. Therefore, this architecture does not suggest replacing the existing systems, rather advocates complement the existing system by adding a new system/network of blockchain.

d) **Blockchain Network:** This is the new system in place which aims at supporting complete supply chain of wind turbine in a distributed sharing, trustable, immutable, transparent, and secure manner by design. Blockchain systems perfectly fit in this context as they offer the same by design and that is the reason it has been chosen as an integral part of this architecture. Additionally, with the advent of modern technologies like Blockchain, IoT and edge computing and their integration is expected to benefit [15] the traditional way of managing the wind turbine supply chain. These technologies integration induce lots of capabilities which includes real time data generation, collection, and processing through IoT, distributed storage, transparency, trust, quality, and traceability among different stakeholders using blockchain and low latency driven decision near the data sources (i.e. wind turbine sites) using edge computing and many more [16].

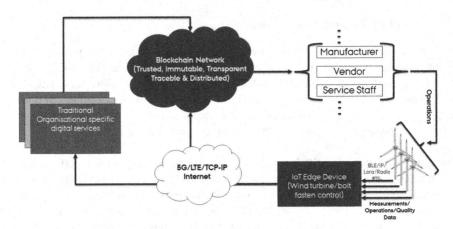

Fig. 2. The overall digital traceability system architecture at high level.

3.2 Demonstrator Realization and Code Snippet

For the demonstrator different digital equipment's were used as illustrated in Table 1.

Table 1: Equipment and services used for the realization of blockchain demonstrator

Item	Purpose
Wind Turbine	A small demo turbine installed in lab upon which the Bolt operations to be performed to replicate the real-world scenario
Bolt	12 mm Bolt that needs to be fasten to the wind turbine
Digital Wrench	To fasten the bolt and digital monitoring of the torque readings
Raspberry Pi+ LCD display	Acted as an edge device to collect the data from different tools during installation or maintenance operation. LCD is used on top of RaspberryPi to display real time data from real time operations
BAR/QR Code Scanner	To scan the QR and Bar codes present on the different components of Wind turbine assembly and to identify them uniquely
QR/BAR Code printers	This is used to print the QR/BAR code for digitalize tagging of the physical assets
Blockchain as a Service	Public Blockchain service (Ethereum [17] based) from Unwind Project that has REST APIs offering over internet to ingest and query data related to supply chain operations
Local blockchain enabled Edge server	Private blockchain service (Hyperledger Fabric [18] - HFabric - based) running at edge server to simulate permissioned blockchain service in a controlled and constrained lab environment
Programming Flow	Node-red based programming flow developed to control/manage devices and related data processing towards blockchain

Following the architecture (Fig. 2), a demonstrator has been developed while focusing only on bolt fastening operation at wind turbine is shown in Fig. 3. The physical components such as wind turbine and the bolt to be fastened is tagged with QR code. These

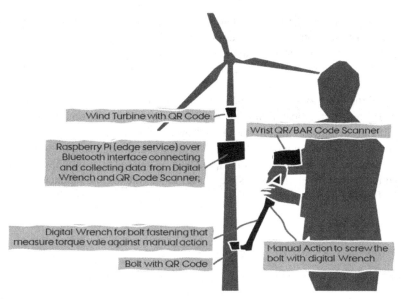

Fig. 3. The digital traceability with HFabric or Ethereum Blockchain demonstrator within the DigiMicrofactory lab at Aarhus University BTECH.

codes are generated by registering the turbine and batch of bolts details in blockchain system beforehand. To read these QR codes, a digital bar code scanner has been used in our demo. This tagging and scanning of QR code is one of the methods to represent identifications of physical systems in digital world in unique manner. In other words, it identifies the specific operation being performed at specific wind turbine with specific component at relevant geolocation. In our case, it establishes a *semantic relationship (one to many type)* [11] *of specific bolt from a specific vendor/supplier associated with the digital wrench (tool/device) operation performed by specific service engineer on specific wind turbine which belongs to a specific owner/operator at specific onsite/offshore location.* An information tied in such semantic relationship model offers semantic search and traceability capabilities with multiple dimensions at ease.

The demonstrator consists of digital wrench device which fastens the bolt to the pre-defined torque threshold. There is a raspberry Pi, which acts as an edge gateway/device providing internet connectivity to upstream systems in order to send them recorded data and as well as radio interfaces connectivity (based on Bluetooth) towards digital wrench and bar code scanner, to monitor onsite component operations. Additionally, the same edge device in the demo has also been used to install and implement a custom programming service flow (based on node-red), as shown in Fig. 4. This service is used to control and manage the bolt screw devices, collect, display, and send data to upstream traditional systems as well as blockchain systems (Hyperledger fabric or Ethereum based) in real time via REST based application programming interfaces (APIs) [19]. The complete operational flow is given as follows:

a) Register the turbine and related batch of bolts with blockchain application. The output of registration event generates a QR code.

b) Tag the turbine and related components with QR code labels.

c) Using programming flow running at edge device, register all the devices (scanner and digital wrench) over Bluetooth interface.

d) Scan all the QR codes (wind turbine and bolt related).

e) Perform bolt fasten operation using digital wrench. This will send torque specific reading in real time to the programming flow running at edge.

f) Metadata (data about wind turbine and bolt identification) and data from specific fasten operation, in semantic relationship manner, is merged in programming flow and send into two different flows upstream traditional systems and blockchain systems via REST APIs.

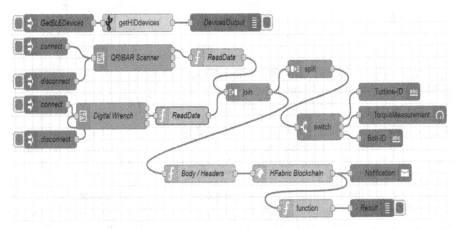

Fig. 4. Code snippet for connecting all reader devices and enabling dataflow and registration with Blockchain

Note: The APIs serves as the interface for storage and retrieval of data related to bolt, wind turbine, and technical operations to/from Hyperledger fabric (used as a private) or Ethereum (used as public) based blockchain. The registration of the bolt batches, wind turbine, documented technical service and recycling data invokes corresponding solidity based smart contracts in the blockchain that validates and stores the respective information. The APIs endpoints process and forward the requests to the smart contract by means of the web3 library. Different stakeholders, choose to be part of the blockchain network, can access the data of their interest based on their privileges (as per the smart contract agreements among the stakeholders) in near real time, shareable, reliable, traceable, secure, and transparent manner. Thus, able to perform the required actions (proactive or course of correction) as per the need of the situational event.

4   Conclusions

Throughout this industry 4.0 case study, we examined with qualitative methods the challenges which wind industry is facing during manufacturing and operational phases for the entire wind turbine life cycle of commodity components. We analyzed the findings and identified the area of the supply chain for commodity products where blockchain technology can contribute significantly as solution to enhance the economy of scale for commodity products in terms of digital traceability, quality, operations with trust and transparency as well as to establish a more sustainable supply chain. Furthermore, we developed a working demo in a controlled lab environment to demonstrate the feasibility of using blockchain in the digital traceability of commodity products such like bolts/fasteners adding value to the entire life cycle of wind turbines in this industry .

Acknowledgements. The authors would like to thank many actors from the wind industry at APQP4wind, Vestas and Simens Gamesa for valuable discussions on various subjects. The study partially funded from the Danish Industries Fund under the grant name "UnWind" (https://indust riensfond.dk/project/unwind-blockchain-i-vindmolleindustrien/).

References

1. Beliatis, M.J., Jensen, K., Ellegaard, L., Aagaard, A., Presser, M.: Next generation Industrial IoT Digitalization for Traceability in Metal Manufacturing Industry: a Case Study of Industry 4.0. Electronics **10**(5), 628 (2021)
2. Treiblmaier, H.: The impact of the blockchain on the supply chain: a theory-based research framework and a call for action. Supply Chain Manag. **23**(6), 545–559 (2018)
3. Cole, R., Stevenson, M., Aitken, J.: Blockchain technology: implications for operations and supply chain management. Supply Chain Manag. **24**(4), 469–483 (2019)
4. Holm, K., Goduscheit, R.C.: Assessing the technology readiness level of current blockchain use cases. In: 2020 IEEE Technology Engineering Management Conference TEMSCON 2020 (2020)
5. Coughlan, P., Coghlan, D.: Action research for operations management. Int. J. Oper. Prod. Manag. **22**(2), 220–240 (2002)
6. Beliatis, M.J., et al.: Slot-Die-Coated V2O5 as Hole Transport Layer for Flexible Organic Solar Cells and Optoelectronic Devices. Adv. Eng. Mater. **18**(8), 1494–1503 (2016)
7. Holm, K.: Blockchain as a Sustainable Service-Enabler: a Case of Wind Turbine Traceability, Lect. Notes Mech. Eng., pp. 516–523 (2022)
8. Saberi, S., Kouhizadeh, M., Sarkis, J., Shen, L.: Blockchain technology and its relationships to sustainable supply chain management. Int. J. Prod. Res. **57**(7), 2117–2135 (2019)
9. Nejad, A.R., et al.: Wind turbine drivetrains: state-of-the-art technologies and future development trends. Wind Energy Sci. **7**(1), 387–411 (2022)
10. Zhao, Y., Xia, S., Zhang, J., Hu, Y., Wu, M.: Effect of the digital transformation of power system on renewable energy utilization in China. IEEE Access **9** (2021)
11. Singh, P., Acharya, K.S., Beliatis, M.J., Presser, M.: Semantic search system for real time occupancy. In. IEEE International Conference Internet Things Intelliigent System (IoTaIS), vol. 2021, pp. 49–55 (2021)
12. Hossain, M.L., Abu-Siada, A., Muyeen, S.M., Hasan, M.M., Rahman, M.M.: Industrial IoT based condition monitoring for wind energy conversion system. CSEE J. Power Energy Syst. **7**(3) (2021)

13. Olaniyan, R., Fadahunsi, O., Maheswaran, M. Zhani, M.F.: Opportunistic edge computing: concepts, opportunities and research challenges. CoRR, vol. abs/1806.04311 (2018)
14. Tziouvaras, A., Foukalas, F.: Edge AI for Industry 4.0: an Internet of Things approach. In: 24th Pan-Hellenic Conference on Informatics, pp. 121–126 (2020)
15. Pan, J., Wang, J., Hester, A., Alqerm, I., Liu, Y., Zhao, Y.: Edge xhain: an edge-IoT framework and prototype based on blockchain and smart contracts. IEEE Internet Things J. **PP**(99), 1 (2019)
16. Seitz, A., Henze, D., Miehle, D., Bruegge, B., Nickles, J., Sauer, M.: Fog computing as enabler for blockchain-based IIoT app marketplaces-a case study. In: 2018 5th International Conference on Internet of Things: Systems, Management and Security, IoTSMS 2018 (2018)
17. Alrubei, S., Rigelsford, J., Willis, C., Ball, E.: Ethereum blockchain for securing the Internet of Things: practical implementation and performance evaluation. In: International Conference on Cyber Security and Protection of Digital Services (Cyber Security) (2019)
18. Foschini, L., Gavagna, A., Martuscelli, G., Montanari, R.: Hyperledger fabric blockchain: chain code performance analysis. In: ICC 2020 - 2020 IEEE International Conference on Communications (ICC) (2020)
19. Alam, M.S., Atmojo, U.D., Blech, J.O., Lastra, J.L.M.: A REST and HTTP-based Service architecture for industrial facilities. In: 2020 IEEE Conference on Industrial Cyber physical Systems (ICPS) (2020)

Sleep Stage Detection on a Wearable Headband Using Deep Neural Networks

Mian Hamza$^{(\boxtimes)}$, Sharmistha Bhadra, and Zeljko Zilic

Department of Electrical and Computer Engineering, McGill University,
Montreal, QC H2X 2G6, Canada
{mian.hamza,zeljko.zilic}@mail.mcgill.ca

Abstract. The flexible PCB medical device developed at our research lab calculates a single-channel EOG. We develop an infrastructure for our device, including an IoT structure for capturing data. As well as an algorithm that can detect Sleep Stages using EOG data from our device. Previous attempts at classifying sleep always use data from double-channel EOG data. Initially, we used a labelled sleep dataset from the University of Wisconsin to train our neural network. We then apply transfer learning to the sleep classifier with data extracted from our device. Overall, we were able to successfully create a model with data from the medical device and obtain a 81.19% sleep stage classification accuracy.

1 Introduction

The Electrooculogram (EOG) measures a potential difference between the cornea and the retina of an eye. This potential relates to eye movements, reflex, and blinking. By measuring the change in the potential we obtain a signal useful in tracking multiple conditions, including the sleep. The magnitude of the EOG potential is correlated with the displacement of the eye from a neutral position during eye movement [1,2]. Usually in EOG measurements the recording electrode placed on the left and right eyes are referred to as E1 and E2 respectively. EOG is the difference between two electrodes, as shown in Fig. 1. If the eye moves towards one electrode it becomes relatively positive, the other relatively negative. The EOG signals can be used to determine wide variety of eye activities, whether it is blinking, winking, moving your eyes and even sleeping.

Sleep is characterized by multiple stages. According to the American Academy of Sleep Medicine's (AASM), there are 5 stages of sleep, and each stage has different types of eye movements:

1. N1 and N2 Sleep
   – Slow Eye Movements (SEM)
2. N3 sleep
   – No Eye Movement
3. REM
   – "conjugate, irregularly, sharply peaked eye movements with an initial deflection lasting <500 ms"

© The Author(s), under exclusive license to Springer Nature Switzerland AG 2022
A. González-Vidal et al. (Eds.): GIoTS 2022, LNCS 13533, pp. 187–198, 2022.
https://doi.org/10.1007/978-3-031-20936-9_15

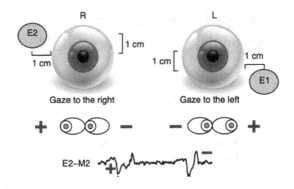

Fig. 1. Electrode placement for EOG recordings [3]

In a nights sleep, a typical person will shift through each of these stages. During sleep the eyes move depending on which stage of sleep we are in. One distinctive stage of sleep, known as Rapid Eye Movement (REM), is characterized by rapid movements of the eyes in multiple directions [4]. Since each stage of sleep has different eye movements, if we record EOG signals while sleeping we are able to determine which stage of sleep the participant is in.

We work with a flexible PCB circuit that calculates the Electrooculography (EOG) signal from both eyes. It calculates the difference between the corneal potential of both eyes, and it is referenced to a neutral site that sits on the center of the forehead. The device will be referred to as "Flex-EOG". It outputs single-channel EOG data. The device when worn while sleeping will record EOG data from the movements of the eyes [1]. Our goal is to be able to classify Sleep Stages with data from Flex-EOG. We will accomplish this by developing an infrastructure to capture and process data from the Flex-EOG. This is significant because: there is a lack of sleep classification studies that use EOG data, especially single-channel. Furthermore, there are few studies that evaluate the effectiveness of using publicly available data to train a prototype medical device; especially for sleep detection.

2   Background

There are several types of sleep tracking devices. Some track the bio-potential signals: such as the brain waves, or the eye movement. In this category we see devices like the Muse, which gives Sleep Stages from EEG signals.

Other devices track your body movement, position, and sleeping noises. There are many commercially available devices in this category; The Google Nest Hub uses a radar sensor to track your movements. This millimeter-wave sensor emits a radio wave, and uses the reflected signal to figure out if someone has moved; their velocity and distance. The radar sensor data is trained on a Machine Learning model for sleep stage tracking [5]. Another similar device that tracks movement has been recently patented by Apple. It is a "layered sensor having multiple laterally adjacent substrates in a single layer". The sensor is piezoelectric, meaning it generates electric signals in response to pressure. It is placed underneath the user like a bed sheet, and can track their movement since the piezoelectric sensor will be sensing their movement [6].

Lastly, there are devices that are a combination of both: fitness watches track the heart rate and the movement.

For this research we are focused on classifying sleep using bio-potential signals. We will develop machine learning models to classify sleep. There are some sleep classification models that have been trained using bio-potential signals. EOGNET is a neural network model that implements sleep tracking using single channel EOG signals. The researchers use deep learning techniques such as CNNs to classify Sleep Stages. The model uses a residual block. The residual block structure is derived from a ResNet model, and is known to produce better accuracy than a normal sequential model [7]. Overall, EOGNET attains a promising classification accuracy of 85% and 82.1% on two separate datasets for sleep stage classification [8].

The work in [9] uses single channel electroencephalography (EEG) captures of brain wave signals for sleep stage classification. It first converts data to the frequency domain, before passing it into a neural processing pipeline consisting of an Autoencoder & CNN. A decent accuracy is achieved, with accuracies above 80% for all Sleep Stages (except N1 Sleep). Overall [9] has a classification accuracy of 88.4% and 87.6% on two separate datasets.

3   Methodology

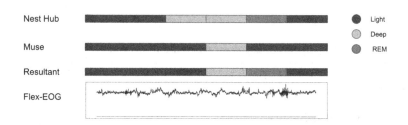

Fig. 2. Technique used to create Flex-EOG dataset

We take overnight recordings of EOG. Participants wear the Flex-EOG device while sleeping. As a ground truth we use two separate sleep stage detection devices, in order to track the participants Sleep Stages. A Muse electroencephalography (EEG) (www.choosemuse.com), and The Google Nest Hub (2nd Gen) [10]. Both Muse and Google have developed sleep scoring algorithms, that allows us to determine the Sleep Stages of participants.

By using the EOG recordings from Flex-EOG, and sleep stage labels from MUSE, Google we are able to create a sleep stage classification algorithm for the Flex-EOG device. Figure 3 shows an overnight recording from the Nest. We can also note from Fig. 3 that the Sleep stages are not close in their duration, especially REM Sleep which happens for only a fraction of the time as Light and Deep Sleep.

As shown in Fig. 2, we obtain two separate ground truth labels from Muse, Nest Hub. Then, for each epoch we randomly choose our sleep stage label from one source to form our resultant sleep stage label. By using data from two different sources, our sleep stage labels are less prone to error. We then combine our resultant sleep stage label with our Flex-EOG data to create a dataset that will be used to update our model.

We propose a sleep stage classification algorithm to work on Flex-EOG device. It is a deep Convolutional Neural Network, that has been trained on data extracted from the University of Wisconsin Sleep study (WSC). Then the model is updated with the dataset we created from our Flex-EOG device.

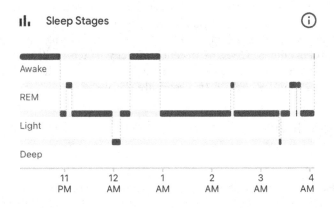

Fig. 3. Overnight sleep recording from Nest Hub

3.1   Experimental Setup

As shown in Fig. 4, both devices are worn at the same time when sleeping. The Muse EEG band is worn above the Flex-EOG band. Since the Flex-EOG band should be positioned right above the eyes, in order to retrieve corneal bio-potentials. The Google Nest Hub is also setup. It is positioned on a bedside table next to the participant, and the radar sensor is pointed towards their torso.

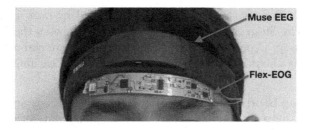

Fig. 4. Placement of Muse and Flex-EOG bands on face.

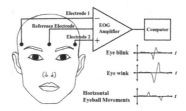

Fig. 5. The Flex-EOG device setup with three electrode configuration [1]

Flex EOG Device. The functionality of the Flex-EOG device is shown in Fig. 5. The eye bio-potentials from the electrode are sent to the EOG amplifier circuit, after which the circuit communicates to an iOS Application via Bluetooth module.

Muse EEG Device. The Muse EEG device is a low cost, portable EEG device. It has been used for numerous research purposes in multiple medical contexts including human visual attention, stroke diagnosis, event-related brain potentials (ERP) research [11–13].

The Muse iOS App has built in sleep tracking with four different Sleep Stages.

1. Awake
2. Light Sleep
   – Corresponds to N1, N2
3. Deep Sleep
   – Corresponds to N3
4. REM

These Sleep Stages are measured using brainwave EEG signals. According to the AASM manual on Sleep Stages, the differences between Sleep Stages can also be measured by brain wave activity using EEG signals [14]. This technique is used by the Muse EEG Device.

Google Nest Hub. Google has trained their own sleep stage detection model, by using data received from a millimeter-wave frequency-modulated continuous wave (FMCW) radar transceiver. It has been trained by over a million hours of sleep data. The Sleep Stages for the Nest are the same as the Muse device: Awake, Light Sleep, Deep Sleep, REM. This means that we can use both labels without worrying about compatibility with the Machine Learning model.

Wisconsin Sleep Study Dataset. Since we are in the early stages of the Flex-EOG project, we have not conducted clinical trials. So our dataset is small in size. Since smaller datasets are prone to overfitting, we populate our model with the Wisconsin Dataset (WSC) dataset. Once we obtain the Flex-EOG recordings, we update our model. This is a technique known as **Transfer Learning**. Like in this paper, for Transfer Learning we train our model with similar data to the classification problem we are trying to solve. This raises the accuracy of our model. Transfer Learning is used in a wide variety of domains, like speech processing, image detection [15–17].

The WSC study currently contains 2570 overnight Polysomnography (PSG) recordings [18], from 1500 participants. Each recording is sleep scored by a technician at an interval of 30 s [19,20]. Compared to other research studies, the WSC dataset has a far superior dataset size. The MIT-BIH dataset used in [9] for example only contains 9 overnight recordings. We use the entire WSC dataset, this can allow the models to reach a higher classification accuracy and prevents the model from overfitting. For Sleep Stage detection using our model, transfer learning is not limited to the WSC dataset but it was chosen because its larger size is beneficial.

From the WSC dataset we extract:

1. EOG values
   - E1 (E_{left}), E2 (E_{right}) which is obtained from left and right eyes.
2. Sleep stage labels
3. Epoch number
4. Seconds elapsed

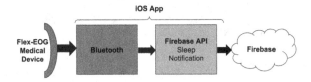

Fig. 6. Structure of Flex-EOG app

IoT Infrastructure. There was a substantial infrastructure and pipeline that had to be developed to be able to receive and synchronize data from three different sources. The Nest, MUSE, and Flex-EOG were concurrently connected to an iPhone device. The Nest and Muse each had their own applications that we used to extract sleep data, so we did not have do develop any infrastructure for them. For the Flex-EOG an iOS application was built.

The iOS application packages the EOG data into a dataset which contains multiple variables necessary for processing the data. All of the added variables correspond to the same measurements found in a majority of sleep studies including the WSC dataset.

1. EOG Value
2. Seconds elapsed
3. Epoch Number
4. UNIX Timestamp

Once the iOS App processes and packages the Flex-EOG data into a datapoint known as a **Sleep Notification**, it sends the data to the Cloud. The Cloud will load the data into a csv formatted dataset.

Figure 6 shows the communication protocol of the iOS app. It is notable that in medical environments, the quality and accuracy of measurements are important. For Sleep detection, having an accurate time measurement accross all three devices was important. In order to maintain synchronization, we attached a UNIX timestamp to our Sleep Notification data structure. This ensured accurate time measurements when adding concurrent sleep labels from the Muse and Nest Hub. Especially, in scenarios where the internet connectivity is poor and data is not being written to the cloud.

One thing we observed was that the Flex-EOG's sampling frequency varied between 115–130 Hz. Standard medical-grade EOG devices had a sampling frequency 100 Hz. To address this discrepancy, the Sleep Notification data structure contained a seconds and epoch measurement. If any given second measurement had more than 100 epochs attributed to it, we would clip the remainder of the output. The epoch variable is used to sort the data. This is important since the Cloud does not sort data chronologically. The seconds measurement allows us to process and label our data in 30-s intervals, which is the standard interval for sleep studies. Overall, we noted that iOS devices are powerful tools that can be used to obtain medical data.

4 Sleep Stage Detection Model

4.1 Data Preprocessing

WSC Data. Most sleep studies have double channel recordings, that need to be converted to single channel. This is because the machine learning model is built for the single channel Flex-EOG. Algorithm 1 lays out the steps taken to convert the WSC dataset from double channel to single channel.

Algorithm 2 lays out the steps we used to preprocess all single channel EOG data. We convert the data to frequency domain and extract the power spectral density from E_{new}. This is done by using the Welch transform. We use the Welch transform, in order to reduce the noise and to extract key patterns from the data

Algorithm 1. WSC Preprocessing: How to create single channel EOG data from double Channel.

1: **if** Double Channel EOG **then**
2:     **for** Every epoch **do**
3:         Create single Channel EOG data: $\mathbf{E}_{new} = E_{left} - E_{right}$
4:     **end for**
5: **end if**

Algorithm 2. EOG Data Preprocessing: Overview of the steps taken to preprocess the datasets from both sources.

1: **for** All single Channel EOG data **do**
2:     **for** Each 30 second interval **do**
3:         Compute Welch Transform using Scipy Welch [21]
4:     **end for**
5:     Apply SMOTE to Training Data [22]
6: **end for**

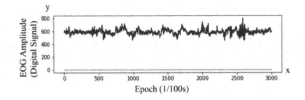

Fig. 7. Sample of the raw Flex-EOG data

[23]. As shown in Fig. 3, Sleep datasets are unbalanced. So, we use a technique called SMOTE to oversample our dataset. SMOTE uses a K-Nearest Neighbors approach to draw new datapoints between two randomly selected neighbors. We use SMOTE to balance our dataset to all have an equal number of samples [22]. Oversampling is a technique only applied to the training dataset to ensure that the model performance is measured against real life recordings. Another technique we use is to conduct more trials, and extract only the minority Sleep Stages. This can be thought of as undersampling, where we discard extra samples from the majority class.

Flex-EOG Data. Figure 7 shows the raw EOG data from the Flex-EOG that is passed through the Algorithm 2. The data we input to the Welch transform is the raw EOG data. Since the Flex-EOG device already outputs single-channel, we do not need to process the data beforehand.

Algorithm 3 is a summary of the steps we take to train the classifier for use on the Flex-EOG device. We first train our model with the WSC dataset. Then we update our neural network with the new data from our Flex-EOG dataset.

Algorithm 3. Steps taken to create Sleep Stage Detection Model

---

1: **for** All processed WSC EOG Data **do**
2:     Train Neural Network (Fig. 8)
3: **end for**
4: **Then** Get Flex-EOG recordings
5: **for** All recorded Flex-EOG data **do**
6:     Add Sleep Stage Labels from Muse, Google Nest
7:     Process using Algorithm 2
8:     Update Neural Network (Transfer Learning)
9: **end for**

4.2 Deep Learning Model

The Deep Learning model is shown in Fig. 8. It contains multiple Batch Normalization layers, this is done in order to bridge the gap between the two different data inputs: Flex-EOG and WSC. Since both the data have corresponding patterns, but have different values and magnitudes.

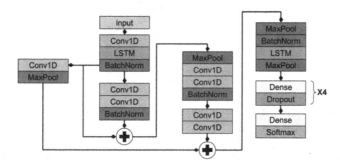

Fig. 8. Neural network structure

The model structure is shown in Fig. 8. The model is inspired by the ResNet architectures [7]. The model has multiple skipped connections that feed earlier outputs to the model. It allows us to create a more deeper model, that can be optimized for higher accuracies. We also have Long Short-Term Memory (LSTM) layers at the start and end. They are used to learn sequential patterns in the data. The excessive use of Batch Normalization is theorized to help the data calibrate accross devices, by constantly re-centering the data and alleviating any variation due to differences in magnitude between the two data sources.

Training on WSC Dataset. In the WSC dataset 70% of the dataset is used for training, 15% is used for test and validation each.

Transfer Learning on Flex-EOG Data. We apply transfer learning to our model. We update it with the Flex-EOG dataset after it is trained on the WSC dataset. Our model is then fine tuned to the Flex-EOG device.

We use recordings from 4 participants taken from the Flex-EOG dataset at different times of the night. Overall, we have around 18 h of data. 55% of the Flex-EOG data is used for training, and 27.5% is used for test and validation each. Given our limited dataset size, we deliberately chose to create a small training dataset. This is because SMOTE is used to add training data.

4.3   Model Results

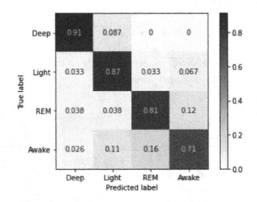

Fig. 9. Confusion matrix for Flex-EOG

The model gives a classification accuracy of **89%** on the WSC dataset. After applying transfer learning to the Flex-EOG dataset, there is an accuracy of **81.19%**. The model has an F-1 Score of 0.8107. It's Precision of 0.8147 shows that it can correctly identify Sleep Stages. A Recall of 0.812 shows that it can differentiate between different Sleep Stages. Overall, the model has a strong performance. One exception is the Awake stage, which has an Recall score of 71%. Meaning that our classification of the Awake stage has many false negatives. This is likely due to the nature of the Awake stage: it varies accross participants. When awake, some participants like to lie in bed with their eyes open, others prefer to close their eyes. Therefore the variability can lead the model to falsely classify the Awake stage as another Stage. A possible remedy for this would be to train the model on more Awake data, and to use data augmentation techniques such as test-time Augmentation [24] (Fig. 9).

5   Conclusion

Overall, we were able to build a model that can detect the different Sleep Stages on a wearable PCB device that measures EOG signals. We show that it is possible to obtain related data from medical datasets to create an initial model and calibrate the model according to data from an experimental medical device.

Transfer learning allows us to obtain a good fit model without the need to conduct medical trials to obtain the necessary data that is required to train the model and prevent overfitting. This finding is impactful since it gives us a low cost, effective and efficient solution for creating viable classification models.

References

1. Debbarma, S., Bhadra, S.: A lightweight flexible wireless electrooculogram monitoring system with printed gold electrodes. IEEE Sens. J. **21**(18), 20931–20942 (2021). https://doi.org/10.1109/jsen.2021.3095423
2. Frishman, L.J.: Electrogenesis of the electroretinogram. In: Retina, pp. 177–201. Elsevier (2013). https://doi.org/10.1016/b978-1-4557-0737-9.00007-2
3. Malhotra, R.K., Avidan, A.Y.: Sleep stages and scoring technique. In: Atlas of Sleep Medicine, pp. 77–99. Elsevier (2014). https://doi.org/10.1016/b978-1-4557-1267-0.00003-5
4. Stages of Sleep: REM and Non-REM Sleep Cycles. https://www.webmd.com/sleep-disorders/sleep-101
5. Dixon, M., Schneider, L., Yu, J., et al.: Sleep-wake detection with a contactless, bedside radar sleep sensing system. Technical report (2021)
6. Rimminen, H., Amin, A.M., Weadon, T.L., et al.: On-bed differential piezoelectric sensor, February 2021
7. He, K., Zhang, X., Ren, S., et al.: Deep residual learning for image recognition (2015). arXiv: 1512.03385 [cs.CV]
8. Fan, J., Sun, C., Long, M., et al.: EOGNET: a novel deep learning model for sleep stage classification based on single-channel EOG signal. Front. Neurosci. **15**, 573194 (2021)
9. Zhang, J., Yao, R., Ge, W., et al.: Orthogonal convolutional neural networks for automatic sleep stage classification based on single-channel EEG. Comput. Methods Programs Biomed. **183**, 105089 (2020). https://doi.org/10.1016/j.cmpb.2019.105089
10. Dixon, M., Lee, R.S.: Contactless sleep sensing in Nest Hub, March 2021. https://ai.googleblog.com/2021/03/contactless-sleep-sensing-in-nest-hub.html
11. Krigolson, O.E., Williams, C.C., Norton, A., et al.: Choosing MUSE: validation of a low-cost, portable EEG system for ERP research. Front. Neurosci. **11** (2017). https://doi.org/10.3389/fnins.2017.00109
12. Wilkinson, C.M., Burrell, J.I., Kuziek, J.W.P., et al.: Application of the Muse portable EEG system to aid in rapid diagnosis of stroke, June 2020. https://doi.org/10.1101/2020.06.01.20119586
13. Krigolson, O.E., Williams, C.C., Colino, F.L.: Using portable EEG to assess human visual attention. In: Schmorrow, D.D., Fidopiastis, C.M. (eds.) AC 2017. LNCS (LNAI), vol. 10284, pp. 56–65. Springer, Cham (2017). https://doi.org/10.1007/978-3-319-58628-1_5
14. Berry, R.B., Brooks, R., Gamaldo, C., et al.: AASM scoring manual updates for 2017 (version 2.4). J. Clin. Sleep Med. **13**(05), 665–666 (2017). https://doi.org/10.5664/jcsm.6576
15. Boigne, J., Liyanage, B., Östrem, T.: Recognizing more emotions with less data using self-supervised transfer learning (2020). https://doi.org/10.48550/ARXIV.2011.05585. https://arxiv.org/abs/2011.05585

16. Kunze, J., Kirsch, L., Kurenkov, I., et al.: Transfer learning for speech recognition on a budget. CoRR abs/1706.00290 (2017). arXiv: 1706.00290
17. Huh, M., Agrawal, P., Efros, A.A.: What makes ImageNet good for transfer learning? (2016). https://doi.org/10.48550/ARXIV.1608.08614. https://arxiv.org/abs/1608.08614
18. Morgan, K.K.: What is Polysomnography (PSG)? https://www.webmd.com/sleep-disorders/what-is-polysomnography
19. Zhang, G.-Q., Cui, L., Mueller, R., et al.: The national sleep research resource: towards a sleep data commons. J. Am. Med. Inf. Assoc. **25**(10), 1351–1358 (2018). https://doi.org/10.1093/jamia/ocy064
20. Young, T., Palta, M., Dempsey, J., et al.: Burden of sleep apnea: rationale, design, and major findings of the Wisconsin Sleep Cohort study. WMJ **108**(5), 246–249 (2009)
21. Virtanen, P., Gommers, R., Oliphant, T.E., et al.: SciPy 1.0: fundamental algorithms for scientific computing in Python. Nat. Methods **17**, 261–272 (2020). https://doi.org/10.1038/s41592-019-0686-2
22. Chawla, N.V., Bowyer, K.W., Hall, L.O., et al.: SMOTE: synthetic minority oversampling technique. J. Artif. Intell. Res. **16**, 321–357 (2002)
23. Welch, P.: The use of fast Fourier transform for the estimation of power spectra: a method based on time averaging over short, modified periodograms. IEEE Trans. Audio Electroacoust. **15**(2), 70–73 (1967). https://doi.org/10.1109/tau.1967.1161901
24. Shanmugam, D., Blalock, D., Balakrishnan, G., et al.: When and why test-time augmentation works. arXiv e-prints, arXiv-2011 (2020)

A Comparative Study on Energy Consumption Models for Drones

Carlos Muli[1], Sangyoung Park[2], and Mingming Liu[1(✉)]

[1] School of Electronic Engineering, Dublin City University, Dublin, Ireland
`carlos.muli2@mail.dcu.ie`, `mingming.liu@dcu.ie`
[2] Einstein Center Digital Future, Technical University of Berlin, Berlin, Germany
`sangyoung.park@tu-berlin.de`

Abstract. Creating an appropriate energy consumption prediction model is becoming an important topic for drone-related research in the literature. However, a general consensus on the energy consumption model is yet to be reached at present. As a result, there are many variations that attempt to create models that range in complexity with a focus on different aspects. In this paper, we benchmark the five most popular energy consumption models for drones derived from their physical behaviours and point to the difficulties in matching with a realistic energy dataset collected from a delivery drone in flight under different testing conditions. Moreover, we propose a novel data-driven energy model using the Long Short-Term Memory (LSTM) based deep learning architecture and the accuracy is compared based on the dataset. Our experimental results have shown that the LSTM based approach can easily outperform other mathematical models for the dataset under study. Finally, sensitivity analysis has been carried out in order to interpret the model.

Keywords: Unmanned aerial vehicle · Drone energy model · Energy consumption · Deep learning · Long short-term memory

1 Introduction

Unmanned Aerial Vehicles (UAVs) are being used in many diverse operations in a range of fields at present, including but not limited to aerial surveillance, search and rescue operations, parcel delivery, and agriculture [1,2]. However, one of the most critical design issues for UAVs is that they often suffer from short flight time, typically tens of minutes, mainly due to their high power requirements and limited battery capacity [3,4]. Thus, it is important to correctly estimate the flight time and range to ensure reliable operation and energy-efficient path planning. To accomplish this, an accurate drone energy consumption model is essential, which enables quantifying the impact of different factors, i.e., wind speed, payload, ground speed, altitude, etc., affecting the energy consumption of drones in various scenarios.

A. González-Vidal et al. (Eds.): GIoTS 2022, LNCS 13533, pp. 199–210, 2022.
https://doi.org/10.1007/978-3-031-20936-9_16

However, it is a challenging task to incorporate all such factors into a single energy consumption model. There are numerous factors related to the drone design (weight, number of rotors, battery weight/efficiency, avionics), the environment (wind conditions, weather, ambient temperature), drone dynamics (acceleration, angle of attack, flight angle/altitude), and operational requirements (flight time, payload). Existing models on drone energy consumption focuses on certain aspects of drones and usually consider a subset of factors [5]. Some models can only be applied to particular conditions such as hovering largely ignoring the impact of the air speed [6]. There are models focusing more on drones acting like fixed-wing aircrafts [7] or more like helicopters [6]. This results in conflicting predictions across different energy consumption models despite same input parameters and trajectories [5]. Apart from the models taking theoretical approaches [6–9], there have been attempts to use regression models [10,11] to match the model better to the realistic measurements. In particular, black box modeling of drones also reports decent results across the missions starting from take-off to return [11]. The work also reports that to account for impacts of control profiles, which is often ignored in other models, a time-series machine learning methods needs to be investigated.

In this paper, we aim at comparing some prominent drone energy consumption models in the literature and propose a long-short term memory (LSTM) deep learning-based architecture, useful for prediction of time-series data, for energy consumption model of drones. Despite such efforts to accurately model the drone energy consumption and decent accuracy reported in the literature, there has been few works on directly comparing different types of models on a real measured data. Our efforts to apply the energy consumption models to a recently published measurement data [12], have shown that significant discrepancies exist between the predicted values and the independently-collected real-world measurement. Therefore, we consider a deep learning approach to create an energy consumption model that considers all aspects of flight (take-off, landing, cruising, hovering) from empirical data and the prediction results have been compared with model-based approaches fitted to the real-world data.

The key contributions in this paper can be summarized as follows:

– We evaluate the performance of several existing drone energy consumption models using the specific realistic dataset [12].
– We propose a learning-based approach using the Long-Short Term Memory (LSTM) deep learning based architecture for power consumption prediction of drones.
– We carry out sensitivity analysis on the trained LSTM model to give some insights on feature importance, i.e., interpretability of the model.

The remainder of this paper is organised as follows. Section 2 elaborates the technical background on some prominent drone energy consumption models in the literature. Section 3 presents our key research problem and propose the LSTM-based system architecture to address the design issue. Section 4 discusses our evaluation results using different models. Finally, Sect. 5 concludes the paper.

2   Background: Drone Power Models

In this section, we introduce drone energy models used in the literature. Prior works on path planning algorithms assume drone energy models for evaluating battery usage. As the flight distance and the number of turns a drone makes determines the paths, energy consumption models regards the factors important in estimating the energy consumption [13].

Other factors such as wind speed, wind angle, and altitude are not considered in the work. More elaborate models consider the impact of acceleration and deceleration [14]. Several tests were performed in this study which focuses on three main performance metrics: straight line distance, the effects of velocity, and the effects of turning. The study has shown that higher speeds result in lower overall energy consumption and higher turning angles resulted in higher overall energy consumption. Analysis of all aspects of on-board electronics to form total energy consumption is also explored and is validated using empirical data from a commercial drone [15]. Energy consumption primarily comes from the motors, followed by communications, processors, and sensors. Communications, processors, and sensors were discovered to be minimal in contribution but not negligible in total energy consumption.

Among such models, we selected representative ones to be investigated in this paper also designated as "five fundamental models for drone energy consumption of steady level flight' in a recent survey [5], dubbed D'Andrea, Dorling et al., Stolaroff et al., Kirchstein, and Tseng energy models.

2.1   D'Andrea Energy Model

The D'Andrea energy model is based on the drone's lift-to-drag ratio [5,16]. The formula is optimised for steady drone flight and uses the drone's mass, airspeed, lift-to-drag ratio, and the power transfer efficiency of the battery. The model comes in two variations; a standard variation with no account for wind, and one that does account for wind in terms of headwind experienced by the drone. The model is further expanded by implementing "empty returns", which occurs when the drone drops off the payload before taking the return flight [7]. The model makes several assumptions to create their energy consumption model. The payload of the drone is no heavier than 2 kg and has an operating range of 10 km. A lift-to-drag ratio of a constant value is selected, inspired by helicopter lift-to-drag ratios and used for comparison with them. Variables such as cruising speed during missions are set to a predetermined value of 45 km/h. The power transfer efficiency is set to 0.5 [16]. A constant p_{avio} is added to account for vehicle avionics.

$$P = \frac{\sum_{k=1}^{3} m_k v_a}{370\eta r} + p_{avio}, \tag{1}$$

where m_k represents the mass of each drone component including drone weight ($k = 1$), battery weight ($k = 2$) and payload weight ($k = 3$). v_a is the drone airspeed, i.e., the speed of drone relative to air, η is the power transfer efficiency, r is the lift-to-drag ratio, and p_{avio} is the power required for drone avionics [5].

2.2 Dorling et al. Energy Model

The Dorling energy model only takes into consideration drone hovering, and thus, cannot detail energy consumption for the take-off, cruising, and landing [5,6]. However, this model does consider the components used in the drone such as the number of rotors and propeller area. Through testing, the equations that dictate the energy consumption was reduced to a linear function dependent on the battery and payload of the drone. The model is derived from the equation used to calculate the power of a helicopter and is adapted for multi-rotors. The mass components of drone m_k are used as parameters alongside gravity (g), air density (ρ), number of rotors (n), and propeller area (ζ).

$$P = \frac{g(\sum_{k=1}^{3} m_k)^{\frac{3}{2}}}{\sqrt{2n\rho\zeta}} \tag{2}$$

2.3 Stolaroff et al. Energy Model

The Stolaroff energy model designs its model using the physics of drone flight including the forces experienced by the drone due to its weight, parasitic drag, and induced drag [5,8]. The model accounts for heavy winds by utilising an adapted version of the previous model by using the angle of attack of the drone. However, it was noted that large values of the angle of attack resulted in unstable results. The model consists of the thrust produced (T), angle of attack (α), power transfer efficiency (η), and the induced speed caused by the drone (v_i). It can be presented as follows:

$$P = \frac{T(v_a sin(\alpha) + v_i)}{\eta} \tag{3}$$

where $T = g\sum_{k=1}^{3} m_k + 0.5\rho \sum_{k=1}^{3} C_{D_k} A_k v_a^2$ with the drag coefficient C_{D_k}, and the projected area perpendicular to travel of each drone component A_k [5].

2.4 Kirchstein Energy Model

The Kirchstein energy model is based on the drone's environmental conditions and flight trajectory [5,9]. It is another component model with a focus on optimised take-off angle, cruising altitude, level flight, descent, and landing. This model takes into consideration a wide range of factors such as the power required for climbing, avionics, and different power losses resulting from the electric motor and power transmission inefficiencies. The model covers the power consumption from air drag from the drone's profile and the rotor profile, the lift required for flight, the climb to the designated altitude, and power supplied to any electronics on-board.

$$P = \frac{1}{\eta}(\kappa T w + \frac{1}{2}\rho(\sum_{k=1}^{3} C_{D_k} A_k)v_a^3 + \kappa_2(g\sum_{k=1}^{3} m_k)^{1.5} + \kappa_3(g\sum_{k=1}^{3} m_k)^{0.5}v_a^2) + \frac{P_{avio}}{\eta_c}, \tag{4}$$

where κ, κ_2, κ_3 are constants, w is the downwash coefficient, and η_c is the battery charging efficiency [5].

2.5   Tseng Energy Model

The Tseng energy model differs from the other energy models as it consists of a nine-term nonlinear regression model created from collected data [10]. This model was created from horizontal and vertical speeds and accelerations, payload, mass, and wind speed data gathered from empirical testing. The drone used for data collection was a DJI Matrice 100 and tested for payloads of 0, 0.3, and 0.6 kg. The drone used for testing consisted of three experiments that recorded the drone's ability to hover without any input or movement, ability to climb and descend, and ability to move horizontally. The model assesses the impact of motion through these tests and the payload weights to create the model. A 3DR Solo drone was also used to create an alternative version of the model for smaller sized drones with the expression for energy consumption shown below. Note that the model is essentially a function of payload mass m_3 and the airspeed v_a [5].

$$P = -2.595v_a + 0.197m_3 + 251.7. \tag{5}$$

3   Data-Driven Model and Proposed LSTM Architecture

In this section, we introduce the data-driven model to fit the realistic dataset [12]. We first present the problem statement for the model fitting task, then we present details for the dataset, and finally we demonstrate the proposed architecture.

3.1   Problem Statement

The key problem that we are considering here is to build an energy consumption model which can take a sequence of input feature data from a drone and predict the corresponding energy consumption of the drone as output. More specifically, the input data essentially captures the characteristics, dynamics and environmental context, e.g., wind speed, payload, ground speed, for the drone under test in a given scenario.

Mathematically, let $F_t \in \mathbb{R}^N$ be the feature vector consisting of the N features for the drone at time t. Let $E_t \in \mathbb{R}$ denote the energy consumption of the drone at time t. For a given time window $\mathcal{T} := \{1, 2, \ldots, T\}$, our objective is to find a learning function $H(.)$ which is able to address the following problem:

$$\min_{H} \quad \sum_{t \in \mathcal{T}} (E_t - \hat{E}_t)^2 \tag{6}$$
$$\text{s.t.} \quad \hat{E}_t = H(F_t)$$

where $\hat{E}_t$ denotes the predicted energy consumption of the drone at time t with respect to the input feature vector F_t.

3.2   Experimental Dataset

The experimental dataset used in this work is from the paper [12]. The dataset presents some very recent energy consumption information for a DJI Matrice 100 drone that consists of a total of 195 test flights with variations in payload, speed, and altitude. A total number of 28 features were recorded onboard which were taken from the battery state, Global Positioning System (GPS), Inertial Measurement Unit (IMU), and the wind measurement unit. A total number of 21 features was included from the dataset in order to create our energy prediction model, the details of which are summarized as follows:

- Wind Speed: Speed of wind recorded by the anemometer in meters per second (m/s).
- Wind Angle: Angle of the airspeed recorded by the anemometer with respect to north in (degrees).
- Position X, Y, Z: Longitude, latitude and altitude recorded by the GPS (degrees).
- Orientation X, Y, Z, W: Orientation as recorded by the IMU in (quarternions).
- Velocity X, Y, Z: Ground speed recorded by the GPS and IMU in meters per second (m/s).
- Angular X, Y, Z: Angular velocity recorded by the IMU in radians per second (rad/s).
- Linear Acceleration X, Y, Z: Linear acceleration recorded by the IMU in meters per second squared (m/s^2).
- Speed: Input ground speed before flight in meters per second (m/s).
- Payload: Payload mass attached to the drone prior to a test in grams (g).
- Altitude: Input altitude the drone rises to before following flight route in meters (m).

3.3   System Architecture

To find out the learning function H, we propose the LSTM architecture which is shown in the Fig. 1 below. Specifically, the proposed LSTM architecture consists of two bidirectional LSTM layers stacked together with a dropout layer attached to the second LSTM layer before connecting to a dense layer for output. Some details for model and network setup are reported as follows:

- The activation function used for the output layer was a tangent function.
- The number of hidden cells for each LSTM layer was defined as 128.
- The Adam optimizer was chosen for model training.
- The proposed model was assembled using Keras at the backend.

In order to achieve the optimal performance for energy prediction using the proposed architecture, we considered dropout, batch size and learning rate as hyperparameters for model tuning through grid search. For each setting of the hyperparameters, a 5-fold cross-validation was carried out on the dataset to evaluate the performance of the resulting model. The best set of parameters which results in the minimum averaged mean square error (MAE) was chosen as the optimal hyperparameters for the proposed model. Table 1 presents our results for the hyperparamters tuning in different settings. We also present the calculation results for the root mean square error (RMSE) in the table for reference, and it can be seen that the optimal hyperparameters for the model are presented in the third row of the table, and this finding is consistent with both performance metrics, i.e., averaged RMSE and averaged MAE. Finally, the training and validation loss under the optimal configuration are shown in Fig. 2, where two curves are converging gradually in a few number of epochs.

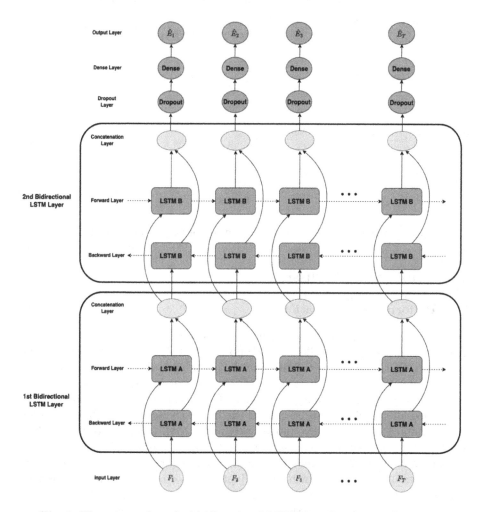

Fig. 1. The proposed stacked bidirectional LSTM-based system architecture.

Table 1. Hyperparameter tuning for the proposed model

Dropout	Learning rate	Batch size	Avg. RMSE	Avg. MAE
0.2	0.001	128	47.4891	5.7213
0.2	0.0001	128	50.7283	6.0008
0.5	0.001	128	46.9918	5.6942
0.5	0.0001	128	48.3828	5.8538
0.5	0.01	128	63.1021	6.8779
0.5	0.001	64	51.3855	5.9844

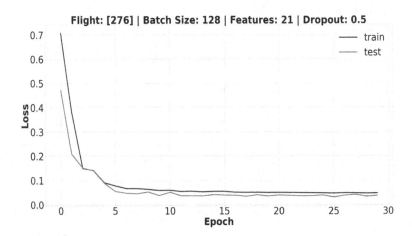

Fig. 2. Training and validation loss curves using the optimal configuration.

4   Results and Discussion

4.1   Performance Evaluation

In this section, we present our experimental results using the five prominent mathematical models as well as the proposed LSTM model in its optimal configuration. Our objective is to illustrate the differences of model prediction performance based on the realistic dataset [12], and reveal the superiority of the model performance using our proposed LSTM-based architecture. Specifically, we applied all models to a specific flight (flight 276) which had not been used for model training. While the five models originated from different studies, unified notation between parameters was used for fair comparison similar to the approach used in [5]. Input parameters from the dataset were airspeed and the weight components of the drone, which were adapted to use in all models. The prediction results for different models under test are illustrated in Fig. 3 and Fig. 4, where Fig. 3 compared the performance for all mathematical models and Fig. 4 compares performance for the LSTM-based model only. The key performance metrics are also summarised and reported in Table 2 for ease of comparison.

Table 2. Energy model comparison

Author	Avg. RMSE	Avg. MAE
D'Andrea	745.9512	21.7650
D'Andrea (With Headwind)	919.2040	23.7520
Dorling	365.1678	18.3391
Stolaroff	291.6590	16.2421
Kirchstein	275.8223	13.8690
Tseng	131.3750	9.5263
Proposed LSTM model	36.2770	4.9080

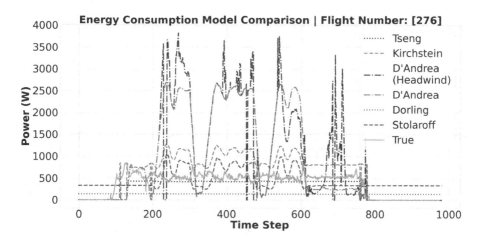

Fig. 3. Comparison of the five mathematical models for energy consumption.

Among the five fundamental models, the D'Andrea model performs poorest with the highest averaged RMSE found for the model variant with the headwind being factored in. In contrast, the Tseng energy model achieves the best prediction result in that both performance metrics, i.e., averaged RMSE and averaged MAE, are lowest. This conclusion can also be further validated in Fig. 3 where the Tseng model maintains a flat prediction throughout the duration of the evaluation which is clearly closest to the ground truth. However, none of these fundamental models achieves a promising result when compared with the proposed LSTM model where the averaged MAE is found as low as 4.908. In practice, this simply implies that on average the predicted energy only incurs 4.9080 W bias compared with the realistic energy consumption.

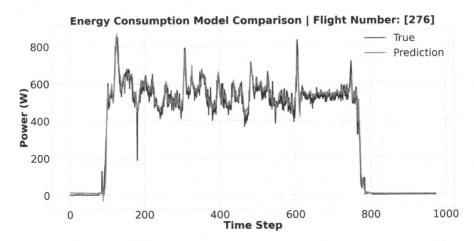

Fig. 4. Comparison of the proposed LSTM model with the ground truth.

4.2 Sensitivity Analysis

To further illustrate some interpretability of the trained LSTM model, we now carry out a sensitivity analysis for the learned model. In particular, we are interested in answering the following question, that is how the altitude, payload and speed as input features can contribute to the energy consumption for drones. Our results are shown in Table 3 and Fig. 5. More specifically, the divergent bar chart in Fig. 5 takes intervals at steps and half steps, where steps are taken as the minimum or maximum value of the input parameter, and half steps are the midpoints from the mean. Table 3 shows the steps taken for each feature of interest. Figure 5 shows payload contributing the most towards change in overall power consumption followed by speed and altitude. Interestingly, the figure also demonstrates that the speed factor is negatively correlated to power consumption of the drone while the altitude factor can positively contribute to the power consumption. Such insight on speed is consistent with what we found in the Tseng model where airspeed is also negatively correlated with power consumption.

Table 3. Power Consumption Sensitivity Data Table

	Step-1	Step-1/2	Step 0	Step+1/2	Step+1
Altitude (m)	25.00	43.75	62.50	81.25	100.00
Payload (g)	0	187.50	375.00	562.50	750.00
Speed (m/s)	4.00	6.00	8.00	10.00	12.00

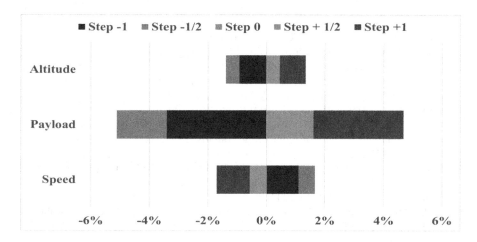

Fig. 5. Sensitivity of power consumption to key features

5 Conclusion

In this paper, we propose a learning-based approach using the LSTM-based deep learning architecture for accurately modelling energy consumptions of drones. We have revealed the efficacy of the proposed model by comparing its performance with the five fundamental mathematical based energy models using a realistic dataset that can be publicly accessed in [12]. Finally, we have also implemented a sensitivity analysis on the trained model with a view to provide some insights and explainability for the fine-tuned model. To conclude, we believe that the work presented in this paper is an important step towards using a data-driven method to understand energy consumption pattern for drones. However, we note that one obvious limitation in our current work is that the proposed deep learning model has not been validated comprehensively across different energy datasets. This challenge will be addressed as part of our future work. In addition, we shall investigate the effectiveness of using a federated learning based framework [17] to further improve accuracy of the proposed model.

Acknowledgements. The author Carlos Muli would like to thank the ide3a team for kindly accommodating a scholarship which has made this research work possible. This work has also emanated from research supported in part by Science Foundation Ireland under Grant Number SFI/12/RC/2289_P2, and the Entwine Research Centre at Dublin City University.

References

1. Merkert, R., Bushell, J.: Managing the drone revolution: a systematic literature review into the current use of airborne drones and future strategic directions for their effective control. J. Air Transp. Manag. **89**, 101929 (2020)

2. Zaheer, Z., Usmani, A., Khan, E., Qadeer, M.A.: Aerial surveillance system using UAV In: Thirteenth International Conference on Wireless and Optical Communications Networks (WOCN), pp. 1–7. IEEE (2016)
3. Thibbotuwawa, A., Nielsen, P., Zbigniew, B., Bocewicz, G.: Energy consumption in unmanned aerial vehicles: a review of energy consumption models and their relation to the UAV routing. In: ISAT 2018. AISC, vol. 853, pp. 173–184. Springer, Cham (2019). https://doi.org/10.1007/978-3-319-99996-8_16
4. Hu, S., Wu, Q., Wang, X.: Energy management and trajectory optimization for UAV-enabled legitimate monitoring systems. IEEE Trans. Wireless Commun. **20**(1), 142–155 (2020)
5. Zhang, J., Campbell, J.F., Sweeney, D.C., II., Hupman, A.C.: Energy consumption models for delivery drones a comparison and assessment. Transp. Res. Part D: Transp. Environ. **90**, 102668 (2021)
6. Dorling, K., Heinrichs, J., Messier, G.G., Magierowski, S.: Vehicle routing problems for drone delivery. IEEE Trans. Syst. Man Cybern. Syst. **47**(1), 70–85 (2016)
7. Figliozzi, M.A.: Lifecycle modeling and assessment of unmanned aerial vehicles (drones) co2e emissions. Transp. Res. Part D Transp. Environ. **57**, 251–261 (2017)
8. Stolaroff, J.K., Samaras, C., O'Neill, E.R., Lubers, A., Mitchell, A.S., Ceperley, D.: Energy use and life cycle greenhouse gas emissions of drones for commercial package delivery. Nat. Commun. **9**(1), 1–13 (2018)
9. Kirschstein, T.: Comparison of energy demands of drone-based and ground-based parcel delivery services. Transp. Res. Part D Transp. Environ. **78**, 102209 (2020)
10. Tseng, C.-M., Chau, C.-K., Elbassioni, K.M., Khonji, M.: Flight tour planning with recharging optimization for battery-operated autonomous drones, CoRR, abs/1703.10049 (2017)
11. Prasetia, A. S., Wai, R.-J., Wen, Y.-L., Wang, Y.-K.: Mission-based energy consumption prediction of multirotor UAV. IEEE Access **7**, 55–63 (2019)
12. Rodrigues, T.A., et al.: In-flight positional and energy use data set of a DJI matrice 100 quadcopter for small package delivery. Sci. Data **8**(1), 1–8 (2021)
13. Fu, Z., Yu, J., Xie, G., Chen, Y., Mao, Y.: A heuristic evolutionary algorithm of UAV path planning. Wireless Commun. Mob. Comput. **2018**, 1–11 (2018)
14. Modares, J., Ghanei, F., Mastronarde, N., Dantu, K.: UB-ANC planner: Energy efficient coverage path planning with multiple drones. In: IEEE International Conference on Robotics and Automation (ICRA), pp. 6182–6189. IEEE (2017)
15. Çabuk, U.C., Tosun, M., Jacobsen, R.H., Dagdeviren, O.: A holistic energy model for drones. In: 28th Signal Processing and Communications Applications Conference (SIU), pp. 1–4. IEEE (2020)
16. D'Andrea, R.: Guest editorial can drones deliver? IEEE Trans. Autom. Sci. Eng. **11**(3), 647–648 (2014)
17. Liu, M.: Fed-BEV: a federated learning framework for modelling energy consumption of battery electric vehicles. In: IEEE 94th Vehicular Technology Conference (VTC2021-Fall), pp. 1–7. IEEE (2021)

ConQeng: A Middleware for Quality of Context Aware Selection, Measurement and Validation

Kanaka Sai Jagarlamudi$^{(\boxtimes)}$ (ID), Arkady Zaslavsky (ID), Seng W. Loke (ID), Alireza Hassani (ID), and Alexey Medvedev (ID)

School of Information Technology, Deakin University, Geelong, Australia
{kjagarlamudi,arkady.zaslavsky,seng.loke,ali.hassani,
alexey.medvedev}@deakin.edu.au

Abstract. A set of quality metrics (e.g., timeliness, completeness) together represent the Quality of Context (QoC); their values determine the usability of context to context consumers (IoT applications). Therefore, obtaining adequate 'QoC from the context providers (context sources) represents a significant research challenge. This paper presents a framework called conQeng that addresses such a challenge through novel approaches in QoC-aware selection, QoC measurement and validation. ConQeng selects the potential context providers that deliver an adequate QoC during runtime, assesses their performance - for further selection, and transfers QoC-assured context to the context management platforms (CMPs). We have implemented conQeng in a simulated scenario involving autonomous cars, marketing service agencies as context consumers, and thermal and video cameras as context providers. The results demonstrate that it outperforms three heuristic approaches in reducing context acquisition cost and improving effectiveness and performance efficiency while obtaining adequate QoC.

Keywords: Context management platforms · QoC-aware selection · QoC measurement · Selection framework

1 Introduction

Current IoT applications collect and infer raw data from data sources (e.g., sensors), through which they analyse situations and deliver relevant services to the end-users. Such inferred IoT data is referred to as 'context'. The work in [1] defined it as '*any information that is used to characterise the situation of an entity*' (entity represents a real-word item). IoT applications that use context and the data sources at the entities that generate context are known as the context consumers and context providers, respectively. CMPs emerged to abstract and mediate between context consumers and providers to quash concerns in IoT environments (e.g., context provider's availability and privacy). Through CMPs, context consumers can publish, monitor and query the context without discovering the potential providers. Most advanced CMPs possess similar architecture

A. González-Vidal et al. (Eds.): GIoTS 2022, LNCS 13533, pp. 211–225, 2022.
https://doi.org/10.1007/978-3-031-20936-9_17

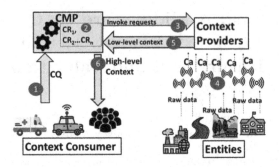

Fig. 1. Overview of context-aware IoT environment; numbers indicate the data flow among the involved systems.

and functionalities [2]. As Fig. 1 depicts, the CMP, associated context consumers and providers form a context-aware IoT environment.

The data flow in a context-aware IoT environment occurs as in Fig. 1. In step 1, a context consumer conveys its requirements to CMP through a context query. Such queries are pre-defined in context consumers by forming them using languages such as 'Context Definition Query Language' [3]. In step 2, the CMP parses it as context requests (CR); each CR contains the entity details, respective context attribute and Quality of Context (QoC) requirements. The context attributes (Ca) represent the entity's specific characteristic (e.g., temperature), also called low-level context. The QoC was defined as *'any information that describes the quality of information that is used as context'* [4]. In simple terms, QoC represents the quality of a context attribute. In step 3, the CMP discovers, selects, and invokes the relevant context provider for each CR. The invoked providers then collect and send the context attributes to the CMP in steps 4 and 5. Next, the CMP aggregates them as high-level context, representing the entity's inferred situation. Finally, the CMP completes the context query by delivering it to the consumer in step 6.

Metrics such as timeliness and completeness—to name a few, represent the QoC of a context attribute. Context providers' owners guarantee such metrics during registration with the CMP. The model in [5] selects appropriate context providers by matching such guarantees with the context request's QoC requirements. Proactively selecting context providers that deliver adequate QoC is known as QoC-aware selection. Most QoC-aware selection models rely on context providers' design time characteristics (e.g., hardware, QoC guarantees), which are vulnerable to runtime inconsistencies (e.g., faulty hardware), leading to selection uncertainties. Using QoC measurement models alongside the QoC-aware selection models handles such uncertainties, as they measure the QoC metrics and discard inappropriate context responses. However, such a system requires re-selecting the context providers when obtaining inadequate QoC, affecting the cost and CMP's credibility. Therefore, a CMP requires a QoC-aware selection model that selects the context providers based on their runtime QoC outcomes.

Furthermore, QoC-measurement models rely on context-response annotations to measure QoC metrics. For instance, using 'timestamp at which context is generated' measures the 'timeliness'. However, these models limit measuring the 'correctness'—a QoC metric representing context accuracy. This metric's adequacy heavily relies on context providers' vulnerability to the associated entity's situations (e.g., weather patterns). Such uncertainty due to external factors hinders the provisioning of correctness guarantees on the service level agreements (SLAs). Besides, annotating the context with the ground truth to measure correctness requires human intervention in the IoT environment. Hence, the related work (e.g., [6]) is bound to measure its probable values instead of exact correctness. Nevertheless, considering that the context consumer's decision-making relies on the correctness of the context: a QoC-aware selection approach must also include the provision of adequate correctness as a selection requirement.

This paper presents a framework called conQeng (context Quality engine) that performs QoC-aware selection, QoC measurement and validation. These processes respectively enable appropriate context providers selection, their runtime performance assessment, and determination of the contexts' alignment to complete context requests in CMPs. ConQeng relies on two metrics associated with context providers: overall QoC (or 'OQoC') and 'relative reputation-value' (or 'RR-value') to perform QoC-aware selection. The OQoC and RR-value refer to the context provider's rate in delivering QoC aligning with its guarantees and the correct context to a particular context consumer. ConQeng uses a novel feedback-based approach to assess RR-value. Correctness requirements vary based on the context consumer; for instance, consumers related to emergency services may require higher correctness than recreational services. Therefore, conQeng obtains feedback on correctness delivered by the invoked providers from the context consumers; then builds context providers' reputation (RR-value) exclusive to each context consumer type.

This paper's organisation is as follows: Sect. 2 provides a motivating scenario elaborating our contributions' significance. Section 3 presents related work. Section 4 discusses key definitions, conQeng's overview and functioning. Section 5 discusses implementation and simulation details. Section 6 discusses the evaluation procedure and results. Section 7 presents conclusion and future work.

2 Motivating Scenario

Using the context 'pedestrian count' at locations, the autonomous cabs (Didi aims to launch autonomous cabs [7]) and marketing service agencies can analyse driving conditions and advertising opportunities. Currently, the sensors deployed at entities (e.g., busy streets) in major metropolitan cities (e.g., Melbourne) generate the pedestrian count, which the CMPs can access through APIs [8]. Nevertheless, the context consumers vary in requirements for QoC and cost of context. For instance, an autonomous cab would require a context with a higher QoC whilst not concerning cost, but a marketing service would be more concerned with cost. As discussed below, for fulfilling such varying expectations

Fig. 2. Use-case– Cc 1 and Cc 2 are the marketing service agency and autonomous car respectively. Crowd icons indicate entities, and cameras to their left and right indicate video and thermal cameras. Blue and yellow arrows represent the autonomous car's main and alternative route to reach 'Cinema nova' (the destination). (Color figure online)

requires context providers with various QoC and cost characteristics that produce similar context.

Popular devices for counting people include image processing video [9] and thermal [10] cameras. The video camera has lower context cost due to the lower initial (device) and maintenance (power consumption) costs; simultaneously, their data quality is more vulnerable to external factors (e.g., weather). On the other hand, thermal cameras have a higher cost and produce context with a higher QoC. Therefore, deploying these context providers at each entity suffices the requirements of context consumers mentioned above. Assuming that such deployment is in place, we have formed the use-case in Fig. 2.

Use-case: The autonomous cab (Cc 2) aims to reach Cinema Nova (destination icon) by selecting one of two available routes: (i) The main route (blue arrow) - a shorter route with more crowded entities; (ii) an alternative route (yellow arrow) - a longer route with less crowded entities. The cab requires the pedestrian count from entities on these routes to find the route with the shortest travel time. Concurrently, the marketing service agency requires such context to determine the advertising opportunities.

Each entity contains an image processing video and a thermal camera that relays the pedestrian count to the CMP upon request. Consider that timeliness, completeness, representation, and correctness are required QoC metrics for both consumers. These metrics define the context's value regarding time, number of context attributes, representation format, and accuracy. Context providers' internal factors affect all metrics except correctness. For instance, network latency delays the context delivery, affecting timeliness. These metrics' outcomes are within context providers' control; hence they guarantee these metrics' to the CMP through SLAs. However, despite such guarantees, these metrics may vary during runtime (e.g., due to malicious context providers). Furthermore, the correctness is omitted from such guarantees because, as Sect. 1 discusses, the context providers' external factors also affect it. We made the following assertions on the given context providers' correctness outcomes based on their sensing characteristics: The thermal camera's sensing approach (thermal imaging) produces higher correctness than a video camera; because data accuracy in such an approach is less vulnerable to external factors (e.g., adverse weather). On the other hand, a video camera produces relatively lower correctness as it relies on regular images; their accuracy is more vulnerable to external factors.

A CMP would not know the context providers' runtime QoC outcomes, and the context consumers' required QoC and cost vary. Therefore, a CMP must perform QoC-aware selection (including cost as a factor) to select and invoke the context providers that satisfy each context consumer's requirements during runtime. Furthermore, it should perform QoC measurement and validation followed by QoC-aware selection to ensure adequate QoC acquisition. These processes measure and compare the QoC metrics in context responses with context requests' requirements and discard the responses with inadequate QoC. Besides this, the QoC metrics in context responses represent its provider's near real-time performance - thus, their aggregate can be used as a metric for QoC-aware selection. Therefore, conQeng enables the functionalities mentioned above in CMPs to obtain adequate context responses in the metrics in (e.g., timeliness) and out (e.g., correctness) of context providers' control.

3   Related Work

According to Li et al. [11], most CMPs exhibit high-level mechanisms (e.g., interoperability and fault tolerance); despite such advancement, they lack standard models related to QoC. This section reviews the current QoC-aware selection and QoC measurement models—discussing their applicability in CMPs.

The popular QoC-aware selection models are based on reputation in social IoT (SIoT), design time QoC characteristics, and filtering incoming context streams. The works in [12,13] discuss the reputation-based QoC-aware selection models in SIoT, where the context consumers maintain context providers' reputations, indicating their rate of delivering adequate QoC. The context consumers find suitable providers in their repositories; upon not finding them, they rely on other context consumers' recommendations. However, CMPs abstract the context providers and consumers, limiting the implementation of SIoT based models. Furthermore, the model in [12] maintains the context providers' reputations at the CMP and context consumer levels. Therefore, the context consumers rely on the CMP upon not finding the suitable context provider through their peers. However, the reputation at the CMP level is assessed based on feedback from various context consumer types—making it coarse-grained. On the other hand, the acceptance levels for correctness vary based on the consumer type; thus, this model may invoke unsuitable providers.

The work in [5] discussed the QoC-aware selection models based on design time QoC characteristics; works in [14,15] discuss the models based on filtering incoming context streams. Both these models select the context providers based on the match of context providers' QoC characteristics (e.g., hardware, QoC guarantees) with the context requests' QoC requirements. However, the model in [5] invokes one context provider at a time, then measures the QoC, and invokes the next provider upon obtaining inadequate QoC. At the same time, the models in [14,15] invoke all the context providers that possess the required QoC characteristics, measure and filter the context responses with inadequate QoC. These models' repetitive and redundant context provider invocations lead to time and cost-inefficiencies.

Popular QoC measurement models include OWL-DL ontology [16], QoCIM Meta-Model [17], and other models [5,14]. These models measure the QoC in a low-level context using annotations; the measurement outcomes indicate the QoC metrics' alignment with the context request. However, due to abstraction between the actors, the context providers negotiate their QoC guarantees and cost with CMP. So, the QoC should be measured to determine its alignment with provided guarantees - to measure the context acquisition cost (as the cost of context depends on SLA satisfaction rate [18]); then, the context should be validated for compliance with the context request. Furthermore, works in [6,19] have discussed the approaches to measure context correctness. Both models are bound to measure the probable correctness. The model in [6] uses Bayesian theory and [19] analyses the context produced by similar context providers. The 'correctness' in the model [6] indicates the probability of the event represented by the context to occur. Therefore, it does not show the accuracy of the information in such an event, which is prime for decision-making using context. Furthermore, the model in [19] requires the invocation of multiple providers to measure correctness—causing cost-inefficiencies.

4   ConQeng's Design and Process

As Fig. 3 depicts, conQeng contains QoC-aware selection, QoC measurement and validation modules. Components in the former module include the Initiator, Selector, Selection Repository, Reputation and RR processors. The latter contains the QoC Evaluator and RR Evaluator. ConQeng interacts with the CMP's processes and context providers for functioning. The yellow and grey arrows represent the data collected/sent by conQeng's components and CMPs processes (represented by gear icon).

Key Definitions. The following are the external concepts related to conQeng's functioning. (i) Context consumer type: a specific type of context-aware IoT application. (ii) Context request: as Sect. 1 defines, a context request

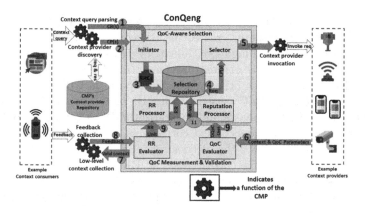

Fig. 3. Process flow in conCQeng (yellow arrows) occurred among its components and with the CMPs processes. The CMPs data flow with the context consumers and providers, which is relevant to conCQeng (grey arrows). (Color figure online)

contains the context requirements. (iii) SLA: a contract between the context provider and the CMP; containing the context provider's service details. Our previous work in [18] discusses SLA templates containing three components: Actors, Service Description, and QoC and CoC. The first component contains the CMP and context provider's identities. The next component contains the entity (e.g., a place—represented by geographic coordinates) and generated context attribute(s) details. The last component contains the QoC guarantees (e.g., 'timeliness': '2–4 s', 'representation': 'JSON'), and cost of context per response. (iv) Feedback: context consumer's report, indicating context correctness adequacy.

The following are conQeng's internal concepts. (i) RR-collection: the data indicating potential context providers' adequate QoC delivery rate for a context request related to a particular context consumer type. Each RR-collection is structured by a unique context request and context providers' SLAs that meet QoC requirements. The following metrics indicate each context provider's adequate QoC delivery rate in RR-collections: sum of OQoC units, total number of OQoC units, sum of RR-units, total number of RR-units, R-value, RR-value, and RR. Here, 'OQoC' (overall QoC) indicates the average QoC guarantees fulfilled by a context provider. Further, 'RR-unit' (relative reputation-unit) indicates the correctness adequacy in context to a particular context consumer type. Hence, the total number and sum of OQoC and RR-units indicate the count of OQoC and RR-units related to a context provider and those values' respective sum. R-value (reputation-value) and RR-value indicates the context provider's OQoC delivery rate and the satisfaction rate of a particular context consumer type with the correctness delivered by the context provider. Finally, RR indicates the context provider's rate in delivering adequate OQoC and correctness.

Process Flow in ConQeng. Each of conQeng's components possess a significant functionality: (i) Initiator creates the RR-collections. (ii) Selector selects the context providers with a high QoC adequacy delivery rate for requests, from which it invokes cost-effective context providers. (iii) Selection Repository holds the RR collections, on which other components perform CRUD operations for QoC-aware selection and QoC measurement. (iv) QoC Evaluator measures the QoC metrics in context responses and generates the OQoC units. (v) RR Evaluator collects feedback to assess context correctness and generates RR-units. (vi) Reputation Processor assesses the metrics related to OQoC (vii) RR Processor assesses the metrics related to correctness, and RR.

The process flow among components occurs, as shown in Fig. 3. The CMP sends the context requests (CRs) and suitable context providers (CPs) for each CR to the Initiator in steps 1 and 2, respectively. For each CR, in step 3, the Initiator checks for an RR-collection containing a similar CR from the requesting context consumer type. When such a collection is not found, the Initiator creates a new RR collection; structuring it with the context consumer's id, CR, and suitable context providers' SLAs. Alternatively, on finding a similar RR-collection, the Initiator updates it with the SLAs of context providers not present in the collection. In either case, the metrics related to new context providers' correctness delivery rate (sum and total RR-units) are initiated as '0' - requiring the context consumer's feedback for their assessment. However, their metrics related to OQoC (sum and total OQoC units) are derived from their existing values in other RR-collections or assigned as '0' - for those non-existent in other RR-collections. In step 4, the Selector finds the relevant RR collections for the CRs by matching the context consumer's id and elements in CRs with the same elements in RR-collections. Then, selects the context providers with the highest RR from each matched RR-collection. In step 5, the Selector issues those context providers with a low cost for invocation.

In step 6, from each invoked context provider, the QoC Evaluator obtains context and respective QoC parameters (e.g., timestamp of context generation); using them and the respective provider's SLA, it computes the QoC metrics values. Discussing approaches to compute QoC metrics is beyond this paper's scope. Currently, we are using the approaches discussed in our previous work [18] to compute timeliness, completeness and representation; obtaining these metrics' in the range 0 to 1 - this scale ranges from violation of a QoC guarantee to its complete fulfilment. Furthermore, the QoC Evaluator measures the OQoC using (1). The work in [20] measures OQoC as the weighted average of QoC metrics, where the context consumer specifies the weights. However, OQoC in our work represents the compliance rate of QoC metrics with their guarantees; as these guarantees have similar significance, defining weights is inconsequential, so we have modified OQoC as (1). After measuring OQoC, the QoC Evaluator validates the context; by checking for QoC metrics' miss-match with their requirements. In case of detecting such a miss-match, the context will be discarded, and the framework re-initiates the selection process to replace it with adequate context. Finally, a valid context is delivered to the CMP in step 7.

$$\mathbf{OQoC} = \sum_{i=1}^{n} QoC_i/n \qquad (1)$$

In (1) 'QoC_i' represents the ith QoC metric, 'n' represents the number of QoC metrics and i ranges from 1 to n.

Upon CMP processing valid context and delivering the resultant high-level context to the consumer, the RR Evaluator receives the consumer's feedback from the CMP in step 8. For each context attribute, the context consumer provides the feedback as '0' or '1' - indicating the correctness adequacy (where '0' and '1' indicate the correct and incorrect context attribute, respectively). In step 9, the RR Processor receives such feedback as RR-units; simultaneously, the Reputation processor receives the OQoC-units. These components compute the RR of each context provider in steps 10 and 11 as follows. First, the Reputation processor assesses the R-values using (2); the RR processor assesses the RR-value using (3). The Reputation Processor then computes the RR using (4). Finally, the RR processor re-initiates the selection procedure when receiving negative feedback on context correctness. Re-selection is performed based on the consumer's acceptance of a new context after the context delivery.

$$\mathbf{R\text{-}value} = ((\sum_{i=1}^{n1} OQoC) + OQoC_{new})/(n1 + 1) \qquad (2)$$

$$\mathbf{RR\text{-}value} = ((\sum_{j=1}^{n2} RR - unit) + RR - unit_{new})/(n2 + 1) \qquad (3)$$

$$\mathbf{RR} = (R - value + RR - value)/2 \qquad (4)$$

The R-value and RR apply to all RR-collections that contain the invoked context provider. Whereas RR-value applies to the RR-collection from which the context provider is selected, i.e., the RR-collection between requesting context consumer type and the invoked context provider. The $\sum_{i=1}^{n1} OQoC$ and $\sum_{j=1}^{n2} RR - unit$ indicate the sum of provider's existing (historic) OQoC and RR-units. $OQoC_{new}$ and $RR - unit_{new}$ indicates newly assessed OQoC and RR-unit. The i and j indicate an OQoC unit and RR-unit, $n1$ and $n2$ represent the total number of existing OQoC units and RR-units respectively.

5   Implementation and Simulation Setup

We have developed conQeng's processing components for all modules using Express.JS and implemented the Selection Repository on Mongo DB. ConQeng performs the data transfer via the REST API. We have also developed a React.Js based front-end application to visualise conQeng's context and QoC-related outcomes (e.g., OQoC, RR) and provide inputs (e.g., feedback) to it. We have simulated the use case in Sect. 2 using the 'IoT-data simulator' [21]. It allows customising the data schema (create or use existing data sets), specifying data push-intervals, and target system to deliver such data. The data delivered to a target system from a defined data schema is a 'session'. We have used six types of sessions: two each to produce the autonomous car and marketing service agency's context requests, produce thermal and video cameras' SLAs, and generate these providers' respective context responses. Table 1 depicts the data schema of context requests and SLAs in their sessions.

Table 1. Data schema and the values in the simulated context requests and context providers' SLAs. The first row and column represent the session types and the contained data attributes, respectively. Each field indicates the data value generated for the attribute represented by its row; in the session type represented by its column.

Data/Sess	AC CR	MSA CR	TC SLA	VC SLA
Cc or Cp	AC	MSA	TC	VC
Entity	$E_{i..5}$	$E_{i..5}$	$E_{i..5}$	$E_{i..5}$
Ca	[CP(P),CP(R)]	[CP(P),CP(R)]	[CP(P),CP(R)]	[CP(P),CP(R)]
QoC	**requ:**	**requ:**	**gaur:**	**gaur:**
T(age)	5 sec	10 sec	2–3 sec	2–3 sec
Comp	[Ca_1: 0.3,Ca_2: 0.7]	[Ca_1: 1,Ca_2: 1]	[Ca_1,Ca_2]	[Ca_1,Ca_2]
Rep	CO: JSON,	CO: JSON	CO: JSON,	CO: JSON,
	[Ca_1:Int, Ca_2:Int]	[Ca_1:Int, Ca_2:Int]	[Ca_1:Int, Ca_2:Int]	[Ca_1:Int, Ca_2:Int]
Corr or Cost	90%	80%	10 units	5 units

In Table 1, AC CR and MSA CR represent the session type for autonomous car and marketing service agency's context requests. TC SLA and VC SLA represent the session type for thermal and video camera SLAs. The column values represent the data generated by these session types for respective attributes.

Replicating the use case in Sect. 2 - we have created five sessions for each context consumer to produce context requests related to the entities in Fig. 2. As Table 1 depicts, for the data attribute Cc (context consumer), the sessions related to AC CR produce values 'AC', whereas the MSA CR's sessions produce value 'MSA', representing the autonomous car and marketing service agency, respectively. E_i represents the Entity; the value of i ranges from 1 to 5 (as there are five entities) depending on the Entity represented by the session. 'CP(P)' and 'CP(R)' indicate the Context attributes (Ca) 'count of pedestrians on the pavement' and 'count of pedestrians on the road'. Furthermore, the sessions produce 5 and 10 s as individual context age requirements (timeliness parameter) in AC CR and MSA CR. Here, age represents the time the context must be delivered after production. Next, they produce 90 and 80% as AC CRs and MSA CRs' respective correctness requirements. Finally, AC CRs produce CP(R) with a higher weight, as this context attribute is curtailed in driver and pedestrian safety in autonomous cars. Whereas MSA CRs produce both context attributes with equal weight. Hence, we defined individual completeness requirements for CP(P) and CP(R) as 0.3 and 0.7 for AV CRs, and 1 each for MSA CRs. Lastly, the CMP required the context responses in JSON format; and the contained context attributes as the integer values. Hence they produce CO as 'JSON'; 'Int' for Ca_1 (i.e., CP(P)) and Ca_2 (i.e., CP(R)).

We have initiated five sessions for each context provider to generate their respective SLAs related to the entities. As Table 1 depicts, the SLAs are generated with the values for entity and Ca to match with the context requests. The QoC guarantees contain the age as 2–3 s, two context attributes CP(P) and CP(R) as the completeness guarantees, and JSON as context responses representation in which the Ca1 and Ca2 are represented as integers. Thus, these guarantees align with the context requests QoC requirements to support the RR-collection initialisation. However, the simulated QoC outcomes in context responses vary during runtime.

6   Evaluation and Results

We aim to evaluate conQeng's efficiency and effectiveness in obtaining adequate QoC compared to existing models, which are discussed in Sect. 3. The simulation shows that (i) conQeng effectively obtains adequate QoC than 'naive selection' models that select context providers based on the design time QoC characteristics. 'Effectiveness' is obtaining adequate QoC without having to re-select the context providers; (ii) It delivers the correct context while reducing context-acquisition cost over general reputation (assessed using feedback from different consumer types) based models; (iii) It exhibits higher performance than filtering approaches.

We created the sessions to generate the context responses containing the context provider's id, entity details, context and QoC parameters, and cost of context to evaluate our aims. Furthermore, the generated QoC parameters vary in the range we define. The correctness and cost vary based on the context provider's type. Moreover, conQeng assesses the RR using feedback on the correctness alignment with the ground truth in a real-world deployment. Hence, we have initiated other sessions that generate the ground truth for providers' context responses to generate such feedback.

To realise the aim (i): we produced both consumers' context requests for all entities and SLAs of related context providers, and performed the selection using conQeng and the naive selection model. Then, we collected the results of OQoC and QoC validity from the invoked providers prior to these models re-selecting the context provider when obtaining inadequate QoC. Furthermore, RR maintains the context provider's reputation exclusive to each context consumer type to address the limitation (as discussed in Sect. 2) in general reputation-based approaches that affect the context acquisition cost. To demonstrate the cost-effectiveness obtained by RR while attaining the correctness adequacy, i.e., to realise aim (ii): producing more MSA CRs than AC CRs, we performed the selection using RR and general reputation models. We produced the context responses with consistent QoC outcomes with the given guarantees and degraded context correctness. The level of such degradation varied based on the context provider:

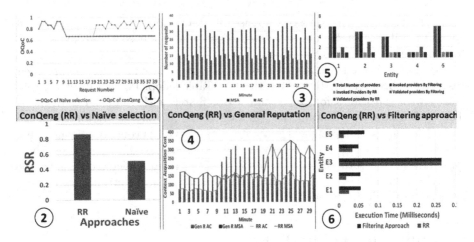

Fig. 4. Results - comparing conQeng with native, general reputation and filtering approaches in terms of effective QoC acquisition, cost and performance efficiency.

the thermal camera (TC) exhibits higher correctness than the video camera (VC); thus, we defined them to produce 90% and 80% correctness, respectively. We performed this procedure for thirty minutes and collected the context acquisition cost in both approaches at each minute.

Furthermore, RR addresses the limitation in the filtering approach (invoking similar context providers) by selecting a potentially better performing provider. To realise aim (iii), assuming that there are a variable number of context providers (up to ten) at each entity, generating a random number between 1–10, we determined their number at each entity and created their sessions to generate SLAs. Next, we selected a few context providers from each entity and had their context outcome sessions produce an adequate QoC—thus, having the highest RR. Finally, by performing QoC-aware selection for AC CRs using the RR and filtering approach, we measured their execution time in obtaining adequate QoC.

Charts 1 and 2 in Fig. 4 indicate the OQoC and Request Success Rate (RSR) of conQeng and naive approaches in forty context requests. Here, *RSR indicates the valid QoC delivery rate from a model in a period, where the period represents a duration of engagement between the context consumer and CMP* [18]. Both models selected the VCs for the initial context requests (five AC and MSA CRs in request numbers 1–10) - as initially, both context providers have a high RR. In turn, they have attained equal and adequate OQoC. However, upon reducing the VC's timeliness outcomes - to violate its guarantees, both models have obtained inferior OQoC in the second repetition (in request numbers 11–20). However, the conQeng has maintained the QoC adequacy from subsequent repetitions (in request numbers 21–30 and 31–40) by selecting the TCs - as VCs possess low RR due to prior QoC violations; hence, exhibiting a higher OQoC at most instances and RSR. According to the results, conQeng reacts to QoC inadequacies to select better providers for future CRs. Therefore, conQeng can potentially act as middleware that effectively obtains adequate QoC.

Charts 3 and 4 depict the number of MSA CRs and AC CRs produced per minute and the associated context acquisition cost. Due to low cost and equal initial Reputation (RR is 1 for new context providers), these models have selected and invoked the video camera for both CRs. Nevertheless, upon reducing the VCs' correctness (from the 10_{th} minute) beyond the AC CRs' tolerance, due to negative feedback, the general reputation (Gen R in Fig. 4) approach selected thermal camera for both CRs from subsequent requests; increasing total context acquisition costs for MSA CRs. In contrast, the RR has only switched the provider in the case of AC CRs; until it has produced the context within MSA CRs' tolerance (till 19_{th} minute), thus having lower context acquisition costs. Therefore, RR enables the CMP to provide correct context to the consumers at a lower cost. Chart 5 depicts the total context providers in each entity that suit the CR, the number of context providers invoked and validated by conQeng and the filtering approach until finding the one with adequate QoC. As depicted, conQeng invoked only one context provider. Filtering invoked all context providers and validated their QoC outcomes until they found an adequate context. Thus, as chart 6 depicts, filtering approach has higher execution times.

7   Conclusion and Future Work

In this paper, we have proposed a framework called conQeng that acquires a cost-effective and QoC aligned context for the CMP through QoC-aware selection, QoC-measurement and validation processes. Through a novel procedure that assesses the context provider's runtime performance in completing QoC metrics that rely on their internal and external factors, we have demonstrated that conQeng effectively selects the context providers delivering an adequate QoC and delivers QoC-assured context to the CMP. Furthermore, our evaluation confirmed that conQeng improves the efficiency and effectiveness in QoC-aligned context acquisition compared to three heuristic approaches. Next, we plan to integrate conQeng with CMPs such as Context-as-a-Service and FIWARE [22,23], implement it in various industry-related projects, and evaluate its performance using real-time data streams.

References

1. Dey, A.: Understanding and using context. Pers. Ubiquit. Comput. **5**, 4–7 (2001) https://doi.org/10.1007/s007790170019
2. Perera, C., Zaslavsky, A., Christen, P., Georgakopoulos, D.: CA4IOT: context awareness for Internet of Things. In: 2012 IEEE International Conference on Green Computing and Communications, pp. 775–782. IEEE (2012)
3. Hassani, A., Medvedev, A., Zaslavsky, A., Delir Haghighi, P., Jayaraman, P., Ling, S.: Efficient execution of complex context queries to enable near real-time smart IoT applications. Sensors. **19**, 5457 (2019)

4. Buchholz, T., Küpper, A., Schiffers, M.: Quality of Context: what it is and why we need it. In: 2003 Workshop of the HP Open View University Association, pp. 1–14. (2003)
5. Manzoor, A., Truong, H., Dustdar, S.: Quality of Context: models and applications for context-aware systems in pervasive environments. Knowl Eng. Rev. **29**, 154–170 (2014)
6. Brgulja, N., Kusber, R., David, K., Baumgarten, M.: Measuring the probability of correctness of contextual information in context aware systems. In: 2009 IEEE International Symposium on Dependable, Autonomic and Secure Computing, pp. 246–253. IEEE (2009)
7. https://www.didiglobal.com/science/intelligent-driving. Accessed May 2022
8. https://www.pedestrian.melbourne.vic.gov.au/. Accessed May 2022
9. Ma, H., Zeng, C., Ling, C.X.: A reliable people counting system via multiple cameras. ACM Trans. Intell. Syst. Technol. **3**, 1–22 (2012)
10. Kristoffersen, M.S., Dueholm, J. V., Gade, R., Moeslund, T.B.: Pedestrian counting with occlusion handling using stereo thermal cameras. Sensors (Switzerland). **16**, 62 (2016)
11. Li, X., Eckert, M., Martinez, J.F., Rubio, G.: Context aware middleware architectures: survey and challenges. Sensors (Switzerland) **15**, 20570–20607 (2015)
12. Javaid, S., Afzal, H., Arif, F., Iltaf, N., Abbas, H., Iqbal, W.: CATSWoTS: context aware trustworthy social web of things system. Sensors (Switzerland) **19**, (2019)
13. Kowshalya, A.M., Valarmathi, M.L.: Trust management in the social internet of things. Wirel. Pers. Commun. **96**, 2681–2691 (2017)
14. Sicari, S., Rizzardi, A., Miorandi, D., Cappiello, C., Coen-Porisini, A.: A secure and quality-aware prototypical architecture for the Internet of Things. Inf. Syst. **58**, 43–55 (2016)
15. Marie, P., Lim, L., Manzoor, A., Chabridon, S., Conan, D., Desprats, T.: QoC-aware context data distribution in the internet of things. In: 2014 Proceedings of the 1st ACM Workshop on Middleware for Context-Aware Applications in the IoT, pp. 13–18. (2014)
16. Filho, J., Miron, A., Satoh, I., Gensel, J., Martin, H.: Modeling and measuring quality of context information in pervasive environments. In: 2010 24th IEEE International Conference on Advanced Information Networking and Applications, pp. 690–697. IEEE (2010)
17. Marie, Pierrick, Desprats, Thierry, Chabridon, Sophie, Sibilla, Michelle: QoCIM: A Meta-model for Quality of Context. In: Brézillon, Patrick, Blackburn, Patrick, Dapoigny, Richard (eds.) CONTEXT 2013. LNCS (LNAI), vol. 8175, pp. 302–315. Springer, Heidelberg (2013). https://doi.org/10.1007/978-3-642-40972-1_23
18. Jagarlamudi, K.S., Zaslavsky, A., Loke, S.W., Hassani, A., Medvedev, A.: Quality and cost aware service selection in IoT-context management platforms. In: 2021 IEEE International Conferences on Internet of Things (iThings) and IEEE Green Computing & Communications (GreenCom) and IEEE Cyber, Physical & Social Computing (CPSCom) and IEEE Smart Data (SmartData) and IEEE Congress on Cybermatics (Cybermatics), pp. 89–98. IEEE (2021)
19. Hossain, M.A., Atrey, P.K., El Saddik, A.: Learning multi-sensor confidence using difference of opinions. In: 2008 IEEE Instrumentation and Measurement Technology Conference, pp. 809–813. IEEE, (2008)
20. Yasar, A.U.H., Paridel, K., Preuveneers, D., Berbers, Y.: When efficiency matters: towards quality of context-aware peers for adaptive communication in VANETs. In: 2011 IEEE Intelligent Vehicles Symposium (IV), pp. 1006–1012. IEEE, (2011)

21. https://github.com/IBA-Group-IT/IoT-data-simulator . Accessed May (2022)
22. Hassani, A., et al.: Context-as-a-Service Platform: exchange and share context in an IoT ecosystem. In: 2018 IEEE International Conference on Pervasive Computing and Communications Workshops (PerCom Workshops), pp. 385–390. IEEE, (2018)
23. FIWARE - Open APIs for Open Minds. https://www.fiware.org/. Accessed 27 (2022)

Automating Heterogeneous IoT Device Networks from Multiple Brokers with Multiple Data Models

Pierfrancesco Bellini, Chiara Camerota, and Paolo Nesi[(✉)]

Distributed Systems and Internet Technology Lab DISIT,
University of Florence, 50139 Florence, Italy
{pierfrancesco.bellini,chiara.camerota,paolo.nesi}@unifi.it
https://www.disit.org

Abstract. The Internet of Things (IoT) is becoming pervasive and at each new installation of IoT platform legacy internal and external brokers have to be integrated. Internal brokers are those under control of the platform, while external brokers are managed by third parties. Both brokers kind may be multiservice/multi-tenant, and may manage multiple Data Models. The interoperable management of these complex network has to pass from the IoT device registration which is typically a recurrent operation since the IoT networks are in continuous evolution. In this paper, the above-mentioned problems have been addressed by the introduction of our concept of IoT Directory and reasoning tools to (i) manage Internal and External brokers, (ii) perform the automated registration by harvesting and reasoning of devices managed into external brokers single- or multi-tenant services, (iii) perform the automated registration and management of Data Models, and any custom Data Model. The solution has been developed and tested into Snap4City, an 100% open source IoT platform for Smart Cities and Industry 4.0, official FIWARE platform, EOSC, and lib of Node-RED. The specific IoT Directory has been developed in the context of Herit-Data Project, the results have been validated in wide condition of the whole Snap4City network of more than 18 tenant, and billions of data.

Keywords: Internal and external IoT brokers · Automated IoT device registration · Smart data model · IoT network · Snap4city

1 Introduction

The Internet of Things (IoT) defines a paradigm for the computation and communication among things that everyone uses more and more daily. It is due to the intense deployment campaign worldwide about Low-Power Wide Area Network technologies [1]. Nowadays, the user's environment includes a wide variety of devices (such as bulbs, fridges, benches, pole, totems) connecting them to an IoT infrastructure. In this scenario, the real world and IoT devices are integrated tother with some human in the loop. Communication among devices may support various protocols (e.g., MQTT, NGSI, AMQP,

© The Author(s), under exclusive license to Springer Nature Switzerland AG 2022
A. González-Vidal et al. (Eds.): GIoTS 2022, LNCS 13533, pp. 226–238, 2022.
https://doi.org/10.1007/978-3-031-20936-9_18

COAP) thus, the cloud-fog infrastructures are exploited, as well as the management of the information [2]. In terms of data management, the complexity is growing, not only for the huge amount of data but also for the needs of interoperability and abstraction. The **Gateway** concept is a relevant entity to manage IoT devices into an **IoT Platform**. It may be integrated with one or several **IoT Brokers** to send/receive data to/from devices. The Gateways and its IoT Brokers are typically based on a single protocol and managed by third parties as a public service for several customers interested in the same area (for example LoraWAN services [3]). A Gateway may abstract from the IoT Broker level managing them for multiple organizations/tenant (which can be regarded as customers of Gateway services to manage a number of **IoT Devices**), via some API and/or Web user interface. Typical IoT Brokers are capable to manage only one organization, and thus they are single-tenant, in the sense that they broker messages using the topic concepts (which can be regarded as the key for subscription) without any internal partition of services as a sort of family of devices and subscriptions. Some IoT Brokers can be multi-tenant, such as the FIWARE **Orion Broker**, which provides a partition of the devices in groups, and each of them may have a dedicated service/path for a specific scope (or of a specific customer), devices of different tenants could exist physically in different places (even having identical ID), and the subscription to the broker's tenant may imply to get all messages/services in the partition, and it is feasible only if the subscriber knows the identifier of the service path and, in the cases of access control, has the grant to access at the services. The complexity of **IoT Platforms** grows with the needs of managing multiple IoT Brokers which can be managed by third parties different from the IoT Platform manager, i.e., **IoT External Brokers**, and/or directly managed by the IoT Platform tools, i.e., **IoT Internal Brokers**, may be adopting different protocols, formats.

For the **IoT External Brokers**, the entities (IoT Devices) are directly registered on the IoT Broker which is not under the control of the IoT Platform. Thus, the IoT Platform does not know the IoT Device data structure nor the composition of messages and services. A multi-tenant External Broker could have many partitions referring to different Organizations (customers, service areas), so that the IoT Platform to interact with them must be capable to cope with this complex scenario. Most of the IoT Platforms neglect these interoperability and integration aspects and provide simplified solutions. They do not care about Internal/External Brokers, just providing the possibility to set up end-to-end solutions with some restricted usage, for example using only internal brokers they provide. Thus, AWS IoT by Amazon (https://aws.amazon.com/iot) and Siemens MindSphere (https://siemens.mindsphere.io/en) make the broker structure transparent to their users unless they buy a specific add-on. While IoT Platform like Google IoT Cloud (https://cloud.google.com/solutions/iot) shows the Broker architecture but allows the usage of only one kind of protocol (e.g., MQTT). At least, solutions like MS Azure IoT (https://azure.microsoft.com/en-us/overview/iot) or IBM Watson (https://www.ibm.com/watson) are more flexible. MS Azure does not provide to cluster their objects, in other words, supporting only one organization on broker; the IBM solution does not allow the connection of External Brokers. In summary, most of the solutions provide simple scenario, and mainly assume to have customers starting to use their solution from scratch (on cloud or on premise), offering limited capabilities to deeply integrate the platform with legacy IoT Broker and Network. Nevertheless, all of them provide the possibility of connecting to other IoT Brokers and Network by means of REST Call on API. Thus, the developer has to know the entities to be connected and the API to be called. Naturally, in those scenarios, the third-party brokers are not directly connected and neither managed in terms of IoT Device registration, subscription, data storage, search, etc.

The IoT Devices may be registered to one or more IoT Brokers and communicate by using simple or mutual authentications. The IoT Device identifier is typically called Topic for the Broker, to which clients can be subscribed. IoT Devices connected to a broker adopt the same protocol and may use different data models. If the message format is based on JSON, the corresponding schema may be defined and used for validation, while variables/attributes can be differently defined. For example, FIWARE Orion Broker adopts the NGSI protocol with the possibility of managing the so-called **Smart Data Models** from which IoT Devices can be templated out [4]. The IoT Devices of a Broker may provide different message schema (data models). Hence, the IoT Platform or Gateway must recognize these **IoT Device Models** and manage them (registering, processing, producing, storage, etc.), especially in the case of **IoT External Brokers**, in which the IoT Platform may not know the IoT device models, and neither the identifier (topic) of the IoT Devices managed by the IoT External Broker. In this case, at the arrival of a message from a unknown device (which can partially provide information in its body, typically not the metadata, since most of the devices minimize the data transmission), the IoT Platform is not in the condition of registering the device, and neither to correct link the message to the former devices. Thus, the adoption of standard Data Models can be a way to make the IoT network more interoperable. The devices and messages are easily managed when a new external device is added to the IoT Platform if the data model adopted is known. In other words, if the IoT Platform knows the data model adopted by a device it is easier to identify the data structure and so it could automatically manage the relationships among data entities and verify coherence. For all these reasons, the Data Model concepts and formalisms are crucial.

In this paper, the above-mentioned problems and other aspects have been addressed to design and implement a solution for leveraging IoT network interoperability and the management of Data Models. To this end, we have created the concept and tool named **IoT Directory** in the Snap4City architecture (https://www.snap4city.org). The **IoT Directory** supports: (i) **Internal** and **External** brokers, (ii) the automated registration of devices managed into External Brokers single- or multi-tenant services, (iii) automated registration by harvesting and reasoning of IoT Devices compliant with standard models such as FIWARE Smart Data Model, and any custom Data Model in Snap4City IoT Device Model providing a formal semantic definition of attributes. The research presented in this paper has been developed for Snap4City architecture presently quite diffuse in Europe as 100% open source IoT platform for Smart Cities and Industry 4.0 and it is an official FIWARE platform and solution, and of EOSC, Node-RED [5, 6]. The specific IoT Directory has been developed in the context of Herit-Data Project which promotes the use of smart and open data to better manage tourism flows in natural and cultural heritage sites, the results have been validated in wide condition of the whole Snap4City network of more than 18 tenant, and billions of data.

The Paper is Organized as Follows. Section 2 presents the major requirements for data model and broker interoperability in IoT Platforms. Section 3 shows the role of IoT Directory in IoT architecture for managing internal/external brokers with the aim of automated registration, management vs data models and formal definition of their attributes. In Sect. 4, some details regarding the validation of the solution are reported. The validation included verifying the processing timing and giving a general numeric KPI about the shape of the entities. In Sect. 5, the conclusions are drawn.

2 Requirements Analysis and Related Work

In this section, the requirements that an IoT Platform for IoT Network management and exploitation should satisfy are reported and commented. They have been identified in the context of analysis for the development and exploitation of the Snap4City platform covering smart city and Industry 4.0 domains. The requirements for the IoT Platform are presented in logical order from R1 to R10 as follows. The following list of the requirement refer also to a set of well-known platforms: AWS IoT by Amazon (AWS), Google IoT Cloud (Google IOT), MS Azure IoT (MS Azure), Siemens MindSphere and IBM Waston. Therefore, an **IoT Platform** should provide support to:

1. **Manage different kinds of IoT Brokers, IoT Devices and IoT Edge Devices.** They should be based on different protocols, formats, and modalities to establish connections with the IoT Platform. Focusing on the Platform considered, all of them support MQTT and HTTP, while Google IoT and Azure IoT support only MQTT Broker. It is important to highlight that most of the platforms provide specific components for different protocols, for instance: Amazon MQ that supports Broker with AMPQP, MQTT, OpenWire and STOMP protocol.
2. **Connect External and Internal Brokers.** They could be multiservice and could provide different protocols. Internal Brokers should be deployed and registered by the IoT Platform, while the External Brokers would be only registered to use them. In the Platform considered, the brokers are the products' core of stakeholders offers, for this reason the requirement is partially satisfied. In that sense, AWS IoT and Siemems MindSphere offer a paid add-on.
3. **Register, manage and use messages conformant to any Data Model with any data type.** Providing, receiving, managing, storing, and retrieving messages for any IoT Device of any Data Model with its attributes and data types, and related access control. A Data Model provides a model format for IoT Device messages with several variables/parameters/attributes with their specific data types. For the listed Platforms, the messages from the IoT Devices are freely shaped, so to assure the data flexibility to the detriment the data model. For example, Google IoT and IBM Watson use formats as JSON or XML.
4. **Verify the correctness of IoT Messages of IoT Devices.** The platform should be capable of verifying correctness of messages in terms of model and format including verification at level of attributes, before accepting/sending them. Please note: this requirement is satisfied by each solution considered since the IoT Devices are formally defined at the registration phase.

5. **Semantic Interoperability.** This requirement is fundamental to achieve the coherence among different IoT Devices (e.g., provided by different builders, addressing the same concepts, information on attributes). An IoT Platform should be capable to *recognize/classify/retrieve* information/attributes and behave accordingly to the semantic data model and types. For example, an IoT application should not risk misunderstanding the unit of measure assigned to attributes of different devices which have the same name, but different units. Thus, to set the temperature of an air conditioner (expecting it in Celsius), while the sensor is just providing temperature in Fahrenheit, thus a direct exploitation is not possible.

6. **Support automatics deploy of Internal IoT Brokers.** The IoT Platform should provide support for the automated deployment of IoT Broker internally managed. And thus, Internal Brokers are directly managed by the Platform which directly perform the registration of IoT Devices on them. The result is an easy experience for the user and an easy way to populate the network. This requirement can be implemented only if the Platform allows the registration and the management of new IoT Brokers. For this reason, this requirement is satisfied only in the Core of Siemens MindSphere and by all FIWARE Platforms for definition.

7. **Register External Brokers.** The platform must support the registration of IoT External Brokers. This means that the IoT Platform should be capable of registering IoT Devices/Services of the External Broker into the IoT Platform. In other words, this is a specification of abstraction requirement. Brokers can be single- or multi-tenant and to recover the IoT Devices data model managed by the Broker is the first step to perform their registration. In the case of External Broker, the endpoint URL and the service and/or service path specifications would be needed to subscribe. None of the commercial platforms considered provides a solution for registering External Brokers, and thus making automated registration of their devices.

8. **Discover IoT Devices on IoT Brokers.** The platform must be capable to abstract IoT Devices from their IoT Brokers and protocols. This is needed for the registration of them and for their **classification and search**, which is based on their position, nature, value types and units, etc. In other words, it should be possible to discover/search (subscribe, get, send data) to/from IoT Devices independently from their position/connection in the IoT Network. The process of discovery must be manageable in the sense that its execution time can be scheduled, and possible with brokers that support a process for device discovery. The result should consist of an automated or semi-automated registration process of IoT Devices.

9. **Easy management graphic interface to list and test IoT Brokers, and IoT Devices** and query them. For each IoT Device, it has to be possible to perform testing activities such as: seeing all details including those regarding setting on authorization, seeing the last message, sending a new message in the broker. As seen before, not all the above-mentioned Platforms manage the IoT Broker, unless they use a specific add-on. So, this requirement is satisfied by each of them only for the kind of Devices they put in the offer.

10. **Manage IoT Device Model and Device Data Type ownership and access grant.** This permits assignment/changing of the ownership and the creation of access grant to the entities (Brokers, Devices, Models, etc.). In delegation management, it must be possible to list them (check the grants provided) and revoke the delegations.

According to GDPR, any entity must start as private of the owner, which is the only one that may decide to change ownership and provide access grant. The delegation should be possible for organizations, groups of users, and single users.

On other aspects, surveys about IoT Platforms are provided in [6–8].

3 The Role of IoT Directory in Snap4City Architecture

In order to enforce the above-described requirements into Snap4City IoT Platform we have designed and developed a new concept that we have called IoT Directory. It extends the features of generic IoT Platforms with the management of (i) IoT Data Models, (ii) IoT External Brokers, (iii) discovery of IoT Devices of External Brokers, (iv) support the multi-tenancy, (v) support several organizations, (vi) GDPR compliance, etc. In order to fully understand the capabilities and role of the IoT Directory, three different scenarios are described, in Fig. 1: -) the registration of an IoT Broker, -) the registration of Internal Devices, -) the automated registration of Devices of External Brokers, and in Fig. 2 the message communication flow.

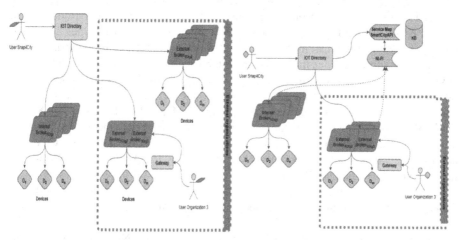

Fig. 1. (left) registration of an IoT Broker, (right) registration of an IoT Device. The solid lines indicate the registrations, while the dashed lines indicate the data flow of the subscriptions.

In Fig. 1(left), the registration process of IoT Brokers (**Internal or External**) in the Snap4City Platform is reported, where the organization is denoted by the subscription in the Broker name. At the Broker registration into the IoT Directory, a number of parameters are needed including: the end point, security, name, External/Internal, single/ multiple-tenant, etc. The most important difference for Internal/external Brokers consists in the IoT Device management as explained in the following. The broker to be usable has to be granted to each specific user or public [6]. An user only belongs to a single organization for security and privacy aspects.

Once a Broker is registered, the IoT Directory automatically performs the subscription of the data platform to the new Broker for all its devices/topics, so that each new message that will be generated by the broker would be directly brokered to the data storage. In Fig. 1(**right**), the subscriptions are denoted by dashed lines, while the registrations are shown as solid lines. In most of the IoT Platforms, the storage is called Data Shadow, and allows to create the historical data of the IoT Devices. In Snap4City, the data storage feeding is performed by Apache NiFi, so that, the IoT Directory automatically performs the association between NiFi and the topics of the new **Internal or External** Broker. This is due to the necessity of having a robust, scalable tool with low latency to handle huge volume of data entering on the storage and coming from several devices and brokers. In Fig. 1(**right**), the processes of **IoT Device registrations** are depicted in both cases. In the case of **Internal Brokers,** the IoT Device registration is performed on the IoT Directory. The user may select the IoT Broker among those of the Organization and set a number of details. The registration may start with the exploitation of an IoT Device Model, the device ID, and then with the definition of GPS location, and all instance details. In Snap4City, the process can be performed: (i) on the IoT Directory via the user interface exploiting a model or not, (ii) exploiting API of the IoT Directory, (iii) using MicroServices in Node-RED which are based on the same API of (ii), (iv) using a set of automated registration processes starting from Excel Files/tables. Each registered IoT Device is registered on the **Knowledge Base**, KB, (implemented with Virtuoso on the basis of Km4City Ontology [10] for the semantic relationships and with Open Search for the time Series data) with all its information and metadata (static information). The KB management allows to index the device and establish all the relationships with the other city entities located in the same area, place, city, region, road, GPS position, etc. This information would be very useful when new messages arrive from a IoT Device in the storage via NiFi (which is represented by the ServiceMap in Fig. 1(**right**), with **Smart City API** for providing access to the storage) they are connected to the right IoT Device description and relationships. The correct and complete indexing and **Smart City API** are fundamental to enable the exploitation of IoT data by IoT Applications (Node-RED microservices [7]) and Dashboards [9].

Finally, Fig. 2 shows the data flow during the usage, it illustrates the event-driven data flows. There are four ways for generating new IoT Messages, from:

- **IoT Devices** pass from a Broker and are passed to: (a) the NiFi, thus reaching the KB and storage, becoming part of historical data which can be accessed and queried from IoT App, Data Analytic and Dashboards; (b) Kafka to directly reach subscribed Dashboards via WebSockets, and IoT App.
- **IoT Apps** may be sent to IoT Broker or to Kafka front end broker. Thus, the message can reach: IoT Device for acting on it, storage, IoT App, Dashboards, etc. If a message is sent by a sensor-actuator (Internal or External), his Broker broadcasts it to Ni-Fi, which spreads it in turn. The IoT Apps are also used for massive registration of IoT Devices, and to perform data adaptation, ETL/ELT (Extract Transform/Load) processes.
- **Dashboards** are passed via Kafka toward the IoT App, or to an Internal Broker or direly into the storage. These messages can be regarded as Virtual IoT Devices to act

on some sensors/actuators IoT Device, or even to simulate it. The produce messages may be sent to Internal/External Brokers, and so on.

- **IoT Directory** may generate a new message towards an IoT Broker (and may also read the last message from the broker). The generation of messages from the IoT Directory is typically used to check if the Internal Broker is alive and works correctly, and if the IoT Device messages are accepted.

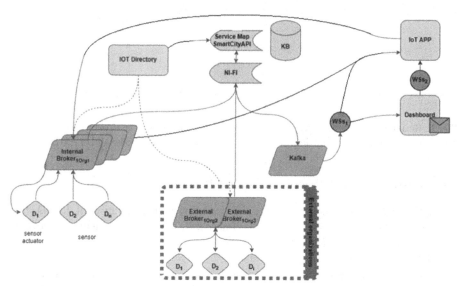

Fig. 2. IoT Messages exchanged among entities: continuous lines are data flows, dashed lines indicate the tests that the user can perform to verify the IoT Devices/Brokers.

In the case of **registration of IoT Devices on an External Broker**, the Broker is not managed by the IoT Directory, and thus the Devices are registered in the External Broker by the third-party gateway manager without informing the IoT Directory. Thus, the IoT Directory need to recover the information needed for registering and indexing the devices into the KB. Then, the IoT Directory queries/harvest the external broker to get the structures of the IoT Devices (also called Discovery has to be started). The harvesting process may start having the broker API end point and also the service path in the case of the multi-tenancy broker. The harvesting has to be performed at the broker registration and every time a new Device is added, thus a periodic Discovery is needed. Figure 3 shows the results of the harvesting process. For the harvesting, the IoT Directory recognizes the Data Model and Data Types of the attributes to register them in KB in proper manner, to validate them. In the following subsections, the registration of IoT Devices on Internal and External Brokers are discussed. Please note that the registration of devices from External Brokers is one of the innovative aspects addressed by the IoT Directory which is capable to harvest the brokers and resolving semantic gaps on IoT device attributes/variables, see Sect. 3.2.

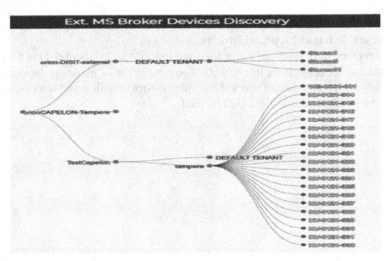

Fig. 3. Result of the discovery process into a multi service/tenant External Broker. Devices marked in Green are registered. New devices are marked in yellow when they are invalid or partially valid.

3.1 Registration of IoT Devices on Internal Brokers

The IOT Directory is fundamental for the definition and registration of IoT Device Models, i.e., data models. Focusing on the Internal IOT Brokers, the platform provides three ways to deploy IoT Devices:

- *Manual process:* the user can register an IoT Device by using a graphic interface, to input information. It is possible to register a device on the basis of a specific IoT Device Model, and to refer at a specific IoT Broker.
- *Bulk process:* the user can upload a file with a list of Devices, defining the IoT Broker, Model and Edge.
- *IoT App process:* The user can build an IoT APP using Node-RED on which specific nodes can be used. The nodes accept JSON with parameters related to the chosen Device Model to register new Devices.

The registered IoT Devices are shown in a table (see Fig. 4) in which the users can manipulate only those he/she created, no matter of the generation process. The users can also see in the list the public devices of the same organization, while the general administrator has a full visibility of all devices of all the organizations.

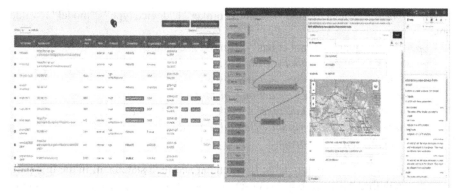

Fig. 4. On the left, the list of IoT device is shown. On the right, the creation of the device by IoT App is shown.

3.2 Discovering and Registering IoT Devices from External Brokers

The Snap4City Platform allows the registration of External Brokers using the broker URL or the couple URL and service identifier in the case of multi-tenancy. After the registration of an External Broker, the user can start the harvesting process and choose the time period for the update. It is important to highlight that Snap4City Platform may know a set of IoT Device Model (data models). Thus, in the best case, when the harvesting starts, it can recognize the device and its model (message format and device ID).

If the IoT Directory does not recognize the Device, the Device has to be Registered. To this end the IoT Directory can query the Broker to have more information to register it. On the other hand, the IoT Device may be compliant with a Data Model or not. If it is compliant the registration is straight forward. It is not compliant, each single attribute has to be recognized in terms of Value Type, Value Unit and Data Type (e.g., Temperature, Celsius, Float). The list of recognized/registered and non recognized/non registered Devices is presented. Through this interface, the user can resolve the problems manually defining the missing data and enabling the registration.

The most common harvesting (automated registration process) problem are due to the lack of matching with known attributes. The IoT Platform tries to identify the attribute kind in terms of value type, value unit and data type by performing query on data Dictionary and Km4City Ontology (via the connection from IoT Directory and ServiceMap by using Smart City API, and Dictionary API, Fig. 2). The recognition may have success in two cases: the data model is known but not this specific attribute or the model is not known, so all the attribute values of the Device are not recognized. In the first case is easy to fix the problem by applying a specific rule. In the second case, the Platform needs to learn a Rule for solving the attributes, thus defining a new Data Model in IoT Directory. Formally, the processing rule R is defined in EBNF as following:

$R: = IF <condition\ list> THEN <action\ list>$
$<condition\ list> := <c> | <c> AND <condition\ list>$
$<c> := <variable> <op> <constant>$

<variable> := "device name" | "context broker" | "device type" | "model" | "value name"

<op> := "is equal" | "is not equal" | "Is null" | "contains".

<constant> := *integer | float | string | list.*

<action list> := *<a>* | *<a>, <action list>*

<a> := *<action variable>: <action constant>*

<action variable> := "Data type" | "Value type" | "Value unit" | "Editable" | *<Coded Healthiness criteria>* | *<Healthiness value>*

< action constant >: = *string.*

The rule is divided into two parts: If statement and then statement. In the first part, the user can define the condition that describes a set of devices, e.g., a device name in common. The *<op>* defines the operators, two of them ("is/is not equal") can apply only on the number constant, others ("Is null" or "contains") only on the string constant. In the second part, the user can establish the action that makes devices or values valid. In other words, for the subset of Devices identify by the <condition list>, the *<action variable>* is modified as defined by *<action constant>*. An example of Rule can be:

IF "context broker" is equal "CONTEXTBROKER".
AND "value name" is equal "activePower".
THEN "value type":"power", "value unit":"W", "data type":"float".

In this case, the rule's builder selects a subset of invalid attributes named activePower, which have the Device subscripts a Broker named CONTEXBROKER which allows to manage the multi-tenancy aspects. Then, it changes the value type, the value unit and the data type in power, W and float (see Fig. 5).

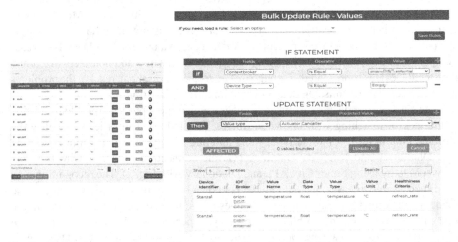

Fig. 5. (a) illustrates the output of harvesting: a list of external Devices; (b) shows the Rule Building/editing tool.

In the IoT Directory, it is possible to search and edit the saved rules. When the user saves a rule, must choose the broker to which is applied. It is also possible to define a specific subset of service or service and service path to cope with multiservice brokers. Thus, the application of a rule is associated to each specific Broker or Organization since a Rule can be suitable for an organization and not functional for the others. Figure 5 illustrates the form of the rule builder.

4 Validation Experiments

As above discussed, the harvesting of External Brokers may take into account one or more rules to recognize the attributes and data models, and thus to indexing the IoT devices in the right manner, and shortening time to registration, dynamically add new IoT Devices registered on the Broker, thus reducing the gap from using Internal and External Brokers. Focusing on the timing of the various processes, the user spends around 1 min and a half on average to fill the form to add a new device with 10 attributes, and the system spends around 3 s to register the device. Meanwhile, if the user builds a device from a model, these timings are less than 1 min on average to fill the form and around 1,35 s on average to submit the new device. Furthermore, if the user records a new device through IOT App, the system registers it in 623 ms on average.

Focusing on the registration timing and considering an external multi-tenant broker with 37000 devices, the harvesting time is 25 min and 50 s on average. Meanwhile, the process's timing of the attributes of a specific FIWARE data model (Streetlight) ingestion is 37.1406 ms on average, which results in the addition of 432 new Streetlight devices automatically. Of course, the user can make changes to IoT Devices structure after their automated or manual registration.

5 Conclusions

The proliferation of the IOT devices, brokers, networks, data models, operators and tenant, make the harmonization and management for IoT Platform a hard goal. This paper offers an analysis and a comparison among relevant existing platforms and delineates the basics requirements to achieve these aims. These identified requirements are in most cases not addressed by major platform which prefer to stay on their own end-to-end solutions with limited interoperability and capacity of exploiting the legacy IoT networks in place. The interoperable management of complex network has to pass from the IoT device registration which is typically a recurrent operation since the IoT networks are in continuous evolution. In this paper, the above-mentioned problems have been addressed introducing our concept of IoT Directory and reasoning tools to (i) manage Internal and External brokers, (ii) perform the automated registration by harvesting and reasoning of devices managed into external brokers single- or multi-tenant services, (iii) perform the automated registration and management of Data Models, and any custom Data Model. The solution has been developed and tested into Snap4City, an 100% open source IoT platform for Smart Cities and Industry 4.0, official FIWARE platform, EOSC, and lib of Node-RED. Thus, the resulting platform is more flexible than the others considered (Google IOT Cloud, MS Azure, AWS, Siemens Mindshare and IBM Watson). Furthermore, the proposed solution is also compliant with Smart Data Model of FIWIRE. The semantic interoperability of the platform can be improved by automatic generation of rules and completing the automation of the ingestion process. Furthermore, the process is helped by Km4City ontology and Data Dictionary to recognize the new or model data's semantic domain. The specific IoT Directory has been developed in the context of Herit-Data Project, the results have been validated in wide condition of the whole Snap4City network of more than 18 tenant, and billions of data.

Acknowledgement. The authors would like to thank the MIUR, the University of Florence and the companies involved for co-founding the Herit-Data project. Km4City and Snap4City (https://www.snap4city.org) are open technologies and research of DISIT Lab. Sii-Mobility is grounded and has contributed to the Km4City open solutions.

References

1. Mekki, K., et al.: Overview of cellular LPWAN technologies for IoT deployment: Sigfox, LoRaWAN, and NB-IoT. In: 2018 IEEE International Conference on Pervasive Computing and Communications Workshops (Percom Workshops). IEEE (2018)
2. Yousefpour, A., et al.: All one needs to know about fog computing and related edge computing paradigms: a complete survey. J. Syst. Archit. **98**, 289–330 (2019)
3. Adelantado, F., et al.: Understanding the limits of LoRaWAN. IEEE Commun. Mag. **55**(9), 34–40 (2017)
4. Cheng, B., Solmaz, G., Cirillo, F., Kovacs, E., Terasawa, K., Kitazawa, A.: FogFlow: easy programming of IoT services over cloud and edges for smart cities. IEEE Internet Things J. **5**(2), 696–707 (2018). https://doi.org/10.1109/JIOT.2017.2747214
5. Badii, C., Bellini, P., Difino, A., Nesi, P., Pantaleo, G., Paolucci, M.: Microservices suite for smart city applications. Sensors **19**, 4798 (2019). https://doi.org/10.3390/s19214798
6. Badii, C., Bellini, P., Difino, A., Nesi, P.: Smart city IoT platform respecting GDPR privacy and security aspects. IEEE Access **8**, 23601–23623 (2020). https://doi.org/10.1109/ACCESS.2020.2968741
7. Ammar, M., Russello, G., Crispo, B.: Internet of things: a survey on the security of IoT frameworks. J. Inf. Secur. Appl. **38**, 8–27 (2018)
8. Ray, P.P.: A survey of IoT cloud platforms. Future Comput. Inform. J. **1**(1–2), 35–46 (2016)
9. Bellini, P., Cenni, D., Marazzini, M., Mitolo, N., Nesi, P., Paolucci, M.: Smart city control room dashboards: big data infrastructure, from data to decision support. J. Vis. Lang. Comput. (2018). https://doi.org/10.18293/VLSS2018-030, https://ksiresearchorg.ipage.com/vlss/journal/VLSS2018/paper%2030.pdf
10. Bellini P., Nesi, D., Nesi, P., Soderi, M.: Federation of smart city services via APIs. In: Proceedings of 6th IEEE International Workshop on Sensors and Smart Cities, with IEEE SmartComp, 14–17 September 2020, Bologna, Italy (2020). http://ssc2020.unime.it/

A Persuasive System for Stress Detection and Management in an Educational Environment

Pablo Calcina-Ccori[(✉)] [iD], Eduardo S. Rodriguez-Canales[iD], and Edgar Sarmiento-Calisaya[iD]

Universidad Nacional de San Agustín de Arequipa, Arequipa, Peru
{pcalcinacc,erodriguezca,esarmientoca}@unsa.edu.pe

Abstract. This paper addresses the development of a persuasive IoT system for stress detection and management in students during classroom situations. An emotion-aware persuasive architecture is developed with four modules: Context Acquisition, Context Manager, Persuasion Manager and Context-Aware Applications. By using the galvanic skin response biomarker, the real-time stress level is measured by the wearable wristband Empatica E4. The data, processed and classified on discrete stress levels from 0 to 5, is sent to the context module that identifies situations of interest where the students need positive reinforcement from the persuasive system. Based on the situation of interest and the user's profile, the persuasive module composes personalized persuasive messages displayed in a mobile application. The persuasive system was evaluated through an exploratory study during a class session, with encouraging results in detecting stress levels and the positive effect of persuasive messages on students.

Keywords: Persuasive system · Internet of Things · Wearable electronics · Student's stress management · Emotion-awareness · Affective computing

1 Introduction

Students are exposed to various stressful situations, from homework to their relationships [11]. Continuous stressful situations can cause psychological and physiological problems in students, leading to reduced academic performance and even school dropout. In the pandemics scenario, conditions causing stress have been accentuated, while others have appeared, such as confinement and remote education [3,18].

In this context, it is necessary to identify and mitigate these stressful situations in order to improve the academic performance of students. Usually, clinical

This research was founded by Concytec - World Bank: "Improvement and extension of services of the National System of Science, Technology and Innovation" 8682-PE. through its executive unit ProCiencia. Contract Nro: 014–2019-FONDECYT-BM-INC.INV.

laboratories and specialized professionals are in charge of performing these tasks, but permanent supervision of each student is unfeasible. In recent years, IoT-based wearable health monitors have been presented as an alternative accessible and portable for detecting and monitoring physiological signals, receiving significant attention from the academic community [5,24].

Several works have addressed stress measurement using wearable health monitors with an IoT-based approach. As a sample of these works, we can mention [19], which presents an algorithm to detect the stress level of pregnant women based on heart rate variations using an online k-means clustering algorithm and an edge-enabled IoT system. In [29] the authors design a system monitor of health parameters such as electrodermal activity and heart rate that sends the data to a cloud-based server and by an application allows visualizing a stress report. [31] deals with the student stress monitoring using a Bayesian Belief Network (BBN) to classify stress events based on physiological measures and a Temporal Dynamic Bayesian Network (TDBN) model to compute the stress index. The work [16] addresses the modeling of mental stress, a wireless network sensor platform detects various signals, and a convolutional neural network (CNN) validates the severity of the stress activities. In [25], is presented an IoT system to detect the degree of stress level using a prediction model algorithm based on a machine learning approach. A Photoplethysmography (PPG) quality assessment approach for IoT-based health monitoring system is proposed in [17] using a CNN to discard the unreliable data. In [10], the authors deal the stress state detection proposing a multi-level deep neural network with hierarchical learning based on IoT biomarkers.

Currently, IoT-based healthcare systems are not limited only to detecting health conditions; recent studies include systems to improve the user well-being by various methods. For instance, an IoT system for student stress management based on a mobile health app with relaxation content is presented in [23]. [7] develop an Internet of Body (IoB) platform capable to measures the stress level in firefighters and providing virtual assistance to Chronic-Obstructive-Pulmonary-Disease (COPD) patients. In [4], the authors explore the benefits of wearable devices and persuasion methods to motivate healthy behavior change. [9] develops a mood tracking application and tested its effect on stress reduction of employees. [13] addresses stress detection by using an EEG device to capture the brain waves activity and music therapy for several stress cases. In [2], the authors propose a framework for transmitting stress control messages based on IoT that monitors the patient's heartbeat remotely. [1] deals with the overuse of smartphone among university students by persuasive messages from a conversational mobile agent.

Inspired by the above discussions, the development of emotion-aware systems able to positively influence students through persuasive messages designed for stressful situations is a challenging issue from the point of view of the IoT and the scientific community in general. To date, the authors have not been aware of the use of psychology-based techniques for the development and evaluation of persuasive messages. Compared to other works such as [1,23], we have used methods such as thought listing and the elaboration likehood model (ELM) for the design and evaluation of the experimental case studies.

In this work, we propose an emotion-aware persuasive system that aim to reduce the stress level in educational environments. The student's physiological signals to measure the stress level are detected by the largely used Empatica E4 wristband [6,22,30]. Using signal processing algorithms it is possible to classify these signals to detect negative emotions related to the stress level. The implemented architecture generates persuasive notifications based on multimodal (text, audio, video or comic) content to the students and teachers in real-time. The persuasive system is validated through experimental results in real classroom situations. This work is organized as follows. Section 2 presents the methodology used to implement the emotion-aware persuasive system, including the hardware, architecture, and software. Section 3 describes the study design to verify the effectiveness of the system. In Sect. 4, we present the experimental results on stress detection and management in students. The paper is concluded in Sect. 4 with some final remarks.

2   Persuasive System

In order to deal with stressful classroom situations in the right time, we propose an IoT-based persuasive system, which continuously monitors and identifies students' stress levels.

2.1   Architecture

The proposed architecture flow is shown in Fig. 1. Two context acquisition modules provide the information to the persuasive system: the context of the student in some situation of interest such as a stress level detected and the context of the teacher in a situation of interest related to the classroom environment [26]. The context manager processes the collected information inferring the situation of interest and sends it to the action manager that generates the persuasive message. Finally, the notifications are visualized in the notification presentation module.

The four main modules and their relationships of the proposed architecture, are based on layered (context acquisition) and event-based (notification) patterns, and described as follows:

- *Context Acquisition:* It includes the set of sensors connected to the mobile device to obtain data about the user's context and environment, such as emotion, location, activity and time.
- *Context Manager:* The data is processed in this module, identifying the situation of interest from the user's context and making it available to the persuasion module.
- *Persuasion Manager:* This module determines the type of notification based on the situation of interest and the user's profile and composes the messages to be sent to the notification presentation module.

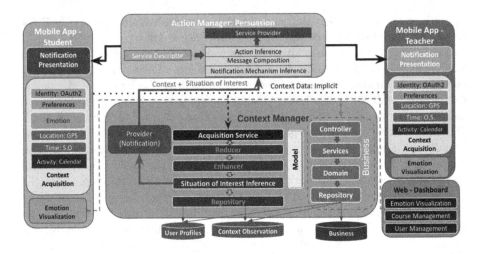

Fig. 1. Kusisqa persuasive system arquicture.

- *Context-Aware Applications:* This module contains the applications that allow the visualization and interaction of the user with the persuasive system (notification presentation module).

2.2 Methodology

Several physiological signals can be used to identify mental stress in students. In this work, we consider the galvanic skin response (GSR) biomarker through the wearable, unobtrusive, and non-invasive wristband "Empatica E4" shown in Fig. 2. This device, dedicated to clinical and research applications, allows real-time biomarkers data acquisition and is equipped with blood volume pulse (BVP), electrodermal activity (EDA), body temperature, and three-axis acceleration sensors. The output GSR signal is measured by two silver-coated (Ag) electrodes with [0.01, 100] µS range with a default sampling rate 4 Hz. The digital resolution is 1 digit per 900 picoSiemens. The E4 measures precisely the skin conductance level (SCL) while maintaining sufficient sensitivity to distinguish the skin conductance response (SCR) under any condition. The EDA signal is sent via bluetooth connection to the *Kusisqa Mobile App*, an application for teachers and students implemented on Android SDK. The steps used to the real-time process of the GSR signal based on [15,28] are briefly described as follows:

- *Noise reduction:* Weak contact between the skin user and the wristband sensors generates noise in the GSR signal. A noise filter to clean data is implemented to reduce this effect by applying a median filter to the signal over a moving window of size $n = 100$ samples.

- *Aggregation:* An aggregation step is applied on the output signal considering a moving window x' of size 240 (samples per minute), where $x_1, \ldots, x_n$ is aggregated to a single value $x'' = max(x')$.
- *Discretization:* The signal is discretized by using the SAX algorithm [12] in a discrete-time series from 1 to 5 to represent the student's stress level. The measure shows local relative stress levels. It is necessary to normalize the signal to obtain a global stress level applying two steps: transforming the original time-series into a piecewise aggregate approximation (PPA) and transforming the PPA data into a string.

These results were validated by using WESAD [27], a publicly available data set for variable stress and affects detection collected from wrist and chest monitor devices during a lab study of 15 subjects. The stress report of the students can be visualized in the mobile application and sent to the context management system.

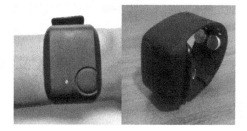

Fig. 2. Wristband Empatica E4.

The context manager module, implemented as a web service, identifies the situations of interest where the students need the intervention of persuasive messages during lectures, evaluations and homework. The module collects and processes the students' stress data, averages each student's measurement, and sends the discrete mean stress level to the persuasive module to generate the respective persuasive messages, as shown in Fig. 3. The messages were created through teaching-learning activities by using the following persuasion principles [8]: Commitment, reciprocity, social proof, authority, liking and scarcity. By using the elaboration likelihood model (ELM) [21], it is possible to evaluate the attitude changes through persuasion considering the processing of the central route and processing of the peripheral route. These two processing strategies constitute the two extremes of continuous processing. That is, the process by which"cognitive responses" are generated as a consequence of exposure to a persuasive message. The ELM predicts the following:

- High-probability processing situation. When the motivation and ability to process a persuasive communication is high, the probability of elaboration will also be high. If the elaborated arguments are more favorable than unfavorable, a positive attitude will develop.

- Low-probability processing situation. When motivation and processing capacity are low, the probability of elaboration will also be low, so that the peripheral processing route will be activated.

Fig. 3. Kusisqa mobile app.

3   Study Design

In order to verify the performance of our persuasive system to manage students' stress levels, an exploratory study was designed to collect and evaluate students' cognitive responses after receiving a persuasive message during class. Seven volunteer students from the Computer Science program of the *Universidad Nacional de San Agustín de Arequipa* participated in the study. The small number of participants was due to restriction during the COVID-19 pandemic. We used the thought listing technique that addresses the analysis of cognitive responses (CR) to identify the level of persuasion [20]. During a 55-min class session, students are asked to use the persuasive system (wristband and mobile application). At the end of the class, each student is sent a persuasive message according to their measured stress level, with values from 0 to 5. Then the students have 3 min to fill out index cards with all the ideas, reflections and thoughts caused by the persuasive messages. Finally, students rated their thoughts by the level of belief (where 1 is *not at all* and 5 is *totally*) and the polarity (P = Positive, N = Negative and X = Neutral) [14].

4 Results

Figure 4 shows an overview of the *Kusisqa Dashboard* that helps visualizing real time stress levels of students during the class session, through a red heat map with measurements in time units of 5 min. The teacher can select the course, data and time interval to improve the flexibility in the stress level visualization.

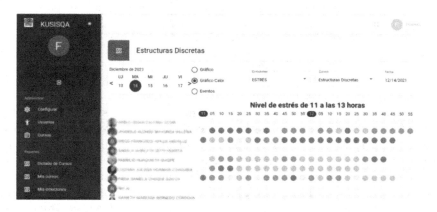

Fig. 4. Kusisqa Dashboard.

Table 1. Persuasive messages evaluation.

Voluntary code	No. CR	Level of belief		Polarity			Polarity index
		Positive	Negative	P	N	X	
P01	3	3.00	3.00	1	1	1	0.00 X
P02	8	4.50	3.00	4	4	0	0.00 X
P03	7	4.00	2.50	3	2	2	0.20 P
P04	5	4.00	6.67	2	2	1	0.00 X
P05	10	4.60	0.00	5	3	2	0.25 P
P06	5	4.00	4.00	3	0	2	1.00 P
P07	8	4.00	4.45	3	2	3	0.20 P
Average	6.6	4.01	3.45	3.00	2.00	1.57	

The average stress level is shown in Fig. 5. These values were the mean of measuring the students' stress levels during a class session of the discrete structures course. The values captured during 55 min of the seven volunteers are shown in a graph bar, with average values ranging from 1.8 to 3.1, which are consistent results considering the range of stress levels between 0 and 5 that the system is capable of measuring.

The results of the exploratory study for persuasive messages validation are summarized in Table 1, which shows the students identified by a code, then

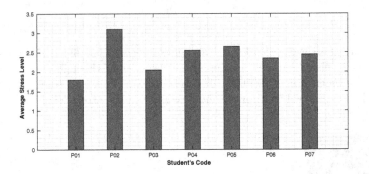

Fig. 5. Students' average stress level.

the column that records the number of cognitive responses or thoughts (No. RC). Next there are the columns that correspond to the level of belief and the polarity of their responses. The computation of the mean belief was elaborated for both positive and negative thoughts. The positive belief values are added and divided by the total of positive thoughts, in the same way for calculating negative thoughts. The polarity index, which has 3° (positive, negative and neutral), was calculated using the following formula: *(number of positive thoughts - number of negative thoughts)/(number of positive thoughts + number of negative thoughts).* The results obtained range between −1 and 1, where −1 indicates an entirely negative degree, 0 is a neutral degree, and 1 is an entirely positive degree.

Table 1 indicates that the students had an average of 6 cognitive responses (CR), with a minimum of 3 and a maximum of 10. Regarding the mean belief, three volunteers had a greater belief in their positive thoughts (P03 = +1.00, P04 = +1.50 and P06 = +4.00), two a greater belief in their negative thoughts (P02 = −0.50 and P05 = −2.07), and the rest did not show differences (0.00). This indicator was obtained by subtracting the average belief in the positive thoughts of each participant from the average belief in the negative thoughts. The average belief are evaluated by using the Likert scale [14]; in positive thoughts was 4.01 or 'Very', and in negative thoughts, it was 3.45 or 'Moderately'. Concerning polarity, three participants had the same number of positive and negative thoughts and four had a higher number of positive thoughts. The average number of positive thoughts (3) is higher than the average number of negative thoughts (2) and in last place are neutral thoughts (1.43). A polarity index was calculated, with values varying from −1 to 1, and it was shown that four students have a positive polarity index and three a neutral index. No negative indexes were found. We consider these results to be promising for the development of our persuasive system and can be complemented with future experiments.

5   Conclusions

In this paper, we present the development of a persuasive system for the detection and management of stress in students during classroom situations using IoT and wearable health technologies. An architecture based on layered and event-based patterns was implemented with four main modules: *Context Acquisition, Context Manager, Persuasion Manager, Context-Aware Applications* to manage the situations of interest of students and teachers. The Empatica E4 wristband was used for the acquisition of physiological signals. The GSR biomarker was processed and discretized by the *Context Manager*, implemented as a web service, to obtain students' stress levels. The students' context (stress level and profile) is sent to the *Persuasion Manager* that generates the persuasive messages that can be visualized in the *Kusisqa Mobile App* and the *Kusiqa Dashboard*, a web application developed to manage and visualize the system data with different functionalities for teachers and students. The performance of the persuasive system was evaluated through an exploratory study in seven volunteer students, who after a class session using the persuasive system rated the effect of the persuasive messages through the thought list technique based on the elaboration likehood model, having mostly positive results. These results encourage us to perform large-scale experiments combining computational and social methodologies to improve the performance of our persuasive system. Thus it would be interesting, as future work the development of low-cost prototypes to GSR measuring, evaluating its performance against clinically certified devices. In addition, other physiological signals such as voice, blood pulse and respiration can be combining and used to measure stress levels in classroom situations.

References

1. Abreu, C., Campos, P.F.: Raising awareness of smartphone overuse among university students: a persuasive systems approach. MDPI Informatics **9**, 15 (2022)
2. Akanksha, E.: Framework for propagating stress control message using heartbeat based IoT remote monitoring analytics. Int. J. Electr. Comput. Eng. (IJECE). **10**, 4615 (2020)
3. Alhasani, M., Alkhawaji, A., Orji, R.: Mental health and time management behavior among students during covid-19 pandemic: Towards Persuasive Technology Design. medRxiv (2021)
4. Ananthanarayan, S., Siek, K.A.: Persuasive wearable technology design for health and wellness. In: 2012 6th International Conference on Pervasive Computing Technologies for Healthcare (PervasiveHealth) and Workshops, pp. 236–240 (2012). https://doi.org/10.4108/icst.pervasivehealth.2012.248694
5. Balakrishna, C., Rendon-Morales, E., Aviles-Espinosa, R., Dore, H., Luo, Z.: Challenges of wearable health monitors. In: A Case Study of Foetal ECG Monitor, pp. 1–6. IEEE (2019)
6. Brick, T.R., Mundie, J., Weaver, J., Fraleigh, R., Oravecz, Z.: Low-burden mobile monitoring, intervention, and real-time analysis using the wear-it framework: example and usability study. JMIR Formative Res. **4**(6), e16072 (2020)
7. Brunschwiler, T., et al.: Internet of the body - wearable monitoring and coaching. In: 2019 Global IoT Summit (GIoTS), pp. 1–6. IEEE (2019)
8. Cialdini, R.B., Cialdini, R.B.: Influence: The Psychology of Persuasion, vol. 55. Collins, New York (2007)

9. Ghavanini, S.A., Homayounvala, E., Rezaeian, A.: Mood-tracking application as persuasive technology for reduction of occupational stress. Int. J. Mobile Learn. Organ. **12**(2), 143–161 (2018)

10. Kumar, A., Sharma, K., Sharma, A.: Hierarchical deep neural network for mental stress state detection using IoT based biomarkers. Pattern Recogn. Lett. **145**, 81–87 (2021)

11. Li, Q., Xue, Y., Zhao, L., Jia, J., Feng, L.: Analyzing and identifying teens' stressful periods and stressor events from a microblog. IEEE J. Biomed. Health Inform. **21**(5), 1434–1448 (2016)

12. Lin, J., Keogh, E., Wei, L., Lonardi, S.: Experiencing sax: a novel symbolic representation of time series. Data Min. Knowl. Disc. **15**(2), 107–144 (2007)

13. Llerena, D., Delgado, R., Ubilluz, C., Lopez, R.: A prototype proposal for detection and reduction of stress by using brain waves and IoT. In: 2020 International Conference of Digital Transformation and Innovation Technology (Incodtrin), pp. 12–16. IEEE (2020)

14. López, A.B.: Modelo de registro y modos de cuantificación para la técnica de listado de pensamientos. Anuario de psicología/The UB Journal of psychology 41–50 (1987)

15. Mamani, Y.: Deteccion de estres en tiempo real a partir de señales de voz y datos fisiologicos. Universidad Nacional de San Agustin de Arequipa, Arequipa, Peru, degree project (2021)

16. Masood, K., Alghamdi, M.A.: Modeling mental stress using a deep learning framework. IEEE Access **7**, 68446–68454 (2019)

17. Naeini, E.K., Azimi, I., Rahmani, A.M., Liljeberg, P., Dutt, N.: A real-time ppg quality assessment approach for healthcare Internet-of-Things. Procedia Comput. Sci. **151**, 551–558 (2019)

18. Onyema, E.M., Eucheria, N.C., Obafemi, F.A., Sen, S., Atonye, F.G., Sharma, A., Alsayed, A.O.: Impact of coronavirus pandemic on education. J. Educ. Pract. **11**(13), 108–121 (2020)

19. Oti, O., Azimi, I., Anzanpour, A., Rahmani, A.M., Axelin, A., Liljeberg, P.: IoT-based healthcare system for real-time maternal stress monitoring. In: 2018 IEEE/ACM International Conference on Connected Health: Applications, Systems and Engineering Technologies, pp. 57–62. ACM (2018)

20. Perosanz, J.J.I.: La técnica del listado de pensamientos como método de investigación en comunicación publicitaria. Comunicación & cultura **3**, 43–62 (1998)

21. Petty, R.E., Cacioppo, J.T.: The elaboration likelihood model of persuasion. In: Communication and persuasion, pp. 1–24. Springer, New York (1986). https://doi.org/10.1007/978-1-4612-4964-1_1

22. Pollreisz, D., TaheriNejad, N.: A simple algorithm for emotion recognition, using physiological signals of a smart watch. In: 2017 39th Annual International Conference of the IEEE Engineering in Medicine and Biology Society (EMBC), pp. 2353–2356. IEEE (2017)

23. Rodic-Trmcic, B., Labus, A., Bogdanovic, Z., Despotovic-Zrakic, M., Radenkovic, B.: Development of an IoT system for students' stress management. Facta Univ. Ser. Electron. Energ. **31**, 329–342 (2018)

24. Romine, W.L., Schroeder, N.L., Graft, J., Yang, F., Sadeghi, R., Zabihimayvan, M., Kadariya, D., Banerjee, T.: Using machine learning to train a wearable device for measuring students' cognitive load during problem-solving activities based on electrodermal activity, body temperature, and heart rate: development of a cognitive load tracker for both personal and classroom use. Sensors **20**(17), 4833 (2020)

25. Safa, M., Pandian, A.: Applying machine learning algorithm to sensor coupled IoT devices in prediction of cardiac stress - an integrated approach. Mater. Today: Proc. (2021)
26. Sarmiento-Calisaya, E., Calcina, P., Cuno, A.: An emotion-aware persuasive architecture to support challenging classroom situations. In: 2022 IEEE International Conference on Consumer Electronics (ICCE). IEEE (2022)
27. Schmidt, P., Reiss, A., Duerichen, R., Marberger, C., Van Laerhoven, K.: Introducing wesad, a multimodal dataset for wearable stress and affect detection. In: Proceedings of the 20th ACM International Conference on Multimodal Interaction, pp. 400–408 (2018)
28. Suni Lopez, F., Condori-Fernandez, N., Catala, A.: Towards real-time automatic stress detection for office workplaces. In: Lossio-Ventura, J.A., Muñante, D., Alatrista-Salas, H. (eds.) SIMBig 2018. CCIS, vol. 898, pp. 273–288. Springer, Cham (2019). https://doi.org/10.1007/978-3-030-11680-4_27
29. Uday, S., Jyotsna, C., Amudha, J.: Detection of stress using wearable sensors in IoT platform. In: 2018 Second International Conference on Inventive Communication and Computational Technologies (ICICCT), pp. 492–498. IEEE (2018)
30. Vallès-Català, T., Pedret, A., Ribes, D., Medina, D., Traveria, M.: Effects of stress on performance during highly demanding tasks in student pilots. Int. J. Aerosp. Psychol. 31(1), 43–55 (2021)
31. Verma, P., Sood, S.K.: A comprehensive framework for student stress monitoring in fog-cloud IoT environment: m-health perspective. Med. Biol. Eng. Comput. 57(1), 231–244 (2018). https://doi.org/10.1007/s11517-018-1877-1

Domain Generalization on Constrained Platforms: On the Compatibility with Pruning Techniques

Baptiste Nguyen[1,2(✉)], Pierre-Alain Moëllic[1,2], and Sylvain Blayac[3]

[1] CEA Tech, Centre CMP, Equipe Commune CEA Tech - Mines Saint-Etienne, 13541 Gardanne, France
{baptiste.nguyen,pierre-alain.moellic}@cea.fr
[2] Univ. Grenoble Alpes, CEA, Leti, 38000 Grenoble, France
[3] Mines Saint-Etienne, CMP, Department of Flexible Electronics, 13541 Gardanne, France
blayac@emse.fr

Abstract. The wide deployment of Machine Learning models is an essential evolution of Artificial Intelligence, predominantly by porting deep neural networks in constrained hardware platforms such as 32 bits microcontrollers. For many IoT applications, the deployment of such complex models is hindered by two major issues that are usually handled separately. For supervised tasks, training a model requires a large quantity of labelled data which is expensive to collect or even intractable in many real-world applications. Furthermore, the inference process implies memory, computing and energy capacities that are not suitable for typical IoT platforms. We jointly tackle these issues by investigating the efficiency of model pruning techniques under the scope of the single domain generalization problem. Our experiments show that a pruned neural network retains the benefit of the training with single domain generalization algorithms despite a larger impact of pruning on its performance. We emphasize the importance of the pruning method, more particularly between structured and unstructured pruning as well as the benefit of data-agnostic heuristics that preserve their properties in the single domain generalization setting.

Keywords: Deep learning · Neural network pruning · Single domain generalization · Embedded systems

1 Introduction

For many IoT domains and applications, *edge computing* enables to reduce bandwidth requirements and unnecessary network communications that may raise critical security threats. Due to its success across a large variety of application domains, deploying state-of-the-art deep neural network models on edge devices is a growing field of research [22]. However, this deployment faces several challenges of different nature, with critical ones related to the training data and hardware constraints.

A. González-Vidal et al. (Eds.): GIoTS 2022, LNCS 13533, pp. 250–261, 2022.
https://doi.org/10.1007/978-3-031-20936-9_20

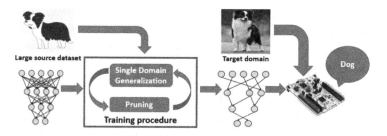

Fig. 1. Illustration of the scope of our study. Pruning and single domain generalization techniques are jointly used to train a model on a source domain and test on an unseen target domain. The model must fit in a constrained MCU.

First, collecting and managing large-scale real-world datasets can be challenging [12], extremely time-consuming and may require large infrastructure and human expertise. These difficulties prevent the use of neural networks, which require large amount of data for their training. A common solution is to train a model on a publicly available dataset similar to the target use case or to create simulated data. Since these datasets cannot perfectly substitute real-world data, techniques such as *domain adaptation* or *generalization* are extensively studied in the AI community. These approaches aim at learning from a source data distribution a well-performing model on a different (but related) target data distribution.

Second, the necessary memory and computational requirements for an inference limit the deployment on typical IoT platforms such as 32 bits MCUs. For example, the state-of-art InceptionTime model [8] for time series classification has 400K parameters and requires approximately 100 MFLOPS for an inference which may be prohibitive for most ARM Cortex-M MCUs for real-time applications. This incompatibility led to the emergence of more efficient architectures (e.g. MobileNet [6]) and compression techniques such as *quantization* or *pruning* that aim at removing parameters from an over-parameterized model.

This work focuses on the evaluation of the compatibility of model pruning under the scope of the single domain generalization problem, as illustrated in Fig. 1: training a neural network on a unique source dataset and testing it on multiple unseen but related datasets. **Our contributions are as follows:**

- We perform several experiments on two typical benchmarks (digit recognition and human activity recognition) with state-of-the-art pruning and domain generalization techniques.
- We show that – on a whole – pruning is efficient in the domain generalization setting even with strong compression rate.
- However, we highlight the importance of the type of the pruning as well as the pruning heuristics, more particularly between structured/unstructured pruning and data agnostic/dependent heuristics.

To the best of our knowledge, this work is the first to focus on model compression techniques in a single domain generalization setting, yet two essential challenges for modern AI-based IoT systems. For reproducibility purpose and further experiments, codes and experiments are publicly available[1].

2 Background

2.1 Single Domain Generalization

Single domain generalization (hereafter, SDG) is a challenging setting where a model is trained on a single source dataset with the objective to generalize to unseen but related target datasets. Traditionally, the target domain represents a real-world application with very few available training data (e.g. anomaly detection from sensors). A source domain is selected according to its closeness to the target domain and the ability to gather sufficient amount of labelled data (e.g. simulated data). The most common method to tackle SDG is data augmentation, for example with a combination of standard input transformations found with an evolution algorithm, as in [21]. *Adversarial data augmentation* is the most popular approach for SDG: it consists of alternating between training and data augmentation phases where the dataset is augmented with samples from a fictitious target domain that is "hard" under the current model [14].

As a reference method, we use the work from Xu *et al.* [23] that recently reaches state-of-the-art performance with a scalable approach. For image classification, the authors start from the observation that semantics often relies more on object shapes than local textures, while local textures are one of the main sources of difference between domains (as the dogs in Fig. 1). To learn texture-invariant representations, they augment the training dataset thanks to random convolutions that *"create an infinite number of new domains"* [23]. At each training iteration, images are augmented with a probability p up to three times. Each augmentation is done by convolving the image with a randomly (size, value) generated kernels. This augmentation creates copies of the input image with different textures. Furthermore, they introduce a consistency loss (based on Kullback-Leibler divergence) to encourage the model to predict the same output for all augmented images. A parameter λ tunes the contribution of the consistency loss to the global loss.

2.2 Neural Network Pruning

Nearly all pruning methods derive from [2] that removes parameters according to a score based on a *pruning heuristic*. Therefore, pruning approaches can be distinguished between four features:

- *Sparsity structure*: unstructured pruning [3] removes individual parameters producing highly efficient sparse neural networks. Rather, structured pruning [11] removes weights in groups, e.g. by removing entire neurons or filters. Furthermore, some methods [2,10] prune a fixed fraction of weights across the whole model (*global pruning*) while other methods [3,5] prune a fraction of weights across each layer of the network (*local pruning*).

---

[1] https://gitlab.emse.fr/b.nguyen/randconvpruning.

Table 1. Mapping of the pruning algorithms used in our study.

Pruning techniques	Types	[11]	[5]	[3]	[2]	[15]	[10]	[20]	[17]
Sparsity structure	Structured	✓	✓						
	Unstructured			✓	✓	✓	✓	✓	✓
	Local	✓	✓	✓					
	Global				✓	✓	✓	✓	✓
Pruning heuristic	Magnitude-based	✓			✓	✓	✓		
	Gradient-based						✓	✓	✓
	Others		✓						
	Iterative scoring							✓	✓
	Data-agnostic	✓	✓	✓	✓	✓			✓
Pruning schedule	One-shot						✓	✓	✓
	Iterative	✓	✓	✓	✓	✓			
Retraining procedure	Fine-tuning	✓	✓	✓					
	Weight Rewinding				✓				
	Learning rate rewinding					✓			

- *Pruning heuristic*: due to its empirical success, estimating the importance of an individual parameter by its magnitude [3,11] is the standard heuristic. Gradient-based heuristics [10,17] are another popular approach. Other heuristics propose to tackle different issues like FPGM [5] which handles redundancy between filters in structured pruning. An important factor in the choice of a heuristic is its use of training data for its computation (data-dependent or data-agnostic).
- *Pruning schedule*: some methods [10,17] prune the weights in one iteration, mainly before training. Others [3] follow an iterative procedure which alternates between prune a small fraction of weights and retrain the model.
- *Retraining procedure*: the most common technique, *fine-tuning*, refers to keep training the network using the trained weights and the last learning rate. Some recent alternatives proposed weight [2] and learning rate [15] *rewinding* in which the weights and/or the learning rate are reset at an early state before the retraining phase.

Table 1 sums up the different approaches and the state-of-the-art references used in this work.

The challenge of porting neural networks to constrained platforms such as microcontrollers has led to the creation of embedding tools (e.g. TFLM[2] or STM32CubeMX-AI[3]) with which structured pruning is generally effortless. However, unstructured pruning (that leads to sparse structures) is more challenging

---

[2] https://www.tensorflow.org/lite/microcontrollers.
[3] https://www.st.com/en/embedded-software/x-cube-ai.html.

and requires the use of a specific sparse computation library (e.g. [19]) to decrease the model's consumption and storage.

We focus our experiments on three common pruning settings. The first setting is the one-shot global unstructured pruning at initialization. Global unstructured pruning algorithms are known to be the most efficient methods to produce sparse neural networks and, one-shot techniques do not increase the training budget. The second is the iterative global unstructured pruning that reduces the loss of accuracy at the cost of a bigger training budget. The third is the iterative local structured pruning since structured methods are easily compatible with standard development platforms.

3   Experiments on Digit Recognition Benchmark

3.1   Datasets and Setup

As in [23], we use digit recognition datasets: MNIST [9], SVHN [13] and USPS [7]. We use two classical CNN architectures: ResNet20 [4] and a variant of Lenet [9] composed of two convolution layers (32 and 64 filters of 5×5 kernels) followed by max-pooling layers and three fully connected layers (128, 128 and 10 neurons). Both models have about the same number of parameters (273K and 276K respectively). The models are trained on MNIST (the source domain). We follow the experimental setting in [23] with random kernels of various sizes within [1–7]. The original data fraction parameter p and the consistency loss factor λ are fixed at 0.5 and 5 respectively. Unless specified, the models are trained on 150 epochs with Adam optimizer, a learning rate of 10^{-4}, a batch size of 32 and 50 epochs of retraining for iterative pruning. Our results are averaged on three training seeds[4].

3.2   Unstructured Pruning at Initialization

Influence of Iterative Ranking. Before training, pruning a network iteratively (i.e. at each iteration, the heuristic is computed and a small fraction of the network's parameters is pruned) improves the performance of the pruned network [20]. This procedure also avoids potential layer collapse (i.e. the premature pruning of a layer that leads to an abrupt drop of accuracy [17]). To check if this property is valid with SDG, we used two state-of-the-art algorithms, SNIP [10] and SynFlow [17] that are applied at initialization with two ranking budgets:

- computing the parameters' score and prune the model in one pass with a single batch (referred as *one batch, one iteration* in Fig. 2),
- computing the parameters' score and pruning the neural network using 100 iterations [17] with a single batch (*one batch, 100 iterations*).

As shown in Fig. 2, iteration helps SynFlow to avoid layer collapse for all domains. But for SNIP, iterations do not affect the accuracy on the different

---

[4] Setups are detailed in https://gitlab.emse.fr/b.nguyen/randconvpruning.

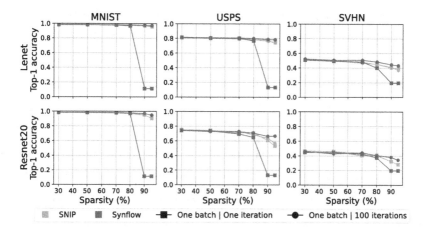

Fig. 2. Influence of iterative ranking on SNIP and SynFlow heuristics.

domains. The data agnosticism of SynFlow can explain this difference. With enough iterations, and independently of the dataset, SynFlow is designed to satisfy the Maximal Critical Compression axiom that implies that Synflow algorithm does not prune a parameter if it leads to layer collapse and there exists another prunable parameter which can avoid layer collapse (see [17]). Meanwhile, SNIP heuristic is designed to discover the important connections of the network for its training on the *source* task. Xu *et al.* [23] relax this task thanks to random convolutions. So SNIP is less relevant and using iterative ranking does not improve the network performance.

Influence of Pruning Heuristic. We compare the baseline magnitude pruning to SNIP and SynFlow. The best ranking budget found in Fig. 3 is used for both heuristics. As shown in Fig. 3 and consistent with [17], SynFlow outmatches other heuristics at high sparsity rates on all domains and magnitude heuristic suffers from layer collapse with Lenet networks (at 80% of sparsity). A heuristic which outperforms other heuristics in the source domain is likely to outperform them in other domains. However, the impact of pruning with a given heuristic on a model performance may not be the same on the source and the target domains. On the source domain, the accuracy begins to decrease exponentially at an extreme sparsity rate (around 95%) while the accuracy starts to decrease almost linearly at a high sparsity rate (around 70%) on the target domains.

3.3   Iterative Unstructured Pruning

Influence of Retraining Procedure. We compare fine-tuning, weight [2] and learning rate [15] rewinding as retraining techniques. In order to compare these

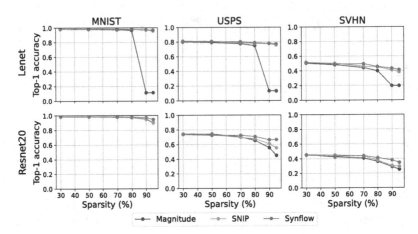

Fig. 3. Comparison of pruning heuristics for one-shot unstructured pruning.

three methods, the learning rate is initialized at 10^{-4} and is reduced by a factor 0.1 at epoch 120. Magnitude heuristic is used for pruning. After each pruning, the network are retrained on 150 epochs.

For all domains and networks, an Occam's hill [18] is observed in Fig. 4: at low sparsity rate, the accuracy increases since pruning acts as a regularization process which forces the model to focus on more important and general aspects of the task [18]. For high sparsity rate, the collapse of the network's performance classically occurs. This local gain of generalization is confirmed with weight rewinding where the network's parameters receive the same number of gradient updates for each sparsity level. Learning rate rewinding outperforms other methods in accordance with [15]. However, the large increase of accuracy is mostly due to the additional training iterations (gradient updates) with high learning rate. For the following experiments, learning rate rewinding will be used.

Influence of Pruning Heuristic. We compare the baseline magnitude pruning to SNIP and SynFlow. Figure 5 shows that there are few differences between pruning heuristics at low sparsity rate. For high sparsity rate, magnitude heuristic underperforms on all domains and networks.

3.4 Iterative Structured Pruning

To study the impact of structured pruning, baseline algorithms such as magnitude pruning [11] and FPGM [5] are used. Furthermore, we adapt SNIP and Syn-Flow to structured pruning by averaging the parameters' score over each filters as in [11]. Our results presented in Fig. 6 do not enable to confirm the superiority of a heuristic. For all domains, the accuracy decreases slightly, then this loss is accelerated at higher sparsity rate. An important observation is that structured pruning is not perfectly suited to domain generalization since this acceleration

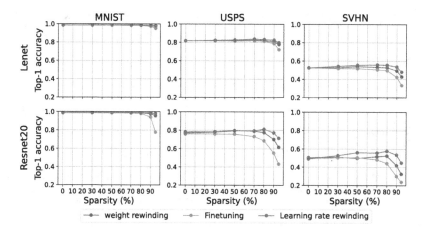

Fig. 4. Comparison of retraining procedures for iterative pruning.

appears earlier in target domains especially on SVHN. Another important, but expected, observation is that structured pruning has a worse accuracy score than unstructured pruning for any sparsity rate.

4 Experiments on RealWorld HAR Dataset

We scale our experiments on a second benchmark dedicated to Human Activity Recognition (HAR) since it is a challenging task, representative of many sensor-based IoT applications that process time series.

4.1 Datasets and Setup

The RealWorld HAR dataset [16] gathers fifteen subjects equipped with smartphones and smartwatches on seven different body positions (head, chest, upper arm, waist, forearm, thigh, and shin) that perform seven activities (climbing stairs down and up, jumping, lying, standing, sitting, running/jogging, and walking). From their devices, accelerometer and gyroscope data are sampled 50 Hz.

We follow the reference procedure of Chang *et al.* [1]. The accelerometer signals are sampled in fixed width sliding windows of 3 s (no overlap). A trace is discarded if it includes a transition of activities, timestamp noise, or data points without labels. The neural network is trained with the data from one body location (chest) then tested on the other body locations.

For our experiments, we use a variant of the model proposed in [1] in which instance normalization layers are replaced with standard batch-normalization

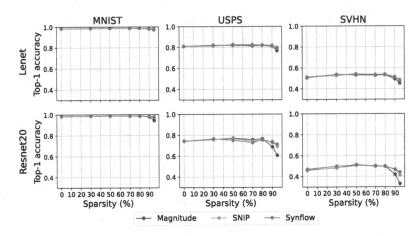

Fig. 5. Comparison of pruning heuristics for iterative unstructured pruning.

layers. We adapt Xu *et al.* [23] technique with temporal convolutions with random kernels of various sizes within [1–7]. The original data fraction parameter p and the consistency loss factor λ are fixed at 0.5 and 5 respectively. We keep SynFlow heuristic since it performs well on all settings of the digit benchmarks. Our results are averaged on three training seeds.

4.2   Impact of the Pruning Settings

For these experiments, the network is trained on 70 epochs with Adam optimizer, a batch size of 32 and an initial learning rate of 0.001 which is divided by a factor 2 at epochs 40 and 60. For iterative pruning, the network is retrained on 50 epochs with learning rate rewinding after each pruning. We also follow the evaluation process of [1] and measure the F1-score with macro-averaging (mean of all the per-class F1 scores).

A first observation from Fig. 7 is the efficiency of our customized version of Xu *et al.* method [23]: for all target domains, random convolutions enable the model to reach a greater f1-score than classically trained model despite a lower F1-score on the source domain. Second, we highlight an interesting compatibility between [23] and pruning techniques, since a compression ratio up to 80% and 50% can be reached without loss of accuracy on the source domains for unstructured and structured pruning respectively, although models trained with random convolutions are more impacted by high compression rate, more particularly for structured pruning (right).

Figure 7 shows that pruning improves the generalization capacity: without random convolutions (bottom), the F1-score of the network increases for target domains at high sparsity score on all pruning settings. Furthermore, with random convolutions, this increase is also observed in the one-shot unstructured pruning

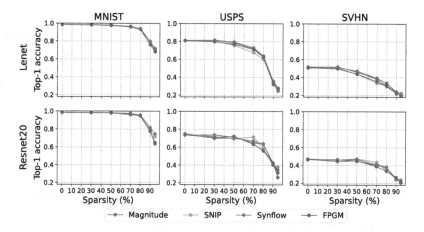

Fig. 6. Comparison of pruning heuristics for iterative structured pruning.

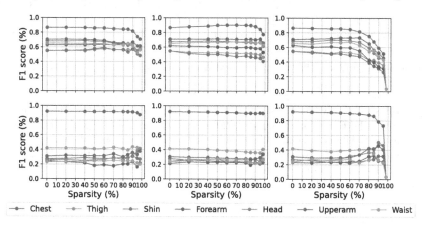

Fig. 7. Pruning on RealWorld HAR: trained with (top) and without (bottom) random convolutions, one-shot at initialization (left) and iterative (centre) unstructured pruning and iterative structured pruning (right).

setting (top-left) for the farthest body positions (thigh, shin) from the source domain (chest). On the contrary, for iterative pruning (top-centre and top-right) pruning increases F1-score on target domains close to the source domain while decreases F1-score on target domains far from the source domains. This effect can be explained by the additional training iterations (gradient updates) caused by iterative pruning with learning rate rewinding.

5   Conclusion

We experimentally evaluate the impact of pruning techniques in the single domain generalization setting with state-of-the-art methods and two benchmarks on image classification and human activity recognition. Our results show an interesting compatibility between pruning methods, that enable to significantly reduce the number of parameters, and single domain generalization approaches. Pruning improves the ability of a model to generalize, especially on domains far from the source domain. Moreover, all properties of pruning techniques are valid in the single domain generalization setting for approaches based on data-agnostic heuristics. Therefore, the combination of these methods represents a powerful tool to ease the deployment of neural network models on constrained platforms like microcontrollers for real-world applications for which the availability of training data is challenging. However, this combination of methods is not free from drawbacks since the impact of pruning on the performance is higher in the single domain generalization setting. More particularly, the additional training steps due to iterative pruning can cause a drop in performance on domains far from the source domain. For pruning algorithms with data-dependent heuristic, some properties like the benefits of using iterative scoring do not apply in the single domain generalization setting. These results highlight the need of developing as well as evaluating advanced domain generalization approaches for embedded applications that use highly compressed models.

Acknowledgments. This work benefited from the French Jean Zay supercomputer thanks to the *AI dynamic access* program. This collaborative work is partially supported by the IPCEI on Microelectronics and Nano2022 actions and by the European project InSecTT (www.insectt.eu: ECSEL Joint Undertaking (876038). The JU receives support from the European Union's H2020 program and Au, Sw, Sp, It, Fr, Po, Ir, Fi, Sl, Po, Nl, Tu. The document reflects only the author's view and the Commission is not responsible for any use that may be made of the information it contains.) and by the French National Research Agency (ANR) in the framework of the *Investissements d'Avenir* program (ANR-10-AIRT-05, irtnanoelec).

References

1. Chang, Y., Mathur, A., Isopoussu, A., Song, J., Kawsar, F.: A systematic study of unsupervised domain adaptation for robust human-activity recognition. Proc. ACM Interact. Mobile Wearable Ubiquit. Technol. **4**(1), 1–3 (2020)
2. Frankle, J., Carbin, M.: The lottery ticket hypothesis: finding sparse, trainable neural networks. In: International Conference on Learning Representations (2019)
3. Han, S., Pool, J., Tran, J., Dally, W.: Learning both weights and connections for efficient neural network. Adv. Neural Inf. Proc. Syst. **1**, 1135–1143 (2015)
4. He, K., Zhang, X., Ren, S., Sun, J.: Deep residual learning for image recognition. In: Proceedings of the Conference on Computer Vision and Pattern Recognition (2016)
5. He, Y., Liu, P., Wang, Z., Hu, Z., Yang, Y.: Filter pruning via geometric median for deep convolutional neural networks acceleration. In: Proceedings of the Conference on Computer Vision and Pattern Recognition (2019)
6. Howard, A.G., et al.: MobileNets: efficient convolutional neural networks for mobile vision applications. arXiv preprint arXiv:1704.04861 (2017)
7. Hull, J.J.: A database for handwritten text recognition research. IEEE Trans. Pattern Anal. Mach. Intell. **16**(5), 550–554 (1994)

8. Ismail Fawaz, H., et al.: InceptionTime: finding AlexNet for time series classification. Data Min. Knowl. Disc. **34**, 1–27 (2020)
9. LeCun, Y., et al.: Backpropagation applied to handwritten zip code recognition. Neural Comput. **1**(4), 541–551 (1989)
10. Lee, N., Ajanthan, T., Torr, P.: Snip: single-shot network pruning based on connection sensitivity. In: International Conference on Learning Representations (2018)
11. Li, H., Kadav, A., Durdanovic, I., Samet, H., Graf, H.P.: Pruning filters for efficient convnets. In: International Conference on Learning Representations (2017)
12. Munappy, A., Bosch, J., Olsson, H.H., Arpteg, A., Brinne, B.: Data management challenges for deep learning. In: 2019 45th Euromicro Conference on Software Engineering and Advanced Applications (SEAA). IEEE (2019)
13. Netzer, Y., Wang, T., Coates, A., Bissacco, A., Wu, B., Ng, A.Y.: Reading digits in natural images with unsupervised feature learning. NIPS (2011)
14. Qiao, F., Zhao, L., Peng, X.: Learning to learn single domain generalization. In: Proceedings of the Conference on Computer Vision and Pattern Recognition (2020)
15. Renda, A., Frankle, J., Carbin, M.: Comparing rewinding and fine-tuning in neural network pruning. In: International Conference on Learning Representations (2020)
16. Sztyler, T., Stuckenschmidt, H.: On-body localization of wearable devices: an investigation of position-aware activity recognition. In: 2016 IEEE International Conference on Pervasive Computing and Communications (PerCom). IEEE (2016)
17. Tanaka, H., Kunin, D., Yamins, D.L., Ganguli, S.: Pruning neural networks without any data by iteratively conserving synaptic flow. Adv. Neural Inf. Proc. Syst. **33**, 6377–6389 (2020)
18. Thodberg, H.H.: Improving generalization of neural networks through pruning. Int. J. Neural Syst. **1**(4), 317–326 (1991)
19. Trommer, E., Waschneck, B., Kumar, A.: dCSR: a memory-efficient sparse matrix representation for parallel neural network inference. In: 2021 IEEE/ACM International Conference On Computer Aided Design (ICCAD). IEEE (2021)
20. Verdenius, S., Stol, M., Forré, P.: Pruning via iterative ranking of sensitivity statistics. arXiv preprint arXiv:2006.00896 (2020)
21. Volpi, R., Murino, V.: Addressing model vulnerability to distributional shifts over image transformation sets. In: Proceedings of the IEEE/CVF International Conference on Computer Vision (2019)
22. Wang, X., Han, Y., Leung, V.C., Niyato, D., Yan, X., Chen, X.: Convergence of edge computing and deep learning: a comprehensive survey. IEEE Commun. Surv. Tutorials **22**, 869–904 (2020)
23. Xu, Z., Liu, D., Yang, J., Raffel, C., Niethammer, M.: Robust and generalizable visual representation learning via random convolutions. In: International Conference on Learning Representations (2021)

IoT Security, Privacy and Data Protection

A Low-Overhead Approach for Self-sovereign Identity in IoT

Geovane Fedrecheski[1]([⊠]), Laisa C. P. Costa[1], Samira Afzal[1], Jan M. Rabaey[2], Roseli D. Lopes[1], and Marcelo K. Zuffo[1]

[1] Department of Electronics Systems Engineering, University of Sao Paulo, Sao Paulo, Brazil
{geovane,laisa,roseli,mkzuffo}@lsi.usp.br, afzal.samira@usp.br
[2] Berkeley Wireless Research Center, University of California, Berkeley, USA
jan_rabaey@berkeley.edu

Abstract. We present a low-overhead mechanism for self-sovereign identification and communication of IoT agents in constrained networks. Our main contribution is to enable native use of Decentralized Identifiers (DIDs) and DID-based secure communication on constrained networks, whereas previous works either did not consider the issue or relied on proxy-based architectures. We propose a new extension to DIDs along with a more concise serialization method for DID metadata. Moreover, in order to reduce the security overhead over transmitted messages, we adopted a binary message envelope. We implemented these proposals within the context of Swarm Computing, an approach for decentralized IoT. Results showed that our proposal reduces the size of identity metadata in almost four times and security overhead up to five times. We observed that both techniques are required to enable operation on constrained networks.

Keywords: Decentralized identity · Secure communications · Constrained networks · Secure Envelope Overhead · CBOR

1 Introduction

Self-sovereign identity (SSI), also referred to as decentralized identity, is an emerging approach that enables subjects to be in full control of their own digital identities [6]. When applied to IoT environments, SSI facilitates device ownership, enhances privacy, and reduces dependency on third parties [5]. IoT approaches that rely on decentralized architectures, such as the Swarm [4], are expected to greatly benefit from these new capabilities enabled by SSI.

Once devices are put in charge of their own identity, new challenges arise, mainly due to the limitations of constrained devices and networks. In this paper, we focus on reducing the overhead of self-sovereign identity in IoT networks. We extend existing standards to reduce message footprint and propose a new serialization method that significantly reduces the transmitted bytes.

The current approach to implement self-sovereign identity relies on the use of Decentralized Identifiers (DIDs) [15]. A DID is a new form of identifier that

A. González-Vidal et al. (Eds.): GIoTS 2022, LNCS 13533, pp. 265–276, 2022.
https://doi.org/10.1007/978-3-031-20936-9_21

does not depend on trusted third parties and has an associated set of cryptographic metadata referred to as a DID Document (DDo). This way, beyond simple identification, a DDo enables the establishment of an end-to-end secure channel, which can be done using a transport-agnostic protocol called DIDComm [9]. The DID data model is extensible, and by May 2022 there are around 110 registered extensions (referred to as "DID methods") [17].

Most works on DIDs, however, overlook the overhead of transmitting DDos, a crucial aspect in bandwidth-constrained networks. For example, while the LoRa network only allows packets of up to 242 bytes, the most compact of the registered DID extensions requires DDos in the order of 500 bytes. Even the works applying DIDs in the IoT context did not consider size limitations imposed by network bandwidth [7,18]. In one approach that does consider resource constraints, DIDs transmission is avoided by using OAuth tokens in a centralized architecture [12]. Furthermore, the overhead on secure communications imposed by the DIDComm protocol also has not been addressed in the literature.

Considering the potential benefits of the self-sovereign approach for the IoT, and the drawbacks of existing solutions, this paper proposes a low-overhead method for DID-based identification and secure communication. The contributions of this paper are as follows:

- A new DID method suitable for IoT networks referred to as *DID Swarm*, which has smaller DID and DDo sizes when compared to existing methods.
- CBOR-based DID Documents for IoT (CBOR-DI), a novel serialization mechanism that can reduce DDo sizes by almost four times.
- DIoTComm, a binary envelope to replace DIDComm in IoT networks that reduces overhead up to five times.
- Integration with the Swarm framework, a decentralized IoT approach that enables spontaneous resource sharing.

2   Related Work

Several works have proposed identity solutions for the IoT, however, many of them require centralized management. The Open Connectivity Foundation [8] uses Fully Qualified Domain Names and relies on certificates for identity management, two centralized approaches. The Web of Things framework [13] relies on Uniform Resource Identifiers (URIs), which can be decentralized, however, the identity management is still done via certificates.

Our previous work shows the potential of DIDs as an owner-centric, privacy-aware and decentralized identification mechanism for IoT applications [5]. One of the challenges for DID adoption in the IoT, however, is communication overhead, since none of the currently registered DID methods [17] has been designed to work in constrained networks. For example, the Sovrin DID method [10] uses approximately 500 bytes to encode a DID Document.

Existing works have applied self-sovereign identity to IoT. In one case [18], authors propose an architecture for machine identifiers based on DIDs, along with a storage layer based on Blockchain and IPFS. Another approach [7] combines DIDs with Verifiable Credentials, a data model for signed attributes in SSI, to manage identification in the IoT. Others [12] have used newly generated DIDs to populate access control lists and enable guests to access smart home devices. None of these works, however, considered the size of the documents associated with implementation of SSI in low-power IoT networks. Moreover, it is not clear how these works protect the communication between agents.

To enable secure communications based on DIDs, the DIDComm protocol has been proposed [9]. DIDComm supports authenticated message exchanges and message routing over loosely trusted routers, and is independent of transport protocol. Nevertheless, DIDComm uses JSON for serialization, which implies an overhead prevents its use in low-power IoT networks. Currently there is no known low-overhead alternative to DIDComm.

3   Background

3.1   Self-sovereign Identity

In the SSI approach each entity has full control of its own identity. Formally, the complete self-sovereign identity of an agent is the union of all of its identifiers and attributes across different domains [6]. The Decentralized Identifiers (DID) specification [15] defines a new format for self-sovereign identifiers and related metadata. A DID is composed of a DID method[1] prefix and a namespace-specific identifier (NSI) [15]. The prefix always start with the string `did:` and is followed by a method name and a colon, e.g., the prefix for the Tangle DID method is `did:tangle:` [2]. The NSI is a globally unique identifier, usually randomly generated, whose size and other parameters are specified by the DID method. A truncated example of a DID is: `did:tangle:WILTZRG...Q99NA9999`. Thus, the primary use for DIDs is to uniquely identify an entity in a decentralized way.

Another use for DIDs is to associate it with related metadata, such as public keys and service endpoints. This association is referred to as a DID Document [15], and it is useful since it enables remote agents to securely message a DID owner. DDos are usually serialized in JSON. Although a binary serialization is specified [15], none of the currently registered DID methods uses it.

3.2   Swarm

Swarm is a distributed collection of cooperating things [4]. In the Swarm architecture, IoT agents interact by exchanging messages through RESTful interfaces. Two key aspects needed to guarantee a cooperative Swarm are agent identification and message security. Agents need to be uniquely identified so that they can be told apart from each other, and since the Swarm is distributed and may have trillions of devices, agent identification must be decentralized and scalable. Messages exchanged between Swarm agents must be protected against attacks such as spoofing and information disclosure, in a network-agnostic way.

---

[1] A "DID method" is an extension of the DID specification;

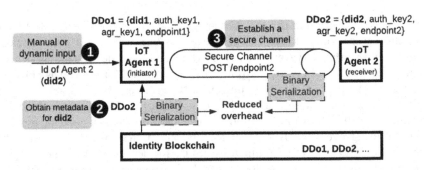

Fig. 1. Architecture of the proposed system.

4 Proposal

This section presents our proposal to enable self-sovereign identification and communication of IoT agents with low overhead for heterogeneous networks.

4.1 Self-sovereign Identification and Communication of IoT Agents

Our proposal is divided into the functions of agent identification and agent communication. We propose agent identification as a fully self-sovereign procedure. Each agent generates its own identifier, in the format of a DID, as well as its own identity metadata, in the format of a DDo, which contains service endpoints and public keys. This approach allows devices to fully own and control their identity without depending on third parties [5]. To enable discoverability, though, agents may choose to anchor their DDos on an Identity Blockchain, which acts as a decentralized source of truth for identity metadata. This allows agents to dynamically resolve the DDo associated with a specific agent, given that its DID is known. For example, if Agent 1 knows the DID of Agent 2, the DDo of Agent 2 can be obtained by querying the blockchain, as shown in Fig. 1.

Once agents are identified, they can begin to communicate securely. We consider interactions to involve an initiator agent and a receiver agent, and optionally the Identity Blockchain. If initiator and receiver are pre-provisioned with each other's DDo, communication can begin immediately, without the need to contact a third party. If, on the other hand, an agent is only given the DID of another agent, it needs the blockchain to retrieve its respective DDo[2]. The latter case is shown in Fig. 1. Then, once the initiator has the DDo of the receiver, it can extract the endpoint to find out where to send the messages and use the public key to protect the messages, i.e., derive a session key for encryption.

These procedures, however, may be of limited use in constrained IoT networks due to the overhead of (1) DID resolution and (2) message protection, as discussed in Sect. 1. Existing works adopting Self-Sovereign Identity in IoT either do not consider the limitations of constrained networks, or address it by

---

[2] Note that the DDo can be cached after the first use.

creating a centralized adaptation layer. In this work we propose a set of extensions and optimizations to reduce the overhead of both transmitting DDos and protecting interactions between self-sovereign IoT agents. First, we propose a lean DID method that specifies the minimum needed metadata for DDos in the IoT. Then, we propose an alternative serialization mechanism for DDos, named CBOR-based DID Documents for IoT (CBOR-DI), that can reduce DDo size up to four times. Finally, we present a binary alternative to DIDComm, named DIoTComm, that significantly reduces overhead of DID-aware communications.

4.2 The Swarm DID Method

A *DID method* consists of a set of definitions about the format of DIDs and DDos, as well as on how to perform management operations [15]. In this section, we present the Swarm DID Method (`did:sw:`), which will enable self-sovereign identification of IoT agents. Although it was motivated by the Swarm architecture, it is sufficiently generic to be used in general IoT architectures.

Requirements. Previously, we established that the self-sovereign approach can satisfy the requirements of privacy and decentralization for IoT devices [5]. We now specify the remaining requirements that need to be tackled in order to enable self-sovereign identification of devices in heterogeneous networks. First, both the DID and the DDo must be short since they may be carried over constrained networks. Second, the DID should carry enough randomness to be able to identify trillions of devices. And third, the DDo should support at least one service URL, needed to allow remote service invocations. The next sections specify the DID and DDo according to these requirements.

DID. In the Swarm DID method, each device is responsible for autonomously generating its own DID. A DID is composed of a prefix and a namespace-specific identifier (NSI). For the part of the prefix that identifies the DID method in use, we chose the two-letter string `sw`. Thus the full prefix is `did:sw:`. Next, we define the NSI as a short byte array of size 16, that must be generated using a strong random number generator. The address space is 2^{128}, what leaves more than 2^{88} unique identifiers for each device, considering 1 trillion devices and a uniform distribution. A full example of a Swarm DID with a Base58-encoded NSI is `did:sw:TTbs19FJKYf6jXzS1dbnqe`.

DID Document. Additional metadata about a DID can be stored in a DID Document. The DDo usually carries the DID itself, one ore more public keys, and zero or more endpoints [15]. Existing DID methods define that the DDo will contain the DID itself and at least one authentication key [1,10]. We adopt this design for the Swarm DID method, since it provides identification and authentication. Next, unlike most DID methods, we propose the use of at least one static agreement key, since it enables the creation of a secure channel without transmission of ephemeral keys, thus saving bandwidth in constrained networks.

One consideration we take in order to shorten the DDo is that both the authentication and the agreement keys must use an optimized cipher suite with respect to public key sizes. While many elliptic curves satisfy this requirement, we adopt the curves X25519 and Ed25519 [17], which have the smallest public keys, i.e., 32 bytes. To allow referencing specific keys within a DDo, keys may have an arbitrary identifier that is unique in the scope of the DDo. We define the following automated way to generate a short locally-unique key id: compute the SHA-2 of the public key, and truncate it to the first eight bytes.

Finally, a DDo in the Swarm must support at least one service endpoint to allow remote service invocations. The main parameter for each endpoint is an URL, which enables remote agents to message the owner of the DDo. Optionally, endpoints can also have a type tag and an id that shall be unique within the DDo. Both the service type and the id are application-dependent, and if used, they should be short.

4.3 Optimized DDo Serialization with CBOR-DI

Serialization mechanisms have direct impact on the size of messages transferred across a network, and range from simple raw bytes encoding to complex structured data, such as the eXtensible Markup Language (XML)[3]. While the binary approach has the benefit of conciseness, a structured approach facilitates arbitrary manipulation. Other formats, such as the JavaScript Object Notation (JSON), have provided a reasonable trade-off, with the benefit of being human-readable. The general specification for DIDs [15] uses JSON as its main format, and most existing DID methods rely on JSON as well.

We provide a JSON-based serialization for the Swarm DID method, as shown in Fig. 2 (a). It contains an identifier (DID), two public keys, and a service endpoint. The random part of the DID is serialized in Base58, since JSON does not allow encoding of raw bytes. The keys have each an id and a value, both encoded in Base58, and a type indicating its format and usage. Similarly, the service contains an id, a type, and an endpoint URL. After trimming white spaces, the JSON document occupies 497 bytes.

Although human-readable and relatively short, the JSON-based DDo still cannot be transmitted over low-power IoT networks, e.g., the LoRa[4] network only supports packets of up to 240 bytes. Fragmentation could be used, at the expense of increased spectrum usage and latency. What is needed is a more concise representation for DDos that allow transmission on constrained networks.

The Concise Binary Object Representation (CBOR) is a JSON-compatible serialization mechanism that uses a binary encoding. Although the DID specification considers direct conversion from JSON to CBOR [15], on average this approach only reduces document size in 20%, i.e., achieving 415 bytes.

Considering this limitation, we present a novel serialization method named CBOR-based DID Documents for IoT (CBOR-DI) that reduces size of DDos

---

[3] https://www.w3.org/TR/2008/REC-xml-20081126/.

[4] https://lora-alliance.org/resource_hub/lorawan-specification-v1-1/.

```
{
  'id': 'did:sw:QmH8UDyHoWFYuntspvkLuZ',
  '@context': ['https://www.w3.org/ns/did/v1'],
  'authentication': [{
    'id': '#MvR5AocE',
    'type': 'Ed25519VerificationKey2018',
    'publicKeyBase58': '7c4...5uQ'
  }],
  'keyAgreement': [{
    'id': '#rUSavwkN',
    'type': 'X25519KeyAgreementKey2019',
    'publicKeyBase58': 'Fph...Tiw'
  }],
  'service': [{
    'id': '#main',
    'serviceEndpoint': 'http://192.168.0.107/',
    'type': 'swarmService'
  }]
}
```

(a) JSON serialization (497 bytes)

```
[
  '73773a4b13...19cf4fd5f4',
  [{-2: '3c0...b87', -1: 6}],
  [{-2: 'c48...b4c', -1: 4}],
  ['http://192.168.0.107/']
]
```

(b) CBOR-DI serialization (128 bytes)

Fig. 2. Example of Swarm DID Document serialized in JSON and CBOR-DI.

in up to 75%. The technique consists in transmitting only the strictly necessary parts of a DID Document, as exemplified in Fig. 2 (b). Specifically, we implement the following modifications when comparing to the JSON serialization:

- Use CBOR as serialization mechanism.
- Use an array instead of a key-value mapping so that the elements have a fixed order: DID, verification keys, agreement keys, and service endpoints.
- Remove the did: prefix of the DID, and only use the method designator, e.g., use sw: instead of did:sw:.
- Encode the DID and the key values as raw bytes instead of Base58. Note that the average overhead of Base58 is close to 30%[5].
- Use the key format defined in the CBOR Object Signing and Encryption (COSE) specification [14]. It defines keys as a mapping that uses integers instead of strings to reduce size. For example, instead of writing "type: Ed25519VerificationKey2019", we write "−1: 6". Also, in Fig. 2 (b), the integer −2 points to the public part of the key. The full table with rules for key representation is available in the Key Objects section of COSE [14].
- Finally, ignore optional fields in service endpoints and only include the URL.

As shown in Fig. 2 (b), CBOR-DI achieves a DDo size of only 128 bytes, enabling DDo transmission in constrained networks, while losing no essential information. Also, by leveraging existing standards, such as CBOR and COSE, it fosters interoperability. Furthermore, the conversion process between JSON and CBOR-DI can be automated by applying a small set of mapping rules, e.g., convert between JSON and CBOR, Base58 and binary, and JSON keys and COSE keys. Finally, although we proposed CBOR-DI in the context of the Swarm DID method, the technique is generic and could be easily extended to reduce DDo size in other methods as well.

---

[5] https://tools.ietf.org/id/draft-msporny-base58-01.html.

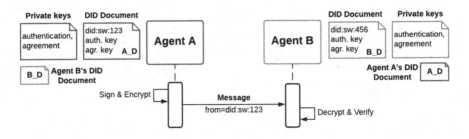

Fig. 3. An overview of the DIoTComm protocol.

4.4   Secure Communication with DIoTComm

Once two agents are identified and have access to each other's DDo, they can exchange messages securely. The DIDComm protocol has been proposed as a way to protect communications between self-sovereign agents [9]. It adopts the structure and algorithms defined in the JSON Object Signing and Encryption (JOSE) standard [11], which allows use of existing schemes for message encryption and authentication. Furthermore, it is agnostic of both DID method and transport protocol. DIDComm also defines a set of message headers to identify a message sender and receiver, as well as a message type, a unique message identifier, and other optional metadata. One downside of DIDComm, however, is its reliance on JSON which causes overhead in constrained networks.

In this section we propose DID-based IoT Communication (DIoTComm), an alternative to DIDComm that is tailored for the IoT, i.e., it uses a more concise serialization method and simpler message headers. While in DIDComm a JSON-based format is used for message protection, DIoTComm uses COSE, which defines both a message format and a set of lightweight security algorithms, leading to small-footprint protected messages. In DIoTComm the only message header used is the sender id, as shown in Fig. 3. We are able to omit the receiver id since the decryption by a receiver other than the intended one will fail. We also consider that message type and unique id, if needed, will be handled at the payload layer, e.g., if the payload is a CoAP message, its header would include a method and path, and an id.

DIoTComm leverages the structure defined by COSE messages which have one integrity-protected header, an unprotected header, a payload, and optional extra fields. We define that the sender id in DIoTComm must be binary-encoded and carried within the "key id" field of the protected header. If the message must be encrypted, the payload will contain the cipher-text. If it must be signed, the payload will contain the plain-text, and the message will have the signature as a fourth parameter. In cases where a message must be protected both for non-repudiability and confidentiality, the plain-text is first signed then encrypted. Creation of such protected envelopes is described as follows.

For message signature, the sending agent will sign the message with its private authentication key. The receiving agent can verify the signature using the key available in the sender's DDo. The COSE algorithm used is EDDSA, which consists in the Edwards Curve Digital Signature Algorithm that is applied over curve Ed25519 keys.

Regarding encryption, the sending agent will obtain an encryption key using its private agreement key that is locally stored, along with the public agreement key available in the receiving agent's DDo. A similar process is then executed by the receiving agent to decrypt the message, wherein the receiving agent uses its private agreement key and the sending agent's public agreement key to obtain the decryption key. The COSE algorithm used for key derivation is the ECDH-SS-HKDF-256, which uses an elliptic curve Diffie-Hellman with two static keys, along with a key derivation function based on SHA-256. The COSE algorithm used for content encryption is AES-CCM-16-64-128, that is the Advanced Encryption Standard in CCM mode with a 64-bit tag and a 13-bytes nonce.

4.5 Implementation

We implemented the proposed system in the SwarmLib, a library for building Swarm agents, using the Python programming language. To construct COSE messages, we used the cose library. We also modified the SwarmLib and added several new routines to create DIDs and DDos, to register and resolve DDos, and to protect messages before sending them to remote agents. Routines for DDo serialization in different formats, including JSON, CBOR, and CBOR-DI were also added to the SwarmLib. We used unit tests to validate the newly added routines. We also implemented a blockchain mock, i.e. an API to create and query DID Documents. The API supports DDos in three different formats: JSON, CBOR, and CBOR-DI. It also validates the signature during the creation of new DDos using the authentication keys from the DDos themselves, ensuring that the DDo was registered by its own agent.

5 Evaluation

5.1 DID and DDo sizes

In this section we measure the size of our proposed DID and DID Document, and compare it to five existing DID methods, as shown in Table 1. The methods did:ockam [1], did:io [3], and did:tangle [2] were selected since they are specifically tailored for IoT applications. The other two, did:sov [10] and did:v1 [16], were selected as references since they provide both a complete specification and a mature open source implementation.

As shown in Table 1, our proposed method, did:sw, has the smaller DID size, occupying only 19 bytes when using the binary serialization described in Sect. 4.3. Among the methods tailored for IoT, did:ockam has the second smaller DID, requiring 39 bytes. In order to compare DID Documents, we built documents with equivalent configurations, i.e., having two public keys and, when applicable, one service endpoint[6]. The measured DDos were extracted from the specification

---

[6] Some DID methods do not use endpoints.

Table 1. Comparison with existing DID Methods.

Prefix	Focus on IoT?	DID serialization	DID size	DDo ser.	DDo size
did:sw:	Yes	binary	**19**	Binary	**128**
did:sov:	No	text	30	JSON	499
did:ockam:	Yes	text	39	JSON	779
did:io:	Yes	text	49	JSON	1112
did:v1:	No	text	54	JSON	1182
did:tangle:	Yes	text	92	JSON	853

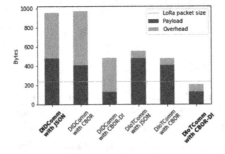

Fig. 4. Size and overhead for DID Documents sent within a signed message (step 2 of Fig. 1).

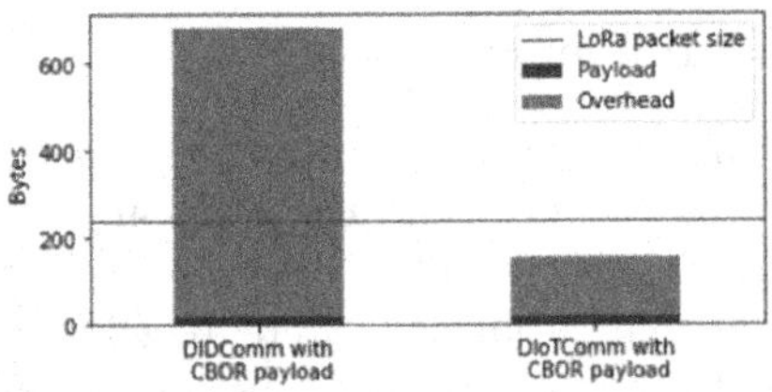

Fig. 5. Size and overhead for regular messages sent within a signed and encrypted message (step 3 of Fig. 1).

of each DID method, and a second public key was added when the example contained only one. As shown in Table 1, the `did:sw` method has the smallest DDo size, which represents a reduction of almost 75% when comparing to the second smallest DDo. These results confirm that the methods proposed in Sects. 4.2 and 4.3 indeed reduced DID and DDo sizes when comparing to previous works.

5.2 Secure Envelope Overhead

In this section, we compare the overhead of using DIDComm and DIoTComm to protect DID Documents and application messages for transmission in constrained networks.

We start by measuring the size of a signed message containing a DID Document, using both DIDComm and DIoTComm. In doing this, we use different DDo serializations: JSON, CBOR, and CBOR-DI. Fig. 4 shows the results. The three leftmost bars use the DIDComm message envelope[7], while the three rightmost bars use DIoTComm. We also highlight the threshold for transmission of LoRa packets when considering Data Rate 6, which allows packets of up to 242

---

[7] The size of DIDComm with CBOR is larger than DIDComm with JSON due to overhead of Base64 encoding.

bytes. Note that, although the overhead is significantly reduced when adopting DIoTComm, the only scenario in which a DDo can be transmitted over a LoRa network is when DIoTComm and CBOR-DI are combined.

In the next chart, shown in Fig. 5, we consider a 21-bytes application message serialized in CBOR and sent over DIDComm and then over DIoTComm. Differently from the previous chart, this message is not only signed, but also encrypted, i.e. the messages are nested with two layers of headers. This confers the DIoTComm version an even higher compression rate, with an overhead at least five times smaller.

6 Conclusion

This paper presented a solution for self-sovereign identification and communication of IoT agents in constrained networks. While previous works either did not consider constrained networks, or proposed centralized solutions, we proposed a set of techniques to enable native self-sovereign identity in IoT environments. First, we presented a specification for Decentralized Identifiers (DIDs) that focus on reduction of metadata size by using shorter identifiers and optimized cipher suites. We then introduced a novel serialization mechanism named CBOR-based DID Documents for IoT (CBOR-DI), which reduces DID Documents up to four times when compared to a JSON serialization. Finally, we proposed DIoTComm, an optimized layer for protection of messages exchanged between self-sovereign agents which uses a binary encoding, thus achieving five times reduction for signed and encrypted messages. We implemented these proposals within the Swarm framework and evaluated them with respect to metadata size and overhead. Regarding identity metadata, we achieved a reduction of 3.89 times when compared to related works. With respect to secure communication, we achieved a reduction of almost five times. The combination of these techniques enable the native use of self-sovereign identity in constrained IoT networks such as LoRa. Future work includes evaluation in a real network scenario and integration with a system for authentication and authorization.

Acknowledgments. We would like to thank researchers at the Laboratory for Integrated Systems at POLI USP, the Interdisciplinary Center of Interactive Technologies at USP, and the Berkeley Wireless Research Center. Authors would also like to thank for the funding provided by LSITEC.

References

1. Ockam DID Method Specification, November 2018. https://github.com/ockam-network/did-method-spec/blob/master/README.md
2. Tangleid DID Method Specification, June 2019. https://github.com/TangleID/TangleID/blob/develop/did-method-spec.md
3. Iotex DID Method Specification, August 2020. https://github.com/iotexproject/iotex-did/blob/master/README.md

4. Costa, L.C.P., Rabaey, J., Wolisz, A., Rosan, M., Zuffo, M.K.: Swarm OS control plane: an architecture proposal for heterogeneous and organic networks. IEEE Trans. Consum. Electron. **61**(4), 454–462 (2015). https://doi.org/10.1109/TCE. 2015.7389799

5. Fedrecheski, G., Rabaey, J.M., Costa, L.C., Ccori, P.C.C., Pereira, W.T., Zuffo, M.K.: Self-sovereign identity for IoT environments: a perspective. In: Proceedings of the Global IoT Summit 2020, pp. 1–6(2020)

6. Ferdous, M.S., Chowdhury, F., Alassafi, M.O.: In search of self-sovereign identity leveraging blockchain technology. IEEE Access **7**, 103059–103079 (2019)

7. Fotiou, N., Pittaras, I., Siris, V.A., Polyzos, G.C.: Enabling opportunistic users in multi-tenant IoT systems using decentralized identifiers and permissioned blockchains. In: Proceedings of the 2nd International ACM Workshop on Security and Privacy for the Internet-of-Things, pp. 22–23 (2019)

8. Foundation, O.C.: OCF (2020). https://openconnectivity.org/developer/

9. Hardman, D.: DIDcomm messaging. DIF draft, DIF, December 2020. https:// identity.foundation/didcomm-messaging/spec/

10. Hardman, D., Lodder, M.: Sovrin DID Method Specification, December 2020. https://sovrin-foundation.github.io/sovrin/spec/did-method-spec-template.html

11. Jones, M.B.: JSON Object Signing and Encryption (JOSE). RFC 7518 May 2015. https://doi.org/10.17487/RFC7518. https://tools.ietf.org/html/rfc7518

12. Lagutin, D., Kortesniemi, Y., Fotiou, N., Siris, V.A.: Enabling decentralised identifiers and verifiable credentials for constrained Internet-of-Things devices using oauth-based delegation. In: Workshop on Decentralized IoT Systems and Security (DISS) (2019)

13. Reshetova, E., McCool, M.: Web of Things (WoT) Security and Privacy Guidelines, April 2021. https://rawgit.com/w3c/wot-security/master/index.html

14. Schaad, J.: CBOR Object Signing and Encryption (COSE). RFC 8152, July 2017. https://doi.org/10.17487/RFC8152. https://rfc-editor.org/rfc/rfc8152.txt

15. Sporny, M., Longley, D., Allen, C., Sabadello, M., Reed, D.: Decentralized identifiers (DIDs) v1.0. W3C working draft, W3C, December 2013. https://www.w3. org/TR/did-core//

16. Sporny, M., Longley, D., Webber, C.: Veres One DID Method Specification, November 2019.https://w3c-ccg.github.io/did-method-v1/

17. Steele, O., Sporny, M.: Did specification registries. W3C wg note, W3C, November 2020.https://w3c-ccg.github.io/did-method-v1/

18. Su, Y., Wu, J., Long, C., Wei, L.: Secure decentralized machine identifiers for Internet of Things. In: Proceedings of the 2020 the 2nd International Conference on Blockchain Technology, pp. 57–62 (2020)

An Analysis of Process Parameters for the Optimization of Specific Emitter Identification Under Rayleigh Fading

Mohamed K. M. Fadul, Jordan T. Willis$^{(\boxtimes)}$, Donald R. Reising$^{(\boxtimes)}$,
and T. Daniel Loveless

University of Tennessee at Chattanooga, Chattanooga, TN 37403, USA
{lzw784,dsh155}@mocs.utc.edu, {donald-reising,daniel-loveless}@utc.edu

Abstract. Specific Emitter Identification (SEI) was introduced over twenty-five years ago to grant electronic warfare systems the ability to uniquely, distinguish between RADARs of the same type using intra-pulse modulation features. The demonstrated success of RADAR SEI led to its application in the identification of wireless transmitters for the purpose of augmenting digital security measures within public and private communication networks. The majority of SEI work has focused on wireless channels comprised of noise only, unknown multipath fading conditions, or fixed fading channels. Our recent works focused on SEI performance within multipath fading channels that conform to a known model/behavior and change from one transmission to another. However, these works did not design the SEI process (i.e., from waveform collection to final radio identification decision) with the singular purpose of maximizing SEI performance under multipath fading. In order to maximize SEI performance under Rayleigh fading, this work analyzes the impacts of the: (i) filter type, order, and bandwidth; (ii) Gabor Transform analysis window width; as well as (iii) the number of candidate signals used by the Nelder-Mead (N-M) channel estimator. The result is a 11.9% average percent correct classification performance improvement for a length five Rayleigh fading channel at a signal-to-noise ratio of 9 dB.

Keywords: Specific emitter identification · RF-DNA fingerprint · Rayleigh fading · Multipath · OFDM · IoT security

1 Introduction

Specific Emitter Identification (SEI) was introduced over twenty-five years ago to provide Electronic Warfare (EW) systems the ability to uniquely, distinguish between RADAR systems of the same type or class using intra-pulse modulation features. These features are a byproduct of Unintentional Modulation On Pulse (UMOP) that is attributed to the systems, sub-systems, and components (e.g., antenna, local oscillator, power amplifier, filters, etc.) that comprise the RADAR emitter. The appeal of SEI lies in its: (i) passive nature, which means that the

© The Author(s), under exclusive license to Springer Nature Switzerland AG 2022
A. González-Vidal et al. (Eds.): GIoTS 2022, LNCS 13533, pp. 277–291, 2022.
https://doi.org/10.1007/978-3-031-20936-9_22

targeted emitter generates signals, as part of its intended mission, without external stimulation, (ii) exploitation of distinct and unique features that are unintentional and organic to the transmission process, (iii) ability to quantitatively measure the exploited features present within the signal, and (iv) exploitation of persistent features across time, location, and environments [1]. The success of RADAR SEI has led to its application in the identification of wireless transmitters for the purpose of augmenting digital security measures (e.g., encryption, username & password) within public and private communication networks. The application of SEI to the identification of wireless transmitters is often referred to as Radio Frequency (RF) or RF-Distinct Native Attributes (RF-DNA) fingerprinting due to the unique 'fingerprint' that is imparted upon the radio signal during its generation and transmission by the components (e.g., mixers, filters, amplifiers, etc.) comprising the RF front-end. RF fingerprinting has demonstrated success in achieving serial number (i.e., same manufacturer and model) discrimination, which represents the most challenging case.

The preponderance of RF fingerprinting work has been focused on wireless channels comprised of Additive White Gaussian Noise (AWGN), unknown multipath fading conditions, or fixed fading channels [8,10,11]. Our recent works presented the first cases in which the multipath fading conditions are known (e.g., Rayleigh versus Rician fading) and change from one transmission to another [4–6]. However, the process presented in our previous works was not designed to maximize RF fingerprinting performance under multipath fading. In this work we analyze the impacts of the: (i) filter type, order, and bandwidth; (ii) Gabor Transform analysis window width; as well as (iii) the number of candidate signals used by the Nelder-Mead (N-M) channel estimator with the goal of maximizing SEI performance under Rayleigh fading. The result is a 11.9% average percent correct classification performance improvement for a length five ($L = 5$) Rayleigh fading channel at a Signal-to-Noise Ratio (SNR) of 9 dB.

The remainder of this paper is organized as follows. Section 2 describes signal collection, detection, and the pre-processing steps. Section 3 presents the methodology, which includes: filter design, the multipath channel model, N-M channel estimation & equalization, RF fingerprint generation, and radio classification. The results and corresponding analysis are presented in Sect. 4 and the paper is concluded in Sect. 5.

2   Background

2.1   Signal Collection, Detection & Pre-processing

This work uses the set of IEEE 802.11a Wireless-Fidelity (Wi-Fi) signals transmitted by $N_D = 4$ Cisco AIR-CB21G-A-K9 radios that operated in a peer-to-peer connection and office environment, which is the same set of signals used in [4–6]. For each radio, a total of 2,000 signals were collected using an Agilent spectrum analyzer. Following signal collection, (i) amplitude-based variance trajectory detection was used to remove individual signals from the overall collection record, (ii) the corresponding Wi-Fi preamble extracted, (iii) carrier frequency

offset estimation and correction performed, and (iv) down-sampled to a rate of
20 MHz.

3   Methodology

3.1   Filter Design

The work in [4–6] used a fourth order, low-pass Butterworth filter, with a
7.7 MHz bandwidth, that was selected and configured based upon successfully
published RF fingerprinting efforts [16,17]. However, the work in [16,17] used
an AWGN channel model, thus the selected filter and its configuration may not
be optimal for maximizing SEI performance under Rayleigh fading conditions.
Therefore, this work analyzes the impact of filter type, order, and bandwidth
on N-M channel estimation and SEI performance. Assessed filter designs consist of: Butterworth, Chebyshev Type I, Chebyshev Type II, and Elliptic Infinite
Impulse Response (IIR) filters using bandwidths of 7.4 MHz to 8.6 MHz in 5 kHz
increments, as well as orders of four, six, and eight [14].

3.2   Multipath Channel Model

This work uses Rayleigh fading to model an indoor 802.11a Wi-Fi multipath
channel [13]. Multipath occurs when attenuated and delayed copies, that are
due to objects within the propagation environment, of the transmitted signal
combine and destructively interfere at the receiver. Each reflection is associated
with a delay and a coefficient (a.k.a., gain), which corresponds to a tap within
the Tap Delay Line (TDL) channel model. The delay spread of the multipath
components depends on the propagation environment. The coefficients for a
length L Rayleigh fading channel are given by,

$$\alpha_k = A_k + jB_k, \tag{1}$$

where $k = 1, \ldots, L$ is the index of the multipath component, A_k and B_k are zero
mean independent and identically distributed random variables with variances
given in [13]. The TDL representation of the channel is,

$$h(t) = \sum_{k=1}^{L} \alpha_k \delta(t - \tau_k T_s), \tag{2}$$

where τ_k is the time delay associated with the kth component normalized by T_s,
where T_s is the sampling period [7,13]. The received signal $r(t)$ for a transmitted
802.11a signal $x(t)$ is given by,

$$r(t) = x(t) * h(t) + n(t), \tag{3}$$

where $n(t)$ is white Gaussian noise, and $*$ denotes convolution. Rayleigh fading
channels of length $L = [2, 3, 5]$ are generated using the time delays and coefficient
variances presented in Table 1. A unique Rayleigh fading channel is generated
and convolved with each collected preamble.

Table 1. The delay, τ_k, and normalized variance, σ_k, values used to generate length L Rayleigh fading channels.

k L	Path Values: τ_k (σ_k)				
	1	2	3	4	5
2	50 ns (0.8)	----	----	200 ns (0.2)	----
3	50 ns (0.8)	----	150 ns (0.13)	----	250 ns (0.07)
5	50 ns (0.865)	100 ns (0.117)	150 ns (0.016)	200 ns (0.002)	250 ns (0.0003)

3.3   Nelder-Mead Channel Estimation and Equalization

Estimation begins by determining the delay, τ_1, of the first tap and all subsequent delays with respect to the first [6,15]. After estimation of the time delays, the N-M estimator, from [5], is used to estimate the coefficients α_k. The N-M estimator is built using the N-M simplex algorithm that uses function values to minimize a d-variable function through the use of four operations: reflection, contraction, expansion, and shrinkage [9,12]. After these four operations and using conditions detailed in [9], the algorithm compares the newest set of function values to the best and worst points of the current simplex denoted as x_1 and x_{d+1}, respectively. The algorithm is terminated when the function values satisfy specific conditions. This work adopts the same stopping criterion presented in [5]. For channel coefficient estimation, the N-M algorithm is used to minimize the squared error function given by,

$$f(h) = \sum_{m \in T} \left| r(m) - \sum_{k=1}^{L} \alpha_k x(m - \tau_k) \right|^2, \tag{4}$$

where $r(m)$ is the received preamble, $x(m)$ is a "candidate" preamble, α_k is the kth coefficient, and τ_k is the kth delay, which is consistent with the work in [5,6]. For each radio N_p candidate preambles are randomly selected (i.e., $4 \times N_p$ total) from the set of collected preambles described in Sect. 2. An estimate of the channel's coefficients is obtained using each of the candidate preambles. The residual power is then calculated for each of the N_p, estimated channels and corresponding candidate. The estimated channel that results in the lowest residual power value is selected as the "best" estimate and used for subsequent channel correction. As in [6], channel correction is performed using an MMSE equalizer because it accounts for the channel statistics (e.g., noise power), which provides superior performance under degrading SNR conditions.

3.4   RF Fingerprint Generation

RF fingerprints are generated from the Time-Frequency (T-F) representation of each radio's preambles. The T-F representation is the normalized magnitude-squared coefficients of the Gabor Transform (GT) given by,

$$G_{\eta\xi} = \sum_{m=1}^{MN_\Delta} s(m)W^*(m - \eta N_\Delta)\exp\left(-j\frac{2\pi\xi m}{K_G}\right),\tag{5}$$

where $G_{\eta\xi}$ are the coefficients, $s(m) = s(m+lMN_\Delta)$ is the input signal, $W(m) = W(m+lMN_\Delta)$ is the analysis window, $N_\Delta = 1$ is the number of shifted samples, $\eta = 1, 2, \ldots, M$ for $M = 320$ total shifts, $\xi = 0, 1, \ldots, K_G - 1$ for $K_G = 320$, and the modulo of $(M\cdot N_\Delta)$ and K_G is zero. The analysis window is,

$$W(m) = \exp\left\{\left(-\frac{\pi}{pN_s^2}\right)\cdot\left[m - \frac{1}{2}(N_s - 1)^2\right]\right\},\tag{6}$$

where the width of the window is approximately $N_s\sqrt{p}$ (i.e., as p increases in the time-domain the bandwidth of the Gaussian window decreases) and N_s is the number of discrete-time samples comprising the input signal $s(m)$ [2]. RF fingerprint generation begins by subdividing the T-F representation into N_R two-dimensional patches. Each patch is comprised of $N_T \times N_F$ values, where N_T and N_F represents the length of the patch along the time and frequency dimension, respectively. The variance, skewness, and kurtosis are calculated over the one-dimensionally reshaped patch. In addition to calculating these features for each patch, they are also calculated over the entire T-F representation and appended to the end of the RF fingerprint. For the RF fingerprints used to generate the results in Sect. 4, $N_T = 53$ and $N_F = 4$, which results $N_R = 420$ total patches per T-F representation and RF fingerprints comprised of $N_f = 1,263$ features.

3.5   Radio Classification

RF fingerprint-based SEI is conducted using the Multiple Discriminant Analysis/Maximum Likelihood (MDA/ML) classifier to permit comparative assessment with the results presented in [6]. MDA linearly projects the N_f-dimensional fingerprints into an N_D-1 dimensional subspace that reduces within class variance while concurrently maximizing between class distance [3]. A multivariate Gaussian distribution is then applied to represent the projected RF fingerprints' distribution. An unknown, projected RF fingerprint (i.e., one not previously seen by the classifier) is determined to have originated from the class (a.k.a., radio) associated with the largest likelihood value. Percent correct classification is calculated by tracking the number of times the classifier assigns the unknown, projected RF fingerprints to the correct class over all Monte Carlo trials.

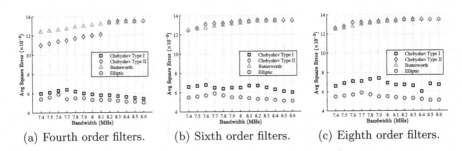

(a) Fourth order filters.   (b) Sixth order filters.   (c) Eighth order filters.

Fig. 1. The average squared error computed between the actual and N-M estimated channel coefficients for the four selected IIR filter types using bandwidths of 7.4 MHz to 8.6 MHz in 100 kHz steps.

4   Results

4.1   Filter Analysis: Average Squared Error

Comparative assessment of the selected IIR filters: Butterworth, Chebyshev Type I, Chebyshev Type II, and Elliptic, is conducted using 1,000 ideal 802.11a Wi-Fi preambles sampled at 20 Mhz. The assessment is conducted using: bandwidths of 7.4 MHz to 8.6 MHz in 100 kHz increments, filter orders of four, six, and eight, as well as AWGN to simulate an SNR of 9 dB. Each instance of AWGN is scaled and added to a preamble prior to filtering and Monte Carlo analysis enabled by repeating this process ten times per ideal preamble. A unique Rayleigh fading channel is generated for each preamble using a TDL comprised of $L = 5$ coefficients and the corresponding values in Table 1. The coefficients of each fading channel is stored to permit analysis of a specific filter implementation through use of the squared error measure,

$$\epsilon = \sum_{m \in L} \left| h(m) - \hat{h}(m) \right|^2, \tag{7}$$

where $h(m)$ and $\hat{h}(m)$ are the actual and N-M estimated channel coefficients, respectively.

The results associated with this assessment are shown in Fig. 1. When considering the four IIR filter types, it is clear that the Chebyshev Type I and Elliptic filters result in the lowest average squared error across all orders and bandwidths with the Elliptic resulting in the lowest average square error in all cases. When comparing fourth (Fig. 1(a)), sixth (Fig. 1(b)), and eighth (Fig. 1(c)) order filter implementations, it can be seen that increasing the filter order does not appreciably reduce the average squared error. This is important, because as the filter order increases so does the computation time and memory storage requirements. Thus, the use of a lower filter order proves beneficial for resource constrained devices without negatively impacting performance. For the fourth order Chebyshev Type I and Elliptic filters, average squared error decreases as the bandwidth of the filter increases with the lowest error occurring at a bandwidth of 8.6 MHz.

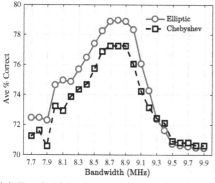
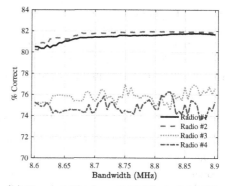

(a) Bandwidths from 7.7 MHz to 9.9 MHz in increments of 100 kHz.
(b) Bandwidths from 8.6 MHz to 8.9 MHz in increments of 5 kHz.

Fig. 2. Average percent correct classification performance generated using an MDA/ML classifier and RF fingerprints extracted from 802.11a preambles that are filtered using either a fourth order Chebyshev Type I or Elliptic filter prior to N-M channel estimation and MMSE correction at an SNR of 9 dB.

4.2 Filter Analysis: Average Percent Correct Classification

Based upon the results and analysis in Sect. 4.1, additional assessment is conducted to determine the filter bandwidth that optimizes N-M channel estimation and SEI performance under Rayleigh fading conditions. Only the fourth order Chebyshev Type I and Elliptic filters are used in this assessment and SEI performance is used in lieu of average squared error. Specifically, percent correct classification performance is used. This is facilitated by randomly selecting 1,000 preambles from each of the Wi-Fi radios' 2,000 collected preambles, Sect. 2. A unique Rayleigh fading channel is convolved with every chosen preamble and white Gaussian noise generated, scaled, and added to achieve an SNR of 9 dB. The addition of scaled Gaussian noise is repeated ten times to facilitate Monte Carlo analysis. The resulting set of preambles are then filtered by fourth order Chebyshev Type I and Elliptic filters using bandwidths of 7.7 MHz to 9.9 MHz in 100 kHz steps prior to N-M channel estimation and MMSE equalization, Sect. 3.3. Figure 2(a) presents the average percent correct classification performance generated using RF fingerprints, Sect. 3.4, and the MDA/ML classifier, Sect. 3.5, at an SNR of 9 dB. Average percent correct classification is superior when the preambles are filtered using a fourth order Elliptic filter with bandwidths less than or equal to 9.2 MHz. Maximum performance is achieved for bandwidths of 8.6 MHz to 9 MHz. Based upon the results in Fig. 2(a), additional analysis is conducted using only fourth order Elliptic filters with bandwidths of 8.6 MHz to 8.9 MHz in 5 kHz increments and percent correct classification performance for the individual radios. The "best" bandwidth value is designated as the one that maximizes individual radio classification performance overall. In other words, there may be bandwidths that achieve higher classification performance for a given radio, but at the expense of another. For example, Radio #4's classification performance is maximized at a bandwidth of 8.82 MHz, but this same bandwidth is associated with one of Radio #3's lowest correct classification performance values. Based upon the percent correct classification performance in Fig. 2(b), a fourth order Elliptic filter with a bandwidth of 8.865 MHz is selected and used for all subsequent analysis and results.

4.3 Gabor Analysis Window Width

In an effort to maximize SEI performance under Rayleigh fading conditions, the impact of the analysis window width, in (6), is investigated. To the best of our knowledge, this work is the first to conduct such an investigation for GT-based SEI. The analysis window width is controlled by the value of N_s and p, however N_s is fixed since it is the number of discrete-time samples comprising a Wi-Fi preamble. In [5,6], the value of p was set equal to 0.015, which is the same value used in prior GT-based SEI works [16,17]. Our investigation is conducted using preambles that: (i) have undergone $L = 5$ Rayleigh fading, (ii) are at an SNR of 9 dB through the addition of scaled white, Gaussian noise, (iii) are filtered using a fourth order Elliptic filter with a bandwidth of 8.865 MHz, as well as (iv) N-M channel estimation and MMSE correction. As in Sect. 4.2, Monte Carlo simulation is facilitated by adding ten unique, scaled noise realizations to each radio's 2,000 preambles. For each Monte Carlo trial, the set of RF fingerprints are subdivided into a training and blind test set using random selection. The test set is comprised of 20% (i.e., 400) of a given radio's 2,000 RF fingerprints. During MDA/ML classifier model development, the training set is further subdivided into five subsets to facilitate k-fold cross validation. The percent correct classification performance, computed across all trials, associated with the test

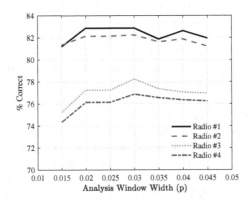

Fig. 3. Percent correct classification performance for each of the four Wi-Fi radios generated using an MDA/ML classifier, RF fingerprints extracted from 802.11a preambles using for $p \in [0.01, 0.045]$. All preambles undergo $L = 5$ Rayleigh fading, have scaled, white Gaussian noise added to them to achieve an SNR of 9 dB and are filtered using a fourth order Elliptic filter using a bandwidth of 8.865 MHz prior to N-M channel estimation and MMSE correction.

set is used as the measure to assess the selected analysis window width, p. The values of p range from 0.015 to 0.045 using a step size of 0.0005. Figure 3 shows percent correct classification performance for each of the four Wi-Fi radios and the "best" value of p chosen using the same criterion described in Sect. 4.2. Thus, the "best" analysis window width is selected as $p = 0.03$.

4.4   Candidate Signal Set Analysis

Using the results in Sect. 4.2 and Sect. 4.3, the number of candidate preambles, N_p, used within the N-M estimator is investigated. As with the previous two sections, analysis is conducted using preambles that: (i) undergo $L = 5$ Rayleigh fading, (ii) have white Gaussian noise added to them to produce an SNR of 9 dB, (iii) are filtered using a fourth order Elliptic filter with a 8.865 MHz bandwidth, and (iv) use an analysis window width for $p = 0.03$ when calculating the Gabor Transform for RF fingerprint generation. For consistency with Sect. 4.2 and Sect. 4.3, Monte Carlo analysis is conducted through the use of ten noise realizations per preamble of each radio. Once again the RF fingerprints are subdivided into training and testing sets with k-fold cross validation used during MDA/ML model development. When classifying the RF fingerprints test set for a specific value of N_p, the MDA/ML model that results in the highest average percent correct classification performance across all Monte Carlo trials and k-folds is selected as the "best" model and used to generate the results in Fig. 4. As the number of candidate preambles increases, percent correct classification performance also increases until $N_p = 20$ candidates are used by the N-M estimator. Thus, the number of candidate preambles is set to $N_p = 15$, because (i) this

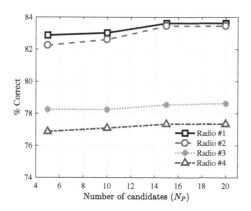

Fig. 4. Percent correct classification performance for each of the four Wi-Fi radios generated using an MDA/ML classifier, RF fingerprints extracted from 802.11a preambles using $N_p = 5$, 10, 15, or 20 candidates within the N-M estimator. All preambles undergo $L = 5$ Rayleigh fading, have scaled, white Gaussian noise added to them to achieve an SNR of 9 dB and are filtered using a fourth order Elliptic filter using a bandwidth of 8.865 MHz prior to N-M channel estimation and MMSE correction.

amount of candidates appears to sufficiently capture the nuances of each radio's SEI features and (ii) the N-M channel estimation computational complexity is lower than the $N_p = 20$ case. If the first claim was not true, then one would expect the classification performance to have increased when N_p is set to 20.

4.5 Parallel Optimization

Up to this point, the SEI process is optimized using sequentially chosen values. In other words, the SEI performance is optimized per stage (e.g., filter bandwidth) and a given stage's optimal values are selected in isolation of those selected for the other stages. Thus, it is possible to optimize a given stage and achieve an SEI performance that is sub-optimal overall. This possibility is attributed to the fact that when optimizing the values of an early stage (e.g., filter bandwidth), the latter stages (e.g., GT analysis window width) may be configured using sub-optimal values that can negatively influence selection of the current stage's optimal value. This possibility is alleviated through the use of parallel optimization. In parallel optimization an exhaustive search is performed across the values of all stages simultaneously and recording the average percent correct classification performance for each of the chosen values. For the results presented in Fig. 5, parallel optimization is performed using settings and values of: (i) Elliptic filter bandwidths from 7.7 MHz to 9.9 MHz in increments of 100 kHz, (ii) GT analysis window widths p from 0.015 to 0.045 in steps of 0.5×10^{-3}, and (iii) number of N-M candidate preambles N_p from 5 to 20 candidates in increments of 5 candidates.

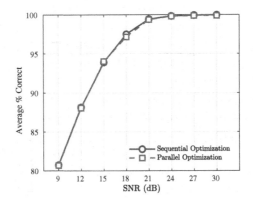

Fig. 5. Average percent correct classification performance for the sequential and parallel optimization approaches generated using an MDA/ML classifier, RF fingerprints extracted from 802.11a preambles that undergo $L = 5$ Rayleigh fading, have scaled, white Gaussian noise added to them to achieve an SNR in the range of 9 to 30 dB and are filtered using a fourth order Elliptic filter prior to N-M channel estimation and MMSE correction (Color figure online).

The highest, overall average percent correct classification performance is achieved when the parallel optimization process sets the: (i) Elliptic filter bandwidth to 8.8 MHz, (ii) GT window width p to 30×10^{-3}, and (iii) number of candidate preambles N_p to 20. These are the same values selected by the sequential optimization approach without the use of the smaller 5 kHz bandwidth increment.

Figure 5 presents the overlay of the average percent correct classification performance when the filter bandwidth, GT analysis window width, and number of candidate preambles are chosen using either sequential (solid, blue line, o) or parallel optimization (broken, red line, □). For the sequential optimization results the: (i) Elliptical filter bandwidth is 8.865 MHz, (ii) GT analysis window width is the same as that of the parallel selected value of 30×10^{-3}, and (iii) number of candidate preambles is set to 15 per radio. The results reflect very little (i.e., at an SNR of 18 dB) to no difference between the classification performance achieved using the parallel optimization selected values and those selected by the sequential optimization approach. Based upon the results in Fig. 5 the final set of results are generated using values chosen via sequential optimization.

4.6   SEI Performance

A final set of individual radio classification performance results are generated using preambles that: (i) represent channels consisting of noise only and $L = [2, 3, 5]$ Rayleigh fading paths, (ii) have white Gaussian noise added to them to produce SNR values from 9 dB to 30 dB in 3 dB steps, (iii) are filtered using a fourth order Elliptic filter with a 8.865 MHz bandwidth, (iv) use Gabor-based RF fingerprints that are generated using an analysis window width for $p = 0.03$, and (v) N-M channel estimation performed by selecting $N_p = 15$ candidate preambles per radio. For the results shown in Fig. 6, a total of ten noise realizations are used for every preamble within a radio's set to facilitate Monte Carlo based analysis. For each channel condition and SNR, an MDA/ML model is developed for each noise realization by dividing the associated RF fingerprints into training and testing data sets comprised of 80% and 20% of the total 2,000 fingerprints, respectively. During training, k-fold cross validation is implemented using $k = 5$ and the validation performance tracked. The training model that results in the highest validation performance across all k-folds and noise realizations is designated as the "best" MDA/ML classifier model for the select SNR and channel condition. The "best" MDA/ML classifier model is used to classify the corresponding test set of RF fingerprints. It is the percent correct classification performance associated with the classification of these test sets that is shown in Fig. 6. Additionally, the final set of results from [6] are included, designated using dashed lines and the word 'Butterworth', to enable direct comparative assessment.

For the results shown in Fig. 6, percent correct classification performance is the same for SNR values of 21 dB or higher across all radios when compared to the results in [6]. These results are not surprising due to the low noise power, thus allowing for accurate N-M estimation of the channel coefficients and

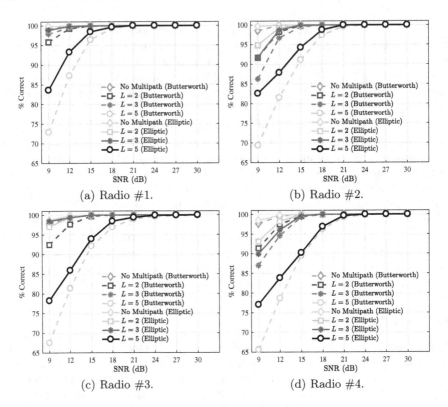

(a) Radio #1. (b) Radio #2.

(c) Radio #3. (d) Radio #4.

Fig. 6. MDA/ML percent correct classification performance generated using a fourth order Elliptic filter with a 8.865 MHz bandwidth, N-M channel estimator, and T-F RF fingerprints. The channel conditions represent the cases of: no multipath ($\diamond$) or multipath channels of length: $L = 2$ ($\square$), $L = 3$ ($*$), or $L = 5$ ($\circ$) for SNR$\in$[9, 30] dB. MDA/ML classification results from [6] are included (Butterworth, dashed lines) to facilitate direct comparative assessment.

preservation of the distinct and unique features that are exploited within the RF fingerprinting process. However, for SNRs of 18 dB and lower, our optimized RF fingerprinting process results in improved percent correct classification performance for all four radios across all four channel conditions: noise only, as well as L equal 2, 3, and 5 Rayleigh fading channels when compared to the results in [6]. As SNR decreases, noise inhibits the N-M estimator's ability to accurately estimate the channel coefficients, thus reducing out of band noise power becomes increasingly important. The greatest amount of improvement is associated with the $L = 5$ Rayleigh fading channel case. This is also the most challenging case, because five delayed and attenuated copies of the same signal are combined at the receiver resulting in constructive and destructive interference that corrupts the SEI exploited features. The largest improvement in percent correct classification performance is for Radio #2, which achieves a 14% improvement at an SNR of 9 dB. The smallest improvement in percent correct classification performance is for Radio #1, which achieves a 10.8% improvement at an SNR of 9 dB. The average improvement is 11.9% across all four radios for the $L = 5$ fading channel when the SNR is equal to 9 dB.

4.7   Comparison with State of the Art

The RF fingerprinting results–shown in Fig. 6–are compared against the Deep Learning (DL) based approach of [4]. In [4] a Convolutional Auto Encoder (CAE) is used to pretrain the Convolutional Neural Network (CNN) to improve classification accuracy. For specifics on the CAE-CNN approach, the reader is referred to [4]. Use of the DL-based approach in [4] is motivated by its use of the same IEEE 802.11a dataset. Table. 2 shows each radio's percent correct classification results for an $L = 5$ Rayleigh fading channel and SNRs of 9 dB to 30 dB in 3 dB steps. For Radio #1 and Radio #3, our approach achieves superior performance for SNR$\geq$12 dB. Our approach outperforms that of [4] when classifying Radio #4 at SNR$\geq$15 dB. When classifying Radio #2, the two approaches are comparable for SNR of 15 dB or higher. However, for low SNRs (i.e., below 15 dB) the DL-based approach achieves superior performance, which is attributed to the large number of tunable parameters that permit optimization of the CAE-CNN architecture. The large number of tunable parameters comes at the cost of higher computational time and power, which can limit the applicability of DL-based RF fingerprinting as an IoT security solution, Table. 3. Table. 3 shows that the DL-based approach requires tuning of 135,619 parameters and a total training time of over 17 h. In contrast, the approach presented herein only requires a total of 12 training hours. The approach chosen depends on the IoT device(s), their use, and the resources available.

Table 2. Percent correct classification performance of our optimized, Feature-Engineered RF fingerprinting approach versus the DL-based approach of [4].

Device	RF Fingerprinting Approach	SNR (dB)							
		9	12	15	18	21	24	27	30
Radio #1	Feature-Engineered	84.30%	93.70%	98.10%	99.70%	99.90%	99.90%	99.90%	99.90%
	Deep Learning-based [4]	87.50%	91.10%	95.10%	97.70%	97.70%	98.50%	100%	100%
Radio #2	Feature-Engineered	82.70%	87.90%	94.80%	98.90%	99.90%	99.90%	99.90%	99.90%
	Deep Learning-based [4]	90.60%	92.30%	95.50%	98.90%	99.70%	99.90%	100%	100%
Radio #3	Feature-Engineered	78.20%	85.80%	94.50%	98.20%	99.40%	99.70%	99.90%	99.90%
	Deep Learning-based [4]	80.40%	85.40%	89.90%	94.80%	96.10%	97.90%	98.80%	99.20%
Radio #4	Feature-Engineered	77.50%	84.40%	90.50%	96.90%	99.50%	99.90%	99.90%	99.90%
	Deep Learning-based [4]	85%	89.80%	94.10%	96.40%	96.80%	97.60%	99.50%	99.50%

Table 3. Number of parameters and training times for our RF fingerprinting approach versus the DL-based approach in [4].

Architecture	Parameters	Training Time
1D CNN	81,918	11 h
1D CAE	53,701	6 h
MDA/ML	–	12 h

5   Conclusion

This work analyzed the impacts of: (i) filter type, order, and bandwidth; (ii) Gabor Transform analysis window width; as well as (iii) the number of candidate signals used by the Nelder-Mead (N-M) channel estimator within the developed process with the goal of maximizing SEI performance under Rayleigh fading and degrading SNR conditions. This results in an optimized SEI process that achieves a 11.9% average percent correct classification performance improvement, when compared to the results in [6], for $L = 5$ Rayleigh fading at an SNR of 9 dB.

References

1. Baldini, G., Steri, G.: A survey of techniques for the identification of mobile phones using the physical fingerprints of the built-in components. IEEE Commun. Surv. Tutorials **19**(3), 1761–1789 (2017)
2. Bastiaans, M.: Discrete Gabor transform and discrete Zak transform. In: IEEE International Conference on Signal and Image Processing Applications (1996)
3. Duda, R., Hart, P., Stork, D.: Pattern Classification, 2nd edn. Wiley, New York (2001)
4. Fadul, M., Reising, D., Sartipi, M.: Identification of OFDM-based radios under rayleigh fading using RF-DNA and deep learning. IEEE Access **9**, 17100–17113 (2021). https://doi.org/10.1109/ACCESS.2021.3053491
5. Fadul, M., Reising, D., Loveless, T., Ofoli, A.: RF-DNA fingerprint classification of OFDM signals using a Rayleigh fading channel model. In: IEEE Wireless Communications and Networking Conference (WCNC) (2019)
6. Fadul, M., Reising, D., Loveless, T., Ofoli, A.: Nelder-mead simplex channel estimation for the RF-DNA fingerprinting of OFDM transmitters under Rayleigh fading conditions. IEEE Trans. Inf. Forensics Secur. **16**, 2381–2396 (2021). https://doi.org/10.1109/TIFS.2021.3054524
7. Hijazi, H., Ros, L.: Polynomial estimation of time-varying multipath gains with intercarrier interference mitigation in OFDM systems. IEEE Trans. Veh. Technol. **58**(1), 140–151 (2009)
8. Kennedy, I., Kuzminskiy, A.: RF fingerprint detection in a wireless multipath channel. In: International Symposium on Wireless Communication Systems (2010)
9. Lagarias, J., Reeds, J., Wright, M., Wright, P.: Convergence properties of the nelder-mead simplex method in low dimensions. SIAM J. Optim. **9**(1), (2006)
10. Liu, M., Doherty, J.: Specific emitter identification using nonlinear device estimation. In: IEEE Sarnoff Symposium (2009)

11. Liu, M., Doherty, J.: Nonlinearity estimation for specific emitter identification in multipath channels. IEEE Transctions Inf. Forensics Secur. **6**(3), 1076–1085 (2011)
12. Nelder, J., Mead, R.: A simplex method for function minimization. Comput. J. **7**(4), 308–313 (1965)
13. O'Hara, B., Petrick, A.: IEEE 802.11 Handbook: A Designer's Companion. Standard Information Network. IEEE Press (2005)
14. Oppenheim, A., Schafer, R.: Discrete-Time Signal Processing, 3rd edn. Pearson Higher Education, Edinburgh (2011)
15. Wang, K., Faulkner, M., Singh, J., Tolochko, I.: Timing synchronization for 802.11a WLANs under multipath channels. In: Australian Telecommunications, Networks and Applications Conference (2003)
16. Wheeler, C., Reising, D.: Assessment of the impact of CFO on RF-DNA fingerprint classification performance. In: International Conference on Computing, Networking and Communications (2017)
17. Wilson, A., Reising, D., Loveless, T.: Integration of matched filtering within the RF-DNA fingerprinting process. In: IEEE Global Telecommunications Conference (GLOBECOM), pp. 1–6 (2019)

Secure Image Data Storage and Transmission Using ESP32-Cam and Raspberry Pi with Steganography

Hrishikesh Gokhale$^{(\boxtimes)}$, Chirag Satapathy, and Ali Zoya Syed

Vellore Institute of Technology, Vellore, India
`hrishikesh.gokhale2019@vitstudent.ac.in`

Abstract. Industries across the world produce thousands of confidential images and other data that needs to be secured on a daily basis. With the onset of the information era and the exponential growth of technologies like big data, security of private and confidential information in any form has become a challenge. Many times, these images need to be transmitted over public networks to facilitate wireless monitoring and sharing testing results with remote operators. This transmission needs to be secure to ensure the safety and confidentiality of the images, thus cryptography techniques like image steganography are required. In this prototype, we have designed, developed and tested a Raspberry Pi LAMP web server which stores images locally which are obtained using an ESP32-Cam, and which facilitates transmission using the steganography technique. There is also an option to store these images on any other widely used cloud server, and the transmission can still use steganography encryption for an extra layer of security. The stored images can only be accessed by authorized users.

Keywords: ESP32-CAM · Raspberry Pi · Security · Steganography

1 Introduction

In today's digital age, the need for security of images has become paramount. This need for security has only increased because there has been an exponential rise in the communication of digital products over open networks. Apart from the obvious requirement in everyday use cases, digital image encryption and security also finds applications in many specialized fields like medical imaging systems and military image communications [1]. These applications also require secure image storage, which will ensure image security before and after the transmission is completed. To ensure secure image transmission and storage, we have decided to use the image steganography technique. Steganography is a technique used to embed information into some sort of covering media. The covering media is usually an image, while the embedded information can vary between text, images, or even audio and visual data. For our purpose, we have chosen both - the covering media and the hidden information to be image data. In order to fulfil the task of encryption, multiple algorithms have been proposed. In this study, we have considered the following:

© The Author(s), under exclusive license to Springer Nature Switzerland AG 2022
A. González-Vidal et al. (Eds.): GIoTS 2022, LNCS 13533, pp. 292–301, 2022.
https://doi.org/10.1007/978-3-031-20936-9_23

1.1 BPCS (Bit Plane Complexity Segmentation)

BPCS is a steganography technique that can replace all "noise-like" regions in all bit-planes of the cover image with secret data while maintaining image quality. According to multiple experiments [2], text images can be embedded and camouflaged successfully in the cover image. The steganography images also have satisfactory quality.

1.2 LSB (Least Significant Bit)

According to the Least Significant Bit embedding approach, data can be concealed in the cover picture's least significant bits, and the human eye would be unable to detect the hidden image in the cover file. This technique is used for embedding images in 24-bit, 8-bit or gray-scale format [3].

1.3 Haar Discrete Wavelet Transform

In the Haar discrete wavelet transform technique, data is hidden in the frequency domain. This is done because the frequency domain is the most robust area. To avoid the loss of data from the floating point, the embedding is done in the integer part of the transform coefficients. This is done in such a way that it increases both, the imperceptibility and the capacity of hiding [4].

1.4 AES (Advanced Encryption Standard)

AES is a symmetric encryption algorithm. In this algorithm, only one key is used for both encryption and decryption that can be used by the sender and the receiver. AES can be used for 128, 192 or 259 bits long, with each of them containing 2128, 2192 and 2256 combinations. The data maintained by the key is secured and authentication is maintained by the key itself [5].

1.5 RGB (Red, Green and Blue)

The RGB steganography algorithm uses the same principle as LSB. As done in the LSB algorithm, the secret algorithm is hidden in the least significant bits of the pixels. Randomization techniques are used in the selection of the number of bits used and the colour channels that are used. Randomization is supposed to increase both - the security of the system and also its capacity [6]. This technique is applied to RGB images where each pixel is represented by three bytes which indicate the intensity of red, green and blue in that pixel.

In this paper, we have created a local server using the Raspberry Pi LAMP functionality. We have taken live images using an ESP32-CAM and stored them securely on the server, from which they can be accessed by authorized personnel only. We have also used image-in-image steganography to ensure secure transmission and storage of the images.

2   Literature Review

An option to be considered for image capture and transfer is ESP32 SoC Integrated Bluetooth with low power 4.2 and Wi-Fi [7]. This is used to design the sensor and gateway nodes. The sensor node captures images using the OV2640 2 MP camera module and transmits image data to Gateway via Energy in Bluetooth. The gateway then stores the collected images and uploads to Firebase via nearby Wi-Fi network connections. This image data is processed and analyzed by computer vision and a machine learning algorithm for estimating crop growth and predicting other useful information. Google Firebase is used as a cloud based storage for image data collected by the sensor. The sensor nodes are designed with ESP32 SoC, a dual core Tensilica Xtensa LX6 module. It has a microprocessor, and is Wi-Fi and Bluetooth 4.2 capable.

Feature point extraction can be required for most computer vision and machine learning algorithms, and an Android-based application with ESP32-CAM and PIR sensors [8] was considered for the same. PCB on-board antenna can be used independently and extend sensitivity by connecting an external antenna separately. The proposed unauthorized intrusion detection system requires a connection between Arduino Uno, ESP32-CAM and the smartphone application. The pre-processing algorithms used include Grayscale, Binarization, Zoom, Rotation/Transformation etc.

The ESP32-CAM can be used remotely and including this possibility in our work was explored. A remote access surveillance device [9] is a perfect example to showcase the module's remote operation capabilities. Apart from the surveillance function, it is also possible to link various other peripherals to the ESP modules. These can be soil moisture sensor, tube light, fan, water pump which basically makes the unit fully automated. The IoT interface used in this case is the Blynk application, which relays real time data from all sensors attached to an IoT capable device.

Steganography is the process of hiding confidential information. There are some security challenges revolving around harsh environments, threats from equipment, unauthorised access and interception of node communication along with malicious data attacks. Messages need to be encrypted so that no one other than the sender and the intended recipient can access them. This method of cryptography was considered because it enables secure transmission of highly confidential information in multiple formats - images, text, audio and video. The technique used in this case was Holding Image Encryption [10].

A new method of integrating steganography and cryptography together was considered [11]. The strength of the system lies in the new concept of the main image. Adding two images (cover and key) in only one (cover) position overs can change modules randomly. This possibility does not provide a steganolytic device but there is a possibility to find a set of predictable changes. The proposed approach has several applications such as hiding and coding messages in standard media, such as pictures or videos.

For any IoT system, data acquisition, storage, analysis and privacy are a major concern [12]. Thus, using cryptography and key management, a symmetric encryption/decryption together with cryptographic hash function to design a secure, user-authenticated key management protocol can be applied in smart agriculture. The network model proposed protocol consists of three different nodes, including sensor nodes, gateway nodes, and cluster head nodes. To verify biometric authentication, the proposed protocol uses fuzzy extraction technique and to provide privacy with end-to-end security assurance a distributed and clustered key management framework, based on group-based keys, specifically consisting of cluster nodes with cluster heads and edge nodes. There are some security challenges revolving around harsh environments, threats from equipment, unauthorised access and interception of node communication along with malicious data attacks do exist.

Fog provides storage, computing, and networking services between edge devices and traditional cloud computing data centres. It primarily solves low latency, mobility support, and location awareness issues in many cyberphysical systems. However, the decentralised and open structure makes it vulnerable and vulnerable to security threats [13]. Due to the high degree of distribution of fogs, implementing a security mechanism for data-centric integrity can have a serious impact on its QoS. Therefore, we need to find new ways to improve the security of the and the trust of the mist. Fog nodes are required to interact with different hardware platforms from different vendors, so a new interface to the Fog software is needed to ensure reliable computing.

3   Construction

The setup of the project involves two parts. The first part consists of the hardware and software required to set up a basic web server to store the uploaded the images, and the second part consists of the same for capturing images and uploading them to the server.

A Raspberry Pi 4 Model B is used to host a local server. This is done using a Raspberry Pi LAMP server [14]. LAMP involves Linux, Apache, MySQL and PHP and is essential for building a basic local server to store images.

To capture images and upload them to the local server, an ESP32-CAM module [15] is used. This module consists of a Wi-Fi module and a camera module. ESP32-CAM can be programmed using the Arduino IDE, which is an open source programming platform for certain development boards. An FTDI programmer [16] is used as an interface between the host computer's USB port and the ESP32-CAM module. The camera module captures images every 5 s (can be changed according to the application) and uploads them to the local server.

Apache's Debian-based web server service is used to local server on the Raspberry Pi. PHPMyAdmin is used to create the local server using PHP, and MongoDB is used as the database service to store the images. Since all the images are stored locally, it is necessary that both - the Raspberry Pi and the ESP32-CAM module are connected to the same network. This is done by configuring Wi-Fi in the Raspberry Pi's terminal and the Arduino IDE for the ESP32-CAM.

The steganography encryption can be performed at two stages of the process. This can either be done when the camera module has captured the image, or when the image has been uploaded to the local web server. This means that steganography can be performed in either the C++ programming language [17], in PHP, or in Python (which was chosen in this case) [18]. The encryption algorithm is written in a Linux-based machine and takes effect before the image is uploaded to the local web server.

Since the entire process takes place on a single network connection, the database of images can be accessed by using a web browser and the Raspberry Pi's IP address [19]. This allows authorized users to access, download and delete files stored on the server. The IP address is secured using a password login.

If the contents of the database need to be accessed by users that are not connected to the same wireless/wired network as the host, it can be made possible by hosting the Apache server on a website dedicated to it. This will allow authorized users from across the world to access and make changes to the database.

The images used as input (cover image and embedded image) are in the JPG format. This format was chosen because they have a small file size, have good colour range, are compatible and are widely supported. The encryption algorithm gave the best results with pictures in the JPG format. The image received as output (final image) is in the PNG format. This is because the PNG format has lossless images and transparency support, while also being widely supported.

The workflow of the project is shown in Fig. 1

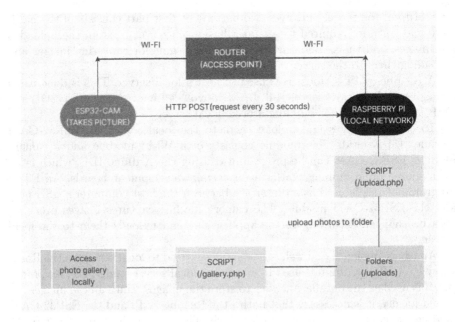

Fig. 1. Project workflow

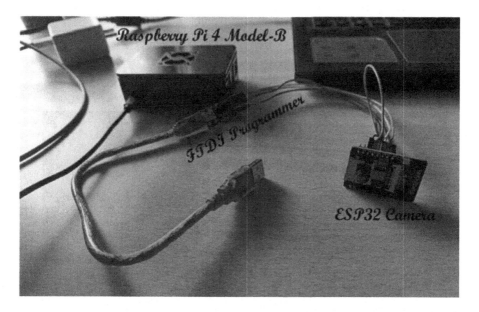

Fig. 2. Hardware components

4 Result

The Raspberry Pi 4 and the ESP32-CAM are connected to the same network connection and a local server is built using Apache's Debian-based web server service. The setup is shown in Fig. 2. This maximum amount of data that this server can store is restricted by the amount of storage the Raspberry Pi 4 is provided with. In the case of this setup, the maximum storage space was 15.4 GB. The server and the data stored on it can be accessed by authorized personnel logged on to the same network connection, and the stored images can be modified, downloaded or deleted (as shown in Fig. 3). The storage system hence created is very secure, allows multiple user access and allows the data to be modified.

To enable secure transmission of the stored images, image steganography has been used. Specifically, the RGB algorithm in image steganography algorithm has been used. In the RGB algorithm, the embedded image (shown in Fig. 5) is hidden in the least significant bits of the pixels of the cover image (shown in Fig. 4). As can be seen with the help of the above images, the test image is completely embedded into the cover image and is hidden from our eyes (shown in Fig. 6). It can only be retrieved using reverse steganography techniques to unmerge the two images.

ESP32-CAM Photo Gallery

Delete file - 2022.03.01_11:26:27_esp32-cam.jpg   Delete file - 2022.03.01_11:19:32_esp32-cam.jpg

Fig. 3. ESP32-CAM gallery

Fig. 4. Cover image

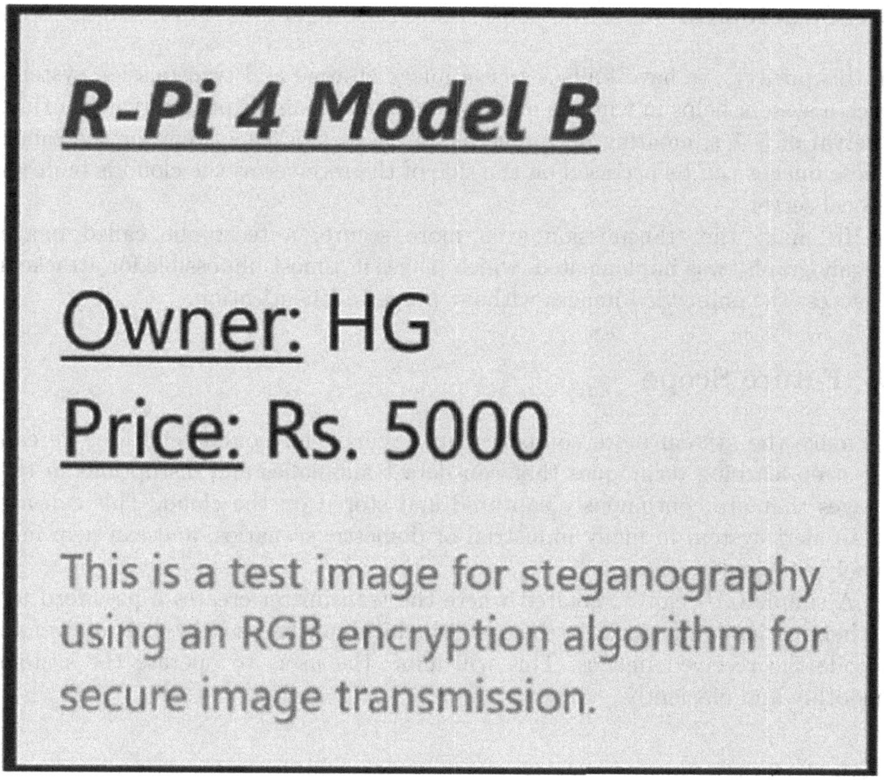

R-Pi 4 Model B
Owner: HG
Price: Rs. 5000
This is a test image for steganography using an RGB encryption algorithm for secure image transmission.

Fig. 5. Test image (To be embedded in the cover image)

Nocturnal
CONAN
WICKED
sbarro
sbarro
sbarro

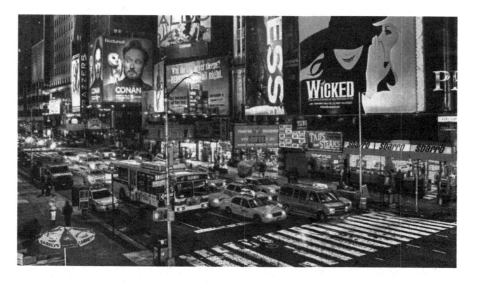

Fig. 6. Final image (Test embedded into cover)

5   Conclusion

In this project, we have built a secure image storage and transmission system. Such a system helps in wireless monitoring and takes multiple interval in a time interval of 5–7 s, creating an online cloud based storage system for the same. These images can be accessed on the side of the receiver as the cloud is built on a local server.

To make the transmission even more secure, a technique called image steganography was implemented, which makes it almost impossible for attackers to access the embedded images without proper authentication.

6   Future Scope

To make the system more competent and precise for commercial use, we can use deep learning techniques that can detect anomalies and disruptions in the images that are continuously captured and stored on the cloud. This can act as an alert system in many industrial or domestic scenarios, and can help in a timely emergency response.

A simple GUI can be created where the transmitter creates a password for authentication while sending the images which can be used by the receiver to decode the received images. This will allow the users to operate the system smoothly and efficiently.

References

1. Li, S., Zheng, X.: On the security of an image encryption method. In: Proceedings International Conference on Image Processing, vol. 2, p. II. IEEE (2002)
2. Bansod, S.P., Mane, V.M., Ragha, R.: Modified BPCS steganography using hybrid cryptography for improving data embedding capacity. In: 2012 International Conference on Communication, Information Computing Technology (ICCICT), pp. 1–6. IEEE (2012)
3. Neeta, D., Snehal, K., Jacobs, D.: Implementation of LSB steganography and its evaluation for various bits. In: 2006 1st International Conference on Digital Information Management, pp. 173–178. IEEE (2006)
4. Alharbi, A., Kechadi, T.M.: A novel steganography algorithm based on alpha blending technique using discrete wavelet transform (ABT-DWT). In: Rocha, Á., Serrhini, M. (eds.) EMENA-ISTL 2018. SIST, vol. 111, pp. 342–351. Springer, Cham (2019). https://doi.org/10.1007/978-3-030-03577-8_38
5. Indra Sena Reddy, M., Siva Kumar, A.P.: Secured data transmission using wavelet based steganography and cryptography by using AES algorithm. Procedia Comput. Sci. **85**, 62–69 (2016)
6. Gutub, A., Al-Qahtani, A., Tabakh, A.: Triple-a: secure RGB image steganography based on randomization. In: 2009 IEEE/ACS International Conference on Computer Systems and Applications, pp. 400–403. IEEE (2009)
7. Wahl, J.D., Zhang, J.X.: Development and power characterization of an IoT network for agricultural imaging applications. J. Adv. Inf. Technol. **12**(3), 214–219 (2021)

8. Myung-Jae, L.I.M., Dong-Kun, J.U.N.G., Young-Man, K.W.O.N.: An image analysis system design using Arduino sensor and feature point extraction algorithm to prevent intrusion. Korea J. Artif. Intell. 9(2), 23–28 (2021)
9. Shukla, A., Diwan, R.: IoT based load automation with remote access surveillance using ESP 32 Camand ESP 8266 module. Ann. Romanian Soc. Cell Biol. 25(3), 6904–6914 (2021)
10. Rasras, R.J., AlQadi, Z.A., Abu Sara, M.R.: A methodology based on steganography and cryptography to protect highly secure messages. Eng. Technol. Appl. Sci. Res. 9(1), 3681–3684 (2019)
11. Bloisi, D.D., Iocchi, L.: Image based steganography and cryptography. In: VISAPP (1), pp. 127–134. CiteSeer (2007)
12. Yang, X., et al.: A survey on smart agriculture: development modes, technologies, and security and privacy challenges. IEEE/CAA J. Automatica Sinica, 8(2), 273–302 (2021)
13. Zhang, P.Y., Zhou, M.C., Fortino, G.: Security and trust issues in fog computing: a survey. Futur. Gener. Comput. Syst. 88, 16–27 (2018)
14. Prabha, S.S., Paul Antony, A.J., Meena, M.J., Pandian, SP.: Smart cloud robot using raspberry pi. In: 2014 International Conference on Recent Trends in Information Technology, pp. 1–5. IEEE (2014)
15. Kumar, S., Sharma, K., Raj, G., Datta, D., Ghosh, A.: Arduino and ESP32-CAM-based automatic touchless attendance system. In: Proceedings of the 3rd International Conference on Communication, Devices and Computing. LNEE, vol. 851, pp. 135–144. Springer, Singapore (2022). https://doi.org/10.1007/978-981-16-9154-6_14
16. Soni, G., Saini, S.S., Malhi, S.S., Srao, B.K., Sharma, A., Puri, D.: Design and implementation of object motion detection using telegram. In: 2021 International Conference on Technological Advancements and Innovations (ICTAI), pp. 203–206. IEEE (2021)
17. AbdelRahim, S., Ghoneimy, S., Selim, G.: Adaptive security scheme for real-time VoIP using multi-layer steganography. In: Proceedings of the 7th International Conference on Software and Information Engineering, pp. 106–110, (2018)
18. Osama Hosam and Muhammad Hammad Ahmad: Hybrid design for cloud data security using combination of AES, ECC and LSB steganography. Int. J. Comput. Sci. Eng. 19(2), 153–161 (2019)
19. Rohadi, E., et al.: Internet of Things: CCTV monitoring by using raspberry pi. In: 2018 International Conference on Applied Science and Technology (iCAST), pp. 454–457. IEEE (2018)

Modelling of Resource-Aware Information Flows for Resource Constraint IoT Devices

Marten Fischer[✉] and Ralf Tönjes

University of Applied Sciences Osnabrück, Osnabrück, Germany
{m.fischer,r.toenjes}@hs-osnabrueck.de

Abstract. The Internet of Things (IoT) is the enabler for new innovations in several domains. It allows the connection of digital services with real, physical entities. These entities are devices of different categories and range in size from large machinery to tiny sensors. In the latter case, devices are typically characterized by limited resources in terms of computational power, available memory and sometimes limited power supply. As a consequence, the use of security algorithms requires expert knowledge in order for them to work within the limited resources. That means to find a suitable configuration for the algorithms to perform properly on the device. On the other side, there is the desire to protect valuable assets as strong as possible. Usually, security goals are captured in security policies, but they do not consider resource availability on the involved device and their consumption while executing security algorithms. This paper presents a resource aware information exchange model and a generation tool that uses high-level security policies as input. The model forms the conceptual basis for an automated security configuration recommendation system.

1 Introduction

In the Internet of Things (IoT), small devices provide real-world data to applications and services in the virtual world. Protecting this data means to apply some form of security algorithm, usually even a combination of multiple algorithms, depending on the security goals. The execution of such algorithm requires resources on the IoT device, depending on the algorithm and its configuration. As a consequence, inappropriate configurations can have a negative influence on the runtime of, especially battery-powered IoT systems.

A number of security measures to protect IoT data are available. However, selecting and configuring them is not trivial. First, the assets and the necessary security goals need to be identified through talks with the stakeholder and recorded in Security Policies (SPs). The purpose of SPs is to communicate security goals among stakeholders and developers in an easy and understandable way. They should be written in a brief, but at the same time precise manner. However, at the point of creating a SP, no information about the involved IoT devices is present nor its available resources and capabilities are considered in relation to the overhead of applying the security measures.

A. González-Vidal et al. (Eds.): GIoTS 2022, LNCS 13533, pp. 302–314, 2022.
https://doi.org/10.1007/978-3-031-20936-9_24

This paper addresses the problem by a) defining a resource-aware Information Exchange Model (IEM) meta-model to describe the transport of data in a typical IoT scenario. Then a high-level Security Policy Language (SPL) is extended to describe the information exchange between the stakeholders in an abstract and easy understandable way. We show how these policies can be used to derive individual information flows of the IEM, which combine security goals and resource constraints at the same time. Finally, we discuss how the IEM can be used to find optimal security configurations. The main contributions of the paper are:

- We define a meta-model to capture message flows, its security goals, and available resources and capabilities of the participants, e.g. (IoT), at the same time.
- We extend an existing SPL and define transformation rules into the former mentioned IEM.
- We explain the transformation of SPs into an instance of the IEM in an environmental monitoring system, including different grouping modes of data assets.

The rest of this paper is organized as follows: Sect. 2 addresses the topics of security policies and security measures in the IoT domain. In Sect. 3 the model for a secure, resource-aware information exchange is introduced followed by a set of instructions to transform high-level policies into an instance of the IEM model in Sect. 4. Section 5 presents an exemplary transformation of SP into information flows with different data assets and security goals.

2   Related Work

Applying appropriate security measures in the IoT domain is a challenging task due to the resource constraints [1]. The authors of [2–4] compared the resource consumption of cryptographic algorithms for both, software implementations and hardware accelerators. They show that even small priced Micro-Controller Units (MCUs) can provide satisfactory security in scenarios such as the environmental monitoring system. They also indicate that the resource consumption depends on the parametrization and that hardware implementations are not always the fastest solutions.

Other researcher approaches try to avoid large resource consumption on the IoT device. One proposal is to use lightweight security algorithms, also known as Light Weight Cryptography (LWC), on constrained devices. Dhanda et al. [5] discussed and compared the applicability of different primitives. They compared a total of 54 implementations in the classes block cipher, stream cipher, hash function and Elliptic Curve Cryptography (ECC). To compare the "lightweightness" they used, among others, the chip area of the algorithm as a metric, i.e. how many logic gates are required to implement the algorithm in hardware. With the number of gates required, the chip area can be calculated in dependence of the internal feature size of the CMOS technology. The chip area is expressed as

Gate Equivalence (GE) and directly proportional to the energy consumption. Another survey was conducted by the authors of [6], but is limited to a comparison between symmetric and asymmetric encryption algorithms. Gunathilake et al. [7] differentiate between Ultra LWC and Ubiquitous LWC, where the former applies only to specific areas, e.g. selective microcontrollers, and the latter is applicable to a wider range of platforms. In contrast to other works, they included hardware crypto accelerators into their study. An example for Ultra LWC is given by [8], where the Advanced Encryption Standard (AES) algorithm is optimized for Long-Range Wide Area Network (LoRaWAN) communication. Batina [9] studied the energy consumption of various AES implementations and showed that significant differences may exist, depending on the configuration of the security algorithms.

Another proposal to handle the resource constraints of IoT devices is to outsource (parts of) the security algorithms to non-constrained devices. The authors in [10] proposed a "Security Agent" in an edge-computing scenario to outsource complex cryptographic algorithms. A survey of edge-computing based security designs for the IoT is given by Sha [11]. Safa et al. [12] investigated the positive effects of fog and cloud computing on the security of IoT systems and presented a decision-making model for selecting the best fog nodes based on the available resources at the fog node. As such, it can be seen as resource-aware routing protocol for data through fog/edge nodes with integrated load balancer. However, they have not investigated the effects of different security algorithms and their configuration on the IoT device itself. Green et al. [13] introduced an entity named "proxy" that transforms Attribte-based Encryption (ABE) cipher-texts into less complex El-Gamal [14] style cipher-texts to be decrypted on constrained mobile devices. Manzoor et al. [15] combined Proxy Re-Encryption (PRE) algorithms with blockchain technology to implement a secure IoT data trading system. In [16], the authors propose a PRE based encryption scheme to reduce the computational costs in fog/edge nodes caused due to the offloading of away from the IoT device.

3   Information Exchange Model

This section presents the developed model to describe the information exchange between stakeholders, including the measure to secure the exchanged data in combination with the consequent additional resource consumption. The model is divided into the four concepts *Information Flow*, *Devices and Resources*, *Performance* and *Security Policy Specification*. The following Subsects. 3.1 to 3.4 describe each concept with focus on the aspects that influence the resource consumption caused by executing security mechanisms.

3.1   Information Flow $\mathcal{F}$

An Information Flow $\mathcal{F} = (\{A^*\}, M, P_P, P_R, P^*, L, \mathcal{P})$ describes the exchange of an information in the form of a message M between at least two participants , a data provider P_P and a receiver P_R. In between, other participants P^* may assist in the transport by forwarding M. Participants are connected to one another by a set of communication links L. M contains at least one asset A, which must be protected according to the required security services as stated in the security policy $\mathcal{P}$. In the context of information flows, an asset is a piece of information, e.g. sensor data. In the following, the individual components of an information flow $\mathcal{F}$ are explained in detail.

Asset. In the context of secure information exchange, we define an asset as digital information that can be transferred between the participants of an information flow. The asset is the entity that needs to be protected and which is of interest to an attacker. The loss/disclosure of the asset has negative effects for at least one stakeholder, e.g. loss of money and/or reputation or the revealing of confidential information.

With respect to the resource consumption in $\mathcal{F}$, an asset A can be characterized by two properties: the frequency A_f of its collection and its size. The frequency describes how often A needs to be sent, which depends on the report-strategy implemented in the use-case. Three principle strategies can be identified: a) *Pull* the data is requested by a consumer; b) *Push* the data is sent by the IoT device, if needed or not; and c) *Event-based* data is sent only when its value changes. In an IoT scenario, the size of an asset can vary between a few bits for numerical sensor readings to several megabytes for high-quality video streams.

Message. The message is used to transfer one or more assets within an information flow $\mathcal{F}$ using a specific communication protocol (including protocol overhead). As mentioned before, a message M is transferred from one participant (a data provider P_P) to at least one other participant (a receiver P_R), but may be routed through/processed by, any number of participants (P^*) in between. The frequency to send a message M_f may be determined by the measurement frequency of the asset A_f. In the simplest case, all assets are measured at the same time and transferred in one message. In this case, both frequencies are the same ($M_f = A_f$).

Participant. Participants are any number of entities involved in $\mathcal{F}$. Two participants are mandatory: a *Provider* (P_P) that transmits M to a *Receiver* (P_R). During transfer, M may pass additional entities, which can be classified as active or passive. Passive participants will be called *Gateway* and active participants *Proxy*. With regard to security mechanisms, the difference between both classes is that gateways just forward a message to the next participant, while proxies employ additional security mechanisms. The name proxy was chosen to relate to the PRE [17] schemes.

Communication Link. In an information flow $\mathcal{F}$, each participant is connected to the next one through a Communication Link. The Participants may support different communication technologies, such as Wi-Fi, and establish multiple links, e.g. to separate signalling and payload messages. The Communication Technology influences the resource consumption while sending or receiving M.

3.2   Devices and Resources Concept

The second concept of the IEM describes the devices and their resources available to receive or transmit messages M of the participants involved in a flow $\mathcal{F}$. Each device has a set of Resources (and Capabilities) that can be used in $\mathcal{F}$. In the context of secure message exchange in a flow $\mathcal{F}$ using resource constrained IoT devices the most relevant resources are: computational power, memory, the available communication technologies, the general energy consumption and as non-technical metric the financial cost. Capabilities include hardware accelerators for cryptographic algorithms. In addition to the resources provided by the device, the use-case itself provides resources. In the context of an information exchange, these are typically described in the form of use-case requirements and include: real-time requirements, the available energy source and the financial budget.

3.3   Performance Concept

A P_M indicates the ability of a device to perform a security algorithm and the resulting resource consumption. P_M can be determined and saved into a knowledge-base by either analysing the security algorithm itself or by experimentally executing the algorithm on the target device. Alternatively, the execution of the algorithms can be emulated in order to evaluate that the avail resources are sufficient. There are two types: a P_M either describes the amount of resources that are going to be consumed when executing the algorithm, or it describes the amount of data (assets) that can be processed in time, e.g. how many bytes of data can be encrypted/decrypted per second.

In addition, we define P_Is as a combination of all relevant P_M that influence an algorithm for a specific use-case. The P_M can be weighted to reflect use-case resources that describe a hard threshold, e.g. real-time requirements. An ideal solution would be, if the P_I could be a normalized value, ranking suitable algorithms in terms of resource consumption on the one hand and the security level on the other.

3.4   Security Specification and Configuration Concept

To capture all security requirements, a system designer consults with the stakeholder. At this stage, a security policy is described at high-level. Later on, the policies are refined and concretized into lower levels. To reflect this, the security specification in the IEM is also done at different levels, which are explained in the following. The terminology used follows the definition of [18].

Security Service (S_S) is the most abstract specification. Here, together with stakeholders, security goals are formulated. For example, a stakeholder may specify that the information exchange shall be *Confidential* or that the asset(s) shall be protected from manipulation (*Integrity*).

Security Mechanism (S_M) is a mechanism to map a S_S. There may be multiple mechanisms to implement one S_S. For example, the S_S Confidentiality can be achieved using the S_Ms *Encryption* or *Steganography*. The security mechanisms *Digital Signature* or *Message Authentication Code (MAC)* can be used to achieve the S_S *Integrity*.

Security Implementation (S_I) name specific algorithms to implement a S_M, a set of parameters for the algorithm and also references additional S_I, if necessary. For example, the S_M *Encryption* can be implemented with symmetric (e.g. AES, Twofish, Blowfish) or asymmetric (e.g. RSA, ABE) algorithms. The reference to any additional S_I is required, because implementing a S_M may require multiple algorithms, e.g. *Digital Signatures* use an asymmetric encryption algorithm and a hash function to "reduce" the amount of data to be signed.

Security Configuration (S_C) is a set of S_I and their configurations, that are usable in an information flow, that is, they are within the boundaries of the available resources of the IoT devices. Example configuration parameters for the S_M encryption include key length, padding mechanism, specific curves in ECC, and for block ciphers the mode of operation.

4 High-level Security Policy Language (HSPL) to IEM Transformation

This section describes the transformation from a SP to an instance of the IEM. We decide to use and extend the High-level Security Policy Language (HSPL) developed in the projects SECURED [19] and ANASTACIA [20]. ANASTACIA investigated ways to define security requirements for Software Defined Networks (SDN). They developed a SPL, named High-level Security Policy Language (HSPL), to be used by typically non-technical end-users and is based on a set of predefined high level syntax. The syntax follows a subject - predicate/action - object scheme, followed by the possibilities to add further conditions and restrictions in the form of key-value pairs. The SPL can be extended by re-defining or adding own expressions.

After the security requirements have been recorded within the high-level SPs, the individual message flows need to be extracted. For this, the policies are transformed into an IEM instance as introduced in Sect. 3. The overall approach is as follows: every time a certain action type is identified, a new flow $\mathcal{F}$ is assumed. Policies using the same HSPL-object are assumed to belong to the same flow. This way, by iterating over all policies, the participants can be added to the flows. At the end, possibilities to merge flows together are searched. That is the case when all participants and their order are identical in different flows. A practical example for such two flows could be a temperature/humidity sensor, which provides both measurements at the same time. The following subsection give details about the different steps.

4.1   Element Identification

In a first step of the transformation, the elements, as described in Sects. 3, need to be identified. More specifically, the Participants and their roles as well as the asset(s) must be found within the HSPL policies. To identify an asset A, we define a special type of action named *protective*. A HSPL-object affected by a protective action is classified as an asset. We defined four actions as protective actions: protects, converts (not) authorized to access. While the "protect" action is trivial, the others imply the security requirements indirectly. For example, the "not authorised to access" action indicates that the following object was protected at the provider's side.

In order to identify the participants of a flow within HSPL policies, we introduce a mapping from HSPL-subjects to the participants of an information flow through a set of predefined HSPL-actions. In other words, we predefine the available actions for a subject depending on its later role. This is in contrast to the original HSPL definition by the ANASTACIA project, where in theory each subject could execute each action. Table 1 shows the mappings between the HSPL-actions and the participants. A special meaning has the "requests" action of a receiver, as it indicates that the report-strategy Pull is to be used. In addition, the HSPL-object in a policy using one of the predefined actions can be interpreted as an asset in an information flow, as shown in the column far to the right of the table.

4.2   Grouping Modes

After the participants and their roles have been identified, the question of how to apply the security measure S_M needs to be addressed. Different strategies can be considered, relevant for the consumption of resources. For example, if the flow $\mathcal{F}$ contains multiple assets, but all are treated the same, these assets can be grouped before the security measure is applied. This may be beneficiary with regard to the resource consumption, since certain operations don't need to be executed multiple time, e.g. initialising cryptographic routines or padding the data for block ciphers. Different grouping modes are possible. The grouping modes are: no grouping (each S_S is applied to each asset separately); grouping by S_S (all S_S that can be applied to one or more assets are grouped); grouping by asset (all assets requiring the same S_S are grouped); .

4.3   Resource Annotation

Although not explicitly stated by the ANASTACIA project [21,22], the examples for HSPL-fields as provided in the documentation indicate that they only allow to specify characteristics and limitations for HSPL-objects. To be able to annotate

Table 1. Participant identification based on HSPL Actions

Type → Action ↓	Provider	Gateway	Receiver	Proxy	Asset
Provides	✓	–	–	–	–
Publish	✓	–	–	–	–
Protects	✓	–	–	–	✓
(not)authorised to access	–	-	✓	–	(✓)
Receives	–	–	✓	–	–
Subscribes	–	–	✓	–	–
Requests	–	–	✓	–	–
Forwards	–	✓	–	–	–
Converts	–	–	–	✓	(✓)

the HSPL policies with additional information required in the IEM, we introduce a set of specific HSPL-fields that affect the HSPL-subject as well. In that respect, we extend the original concept with the following HSPL-fields to further describe HSPL-subjects.

is a: This field key is used to specify a device type for the corresponding HSPL subject.

every: This field key is used to specify the update frequency of the IoT device in which new data is provided. The field value has to be some sort of time value, such as $1\,s(s)$.

within: With this field key, real-time requirements in the provision of data can be specified. In contrast to **every**, this field describes the maximum transfer time of the message M from provider P_P to receiver P_R.

has energy source: This field key is important for IoT devices with a limited energy source, i.e. that are battery powered. Its value describes the amount of energy stored within the battery in mAh (mill-amp-hour).

has size: With this field, the size of an asset (i.e. the object) can be specified.

with topic: This field describes the message's topic in a publish/subscribe pattern. The topic's size has to be added to the size of the message.

5 Implementation

For the previously presented concept, we implemented a transformation tool applying the transformation rules, as presented in Sect. 4, from the high-level SPs into an instance of the IEM. To visualize the information flows in an IEM, we choose to use Business Process and Modelling Notation (BPMN) as representation format. The use of an existing BPMN extension would benefit from recognizability and available experience. In [23], Zarour et al. provide an extensive overview over several available BPMN extensions and give a statistical evaluation about types of extensions. They show that the majority of BPMN extensions introduce new graphical elements to represent special, usually domain specific, process behaviour. Chergui Provides in [24] an overview of security related BPMN extensions. Bocciarelli [25,26] developed BPMN extensions to model task resources in the context of Cyber Physical Systems (CPS) and the industry 4.0. However, since no extension covers both aspects, security <u>and</u> resource limitations, at the same time, the use of a combination of two extensions is necessary.

For the IEM, the modelling of the operations of the individual participants can be done in a very simplified way. As depicted in Fig. 1, each participant operates in an endless loop, where at least one operation is related to the transfer of a message. With the exception of a participant of type Gateway, another operation is to apply/remove the security measure. Between loop iterations, the participant of type Receiver delays for a specific amount of time to match a message's frequency M_f. Meanwhile, the other participants start their operations upon reception of message M.

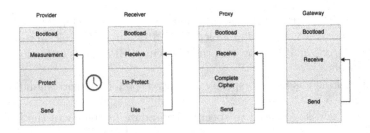

Fig. 1. Participant operations

The transformation is illustrated on an example with a sensor providing temperature, humidity and air pressure readings (e.g. the BME280[1]). The S_S for the temperature and humidity shall be *confidentiality* and *integrity*. The S_S for the asset "air pressure" is only *integrity*. Within the information flow, the message shall pass through a gateway (Access Point). For the purpose of better visibility, the tasks to read out the sensor and use this data, have been merged into a single subprocess. This results in the following 9 HSPL policies:

1. Sensor; protects Confidentiality, Integrity; temperature; has size $\rightarrow$ 16 bytes; every $\rightarrow$ 1 s
2. Sensor; protects Confidentiality, Integrity; humidity
3. Sensor; protects Integrity; air pressure
4. Bob; authorized to access; temperature
5. Bob; authorized to access; humidity
6. Bob; authorized to access; air pressure
7. Access Point; forwards; temperature

---

[1] https://www.bosch-sensortec.com/products/environmental-sensors/humidity-sensors-bme280/.

8. Access Point; forwards; humidity
9. Access Point; forwards; air pressure

Figure 2 shows the BPMN representation of the resulting information flow with grouping mode "grouping by asset". As all assets have the same P_P, P_R, and the gateway, only one single flow is generated. The participants P_P and P_R (top and bottom) contain four tasks each, two of which to apply the security services. The security tasks are depicted with a padlock symbol, as suggested by [27]. Furthermore, we also acknowledge the need to "undo" or validate a security measure at the receiver side, which will be represented with an open padlock. The S_S applied in the task is illustrated with orange symbols. Here, we use the symbols defined in SecBPMN [28]. That is a symbol with two hands shaking for *confidentiality* and a symbol with a white document for *integrity*.

The sequence flows (chain of tasks within a BPMN pool) relate with the operations for the different types of participant, as introduced in Fig. 1. On the P_P's side, it covers the gathering of the assets from the sensors. The tasks should be annotated with the resource consumption to read out the hardware sensor. Like with the BME128 sensor, this is often a single, integral step for all assets. Thus, from a resource consumption point of view, it is possible to merge all these tasks into one task/subprocess. In general, as a detailed sequence flow is not necessary as long as the resource consumption is known, the same merging can be done on the P_R's side.

The Access Point in the middle simply receives the message and directly afterwards sends it to the P_R Bob. The resource properties are provided via an input form in a property-panel. The implementation is an extension to the bpmn-js project [29], an open source BPMN modeller written in JavaScript. The transformer tool is implemented in Swift and is still a work in progress. The GUI allows constructing new HSPL policies out of the redefined sets of HSPL elements, i.e. subjects, actions, objects and fields.

Figure 3 shows the tasks of the participant P_P when using the grouping mode "grouping by S_S". As before, two tasks are generated to protect all three assets. However, in contrast to the first example, protecting the *Integrity* in the later task only processes one asset, namely the air pressure.

6   Conclusion and Future Work

This paper addressed the topic of applying security measure while providing data with resource constrained devices in an IoT environment. Furthermore, the paper presented an IEM capable of capturing available/required resources. As these policies are used by non-expert stakeholders, the use of a high-level SPL was proposed, together with a set of transformation rules to derive individual information flows as part of the resource-aware Information Exchange Model (IEM).

As a next step to realize the envisioned security configuration recommendation system is to determine the P_I. That means to determine relevant sets of P_M for available IoT devices. Here, an extendable emulation framework is planed,

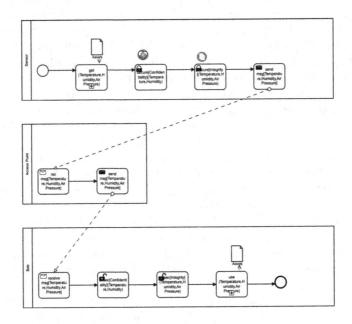

Fig. 2. Information flow represented as BPMN process

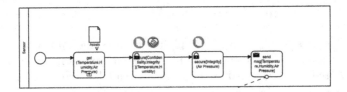

Fig. 3. Information flow with grouping by Security Service

able to emulate the resource consumption of an information flow on a microcontroller. More precisely, the resource consumption during the execution of various security algorithms and configurations is in the focus. First experiments with the QEMU emulator for the ESP32 microcontroller showed mixed results with respect to the runtime when compared with the real device.

Acknowledgement. This work is part of the research project "I4sec - Sichere Maschinenkommunikation und Fernwartung von Sensoren in der Produktion", funded by the Federal Ministry of Education and Research of Germany (BMBF).

References

1. Zhang, Z.-K., Cho, M.C.Y., Wang, C.-W., Hsu, C.-W., Chen, C.-K., Shieh, S.: IoT security: ongoing challenges and research opportunities. In: IEEE 7th International Conference on Service-Oriented Computing and Applications, pp. 230–234 IEEE (2014)
2. Pearson, B., et al.: On misconception of hardware and cost in IoT security and privacy. In: ICC 2019-2019 IEEE International Conference on Communications (ICC), pp. 1–7, ISSN: 1938–1883
3. Kietzmann, P., Boeckmann, L., Lanzieri, L., Schmidt, T.C., Wählisch, M.: a performance study of crypto-hardware in the low-end IoT. In: Proceedings of the 2021 International Conference on Embedded Wireless Systems and Networks, ser. EWSN '21. Junction Publishing, pp. 79–90
4. Munoz, P.S., Tran, N., Craig, B., Dezfouli, B., Liu, Y.: Analyzing the resource utilization of AES encryption on IoT devices. In: 2018 Asia-Pacific Signal and Information Processing Association Annual Summit and Conference (APSIPA ASC), pp. 1200–1207 ISSN: 2640–0103
5. Dhanda, S.S., Singh, B., Jindal, P.: Lightweight cryptography: a solution to secure IoT. Wireless Pers. Commun. **112**(3), 1947–1980 (2020). https://doi.org/10.1007/s11277-020-07134-3
6. Dutta, I.K., Ghosh, B., Bayoumi, M.: Lightweight cryptography for internet of insecure things: a survey. In: 2019 IEEE 9th Annual Computing and Communication Workshop and Conference (CCWC), pp. 0475–0481 (2019)
7. Gunathilake, N. A., Buchanan, W.J., Asif, R.: Next generation lightweight cryptography for smart IoT devices Implementation, challenges and applications. In: 2019 IEEE 5th World Forum on Internet of Things (WF-IoT), pp. 707–710 (2019)
8. Tsai, K.-L., Huang, Y.-L., Leu, F.-Y., You, I., Huang, Y.-L. Tsai, C.-H.: AES-128 based secure low power communication for Lora WAN IoT Environments. IEEE Access **6**, 45325–45334 (2018)
9. Batina, L.: Dietary recommendations for lightweight block ciphers: power, energy and area analysis of recently developed architectures. In: Hutter, M., Schmidt, J.-M. (eds.) RFIDSec 2013. LNCS, vol. 8262, pp. 103–112. Springer, Heidelberg (2013). https://doi.org/10.1007/978-3-642-41332-2_7
10. Hsu, R.-H., Lee, J., Quek, T.Q.S., Chen, J.-C.: Reconfigurable security: edge-computing-based framework for IoT. In: Conference Name: IEEE Network vol.32 (5), pp. 92–99
11. Sha, K., Yang, T.A., Wei, W., Davari, S.: A survey of edge computing-based designs for IoT security, **6**(2), pp. 195–202. https://www.sciencedirect.com/science/article/pii/S2352864818303018

12. Safa, N.S., Maple, C., Haghparast, M., Watson, T., Dianati, M.: An opportunistic resource management model to overcome resource-constraint in the Internet of Things, 31(8), pp. e5014, eprint: https://onlinelibrary.wiley.com/doi/pdf/10.1002/cpe.5014. https://onlinelibrary.wiley.com/doi/abs/10.1002/cpe.5014

13. Green, M., et al.: Outsourcing the decryption of ABE ciphertexts. In: USENIX Security Symposium, pp. 34-34 (2011)

14. Elgamal, T.: A public key cryptosystem and a signature scheme based on discrete logarithms. IEEE Trans. Inf. Theory 31(4), 469–472 (1985)

15. Manzoor, A., Liyanage, M., Braeke, A., Kanhere, S.S., Ylianttila, M.: Blockchain based proxy re-encryption scheme for secure IoT data sharing. IEEE Int. Conf. Blockchain Cryptocurrency (ICBC) 2019, 99–103 (2019)

16. Khashan, O. A.: Hybrid lightweight proxy re-encryption scheme for secure Fog-to-Things Environment. IEEE Access 8, 878–887 (2020)

17. Suksomboon, K. Tagami. A., Basu, A., Kurihara, J.: In-device proxy re-encryption service for information-centric networking access control. In: 2018 IEEE 43rd Conference on Local Computer Networks (LCN), pp. 303–306 (2018)

18. Patz, G., Condell, M., Krishnan, R., Sanchez, L.: Multidimensional security policy management for dynamic coalitions, In: Proceedings DARPA Information Survivability Conference and Exposition II. DISCEX'01, vol. 2, pp. 41–54

19. Vallini, M.: Fp7 project secured deliverable d4.1 policy specification (2015)

20. Zarca, A.M., Bernabé, J.B., Ortíz, J., Skarmeta, A.: H2020 project Anastacia deliverable d2.5 policy-based definition and policy for orchestration final report. (2018)

21. ANASTACIA Project - advanced networked agents for security and trust assessment in CPS / IOT architectures. http://www.anastacia-h2020.eu/

22. AANASTACIA Project - GitLab repsitory. https://gitlab.com/anastacia-project

23. Zarour, K., Benmerzoug, D., Guermouche, N., Drira, K.: A systematic literature review on BPMN extensions, publisher: Emerald Publishing Limited. https://www.emerald.com/insight/content/DOI/10.1108/BPMJ-01-2019-0040/full/html

24. Chergui, M.E.A., Benslimane, S.M.: A valid BPMN extension for supporting security requirements based on cyber security ontology. In: Abdelwahed, E.H., Bellatreche, L., Golfarelli, M., Méry, D., Ordonez, C. (eds.) MEDI 2018. LNCS, vol. 11163, pp. 219–232. Springer, Cham (2018). https://doi.org/10.1007/978-3-030-00856-7_14

25. Bocciarelli, p., D'Ambrogio, A., Giglio, A., Paglia, E.: A BPMN extension to enable the explicit modeling of task resources

26. Bocciarelli, p., D'Ambrogio, A., Giglio, A., Paglia, E.: A BPMN extension for modeling cyber-physical-production-systems in the context of industry 4.0, In: IEEE 14th International Conference on Networking, Sensing and Control (ICNSC), pp. 599–604 (2017)

27. Sang., K. S. Zhou, B.: BPMN security extensions for healthcare process. In: IEEE International Conference on Computer and Information Technology; Ubiquitous Computing and Communications; Dependable, Autonomic and Secure Computing; Pervasive Intelligence and Computing, pp. 2340–2345 (2015)

28. Salnitri, M., Dalpiaz, F., Giorgini, P.: Modeling and verifying security policies in business processes. In: Bider, I., Gaaloul, K., Krogstie, J., Nurcan, S., Proper, H.A., Schmidt, R., Soffer, P. (eds.) BPMDS/EMMSAD -2014. LNBIP, vol. 175, pp. 200–214. Springer, Heidelberg (2014). https://doi.org/10.1007/978-3-662-43745-2_14

29. BPMN-JS - BPMN 2.0 for the web, original-date: 2014–03-10T12:57:00Z. https://github.com/bpmn-io/bpmn-js

IRIS Advanced Threat Intelligence Orchestrator- A Way to Manage Cybersecurity Challenges of IoT Ecosystems in Smart Cities

Vasiliki-Georgia Bilali[✉] [iD], Dimitrios Kosyvas[iD], Thodoris Theodoropoulos[iD], Eleftherios Ouzounoglou[iD], Lazaros Karagiannidis[iD], and Angelos Amditis[iD]

Institute of Communication and Computer Systems (ICCS), 9, Iroon Politechniou Str. Zografou, 15773 Athens, Greece
giovana.bilali@iccs.gr

Abstract. This paper provides an overview of the Advanced Threat Intelligence Orchestrator in assisting organizations and society's first responders in managing, prioritizing, and sharing information related to cyber security incidents. In order to accomplish this, the capabilities and benefits of security, orchestration, automation, and response (SOAR) systems, on which Orchestrator is based, were promoted. The results of this survey conducted as part of the IRIS EU-funded project to protect Internet of Things (IoT) and Artificial Intelligence (AI)-driven ICT-enabled systems from cyber threats and attacks on their privacy facilitating SOC/CSIRTs/CERTs.

In this context, the tool is explored in methods of orchestrating and automating cyber security processes and routines. The open-source tool that was chosen for the creation of Advanced Threat Intelligence Orchestrator was SHUFFLE. SHUFFLE gives a wide variety of functionalities as it can be integrated with numerous tools and APIS. Furthermore, the provision of schematic workflows with action steps makes the stakeholders' interface more intuitive.

Keywords: Orchestration · SOAR · Information management · Automation · CSIRTs · Threat management · SHUFFLE

1 Introduction

Security operational centers (Socs) and enterprise experts spend hours in security departments monitoring processes, waiting for alerts and searching for clues that something unusual is happening identified among massive amount of data. Many times, these alerts either do not reach security centers or misinterpreted by the system for immediate action, causing uncertainty and anxiety both within the organization and in a smart city. Even if the alerts are received, the process of sending the information to the appropriate "place" is time-consuming, as well as managing a massive amount of data necessitates multiple decision-making processes. As a result, in many cases, implementing automation and orchestration is the answer when it comes to managing and, ultimately, combating cyber security threats.

A. González-Vidal et al. (Eds.): GIoTS 2022, LNCS 13533, pp. 315–325, 2022.
https://doi.org/10.1007/978-3-031-20936-9_25

Advanced Threat Intelligence Orchestrator can be provided as a drastic solution in a cyber-threat challenging world since it not only manages cyber-threat information and processes in IoT and AI-enabled infrastructures, but it also secures smart ecosystems by facilitating vulnerability management, security incident response, and security operations automation. This technical solution adheres to the capabilities of security, orchestration, automation, and response (SOAR). SOAR capabilities can benefit from relying on and leveraging security information and event management (SIEM) system information through automation and orchestration.

1.1 Data Sources in Smart Cities

IoT implementation in urban areas improves citizens' daily lives and society's operations by providing safety and operational stability. These ecosystems consume static and real-time data from a wide range of sources, such as sensors, adaptors, actuators, IDs, SIEM alerts, CCTV cameras, and so on. Nonetheless, as IoT and AI smart ecosystems become more complex, their capabilities increase, making them more vulnerable to malicious actors.

1.2 State of the Art of Tools Used into SOAR

As it is mentioned by Gartner Glossary[1] "SOAR refers to technologies that enable organizations to collect inputs monitored by the security operations team. For example, alerts from the SIEM system and other security technologies—where incident analysis and triage can be performed by leveraging a combination of human and machine power— help define, prioritize and drive standardized incident response activities. SOAR tools allow an organization to define incident analysis and response procedures in a digital workflow format".

SOAR platforms (SOARP) interact with several technologies such as threat detection technology tools, vulnerability detection tools, AI/ML-powered cyber defense systems etc. Indicatively some of them are **SIEM** is a piece of software that allows users to log, monitor, alert, anticipate, correlate, and display security-related events and data collected from networked devices [1]. **Unified Threat Management (UTMs),** contains a software or a hardware gathering security management information displaying security logs in a console. **Next-gen firewalls,** include traditional firewalls, combine them with filtering capabilities, network- and port-address translation (NAT), VPN support, and other features. According to [2], the threat detection technology tools mentioned above are unaware of an organization's entire IT ecosystem. **Vulnerability detection tools** is a software tool that according to the bibliography, there are three major types of analysis tools and techniques for detecting software vulnerabilities: a) static analysis, which examines the system/software without executing it, including examining source code, bytecode, and/or binaries, b) dynamic analysis, which examines the system/software by executing it, giving it specific inputs, and examining results and/or outputs, c) hybrid

---

[1] https://www.gartner.com/en/information-technology/glossary/security-orchestration-automation-response-soar.

analysis, combining a, b [3]. **AI/ML-powered cyber defense systems** [2], using deep learning and cutting-edge algorithms.

Despite the fact that the implementation of SOAR capabilities into a variety of technical solutions is a relatively new phenomena, a literature study has begun to revolve around this subject [4–7].

1.3 SOAR Solutions

There are many already existed market-oriented and Open-Source solutions. Gartner's 2020 SOAR market guide[2] entails a list of representative vendors and their products, including the following: Anomali ThreatStrecam, Cyware Virtual Cyber Fusion Center, D3 Security D3 SOAR, DFLabs IncMan SOAR, EclecticIQ Platform, FireEye Helix, Fortinet FortiSOAR, Honeycomb SOCAutomation, IBM Security Resilient, LogicHub SOAR+, Micro Focus ArcSight SOAR, Palo Alto Networks Cortex XSOAR [8], Rapid7 InsightConnect, ServiceNow Security Operations, Siemplify SOAR Platform, Splunk Phantom, Swimlane SOAR, ThreatConnect SOAR Platform, ThreatQuotient ThreatQ, Tines. The open source community is also providing solutions for the security Orchestration domain.

Some of the common elements of SOAR enabled tools include using machine learning algorithms, workflow automation, incident response playbooks, an open plugin framework, a case management visual environment, an intuitive user interface, a command line console, and so on. Some of the products, indicatively,

Cortex XSOAR [9] unifies security automation, case management, real-time collaboration and threat intelligence management, it also includes a registration fee.

DFLabs IncMac SOAR [2, 4] enable the planning and recovery phases through features such as knowledge bases, key performance indicators, and advanced reporting.

Anomali ThreatStream [10], converts raw data into actionable information by automating the collection and processing of data. This product is oriented to security teams' experts.

As a result, of cutting-edge research conducted through the IRIs project, SHUFLLE open source tool was the more interesting and mature since it facilitates to achieve project goals. More specifically, it supports thousands of premade integrations (see Table 1) using open frameworks such as OpenAPI to ease migration. Provides options for automating the digestion of trigger points. Possess a diverse set of cyber incident use cases (see Table 1), including MISP and HIVE cases that will be used in the project.

We also considered various user-oriented criteria, which resulted in the following benefits.

a. Maintains a well-organized GitHub repository and community
b. Contains useful documentation
c. Encourages creativity since the visual design allows you to personalize the dashboards.
d. It has the ability to integrate a wide range of tools from various categories
e. It is available in a free version.
f. It caters to the needs of both experts and non-experts.

---

[2] https://www.splunk.com/en_us/form/gartner-soar-market-guide-2020.html.

1.4 SOAR Benefits

Automate Critical Use Cases: The automatic definition of emergency cases, can be proved as savior in cases where the time is a valuable parameter for tackling an incident. In any case automating any kind of use cases indicates preparedness in operational and decision-making processes.

Streamlined Operations: Each element of SOAR contributes to the streamlining of security operations. Security orchestration aggregates data incoming from a variety of sources. Security automation, meanwhile, can easily handle low-priority alerts and incidents through the use of automated playbooks.

Immediate Incident Detection and Automating Response: This capability ensures that the system responds on time and without delay during the decision-making process of multiple data aggregation.

Faster Response Time: Security orchestration combines multiple alerts from different systems into a single incident. Security automation saves even more time by allowing the system to respond to alerts without the need for human intervention whenever possible. Adding context to textual data and automating the decision-making process allows for faster alert handling[3].

Elevating SIEM: A SOAR solution that integrates with a Security Information and Event Management (SIEM) is required to automate Security Operational Centers (SOCs). A SIEM with an integrated SOAR solution allows teams to respond to threats more quickly because all of the information they require is in one location. It also reduces the possibility of human error and the time analysts spend switching between tools because they can all be accessed through a unified interface.

Systems Scalability: The scalability of the system is achieved by the Web based application of SHUFFLE solution.

2 Specifications of Advance Threat Intelligence Orchestrator

In IRIS context, Advanced Threat Intelligence Orchestrator will be a facilitator of the communication among the external data sources and stakeholders. The end-user categories are composed by SOC teams, CSIRTS/CERTS and AI infrastructure providers. In particular, Orchestrator will create workflows to respond to incident information sent from infrastructures by implementing expert knowledge and processes. Each workflow's knowledge can be updated based on the most recent laws and processes.

2.1 Orchestrator's Subcomponents

The Advanced Threat Intelligence Orchestrator is made up of six sub-components, including two visual environments and four backend tools. The structure of the integrated tool is presented below (Fig. 1):

---

[3] https://www.siemplify.co/blog/security-orchestration-automation-response-benefits/

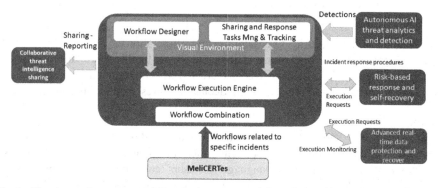

Fig. 1. The internal structure of the Orchestrator and its relationship to input and output information.

The visual environment consisting of a) the Workflow Designer as well as b) the Sharing, and Response Tasks Management & Tracking will be based on the Shuffle visual environment, while the backend tools will provide extra functionalities to imported and exported information.

Workflow Designer/Manager is a graphical environment that allows the creation of multiple scenario workflows. In particular, the definition of various incident response scenarios is the digitized form of the associated runbooks/playbooks that are executed. The runbooks are documents comprising proper background information and procedures to successfully execute security-related tasks, or address incidents, while the playbooks are documents comprising workflows, operating procedures, and cultural values required to approach and complete tasks in a consistent way. Finally, the Workflow Designer/Manager will include all the steps that should be automatically or manually executed based on the defined workflows.

Workflow Execution engine is the engine that implemented on the defined workflows, executes the data exchange steps and realizes the command execution requests to components.

Workflow combination engine will take the already existing workflow procedures connected to cyber-incidents and will automatically combined them with expert input from the MeliCERTes platform to enable proactiveness.

Threat Sharing and Response Tasks management and Tracking is a visual environment, which a part of this provides information on the tools related to threat sharing and response tools that have been automatically applied or should be manually/semi-automatically applied based on the risk levels.

Data exchange framework is a framework facilitating the data exchange among the orchestrator and intercorrelated components through APIs.

Command execution requests framework (based either on existing solutions of components or definition based on the OpenAPI specifications) is a framework facilitating the execution requests from the orchestrator to the components through APIs as well as the sharing of information for automatically applied/executed processes.

2.2 Technologies

SOAR tools combine Security, Orchestration and Automation capabilities (SOA), with Security Incident Response Platform (SIRP), and Threat Intelligence Platform (TIP) to seamlessly manage all the data received and created workflows in real time. A scenario workflow, referred to as a Failed ssh login Scenario, is presented in this section.

Shuffle

Within this section, SHUFFLE documentation is presented, to imprint potential SOAR capabilities that Orchestrator could perform in IRIS information sharing and awareness platform, as well as to perform a "language" for users' common understanding.

SHUFFLE is developing workflows for a variety of use case categories. SHUFLE has clustered these use cases into 8 groups, which namely are a) Communication, b) Case Management, c) SIEM, d) Assets, e) IAM, f) Intelligence, g) Network, h) Eradication cyber incident detection, prevention, remediation, case management, communication etc., more information on Table 1 below. The below use case categorization has been depicted from GitHub repository.[4] Based on the case scenarios, specific SOC tools are involved.

SHUFFLE open source tools have a wide range of capabilities, including integration and communication with a plethora of tools, including (e.g. Hashdd, Elastic Search, the Hive, MISP, Keycloak IAM, etc.), managing cyber-security issues, related to threat and vulnerability management, authority management, security incident response and security operations automation.

APIS Integration

The SHUFFLE platform makes third-party API integration straightforward by utilizing trigger-based communication techniques such as Webhook, which can be quickly activated by a POST request from the backend. Using this way, the synchronization of the workflow and the incoming input can be defined from the REST-API, and the necessary automated process can be simply configured in SHUFFLE.

2.3 Failed SSH Login Scenario

The example of a failed remote authentication login was chosen to demonstrate a small portion of SHUFFLE's capabilities and to familiarize the user with the platform's consensus and visual output. So, to establish an input data pipeline for the SHUFFLE procedure, Wazuh, an open-source platform for thread identification, security monitoring, and incident response, was used. As a result, a Wazuh manager was set up and agent in virtual machines and integrate SHUFFLE to monitor for failed ssh authentication. The Wazuh manager checks the security logs produced by the manager itself and the agent that controls and when it detects a password failure it sends a HTTP-POST request to the SHUFFLE Webhook.

This request is essentially a JSON message containing information about the authentication attempt and the configuration rules from Wazuh. By sending this message we trigger the SHUFFLE Webhook and kickstart the flow of our use case.

---

[4] https://github.com/Shuffle/python-apps.

Table 1. SHUFFLE use case categories correlated with capabilities and tools

Use case category	Use case capabilities	Tools
Communication	• Write text to someone • Read chats • List chats • Send actionable buttons • Send a file • Search through chat • Send a chat (comms) for every new email found (comms) every 5 min. Look for any IoC in it (SHUFFLE tools) and analyze it with Threat Intel	Chat: • Discord • Slack • MS Teams • SMS Email: • Gmail • Outlook • AWS SES
Case management	• Open ticket • Update ticket • Comment ticket (if not an update) • List Tickets • Merge ticket • Search for ticket(s) • Upload file(s) • Download file(s) • Add artifact/Indicator like IP and domain (security specific) • Syncronize tickets with another ticketing system (cases) every 5 min. When a new ticket comes, send a message to messaging app (communication)	• GitHub Notifications • TheHive • Service Now • Jira • Secureworks • HappyFox • PagerDuty • Zoho • ConnectWise
SIEM	• Search • Send event TO SIEM • Get Search results • Create Saved Search • Create Alert from Search (sends webhook/something else) • List Incidents • Get Incident • Update incident • Add comment	• Splunk • QRadar • Elasticsearch (ELK) • MDATP • Azure Sentinel • Logz.io • Security Onion

(continued)

Table 1. (*continued*)

Use case category	Use case capabilities	Tools
Assets	• Find hostname • Find Software by name • Find IP • Find hostname's owner • Search for CVE • List vulnerabilities by severity • List vulnerabilities by host • Get vulnerability • Edit vulnerability • Generate report	VMS systems: • Nessus • TenableVMS • Tenable Container Security • Snyk • Gitguardian Asset Management • McAfee CHS
IAM	• Access Management • Active Directory • Single Sign-on	• Microsoft Identity and Access • Sailpoint IdentityQ • CISCO Identity Services Engine • Keycloak IAM • AWS IAM
Intelligence	• Search for IP • Search for Domain • Search for URL • Search for hash (md5, sha256…) • Add IP/domain/url/hash to have been seen (sighted MISP) • Search for CVE • Search for Threat actor • Get incidents	• MISP • Passivetotal • Recorded Future • Secureworks • Shoden • Virustotal • IBM xforce • IPInfo
Network	• Block IP • Block domain • Block URL • Sinkhole IP • Sinkhole domain • Unblock (all of the above) • Search for status with IP/domain	• AWS WAF • Cisco • Check point • Palo Alto • Fortinet • AWS VPC FW
Eradication	• Ticketing system (list/create/edit alert) • Search • Find hostname • Ban hash/ip/url/domain • Isolate host • Execute script on host • Create rulE	• VMware Carbon Black • GoSecure • Cylances • InfoCyte • Waxuh • Windows Defender • Windows Defender ATP • CrowdStrike Falcon • Velociraptor • Qualys EDR • Trend MicroXDR

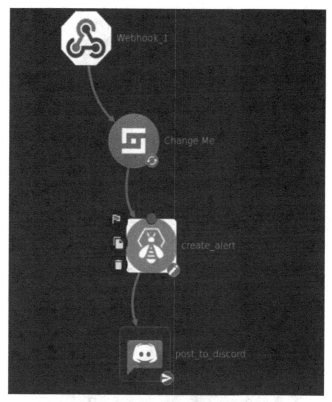

Fig. 2. Orchestrator's Workflow Designer visual environment relying on SHUFFLE design environment

In Fig. 2 the pointing arrow shows the direction of input data in SHUFFLE and all the blocks have access to that information.

In this example we have also used TheHive that is an incident response platform to create an alert regarding the failed connection by filtering some fields of the original message. At the end of the flow we post in a Discord channel some results like the IP and port used in the login attempt to notify the user.

The results of the execution workflow are indicated to the figure above (Fig. 3). These outcomes can be viewed in either the related tools or in this visual environment. As a result of the scenario, users reported that the Orchestrator processes flowed smoothly and that it was user-friendly.

2.4 Stakeholders Communication Through Orchestrator

The Advanced Threat Intelligence Orchestrator will be accessible to stakeholders via a user management interface. Begin by deciding whether to use a predefined or custom workflow. End users are thus able to seek and execute an already existed workflow or create a sequence of steps implementing tools based on use case categories (see Table 1), based on the triggering information received (e.g. alerts and events etc.). Orchestrator

Fig. 3. Orchestrator's Sharing and Response Track Management and Tracking visual environment relying on SHUFFLE design environment.

will be able to interface with the MeliCERTes platform and seek expert knowledge for response, improving default workflows and recommended response actions. The combination of multiple data sources gathered from other tools and MeliCERTes platform will improve the ability to compute efficient proactive response steps. As a result of the foregoing, security operations teams will benefit from automating iterative response processes, saving time for higher priority sorting tasks, and providing a standardized, easy-to-follow response.

3   Conclusions

In a nutshell, the numerous threats of security operational centers business face on a daily basis are draining resources and slowing incident response time, whether it is called alert fatigue or information overload. Here it comes SOAR platforms to give the solution by relieving SOC analysts of remedial and low-priority tasks, allowing them to focus on improving the overall effectiveness of SOC in responding to incidents. IRIS will take a step forward in this direction by implementing Orchestrator, which will assist stakeholders in lowering smart city risks while automatically managing, prioritizing, and sharing information related to cyber security incidents.

Acknowledgement. This work is a part of the IRIS project. This project has received funding from the European Union's Horizon 2020 research and innovation programme under grant agreement No 101021727. This content reflects only the authors' view and the European Commission is not responsible for any use that may be made of the information this publication contains.

References

1. Redlegg Managed Security Services: What is SIEM?
2. Johnson Kinyua, L.A.: AI/ML in security orchestration, automation and response: future research directions, vol. 28, no. 2, p. 19 (2021)
3. Larsen, G., Fong, E.K., Wheeler, D.A., Moorthy, R.S.: State-of-the-art resources (SOAR) for software vulnerability detection, test, and evaluation 2016 (2016)
4. DFLABS- Cyber Incidents under control: The most comprehensive ebook on soar use cases. https://dflabs.com/wp-content/uploads/2020/12/The-Most-Comprehensive-eBook-on-SOAR-Use-Cases.pdf
5. LogRhythm: Practical Use Cases for SOAR. https://logrhythm.com/practical-use-cases-for-soar-white-paper-2019/. Accessed February 2022
6. Palo Alto: Top Security Orchestration Use Cases
7. Logsign: Security orchestration, automation and response (SOAR) buyer's Guide- an ultimate guide for SOAR
8. Cortex: The state of SOAR 2020- the fourth annual survey report on incident response (2020)
9. CORTEX: Security automation for everyone. https://www.paloaltonetworks.com/cortex/cortex-xsoar
10. ANOMALI: Big data security. actionable intelligence. Relevant insights

Federated Learning-Based IoT Intrusion Detection on Non-IID Data

Wenxuan Huang$^{(\boxtimes)}$, Thanassis Tiropanis⊕, and George Konstantinidis⊕

Electronics and Computer Science, University of Southampton, Southampton, UK
{wh1g19,t.tiropanis,g.konstantinidis}@soton.ac.uk

Abstract. Federated learning allows multiple parties to jointly train and update machine learning models without shared data to a central server, which is particularly suitable for intrusion detection in IoT environments. However, data on each node in the IoT scenario are usually not independently and identically distributed (IID), which poses an additional challenge to the convergence and speed of federated learning. To address this problem, there have been proposals to have nodes share a portion of their data centrally, which can still raise privacy concerns. In this paper we propose a strategy to improve the training of non-IID data by allowing mutually trusted nodes to self-aggregate into clusters of trust that will participate in federated learning as peers. We experiment with an up-to-date IoT dataset, Aposemat IoT-23 (IoT-23 for short) and show that using this strategy is considerably more accurate federated learning, comparably accurate to proposals that envisage central sharing a portion of node data, and comparable to centralised machine learning accuracy.

Keywords: Federated Learning · Intrusion Detection · Internet of Things

1 Introduction

In recent years, the proliferation of smart devices and network technology has triggered a new era where the Internet of Things (IoT) is being more widely used in people's lives, including logistics, industrial processes, public safety, home automation, environmental monitoring and healthcare [2]. At the same time, the number of cyber-attacks against IoT is also increasing, such as distributed denial of service attacks, botnets, and other intrusions [10]. The intrusion detection systems (ID) [3] that monitor networks and detect malicious activity become more and more critical as cyber-attacks are increasing and devices are highly vulnerable to malicious activities. The IDS plays a vital role in the network defence process, with the aim of alerting security administrators to malicious behaviour.

One approach to implementing IDS in the IoT is based on anomaly detection. Models are built from the characteristics of normal samples to detect outliers and identify suspicious behaviour on devices. Machine learning algorithms have proven to be very effective in building models that distinguish between normal

© The Author(s), under exclusive license to Springer Nature Switzerland AG 2022
A. González-Vidal et al. (Eds.): GIoTS 2022, LNCS 13533, pp. 326–337, 2022.
https://doi.org/10.1007/978-3-031-20936-9_26

and malicious traffic [8]. In this paper, our research implements anomaly-based intrusion detection in an IoT environment through a multi-layer perceptron.

However, traditional machine learning training requires data to be stored in a central node to train the model. Applying traditional machine learning algorithms to implement an IDS means that the training data generated by IoT devices at the edge of the network is aggregated to a central server for computation, to train a model that can detect malicious attacks, and the trained model is then transferred to the user device for task inference. While such an approach can detect intrusions with high accuracy, there are a number of problems. First, latency becomes an important issue since large amounts of data are generated by end devices and transferred to a data centre. Due to the distance between the geographical location of the IoT devices and the intrusion detection system, this can lead to longer processing times that do not meet the timeliness required for anomaly reporting. Second, privacy and security are at risk whenever the original data leaves its host. Data leakage can occur during data storage, data transfer and data sharing, which can cause serious problems for owners and providers. In fact, data from some devices cannot be shared at all, for privacy reasons, and cannot be used for the training of machine learning models [13]. Another approach to train models in a distributed environment is to use local data to train and update models on each device, isolated from other devices. However, insufficient data samples and local data bias can lead to poorer models. One solution for dealing with such distributed data training is federated learning, which enables the collaborative training of high-quality shared models by aggregating and averaging local computational updates uploaded by IoT devices [16].

Unlike traditional machine learning, data for federated learning is distributed on edge devices rather than on centralised data servers. Data samples are trained locally and parameters (such as weights and biases of deep neural networks) are are updated after aggregation between these local nodes with some frequency to produce a global model that is shared by all nodes. The main advantage of this approach is that the training of the global model does not require direct access to the data, so that federated learning can learn satisfactory global models without compromising the privacy of user data.

A common assumption for federated learning is that the data is independent and identically distributed(IID), and it has been shown that when trained with IID data, the accuracy of FedAvg [9] can be well approximated to centralised models. However, in practice, it is unrealistic to assume that the local data on each edge device is always IID. In particular, in an IoT environment, the distributions of data across devices are often non-IID due to different user preferences, devices and network environments. When the data distribution is non-IID, the FedAvg model converges erratically and the loss of the model may even diverge with training [17]. In [1] the authors present experiments that show much lower experimental performance on non-IID data than on IID data in an IoT intrusion detection scenario. This is caused by divergence between the stochastic gradient descent (SGD) performed locally by different nodes, which aims to minimise the loss value of local samples on each device, and the global model, which aims to minimise the overall loss on all devices. As we continue to train the model with heterogeneous local data on different devices and fit it to the global model, the differences between the weights of these local models will accumulate and eventually degrade the performance of learning [12], resulting in more communication rounds needed for training convergence. And given that the individual nodes in a federated learning scenario are usually devices with limited computational power and communication bandwidth, it is crucial to reduce the number of communication rounds in federated learning in order to improve the convergence speed of the global model. One approach to address this issue is that of [17] which proposes that each node places a portion of their data into a globally shared central repository; this results in performance that sometimes approaches that of centralised machine learning, coming however at a privacy cost.

In this paper, we propose an alternative strategy to address the above limitations and improve the performance of federated learning-based IoT intrusion detection in non-IID data. Our approach is to add clusters of servers between the aggregation server and local nodes. Namely, we consider the aggregation of mutually trusted nodes, into a single cluster of trust, who acts as a single peer for federated learning. Therefore, each cluster is trained as the client in federated learning. The goal of the proposed scheme is to achieve detection accuracy as close to that of a centralised IDS, while maximising data privacy and security and reducing communication overhead. Our contributions include:

- We perform a structural comparison of the performance of general federated learning (FedAvg) on different IoT IDS scenarios for the Aposemat IoT-23 dataset.
- We implement a strategy that uses clusters of trust instead of the original nodes as clients for federated learning training to improve IoT IDS performance on non-IID data.
- We compare the performance between clusters of trust of different sizes and with different threat coverage, with the globally shared data approach exploring the trade-offs for the Aposemat IoT-23 dataset.

2   Background

2.1   Internet of Things

The Internet of Things (IoT), is a new technological paradigm envisioned as a global network of machines and devices capable of interacting with each other [6]. As the Internet of Things grows and the number of potential devices that can be connected to it runs into the hundreds of billions, the potential security threats are escalating [14]. While the IoT increases productivity for companies and improves the quality of life for people, the IoT will also increase the potential attack surface for hackers and other cyber criminals. a study in [6] shows that 70% of the most commonly used IoT devices have serious vulnerabilities. IoT devices are vulnerable due to a lack of transmission encryption, insecure web interfaces, inadequate software protection and insufficient authorisation. In recent years, positive progress has been observed in academic research addressing privacy and security issues in IoT systems. The technologies and security approaches currently proposed are largely based on traditional network security methods. However, applying security mechanisms in IoT systems is more challenging than traditional networks due to the heterogeneity of devices and protocols and the size or number of nodes in the system. In [11] the authors extensively explain the challenges of applying IoT security mitigation due to physical coupling, heterogeneity, resource constraints, privacy, large scale, trust management, and inadequate security readiness.

2.2 Federated Learning

Federated learning [5] is a machine learning solution to decentralise training data, which aims to learn high-quality centralised machine learning models by training distributed data stored in a large number of endpoints. The approach's distributed data architecture reduces the strain on centralised data storage and solves the problem of data silos. In addition, it protects privacy as the central server does not access user data.

The algorithm that implements federated learning is FedAvg [9]. FedAvg coordinates training through a central server that hosts a shared global model. Federated learning trains the shared global model by iteratively aggregating model updates from multiple client devices, which may have slow and unstable network connections. Initially, client devices are first signed in using a remote server. The remote servers then take turns to synchronise federated learning. Each round of FedAvg has four steps. First, the server sends a global model to all parties. Second, the parties perform stochastic gradient descent (SGD) to update their local models. Third, the server randomly selects a subset of available client devices to participate in the training. The parameters of the local model are sent to the central server. Finally, the server averages the weights of the models to produce a global model for the next round of training.

2.3 Intrusion Detection

An intrusion detection system(IDS) is a device or software application that detects the activities of an intruder performing operations on an information system. These actions, known as intrusions, are designed to gain unauthorised access to a computer system [15]. A typical IDS consists of sensors, an analysis engine and a reporting system. The sensors are deployed at different network locations or on hosts. Their task is to collect network or host data, such as traffic statistics, packet headers, service requests, operating system calls and file system changes. The sensors send the collected data to the analysis engine, which is responsible for investigating the data and detecting ongoing intrusions. When the analysis engine detects an intrusion, the reporting system alerts the network administrator or collects intrusion activities by the security event management system.

Depending on the detection mechanism used in the system, intrusion detection techniques are usually classified as anomaly-based and signature-based. In the signature-based approach, the IDS detects threats by comparing system or network behaviour with signatures stored in the IDS internal database. When any system or network activity matches the stored threat pattern/signature, the IDS will trigger an alert. Signature-based IDSs are very precise and effective in detecting known attacks, and their mechanisms are easy to understand. However, this approach is not effective in detecting unknown attacks such as zero-day attacks or variations of known attacks where the matching pattern is still unknown [7]. Anomaly-based IDS evaluates the system's activity in real time and triggers an alert if the current behaviour deviates from normal behaviour by more than a threshold. This approach can be effective in detecting new attacks, especially those related to resource misuse. However, any behaviour that does not match normal behaviour is considered an intrusion and previously unknown legitimate activity may also be classified as malicious. As a result, this method usually has a high false alarm rate [4]. To assess whether a system or network activity is normal or not, researchers often use machine learning to create a trustworthy model of the activity and then compare the new behaviour with this model [10].

3 A Data Sharing Strategy for IoT IDS Based on Federated Learning

In the IoT intrusion detection problem, different nodes are often heterogeneous and exposed to different network attacks, making it even more important to consider the problem of training on non-IID data. To address the above limitations, we propose a strategy based on clusters of trust to reduce the weight divergence to improve the performance of federated learning-based IoT IDS on non-IID data. Figures 1 and 2 visualise the structure of FedAvg and Clusters of Trust respectively.

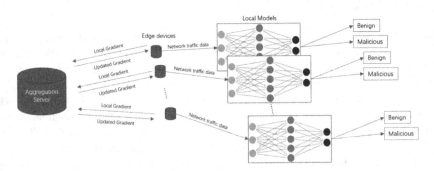

Fig. 1. Structure of the FedAvg.

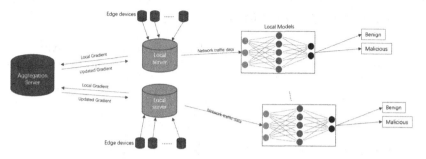

Fig. 2. Structure of clusters of trust.

Unlike the FedAvg algorithm, our proposed algorithm shown in Algorithm 1, adds cluster servers between the aggregation server and local nodes. In cluster servers, we aggregate mutually trusting nodes into a single aggregated cluster node. Each cluster is trained as a separate client in federated learning. We use this algorithm and the IoT-23 dataset presented in the next section to improve the performance of federated learning-based IoT IDS on a distribution of non-IID data, natural for the IoT setting.

Algorithm 1. Federated Averaging Algorithm based on Clusters of Trust

---

Input: Mini-batch size (B), Participants (k),
Participants per epoch (m), Total epochs (E).
Output: Global model W_{GM}

Cluster Service Execution:
Integrating mutually trusted nodes into clusters $C\{C_1, C_2, \ldots, C_i\}$

Aggregation Service Execution:
Initialise W_{GM} :
for each epoch $=1,2,3 \ldots E$ **do**
  $S_t \leftarrow$ (random set of m clients from C)
  for each participant k in S_t **do**
    $w_{GM}k^{t+1} \leftarrow$ Update $(k, w_{GM}k^t)$
    $w_{t+1} \leftarrow \sum_1^k \frac{m_k}{m} w_{GM}k^{t+1}$ (Averaging Aggregation)

Client Update:
$\beta \leftarrow$ mini-batches creates through splitting local datasets D_L
for each epoch $=1,2,3 \ldots E$ **do**
  for local mini-batch $b \in \beta$ **do**
    $w_{GM} \leftarrow w - \eta \triangle l(w, b)$
    ($\triangle l$ is the gradient of l on b and η is the learning rate

---

4   Evaluation Methodology

In this section we describe the dataset used in our experiments, our experimental scenarios, the pre-processing stages performed on the data and the metrics used for evaluation.

4.1   Data Description

In this paper, we use the Aposemat IoT-23 dataset, a new dataset of IoT network traffic captured by Stratosphere Laboratorycite IoT-23, first released in January 2020. It aims to provide researchers with a large-scale, labelled dataset of IoT traffic for the development of machine learning algorithms. IoT-23 contains 23 sub-datasets consisting of network data collected by the capturers in 23 scenarios, including network traffic data (pcap format) and labels for malicious behaviour. The 23 scenarios include 20 malicious scenarios and 3 benign scenarios. In each malicious scenario, the experimenter executes a specific malware sample that uses multiple protocols and performs different actions to generate malicious traffic. The benign scenarios were created by capturing network traffic data from uninfected real IoT devices.

4.2   Experimental Setup

To analyse the performance of our proposed strategy, we implemented the IoT IDS in different scenarios and approaches.

Baseline Scenarios. We apply the IoT IDS in basic scenarios as the comparison of our proposed strategy. The scenarios implemented include:

1. We clustered the sub-data sets of IoT-23 into an aggregated dataset, in order to implement IDS by centralised machine learning.
2. Since each sub-dataset is generated in a highly non-homogeneous distribution, each sub-dataset contains a different type and amount of malicious traffic. We trained the original IoT-23 data using the FedAvg algorithm, by maintaining 23 nodes each one containing data captured in a single scenario. This measures the performance of federated learning on non-IID datasets.
3. We reshuffled the data amongst the 23 nodes as follows. We obtained 23 sub-datasets of the same size by random sampling from the aggregated IoT-23 dataset, which eliminated statistical heterogeneity between the individual sub-datasets. This results in an IID distribution of the data. We trained the FedAvg algorithm on this dataset to measure federated learning performance on the IID dataset.

Globally Shared a Portion of Data. Addressing the decline in performance of federated learning on non-IID, we include the data sharing strategy proposed by [17] in our scenarios. A globally shared dataset G is first sampled from the overall aggregated dataset. Each client's local model is trained on both the shared data of G and each client's private data (the original 23 captures of IoT-23 each one to one of the 23 nodes). The framework then aggregates the local models from the clients and trains a global model using FedAvg. Experiments have previously shown that this strategy can improve accuracy by 30% for non-IID image classification tasks with 5% globally shared data [17]. In this paper, we add 5% and 10% global data to each subset of IoT-23 to measure the improvement of this strategy on IoT IDS for non-IID data and we show an improvement of 17.5% and 32.1% respectively.

Clusters of Trust - Data Sharing within Clusters. The intuition behind this method is it is natural to assume that in some IoT settings different nodes "trust" each other more or belong to the same "privacy class", e.g., fire detector sensors in a particular corridor. Our idea is that if we can sacrifice privacy just between these small clusters of nodes we might be able to reduce statistical heterogeneity between nodes by combining clusters; in this case the federated learning model will have better accuracy when the data is closer to IID. We have implements the Clusters of Trust method containing 2, 4, 7, 10 nodes respectively. For each size of clusters we compare two limit cases where the clusters have maximum label coverage and minimum label coverage for threats. We achieve this by either assuming a cluster is composed of nodes with very different types of threats (and choosing among nodes to form our clusters appropriately) or we chose to form clusters where the nodes have very similar threats.

4.3   Evaluation Metrics

In order to assess the performance of the model, the following indicators were used.

- Loss curve: the curve of losses during training, used to observe the convergence of the model.
- Accuracy: the ratio of correctly classified data instances relative to the total number of data instances.
- Recall: the ratio of the true positives to the union of true positives and false negatives. For IDS, the high recall rate reflected that the model alerts have a strong sensitivity.
- Precision: the ratio of the true positives to the union of true positives and false positives. For IDS, The high accuracy indicates that the model is not prone to false alarm.
- F1 score: F1 = $\frac{2*P*R}{P+R}$. For IDS, we need a model that is sensitive to malicious attacks and has a low false alarm rate. We can find a balance between model accuracy and recall by measuring the F1 score.

5   Experimentation Result

5.1   Federated Learning in IoT Intrusion Detection Baseline Scenarios

We tested the performance of the IDS on baseline scenarios for comparison. The results of the training are shown in Fig. 3 and Table 1. The red line indicates the loss curve for centralised machine learning; the blue line indicates the loss curve for federared learning trained with IID data; and the green line indicates the loss curve for federared learning trained with non-IID data.

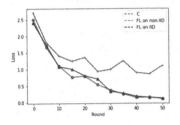

Fig. 3. Loss on baseline scenarios. (Color figure online)

Table 1. Performance metrics.

	Recall	Precision	F1 score
Centralised	92.3%	91.0%	91.7%
Federated	86.3%	90.7%	88.4%

We can see that centralised machine learning and federated learning on IID dataset perform more accurately and converge faster. In contrast, the loss curves show the erratic loss convergence and lower model accuracy of the federated learning model on non-IID dataset during gradient descent. This is due to the fact that each subset of the IoT-23 data (except for the 3 conscientious datasets) is a dataset of traffic generated by different malware, each containing different types of attacks. And different attacks have different behavioural patterns, which causes different subsets of data to be non-IID. In contrast, in federated learning, the SGD algorithm performed locally at each node aims to minimise the loss value of local samples on that device, i.e., the local model tends to differentiate between the types of attacks contained in that dataset. As we continue to fit models on different devices to the global model, the differences between the weights of these local models will accumulate and eventually degrade the performance of global learning.

5.2   Clusters of Trust vs Globally Shared Data

For the global shared data method, the results show that the accuracy of the federated learning model is 55.7%, 73.2% and 87.8% when the percentage size of the global dataset is 0%, 5% and 10%, respectively. Figure 4 reflects the loss convergence curves of the 2 two models; with light blue and legend 'C' we plot the loss convergence of the centralised solution.

We can see that as the size of the global dataset increases, federated learning converges faster, which means fewer rounds of communication are required, which is a significant improvement for IoT environments where communication bandwidth is constrained. For the IoT dataset, about 15% accuracy improvement can be achieved with just 5% of the globally shared data, while about 15% accuracy improvement can be achieved with 10% of the globally shared data, achieving similar accuracy to the centralised machine learning training.

For the clusters of trust method, the results are shown in Fig. 5 and Table 2. Figure 5 shows accuracy when clusters have minimum threat coverage tagged with 'A' and shown in blue and accuracy when clusters have maximum threat coverage tagged with 'B' and shown in orange. Table 2 shows the accuracy in each case of clustering (based on the size of nodes in a cluster, i.e., the size of clustering); For each clustering size the first line of the table shows the limit case of having similar kinds of threats in the cluster while the second line shows wider threat coverage per cluster.

The results of our Clusters of Trust experiments show that the accuracy of the model increases as the cluster contains more nodes and its label coverage increases. When the cluster contains 4 nodes and has maximum label coverage, the accuracy of the model exceeds 70%. And when the cluster contains 10 nodes even with minimum label coverage, the accuracy of the model exceeds 90%, which is very close to the performance of centralised machine learning.

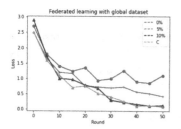

Fig. 4. Loss on non-IID data with global dataset.

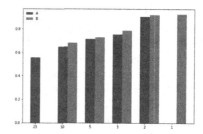

Fig. 5. Accuracy histograms for different size clusters.

In terms of accuracy, we can see that for the clusters of trust strategy, the accuracy of the model exceeds the accuracy of the strategy with 5% and 10% of globally shared data added when the cluster size is 7 and 10 respectively. In terms of cost, adding 5% and 10% of the globally shared dataset equates to an average of 110% and 220% more data per node, which increases the communication costs, as well as requirements of devices' memory and computation power. For clusters of trust strategy, additional cluster servers are required, but there is no need to worry about the lack of memory or computing power of the edge devices. Furthermore, the globally shared dataset is obtained by sampling from the original dataset, which makes the model sacrifice privacy. In contrast, in the cluster of trust approach, nodes only send their own data to the trust cluster

Table 2. Accuracy for different clusters.

Size of cluster	Coverage of malicious label	Accuracy
1	19.7%	55.7%
2	26.0%	59.7%
	31.0%	65.0%
4	36.7%	68.3%
	48.3%	72.7%
7	53.3%	75.3%
	67.7%	78.5%
10	83.3%	90.5%
	100%	91.9%
23	100%	92.5%

server for training, which is more in line with the limited communication bandwidth and computing power of edge devices in the IoT environment. Moreover, as the clusters are divided according to the trust relationship of the nodes, there is no risk of privacy leakage.

6 Conclusions

Federated learning will play a key role in IoT intrusion detection. However, due to the heterogeneity of devices and the diversity of attacks in IoT scenarios, edge devices that are in different networks are often subject to different attacks. As a result, edge devices generate non-IID data, and then the quality of model training is degraded. To make federated learning mainstream, however, improving model training on non-IID data is key to making progress in this area. In this work, we first show that for neural networks trained on non-IID data, the accuracy and convergence rate of federated learning is greatly reduced, with an accuracy of down to 55%. We validate a strategy to improve the training of non-IID data by allowing mutually trusted nodes to aggregate into a cluster that is updated as a new federated learning client. Experiments on the Aposemat IoT-23 dataset show that federated learning-based IDS models using this strategy are considerably more accurate and can ideally achieve performance comparable to centralised machine learning when there is good coverage of threats in each cluster of trust. In terms of communication and computational costs and privacy, the clusters of trust strategy is more suitable for IoT intrusion detection scenarios than the global data sharing strategy.

Given these promising results, we aim to experiment further in the direction of smart composition of clusters of trust for federated learning, and with partial aggregation of data within those clusters of trust. This would enable clustering among nodes that do not have a high level of trust that would allow them not to share their complete traffic data within the cluster, but would enable to share just a portion of it; privacy-wise, this later option offers advantages over sharing a portion of data globally. In addition, we plan to measure the efficiency and scalability of the strategy, for example, the communication costs and computational costs of the model.

References

1. Evaluating federated learning for intrusion detection in internet of things: review and challenges. Comput. Netw. **203**, 108661 (2022). https://doi.org/10.1016/j. comnet.2021.108661
2. Borgia, E.: The internet of things vision: key features, applications and open issues. Comput. Commun. **54**, 1–31 (2014)
3. Chawla, S., Thamilarasu, G.: Security as a service: real-time intrusion detection in internet of things. In: Proceedings of the Fifth Cybersecurity Symposium, pp. 1–4 (2018)
4. Debar, H.: An introduction to intrusion-detection systems. In: Proceedings Connect (2000)
5. Konečný, J., McMahan, H.B., Yu, F.X., Richtárik, P., Suresh, A.T., Bacon, D.: Federated learning: Strategies for improving communication efficiency (2017)
6. Lee, I., Lee, K.: The internet of things (IoT): applications, investments, and challenges for enterprises. Bus. Horiz. **58**(4), 431–440 (2015). https://doi.org/10.1016/ j.bushor.2015.03.008
7. Liao, H.J., Lin, C.H.R., Lin, Y.C., Tung, K.Y.: Intrusion detection system: a comprehensive review. J. Netw. Comput. Appl. **36**(1), 16–24 (2013)
8. Liu, Z., Thapa, N., Shaver, A., Roy, K., Yuan, X., Khorsandroo, S.: Anomaly detection on IoT network intrusion using machine learning. In: 2020 International Conference on Artificial Intelligence, Big Data, Computing and Data Communication Systems (icABCD), pp. 1–5. IEEE (2020)
9. McMahan, B., Moore, E., Ramage, D., Hampson, S., y Arcas, B.A.: Communication-efficient learning of deep networks from decentralized data. In: Artificial Intelligence and Statistics, pp. 1273–1282. PMLR (2017)
10. Mitchell, R., Chen, I.R.: A survey of intrusion detection techniques for cyber-physical systems. ACM Comput. Surv. (CSUR) **46**(4), 1–29 (2014)
11. binti Mohamad Noor, M., Hassan, W.H.: Current research on internet of things (IoT) security: a survey. Comput. Netw. **148**, 283–294 (2019). https://doi.org/10. 1016/j.comnet.2018.11.025
12. Mohri, M., Sivek, G., Suresh, A.T.: Agnostic federated learning. In: International Conference on Machine Learning, pp. 4615–4625. PMLR (2019)
13. Mothukuri, V., Parizi, R.M., Pouriyeh, S., Huang, Y., Dehghantanha, A., Srivastava, G.: A survey on security and privacy of federated learning. Future Gener. Comput. Syst. **115**, 619–640 (2021). https://doi.org/10.1016/j.future.2020.10.007
14. Raza, S., Wallgren, L., Voigt, T.: Svelte: real-time intrusion detection in the internet of things. Ad Hoc Netw. **11**(8), 2661–2674 (2013). https://doi.org/10.1016/j. adhoc.2013.04.014
15. Vacca, J.R.: Computer and information security handbook. In: Newnes (2012)
16. Yang, Q., Liu, Y., Chen, T., Tong, Y.: Federated machine learning: concept and applications. ACM Trans. Intell. Syst. Technol. (TIST) **10**(2), 1–19 (2019)
17. Zhao, Y., Li, M., Lai, L., Suda, N., Civin, D., Chandra, V.: Federated learning with non-iid data. arXiv preprint arXiv:1806.00582 (2018)

A Holistic Approach for IoT Networks' Identity and Trust Management – The ERATOSTHENES Project

Konstantinos Loupos[1]([✉]), Christos Kalogirou[1], Harris Niavis[1], Antonio Skarmeta[2], Elena Torroglosa-Garcia[2], Angel Palomares[3], Hui Song[4], Paul-Emmanuel Brun[5], Francesca Giampaolo[6], Dimitri Van Landuyt[7], Sam Michiels[7], Blaž Podgorelec[8], Christos Xenakis[9], Michail Bampatsikos[9], and Konstantinos Krilakis[10]

[1] Inlecom Innovation, Kifisia, Greece
Konstantinos.loupos@inlecomsystems.com
[2] Universidad De Murcia, Murcia, Spain
[3] Atos IT Solutions and Services Iberia SL, Madrid, Spain
[4] Sintef AS, Oslo, Norway
[5] Airbus Cybersecurity SAS, Elancourt, France
[6] Engineering - Ingegneria Informatica SPA, Rome, Italy
[7] Katholieke Universiteit Leuven, Leuven, Belgium
[8] Technische Universitaet Graz, Graz, Austria
[9] University of Piraeus Research Center, Piraeus, Greece
[10] Eulambia Advanced Technologies, Athens, Greece

Abstract. The ERATOSTHENES project is driven by recent security challenges of IoT networks being today embedded into our day to day lives. The high increase of connected devices, their inhomogeneous nature, high penetration, as well as different manufacturing and vendor characteristics have created a vast attack surface that is prone to increase in the next years. This has already created challenges such as: confidentiality access control, privacy for users and things, devices' trustworthiness and compliance that require lifecycle considerations of IoT devices and networks. ERATOSTHENES will devise a novel distributed, automated, auditable, yet privacy-respectful, Trust and Identity Management Framework intended to dynamically and holistically manage the lifecycle of IoT devices, strengthening trust, identities, and resilience in the entire IoT ecosystem, supporting the enforcement of the NIS directive, GDPR and Cybersecurity Act. This publication positions the project into the internet of things and applications and describes the project concept, requirements, first architectural decisions and outcomes.

Keywords: Digital identity · Identity management · Privacy preservation · Cybersecurity · IoT lifecycle · Self-sovereign identity

© The Author(s), under exclusive license to Springer Nature Switzerland AG 2022
A. González-Vidal et al. (Eds.): GIoTS 2022, LNCS 13533, pp. 338–347, 2022.
https://doi.org/10.1007/978-3-031-20936-9_27

1 Introduction

1.1 Internet of Things, Status and Applications

The Internet of Things (IoT) can be nowadays defined as a system of inter-connected or inter-related devices as well as other machines with the ability to transfer and communicate data over the internet or other networks, usually in an autonomous nature. In this, 'things' can be various network components that communicate with each other and transfer data over their related networks. Such formed ecosystems of devices are usually formed by web-enabled capabilities using embedded systems, sensors and communication devices to acquire data and exchange them within their environment. IoT today shows a significant penetration and introduction in our day to day lives, including mobile phones, smart appliances, smart security systems, smart home hubs, smart assistants, health care, industrial applications, activewear, and many more. In this dimension, IoT supports smarter working and living, gaining complete control over our lives while supporting automation and wellbeing behind the scenes [1–4]. This is supported by a large business and industry umbrella on related technologies with a market of 212b$ worldwide. The number of connected IoT devices is today growing by 9% to 12.3 billion globally, with a trend to rise to more than 27 billion IoT nodes (connections) [5] and potential to generate 4–11 t$ of economic value by 2025 [6].

Such a vast penetration of IoT devices and networks in our day-to-day lives creates a significant attack vector that can dramatically risk peoples' personal data, privacy, data ownership, safety and security, directly (personal lives) or indirectly (via critical infrastructures etc.). Good examples include the Mirai IoT botnet (October 2016) that caused significant DDOS (Distributed Denial of Service) service interruptions while it supported the creation of different variations (Torii, Hajime or BrickerBot) in turn infecting and affecting other services. With the above in mind, the IoT leap brings together a lot of challenges relating to confidentiality, access control, device and user privacy, devices' trustworthiness and compliance. However, there are initiatives at the European level that strongly support cyber security challenges aligned to the above. The Cybersecurity Act framework is the regulation 2019/881 of the European Parliament and of the Council of April 17, 2019, on the European Union Agency for Cybersecurity (ENISA) on information and communications technology (ICT) cybersecurity certification with an objective to guarantee a minimum-security level for ICT/IoT components towards an EU cybersecurity framework. On top, a key element in Europe to address privacy threats is the GDPR, a European regulation on data protection and privacy for all individuals within the EU in force since March 2018. The Network and Information Security (NIS) focuses on the cooperation and exchange of security information among the Member States. Finally, the Cybersecurity Act (CSA), along with GDPR and NIS directive, conform to the three main pillars of the EU perspective on cybersecurity. On top, European Union research programmes (Horizon 2020, Horizon Europe etc.) have strongly supported the acceleration of technological progress and systematically addressed resulting scientific and technological challenges to achieve the EU objectives.

ERATOSTHENES will devise a novel distributed, automated, auditable, yet privacy-respectful, Trust and Identity Management Framework intended to dynamically and holistically manage the lifecycle of IoT devices, strengthening trust, identities, and resilience in the entire IoT ecosystem, supporting the enforcement of the NIS directive, GDPR and Cybersecurity Act. Other changes relating to language Rectify the order of the currency figure to scientific writing and to be consistent in ordering.

1.2 Risk Impediments to IoT Evolution

Risk identification in modern IoT systems requires a deep and constant effort in managing and controlling risks that are typically found in an internet system, specific risks of IoT devices as well as general safety considerations to ensure that the application of the device follows the safety requirements intended. Such considerations include scalability, connectivity, end-to-end security as well as authentication and trust, identity management and attack-resistant security applications [7].

Table 1. IoT devices Threats [7].

Threats	Attack Procedure	Security Requirement	Examples
Physical attacks	Tamper with the hardware and other components.	Tamper resistance	Layout reconstruction, micro-probing
Environment attacks	The device encryption key can be discovered by the attacker by recovering the encryption information.	Secure encryption scheme	Timing attack, side-channel attack, fault analysis attack
Cryptanalysis attacks	Find ciphertext to break the encryption.	Secure encryption scheme	Known-plaintext attack, chosen plaintext attack
Software attacks	Exploit vulnerabilities in the system during its own communication interface and inject malicious codes.	Proper antivirus update	Trojan horse, worms, or viruses

The top ten vulnerabilities as identified by the IoT security: challenges, solutions and future prospects document by DELL EMC include the following [7]:

- Web interfaces that include insecure components
- Transport encryption lack or other limitations
- Unsatisfactory and inappropriate authorization mechanisms
- Uncontrolled/unmanaged and maybe insecure firmware
- Concerns regarding privacy content
- Cloud and mobile interfaces with insecure components
- Limited physical security
- Nework services with linited security capabilities

1.3 The ERATOSTHENES Project

ERATOSTHENES, inspired by Eratosthenes of Cyrene (c. 276—194 bc) (Greek scholar, geographer, and astronomer, Founder of scientific chronography) and related to the critical challenges in IoT lifecycle management, is a Research and Innovation Action (RIA) project, funded by the European Commission under the topic SU-DS02–2020 (Intelligent security and privacy management), subtopic (d) Distributed trust management and digital identity solutions. The project is coordinated by INLECOM INNOVATION (Athens, Greece), and its consortium consists of 14 partners from 8 countries. With a total budget of around 6M€, the project formally started its activities on October 1, 2021, and is finishing in March 2025.

The project provides compelling innovation on recent challenges of IoT security such as: i) Lack of security visibility gaps of IoT devices and large heterogeneity as extremely challenging to establish a trustworthy environment among objects and persons, ii) lack of a common trust enforcement mechanisms and relevant standards, iii) infrequent IoT devices' firmware and security updates, iv) lack of a transparent identity and privacy frameworks to allow users' full control of identity and data at IoT device level, v) lack of security training and security protocols' adoption for persons and devices and vi) limited effectiveness of information sharing to CERTs/CSIRTs (Computer Emergency Response Teams/Computer Security Incident Response Team).

ERATOSTHENES devises a novel distributed, automated, auditable, yet privacy-respectful Trust and Identity Management Framework intended to dynamically and holistically manage the lifecycle of IoT devices, strengthening trust, identities, and resilience in the entire IoT ecosystem, supporting the enforcement of the NIS directive, GDPR and Cybersecurity Act. ERASTOSTHENES leverages breakthrough solutions: (a) the first-ever enclosure of cybersecurity features in IoT devices through deployment of Trust Agents and continuous trust evaluation within the network in a contextual and social approach; (b) decentralised identity management mechanisms to conciliate requirements of self-sovereignty and privacy preservation in a distributed/transparent trust model along with disposable identities; (c) self-encryption/decryption at device-level with a whole system automated recovery process (incl. Software, crypto-key material, identities) after an attack based on a multi-layer recovery model; (d) threat-analysis models based on federated learning and edge execution to continuously monitor devices and detect attacks; (e) collaborative IoT threat intelligence sharing across ledgers to adapt detection/defense mechanism to the evolving security conditions and assist the IoT lifecycle; (f) integration of Physical Unclonable Functions in trust framework and distributed ledgers. Finally, ERATOSTHENES supports the enforcement of the NIS directive with a security information sharing mechanism based on inter-ledger technologies to support the exchange of trust and security information among stakeholders, enhancing collaboration, vulnerabilities' disclosure, and secure management of software updates. The overall vision of ERATOSTHENES is to provide core cybersecurity features to be adopted by manufacturers as baseline certification elements in the production of devices and throughout their entire lifecycle. The solution will be validated in 3 industrial cases: Automotive, Health and Industry 4.0. The ERATOSTHENES holistic solution concept is presented in the following chapters, starting from the industrial requirements and challenges over digital identity and trust that steam behind its technical solution.

2 Industrial Requirements over Digital Identity and Trust

In this chapter, we present an overview of the cybersecurity challenges of IoT that have been considered when designing the ERATOSTHENES solution as well as its system architecture and technical specifications. This has been performed as a form of gap analysis of existing systems and industrial devices/networks.

In the mind of the increasing number of connected IoT devices emerges actions to prevent cybersecurity attacks. However, protecting the users from those attacks requires the analysis and realisation of their needs to provide solutions that will protect their devices efficiently. ERATOSTHENES believes that User needs should primarily drive IoT cybersecurity research. Hence, the project solves critical societal obstacles in IoT, considering "Security of Things" as core to the IoT's future success. Despite the tangible benefits of IoT, the consortium has identified high-risk impediments to IoT evolution [8]:

- Lack of security visibility.
- Lack of effective information sharing and communication.
- Heterogeneity of IoT devices.
- Lack of a common trust enforcement mechanism and relevant standards.
- Quantified "trust" that it can be understood by the artificial agents.
- Firmware and security updates are infrequent and difficult or even impossible.
- Lack of a transparent identity and privacy framework.
- Lack of security training and security protocols' adoption.

The main target of the project is to provide a secure environment for IoT devices. However, such a task emerges special treatment, as there are many open issues and gaps that are already identified. Following, we present these gaps through different categories using as reference the works and reports [9–12]. After an exhaustive gap analysis, only the gaps relating to IoT trust and identity challenges are included below [8].

2.1 Industrial Orientation of ERATOSTHENES

The project develops a holistic solution over several modern cybersecurity challenges in an approach to cover most related industrial requirements and validating the solution into three (3) pilot applications (use cases): 1) Automotive (car on-board units), 2) Health (personal, smart health devices) and 3) Industry 4.0 (disposable IDs and embedded devices). Particular requirements of the automotive sector include identity management for the interaction of the Connected Vehicles and remote software updates. Methods that can ensure secure and distributed asset/devices identification, distributed trust management in vehicle On-board Unit (OBU) and Road Side Unit (RSU) as well as trust policies and recovery ability of trust agents and cyberthreat information sharing to CERTS/CSRTs interface to inform for cyberattacks and threats (IDS events). Moreover, monitoring the device behaviour for suspicious and anomalous indicators in the V2V/V2I communications through trust agents and network-based IDS to identify possible attackers or malfunctioning devices is necessary. The smart health devices' use case requirements include effective and user-friendly identity management combining external authentication services and fine-grained, context-aware trust management for the open platform. The aforementioned is used to assess the trustworthiness of both data consumers and data providers, based on the contexts, faster design, deployment and self-adaptation of the identity and trust management policies and functional components and to prove the

Table 2. Identified gaps [8]

Gap	Description
Support of heterogeneous devices	The support of heterogeneous devices is a big challenge, and, in many cases, there is limited support for heterogeneous devices, or a gateway is necessary
Ecosystem formation	There is low platform expandability. Only open-source platforms can be expanded with new technologies
Manipulation of data	Data are stored on the platform unencrypted, and very little information is provided to the security measures
Secure authentication, identification of management of IoT devices	Security mechanisms should be integrated into platforms
Unreliable and incomplete data	Data protection mechanisms through intrusion detection, prevention and recovery should be developed
Security and Privacy	IoT platforms must ensure data privacy, integrity, and transmission according to information sensibility
Connectivity	If different network technologies and communications protocols are used, secure high network availability
Usability and customisation of the solutions	Address these different market sub-segments and simplify their usage by the large public

satisfaction to standards and regulations for security and privacy both in general and in the healthcare domain. In parallel, the industry 4.0 use case requirements include aspects for generating secure and distributed IDs for smart connected devices, research, implementation and testing of cryptographic methods and algorithms for smart contracts, ID key generation and key sharing, distributed service architectures for asset management and facilitating disposable IDs and actions to demonstrate distributed architecture and applications for heterogeneous Industrial IoT (IIoT) environment with hardware testbed [8].

3 ERATOSTHENES IoT Lifecycle Approach for Trust and Identity Management

ERATOSTHENES includes several highly innovative objectives that serve as high-level components in its system architecture and design assets. They have several internal components that are synthesising its overall system specifications and architecture, including:

- Trust Framework and a Reference Architecture to ensure end-to-end trust and identity management in distributed IoT networks, suited for resource-restricted environments, critical and industrial applications
- A lightweight, distributed, and dynamic Trust Manager enhances trust in large-scale distributed networks of heterogeneous IoT devices covering each layer and cross-layer of the network.
- A decentralised, scalable, efficient, and privacy-preserving IoT identity management conciliates self-sovereignty and privacy preservation requirements in a distributed, interoperable and transparent trust model, including self-encryption/decryption schemes and IoT identity recovery.
- Lifecycle management and the overall governance layer of the trust network on novel Distributed Ledger Technologies and a hybrid consensus protocol. Implement Smart Contracts for enforcing access policies and sharing trustworthiness within the network, guaranteeing their transparency, integrity, authenticity, and authority. Design of Inter-ledger Cyber-Threat Information Sharing and automated Recovery Solutions based on a multi-layer approach
- Integration and Validation of the approach through real-world pilots to assess its effectiveness and organise hands-on training through realistic cybersecurity exercises.

In Fig. 1, a high-level overview of the draft architecture is presented. The solution addresses the lack of trust in large-scale networks of various IoT devices and vendors in complex and real-world scenarios. Following this, a decentralised and contextual Trust and Identity Management Framework for resource-restricted IoT environments well-suited for industrial applications are being developed based on a Self-sovereign approach. An Identity Manager (IdM), Trust Manager and Broker (TMB), as the main components of the architecture, rely on the distributed network itself or on network coordinators (gateways) through an automated deployment of Trust Agents. As shown in the figure below, a Trust Agent is to be deployed and executed on the actual device and forms a containerised or virtualised service ($S\mu V$), depending on the device's processing capabilities. The device network enrolment follows a context-based reputation approach. Its initial trust value score will be adapted to ensure dynamic/automated device deployment in the distributed network. The TMB produces updated trust scores based on the real-time evaluation of device behaviours during established interactions in addition to feedback and recommendations gathered from other devices, based on three core trust computation algorithms and trust evaluation models (network experience, reputation, and contextual attributes). Their trust scores and the access policy and identity management for authentication purposes will be securely stored and publicly shared through an inter-ledger implementation within the IoT network, guaranteeing their transparency, integrity, authenticity, and authorisation.

The solution is based on a next-generation distributed inter-ledger approach focusing on self-aspects and collective threat intelligence in distributed networks of heterogeneous IoT devices. For these, authoritative consensus algorithms are usually deployed that rely on a centralised infrastructure to validate data; however, the validation speed is quite faster than the conventional algorithms.

Thus, we envision applying a novel hybrid consensus model founded on the Proof-of-Importance algorithm. Proof-of-Importance (PoI) algorithms work by judging the "importance" of a party in the operation of the overall DLT "network". If a party has multiple transactions in the network and provides a consistent "influx" of network utilisation, the party is considered pivotal in the network's evaluation. By using a self-sovereign identity approach for the decentralised IdM, the authentication of the different IoT devices will be performed in a distributed manner, and thanks to the functionality associated with this approach, transmission channels will be encrypted and therefore secure based on decentralised identifiers (DID) and Verifiable Credentials (VC). Lastly, the overall framework to support secure lifecycle management (as the core project objective) will be accompanied by a system manager, which will host a series of required added-value services such as: i) Automated recovery after an attack based on a multi-layer approach ii) the aforementioned DLT implementation on a network level, and iii) Blockchain-based (independent from the DLT implementation supporting the trust and identity management) cyberthreat information management.

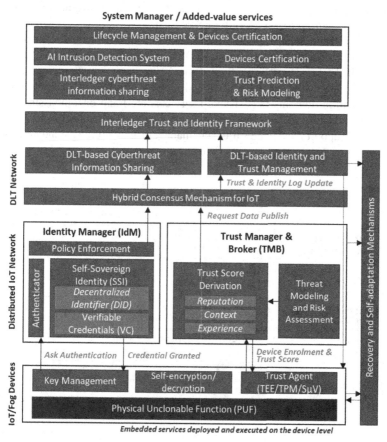

Fig. 1. ERATOSTHENES high level (draft) architecture

Figure 2 includes the layer of management of identities of IoT devices as a key component of the ERATOSTHENES technology stack. ERATOSTHENES will establish means, both in terms of infrastructure, protocols, and components, for device identity management with security and privacy (e.g., minimal disclosure, disposable identifiers) guarantees. The identity management will be supported by Physical Unclonable Function (PUF) based authentication, which provides extra security for device identification and cryptographic fingerprinting. Additionally, the identity framework will be supported by DLTs, specifically enabling interactions in multiple domains through inter-DLTs.

ERATOSTHENES will also focus on providing a trust framework for IoT environments. This will involve infrastructural components but also mechanisms for the devices themselves. In particular, Trusted Execution Environments (TEE) will be used as one of the anchors of trust for devices. Additionally, domains will have trust and reputation services, where the entities involved in the domain will be continuously evaluated. Regarding this, monitoring interactions will be necessary, raising the need for Intrusion Detection Systems in all domains. Finally, operations will be supported by DLTs, which will enable the auditability of processes by acting as verifiable data registries. Moreover, (inter-)DLTs will support the sharing of trust and cyber threat information, improving the security of the entire ERATOSTHENES ecosystem.

Lastly, one of the most important elements when dealing with IoT environments is managing the lifecycle of devices. ERATOSTHENES will provide mechanisms for performing all the key steps throughout device's lifetimes: bootstrapping, enrolment in domains, backup and recovery of data and identity information, decommissioning, etc. Entities within domains (e.g., backup services, etc.) and encompassing multiple domains (eg., software repositories, manufacturer servers, certification services, etc.) will be used to support the device's lifecycle management, including standard protocols like Manufacturer Usage Descriptions (MUDs) [13].

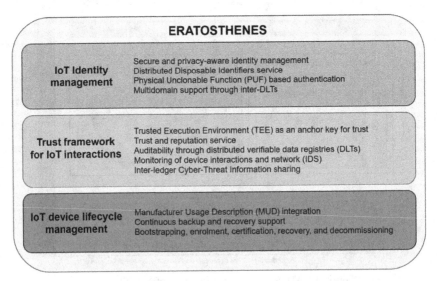

Fig. 2. ERATOSTHENES main system components [13]

4 Upcoming Work and Next Steps

ERATOSTHENES is currently during the stage of requirements finalisation and draft architecture finalisation as the driving steps for the technical efforts that will follow. During this stage, the requirements are being exhaustively studied. The precise system architecture and final system specifications are being defined starting from deployment investigations at the three pilot sites (use cases). Following the ERATOSTHENES work plan, the first results of all the described components will be available by the end of 2022, first delivering the technical solution (proof of concept). Following this, the first deployment to the first pilot (automotive) will start as an iterative mechanism of validating the developed solution in industrial settings and providing feedback to the technical components for their second and updated version.

Acknowledgements. This project has received funding from the European Union's Horizon 2020 research and innovation programme under grant agreement no 101020416. The authors acknowledge the research outcomes of this publication belonging to the ERATOSTHENES (101020416) project consortium.

References

1. Loupos, K., et al.: Cognitive Heterogeneous Architecture For Industrial IoT (The Chariot Project), IERC IoT Cluster Book 2018 IoT European Trust Projects – Security and Privacy: Integration, Architectures and Interoperability, River Publishers (Verlag) (2018) ISBN: 978-87-7022-008-8
2. Loupos, K., et al.: Cognitive Platform For Industrial IoT System Security, Safety And Privacy, Embedded World: Conference and Exhibition, 25–27 Nuremberg, Germany (2020)
3. Loupos, K.: Integrated Solution For Industrial IoT Data Security - The Chariot Solution, Eclipse SAM IoT 2020, Security, Artificial Intelligence and Modelling for the next generation Internet of Things, 17–18 (2020)
4. Vermesan, O., et al.: New Waves of IoT Technologies Research – Transcending Intelligence And Senses At The Edge To Create Multi Experience Environments, Internet of Things – The Call of the Edge - Everything Intelligent Everywhere, River Publishers, DK (2020) ISBN: 9788770221962, e-ISBN - 9788770221962
5. State of IoT—Summer 202, IoT Analytics – Market Insights for Internet of Things (2021)
6. Internet of Things statistics for 2022 - Taking Things Apart, Bojan Jovanovic (2022)
7. Laeeq, K., Shamsi, J.A.: A Study of Security Issues, Vulnerabilities, and Challenges in the Internet of Things. Taylor and Francis, In Securing Cyber-Physical Systems (2015)
8. ERATOSTHENES – D1.2 Use cases, requirements and methodological Framework (2022)
9. SmartM2M IoT LSP use cases and standards gaps, ETSI TR 103 376 (STF 505) (2016). https://docbox.etsi.org/SmartM2M/Open/AIOTI/STF505
10. High Priority IoT Standardisation Gaps and Relevant SDOs (2020). https://aioti.eu/wp-content/uploads/2020/01/AIOTI-WG3-High-Priority-Gaps-v2.0-200128-Final.pdf
11. Mineraud, J., Mazhelis, O., Su, X., Tarkoma, S.: A gap analysis of Internet-of-Things platforms. Comput. Commun. Elsevier **89–90**(0140-3664), 5–16 (2016)
12. Analysis, IoT Security Standards Gap (2019). https://www.enisa.europa.eu/publications/iot-security-standards-gap-analysis
13. ERATOSTHENES – D1.3 - Preliminary ERATOSTHENES Architecture v1.0 – FINAL (2022)

ARCADIAN-IoT - Enabling Autonomous Trust, Security and Privacy Management for IoT

Sérgio Figueiredo[1(✉)], Paulo Silva[1,2], Alfonso Iacovazzi[3], Vitalina Holubenko[1], João Casal[4], Jose M Alcaraz Calero[5], Qi Wang[5], Pedro Colarejo[6], Ross Little Armitt[7], Giacomo Inches[8], and Shahid Raza[3]

[1] Instituto Pedro Nunes, Coimbra, Portugal
sfigueiredo@ipn.pt
[2] University of Coimbra, Centre for Informatics and Systems of the University of Coimbra (CISUC), Coimbra, Portugal
[3] RISE Research Institutes of Sweden, Gothenburg, Sweden
[4] SCNL Truphone S.A., Lisbon, Portugal
[5] University of the West of Scotland, Blantyre, UK
[6] LOAD Interactive, Aveiro, Portugal
[7] ATOS, Madrid, Spain
[8] Martel Innovate, Dübendorf, Switzerland

Abstract. Cybersecurity incidents have been growing both in number and associated impact, as a result from society's increased dependency in information and communication technologies - accelerated by the recent pandemic. In particular, IoT. technologies, which enable significant flexibility and cost-efficiency, but are also associated to more relaxed security mechanisms, have been quickly adopted across all sectors of the society, including critical infrastructures (e.g. smart grids) and services (e.g. eHealth). Gaps such as high dependence on 3rd party IT suppliers and device manufacturers increase the importance of trustworthy and secure solutions for future digital services.

This paper presents ARCADIAN-IoT, a framework aimed at holistically enabling trust, security, privacy and recovery in IoT systems, and enabling a Chain of Trust between the different IoT entities (persons, objects and services). It builds on features such as federated AI for effective and privacy-preserving cybersecurity, distributed ledger technologies for decentralized management of trust, or transparent, user-controllable and decentralized privacy.

Keywords: ARCADIAN-IoT · Cybersecurity · Trust · IoT

1 Introduction

The increased penetration of Internet of Things (IoT) technologies, devices and services has, along with other technologies such as cellular networks or AI, a

This work was carried out in the scope of the ARCADIAN-IoT - Autonomous Trust, Security and Privacy Management Framework for IoT, Grant Agreement Number: 101020259. H2020-SU-DS02-2020.

profound impact in society. Thus, the potential threats associated with IoT and the need to reduce risks are important cybersecurity topics. IoT-related cyber-attacks spiraled in 2021, showing the pandemic has aggravated IoT-based vulnerabilities (e.g. with prolonged multi-device usage in household settings). Recent projections estimate 75.44 billion connected devices will be deployed by 2025, supporting sectors such as education, transport, energy, health and security, which emphasizes how threats and risks associated with IoT devices and systems can have huge consequences on both cyber and physical domains. As the number of IoT devices and the data shared between them grows, so does the number of attacks and vulnerabilities associated with them. A report by Gartner estimates over 25% of cyber-attacks against businesses will be IoT-based by 2025 [1]. Attacks like Mirai [2] highlight that weak security measures in the development, adoption and usage of IoT devices can have a tremendous impact - for instance, attackers can orchestrate a large set of devices to launch Distributed Denial of Service (DDoS).

IoT devices and applications have an increased risk of becoming victims of cyber-attacks due to a lack of security measures in the IoT ecosystem, exposing IoT devices to malicious attacks that leave them vulnerable. This results e.g. from the lack of computational capacity for efficient built-in security mechanisms, limited budget for properly testing and improving firmware security, lack of regular updates due to limited budgets and technical limitations of IoT devices, or discontinued updates, restricting vulnerability patching (e.g. resulting in lack of encryption integrated in end-to-end communications between IoT devices).

Other technological advances (e.g. 5G or AI) will tend to further intensify cybersecurity issues, in particular in SMEs, where skills for managing the security of business-critical IoT systems are limited. The increased dependency on third party IT suppliers (e.g., cloud providers), and IoT device manufacturers puts in evidence the need for trustworthy and secure solutions for future (and current) digital services powered by IoT systems. New attack surfaces are introduced by the evolving IoT ecosystem, caused by the interdependent and interconnected IoT systems, which results in added complexity and challenging security maintenance. IoT devices mostly work in an unattended environment, where an intruder may physically access these devices easily, and are wirelessly connected, where an intruder may access private information from a communication channel through eavesdropping.

The dependency on the aforementioned technologies, the growing complexity of cyberattacks, and the rise in incidents (e.g. ransomware, loss of data, disruption to public or critical services) exposes the need for designing and implementing effective cybersecurity mechanisms spanning threat prevention, detection and mitigation. In order to ensure that the transformation brought by IoT will benefit all citizens in a way that warrants security and privacy, the definition and development of innovative and advanced security and privacy management mechanisms and technologies that can seamlessly be integrated across different sectors and use cases are required.

This paper presents ARCADIAN-IoT, a framework for enabling decentralized management of trust, identity, privacy and security in IoT systems considering persons, objects and services. ARCADIAN-IoT intends to enable security and trust in the management of object's and persons identification, establish a Chain of Trust through distributed and autonomous models for trust, security and privacy, and provide self and coordinated recovery and healing upon threat detection.

The paper is organized as follows: Sect. 2 describes related work on cybersecurity for IoT; the ARCADIAN-IoT framework, its planes and main functionalities are described in Sect. 3; Sect. 4 presents three distinct use cases which demonstrate the framework intended benefits; finally, Sect. 5 concludes the paper and lists future work.

2   Related Work

Cybersecurity in IoT systems has been extensively studied during last decades and several surveys on the achievements, challenges, and open issues in this area have been produced [6,11,12]. As highlighted by Lu et al. [12], IoT systems are susceptible to various security attacks at different levels, and for this reason, most of the measures deal with cyber attacks and protection with layer-level perspectives: "sensing," "network," "middleware," and "application" layers.

Protection of end-nodes/sensors is generally obtained at the sensing layer by providing lightweight tools directly embedded (built-in) into the end-devices for encryption, access control, and node authentication [4,17]. Tiburski et al. defined a security architecture that integrates trust mechanisms with embedded virtualization providing security from hardware to applications [15]. Instead, a lightweight and hybrid system merging Physically Unclonable Functions (PUFs), Arbiter, and Read-Only PUFs was proposed by Sankaran et al. [13].

Cybersecurity at the network layer aims to monitor and protect IoT communications by means of firewalls and Network Intrusion Detection/Prevention Systems (NIDS/NIPSs) [19]. Although lightweight NIDSs can quickly process the huge amount of traffic in IoT networks (e.g., the solution proposed by Jan et al. [9]), the hybrid systems that rely on both pattern matching and deep learning models are more suitable for detecting the more recent and advanced cyber attacks targeting IoT [10,14].

The middleware layer, which is often affected by security and privacy issues, offers an important perspective for cyber protection [7,8]. For example, Da Cruz et al. suggest a reference model for designing IoT middleware platforms based on modules that reflect main IoT requirements: (i) interoperability, (ii) persistence and analytics, (iii) context, (iv) resource and event, (v) security, and (vi) graphical user interface [7].

Finally, cybersecurity at the application layer explores those threats, and corresponding mitigation mechanisms, that relate to the system functionalities and services for the final users [16]. Given the significant amount of use cases and applications in IoT, the state of the art shows a proliferation of domain-specific cybersecurity solutions. An example of a cybersecurity tool for healthcare ecosystem is the architecture proposed by Abie [3]; on the other side Bringhenti et al. provided a personalized cybersecurity approach for smart homes [5], and Vijayakumaran et al. built an architecture for smart industry [18].

3 ARCADIAN-IoT Framework

3.1 Overview

The concept of ARCADIAN-IoT represents an integrated approach to manage identity, trust, privacy, security and recovery of IoT devices, persons and services. It relies on specialised components laid out on vertical and horizontal planes (described in Sects. 3.2 and 3.3) to address those aspects. The vertical planes cover identity, trust and recovery management. The horizontal planes are in charge of managing privacy and security across the framework.

Figure 1 depicts ARCADIAN-IoT Concept, its horizontal and vertical planes, as well as the components that support the framework. The different entities (i.e., persons, IoT devices and apps/services) covered by ARCADIAN-IoT enable a way to interact with IoT systems and its operations (e.g., data collection, data processing, or data transmission) in a safe, secure and privacy-preserving manner.

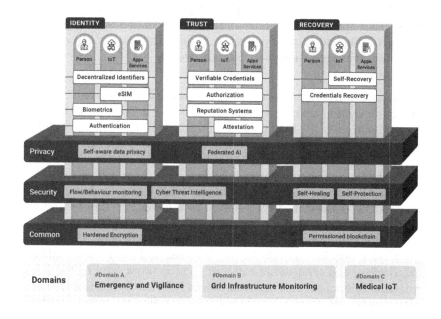

Fig. 1. ARCADIAN-IoT conceptual representation.

The main objective of ARCADIAN-IoT is to enable a holistic framework with components leveraging Federated AI, Distributed Ledger Technologies (DLT), functional encryption, eSIM technologies, Cyber Threat Intelligence (CTI), and several other approaches for autonomous trust, security and privacy management for IoT systems. There are six specific objectives to achieve with the development of ARCADIAN-IoT framework:

1. Enable security and trust in the management of objects' identification.
2. Enable distributed security and trust in management of persons' identification.
3. Provide distributed and autonomous models for trust, security and privacy - enabling a Chain of Trust.
4. Provide hardened encryption with recovery ability.
5. Self and coordinated healing with reduced human intervention.
6. Enable proactive information sharing for trustable CTI and IoT Security Observatory.

3.2 Horizontal Planes

The Privacy Plane aims to provide functionalities for the privacy-preserving management of confidential or sensitive data involving persons' entities, and includes the (i) Self-aware Data Privacy and (ii) Federated AI components. The Self-aware Data Privacy component will enhance the way data privacy is managed by allowing the user to define privacy policies for data, and by crowdsourcing policies specified on similar data. The Federated AI component will provide dependable and privacy preserving federated learning (FL) capabilities to the machine learning (ML)-based components.

The Security Plane contains all the cyber security features required for the monitoring, prevention, management, and recovery; it comprises the (i) Network Flow Monitoring, (ii) Behaviour Monitoring, (iii) CTI, (iv) Network Self-protection, (v) IoT Device Self-protection, and (vi) Network Self-healing components. The Network Flow Monitoring will enhance existing NIDSs to get advanced detection along the entire infrastructure of the IoT network, while the Behavior Monitoring component aims at detecting anomalous behaviours occurring on IoT devices. The CTI system focuses on IoT threats and it will enhance the open source MISP[1] platform with IoT-specific functionalities for automated gathering, producing, elaborating, and sharing cyber threat data. A set of protection policies and rules aiming to safeguard the network infrastructure, IoT devices, and services are enforced (i) at network level by the Network Self-protection component and (ii) locally on IoT devices by the IoT Device Self-protection component. Finally, the Network Self-healing component is designed to mitigate the potential impact of a cyber attacks when there is no protection rule for that specific attack, thus with the potential to penetrate the IoT infrastructure.

---

[1] https://www.misp-project.org/.

The Common Plane includes the two components that provide functionalities that will reinforce other components in both Horizontal and Vertical Planes, i.e., (i) the Hardened Encryption and (ii) Permissioned Blockchain. The Hardened Encryption component aims at providing encryption mechanisms that are more flexible, decentralized, and hardened by an hardware-based Root of Trust (RoT) which can be provided by: (i) the eSIM component, (ii) the crypto chip embedded in the IoT device, or (iii) an independent/external crypto chip module integrated as add-on module by the vendor into existing IoT device. Finally, the framework will provide a Permissioned Blockchain to (i) anchor the trust for decentralized identifiers, (ii) publish and share information in a trusted and immutable fashion with different actors in the IoT ecosystem, and (iii) support the deletion of personal data by the users.

3.3   Vertical Planes

The Identity Plane supports (i) a multi-factor Authentication component that calls upon other components to realise the required authentication as needed for the different use cases, (ii) a Decentralized Identifier component, (iii) an eSIM - Hardware-based Identity and Authentication component, and (iv) a Biometrics authentication component. The Decentralized Identifier (DID) component follows the W3C DID Core Specification[2] to support the Self-Sovereign Identity approach with support for both public and privacy preserving DIDs and supports the Verifiable Credentials in the Trust Plane through cryptographic keys associated with a DID. Proving ownership of a DID itself by cryptographic means also authenticates the user, thing or system as holder of the private key, which can serve to authenticate constrained devices that may not be able to support the whole SSI stack with Verifiable Credentials. The Decentralized Identifier component will make use of the blockchain in the horizontal plane for anchoring the trust in public DIDs that are published in Content Addressable Storage (CAS) off-chain. The eSIM component in the context of identity, will act as a Secure Element (SE) capable of storing identity and authentication credentials at devices hardware level, and use them in network-based authentication with a novel method to authenticate an eSIM-equipped device in a third-party service by leveraging cellular authentication, whose credentials and processes are securely stored at hardware level in the device eUICC. The Biometrics authentication component adds a third factor to identify persons, and will support AI/ML facial matching algorithms to match live video feed against a set of photos for particular persons and in challenging operational conditions (e.g. distance, angle between camera and individual, lighting conditions).

The Trust Plane supports (i) Verifiable Credentials component, (ii) Network-based Authorization component, (iii) Reputation System component and (iv) Remote Attestation component. The Verifiable Credentials component follows

---

[2] https://www.w3.org/TR/did-core/.

the W3C Verifiable Credential Specification[3] and enables trusted identification of users and things through these entities being issued with claims inside a Verifiable Credential (VC) and later being able to present it with secure cryptographic proofs, supported by Decentralized Identifiers in the identity plane. The Network-based Authorization component leverages network-based policy enforcement tools, to enable novel processes of dynamic authorization throughout ARCADIAN-IoT ecosystems with respect to the entities' current trustworthiness (provided by the Reputation System). The latter component dynamically determines the current reputation score of persons, devices and services, where the score is continually updated based on data received from other entities regarding its interactions and represents its current trust level. To enable 3rd party actors that need access to this information in a trusted and distributed manner, the reputation score will be anchored on the blockchain while the actual score is stored off-chain in distributed storage. The Remote Attestation component supports support hardware-based attestation with the ability to leverage Root-of-Trust using a secure element (e.g. eSIM or crypto chip) and aligns with the standardisation effort of the IETF Remote Attestation Procedures (RATS)[4] working group, with respect to standardized formats for describing claims and associated evidence, and procedures to deliver these claims.

The Recovery Plane supports (i) Self-recovery component and (ii) Credentials Recovery component. The Self-recovery component provides a storage server solution, that enable devices to securely store and retrieve backups making use of the ARCADIAN-IoT framework's Authentication and Hardened Encryption components. It supports data to be encrypted in a selective way, by applying a policy that defines which stakeholders, relying on their public keys, can decrypt the data either partially or completely. The Credential Recovery component provides for the scenario where a user's device or IoT device's data was somehow corrupted or wiped and the user or device respectively requests a recovery of credentials and data.

4   Reference Use Cases

ARCADIAN-IoT research is supported by reference use cases from three domains, where concrete IoT solutions allow to better understand requirements, and validate the framework and its components. The selected domains are considerably different to ensure a broad view over the needs of IoT security, trust and privacy management, towards the intended holistic approach of the framework. In the next subsections, are briefly presented the IoT solutions of the three domains, making visible the needs that motivate the project. In Sect. 4.4 is provided a summary of the IoT security, trust and privacy management challenges that are common to the presented solutions.

---

[3] https://www.w3.org/TR/vc-data-model/.
[4] https://www.ietf.org/mailman/listinfo/rats.

4.1   Domain A: Emergency and Vigilance Using Drones

Ensuring security and safety of citizens in urban environments is a complex subject that depends on the availability of considerable resources and, in many cases, the use and manipulation of sensitive data (e.g., when using street vigilance cameras). ARCADIAN-IoT domain A focuses on the use of IoT devices, in this case, drones, in novel citizen centered urban vigilance services.

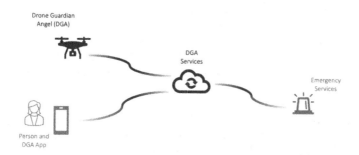

Fig. 2. Drone guardian angel solution

The solution (see Fig. 2) consists of a mobile app where citizens can request a Drone Guardian Angel (DGA) service, e.g., to escort them in their way home. The user needs to supply personal data in the registration phase, like name, address and photos, and, when requesting the service, needs to provide its initial and final location, to ensure that the service is available in both places.

When receiving a service request with a person's data, a drone parked nearby goes to the requested location and identifies the user (e.g., by face recognition). After the identification the service starts and the drone follows the person, aware of the surroundings to detect any threat. If something abnormal is detected (e.g., an attempt of robbery), the drone calls for rescue services according to the incident type (e.g. police in case of robbery, and/or medical emergency in case injuries exist). While the rescue team(s) is/are on its/their way, some details are sent, collected by the drone camera, microphone or other appropriate sensors (e.g., GPS), to optimize the response to the incident.

DGA solution depends on the use of persons sensitive data, like location and photos. Compromised devices can endanger the users safety and their data security. The service itself depends on the trustworthiness of the data gathered and provided by IoT devices. Also, the IoT network, if vulnerable, may endanger the users security and safety (especially in emergency moments). These and other trust, security, and privacy management challenges are summarized in 4.4.

4.2   Domain B: Grid Infrastructure Monitoring

Grid infrastructures are the base for power utilities like electricity, gas or oil. These are critical services for most of the daily urban activities. Monitoring these infrastructures has high importance for providing reliable services and for efficient energy management practices.

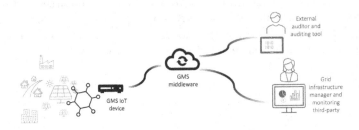

Fig. 3. Grid monitoring services solution

ARCADIAN-IoT domain B features an IoT solution for monitoring grid infrastructures (see Fig. 3). Typically, a grid infrastructure manager needs to be aware of factors that influence the system behaviour, like component degradation, and of aspects that allow to optimize and predict the service performance (e.g. temperature). In this sense, the Grid Monitoring Services (GMS) consist of a solution that collects and aggregates data from a set of sensors using an IoT device that acts as gateway for communication. This IoT device makes the grid data available, through a middleware, to be consumed by grid managers in a monitoring service (e.g., web). GMS also allows a grid manager to change the sensors procedures (e.g., change the reading cycle frequency). Finally, the solution is prepared for external audits, where data from devices/sensors needs to be securely provided to authorized external persons.

GMS solution collects data from a set of devices that inform about grid performance and related factors. The trustworthiness of the data is critical. If corrupted, the system or the manager are prone to have wrong decisions, putting at risk energetic needs of businesses and citizens. It is also confidential data, that can harm the service provider in case of unauthorized access. Furthermore, GMS provides means to interact with the sensor network, action that may compromise the infrastructure performance. The monitoring tool can also be targeted in network attacks, e.g., DDoS, making the service unavailable and delaying/hampering potentially relevant decisions. In Sect. 4.4, these and other trust, security, and privacy management challenges relevant for GMS are summarized.

4.3 Domain C: Medical IoT for Remote Monitoring of Patients

Monitoring patients at their homes, when possible, is important for the sustainability of health systems, and for the comfort of the monitored persons. IoT systems, namely body sensor networks, provide solutions that make this possible.

ARCADIAN-IoT Medical IoT (MIoT) solution (see Fig. 4) focuses on this opportunity, making possible to reduce the number of medical appointments from patients that need to be accompanied. MIoT is able of monitoring patients health considering a treatment protocol (readings frequency, medication, and other medical recommendations). It collects, stores, and presents the evolution of the patient vital signs, captured with medical sensors, and timely provides alerts for medical decision support. To complement these parameters, the patient can enter perceived health status in a mobile app, adding symptoms that can describe the his/her condition. The solution relies in a MIoT kit, provided to the patient at the hospital, that comprises a set of medical sensors and a smartphone that is used as gateway for the sensing devices' communication to the Cloud, and as interface for the patient to enter his/her perceived condition. The solution also includes a middleware for storing the patients' data, to provide it to medical monitoring tools, and for generating health alerts; and a monitoring tool for the medical staff to check the patient's condition and to change the monitoring protocol when needed.

Fig. 4. Medical IoT solution

ARCADIAN-IoT MIoT solution aims to improve the conditions of follow-up of patients at home, in an active treatment process. However, by collecting patient's data and storing it in a centralized Cloud, the system deals with sensitive information security and privacy risks. Also, the trustworthiness of the data is critical for the medical staff to make right treatment decisions. Fake or manipulated diagnostic information can put the patients' well-being, or even their lives, at risk. Furthermore, MIoT provides means to update the patient monitoring protocol, which needs to be secured to avoid unauthorized control over the devices' behaviour. The mobile app and the monitoring tool for the medical staff can also be targeted in attacks that can make the services unavailable and delay/hamper potentially relevant medical decisions. These challenges and others relevant to this domain are consolidated in the next subsection.

4.4   Common Trust, Security and Privacy Management Challenges

The IoT solutions aforementioned share trust, security and privacy management challenges, namely the following:

- Enable security and trust in the management of devices' and persons' identification, ensuring protection to, e.g., impersonation attacks that could endanger persons safety and data security.

- Define trust evaluation models and processes for devices, persons and services, that can trigger and support protection measures, and also keep the user in control his data privacy (who accesses what and when).
- Protect the users' and devices' sensitive data with hardened encryption mechanisms that have recovery ability in case of need.
- Detect anomalous behaviour on IoT devices, IoT network and related services, which can indicate the presence of known or zero-day vulnerabilities or threats.
- In case of an incident with a device, have self-protection, self-recovery and self-healing mechanisms that allow to protect and to recover functionalities and data to pre-defined trust levels with reduced human intervention.
- Have a CTI approach for IoT threat information generation, sharing, analysis, storage, and consumption, able of spreading and using threat knowledge in a efficient way.

ARCADIAN-IoT research aims to provide answers to these challenges. The hypothesis are formulated jointly with the IoT technology providers to ensure viability, and integrated for validation in their IoT solutions. The process includes as well the analysis of the legal, ethical, regulatory and social dimensions associated with the technology.

5   Conclusions

This paper presented ARCADIAN-IoT, a framework aimed at holistically managing identity, trust, privacy security and recovery capabilities in a holistic approach. Its concept and objectives have been described, along with its plane-based structure and corresponding functionalities. The future work includes the research and development of its components, and later on their integration and demonstration by supporting the described use cases.

References

1. Gartner insights on how to lead in a connected world. https://www.gartner.com/imagesrv/books/iot/iotEbook_digital.pdf/. Accessed 26 Apr 2022
2. NETSCOUT: weaponization of internet infrastructure. https://www.netscout.com/use-case/weaponization-internet-infrastructure (2020). Accessed 26 Apr 2022
3. Abie, H.: Cognitive cybersecurity for cps-IoT enabled healthcare ecosystems. In: 2019 13th International Symposium on Medical Information and Communication Technology (ISMICT), pp. 1–6. IEEE (2019)
4. Babar, S., Stango, A., Prasad, N., Sen, J., Prasad, R.: Proposed embedded security framework for internet of things (IoT). In: 2011 2nd International Conference on Wireless Communication, Vehicular Technology, Information Theory and Aerospace & Electronic Systems Technology (Wireless VITAE), pp. 1–5. IEEE (2011)
5. Bringhenti, D., Valenza, F., Basile, C.: Toward cybersecurity personalization in smart homes. IEEE Secur. Priv. 20(01), 45–53 (2022)

6. Burhan, M., Rehman, R.A., Khan, B., Kim, B.S.: IoT elements, layered architectures and security issues: a comprehensive survey. Sensors **18**(9), 2796 (2018)
7. da Cruz, M.A., Rodrigues, J.J.P., Al-Muhtadi, J., Korotaev, V.V., de Albuquerque, V.H.C.: A reference model for internet of things middleware. IEEE Internet Things J. **5**(2), 871–883 (2018)
8. Dhas, Y.J., Jeyanthi, P.: A review on internet of things protocol and service oriented middleware. In: 2019 International Conference on Communication and Signal Processing (ICCSP), pp. 104–108. IEEE (2019)
9. Jan, S.U., Ahmed, S., Shakhov, V., Koo, I.: Toward a lightweight intrusion detection system for the internet of things. IEEE Access **7**, 42450–42471 (2019)
10. Khraisat, A., Gondal, I., Vamplew, P., Kamruzzaman, J., Alazab, A.: A novel ensemble of hybrid intrusion detection system for detecting internet of things attacks. Electronics **8**(11), 1210 (2019)
11. Lee, I.: Internet of things (IoT) cybersecurity: literature review and IoT cyber risk management. Future Internet **12**(9), 157 (2020)
12. Lu, Y., Da, Xu., L.: Internet of things (IoT) cybersecurity research: a review of current research topics. IEEE Internet Things J. **6**(2), 2103–2115 (2018)
13. Sankaran, S., Shivshankar, S., Nimmy, K.: LHPUF: lightweight hybrid PUF for enhanced security in internet of things. In: 2018 IEEE International Symposium on Smart Electronic Systems (ISES)(Formerly iNiS), pp. 275–278. IEEE (2018)
14. Smys, S., et al.: Hybrid intrusion detection system for internet of things (IoT). J. ISMAC **2**(04), 190–199 (2020)
15. Tiburski, R.T., et al.: Lightweight security architecture based on embedded virtualization and trust mechanisms for IoT edge devices. IEEE Commun. Mag. **57**(2), 67–73 (2019)
16. Tweneboah-Koduah, S., Skouby, K.E., Tadayoni, R.: Cyber security threats to IoT applications and service domains. Wireless Pers. Commun. **95**(1), 169–185 (2017)
17. Usmonov, B., Evsutin, O., Iskhakov, A., Shelupanov, A., Iskhakova, A., Meshcheryakov, R.: The cybersecurity in development of IoT embedded technologies. In: 2017 International Conference on Information Science and Communications Technologies (ICISCT), pp. 1–4. IEEE (2017)
18. Vijayakumaran, C., Muthusenthil, B., Manickavasagam, B.: A reliable next generation cyber security architecture for industrial internet of things environment. Int. J. Electr. Comput. Eng. **10**(1), 387 (2020)
19. Zarpelão, B.B., Miani, R.S., Kawakani, C.T., de Alvarenga, S.C.: A survey of intrusion detection in internet of things. J. Netw. Comput. Appl. **84**, 25–37 (2017)

IoT Pilots, Testbeds
and Experimentation Results

GAIA 5G: A Multi-access Smart-Campus Architecture

Jorge Gallego-Madrid[1]([⊠]) [iD], Luis Bernal-Escobedo[1] [iD], Rodrigo Asensio[1] [iD],
Ana Hermosilla[1] [iD], Alejandro Molina Zarca[1] [iD], Jordi Ortiz[2] [iD],
Ramon Sanchez-Iborra[1] [iD], and Antonio Skarmeta[1] [iD]

[1] Department of Information and Communication Engineering, University of Murcia,
Murcia 30100, Spain
{jorgegm,luis.bernal,rodrigo.asensio,ana.hermosilla,
alejandro.mzarca,ramonsanchez,skarmeta}@um.es
[2] University Center of Defense at the Spanish Air Force Academy,
San Javier 30720, Spain
jordi.ortiz@cud.upct.es

Abstract. Smart-campuses are an emerging ecosystem that permit to
enhance the performance and efficiency of academic facilities. Besides,
they are also adopted as research, development, and testing platforms
for the integration of novel management and governance mechanisms in
complex ICT infrastructures. In this line, they are considered as small
smart-city-like scenarios which can be used as a playground prior to
large-scale deployments. This work presents the GAIA 5G smart-campus,
located in the Espinardo campus of the University of Murcia (Spain). In
the first place, its technological architecture is presented, detailing the
multi-access platform that provides 5G, Internet of Things (IoT), and
vehicular communications connectivity. Also, the virtualized computation environment is described. Thanks to these two pillars, GAIA 5G has
the potential to host diverse use cases in multiple verticals, such as 5G
connectivity, Network Function Virtualization (NFV) management and
orchestration, or cybersecurity, which are also described. As discussed
along the paper, GAIA 5G is an operative smart-campus infrastructure
ready to support state-of-the-art research and accommodate novel 5G-
and-beyond (B5G) test cases.

Keywords: Smart-campus · 5G · MEC · SDN · NFV · IoT · B5G

1 Introduction

The convergence of multiple radio access technologies in a single scenario is
fueling the development of smart environments. This is true specially in urban
settings, thanks to the omnipresence of broadband solutions such as Wi-Fi or cellular networks, e.g., 4G/5G, together with the incipient expansion of the Internet
of Things (IoT)-based solutions, e.g., LoRaWAN, Sigfox, or Narrow Band IoT
(NBIoT). Given the different features provided by these technologies, the range

© The Author(s), under exclusive license to Springer Nature Switzerland AG 2022
A. González-Vidal et al. (Eds.): GIoTS 2022, LNCS 13533, pp. 363–374, 2022.
https://doi.org/10.1007/978-3-031-20936-9_29

of enabled applications is huge, including user-centric, vehicular, sensorization services, etc. [2].

Smart-campus spaces are gaining relevance as they provide similar characteristics to those offered by smart-cities but at a lower scale, which is notably interesting for research and development purposes [17]. Thus, different academic institutions are investing important resources and efforts for turning their traditional facilities into a rich smart-campus environment to promote multidisciplinary research among their academics as well as the arrival of visiting researchers [3].

In this line, as depicted in Fig. 1, the University of Murcia (Spain) is developing its own smart-campus infrastructure encompassing different state-of-the-art radio access, virtualization, and computation technologies. As comprehensively detailed in next sections, the GAIA 5G smart-campus provides a private functional 5G infrastructure, which is the pivotal element of its communication architecture. Besides, attached to its core network other radio technologies are also available with different purposes: Wi-Fi for improved indoor coverage, LoRaWAN and NBIoT for IoT applications, and 802.11p-based radio access for vehicular services. From a computational and virtualization perspective, the infrastructure is currently equipped with a Cloud platform which hosts the core network components, as well as Software Defined Networking (SDN), Network Function Virtualization (NFV) and Multi-Access Edge Computing (MEC) deployments. Still under development, since its origins, GAIA 5G has enabled previous research advances [11,13,14] and it is currently being employed in different European projects such as 5G-MOBIX [16], 5GASP [4], or INSPIRE-5Gplus [10], among others.

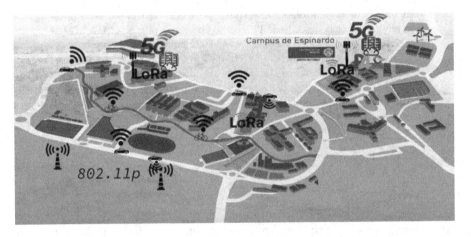

Fig. 1. University of Murcia's GAIA 5G architecture.

The main objective of this work is to present the GAIA 5G smart-campus architecture to the community. Therefore, its principal characteristics will be dissected along the paper and three different illustrative use cases will be also described. Concretely, the aim of these demonstrators is to evidence the functionality of the infrastructure in different planes, namely, 5G connectivity, NFV management, and cybersecurity. Therefore, the contribution of this work is twofold: (i) A detailed overview of the University of Murcia's smart-campus GAIA 5G is given, and (ii) the description of recent functional demonstrators implemented over the GAIA 5G infrastructure are presented.

The rest of the document is organized as follows. Section 2 discusses about other functional smart-campus infrastructures in order to place in context the GAIA 5G one. Section 3 describes the GAIA 5G smart-campus architecture. Three illustrative use cases and their preliminary results are presented in Sect. 4. Finally, the paper is closed in Sect. 5, remarking the most important facts as well as future research lines.

2 Background

The idea of increasing the level of intelligence and automation of university campuses has been explored in the literature during the last years from multiple points of view. From a sustainability perspective, authors in [8] included IoT and data science mechanisms for monitoring and managing university energy-related activities to help efficient decision making in all levels. The presented proposal was focused on enabling good sustainability indicators through the establishment of monitoring systems that permit regular data collection with certain levels of quality, to ease the decision-making processes of involved stakeholders. From a Cloud computing point of view, in [6] a smart-campus service platform based on Cloud computing aiming at promoting the development of smart-campuses was presented. Apart from the infrastructure considerations, this work also focused on teaching-related issues such as course and equipment management and identity authentication access. From an AI perspective, work in [7] explored the creation of an open AI platform to achieve multi-application integrated management. The architecture of this platform can integrate all the services deployed in the smart-campus and enhance its management capabilities with dynamic and sustainable development. From a network infrastructure angle, Njah *et al.* [9] presented a fully-programmable SDN architecture with a multi-flow optimization model to manage the massive number of heterogeneous traffic flows that are typically generated in smart-campuses scenarios. The proposed solution is ready to be implemented in all kind of scenarios and can be integrated also with a large IoT environment. Regarding multi-access infrastructures, work in [5] presented a smart-campus framework based on a 5G test network, sensor technologies, augmented reality, and AI. The framework functioning is oriented towards three main use cases: university key operations, campus services, and campus surroundings. Besides, this research showed that a local micro operator would be an essential action to fulfill the smart-campus requirements. Finally, work in [1] presented a comprehensive review of the research efforts during the last decade and current challenges related to smart-campuses. The survey work pointed out that the main challenges in this field are the interoperability among heterogeneous entities, infrastructure sustainability, and the open data access policies.

In this way, the objective of this work is to present the GAIA 5G smart-campus as a research and development playground. The environment found in smart-campuses is very similar to the one found in smart-cities, but in a reduced scale with less people and buildings. However, it has to offer the same set of characteristics and services. In this way, the introduction of the GAIA 5G research and development smart-campus will pave the way to the design and shaping of new services and applications that could be later directly transferred to smart-cities scenarios.

3   GAIA 5G: A Smart-Campus Architecture

The GAIA 5G smart-campus is an initiative funded by the Spanish Ministry of Science and Innovation through the European Regional Development Fund (ERDF) with the aim of providing the Murcia Region with the necessary technological infrastructure to reach excellence in areas such as logistics and agriculture, in which the Region is already a reference. The University of Murcia is in charge of the deployment and management of the infrastructure and at the same time relies on it to materialize its smart-campus vision. To this end, a multi radio access technology focused on empowering broadband-, IoT-, and vehicular-oriented vertical services is being deployed.

3.1   Technical Description

The already functional GAIA 5G backbone network presents a twofold purpose. On the one hand, the network devices provide a production-ready environment in which a more traditional and well-tested network management approach is used; on the other hand, the backbone devices need to be compliant with state-of-the-art networking technologies, e.g., SDN or NFV, and also be capable of providing advanced network management strategies such as network slicing or dynamic resource allocation, among others. To this end, the employed switches, namely, Delta AG7648 white boxes, run PicOs which is able to manage the Broadcom's data plane as a regular switch but also provide cross-flow ports that can be attached to different OpenVSwitch instances. Therefore, in the future a pure OpenFlow approach can be deployed making use of the same devices.

However, OpenFlow is not the unique solution to manage SDN-based infrastructures and it is regarded as ossified in terms of development of new protocols. Thus, to provide with beyond state-of-the-art protocol match-action capabilities at line-rate, the backbone infrastructure is also provisioned with P4-compliant devices (EdgeCore Wedge 100bf-32X and APS-BF2556X-1T) that permit complete programmability of both the control and data planes, removing the constraints imposed by white boxes with vendor-managed data-planes. Finally, from a capacity point of view, the backbone is provisioned with 40 Gbps trunks between buildings and 10 Gbps service ports, which can be upgraded up to 100 Gbps ports after properly configuring the P4 devices.

Considering the available radio access technologies, firstly it is worth mentioning that GAIA 5G offers 5G Stand Alone (SA) access empowered by a commercial fully functional solution from Amarisoft. Concretely, the 5G infrastructure presents two macro cells (see Fig. 1) enabled by their respective Remote Radio Heads (RHHs), which are connected via Common Public Radio Interface (CPRI) fiber links to a gNB powered by the Amarisoft software. These RRH provide 20 MHz each with a 2x2 MIMO configuration and 20 W of Radio Frequence (RF) power. Besides, GAIA 5G also presents a 5G laboratory, located at the Computer Science faculty that provides small-scale testing via different Software Defined Radio (SDR) devices (various BladeRF x40, Ettus USRP B210, N310) and also an Amarisoft Callbox, with 3 2x2 full duplex SDR elements and an Amarisoft Simbox, capable of simulating up to 64 User Equipments (UEs). This laboratory is connected to the rest of the GAIA 5G backbone via two 10 Gbps dedicated links. This lab testbench is further equipped with assorted RF equipment like spectrum analyzers, signal generators, etc. Other specialized 5G tools like the Keysight Nemo for network performance validation, the Anritsu's MS2090A for New Radio (NR) layer 1 validation, and diverse 5G SA capable modems are available as well as different embedded solutions to deploy and demonstrate multiple IoT scenarios. Besides the professional Amarisoft software, the experimental Free5GC 5G core, which is a full 5G core instance developed as an open source implementation based on microservices, is also deployed and running for researching purposes.

In order to provide long-range IoT connectivity inside the campus, GAIA 5G also provides LoRaWAN access. This infrastructure relies on three Kerlink iStation gateways distributed along the campus (see Fig. 1). These gateways, working in the 868 MHz band, are connected to a self deployed LoRaWAN network server based on the Chirpstack implementation. The data received by the gateways are also forwarded to The Things Network (TTN) servers aiming at enabling an open access to this widespread IoT network. Besides, NB-IoT can also be integrated into the architecture by external providers as to compare different Low Power Wide Area Network (LPWAN) solutions [15]. This unique mix of radio access technologies has enabled the development of solutions like the on-device smart selection of access network [12].

Besides the coverage offered by 5G and IoT radio technologies, a vehicular-specific communication solution has been deployed to evaluate different alternatives in this crucial vertical sector. Concretely, a 802.11p-based infrastructure has been installed at the south area of the campus (see Fig. 1). The adopted 802.11p solution is based on the OpenWRT system, which enables the deployment of both On-Board Unit (OBU) and Road-Side Unit (RSU) software on a variety of hardware platforms such as Raspberry Pi or similar boards, or even more powerful x86-64 devices. As can be seen, with the different available radio access deployments, diverse Intelligent Transportation Systems (ITS) solutions can be evaluated, such as the 802.11p-based ITS-G5 scheme or the cellular-powered C-V2X alternative.

Finally, regarding the computation infrastructure, GAIA 5G is currently equipped with a Cloud platform which hosts core network components, as well as SDN, NFV and MEC deployments. Two Virtual Infrastructure Managers (VIMs) based on OpenStack are currently operative; OpenStack's Rocky version, a full-fledged deployment offering 160 vCPUs and 512 GB RAM split in two Compute nodes; and Openstack's Queens version, a lightweight deployment providing 12 vCPUs with 48 GB RAM and some Raspberry Pi nodes with 4 vCPUs and 8 GB RAM. Additionally, the laboratory offers an Hyper-Converged infrastructure with a 4-node cluster with 128 vCPUs and 4 TB RAM and two Edge clusters with 24 vCPUs and 512 GB RAM each, which extends the VIM capabilities and offers MEC provisioning. All these nodes are interconnected using the aforementioned P4 and SDN-enabled programmable devices. To manage and orchestrate the dynamic deployment of VNFs in this infrastructure, Open Source MANO (OSM) is the chosen orchestrator. Besides, a Kubernetes cluster is deployed and tested to complete the computation infrastructure and offer a different VIM alternative.

4   Use Cases

4.1   5G Connectivity

One of the principal challenges when a new radio-communication infrastructure is deployed is to ensure its connectivity and reachability along the covered area. During the design phase, a series of location were considered in order to place the two 5G base stations described in the previous section. Finally, the two points indicated in Fig. 2 were selected given the joint coverage provided along the campus. Given the importance of having a good 5G coverage for supporting current and present test cases, the first functional demonstrator within the GAIA 5G infrastructure was oriented to validate the 5G deployment.

In this use case, a High Definition (HD) video delivery service was enabled for the local fire brigade. Concretely, a fire truck, a drone, and a firefighter were provisioned with 5G connectivity for allowing the production and reception of several video-flows in real-time. Both, the truck's On-Board Unit (OBU) and the drone made use of a USB 5G modem connected to their Linux-based processing platforms, while the firefighter employed a commercial 5G smart-phone. Besides, a multimedia dashboard where all the video-streams were cast was developed and placed at an Edge node (Fig. 3). The aim of this joint initiative together with the city of Murcia's fire brigade, is to increase the effectiveness and safety of risky operations by making these video-flows accessible to the deployed units (including individuals and vehicles) as well as the emergency control center. This successful preliminary evaluation of the infrastructure 5G connectivity is currently being further developed with the implementation of network slicing mechanisms to ensure the Quality of Service (QoS) offered to this kind of critical applications.

Fig. 2. 5G coverage in the campus calculated as NR RSRQ dBm.

Fig. 3. 5G-enabled video-flows dashboard.

4.2   NFV Management

Regarding Network Function Virtualization (NFV), it is worth mentioning that virtualization technologies and their use as network function enablers resulted in an explosion of alternatives to deal with new and on-demand deployments. These so-called Virtual Network Functions (VNFs) are considered the present and future of new architectures such as 5G. Nonetheless, they can not be regarded as totally independent functions, as their synchronization and coordination (subsumed under the term of NFV Orchestration) is crucial for their proper operation and handling. Furthermore, preparing the underlying infrastructure to be used along with NFV is a fundamental, but also complex and transversal, process that requires a significant effort.

In this line, the H2020 project 5GASP, in which GAIA 5G is involved through a collaboration between the University of Murcia and Odin Solutions (a private company), aims to ease the VNF development and on-boarding processes by offering a "ready-to-use" infrastructure. Its objective is to shorten the idea-to-market process by creating an automated, self-service, European testbed for Small-Medium Enterprises (SMEs) to foster the development and testing of innovative NFVs (NetApps (Network Applications) in 5GASP jergon) using the 5G and NFV-based reference architecture.

The smart-campus architecture presented in this work is one of the physical settings that are being integrated in the 5GASP ecosystem. It provides the experimenters with the underlying infrastructure and tools required to test and validate their NetApps in a real-world 5G network (see Fig. 4). In this case, as mentioned previously, GAIA 5G uses OSM as NFV orchestrator and two OpenStack substrates that serve as VIMs for the facility. Besides, the Murcia testbed offers to 5GASP multiple types of User Equipment (UE) in the form of 5G SA

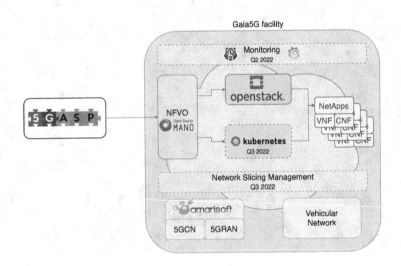

Fig. 4. University of Murcia's 5GASP framework.

smartphones and modems, and vehicular On-Board Units (OBUs) to host the user applications of the NetApps deployed in the framework.

4.3 Cybersecurity

5G is changing the way we interact with services, leaving aside static and rigid configurations and services. 5G networks, interconnect an heterogeneous set of devices and technologies and offer services tailored to the needs of the connection and the constraints of those technologies and devices. This wide diversity becomes a major challenge when it comes to ensuring cybersecurity, as the possible attack surface becomes complex and difficult to manage. This challenge is even greater with the onset of the pandemic, where the flexibility and scalability that characterizes 5G becomes a must. Millions of companies standardize teleworking while users change their habits and are connected to the network 24 h a day. This causes the network congestion to reach unprecedented levels and, together with the increase in the attack surface, cybercrime is finding a perfect place to take place.

In this regard, the University of Murcia-participated INSPIRE-5Gplus project leverages Zero touch network & Service Management (ZSM) architecture (defined by ETSI) to deliver automated E2E policy-based security management driven by a closed-loop of 5G and B5G networks. Figure 5 showcases the INSPIRE-5Gplus high-level architecture, that presents a two-tier hierarchical architecture. On the one hand, it provides Security Management Domains (SMDs) that are horizontally positioned, with self-management capabilities that allow the orchestration of dynamic reactions to security events or security predictions that occur at intra-domain level (inside of the SMD). On the other hand, these SMDs are coordinated, directed and validated through an E2E Security Management Domain (E2E SMD) that orchestrates proactive and reactive E2E security policies by involving multiple SMDs (inter-domain).

The INSPIRE5G-PLUS closed-loop is a combination of the stages of OODA (Orient-Observe-Decide-Act) and MAPE-K (Monitor-Analyse-Plan-Execute Knowledge) models with integration of cognition capabilities leveraging AI/ML techniques. Conceptually there are two interconnected loops, the outer loop which is managed including the E2E SMD orchestration and policy distribution to the different SMDs and the inner loop which is present on each SMD to maintain its self-management capabilities. Each loop is formed by Governance, Action, Observation, Orientation and Decision which heavily relies on the knowledge that is generated and needs to be trustable. This ZSM approach as identified and defined by ETSI, relies on the use of integration fabrics. These fabrics provide communication and security capabilities between and within the SMDs as well as other service management features such as registration, discovery that needs to be performed inter/intra-domain.Isolation features are not only provided within computers but also on the network itself. To this aim, network slicing is also provided across multiple self-managed SMDs.

To validate the implementation of the framework in a real 5G environment, a part of INSPIRE-5GPlus framework has been deployed in GAIA 5G smart

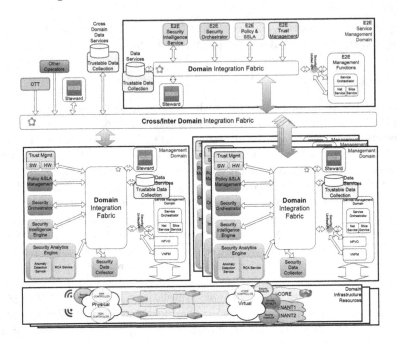

Fig. 5. INSPIRE-5Gplus framework.

campus. Current experiments are specially focused on providing dynamic E2E 5G security involving different SMDs such as 5G Core, transport and RAN by orchestrating dynamically 5G, SDN and NFV resources.

5   Conclusion

Smart-campuses are acquiring great relevance as they permit increasing the automation, monitoring, and control of the complex university infrastructures. Besides, from a research perspective, they are understood as small-scale smart-city environments where bounded and controlled tests may be conducted before their final deployment in larger scenarios. In this work, the University of Murcia's smart-campus infrastructure, so-called GAIA 5G, has been presented. Firstly, the available multi radio access scheme, encompassing 5G, IoT, and vehicular communication technologies, has been described. This range of connectivity alternatives permits the implementation of a plethora of services and vertical use cases. Besides, GAIA 5G presents a rich and powerful computation infrastructure that allows the exploitation of state-of-the-art virtualization schemes considering the different domains within the architecture: Fog, Edge, and Cloud. Finally, a series of demonstrators have been discussed with the aim of evidencing the potential of the infrastructure. Although it is in an advanced deployment status, GAIA 5G will continue evolving to integrate novel B5G technologies and enable the development and evaluation of new application and services.

Acknowledgements. This work has been supported by Fundación Séneca—Agencia de Ciencia y Tecnología de la Región de Murcia—under the FPI Grant 21429/FPI/20, and co-funded by Odin Solutions S.L., Región de Murcia (Spain); by the Spanish Ministry of Science and Innovation under the DIN2019-010827 Industrial PhD Grant, and co-funded by Odin Solutions S.L.; by the European Commission under the 5GASP (Grant No. 101016448) and INSPIRE-5Gplus (Grant No. 871808) projects; by the ONOFRE-3 project (Grant No. PID2020-112675RB-C44) funded by MCIN/AEI/10.13039/501100011033; and by the 5G Huerta project (Grant No. EQC2019-006364-P) funded by the Spanish Ministry of Science, Innovation and Universities, with ERDF funds.

References

1. Chagnon-Lessard, N., et al.: Smart campuses: extensive review of the last decade of research and current challenges. IEEE Access **9**, 124200–124234 (2021). https://doi.org/10.1109/ACCESS.2021.3109516
2. Cirillo, F., Gomez, D., Diez, L., Elicegui Maestro, I., Gilbert, T.B.J., Akhavan, R.: Smart city IoT services creation through large-scale collaboration. IEEE Internet Things J. **7**(6), 5267–5275 (2020). https://doi.org/10.1109/JIOT.2020.2978770
3. Dong, Z.Y., Zhang, Y., Yip, C., Swift, S., Beswick, K.: Smart campus: definition, framework, technologies, and services. IET Smart Cities **2**(1), 43–54 (2020). https://doi.org/10.1049/iet-smc.2019.0072
4. Gallego-Madrid, J., Sanchez-Iborra, R., Skarmeta, A.: From network functions to netapps: the 5GASP methodology. Comput. Mater. Continua **71**(2), 4115–4134 (2022). https://doi.org/10.32604/cmc.2022.021754. https://www.techscience.com/cmc/v71n2/45796
5. Jurva, R., Matinmikko-Blue, M., Niemelä, V., Nenonen, S.: Architecture and operational model for smart campus digital infrastructure. Wireless Pers. Commun. **113**(3), 1437–1454 (2020). https://doi.org/10.1007/s11277-020-07221-5
6. Li, Y.: Research on building smart campus based on cloud computing technology. In: 2020 5th International Conference on Mechanical, Control and Computer Engineering (ICMCCE), pp. 723–726 (2020). https://doi.org/10.1109/ICMCCE51767.2020.00159
7. Liang, W.: Analysis of the application of artificial intelligence technology in the construction of smart campus. In: 2020 International Wireless Communications and Mobile Computing (IWCMC), pp. 882–885 (2020). https://doi.org/10.1109/IWCMC48107.2020.9148200
8. Negreiros, I., et al.: Smart campusô as a living lab on sustainability indicators monitoring. In: 2020 IEEE International Smart Cities Conference (ISC2), pp. 1–5 (2020). https://doi.org/10.1109/ISC251055.2020.9239017
9. Njah, Y., Pham, C., Cheriet, M.: Service and resource aware flow management scheme for an SDN-based smart digital campus environment. IEEE Access **8**, 119635–119653 (2020). https://doi.org/10.1109/ACCESS.2020.3005569
10. Ortiz, J., et al.: INSPIRE-5Gplus: intelligent security and pervasive and Security, pp. 1–10. ACM, New York, NY, USA (2020). https://doi.org/10.1145/3407023.3409219
11. Sanchez-Gomez, J., Gallego-Madrid, J., Sanchez-Iborra, R., Santa, J., Skarmeta Gómez, A.F.: Impact of SCHC Compression and Fragmentation in LPWAN: a Case Study with LoRaWAN. Sensors **20**(1), 280 (2020). https://doi.org/10.3390/s20010280

12. Sanchez-Iborra, R., Bernal-Escobedo, L., Santa, J.: Machine learning-based radio access technology selection in the internet of moving things. China Commun. **18**(7), 13–24 (2021). https://doi.org/10.23919/JCC.2021.07.002

13. Sanchez-Iborra, R., Sanchez-Gomez, J., Santa, J., Fernandez, P.J., Skarmeta, A.F.: IPv6 communications over LoRa for future IoV services. In: 2018 IEEE 4th World Forum on Internet of Things (WF-IoT), pp. 92–97. IEEE (2018). https://doi.org/10.1109/WF-IoT.2018.8355231

14. Sanchez-Iborra, R., Santa, J., Gallego-Madrid, J., Covaci, S., Skarmeta, A.: Empowering the internet of vehicles with multi-RAT 5G network slicing. Sensors **19**(14), 3107 (2019). https://doi.org/10.3390/s19143107

15. Santa, J., Bernal-Escobedo, L., Sanchez-Iborra, R.: On-board unit to connect personal mobility vehicles to the IoT. Procedia Comput. Sci. **75**, 173–180 (2020). The 17th International Conference on Mobile Systems and Pervasive Computing (MobiSPC), The 15th International Energy Information Technology. https://doi.org/10.1016/j.procs.2020.07.027. https://www.sciencedirect.com/science/article/pii/S1877050920317063

16. Serrador, A., Mendes, C., Datia, N., Cota, N., Cruz, N., Beire, A.R.: A Performance measurement platform for C-ITS over 5G. In: Joint European Conference on Networks and Communications & 6G Summit (EuCNC/6G Summit), pp. 478–483. IEEE (2021). https://doi.org/10.1109/EuCNC/6GSummit51104.2021.9482603

17. Villegas-Ch, W., Palacios-Pacheco, X., Luján-Mora, S.: Application of a smart city model to a traditional university campus with a big data architecture: a sustainable smart campus. Sustainability **11**(10), 2857 (2019). https://doi.org/10.3390/su11102857

IoT Device for Reduction of Roe Deer Fawn Mortality During Haymaking

Tilman Leune$^{(\boxtimes)}$ ⓘ, Carsten Koch ⓘ, Stephan Fabry, and Simon Struck

Department of Electronics and Informatics, Hochschule Emden/Leer,
University of Applied Sciences, Emden, Germany
{tilman.leune,carsten.koch}@hs-emden-leer.de

Abstract. In this paper, we propose a novel approach in smart farming with the deployment of centrally controlled IoT-scaring devices in meadows with the goal to reduce the killing of roe deer fawn during haymaking. These deaths are due to fawns not actively avoiding threats in their first two weeks of life, employing a defensive strategy of hiding scentless and motionless in order to avoid predation instead. Currently, they are searched and removed from areas to be mowed by hand. Our approach allows for a reduction of the labour required in advance of a scheduled mowing. During field tests, the effectiveness of the devices has been shown in northern Germany.

Keywords: Smart farming · LoRaWAN · Wildlife protection · IoT · Fawn mortality

1 Introduction

1.1 Motivation

In case of danger, a roe deer fawn (as shown in Fig. 1) presses itself firmly on the ground and remains motionless. The flight instinct only sets in after the second week of life. In nature this is a good strategy against predation, but this behaviour is useless against a mowing machine. The German Wildlife Foundation (Deutsche Wildtier Stiftung) estimates that 92,000 fawns are threatened with mowing death every year on the 2.3 million hectares of grassland in Germany. Besides the obvious ethical reasons to avoid the mowing death of newborn animals, there are also economic and legal reasons.

The grass cuttings harvested from mowing are often processed into silage. If the cuttings are contaminated with carcass parts, it can become a breeding ground for the bacterium *Clostridium Botulinum* [4]. In the anaerobic conditions of silage, this bacterium secretes Botulinum toxin, a neurotoxin that causes botulism [2]. This toxin is considered one of the most potent poisons known to occur in nature and can kill cattle fed this silage within a few days [4].

A. González-Vidal et al. (Eds.): GIoTS 2022, LNCS 13533, pp. 375–384, 2022.
https://doi.org/10.1007/978-3-031-20936-9_30

Fig. 1. Roe deer fawn hiding in meadow (Author: Jan Bo Kristensen) and *Kitzretter* field effector deployed on meadow

Likewise, various German courts have ruled that landowners are liable to prosecution if the mowing death of wild animals is considered possible and no appropriate measures are taken to prevent animals from setting or to scare them away. [1] In Germany, Sect. 17 (1) of the German Animal Protection Act is particularly relevant here: *Whoever kills a vertebrate animal without reasonable cause is liable to a custodial sentence not exceeding three years or to a monetary penalty.*

Unfortunately, the main deer birthing season in May and June coincides with the first grassland cutting, so farmers have to take measures to save the fawns before mowing. However, these measures are very labour- and time-intensive and thus a challenge, especially on large areas.

The solution proposed in this work is designed to reduce the labour required for the saving of fawns while also decreasing mowing deaths. It is proposed to deploy multiple centrally controllable IoT deer-scaring devices. These are to be placed in and around meadows used for haymaking in advance of the mowing season.

The scaring devices are then supposed to be activated the night before a scheduled mowing. Once activated, varying localized audio-visual disturbances are emitted intermittently, running throughout the entire night. This is supposed to decrease the attractivity of the effected meadow, thus giving the doe an incentive to call her fawn and move it to a neighbouring safe hiding area.

1.2 Structure

This paper is structured as follows: In Sect. 2, the approach for protection of wildlife before and during haymaking currently employed by farmers and hunters laboriously are discussed. Additionally, the current state of research on sensory perception of roe deer is explored with regard to the design of scaring cues.

Section 3 describes the implementation of the proposed solution, starting with a high level overview of the entire application and detailing the aspects of all components of the IoT-scaring device.

The effectiveness of the proposed devices and network is discussed in Sect. 4, wherein the results of field tests conducted in northern Germany are evaluated. Finally, in Sect. 5 the results and insights gained for further work are discussed.

2 Related Work

This section describes methods currently employed to reduce fawn mortality in preparation for haymaking with specific focus on the perceptual sensitivity concerning scaring cues of roe deer.

2.1 Available Methods for Detection and Rescue of Fawns

In order to avoid killing breeding and setting animals during haymaking, various approaches are proposed by the *Deutsche Wildtier Stiftung*:

A principle measure is to start mowing as late as possible, completely avoiding the breeding and setting seasons and prevent the mowing death of many animals. During mowing season, choosing daylight hours for mowing can avoid unnecessary animal deaths, as at night the necessary headlights disorientate wild animals [4]. Another measure is the mowing a parcel from the inside out to leave a protected escape route for the animals . Additionally, disc mowers lead to more animals being killed than bar mowers because of their strong suction effect.

Measures to be taken before mowing include searching the meadow with the help of dogs or drones (UAV, equipped with thermal imaging) shortly before mowing and taking them to safety or mark nests and fawns so that they are spared. Also, if a mowing is scheduled, measures can be taken to deter game beforehand. Traditionally, simple scarecrows constructed from wooden poles with large plastic bags attached to the top have been used. Electronic acoustic and visual game scaring devices have also become available in recent years. While both these scaring devices work, they need tight scheduling of deployment because of the roe deer's habituation to the devices, lessening the effect [7].

The deployment itself is labour intensive since many scaring devices must be placed to cover large patches of land. Also, when the weather conditions are suitable for haymaking, many farmers in a given area will want to mow simultaneously. Another problem is that all this work will be in vain if the mowing can not be performed on the scheduled day. In that case, the scaring devices have to be removed from the meadows to avoid habituation and redeployed once the new mowing date arrives, or the labour intensive searching of the meadow with dogs or drones has to be repeated.

2.2 Auditory and Visual Sensitivity of Roe Deer

When designing a stationary device to scare away (roe) deer, the sensory perception of roe deer must be studied to determine which colours and sound frequencies deers can perceive and thus which stimuli can be employed to drive them away. Since roe deer are not a frequent topic in established scientific publications [5], the literature research was oriented towards related species such as the fallow deer (Dama dama) and the white-tailed deer (Odocoileus virginianus).

Vision. In game animal's eyes, more rods (sensitive to brightness) are present than cones (sensitive to colours). In cloven-hoofed game, the ratio is 9 to 1 [8], giving up to 100 times better vision in dark environments compared to humans.

Unlike humans, cloven-hoofed game usually have only two types of cones (dichromacy), one for short-wave light from ultraviolet to blue and one for green to yellow. Green tones can be perceived and distinguished very well, whereas red and brown tones are difficult to differentiate.

Blue stands out in a natural green environment. The most sensitive range is around 500 nm, 497 nm in white-tailed deer and dam deer [6]. The most sensitive short-wave range in both species is 450–460 nm in the mid- and long-wave range 530–550 nm [6]. Wild animals often feel disturbed by visual changes in their territory alone and avoid them. However, the habituation effect occurs quickly if no other negative effects emanate from a change [9]. With regard to this, randomised scare cues seem to be the means of choice.

Hearing. Deer have large auricles that they can turn independently up to 180°. It has been shown that white-tailed deer hear frequencies from about 0.25 kHz to 30 kHz, with the greatest sensitivity in the range between 4 kHz and 8 kHz [3]. The situation is similar for conspecifics. Furthermore, deer tend to focus their attention on low frequencies rather than ultrasound. The longer the wavelength, the lower the intensity needed to reach the sound threshold, the more suitable the signal [10].

3   Implementation

In summary, roe deer fawn mortality during haymaking should be reducable if there exists a way to generate randomized audio-visual cues perceptible by roe deer in and around meadows, which can be activated just in time prior to the mowing to avoid habituation effects and all this with a low workload for setup and retrieval.

Given these design parameters, we propose a centralized networked solution based on smart scaring devices to be placed in the field, communicating wirelessly with a central server application which is itself controlled by users through a web-application.

3.1   Network Overview

The approach of the *Kitzretter* (eng: fawn guard) system to reduce the mortality of fawns during haymaking, designed at the University of Applied Sciences Emden/Leer in cooperation with the Aurich hunters' association, is the use of

IoT devices that can be individually controlled and configured by a central server based on the radio technology LoRaWAN[1].

Field Devices are deployed in advance independent of the mowing schedule. They communicate wirelessly using LoRaWAN with the infrastructure of *The Things Community Stack* (TTN). The TTN forwards requests to a web application (see Fig. 2) and routes replies back to the devices. This enables a user to do monitoring and control and allows the scheduling of scaring effects just prior to the mowing, avoiding any habituation effect on the animals.

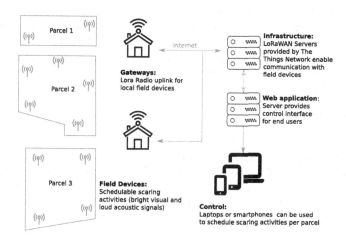

Fig. 2. Architecture and components of the proposed *Kitzretter* network: meadows (parcel 1 ..n) with IoT-scaring Field Devices (FE), and public or private LoRaWAN-Gateways.

3.2 Wireless Communication

A plethora of wireless communication technologies usable for IoT devices exist, such as GSM, Sigfox or LoRaWAN.

Using cellular radio as data connection for the devices was rejected for multiple reasons. First and most importantly, many rural areas in Germany, which are the primary environment for the devices, have notoriously bad cellular network coverage, so a reliable connection cannot be assured. Additionally, mobile operators are in the process of shutting down GSM (2G, 3G) networks in favour of more modern technologies (LTE, 4G, 5G). While LTE provides higher data rates, the maximum range of a cell is limited and coverage in rural Germany is rather sparse. Also, providing each device (about one to two per hectare are required) with a cellular subscription would increase the operating cost substantially.

---

[1] compare https://lora-alliance.org/.

The commercially available network architecture provided by Sigfox provides long range transmission capabilities, but was rejected since Sigfox does not provide built-in authentication nor encryption. Also, no free network plan is available, putting it at a cost disadvantage.

The corporation The Things Industries provides The Things Stack Community Edition, a free, community based deployment of a LoRaWAN network free of charge which has been selected for the *Kitzretter* devices' communication.

The low bandwidth provided by LoRaWAN due to it's diminutive data rate and fair-use airtime restrictions when using the community network plan are not a limitation for the proposed approach since only very little data communication is required as described in Sect. 3.4. If a rural location does not provide a local LoRaWAN Gateway, a private or mobile gateway with a cellular connection can be deployed within reach of the meadows, equipped with a larger cellular antenna if necessary as illustrated in Fig. 2.

3.3   Web Application

The user frontend for control of the scaring activities provides registering of devices and users, monitoring of the devices status and scheduling of scaring activities for clusters of devices, all accessible through the user preferred web browser. The backend communicates with The Things Community Network (TTN) using the web-hook API: Whenever the TTN receives a data packet from a field device, the application receives a HTTP POST request containing the contents of the packet.

Replys generated by the backend are then returned to TTN and delivered to the field devices using TTN's uplink to the local LoRaWAN Gateways. The web application used to control a *Kitzretter* network is written in the Rust programming language. It is self-contained and can easily be deployed to Linux based server of choice, either in house or rented from a public cloud.

3.4   Design of Field Effectors

The battery-operated devices to be placed in meadows are called field effectors (FE, see Fig. 1). Each FE is tagged with an unique QR-code which can be recorded during deployment using a geotagging camera (e.g. any smartphone with GPS receiver) to record it's position.

Hardware. The FE consist of a scaring module called Effectorboard and a logic and communication module called Loraboard as illustrated in Fig 3. The Loraboard is a custom circuit board equipped with a NXP 32-bit Cortex M0 micro-controller unit (MCU) and an integrated LoRaWAN-module *RFM95W*, with the antenna line connecting to an U.FL coaxial connector.

For power supply, the board is equipped with mounting clips for two standard 18650 LiPo-battery cells and a charge control circuit providing an USB 2.0 Micro-B connector as charging port.

 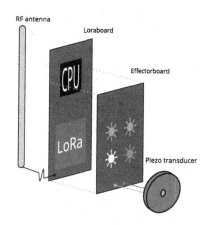

Fig. 3. Components of the proposed *Kitzretter* field effector (FE)

In consideration of the auditory and visual sensitivity of roe deer as discussed in Sect. 2.2, the Effectorboard mounted on top of the Loraboard, is equipped with four high powered LEDs (350mA each) in the colours amber, green, white and blue for visual effects and an amplifier stage driving an external piezo transducer for the emission of audio signals with a sound pressure level of up to 95 dB (square wave, 1 KHz, 0.5 m distance).

The components are bolted to a 3D-printed holder and mounted inside a transparent acrylic pipe with a length of 10 cm and a diameter of 70 mm, sealed rubber rings and 3D-printed screw-on caps. The upper cap carries an external whip antenna while the lower cap contains the piezo transducer firing downward on a conic omnidirectional sound diffuser (compare Fig. 3).

Firmware. The firmware is designed for low power usage during deployment over several weeks. To achieve this, activity is limited to short phases while most of the time, the field effectors are in sleep mode. In following, a short description of the devices behaviour is given.

On power-up, the devices try to connect to a local LoRaWAN Gateway immediately. On connection, the server sends the current time for clock synchronization, followed by any scheduled scaring activities. The current state of the initialization is indicated with coloured LEDs.

Once the initialization phase is over, the LEDs blink three times before going dark, indicating switch-over to standby mode. In standby mode, the CPU and radio are powered down to conserve energy. The internal RTC (realtime-clock), driven by an external oscillator for higher precision, is used to wake up the MCU periodically to send an 'alive' beacon and to be able to receive newly scheduled scaring activities.

This continues until the time of a scheduled scaring activity is reached or power runs out. During a scaring activity, one of several preprogrammed scaring sequences are played back. The available effects are visual and auditory, using the very bright LEDs mounted on the Effector board and the emission of waveforms generated numerically with Direct Digital Synthesis (DDS). This allows for both square wave beeps 100 Hz to 15 kHz or playback as well as digital samples, such as barking dogs or the warning call of the Eurasian jay *(Garrulus glandarius)*[2].

The Firmware is based on a port of the open-source LMIC-driver[3], originally designed for use with Arduino compatible 8-Bit micro-controller boards, to the ARM-based LPC11xx-platform used by this project.

4   Evaluation

In May and June 2019, successful initial tests were carried out with prototypes of the system created as part of student work in the rural municipality of Großefehn in the district of Aurich, Germany, proving the technical viability of the proposed solution. In the springtime of 2020 and 2021, further field evaluations focussing on network, timing and network coverage were conducted with up to 16 of the revised version of the *Kitzretter* field effectors (FE) as described in Sect. 3.

4.1   Scaring Effectiveness

For a field test, FE are deployed all over the target area, leaving a distance of about 40 m to 80 m between them (compare Fig. 4a and b). The deployment is done a week or two in advance of the planned scaring in order to be sure the Effectors scare of the deer and not the deployment activities.

Some of the target areas had LoRaWAN network coverage from gateways several kilometres away, but for reliable synchronous scaring it was necessary to install a local gateway on a barn of the neighbouring farm. In places where no public gateway was within range, a trailer mounted battery powered gateway with an antenna height of 3.5 m was set up.

Scaring activity typically last for several hours of intermittent playback of scaring effects running for a minute or two, followed by 15 to 30 min of silence. Scaring activities can be scheduled remotely at arbitrary times via the web application, and are typically scheduled from dusk the day before a planned mowing until the next dawn in order to maximize the disturbance.

In order to determine the scaring effectiveness, an unmanned aerial vehicle (UAV) with a thermal imaging camera is used to seek out fawns in the meadows prior to and after a test cycle, with the absence of fawns after a scaring cycle considered a successful trial (compare Fig. 4c and d).

Five evaluation trials were conducted in different locations between April and June of 2021. Observation of the trials was performed by members and associates of the Aurich hunting association. The results are promising:

---

[2] A bird common across Eurasia with a harsh, rasping screech that it uses upon sighting of predators.
[3] https://github.com/mcci-catena/arduino-lmic.

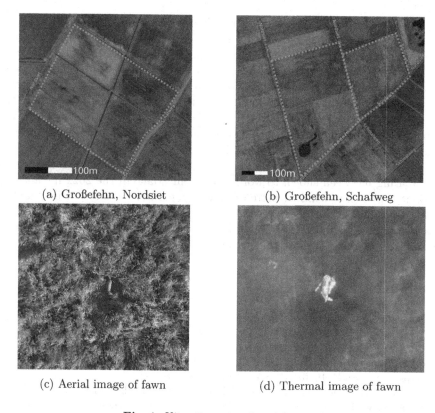

(a) Großefehn, Nordsiet

(b) Großefehn, Schafweg

(c) Aerial image of fawn

(d) Thermal image of fawn

Fig. 4. *Kitzretter* setup in trial areas

In two of the five trial areas, no roe deer and fawns were detected by the drones prior to the scaring activity, probably due to very wet weather in the area and subsequent low growth of vegetation. Four fawns were detected in the third location and further two in the forth. In the fifth trial area, no fawns but two does were present. In all five trial areas, neither adult roe deer nor fawns were present in the morning after scaring activity. This indicates that the doe has led the fawns out of the meadow. Accordingly, no intervention or action by humans was necessary to search for or remove the animals before the upcoming mowing.

5 Conclusion

In this work, the *Kitzretter* network, a smart networked digital scaring device, is presented and shown to have the ability to reduce roe deer fawn mortality during haymaking.

As is evident from this report, it can be difficult to conduct trials in the field since multiple factors may interfere with test arrangements and animal behaviour cannot be planned. Since every scaring activity in locations with roe deer present resulted in the deer leaving, it appears that some effectiveness of the *Kitzretter* devices has been confirmed.

A secondary goal of *Kitzretter* is to reduce the labour required for the rescue of fawns. This is achieved twofold: first, since the deployment is independent from the actual mowing date, a meadow can be prepared in advance, avoiding scheduling conflicts for those conducting the deployment. Second, since the scaring activities decrease the attractivity as a hiding place, the roe does call their fawns from the meadows themselves, such that the step of locating and picking up or marking the fawns is no longer necessary.

In conclusion, the system using LoraWAN in rural environments for synchronised scaring has been shown to work during our trials. In the 2022 haymaking season it is planed to conduct more trials with a greater number of FE in multiple locations across Germany to validate our approach with a larger amount of data points and to find the optimal parameters, such as minimum devices per hectare and selection of most efficient audio-visual scaring cues.

References

1. Biedenkopf, A.: Urteil — Tötung von Tieren (Rehkitze) durch Abmähen einer Wiese, AZ: 40 Ds 4 Js 8205/09 März (2010)
2. Collins, M.D., East, A.K.: Phylogeny and taxonomy of the food-borne pathogen clostridium botulinum and its neurotoxins. J. Appl. Microbio. **84**(1), 5–17 (1998). https://doi.org/10.1046/j.1365-2672.1997.00313.x
3. D'Angelo, G.J., de Chicchis, A.R., Osborn, D.A., Gallagher, G.R., Warren, R.J., Miller, K.V.: Hearing range of white-tailed deer as determined by auditory brainstem response. J. Wildl. Manage. **71**(4), 1238–1242 (2007). https://doi.org/10. 2193/2006-326
4. Genteföhr, S., Kinser, D.A., v. Münchhausen, H.F.: Praxisratgeber mähtod - ein ratgeber zum schutz von jungwild und wiesenvögeln. Deutsche Wildtier Stiftung (2019)
5. Hoffmann, D.: Rehwild - überraschend unerforscht (2019). https://gameconservan cy.de/rehwildgedanken_1/. Accessed 11/2021
6. Jacobs, G.H., Deegan, J.F., Neitz, J., Murphy, B.P., Miller, K.V., Marchinton, R.L.: Electrophysiological measurements of spectral mechanisms in the retinas of two cervids: white-tailed deer (odocoileus virginianus) and fallow deer (Dama dama). J. Comp. Phys. A **174**(5), 551–557 (1994). https://doi.org/10.1007/BF00217375
7. Jarnemo, A.: Roe deer capreolus capreolus fawns and mowing-mortality rates and countermeasures. Wildl. Biol. **8**(1), 211–218 (2002)
8. Junker, E.: Sehvermögen von Wildtieren. Wildbiologie: 9, Physiologie, Wildtier Schweiz (2004)
9. Nolte, D.: Grazing behavior of livestock and wildlife, chap. Behavioral approaches for limiting depredation by wild ungulates. Idaho Forest, Wildlife and Range Exp. Sta. Bull. #70, University of Idaho, Moscow, ID (1999)
10. Scheifele, P.M., Browning, D.G., Collins-Scheifele, L.M.: Analysis and effectiveness of deer whistles for motor vehicles: frequencies, levels, and animal threshold responses. Acoust. Res. Lett. Online **4**(3), 71–76 (2003). https://doi.org/10.1121/ 1.1582071

Latency and Energy Consumption of Convolutional Neural Network Models from IoT Edge Perspective

Sebastian Hauschild[(⊠)] and Horst Hellbrück

Department of Electrical Engineering and Computer Science,
Center of Excellence CoSA, University of Applied Sciences Luebeck,
Mönkhofer Weg 239, 23562 Lübeck, Germany
{sebastian.hauschild,horst.hellbrueck}@th-luebeck.de
http://www.th-luebeck.de/cosa

Abstract. The increase in computing power and integration of specialized hardware for Artificial Intelligence (AI) acceleration like Tensor Processing Units (TPU) enable complex machine learning at edge devices in the Internet of Things (IoT). However, wireless portable systems are limited in computing power and battery lifetime. To increase the battery lifetime of edge devices and accelerate inference of IoT systems, many developments focus on combining or outsourcing AI algorithms to a cloud via wireless links e.g. wireless LAN IEEE 802.11ac or mobile network 4G/5G. Due to limitations of restricted wireless transmissions in rural areas mainly below 50 MBit/s, resulting longer transfer times can significantly affect inference latency and energy consumption from the perspective of the IoT edge device and deteriorate the response time of the application. In this work, we provide a prototype setup for image processing via Convolutional Neural Networks (CNN) and investigate inference latency and energy consumption of an IoT edge device with a varying wireless link. The complexity of selected pre-trained CNN models is between 300 MFLOPs to 19.6 GFLOPs where FLOPs are Floating Point Operations. The first experiments address the latency and energy consumption by processing CNN models on the IoT device with and without TPU as edge AI accelerator. Following experiments address the latency and energy consumption on the IoT device in cloud processing mode with and without Graphics Processing Unit (GPU) as cloud AI accelerator. The edge device sends input data and receives the results via wireless link from 1 MBit/s to 50 MBit/s. For CNN models with ≤564 MFLOPs edge processing with AI acceleration performs better than cloud processing regarding latency and energy efficiency. Even for complex CNN models with 7.6 GFLOPs edge processing can be useful at limited wireless link data rates up to 14 MBit/s. Edge processing without AI acceleration is only an option for low complexity (≤300 MFLOPs) and low expected wireless link data rates.

Keywords: IoT systems · Artificial Intelligence (AI) · Machine learning · Energy consumption · Inference latency

This work is founded by the Joachim Herz Stiftung.

1   Introduction

Internet of Things (IoT) systems are highly scalable distributed systems [1]. Data acquisition, distribution and processing requirements on latency and efficiency are continuously increasing for portable IoT devices. Due to higher computing power of microcontrollers, deep learning methods like Convolutional Neural Networks (CNN) that are executed directly on the individual IoT device become more relevant in distributed systems [2]. One challenge is, that despite the increased computing power, IoT devices are still limited in computing performance and battery lifetime. To increase the performance current work focuses on combining IoT devices with powerful servers or outsourcing the CNN models completely [3]. While many publications consider the inference time and accuracy in deep learning IoT systems, the energy consumption and the resulting battery lifetime are often neglected [3–5]. However, in IoT systems the connection between IoT devices and a high-performing processor (e.g. a cloud server) is often implemented via a wireless link like wireless LAN IEEE 802.11ac or mobile network 4G/5G. Due to limitations of wireless transmissions in rural areas mainly below 50 MBit/s, resulting longer transfer times and system limitations, the wireless link in combination with the CNN models complexity significantly affects the inference latency and energy consumption in the IoT device [6,7].

The contributions of work from Gaddam et al. and Lane et al. showed that large latency causes malfunctions in applications with strict time constrains and also reduces battery run times [8,9]. Energy efficiency in neural networks is influenced by the number of multiply and accumulate operations (MAC) of the CNN models which were investigated by Rodrigues et al. for a regression model for the prediction of the energy consumption of the jetson nano tx2 [10]. They achieved a relative test accuracy between 76% to 84% for a linear energy estimation model by mere summation of MACs depending on respective CNN models [11]. The measurements by Liu et al. show that the MAC related floating point operations (FLOPs) increase the latency linearly [2]. In research of distributed federated learning systems Yang et al. investigate an algorithm to solve the problem of resource allocation in communication during the learning process of multiple heterogeneous agents [7]. Numerical results show up to 60% reduction of energy consumption compared to conventional federated learning methods. In addition Wang et al. discovered the effect of multi user interaction while super-vector-machine based federated learning and could accomplish an optimized model which was able to reduce the users energy consumption up to 20% depending on the simulation model [6].

However, previous works mainly focus on modeling energy consumption of learning processes or the energy consumption on the IoT device itself. Our work investigates and compares the latency performance of an IoT device with respect to the energy consumption including a wireless link, the processing hardware and the complexity of selected pre-trained CNN models. Our contributions are:

– Prototypical IoT test setup (Hard- and Software) for latency and energy measurements of neural networks in a lightweight heterogeneous system.

- Validated system to measure and compare the latency and energy consumption of applied CNN models in edge and cloud processing modes with and without AI acceleration.
- Investigation of latency and energy consumption of CNN models on IoT devices in edge and cloud processing modes with wireless link.
- The scripts and measurements for download on our project repository[1].

The paper is structured as follows. Section 2 briefly describes our System Setup & Methodology to measure and compare energy consumption and latency of an IoT device in edge and cloud processing mode. In Sect. 3, we present and compare results of measurements between edge and cloud processing and summarize the findings. We conclude the paper and present directions for future work in Sect. 4.

2   System Setup and Methodology

2.1   Hardware

To avoid external influences during measurement like Internet traffic, the system is set up on local hardware. The hardware setup shown in Fig. 1 includes a typical IoT device comprising a Raspberry PI 4 with a CPU Advanced RISC Machines Cortex-A72 (ARM), 8 GB RAM and an edge AI accelerator Tensor Processing Unit (TPU) google Coral. As a typical server setup, we choose a CPU Intel i7-11800H (i7), 16 GB DDR4 RAM and a cloud AI accelerator Graphics Processing Unit (GPU) Nvidia RTX 3070 Mobile and 8 GB GDDR6 RAM.

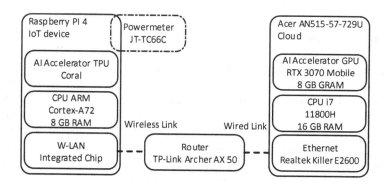

Fig. 1. Overview of the hardware setup.

The wireless link from the IoT device to the cloud is established via the router TP-Link Archer AX 50. The transmission standard is IEEE 802.11ac with 5 GHz band on channel 36 with a channel bandwidth of 40 MHz and a

---

[1] https://www.th-luebeck.de/en/cosa/projekt/pasbadia#cnn-results.

maximum transmission rate of 200 MBit/s. The connection between the wireless router and the server is a direct short cable Ethernet link. A powermeter JT-TC66C measures the energy consumption of the IoT device. The JT-TC66C has a voltage resolution of 0.1 mV at ±0.5% accuracy and a current resolution of 0.01 mA at ±0.1%. The sample rate 2 Hz [12].

2.2 Convolutional Neural Network Models and Classification Patterns

For a fair comparison, we have selected pre-trained standard CNN model graphs from the keras library which are convertible to the TPU according to [13]. The CNN models are pre-trained to the imagenet and have a complexity between 300 MFLOPs and 19.6 GFLOPs (multiply-adds) (Table 1) [14–17].

Table 1. Complexity in FLOPs of selected pre-trained standard CNN model graphs.

Consecutive Number	Parameters	
	Networks	*FLOPs (multiply-adds)*
1	mobilenetv2	$\approx N = 300$ M [15]
2	nasnetmobile	$\approx N = 564$ M [15]
3	resnet50	$\approx N = 3.8$ G [16]
4	resnet101	$\approx N = 7.6$ G [17]
5	vgg16	$\approx N = 15.3$ G [16]
6	vgg19	$\approx N = 19.6$ G [16]

Figure 2 visualizes how models are adapted and prepared for the hardware before the measurements. The cloud processing on the i7 and GPU is executed with frozen CNN models and full precision float32 values. For the edge processing on the ARM, a uint8-bit fixed post-training quantization is applied to the frozen CNN models for fairness. Post-training quantization converts CNN models to reduce model size while improving the CPU ARM latency without compromising model accuracy [18,19]. The TPU classifications are executed with further converted uint8-bit fixed edge-tpu CNN models for compatibility [20,21]. For classification, we select a subset from the imagenet resized to $224 \times 224 \times 3$ byte per image. The resulting average size of an image is about 150 kByte.

2.3 Measurements

The measurements are split into four experiments. The first experiments address the latency and energy consumption of the IoT device by processing CNN models at the edge with (EwA) and without (EwoA) edge AI acceleration.

Following experiments address the latency and energy consumption of the IoT device by processing CNN models in the cloud with (CwA) and without (CwoA)

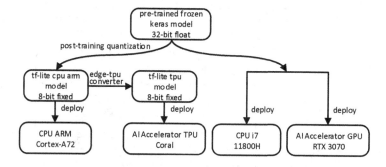

Fig. 2. Quantization and deployment of CNN models [20].

cloud AI acceleration including the data transfer via wireless link. To emulate different quality of the wireless link, data rates are configured via software. The measurements are compared to assess the impact of the data rate and complexity of the processed CNN models to the IoT devices latency and energy consumption. The selected hardware of the experimental is listed in Table 2.

Table 2. Hardware for edge and cloud processing experiments.

Processing Modes (with/without AI acceleration)	IoT Device		Link	Server	
	CPU	Accel.		CPU	Accel.
	ARM	TPU	WLAN	i7	GPU
Edge w.o. Accel. (EwoA)	Pre+**CNN**+Post	–	–	–	–
Edge w. Accel. (EwA)	Pre+Post	**CNN**	–	–	–
Cloud w.o. Accel. (CwoA)	Pre+Post	–	Trans	Pre+**CNN**+Post	–
Cloud w. Accel. (CwA)	Pre+Post	–	Trans	Pre+Post	**CNN**

Edge Processing. The latency and energy measurements for edge processing include the CNN models inference (**CNN**) and the pre- and post-processing steps (loading of image data and extraction of classification) as shown in Fig. 3.

In EwoA mode the CPU ARM runs pre- and post-processing as well as inference of the **CNN**. In EwA the CPU ARM runs pre- and post-processing only. The inference of **CNN** is executed on the AI accelerator TPU.

Cloud Processing. The cloud processing measurements include the CNN models inference (CNN) and the pre- and postprocessing steps loading, decoding, encoding and transmission of the image data via WLAN from the IoT device to the cloud as illustrated in Fig. 4.

In accordance with typical transmission rates in mobile networks, we analyze the latency and energy consumption with alternating data rates between 1 MBit/s and 50 MBit/s [22].

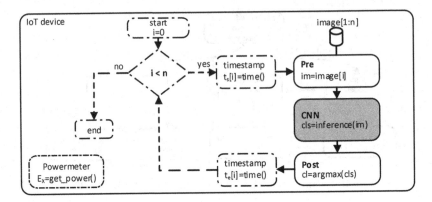

Fig. 3. Flow Diagram of measurements for edge processing with and without acceleration: Inference latency and energy consumption of the IoT device.

In cloud processing without AI acceleration (CwoA), the edge device CPU ARM and server CPU i7 perform the pre- and post-processing and the CNN is executed on the server CPU i7. In cloud processing with AI acceleration (CwA) the CNN is executed on the server GPU.

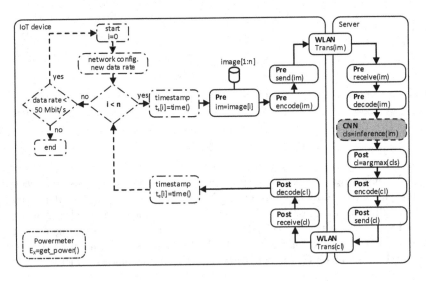

Fig. 4. Flow diagram of measurements for cloud processing with and without acceleration: Inference latency and energy consumption of the IoT device.

Method. In the experiment environments EwoA, CwoA and CwA the measurements are repeated with $n = 100$ images. Due to the fast inference times of the

TPU by executing CNN models with $\leq$564 MFLOPs, the experiment EwA is repeated with $n = 500$ images for more precise measurements. The mean latency t_X per image classification, comprising the pre-, post-processing and inference time of the CNN, is calculated with

$$\bar{t}_X = \frac{1}{n} \sum_{i=1}^{n} t_{e_i} - t_{s_i} \tag{1}$$

which is the mean time difference between the classifications start t_{s_i} and end t_{e_i} time. Afterwords, the energy consumption $\overline{E}_X$ per image classification is estimated with (2), where $\overline{P}_{idle}$ is the constant measured power in idle mode:

$$\overline{E}_X \approx \frac{\bar{t}_x}{(t_{e_n} - t_{s_1})} \int_{t_{s_1}}^{t_{e_n}} (P(t) - \overline{P}_{idle})dt \tag{2}$$

3 Results

We performed the measurements in the following order: First, we compare latency and energy consumption in the edge processing mode with and without AI acceleration. We expect that the acceleration decreases the inference latency and we presume a reduced energy consumption. Secondly, we compare cloud processing with different data rates of WLAN. We expect that with higher complexity of the neural network characterized by FLOPs, cloud processing gains an advantage over edge computing in terms of latency and energy consumption.

3.1 Edge Processing

The measurements show that the latency of edge processing with AI acceleration is in the range between 5.6 ms at 300 MFLOPs and 445 ms at 19.6 GFLOPs and significantly smaller than the case of processing without acceleration which is between 84.5 ms and 2590 ms. The energy consumption is proportional to the latency in the system and is in the range between 14.4 mJ at 300 MFLOPs and 1190 mJ at 19.6 GFLOPs with acceleration and between 91.5 mJ and 2980 mJ without acceleration, respectively.

The advantage in acceleration is higher the fewer FLOPs the CNN model includes and reduces from 15 times at 300 MFLOPs to 5.8 times at 19.6 GFLOPs with a minimum of 4.8 times at 15.3 GFLOPs. The ratio of latency without acceleration vs with acceleration decreases from 6.35 at 300 MFLOPs to 2.5 at 19.6 GFLOPs where the minimum ratio 2.1 is obtained as 15.3 GFLOPs. We assume, that the anomaly between 15.3 GFLOPs and 19.6 GFLOPs depends on the CNN graph structure which provides a slight advantage of the TPU processing against the CPU ARM processing.

With AI acceleration the benefit for energy consumption is less than for the latency because the TPU increases the power consumption by $\approx 2\ W$ compared to ARM only.

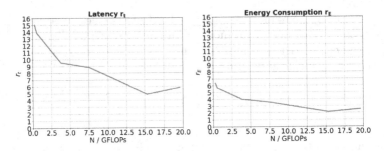

Fig. 5. Advantage of AI acceleration for latency $r_t = \frac{\bar{t}_{EwoA}}{\bar{t}_{EwA}}$ and energy consumption $r_E = \frac{\bar{E}_{EwoA}}{\bar{E}_{EwA}}$ in edge processing mode with respect to the FLOPs N.

3.2   Cloud Processing

In cloud processing mode, the measurement of the latency $\bar{t}_X$ and energy consumption $\bar{E}_X$ of the IoT device is performed in the same way. Additionally, latency for image classification includes the transfer time from the edge device to the cloud server plus en- and decoding. Before performing measurements, we first characterize the influence of the network configuration.

The influence of the networks idle latency on the CNN inference latency is measured by sending 1 byte to the server and receiving a 2 byte answer. The latency is the round trip time on the application layer for messages. The value is about 3 ms at 50 MBit/s and 7 ms at 1 MBit/s per message. The additional round trip time is acceptable compared to the margin between CwoA and CwA characteristics in later measurements as we expect total latency values in the range of hundreds of milliseconds.

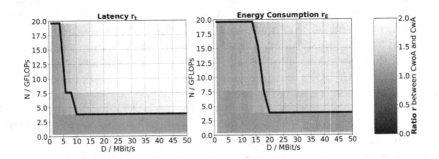

Fig. 6. The right side of the solid line shows the advantage of AI acceleration in cloud processing mode with respect to the FLOPs N and data rate D. (Color figure online)

In cloud processing with and without AI acceleration, we expect an improvement in latency and energy consumption with AI acceleration at higher WLAN data rates and more complex CNN. We choose 3D plots with a color code to visualize the results as rotated 3D plots were hard to interpret. The measurements in Fig. 6 compare the latency $\bar{t}_{CwoA}$, $\bar{t}_{CwA}$ and energy characteristics $\overline{E}_{CowA}$, $\overline{E}_{CwA}$ of the IoT device between CwoA and CwA. The solid line indicates at which data rate CwA is more efficient. At very slow data rates of the WLAN, there is no improvement regardless of neural network complexity. The transmission delay is the main portion of the latency and energy consumption of about 1.3 s and 350 mJ. At faster data rates, starting with 2 Mbit/s, acceleration improves efficiency with more complex CNNs. In terms of latency CwA with 56 ms is 2.75 times faster compared to CwoA with 160 ms and 1.75 times more efficient (43 mJ vs. 79 mJ) at 19.6 GFLOPs.

3.3 Edge Versus Cloud Processing

To evaluate the performance of latency and energy consumption of the IoT device depending on transmission rate, processing mode and CNN models complexity, the relative ratio of the measured values from Sect. 3.1 or Sect. 3.2 is calculated as a function of the data rate D and the FLOPs N with (3) and (4), where $\bar{t}$ represents the latency measurement value and $\overline{E}$ represents the energy value.

$$r_t(D) = \frac{\bar{t}_{cloud}(D)}{\bar{t}_{edge}} \tag{3}$$

$$r_E(D) = \frac{\overline{E}_{cloud}(D)}{\overline{E}_{edge}} \tag{4}$$

Cross validation results for EwoA and EwA versus CwoA and CwA are shown in Fig. 7 and Fig. 8 with respect to latency and energy consumption, respectively. The brighter region points (yellow) to the superiority of edge processing mode, but the darker region (red) emphasizes the preference for cloud processing mode separated by the solid black line.

At low data rates $D = 1$ Mbit/s and $N = 300$ MFLOPs the ARM (EwoA) ratio measurements r_t and r_E show, that the edge processing is at least 15 times faster in latency and three times more efficient in terms of energy consumption than the cloud processing modes CwoA and CwA. With a rising data rate D, the advantage reduces significantly. At a data rate D above 28 Mbit/s, the latency $\bar{t}_{EwoA}$ and at data rates D above 14 Mbit/s the energy consumption $\overline{E}_{EwoA}$ is higher at the edge compared to the cloud processing location. If N is larger than 7.6 GFLOPs the EwoA latency performance is worst compared to cloud processing, in terms of energy consumption cloud processing gets more efficient at $N = 3.8$ GFLOPs.

With acceleration by a TPU (EwA) the ratio measurements r_t and r_E show that the edge processing is up to 230 times faster and 23 times more efficient at slow data rates $D < 1$ Mbit/s than in cloud processing (CwoA and CwA). With increasing data rate D, the advantage reduces but edge processing EwA remains faster and more efficient at $N \leq 564$ MFLOPs than cloud processing. Furthermore, the latency $\bar{t}_{EwA}$ up to $N = 7.6$ GFLOPs and $D = 14$ Mbit/s and the energy consumption $\overline{E}_{EwA}$ up to $N = 3.8$ GFLOPs and $D = 4$ Mbit/s is better on edge processing with acceleration (EwA).

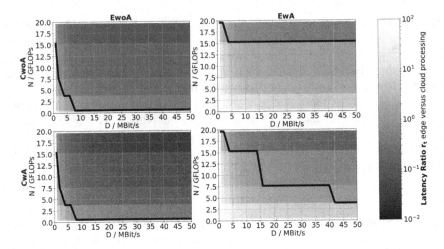

Fig. 7. The left side of the solid line shows the advantage in latency $\bar{t}$ in edge processing mode versus cloud processing mode. (Color figure online)

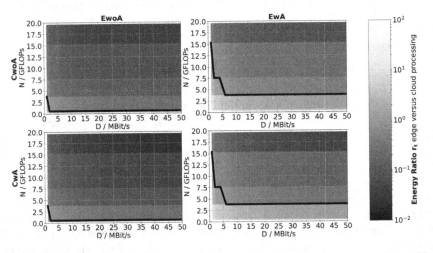

Fig. 8. The left side of the solid line shows the advantage in energy consumption $\bar{E}$ in edge processing mode versus cloud processing mode. (Color figure online)

4   Conclusion and Future Work

In this work, a test system was developed for the examination of latency and energy consumption of CNNs for IoT systems with edge and cloud processing with and without AI acceleration. The investigation results allow for decisions based on the data rate of a wireless link and the complexity in FLOPs of CNN models. The results show that processing CNN models on IoT devices through optimized hardware such as a TPU has latency and power advantages for low complexity CNNs. However, these benefits decrease with increasing complexity and decreasing data rate. When processing the CNN models in the cloud via low data rate wireless links the wireless link dominates the latency and energy consumption. At higher data rates starting with 2 MBit/s cloud processing with acceleration is more efficient than without acceleration when processing complex CNN models with more FLOPs.

For CNN models with less than 564 MFLOPs, edge processing with AI accelerator performs better than the cloud processing solutions. Even for more complex networks with 7.6 GFLOPs edge processing is useful at limited network speeds up to 14 MBit/s. Edge processing without AI accelerator performs better than the cloud processing solutions at low data rates and a small number of FLOPs namely below 300 MFLOPs.

In future, we will start the development of a productive IoT system in a distributed AI medical application based on smartphones with the achieved knowledge. In future work, we will also consider an estimation model of the energy consumption on the wireless link in order to decide at runtime which processing is more appropriate for each situation.

Acknowledgements. This publication results from the research of the Center of Excellence CoSA at the Technische Hochschule Lübeck and is funded by the Joachim Herz Stiftung in the joint project PASBADIA, Germany. Horst Hellbrück is an adjunct professor at the Institute of Telematics of University of Lübeck.

References

1. Figueredo, K., Seed, D., Subotic, V.: Preparing for highly scalable and replicable IoT systems. IEEE Internet of Things Mag. **3**, 94–98 (2020)
2. Liu, D., Kong, H., Luo, X., Liu, W., Subramaniam, R.: Bringing AI to Edge: from deep learning's perspective. Neurocomputing (2021)
3. Cheng, C.-Y.: et al.: Design of a feeding system for cage aquaculture based on IoT and AI technology. In: 2021 International Symposium on Intelligent Signal Processing and Communication Systems (ISPACS). IEEE (2021)
4. Chin, T.-W., Ding, R., Zhang, C., Marculescu, D.: Towards efficient model compression via learned global ranking. In: 2020 IEEE/CVF Conference on Computer Vision and Pattern Recognition (CVPR). IEEE (2020)
5. Ahmad, R.W., Gani, A., Hamid, S.H.A., Xia, F., Shiraz, M.: A review on mobile application energy profiling: taxonomy, state-of-the-art, and open research issues. J. Netw. Comput. Appl. **58**, 42–59 (2015)
6. Wang, S., Chen, M., Saad, W., Yin, C.: Federated learning for energy-efficient task computing in wireless networks. In: ICC 2020–2020 IEEE International Conference on Communications (ICC). IEEE (2020)
7. Yang, Z., Chen, M., Saad, W., Hong, C.S., Shikh-Bahaei, M.: Energy efficient federated learning over wireless communication networks. IEEE Trans. Wireless Commun. **20**, 1935–1949 (2021)
8. Gaddam, A., Wilkin, T., Angelova, M., Gaddam, J.: Detecting sensor faults, anomalies and outliers in the Internet of Things: a survey on the challenges and solutions. Electronics **9**, 511 (2020)

9. Lane, N.D., Bhattacharya, S., Georgiev, P., Forlivesi, C., Kawsar, F.: An early resource characterization of deep learning on wearables, smartphones and Internet-of-Things devices. In: Proceedings of the 2015 International Workshop on Internet of Things towards Applications. ACM (2015)

10. Rodrigues, C., Graham, R., Mikel, L.: SyNERGY: An energy measurement and prediction framework for convolutional neural networks on Jetson TX1. In: Proceedings of the International Conference on Parallel and Distributed Processing Techniques and Applications. PDPTA (2018)

11. Rodrigues, C.F., Riley, G., Lujan, M.: Energy predictive models for convolutional neural networks on mobile platforms (2020)

12. Joy-IT, JT-TC66C. Datasheet (2021). https://joy-it.net/de/products/JT-TC66C. Accessed 05 Apr 2022

13. keras, Keras applications - available models. Website (2022). https://keras.io/api/applications/. Accessed 17 Mar 2022

14. Deng, J., Dong, W., Socher, R., Li, L.-J., Li, K., Fei-Fei, L.: ImageNet: A large-scale hierarchical image database. In: 2009 IEEE Conference on Computer Vision and Pattern Recognition. IEEE (2009)

15. Tan, M., Le, Q.V., MixConv: mixed depthwise convolutional kernels BMVC. arXiv preprint arXiv:1907.09595 (2019)

16. He, K., Zhang, X., Ren, S., Sun, J.: Deep residual learning for image recognition. In: 2016 IEEE Conference on Computer Vision and Pattern Recognition (CVPR). IEEE (2016)

17. Cao, K., Gao, J., Choi, K.-N., Duan, L.: Learning a hierarchical global attention for image classification. Future Internet 12, 178 (2020)

18. Jiang, H., Li, Q., Li, Y.: Post training quantization after neural network. In: 2022 14th International Conference on Computer Research and Development (ICCRD). IEEE (2022)

19. Ignatov, A., Malivenko, G., et al.: Fast and accurate quantized camera scene detection on smartphones, mobile AI 2021 challenge: Report. In: 2021 IEEE/CVF Conference on Computer Vision and Pattern Recognition Workshops (CVPRW). IEEE (2021)

20. Google, Tensorflow models on the edge TPU (2020). https://coral.ai/docs/edgetpu/models-intro/. Accessed 27 Jan 2022

21. Natarov, R., et al.: Artefacts in EEG signals epileptic seizure prediction using edge devices. In: 2020 9th Mediterranean Conference on Embedded Computing (MECO). IEEE (2020)

22. Cisco Systems, Cisco annual internet report. Statistic (2018). www.cisco.com/c/en/us/solutions/collateral/executive-perspectives/annual-internet-report/white-paper-c11-741490.pdf. Accessed 05 Apr 2022

Industry-Academia Cooperation: Applied IoT Research for SMEs in South-East Sweden

Arslan Musaddiq[1], Neda Maleki[1], Francis Palma[1], Tobias Olsson[1],
Daniel Toll[1], David Mozart[1], Mustafa Omareen[1], Johan Leitet[1],
John Jeansson[2], and Fredrik Ahlgren[1]([✉])

[1] Applied IoT Lab, Department of Computer Science and Media Technology,
Linnaeus University, Växjö, Sweden
fredrik.ahlgren@lnu.se
[2] Department of Organisation and Entrepreneurship,
Linnaeus University, Växjö, Sweden

Abstract. This paper presents the activities of the **Applied IoT Lab**
at the Department of Computer Science and Media Technology, Linnaeus University (LNU), Kalmar, Sweden. The lab is actively engaged
in IoT-based educational programs, including a series of workshops and
pilot cases. The lab is funded by the European Union and two Swedish
counties – Kalmar and Kronoberg. The workshops and pilot cases are
part of the research project named IoT Lab for Small and Medium-sized
Enterprises (SMEs). One of the lab's main objectives is to strengthen
and support local companies with IoT. The project IoT Lab for SMEs
also aims to spread knowledge and inspire the local community about
the possibilities of using IoT technologies by organizing open lab days,
in-depth lectures, and seminars. This paper introduces Applied IoT Lab
at LNU, its educational programs, and industry-academic cooperation,
including workshops and a number of ongoing pilot cases.

Keywords: IoT · SME · Pilot cases

1 Introduction

Internet of Things (IoT) is one of the prospective technologies that is predicted
to affect a large number of business models. IoT unifies the physical and digital
worlds and allows controlling the things around us while keeping us updated on
the state of the environment [1]. The main idea of IoT is to provide communication between various devices, apparatuses, and other hardware without human
intervention. Besides, it presents easy access to various information through
enhanced connections within a worldwide network scale. Considering the aforementioned potential benefits, Linnaeus University (LNU) in Sweden has founded
a state-of-the-art Applied IoT Lab [2]. The objectives of this laboratory are to
facilitate applied IoT research, disseminate IoT knowledge among society, and

A. González-Vidal et al. (Eds.): GIoTS 2022, LNCS 13533, pp. 397–410, 2022.
https://doi.org/10.1007/978-3-031-20936-9_32

solve real-world problems by creating a close relationship between higher education and small and medium-sized enterprises (SMEs).

In this era, wireless communication has been considered one of the important aspects of economic growth [3]. Considering the importance of wireless communication, numerous countries are investing time, effort, and money into the growth of the future information and communication technology (ICT) industry. Many countries around the globe established research centers to contribute to the betterment of the world through ICT [4]. Apart from this, it is also important to spread the IoT knowledge into society by creating a close relationship between higher education institutions and industry. Sweden, as one of the dominating ICT countries with the largest ICT sector in the Nordic region, creates numerous business opportunities by converging with more diverse industrial fields [1]. Sweden is actively participating in promoting convergence of industry to introduce a new era like the IoT [5].

IoT is a broad area and generally refers to things that can be connected to the Internet to make our lives easier in many ways. Examples include smart locks, smart scales, smart home appliances such as coffee machines, and so on [6]. Apart from daily-life personal use items, companies and industries leveraging on IoT to automate or simplify the processes to save cost/time and reduce waste [7]. In the long run, at the industrial scale, IoT has the potential to lower consumer goods prices and improve the overall economy of the countries. Similarly, the technological change led by IoT supports sustainability by minimizing energy consumption, reducing waste, and bringing automation to optimize the use of natural resources [8]. According to a World Economic Forum report, around 85% of IoT deployments are addressing the sustainability goals [9].

At present, there is a wide array of activities in Sweden relating to sustainable development at the national, regional, and local levels of government. Besides, there are myriad different environments and sustainable development initiatives in various contexts within Sweden. The importance of sustainability is not beyond question [10]. Sustainability improves the quality of our lives, protects our ecosystem, and preserves natural resources for future generations. Going green and sustainable is not only beneficial for the companies, but it also maximizes the benefits from an environmental focus in the long-term [11].

According to the European Commission, the approach to distinguish small and medium-sized enterprises (SMEs) from large businesses is based on quantitative and qualitative indicators, which mostly refer to the number of employees and characteristics of management, respectively [12]. Thus, there is no unique, universally accepted definition for SMEs. In the project and local context, the definition of an SME is a company with a number of employees less than 250 people, and that accounts for more than 90% of companies in the region. In order for IoT to secure the future of SMEs, promising and best practices need to be made visible, the level of knowledge increased, and experiments carried out. SMEs need to be aware of the benefits of IoT and adopt such solutions with priority to achieve sustainable growth of their businesses [13].

The Applied IoT Lab at LNU has also established a close collaboration with both Kalmar Energy (https://kalmarenergi.se) and Wexnet (https://wexnet.se),

Table 1. Regions, Municipalities, and Number of People [14].

Region	Municipalities	Population	Region	Municipalities	Population
Kalmar Län	Kalmar	69,467	Kronoberg	Alvesta	20,134
	Västervik	36,679		Lessebo	8,733
	Vimmerby	15,647		Ljungby	28,521
	Hultsfred	14,224		Markaryd	10,320
	Oskarshamn	27,102		Tingsryd	12,393
	Högsby	5,921		Uppvidinge	9,588
	Mönsterås	13,430		Växjö	94,129
	Borgholm	10,839		älmhult	17,651
	Nybro	20,318			
	Emmaboda	9,445			
	Torsås	7,125			
	Mörbylänga	15,249			
Total		245,446	Total		201,469

which are local companies providing IoT-infrastructure in Kalmar and Växjö with an extensive experience from the infrastructure perspective. During the project, companies in the Kalmar and Kronoberg region will be given the opportunity to deepen their knowledge linked to IoT: *What can you do with IoT? How do you do it?* To achieve these goals, the Applied IoT Lab has initiated a number of pilot cases and workshops at LNU. In this paper, we introduce regional innovation at the Applied IoT Lab, its educational programs, workshops, and pilot cases. The objective of this paper is to provide characteristics of the IoT lab in terms of educational activities and industrial cooperation.

The rest of the paper is organized as follows. Section 2 introduces the Applied IoT Lab; Sect. 3 focuses on highlighting education and industrial-academic cooperation activities in detail, while Sect. 4 provides lessons learned, and Sect. 5 concludes the paper.

2   The Applied IoT Lab

The Applied IoT Lab started as an outcome of a series of IoT workshop activities that was organised at LNU together with the local energy company Kalmar Energi in 2018. LNU has two campuses in Kalmar (Kalmar county) and Växjö (Kronoberg county). Hence, in this paper, we introduce a number of pilot cases initiated by the Applied IoT Lab in these counties with a goal of sustainability. For the reader's perspective, the list of municipalities and their population sizes in the two counties are shown in Table 1 [14].

The activity 'pilot cases' is a part of the research project IoT lab for SMEs, funded by the European Union and two Swedish counties, Kalmar and Kronoberg. In order to strengthen small companies that today are not using IoT, they are in need of support for testing and evaluating their ideas. One challenge is that there is an overwhelming amount of different design choices in both the architecture and hardware within IoT. For a company that has not yet started working with IoT, there is a need for support early in the process. There is also a broad number of applications that can be applied to current business processes, which makes it a challenge for a company to see the added value.

The Applied IoT Lab located in Kalmar is equipped with state-of-the-art IoT devices and hardware. The lab has a number of Pycom (https://pycom. io) development boards, including Fipy, Lopy4, Gpy, and Wipy 3.0, along with expansion boards such as Pysense, Pyscan, etc. The lab is also equipped with various other microcontrollers including all types of Raspberry Pi and Arduinos. In addition, the lab contains number of sensors, from basic temperature sensors to more complex industrial sensors. Other hardware includes different kinds of components such as motors, cameras, RAK boards, LoRaWAN gateways, solar panels, and so on. Wireless communication technologies, such as WiFi, Bluetooth Low Energy (BLE), Zigbee, Long-Term Evolution (LTE), Long Range (LoRa), and SigFox are currently employed by IoT lab for different applications based on the range, coverage, bandwidth, power consumption, and cost criteria.

3   Education and Industry-Academic Cooperation

The importance of industry-academic cooperation and its impact on regional innovation has been widely acknowledged across the world. Considering the international competition and advancing technological landscape, the European Union have been continuously encouraging industry-academic cooperation to improve regional and international innovation, as well as wealth creation [14]. The Swedish government, including local municipalities, also supports collaboration between academia and industry [15].

IoT has emerged as one of the strongest wireless networking paradigms in the twenty-first century, attracting a wide range of research interests. As the area of IoT is broad and cross-disciplinary, the focus of Applied IoT Lab, from the research and implementation perspective, is on the end-user application and actual use of IoT. The use of IoT in the industrial sector is growing as new services and software are created and implemented around the world [6]. Considering the impact of this ongoing transition, LNU, together with Applied IoT Lab, actively promotes industry-academic cooperation through a number of IoT-based pilot cases. The Applied IoT Lab is carrying out detailed research-oriented tasks and graduate-led creative initiatives for industrial-academic cooperation, mainly in the form of applied projects and workshops.

There is a track record of many different applied projects as an outcome of university courses at the engineering programs in software engineering and computer engineering, also from a yearly distance summer course in applied IoT that is open for applicants from all over the world [16]. In the last two years, several IoT-related projects have been done in close collaboration with the industry, such as digital bee-hives and crowd avoidance in transport [17,18].

3.1   Workshops

The project IoT lab for SMEs organises various skill-enhancing activities to increase IoT competence among SMEs. These activities include lectures, open lab days, and workshops. Such programs are normally divided into two parts. During the first half of the day, in-depth theoretical knowledge is presented, and for the rest of the day, companies are given the opportunity to test their ideas to develop a simple IoT-enabled solution. The in-depth lecture and seminars could be on the topic of IoT hardware and software, product commercialization, ecosystems, sustainability, and business models.

The lab also organizes open lab days to test or develop ideas for educational purposes. The companies in the Linnaeus region in Kalmar, Sweden, together with LNU students and researchers, test their ideas. IoT lab also organizes more formal, detailed workshops with companies where LNU researchers and faculty members work with the companies side by side. The workshops are held physically in place or virtually, depending on the company's invocation, and the sessions are divided into three parts:

- Short introduction to the project and IoT.
- Hands-on activities, where participants learn to connect sensors, program cutting edge hardware, send and visualise sensor data.
- Debugging, troubleshooting, and open discussion.

Some SMEs are interested in IoT basics, while others prefer to work with and read data from the application-specific hardware. In basic workshops, participants learn how to connect a (temperature) sensor to a micro-controller and send the data using LoRaWAN. In cases where LoRaWAN coverage is unavailable, participants use WiFi mostly during virtual workshops.

When planning workshops, the company's business type is taken into consideration. Some companies are only interested in how data can be extracted from their existing systems and sent to the cloud. Other companies with a non-concrete idea, however, participate for inspiration.

3.2   Pilot Cases

The lab established an innovation ecosystem in the Linnaeus region in Sweden by providing technical guidance, consultation, and recommendation for the development of SMEs through IoT. A limited number of SMEs were adopted/admitted as pilot cases within the project.

As a pilot case, an SME is subjected to two main processes. The first has an IoT-technology development focus, where IoT lab researchers and engineers work together with SMEs in order to identify and connect their IoT initiative with relevant hardware and software. The second process has an IoT-business model development focus, where researchers from the School of Business and Economics at Linnaeus University come alongside each pilot case in order to facilitate a discussion on how to create and capture the potential business value of their IoT initiative. This process has two parts. The first part takes place

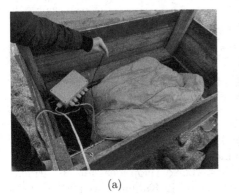 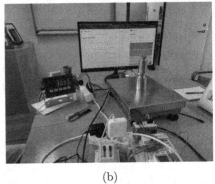

(a)   (b)

Fig. 1. (a) Traditional beehive with Raspberry Pi connected sensors; and (b) An RS-485 enabled scale sending data using LoRaWAN to The Things Network and Datacake.

as soon as an SME is accepted as a pilot case. Its objective is to discuss why the company pursues an IoT initiative and how they perceive potential benefits, competitiveness, and innovation processes. SMEs are also asked to assess their digital transformation readiness during this first part. The second part takes place when SMEs reach the end of their pilot case journey within the IoT lab. The objective is to have a discussion regarding SME's management experience as they navigated impacts, outcomes, and challenges in order to achieve a successful IoT initiative. Discussions are made in light of, and related to, business model frameworks. When SMEs end their time as pilot cases and wish to commercialize the IoT lab recommended solution, they are free to invest and fund any further development.

In the following, we provide an overview of all the pilot cases initiated by the Applied IoT Lab.

Beelab: Beelab Technology Sweden AB (www.beelab.se) develops and manufactures products and services for digitally connected beehives. The objective of Beelab Technology is to introduce eco-friendly communication technology to monitor the bees population and honey production. A sustainable digital beekeeping solution is expected to offer better beehives observation and monitoring.

The company is currently utilizing a Raspberry Pi acting as a gateway to connect sensors to the beehives. Such a system depends on a continuous source of power along with a number of cables. The sensors of interest include weight, temperature, air pressure, and humidity sensors. The company aims to provide battery-powered wireless-communication-based connected hives solutions throughout Sweden. The company also aims to use cutting-edge sensors which can provide additional added value for beekeepers, researchers, and authorities. The Applied IoT Lab developed an energy-efficient wireless connected hives solution using Fipy (pycom.io/product/fipy/) development board which provides five communication modules, i.e., WiFi, BLE, LoRa, SigFox, and dual LTE (CAT-

M1 and NB-IoT). For a long-range battery-operated wireless infrastructure, we propose to utilize LTE CAT-M1 or NB-IoT.

LTE CAT-M1 and NB-IoT use a simplified version of the fourth generation (4G) mobile communication standard, which reduces hardware complexity and cost when the technology is used on a larger scale. LTE CAT-M1 offers better coverage than 4G in, for example, indoor environments and remote locations. LTE CAT-M1 also provides enabling over-the-air (OTA) updates so that IoT devices can continue to update securely for many years. The Fipy boards can be connected to the Pycom expansion board to program the devices. A traditional beehive with Raspberry Pi-based connected sensors is shown in Fig. 1a.

The Fipy acts as a gateway, and a number of sensors with different serial protocols are connected to it, which can go into the power-saving mode or connect less frequently to the network. The data is transmitted each interval via Telia sim card[1]. The devices use constrained application protocol (CoAP). The developed product has been transferred to Beelab technology company and the researchers for the continuity of research and development in this field.

Svenska Våg: Svenska Våg AB (www.svenskavag.com) is one of the main manufacturers and suppliers of weighing machines in Sweden. The company works with everything in weighing, from loose components such as load cells, weighing platforms, and weighing instruments, to advanced weighing systems for manual or automatic weighing/dosing.

The company wants to connect the weighing machine to the Internet for the customers who want to see the weight value without being physically present at the weighing instrument. Figure 1b shows an RS-485 enabled scale sending data using LoRaWAN to The Things Network (https://www.thethingsnetwork.org/) and Datacake (https://datacake.co/).

Sometimes customers need weighing at stations and places that are remote. They can be in hard-to-reach environments or places with no access to the Internet. Examples can be with customers who have one/several silos/containers outdoor for storage of materials. They sometimes need to check and update themselves on how much content is left in the container. In a simple way, monitoring the weight, e.g., via a smartphone, is an option.

The Applied IoT Lab is working to develop a long-range communication mechanism using LPWAN RS485 bridge (https://www.rakwireless.com/). The current setup consists of multiple types of load cells where all the cells use one common communication channel, i.e., Modbus RS485-based protocol. The proposed solution uses Modbus LoRaWAN bridge and the approach of using RS485 instead of TCP/IP is to remove the access point dependency.

QTF: QTF Sweden AB (www.qtf.se) works to ensure that all plumbing systems have system fluid that allows the systems to work energy efficiently, without malfunctions, and without rusting. The company works to identify the status of system fluid, for example, oxygen, pH, pressure, and conductivity level of fluid. The company monitors the fluid system at the facilities, which might be located 30–50 km away from the head office in Kalmar city. To save time and travel costs,

---

[1] https://www.telia.se/.

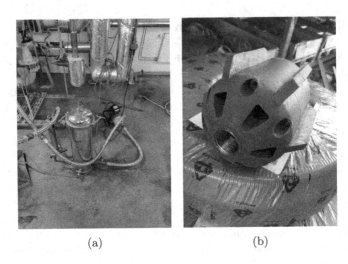

(a)   (b)

Fig. 2. (a) The tube used for filtering heating system liquid; and (b) AquaTeq nozzle for sewage cleaning.

the company aims to have a mechanism that monitors the fluid systems and transmits the information wirelessly, i.e., geographically independent of where the facility is located.

The company is currently measuring three properties: deviation in the magnetic field in a circulation pump, CO_2 levels from a top dehumidifier, and liquid pressure in a filter tube. The deviation in the magnetic field is in the electrical control panel. The monitoring of these values is done in three different stages. The first stage is monitoring the deviation in the magnetic field for approximately two weeks, i.e., if the circulation pump is spinning or not. The second stage is to monitor the CO_2 levels from the top dehumidifier. The third and final stage is to monitor the liquid pressure in the filter tube. It is critical to shut down the system during the first stage if the circulation pump stops. This is done by sending a signal to the PLC. Figure 2a shows the filter tube used by QTF for filtering heating system fluid.

The lab proposes using a Pycom Fipy and a sensor fit for each stage. In the first stage, i.e., when monitoring deviations in the magnetic field, the data is sent from the Fipy to the PLC using Modbus TCP/IP. Data will be transmitted to a remote server using NB-IoT in the remaining two stages. The proposed solution introduces flexibility in terms of mobility.

AquaTeq Sweden AB: When maintaining sewage and stormwater systems, it is a great advantage to know the conditions in and around the nozzle or equipment that unplugs it using high-pressure water. AquaTeq Sweden AB (https:// aquateq.com/) started in 1986 to develop the cleaning nozzles better and faster than its competitors. However, monitoring the operating condition where the target is a 100 mm diameter and up to 150 m long pipe located approximately

Fig. 3. PM & Vänner CPWplus-75 scale.

10m underground is challenging. Figure 2b shows a nozzle that AquaTeq uses for sewage cleaning.

The Applied IoT Lab proposes to initiate the project with an experiment to evaluate LoRa 433 MHz and NB-IoT. In cases where one or both technologies prove to be reliable, AquaTeq may consider integrating sensors into their nozzles. A wireless solution can enable AquaTeq to (1) Reduce water consumption: each flushing nozzle consumes a certain number of liters per minute; (2) Reduce operating time: operators are not immediately aware of potential obstacles such as tree roots, and continuously feeding the hose, resulting in a waste of time; and (3) Reduce diesel consumption: to get water under pressure requires a certain speed on the engine as in turn drives the purge pump, an average cleaning truck consumes between 25–50 l of diesel per hour.

PM & Vänner: PM & Vänner (https://pmrestauranger.se/en/) is a hotel and restaurant group in Växjö, Sweden. In a restaurant environment, food waste is one of the major problems. Environmental impact and sustainability are also related to food waste issues. Reducing food waste in various ways is a priority issue where restaurants need to work broadly and where measuring food waste has proven to be an important factor. Knowing the amount of food that is wasted would be a basis for discussion and motivation for taking appropriate action. The food wastage problems can be solved with the help of current technology, such as IoT.

The Applied IoT Lab is helping PM & Vänner with environmental sustainability by reducing food wastage. The lab proposes two different prototypes: one is based on a load cell driver, load cell amplifier, Raspberry Pi touch interface, and a web service such as Node-RED (https://nodered.org). The load cells are connected to an OpenScale breakout board, which is an easy-to-use board for measuring weight from load cells. The second approach leverages the company's existing scale (CPWplus-75) and reads the weighing measurements through the

(a)   (b)

Fig. 4. (a) Distance Sensor (LDDS75) at Kalmar Dämme; and (b) Wireless Micro-weather Station and Wireless Wind Station at Kalmar Dämme.

RS232 interface. For data visualization, the lab proposes the use of a low-code IoT platform such as Datacake. Figure 3 shows the PWplus-75 scale connected to an IoT device.

Flowbic: Kalmar Dämme has a total water area of about 18 hectares [19]. Through a unique collaboration between the Swedish Civil Aviation Administration and Kalmar Municipality, a large part of nitrogen and phosphorus, which would otherwise be added to the Western Lake (a bay of the Baltic Sea), can be removed in the landscaped wetland park Kalmar Dämme. It is nature's own purification plant, where a whole series of natural processes take place that reduces the nitrogen and phosphorus levels [20].

Therefore, at Kalmar Dämme, there is a need for different measurements, e.g., water properties (level, conductivity, O_2, and pressure) and weather conditions (pressure, CO_2, wind speed, and wind direction). Today, manual collection and compilation of data is time-consuming and results in long intervals between data points. Flowbic is a private web agency that provides digital services. The company aims to automate and facilitate the data measurements and compilation to save time and resources and shorten the intervals between the measurements by providing more data between intervals. For data collection, the IoT lab and Flowbic installed several sensors at Kalmar Dämme.

These sensors include an LDDS75 distance sensor model, a DL-CTD10 pressure, liquid level, temperature, and electrical conductivity sensor model, a DL-LP8P temperature, humidity, CO_2, and barometric pressure sensor model, a DL-OPTOD optical dissolved oxygen and temperature sensor model, a DL-PM particulate matter, temperature, humidity, and barometric pressure sensor model, a wireless micro-weather station with World Meteorological Organization (WMO)

(a)   (b)

Fig. 5. (a) Honestbox unmanned store; and (b) Linnaeus University visiting Stens Chark to discuss how to apply potential IoT solutions.

precision micro-climate measurement, and a WMO conforming wireless wind station. All of these sensors are connected to the Helium network in the region. Figures 4a and 4b show the installation of LDDS75 distance sensor and wireless micro-weather and wind station, respectively, at Kalmar Dämme.

Honestbox: The Honest Box Sweden AB (https://honestbox.se) develops hardware and software for trading, primarily with a focus on unmanned environments. The company's objective is to reinvent the future of retail by selling products and goods at a store without the presence of staff on-site. Honestbox unmanned store is shown in Fig. 5a. The store is open 24/7, and the customer can open the store by authorizing electronically using the recommended mobile web application. Once the cloud server from the web application receives a request, it then forwards data to the service, where a free-of-charge phone call is made to the system box to open the box. Alternatively, there is a control box that constantly polls the cloud server via an HTTP request every three to four seconds to decide whether the lock should be opened or not.

Currently, the company is utilizing a mechanism that makes a call within about 4 s, but if the store is located at a location where the mobile coverage is not good such as a sports hall. In such scenarios, the signal fails completely or takes a long time, which gives a bad experience to the users. The company Honestbox requires 100% faultless control boxes.

The proposed uses a Pycom Fipy to benefit from all its communication abilities, i.e., WiFi, LoRa, and LTE. In addition, there are several platforms that offer OTA update services for ESP32-based MCUs, such as Toit.io and Amazon FreeRTOS.

Stens Chark, Åseda: Stens Chark (https://stenschark.se/) is a company in Åseda that produces meat-based products, mainly sausages. Their objective is to keep a local and small-scale production aimed for the more conscious consumers that value buying from local farmers. They have a low digital readiness, and most of their processes are done manually. The company reports the temperature and humidity readings once a day to update the related authority every week.

Table 2. Summary of all pilot cases at Applied IoT Lab.

Pilot Cases	Problem	Objectives	Proposed Solution	Innovation Type
Beelab	Connected beehives are dependent on power source	Battery driven wirelessly connected beehives	Use LTE CAT-M1 or NB-IoT-based FiPy gateway	Digitalizing beekeeping
Svenska våg	Monitor the weighing scales at stations and places that are remote	Connect the weighing machine to the Internet	Use LPWAN RS485 bridge with weighing machines	Digitalizing weighing stations
QTF	Time consuming and costly to monitor fluid systems at faraway locations	Monitor the fluid systems wirelessly and remotely	Utilize WiFi and CAT M1 or NB-IoT devices for communication	Next-generation plumbing system
AquaTeq	Manage the sewage and stormwater systems blockages	Know the conditions in and around the nozzle, maintaining sewage and stormwater systems	Install a sensor on the nozzle such as pressure sensor, and wirelessly transmit the sensor data from sewage to the operation vehicle or to a cloud platform using LoRa 433 MHz or NB-IoT	Underground sensing and communication
PM & Vänner	Reduce the food waste efficiently	Measure the amount of food waste	Use load cell driver, load cell amplifier, Raspberry Pi touch interface and a web service such as Node-RED	Digitalizing food waste
Flowbic	Time-consuming data collection	Automate and Facilitate the data collection	Install relevant sensors and transmit data over LoRa network	Nature conservation
HonestBox	Unreliable to relay on one communication technology	Make 100% faultless control boxes	Use Pycom devices with three alternatives communication mechanisms: LTE, WiFi, and LoRa for transmission and OTA updates	Resilient systems
Stens Chark	Manually reporting of temperature and humidity	Automate the reporting	Use Pycom device to connect sensors using LoRa gateway and Datacake for visualization	Digitalizing food processing

Fig. 5b shows the LNU representative at Stens Chark to discuss IoT solutions. The company aims to automatically measure temperature and humidity inside the factory to control the production of sausages better. The IoT lab provided one LoRa gateway registered to The Things Network, four LoRa-enabled temperature and humidity sensors, and a configured visualisation platform Datacake. Table 2 shows the summary of all the pilot cases.

4   Lessons Learned

The projects have demonstrated a vast number of different applications comprising IoT that companies can leverage to either make their business more effective or to find new business models. All projects are different in terms of technology and the technological readiness level of the company involved. A company with a low technology readiness can find great value in a simpler approach of just starting to measure processes that have been done manually. In the case of QTF, deploying the proposed solution would "save the company a significant amount of money." On the other end, some companies already have an IoT solution in place but need support in finding new and more effective solutions, using different networks and more energy-efficient hardware. In addition, learning existing systems in the companies and integrating the proposed IoT solutions without any downtime can be challenging.

In general, IoT is a broad area that is also evolving at a high pace, and there is a need for both exploration and lab resources to find new novel solutions. Sometimes, the offered solution might not be pragmatic. It can also be noted that smaller companies often do not have the resources and competence in order to evaluate different options.

5   Conclusion

Since the establishment of the Applied IoT Lab, it has been actively working to provide IoT-based educational programs to the Linnaeus University (LNU) students and local communities. Along with fundamental research and educational programs, the lab has initiated a number of workshops and a series of pilot cases to strengthen small and medium-sized enterprises (SMEs) in the Linnaeus region, Sweden. The activities at the Applied IoT Lab are supported by the European Union and Kalmar and Kronoberg counties in Sweden. In this paper, we highlighted the IoT lab background and its current educational and industry-academic programs, including workshops and pilot cases. One of the main emphases of the lab is to support local businesses and communities and provide researchers and developers a platform to conduct research and development for the next-generation IoT systems.

The Applied IoT Lab aims to continue its efforts to elevate the regional SME's operational capabilities using IoT, create an IoT-aware knowledge-based society, and enhance the research capabilities of the Linnaeus region.

Acknowledgment. This work was supported by the European Regional Fund, Kalmar Region, Kronoberg Region, and Linnaeus University.

References

1. Beyond Numbers: Insights that Makes a Difference. https://marketing.business-sweden.se/acton/fs/blocks/showLandingPage/a/29361/p/p-0075/t/page/fm/0? sid=TV2:wWCt5cMGT. Accessed 22 Feb 2022
2. Linnaeus   University.   https://lnu.se/en/research/searchresearch/research-projects/project-iot-lab-for-sme/. Accessed 22 Feb 2022
3. Toader, E., Firtescu, B.N., Roman, A., Anton, S.G.: Impact of information and communication technology infrastructure on economic growth: an empirical assessment for the eu countries. Sustainability **10**(10), 3750 (2018). https://www.mdpi.com/2071-1050/10/10/3750
4. Carrión-Martínez, J.J., Luque-de la Rosa, A., Fernandez-Cerero, J., Montenegro-Rueda, M.: Information and communications technologies (ICTs) in education for sustainable development: a bibliographic review. Sustainability **12**(8), 3288 (2020)

5. Saarikko, T., Westergren, U., Jonsson, K.: Here, there, but not everywhere: adoption and diffusion of IoT in Swedish municipalities. In: Proceedings of the 53rd Hawaii International Conference on System Sciences (2020)

6. Da Xu, L., He, W., Li, S.: Internet of Things in industries: a survey. IEEE Trans. industr. inf. **10**(4), 2233–2243 (2014)

7. Malik, P.K., et al.: Industrial Internet of Things and its applications in industry 4.0: state of the art. Comput. Commun. **166**, 125–139 (2021)

8. Schneider, A.: Internet of Things and sustainability: a comprehensive framework (2019)

9. World Economic Forum: Internet of Things Guidelines for Sustainability. https://www3.weforum.org/docs/IoTGuidelinesforSustainability.pdf. Accessed 22 Feb 2022

10. Jamieson, D.: Sustainability and beyond. Ecol. Econ. **24**(2–3), 183–192 (1998)

11. Biedenweg, K., Monroe, M.C., Oxarart, A.: The importance of teaching ethics of sustainability. Int. J. Sustain. High. Educ. **14**(1) 2013

12. Berisha, G., Pula, J.S.: Defining small and medium enterprises: a critical review. Acad. J. Bus. Adm. Law Soc. Sci. **1**(1), 17–28 (2015)

13. Tudor, A.I.M., Chiţu, I.B., Dovleac, L., Brătucu, G., et al.: IoT technologies as instruments for Smes' innovation and sustainable growth. Sustainability **13**(11), 6357 (2021)

14. Statistics   Sweden.   https://www.statistikdatabasen.scb.se/pxweb/sv/ssd/. Accessed 22 Feb 2022

15. The Swedish Innovation Strategy. https://www.government.se/contentassets/cbc9485d5a344672963225858118273b/the-swedish-innovation-strategy.   Accessed 22 Feb 2022

16. Projects   summer   course   applied   IoT.   https://web.archive.org/web/20220318141147/https://hackmd.io/@lnu-iot/good-examples. Accessed 18 Mar 2022

17. Hodzic, A., Hoang, D.: Detection of deviations in beehives based on sound analysis and machine learning, p. 48 (2021)

18. Mozart Andraws, D., Thornemo Larsson, M.: Crowd avoidance in public transportation using automatic passenger counter, p. 34 (2021)

19. Wetland Park Kalmar Dämme - For a cleaner Baltic Sea. https://www.ctc-n.org/products/wetland-park-kalmar-d-mme-cleaner-baltic-sea. Accessed 22 Feb 2022

20. Herrmann, J.: Skälby dämme, en dagvatten-våtmark i kalmar; kemi och biologi under de första åren (2011)

Experiment to Scope Low Carbon Electricity Based Additive Manufacturing with IoT

Damian Pokorniecki and Kartikeya Acharya(✉)

PROTO* Lab, BTECH, Aarhus University, Herning, Denmark
ksacharya@btech.au.dk

Abstract. Seeking a potential of low carbon-based energy use for additive manufacturing, we present a preliminary experimental test using open source IoT tools on FDM (Fused Deposit Modelling) type of 3D printing. In our test we determine and categorize the electricity consumption of processes of a commercial grade FDM printer using a custom-built energy monitor. Our tests indicate that this model of FDM type 3D printer consumes between 22%–33% more energy when printing vertical volumes (Z-axis on 3D printing plate). Based on these tests we present a potential for IoT based low carbon FDM 3D printing using open-source data, hardware and software. With this the article's contribution is two-fold. One as a study on energy and environmental impact of additive manufacturing and secondly as a potential and scope for IoT applications for facilitating low carbon additive manufacturing.

Keywords: Additive manufacturing · Low carbon · 3D printing

1 Introduction

Additive manufacturing (AM), commonly known as 3D printing is a matter of growing interest to industrial production due to its unique processes when compared to traditional manufacturing. AM techniques have proven to be useful in various application settings such as automotive, aerospace, electronics dentistry and medicine [1]. Other than customizable prototyping, it offers potential for minimizing environmental impacts of the created goods, because of the reduction in total carbon emissions of the manufacturing process [2]. Furthermore, a large growth in the market size of 3D printing technologies is expected to happen annually with just 3D printing materials being forecasted to reach $23 billion by the year 2029 [1]. These aspects indicate a need for further assessing the environmental impacts from AM.

In terms of energy research of AM, monitoring of energy consumption from 3D printing equipment has been undertaken from a number of approaches. From calculating the ratio of the energy consumption between the specific components of a 3D printer, to preliminary energy analysis based on device and setup specifications [3–6] have been made. Furthermore, earlier research has examined the difference between power consumption of different AM technologies. Yoon et al. [7] have compared the energy requirements of various types of energy consumption for bulk forming from prior

A. González-Vidal et al. (Eds.): GIoTS 2022, LNCS 13533, pp. 411–420, 2022.
https://doi.org/10.1007/978-3-031-20936-9_33

research and have provided energy consumption from different types of AM processes, which we have collated in the table below (Table 1).

Table 1. A comparison of energy consumption of types of AM, based on Yoon et al. 2014

Process	Specific energy consumption $(kWh\ kg^{-1})$
SLS	14.5–66.02
FDM	**23.08–346.4**
SLA	20.7–41.38
3DP	14.7–17.4
DMLS	24.2
SLM	27–163.33
EBM	17–49.17

As seen in the table above it is indicative that FDM type of AM has been shown to have a wide variation in the energy use. It is also indicated to be the highest consumer of energy when compared with other types of AM. Relatedly [8] it has been shown that for EBM (Electron Beam Melting) AM process, the shape complexity of the manufactured product has weak correlation with energy consumption, but to be specific as an energy study of AM this again is for the EBM process and not with the FDM type of printing, which is the focus of our study in this article. More recently Szemeti and Ramanujan [5] undertaking FDM process study point out that there is a lack of detailed process information relating to AM processes and with that provide an layer-wise energy consumption of the heaters of the bed and extruder, material use, and other printing peripherals of large number of shape parts as a benchmark for FDM type of printing. But in this study, it is not evident if there is a variation in the energy consumption based on axes of printing. Thus, based on such a background of prior research our experiment provides insight on the difference in energy consumption in on the axes of FDM printing. For this our study undertook a direct approach in which the specific energy consumption of a FDM type of 3D print equipment was measured during the whole printing process.

Then having undertaken such a process the scope of our study further seeks potential of AM in terms of carbon footprint from the electrical energy used while printing. CO_2 footprint is an important aspect for the energy systems in today's world. It refers to the measurement of total amount of emissions of carbon dioxide and other greenhouse gases such as nitrous oxide and methane caused by products throughout its life cycle [9]. Since electricity accounts for 25% of the global greenhouse emissions [10] the carbon footprint of energy usage should be a necessary consideration in the setting of environmentally friendly products and services. Thus, based on our experiment we indicate potential for using data of CO_2 intensity from electricity used and integrating within AM processes. We indicate that to be able to control printing and minimize the negative environmental impact of 3D printed products, an integration between external data sources and the AM equipment is needed which could be undertaken using open-source hardware. We provide a preliminary possibility for such a setup, indicating how Fused Deposition Modelling (FDM) type AM system could be made to control its process using the carbon dioxide intensity in the electricity grid system.

To convey this the paper is structured in sections and organized in the following manner: first the methodology section covers tools and technologies used in our experimental setup, including our data collection process. In the result section, the gathered data and its analysis are presented. In the discussion section we present the data source for accessing CO_2 data from electricity production, potential ways to integrate it within a similar FDM 3D printing setup and also limitations of such a proposal are presented. After this we conclude with next steps for our research.

2   Methodology

2.1   Deploying the Experimental Setup

To undertake our experiment, we chose a Prusa i3 MK3s to serve as FDM equipment for our experimental setup. Open Energy Monitor, an open-source energy monitoring system with a clip-on current transducing sensor, was used as a tool for monitoring live energy usage of the 3D printer [11, 12]. The device was built with the open-source microcontroller Arduino Uno using the online guide, and calibrated accordingly, with the use of a smart power socket. Data saving was handled via Putty, an open-source terminal emulator, which collected the data from the PC serial port, connected to Arduino, and saved it as a csv file for analysis (Fig. 1).

Fig. 1. The three printed models of cylindrical section pipe type, the full model and the 'split' model with the base and wall separated.

To measure the energy consumption of the above set up FDM printing equipment, we printed six 3D models. All the prints are manufactured with 20% infill, printed with PETG material in 230 °C, with heat bed temperature set to 90 °C. Firstly, two "full" one-hour models were printed, a rectangular cuboid with a base and a cylindrical section pipe with a base, for which the data was collected. Next, each of the models was split into two separate parts, one containing the "base" of the models, and the second containing the "walls" of the models. This was done to determine the energy consumption of 3D printing along the X and Y axis, and to inspect whether printing more vertically focused parts consumes additional energy, compared to flatter parts, due to higher involvement of the z-axis motor of the printer. The split models are also printed individually. The splitting of the models was chosen, instead of creation of new models, to create an exact correlation between the parts in terms of size, thickness of the walls and infill percentage. All the prints are manufactured with 20% infill, printed with PETG material in 230 °C, with heat bed temperature set to 90 °C.

In the energy monitor setup, an Arduino script was written, which collected the data about energy usage of the Prusa 3D printer. The simplified flow of the data collection algorithm was made which started from establishing a serial connection, after which a power consumption was measured, this measurement was collected and saved as data every second.

3   Results

3.1   Energy Consumption Data

Six models were printed with Prusa i3 3D printer and the energy consumption of the printer was measured along the entire duration of the prints. To analyze the energy demand of the printer during different stages of the printing process, as mentioned earlier the base model prints were divided into two separate models, for which energy demand consumption data were also collected. The energy consumption data of the first rectangular-cuboid model can be seen in Fig. 2 in the top row and the data of the two models, that are part of the base model can be seen in the following second and third rows. The energy consumption data of the cylinder-shaped model can be seen in Fig. 2 in the fourth row and the data of the two models, that are part of the base model can be seen in following in the row five and six. The data points were collected each second, and the average power consumption of creation of each of the models was calculated, by dividing the sum of all data points, divided by number of them. The average power consumption was calculated with the accuracy of 1 W.

Splitting of the base models into two separate prints gives an overview of the energy demand changes, based on the involvement level of motors responsible for different printing axes (X, Y, Z). The setup process is present at the beginning of each printing cycle, which corresponds to heating up the nozzle and heat bed, and calibration of the three axes motors, thus the left side of each of the graph is almost identical. Due to the considerably shorter printing time of the cylinder walls model, the setup process is clearly visible and takes almost half of the graph area. The energy consumption of printing the "base" parts tends to fluctuate between around 100–150 W with random energy use spikes – as seen in the middle part of the base model graphs. The rectangle bottom model averaged the power consumption of 130 W, while the cylinder bottom model averaged 127 W. It can be observed that the energy demand tends to rise, when the printing process focuses on manufacturing along the Z axis (the "walls" models), which can be found on the right side of the base models graphs. That corresponds to around 150–200 W of constant energy utilization. The rectangle walls model averaged the power

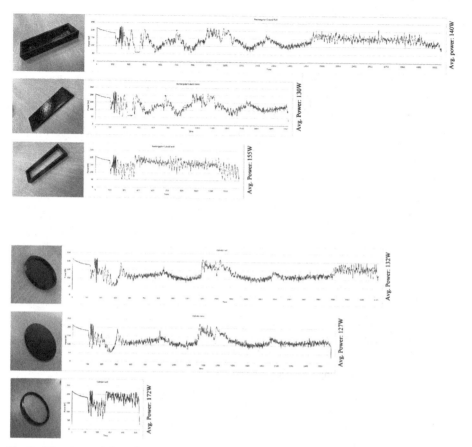

Fig. 2. The six models and their energy use pattern from the FDM printer when printing the models

consumption of 155 W, while the cylinder walls model averaged 172 W, both models being considerably more energy demanding than their bottom models counterparts.

Patterns of different printing processes can be observed on all the graphs. With the cylinder walls model being the one printed in the shortest amount of time, and thus the graph being the widest due to fewer datapoints measured, it is easier to visualize these patterns. The visualization can be seen in Fig. 3, where *A*, *B*, and *C*, mark the processes. These are explained in Table 2.

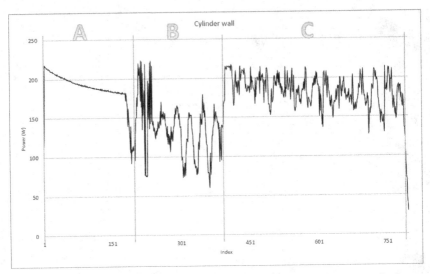

Fig. 3. The three processes of bed heating, motor calibration and printing as seen in the energy use pattern of the 3D printer.

Table 2. The three processes as seen in the energy use pattern

A	Heating up of the heat bed
B	Calibration of axes motors and heating up of the nozzle
C	Printing

4 Discussion

Our research indicated that vertical (Z axis) printing using Fused Deposition Modeling (FDM) technology, consumes more energy than when printing horizontally (XY axis). The exact energy difference may vary, depending on the material used and printing settings, for instance the infill percentage and support layer generation. Several different AM technologies exist, each with various energy requirements, based on specific machines used in the process. Due to this, our research approach may reveal distinct results for each of the technologies. With some of the technologies requiring considerably heavier loads of energy than FDM, for instance Direct Metal Laser Sintering (DMLS) or Electron Beam Melting (EBM). Undertaking such a process with as indicated above with various other types of AM can generate an understanding for optimizing the production process to decrease negative environmental impacts.

4.1 CO_2 Emissions Data for Integration

Towards such a potential for enhancing environmental benefits we further hypothesize the integration of CO_2 emission data with 3D printing, which could result in low carbon AM.

For this we accessed live CO_2 emissions data from a known service called ElectricityMap [13] and looked for ways to integrate this live CO_2 data to work with FDM printer. This provisions scope for getting integrate as an IoT based approach.

Data about carbon intensity of the energy consumed in (our region) was collected using a Python script, and made to run on the open-source microcomputer RaspberryPi. The script collected the data and was made to be saved as a.csv file for analysis. The resolution of data provided by electricityMap is one hour, meaning that the values do not change within the given hour. Furthermore, because of the occurring incidents of delays in data provision, meaning that the data is not always available right at the beginning of each hour, the algorithm collected the data every ten minutes and deleted duplicates if such instance occurs. The simplified illustration of how the algorithm works can be seen in Fig. 4. The data of carbon intensity is presented as gCO2eq/kwh, which indicates emissions as grams of carbon dioxide equivalent per kilo-Watthour of energy consumed.

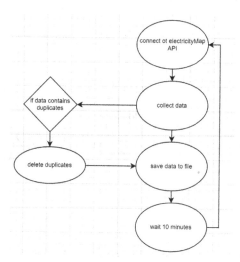

Fig. 4. A simplified illustration of carbon data collection algorithm.

Control of the Prusa printer via Python was established by sending the printer commands to the RaspberryPi attached to the printer. Connection to the printer was handled via OctoPrint, an open-source 3D printer controller application, which connected the local PC or tablet to the RaspberryPi on the printer. All the parameters of the printer, including temperatures, printing job operations and axis adjustments were controlled through OctoPrint. Further control automatization is performed with a Python program, run by Thonny, an integrated development environment for Python, which can run either on local PC or a RaspberryPi.

Such a connection can be used to control the printer based on given variables, for example the level of carbon dioxide intensity in the (our region) energy grid. Possibility of pausing and resuming the printing operation worked without issues. Although because of the inability of the printer to change the heat bed temperature during the printing operation, there is a need of sending the arbitrary commands, as described in the Octoprint manual to the printer, instead of the classic tool commands. Doing that, however, solved the problem. Arbitrary commands send G-code directly to the printer via the serial interface, a raspberryPi on the local network, ordering certain actions to take place, for instance changing the temperature of the tools or pausing and resuming current print.

In this manner carbon dioxide intensity data was collected by using a free API provided by electricityMap. The data provided insights about the energy consumed in (our region), which included the carbon intensity metric, referring to lifecycle greenhouse gas emissions, estimated as grams of carbon dioxide equivalent per kilowatt-hour of electricity (gCO2eq/kWh).

Data about carbon intensity of the energy consumed from (our region) energy grid was collected for one week with hourly resolution. The datapoint visualization can be seen in Fig. 5. From the data collected it is visible that the carbon intensity differs, based on the time during the week. Thus, manufacturing processes requiring greater loads of energy should be scheduled to low carbon intensity times, to minimize their negative environmental impacts.

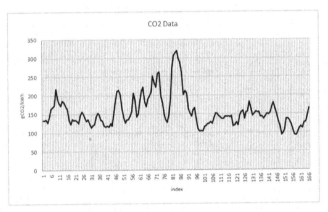

Fig. 5. The CO_2 emissions pattern collected over one week period

Reflecting on the collected CO2 data and the data about the different parts of 3D printing process energy requirements it can be observed, that manufacturing more vertical parts, e.g., the walls of the models, should be performed on the lowest carbon intensity times, while bases of the models could be printed during high carbon intensity times. Including such a control system to the manufacturing setup of numerous 3D printers could significantly lower the carbon footprint of created products and thus minimize its negative environmental impacts.

Furthermore, optimizing the AM processes in terms of their negative environmental impact may be an important aspect for businesses, that base their products on sustainability principles. Examples of such cases may be large 3D printers, manufacturing concrete houses in green areas, or creating sustainable textiles for clothing. Such optimization may provide companies with leverage of calling themselves more sustainable, and documenting that, by mapping the carbon footprint of created products.

Other use cases may include large infrastructure projects, for instance electric vehicles (EV) charging stations in private homes, which could shift the charging times of EVs, for example for specific period during the night, based on the carbon intensity levels in the energy grid. Fast charging stations on highways could also implement such solutions, however that would require more complicated setup, in terms of a large power bank that is charged at specific times, and acts as a power source for the station, so that it may be always used and not interfere with user's needs.

As in the nearest future more and more attention is being paid to the topic of CO_2, and industries need to take definitive action, to live up to the government's regulations, further use cases will arise.

4.2 Limitations

The data about the carbon intensity of the energy consumed in (our region) represents the state of the energy from three hours before the collection time. This is due to the nature of the API provided by ElectricityMap when undertaking the exercise. In the current context this delay is one hour indicating the possibility of lesser delays in the data delivery. With the experiment using the carbon output from electricity we wish to not only indicate the potential if carbon data could go live, but our experiment's applicability gets further validated when typical FDM printing taking more than three hours for a full print.

The two points in the weekly data about carbon intensity collected were missing, corresponding to 166 datapoints being collected instead of 168. This is due to the loss of connection to the API provider, however that does not impact the general goal of the research.

For the FDM technology, the temperatures of the tools used are crucial, thus in future research a special focus should be put into examining the right temperatures of pausing the print and saving energy, so that it does not interfere with quality of the printed models.

5 Conclusion

Additive manufacturing was introduced as a topic of research and experimental setup. The research focused on understanding the FDM process from the perspective of energy consumption, introducing and developing the tools for its optimization, in terms of its negative environmental impacts. We developed a set of tools, using open-source hardware and software, for monitoring the energy consumption of a 3D printer, and collecting data about carbon intensity of the energy consumed in DK1 energy grid. The main finding of our research is that for the FDM process, manufacturing more vertically oriented models requires more energy than for the more horizontally oriented ones. Our analysis indicates that this is due to the fact of greater involvement of the Z-axis motor. Reflecting on the data about the energy consumption of the FDM printer and collected data about carbon intensity of energy consumed in DK1 gave an overview of how the AM process can be scheduled and optimized, to reduce its negative environmental impacts.

Future research may include examining different AM technologies from the perspective of power consumption, collecting carbon intensity data for larger time periods and optimizing other processes with the developed tools.

References

1. Khosravani, M.R., Reinicke, T.: On the environmental impacts of 3D printing technology. Appl. Mater. Today **20**, 100689 (2020). https://doi.org/10.1016/j.apmt.2020.100689
2. Annibaldi, V., Rotilio, M.: Energy consumption consideration of 3D printing. In: 2019 II Workshop on Metrology for Industry 4.0 and IoT (MetroInd4.0 IoT), pp. 243–248 (2019). https://doi.org/10.1109/METROI4.2019.8792856
3. Ajay, J., Rathore, A.S., Song, C., Zhou, C., Xu, W.: Don't forget your electricity bills! An empirical study of characterizing energy consumption of 3D printers. In: Proceedings of the 7th ACM SIGOPS Asia-Pacific Workshop on Systems, Association for Computing Machinery, New York, USA, pp. 1–8 (2016). https://doi.org/10.1145/2967360.2967377
4. Peng, T.: Analysis of energy utilization in 3D printing processes. Procedia CIRP. **40**, 62–67 (2016). https://doi.org/10.1016/j.procir.2016.01.055
5. Szemeti, G., Ramanujan, D.: An empirical benchmark for resource use in fused deposition modelling 3D printing of isovolumetric mechanical components. Procedia CIRP. **105**, 183–191 (2022). https://doi.org/10.1016/j.procir.2022.02.030
6. Simon, T.R., Lee, W.J., Spurgeon, B.E., Boor, B.E., Zhao, F.: An Experimental Study on the Energy Consumption and Emission Profile of Fused Deposition Modeling Process. Procedia Manuf. **26**, 920–928 (2018). https://doi.org/10.1016/j.promfg.2018.07.119
7. Yoon, H.-S., et al.: A comparison of energy consumption in bulk forming, subtractive, and additive processes: review and case study. Int. J. Precis. Eng. Manuf. Green Technol. **1**(3), 261–279 (2014). https://doi.org/10.1007/s40684-014-0033-0
8. Baumers, M., Tuck, C., Wildman, R., Ashcroft, I., Hague, R.: Shape complexity and process energy consumption in electron beam melting: a case of something for nothing in additive manufacturing? J. Ind. Ecol. **21**, S157–S167 (2017). https://doi.org/10.1111/jiec.12397
9. Thøgersen, J., Nielsen, K.S.: A better carbon footprint label. J. Clean. Prod. **125**, 86–94 (2016). https://doi.org/10.1016/j.jclepro.2016.03.098
10. Tranberg, B., Corradi, O., Lajoie, B., Gibon, T., Staffell, I., Andresen, G.B.: Real-time carbon accounting method for the European electricity markets. Energ. Strat. Rev. **26**, 100367 (2019). https://doi.org/10.1016/j.esr.2019.100367
11. Salzillo, G., Rak, M., Moretta, F.: Threat modeling based penetration testing: the open energy monitor case study. In: 13th International Conference on Security of Information and Networks, Association for Computing Machinery, New York, USA, pp. 1–8 (2020). https://doi.org/10.1145/3433174.3433181
12. Rak, M., Salzillo, G., Granata, D.: ESSecA: an automated expert system for threat modelling and penetration testing for IoT ecosystems. Comput. Electr. Eng. **99**, 107721 (2022)
13. Tmrow.co: Live 24/7 CO$_2$ emissions of electricity consumption. http://electricitymap.tmrow.co. Accessed 02 May 2022

Author Index

Printed in the United States
by Baker & Taylor Publisher Services